Pentecost & Sanctification

*In the Writings of
John Wesley and
Charles Wesley*

With a Proposal for Today

Laurence W. Wood

*Asbury Theological Seminary Series:
The Study of World Christian Revitalization Movements in Pietist/Wesleyan Studies*

EMETH PRESS
www.emethpress.com

Pentecost & Sanctification in the Writings of John Wesley and Charles Wesley with A Proposal for Today

Copyright © 2018 Laurence Wood
Printed in the United States of America on acid-free paper

All rights reserved. No part of this book may be reproduced, or stored in a retrieval system or transmitted in any form or by any means, electronic, mechanical, photocopying, recording, scanning or otherwise, except as permitted by the 1976 United States Copyright Act, or with the prior written permission of Emeth Press. Requests for permission should be addressed to: Emeth Press, P. O. Box 23961, Lexington, KY 40523-3961. http://www.emethpress.com.

Library of Congress Cataloging-in-Publication Data

Names: Wood, Laurence W., 1941- author.
Title: Pentecost & sanctification in the writings of John Wesley and Charles Wesley : with a proposal for today / Laurence W. Wood.
Other titles: Pentecost and sanctification in the writings of John Wesley and Charles Wesley
Description: Lexington : Emeth Press, 2018. | Series: Asbury Theological Seminary series: the study of world Christian revitalization movements in Pietist/Wesleyan studies
Identifiers: LCCN 2018009013 | ISBN 9781609471224 (alk. paper)
Subjects: LCSH: Methodist Church--Doctrines. | Methodist Church--History. | Pentecost. | Sanctification--Methodist Church. | Wesley, John, 1703-1791. | Wesley, Charles, 1707-1788.
Classification: LCC BX8331.3 .W66 2018 | DDC 234/.80922--dc23
LC record available at https://lccn.loc.gov/2018009013

Graphic Designer: Jenelyn Camingawan

Front Cover Portrait
John Wesley with a group of friends rushing into
Charles Wesley's room, declaring, "I Believe!"

By Richard Douglas
Used with permisson

Contents

Foreword by J. Steven O'Malley / vii

Preface / ix

Acknowledgments / xiii

Chapter 1. "A Farther Grace—The Spirit of Holiness" / 1

Chapter 2. The Anglican Liturgy of Confirmation and "The Second Blessing" (John Wesley) or "Second Gift" (Charles Wesley) / 9

Chapter 3. John and Charles Wesley's Time-Line for their Developing Theology of Pentecost and Sanctification / 19

Chapter 4. John Heylyn's Pentecost Sermon and Charles Wesley's Pentecost Conversion / 29

Chapter 5. John Wesley's Aldersgate Experience and the Influence of Christian David / 37

Chapter 6. "Holiness *after* Justification" / 49

Chapter 7. "The Indwelling Comforter" / 63

Chapter 8. The Promised Land Motif / 67

Chapter 9. "The Holy Spirit . . . in His Sanctifying Graces / 93

Chapter 10. John Wesley's Day of Pentecost / 121

Chapter 11. Introducing the Reverend John Fletcher, Vicar of Madeley / 137

Chapter 12. "New Baptisms are Necessary from Time to Time" / 151

Chapter 13. "I Do Not Perceive . . . That There is Any difference between Us" / 161

Chapter 14. A Consensus between John Wesley and John Fletcher / 171

Chapter 15. John Wesley's Many Sermons on "Baptized with the Holy Spirit" / 193

Chapter 16. John Wesley's Inner Circle and Other Prominent Leaders / 205

Chapter 17. A Sampling of the Expression of the Baptism with the Spirit in Methodist History / 233

Chapter 18. A Proposal for Today / 245

Appendix 1: John Heylyn's Whitsunday Sermon / 281

Appendix 2: Phillips Brooks's Whitsunday Sermon / 289

Appendix 3: Jeremy Taylor's *Discourse on Confirmation* / 295

Select Bibliiography / 321

Index / 325

Foreword

Pentecost and Sanctification in the Word of John Wesley and Charles Wesley

This volume is published in collaboration with the Asbury Theological Seminary Series in Christian Revitalization Studies. Building on the work of the previous Wesleyan/Holiness Studies Center at the Seminary, the Series provides a focus for research in the Wesleyan Holiness and other related Christian renewal movements, including Pietism and Pentecostal movements, which have had a world impact. The research seeks to develop analytical models of these movements, including their biblical and theological assessment. Using an interdisciplinary approach, the Series bridges relevant discourses in several areas in order to gain insights for effective Christian mission globally. It recognizes the need for conducting research that combines insights from the history of evangelical renewal and revival movements with anthropological and religious studies literature on revitalization movements.

This volume presents Laurence Wood's definitive research bringing to fruition the groundbreaking work he began with the publication in this series of his award winning study of John Fletcher, on the meaning of Pentecost in early Methodism, a decade ago. A thorough demonstration of how the theme of Pentecost and Sanctification is consistently developed through the thought of both Wesleys, along with that of Fletcher, is the theme of this important new study.

The theme is developed with astute and comprehensive use of primary sources and historical context, deployed to demonstrate the distinctive way in which each author nuances a critical theme striking to the core of the evangelistic message of the Wesleys, as well as early through nineteenth century Methodism. Previous paradigms for alternate explanations are effectively deconstructed in the course of this research.

He also opens important new questions, including the interface of Pentecost and confirmation in the traditions of Anglican and Methodist liturgy. Second, he addresses the wider concerns of the relationship between the Wesleys and the Pentecost impulse within the continental revival which antedated Methodism, a larger issue which now awaits further exploration.

It is with honor and gratitude to Professor Wood that this timely study is now available to the public through the venue of this series. Its theme is also readily applicable as a rich resource for personal faith formation.

—J. Steven O'Malley
General Editor
Asbury Theological Seminary Series:
The Study of World Christian Revitalization Movements;
Pietist and Wesleyan Studies

Preface

In his keynote address to the Wesleyan Theological Society in 2004, William Abraham observed that John Wesley was not a systematic theologian, nor an academic theologian.[1] Albert Outler suggested that he could have been called a "folk theologian." Even this term is not quite accurate if by "folk theologian" is meant an attempt to write general theology on a popular level. John Wesley had no intention to offer an explanation of the core doctrines of the church, although he certainly could have done so with distinction, for his knowledge of the history of theology, especially the Early Church Fathers, was comprehensive.

In the "Preface" to his standard sermons, John Wesley said he intended to write for the masses of people so that they could understand simply and clearly the saving message of the Bible. He did not write as a critical Bible scholar, although his knowledge of the biblical language and Latin was excellent. His approach to the Bible was to present its central theme of salvation in an accessible way so that his hearers would be confronted with the call of the gospel.

One reason why he was not a systematic theologian is because he was an Englishmen, and English scholars do not usually write systematic theology. Thomas Cranmer placed the new theology of the reformers in Homilies and in the Book of Common Prayer, not in *Theological Institutes* as John Calvin did. The Anglican focus was upon learning one's theology in worship through sermons and liturgy rather than in abstract doctrinal treatises.

John Wesley was first and foremost an Anglican. Everything he derived from other traditions was filtered through his Anglican heritage. If he and Charles Wesley focused on sanctification, it was because they were Anglicans.

There was a wide range of topics in John Wesley's writings, but in almost all cases he called his readers to experience for themselves justifying and sanctifying grace. Whether you read his sermon on "Scriptural Christianity" or "The Imperfections of Human Knowledge," his call was to "sanctifying grace" and "without holiness no man shall see the Lord." Almost any of his sermons could be captioned as a sermon on salvation with each one being about justifying and sanctifying grace.

Likewise with Charles Wesley's hymns and poems. He penned hymns and poems on a wide range of topics, but his unifying theme was holiness. Specifically, a prominent theme was Pentecost and sanctification. Whatever different nuances between John and Charles Wesley might have emerged in their understanding of Christian perfection in human experience, they agreed on the meaning of Pentecost.

If John and Charles Wesley were not academic theologians and did not write abstract treatises and textbooks on Christian doctrine, this was because they were evangelists and preachers who travelled the British Isles and spoke about pastoral issues as they arose from time to time and in different places.

The primary calling of the Wesleys to be evangelists is too often left out of the writings of contemporary Wesley scholars, but this above else was what they really were about.

It is also unrealistic to expect academic consistency in everything that John Wesley had to say when his sense of urgency was getting people to heaven, as he explained in the preface to his standard sermons. To be sure, John Wesley was as intellectually informed as anyone in his day, and probably the most intellectually gifted evangelist ever. Charles Wesley was the poet laureate of Methodism without an equal in hymn composition. John's sermons and Charles' hymns had one design—to bring persons to justifying and sanctifying faith in Jesus Christ.

The inspiration for this study extends back into the 1970s when I was once president of the Wesleyan Theological Society. A serious discussion emerged in those days about the roots of Pentecostalism in the American Wesleyan holiness tradition. The main issue in this conversation was whether or not John Wesley used the language of the baptism with the Holy Spirit for Christian perfection. Since then, it has been commonplace for many to assume just the opposite of what this study will demonstrate.

This study will show that the language of Pentecost for Christian perfection originated with John Wesley. Charles Wesley's hymns engraved this theology into the hearts of the early Methodists as they sang about Pentecost and sanctification in his hymns.

In the 1760s and early 1770s John Wesley wanted to make sure his preachers understood that the Holy Spirit is given to the justified person in some measure, although the full measure of the Spirit is given in full sanctification. Charles Wesley assumed this distinction, but he mostly reserved Pentecost expressions for Christian perfection.

It will be seen that John and Charles Wesley used "the baptism with the Spirit" and other Pentecost expressions from the beginning right up to the very end of their ministry. We now know from the recent publication of his diaries that John preached on the baptism with the Spirit on multiple occasions (Acts 1:5), but he more often used the expression, "filled with the Spirit" (Acts 2:4). It will be seen that the network of their closest friends, preachers, and band leaders also used Pentecost expressions, especially "the baptism with the Spirit."

My previous book, *The Meaning of Pentecost in Early Methodism,* was focused largely on John Fletcher and his popularizing the Pentecost motif for Christian perfection. I was delighted that it was given "The Book of the Year Award" in 2003 by the Wesleyan Theological Society.

This follow-up book focuses primarily on the writings of John Wesley and Charles Wesley, and it gives the chronological sequence of their development so that their views can be understood in proper context. The historical development is important in order to see the larger whole of their thinking on holiness. For example, critical comments that John Wesley made to John Fletcher March 22, 1775 will be misinterpreted unless his words are followed up by what he said to Fletcher on August 18, 1775, that there was now no difference between them. Significantly, the only criticism of Fletcher's writings occurred when his writings were still in manuscript form; there was never one word of criticism about his published writings, which John and Charles Wesley had edited and approved. Nor was there anyone in Methodist history who imagined there was lack of congruence between John Wesley and John Fletcher—until the 1970s when a view emerged based on incomplete research and an agenda superimposed on statements made by John Wesley that were taken out of context.

My goal was to understand the theme of Pentecost as the Wesley brothers understood it in their developing story. This story also entails understanding the network of their associates and how they understood the Wesley brothers' theology of Christian perfection.

In his Wesleyan Theological Society Keynote Address on "The Death of Wesleyan Theology," William Abraham said that contemporary Wesleyan theology is "dead" because so much of it is written with a specific contemporary agenda that has little to do with John Wesley's interests or perspective. He observed that "there are as many Wesleys as there are Wesley scholars."[2] Among other things, he called for a "revisit" of John Wesley's idea of Christian perfection, noting that it "deserves a fresh, sympathetic visit now that we have had a spirited revision of what happened to the doctrine of the baptism of the Holy Spirit after Fletcher of Madeley—initiated by . . . Laurence Wood,"[3] a reference to my previous work, *The Meaning of Pentecost in Early Methodism*.

My intent in writing this current book is to let the Wesley brothers be who they are in their own context as they understood holiness and not to reconstruct them according to our own contemporary agendas. That is not to say that it might be important to update and adjust some of their ideas for contemporary Wesleyans, even their views on Christian perfection, but at least we should understand their real views on this topic.

There is only a select bibliography at the end of this work because my sources are largely original sources. I have spent much time in archives consulting original and handwritten materials and manuscripts, and my sources are documented in extensive notes. I have of course read the critical literature published on this topic in recent years, and I have learned much from it.

I am aware that the initial opposition in the 1970s to Pentecost expressions for Christian perfection arose out of a concern that John Wesley should not be held theologically responsible for the emergence of twentieth-century pneumatic movements. Hopefully we are no longer driven by that sentiment today and we can move forward with trying to get it right about Pentecost and sanctification as understood by the co-founders of Methodism.

I have modernized the spelling of the 18th century manuscripts and books according to acceptable scholarly practice. I have changed "Holy Ghost" to "Holy Spirit" although not in Charles Wesley's hymns and poems.

One may be surprised by the number of extensive quotations, but this is because I want readers to see the historiography for themselves and thus make their own judgments whether or not the Wesley brothers are being interpreted correctly. I would also encourage readers to read carefully the many quoted hymns of Charles Wesley and not just skip over them. They are devotional and theological at the same time.

I will repeat some comments to make sure the reader catches the significance of a particular reference or expression. These comments will funtion as a running commentary on the writings of John and Charles Wesley.

A promiment feature, especially of Charles Wesley, was the Promise Land motif as the Old Testament anticipation of the meaning of perfect love. This motif will be seen to be not a mere allegory, but is theologically rooted in the promise-fulfilment typology that the Israelites will return to the land and will be enabled to remain there forever because God will circumcize their hearts, thus enabling them to love God with all their heard, mind, and soul—a precondition for living in the Promise Land which the Israelites failed to observe. Its fulfilment occured on the day of Pentecost, according to Joel (which John and Charles everywhere assumed in their writings).

In the last chapter I propose a way to engage others in the experience of holiness for today. I intentional use the term "experience" because this term highlights an important part of the Wesleyan quadrilateral. I believe this proposal is consistent with the Wesley brothers' Anglican heritage with its focus on liturgy and worship, and I believe this proposal will help to preserve their evangelistic intent to make holy love a primary goal and inspiration for all Christians. Paraphrasing John Wesley's comment to William Law, the baptism with the Holy Spirit of Christ means mainly one thing—a baptism of his holy love. Now how can anyone disagree with the baptism of Christ's holy love as the greatest need in today's world.

The appendices contain two Whitsunday sermons—one by John Heylyn which John Wesley heard preached on the very day of Charles Wesley's Pentecost conversion, and one by Phillips Brooks who is one of the most famous preachers in American history. These sermons may serve as models of preaching on Pentecost and especially in preparation for confirmation service. John Heylyn's sermon exactly represents John and Charles Wesley's view of sanctification, and Phillips Brooks' sermon is a beautifully written and spiritually inspiring message on union with Christ through being filled with the Spirit. It nuances all the main points of Christian perfection without using the term itself. Jeremy Taylor's *Discourse on Confirmation* is also in the appendices so that it may be readily accessible to the reader.

Laurence (Larry) Wood
Frank Paul Professor of Systematic Theology/Wesley Studies
Asbury Theological Seminary
March 2, 2018

Notes

1. William J. Abraham, "The End of Wesleyan Theology," *The Wesleyan Theological Journal*, 40:1(Spring, 2005): 7-27.
2. Ibid., 13.
3. Ibid., 21.

Acknowledgments

The Charles Wesley hymns and sacred poems in their entirety are easily accessible online thanks to the scholarly and technical work of Randy Maddox and Aileen F. Maddox in making these materials freely available to anyone. These materials were accessed with permission through The Center for Studies in the Wesleyan Tradition, Duke Divinity School. One cannot overstate the invaluable contributions of Dr. Maddox to Wesley Studies over many years.

Original materials were generously made available to me through the kind services of Peter Nockles and Gareth Lloyd of the Methodist Archives and Research Center (MARC), John Rylands University Library. Gareth Lloyd also made available to me his transcriptions of Charles Wesley's unpublished letters. His writings on Charles Wesley have also been of inestimable value.

Special thanks to Kate Collins and Josh Larkin Rowley of M. Rubenstein Rare Book & Manuscript Library staff for help in providing me with copies of the Elizabeth Ritchie Correspondence in the Frank Baker Collection of Duke University Libraries.

Permissions to draw from my previously published works on this topic have been graciously granted—*The Meaning of Pentecost in Early Methodism* by Scarecrow Press, numerous articles in *The Wesleyan Theological Journal*, and *The Proceedings of the Charles Wesley Society*. Special lectureships in universities and seminaries have also been an important inspiration and source for putting this research together, including the Cowman Lectures at Seoul Theological Seminary. My students have been an invaluable source of inspiration and assistance to me as I have been engaged with them in group discussions and class lectures over many years, as well over lunch and in dinner settings. I must mention James Boetcher, a PhD Intern, whose assistance has been so helpful to me.

Special thanks for the input from so many over the years who have been engaged in conversations with me on this research topic—too many to mention. Some of these conversations have been in private conversation, emails, personal letters, and published critical scholarly responses to my writings on this topic. Of particular importance are the responses to my work edited by Nathan Crawford, *The Continuing Relevance of Wesleyan Theology, Essays in Honor of Laurence W. Wood* with a foreword by Stanley Hauerwas. Many Wesley scholars have also read the manuscript and offered helpful suggestions. They have also provided endorsement statements for which I am most grateful. At the risk of not mentioning others, I must mention Dr. J. Steven O'Malley with his encyclopedic mind in Church History and Wesley Studies. He has been a scholarly, critical source of inestimable value to me over the years. I must also mention Dr. Timothy C. Tennent, President of Asbury Theological Seminary and Professor of World Christianity, whose careful reading of this work and suggestions were invaluable to me. His friendship and encouragement have been a constant source of inspiration. He is a witness to the sanctifying baptism with the Spirit in the Wesleyan tradition.

Chapter 1

"A Farther Grace—The [Pentecost] Spirit of Holiness"

> "Who have the gospel truth believ'd,
> And mercy from the Lord receiv'd,
> And known our sins forgiven,
> We surely need a farther grace,
> We want the Spirit of holiness,
> To seal us heirs of heaven."
> —Charles Wesley

John Wesley said the Methodists had been raised up by God "to spread scriptural holiness over the land."[1] He believed a person needed to be "justified before they are sanctified; but still holiness was their point."[2] Charles Wesley in his sacred poems defined this call to holiness "a farther grace."[3]

By holiness, John Wesley explained that he and his brother Charles meant one thing: the pursuit of believers to be made perfect in love subsequent in time to their moment of justification and "that no man can be thus sanctified till he be justified." Their purpose was "to raise a holy people" within the Church of England and across the nation.[4]

In the final days of his life in 1790, John Wesley said to Adam Clarke that retaining the sanctifying grace of God "should be strongly and explicitly urged on all who have tasted of perfect love. If we can prove that any of our Local Preachers or Leaders, either directly or indirectly, speak against it, let him be a Local Preacher or Leader no longer. I doubt whether he should continue in the society. Because he that could speak thus in our congregations cannot be an honest man."[5]

John and Charles Wesley never wavered in their understanding that the distinctive doctrine of Methodism was Christian perfection. All other things that the Wesley brothers had to say were but tributaries of this central stream of their evangelistic message. In a letter to a friend just months before his death, John Wesley said that "full sanctification . . . is the grand depositum which God has lodged with the people called Methodists."[6] Anyone who opposed the doctrine of full sanctification, he said, was at best only "a half-Methodist."[7] He cautioned his "preachers . . . never to speak against *the Great Salvation*, either in public or private; and never to discourage either by word or deed, any that think they have attained it. No: but prudently encourage them to *hold fast whereunto they have attained*. And strongly and explicitly exhort all believers, to *go on to perfection*; yes to expect full salvation from sin every moment, by mere grace, through simple faith."[8]

John Wesley made a formal distinction between "sanctification" (which is begun with justification) and "entire sanctification," and yet he most always meant entire sanctification when he spoke of "sanctification," as Harald Lindström has shown.[9] Likewise the term, holiness, was used interchangeable with Christian perfection, as Albert Outler has also pointed out: "'Perfection,' 'holiness,' 'sanctification,' 'full salvation,' are simply so many terms to denote one thing—loving God above all else . . . so far as one's *conscious* will and *deliberate* acts are concerned."[10]

Entire sanctification or Christian perfection was never a terminal point for the Wesley brothers. The fullness of sanctification or Christian perfection was a gift to the justified person "by the power of the Holy Spirit,"[11] and it was a never-ending process of further growth and improvement; it meant purity of intent and an increasing capacity of perfect love; but it never meant perfect performance. It was never a finished perfection of performance but growing perfection in love. John Wesley insisted that perfect love is consistent with a "thousand infirmities," honest mistakes, "nervous disorders," and unwitting failures of the perfect law of God. Not even the most saintly person is exempt from praying the Lord's prayer, "Forgive us our trespasses even as we forgive those who trespass against us" because perfect performance is not a possibility.

Jesus' command to be "perfect as your Father in heaven is perfect" (Matthew 5:48) should be interpreted in the light of the Shema: "Hear, O Israel: the Lord our God, the Lord is one. Love the Lord your God with all your heart and with all your soul and with all your strength" (Deuteronomy 6:4-9). This the only kind of perfection required of persons. It was first required of Abraham: "Walk before me and be thou perfect [blameless in heart]" (Genesis 17:1).

Amos Binney in 1839 explained that many expressions came to be used for Christian perfection derived from the Wesley brothers: "It is called full redemption, the abiding witness, the fullness of the Spirit, full assurance, perfection, holiness, sanctification. . . . What is meant by these expressions is, that maturity in grace and participation of the divine nature . . . exclude all sin from the heart, and fill it with perfect love to God and man."[12]

John Wesley's journals and letters contained many instances of people in his meetings who were justified and then later sanctified in a sudden moment of time.[13] This focus on a defining moment of coming to love God with all one's heart, mind, and soul may come as a surprise to some in the Methodist tradition, but it was largely this focus that was the driving force of early Methodism in Britain and America.

Monday, May 5, 1740, John Wesley recorded: "I expounded those words, 'I write unto you, little children, because your sins are forgiven you:' And described the state of those who have forgiveness of sins but have not yet a clean heart."[14]

When he visited Dublin on Monday, July 26, 1762, John Wesley wrote in his journal: "At five in the morning, the congregation was larger than it used to be in the evening. And in these two days and a half, four persons gave thanks for a sense of God's pardoning mercy; and seven, (among whom were a mother and her daughter) for being 'perfected in love'."[15]

One of the leaders in that Dublin society said to Wesley: "The work here is such as I never expected to see. Some are justified or sanctified, almost every day."[16]

John Wesley preached at the Chapel-en-le-Frith on April 1, 1786. He said that "many have been awakened, justified, and soon after perfected in love."[17]

In a letter to Freeborn Garrettson of the Methodist Episcopal Church in America on

June 16, 1785, John Wesley wrote: "Let none of them rest in being half-Christians. Whatever they do, let them do it with their might; and it will be well, as soon as any of them find peace with God, to exhort them to 'go on to perfection.' The more explicitly and strongly you press all believers to aspire after full sanctification, as attainable now by simple faith, the more the whole work of God will prosper."[18]

John Wesley sermons consisted primarily of two themes, calling his hearer to have a personal experience of justifying faith and sanctifying grace. In his chapels, John Wesley reported that he preached for thirty minutes and "his constant doctrine was, salvation by faith, preceded by repentance, and followed by holiness [i.e., entire sanctification]."[19]

The distinction between justification and holiness was also part of the evangelistic, itinerant preaching of Charles Wesley who was the co-founder of Methodism and who had co-ordinate authority with John in supervising the Methodist societies.[20] In his journal for Sunday, July 12, 1741 Charles Wesley wrote: "The power and seal of God is never wanting while I declare the *two great truths* of the everlasting gospel: universal redemption and Christian perfection."[21]

On that same day, Charles recorded in his journal, "At Kingswood I received Jane Sheep into the fold by baptism, which she felt in that moment to be the redemption of sins." The next day he went to Cardiff where he met with a Methodist society there, and on July 15, he "encouraged them to expect salvation from indwelling sin [i.e., Christian perfection]."[22]

On June 24, 1741, Charles visited a woman member of the Society near Bristol who encouraged him to continue preaching "Christ the Saviour of all men, whose blood cleanseth from all sin." She admitted, "I have not yet attained, but know He will fill up what is lacking in my faith."

While Charles was serving the sacrament of holy communion, Charles said "she bore witness of the truth, 'Everyone that is perfect shall be as his Master'." Charles noted in his journal: "God, she said, had then taken away the evil heart and she had no sin remaining in her [i.e., Christian perfection]."[23]

Charles reported that not all of his hearers understand or agreed with his teaching that holiness follows justification. On June 23, 1743, Charles reported that some "did not understand what we meant by talking of holiness *after* forgiveness."[24]

Charles, like his brother, galloped on his horse from town to town through rain and snow, often attacked by mobs, suffered from hunger and exhaustion, while establishing, organizing, and supervising Methodist societies for nearly twenty years until his semi-retirement to Bristol in 1756 and then to London in 1771.[25] The reasons for his semi-retirement are not clear, but it appears in part due to his struggles with health issues as well as his family commitments and personal needs.[26]

In a recent work, *Charles Wesley and the Struggle for Methodist Identity* (Oxford: OUP, 2007), Gareth Lloyd has corrected the dismissive role of Charles Wesley given by earlier Methodist writers who worried about his views regarding the relationship of Methodism to the Church of England. Lloyd has helped to restore a proper and more balanced understanding of the significance of Charles Wesley as the co-founder of Methodism. He was well liked and highly respected, and his hymns were sung every week in Methodist chapels. His view that Methodists should retain their loyalty to the Church of England was the prevailing one among Methodists.[27] As we shall see, if Pentecost was widely understood among early Methodists to be connected with sanctification, Charles' hymns largely accounted for this emphasis.

Despite his health issues, Charles continued with bursts of great energy to be active in his preaching and in supervising the preachers after his semi-retirement until his death in 1788. His "behind-the-scenes activities in the years between 1756 and 1788 represent one of the most fascinating aspects of his contribution to the development of early Methodism," as Gareth Lloyd has shown.[28]

Occasionally Charles attended the annual conference, as he did for the last time in 1786.[29] It is not clear exactly when Charles ceased his full-scale itinerant ministry, but his journal entries ceased on November 5, 1756. He said to his wife in a letter of June 15, 1758, "I shall quite come over to you, and never stir from home—except to visit the sick or to preach."[30] In a letter to the Countess of Huntingdon on September 6, 1766, he mentioned to her that his "few remaining days will be divided between London and Bristol."[31] His comment about his "few remaining days" might indicate his concern over health issues which he was known to struggle with.

In a letter to Michael Callender in 1786, Charles made it clear he "has remained with the Methodists to this day," despite his brother's action of ordaining Methodist preachers in 1784, which Charles vehemently opposed because he perceived it to be a declaration of separation from the Church of England.[32]

His active involvement as the co-leader of Methodism never ceased. For example, he actively sought to recruit someone in 1773 to help his brother lead the Methodist movement.[33] He continued to approve or disapprove who would become a Methodist preacher. In the final months of his life, Charles appealed to John Wesley's designated successor, John Fletcher, to take over the leadership of Methodism, except that Fletcher was himself dying from tuberculosis.[34] Because of his brother's practice of ordaining Methodist preachers, he told John and Mary Fletcher that Methodism was on the verge of being a "wreck" and *Methodism will be broken into 1000 pieces."* He encouraged them to take on the responsibility to salvage what they could.[35] So even in the midst of radical disagreement with his brother, Charles always felt a heavy responsibility for the Methodist cause.

It is doubtful that John Fletcher's influence would have emerged so prominently in Methodism if it had not been for his deep personal relationship with Charles. After his semi-retirement, Fletcher relied upon Charles to read and correct his manuscripts and then to supervise their publications. Fletcher specifically mentioned that he derived his emphasis on the "baptism with the Spirit" from Charles' hymns and they together discussed this theme in numerous letters of correspondence.

So Charles did not simply withdraw from Methodism, but he continued a decision-making role as the co-leader of Methodism until his death in London (Marylebone), March 29, 1788. Samuel Bradburn, one of his preachers and a faithful friend and known as the "Orator of Methodism," preached his funeral at two of the Methodist chapels—

West Street and City Road— "to an inconceivable concourse of people of every description." Bradburn's text was: "A prince and a great man is fallen this day in Israel."³⁶

It is doubtful that Methodism would have emerged as a world-transforming movement without the organizing and supervising efforts of Charles and his hymns. It has been said that John Wesley was the "head" and Charles Wesley was the "heart" of Methodism. The substance of his hymns shows him also to be a serious and thoughtful theologian and a penetrating lyrical commentator on Scripture.

If Charles continued to preach and promote Methodism in his semi-retirement years, he also never lost a passion for the holiness message of Methodism. In a letter to his daughter, Sally, on September 17, 1782, he encouraged her to seek and expect the experience of Christian perfection, encouraging her to read William Law who "is always sacred" on this topic. He told Sally that it is attained "through faith which is the gift of God, given to everyone that asked." He said to her that "all we can do till faith comes, is . . . not to neglect the means of attaining faith . . . especially private prayer and the scripture."

> That you gained by the despised Methodists, if nothing more, the knowledge of what true religion consists in, namely in happiness and holiness; in peace and love, in the favour [and] image of God restored; in paradise regained . . . a kingdom within you; a participation of the divine nature. The principle means, or instrument of this is faith: which faith is the gift of God, given to everyone that asked."³⁷

Charles eventually nuanced the meaning of Christian perfection as a long process of preparation through the discipline of tribulation, suffering and growth in grace before its attainment in this life, but he never abandoned his belief that an experience of perfect love could be, and should be, attained in this life. Even though he emphasized the element of process more so than the instant moment of Christian perfection, his belief in the possibility of perfect love was often expressed in such poetic words as these:

> O let them all thy mind express,
>   Stand forth thy chosen witnesses!
> Thy power unto salvation show,
>   And perfect holiness below.³⁸

Whatever different nuances emerged in the course of their life as the leaders of Methodism, the Wesley brothers remained the same in their interpretation of holiness or Christian perfection, as the pure love of God filling the heart through the Pentecost power of the Holy Spirit received sometime "after" their moment of justification. Interestingly enough, they often disagreed on Methodist-related issues and they did so at times with passionate feelings and harsh comments to each other, but these human foibles were still considered to be consistent with a heart of pure love as entailed in their doctrine of Christian perfection.

When Charles described justification by faith, he normally referred to it as receiving forgiveness of sins. When he described Christian perfection, some descriptions included specific words such as new birth, the second gift, pardon sealed, participation in the divine nature, purifying, holiness, sanctification, love, full assurance, the promise of the Father, the descent of the Spirit, and baptism with the Spirit.

Patrick Eby has recently shown in *The Heart of Charles Wesley's Theology* that Charles' preferred expression for Christian perfection was the "one thing needful, namely the recovery of the image of God."[39] Eby's work showed the main themes in Charles Wesley's overall theology.

My work focuses upon Pentecost expressions for Christian perfection highlighted in Charles Wesley's journal and hymns. The reason for this approach will become apparent in the last chapter where I offer "A Proposal for Today." It will also be seen in this work that the center of Charles Wesley's soteriology is Pentecost as the means of recovering the image of God.

It is also important to recognize that John Wesley at the point of his early developing theology equated being "born again" with Christian perfection, as did Charles Wesley.

These expressions for perfection are typically used in Jeremy Taylor's *Discourse on Confirmation*. When Charles referred to the Pentecost gift of the Spirit in sanctification after justification, the precedent for this twofold understanding was thus already part of his Anglican heritage.

John Wesley insisted his understanding of the doctrine of salvation was consistent with mainstream church teaching. In the 1778 dedication of the City-Road Chapel in London that was the headquarters of the Methodist movement, he said: "Methodism, so called, is the old religion, the religion of the Bible, the religion of the primitive church, the religion of the Church of England."[40]

If the distinctive teaching of Methodism was to promote "scriptural holiness" as a subsequent moment in time to justifying faith, it will be seen in the following discussion that John and Charles Wesley's idea of sanctification was a personal application of the liturgical theology of confirmation in the Church of England in the tradition of Jeremy Taylor.

Notes

1. *The Methodist Societies, The Minutes of the Conference*, ed. Henry D. Rack, in *The Works of John Wesley* (Nashville: Abingdon Press, 2011), 10:875, "The Large Minutes."
2. Ibid.
3. MS Acts, MARC: MA 1977/555 (Charles Wesley Notebooks Box 1), 148.
4. Ibid. Cf. Albert C. Outler, *Sermons* in *The Bicentennial Edition of the Works of John Wesley*, vols. 1-4 (Nashville, Abingdon Press, 1984-1987), 2:491, "General Spread of the Gospel." Cited hereafter as Outler, *Sermons*.
5. *The Works of John Wesley*, ed. Thomas Jackson, 104 (Peabody, Massachusetts: Hendrickson Publishes, Inc., 1984), 13:104, "Letter to Adam Clarke Nov. 26, 1790."
6. *Letters of John Wesley*, ed. George Eayrs (London: Hodder and Stoughton, 1915), 173. "Letter to Robert Carr Brackenbury, September 15, 1790."
7. Ibid., 175, "Letter to Adam Clarke," February 3, 1786.
8. John Wesley, "Editor's Comment," *The Arminian Magazine*, 3 (April, 1780): 207.
9. Cf. Harald Lindström, *Wesley and Sanctification* (Wilmore, KY: Francis Asbury Publishing Company, 1980), 127.
10. *The Wesleyan Theological Heritage*, ed. Thomas C. Oden & Leicester R. Longden (Grand Rapids: Zondervan Publishing House, 1991), 52. Cf. this equation of holiness and entire sanctification in *The Methodist Magazine and Quarterly Review* 23 (January, 1841): 123-124. John Lawson also writes: "Wesley's doctrine is that Christian perfection, or holiness, is to be defined as the divine gift of 'perfect love'." *Introduction to Christian Doctrine* (Francis Asbury Publishing Company, 1980), 232.
11. "Thoughts upon Methodism," *The Methodist Societies, History, Nature, and Design*, 9:528.
12. *The Theological Compend* (New York: G. Lane and Sandford, 1840), 83.

13. *Journal and Diaries IV (1755–65)*, eds. W. Reginald Ward and Richard Heitzenrater, in *The Bicentennial Edition of the Works of John Wesley*, 21:383–84.

14. *Journal and Diaries II*, ed. W. Reginald Ward and Richard Heitzenrater, in the *Works of John Wesley* (Nashville: Abingdon Press, 1990), 19:148.

15. *Journal and Diaries IV (1755-1765)*, 21:374-375.

16. Ibid.

17. *Journal and Diaries VI (1779-1786)*, 23:389.

18. Wesley, *Works* (Jackson edition) 13:70 (to Freeborn Garrettson, June 16, 1785). Cf. Nathan Bangs, *The Life of the Rev. Freeborn Garrettson* (New York : Carlton & Porter, 1832), 202.

19. "Thoughts upon Methodism," *The Methodist Societies, History, Nature, and Design*, 9:528.

20. Thomas Jackson, *The Life of Charles Wesley* (London: John Mason, 1849), 548.

21. *The Manuscript Journal of the Reverend Charles Wesley, M.A*, ed. S. T. Kimbrough, Jr., and Kenneth G. C. Newport, 2 volumes (Nashville: Kingswood Books, 2008), 1:319. Cited hereafter as *Manuscript Journal*.

22. *Manuscript Journal*, 1:319.

23. *Manuscript Journal* 1:315

24. *Manuscript Journal*, 2:354.

25. Cf. Charles Wesley, "Letter to unidentified, 1773," transcribed by Gareth Lloyd, the Methodist Archives and Research Center (MARC), John Rylands University Library of Manchester, England, DDCW 1/93.

26. Gareth Lloyd, *Charles Wesley and the Struggle for Methodist Identity* (Oxford: Oxford University Press, 2007), 159.

27. Ibid., 154.

28. Ibid., 162.

29. Cf. "Letter to Sally Wesley (his wife)," July 29, 1786, transcribed by Gareth Lloyd, MARC: DDWes 4-69; "Letter to Sally Wesley," August, 6, 1786, transcribed by Garth Lloyd, MARC: DDWes 4-50.

30. Charles Wesley, "Letter to Sarah Wesley," June 15, 1738, transcribed by Gareth Lloyd, MARC: DDCW 7/78.

31. Charles Wesley, "Letter to Selina Hastings, Countess of Huntingdon," September 6, 1766, transcribed by Gareth Lloyd. Source: Cheshunt College Archive, Westminster College (#G2/1/125).

32. Charles Wesley "Letter to Michael Callender," November 25, 1786, transcribed by Gareth Lloyd MARC: MA 1977-156 (Colman Collection, JW V.III, 36-37).

33. 34. Cf. Charles Wesley, "Letter to Mark Davis," May 22, 1773, transcribed by Gareth Lloyd, MARC: DDCW 1-62.

34. Charles Wesley, "Letter to John and Mary Fletcher," June 21, 1785, transcribed by Gareth Lloyd, MARC: DDCW 1/75; Cf. Charles Wesley, "Letter to John Fletcher," March 13, 1784, transcribed by Gareth Lloyd, Duke Baker Collection.

35. Charles Wesley, "Letter to John and Mary Fletcher," June 21, 1785, transcribed by Gareth Lloyd, MARC: DDCW 1/75.

36. Frederick G. Gill, *Charles Wesley, the First Methodist* (Nashville: Abingdon Press, 1964). 226.

37. Charles Wesley, "Letter to his daughter, Sarah," on September 17, 1782, transcribed by Gareth Lloyd Source: MARC: DDCW 4-26.

38. Charles Wesley, *Hymns for Those to Whom Christ is All in All* (London: n.p., 1761), 133. http://www.divinity.duke.edu/initiatives-centers/cswt/wesley-texts.

39. Patrick Eby, *The Heart of Charles Wesley's Theology* (Lexington: Emeth Press, 2018).

40. Outler, *Sermons* 3:586, "On Laying the Foundation of the New Chapel."

Chapter 2

The Anglican Liturgy of Confirmation and "The Second Blessing" (John Wesley) or "Second Gift" (Charles Wesley)

> "Five in one band received a second blessing."
> —John Wesley

> "Now the second gift impart,
> Now th' abiding witness give,
> Give us now the perfect heart."
> —Charles Wesley

> "The necessity of confirmation, or receiving the Holy Spirit after baptism, is imitation of the divine precedent of our blessed Saviour."
> —Jeremy Taylor

> "Sanctification . . . is the proper effect of confirmation."
> —Jeremy Taylor

John Wesley often called sanctification "the second blessing." In a letter to Sarah Crosby on February 14, 1761: "The work of God goes on mightily here both in conviction and conversion. This morning I have spoken with four or five who seem to have been set at liberty within this month. I believe within five weeks, six in one class have received remission of sins and five in one band received a second blessing."[1]

Charles referred to it as "the second gift" and "the farther rest."

> A second gift impart,
>   (The sinless mind, the farther rest)
> And stamp thine image on my breast,
> And fill my emptied heart.[2]

Charles believed this "second gift" was to be received in an instant moment of the "now" of personal faith.

> Jesu, Lord, for this we wait,
> Till thine image we regain:
> Wilt thou not our souls create?
> Saviour, shall our faith be vain?
> If we do in thee believe,
> Now the second gift impart,
> Now th' abiding witness give,
> Give us now the perfect heart.[3]

John and Charles Wesley's Idea of Sanctification As a Personalized Interpretation of the Anglican Rite of Confirmation

John Fletcher (who on occasions preached with John and Charles Wesley on their evangelistic tours) preferred to speak of the "second blessing" or "second gift" as a "sanctifying baptism with the Spirit." He believed the doctrine of Christian perfection was a personalized and evangelical meaning of the Anglican rite of confirmation, as will be discussed more fully in the final chapter. The logic of this view naturally follows from the connection between a sanctifying baptism with the Spirit and the rite of confirmation.

This chapter will illustrate that the emphasis of the Wesley brothers on sanctification after justification was embedded deeply in their Anglican heritage and was a natural extension of their heritage, not something merely *de novo*.

John Wesley said in his *Plain Account of Christian Perfection* that he was greatly influenced by Jeremy Taylor's dual book, *Holy Living and Holy Dying*. It was one of the primary influences that launched him on his journey toward Christian perfection ("purity of intent").

Taylor wrote another treatise in 1663 that highlighted the importance of "sanctification and power,"[4] entitled *A Discourse of Confirmation*. It was based on Paul's question to the Ephesian believers in Acts 19:2, "Have you received the Holy Spirit since you believed?"[5]

He traced the Anglican rite back in history to "the many great and glorious expressions which we find in the sermons of the holy fathers of the primitive ages."[6] Perhaps even more significant than his tracing the practice of confirmation back through the Early Church Fathers to the New Testament is that we now have data that precedes the actual writings of the New Testament that shows the laying on of hands (Pentecost) was distinct from water baptism (Easter) and together these two events constituted the baptism liturgy. Only in recent years has the baptism liturgy of most denominations come to include the laying on of hands. Until now, the Pentecost dimension of baptism had been missing in Protestantism. Protestant scholars have often used an abstract exegetical interpretation of the Pentecost passages in the Book of Acts often with the intent to equate water baptism and the baptism with the Spirit. The liturgical practice of the earliest Christian community, having coming to light (thanks to the ecumenical liturgical renewal movement) has now cleared away this confusion. No longer can abstract exegesis take precedence over the actual liturgy of Christian initiation practiced by the primitive church. This new data reinforces the view of confirmation as set forth in Taylor, and it will form the basis for the last chapter on a proposal for understanding confirmation today.

Taylor considered the rite of confirmation as an "ordinance," not as a sacrament, though he deemed it to be an essential part of Anglican liturgy.[7] In defending the rite of confirmation, he pointed out the distinction between water baptism and "the baptism with the Spirit" through a comprehensive study of the theology of the Early Church Fathers.[8]

We do not know if the Wesleys read this treatise, but we know that John Wesley often made references to Jeremy Taylor in his sermons and writings. We know that he exchanged letters with his mother Susanna about Bishop Taylor's writings.[9] If Taylor's *Rule and Exercises of Holy Living* decisively inspired John Wesley in his pursuit of holiness, we know that he probably read Taylor's view about the importance of confirmation. In this book, Taylor urged parents to provide for the catechism and confirmation of their children as part of their spiritual reponsibility.[10] He said that "since God hath given the Holy Spirit to them that are baptized and rightly confirmed and entered into covenant with him, our bodies are made temples of the Holy Ghost, in which he dwells."[11] We also know that in 1784 John Wesley liked the statement of Bishop Warburton: "I have no conception of a greater genius on earth than Dr. Jeremy Taylor."[12] John Wesley mentioned that he found help in reading Taylor's interpretation of Scripture when he was on the way to Georgia in January, 1738.[13] Charles Wesley also mentioned him favorably in his journal.[14]

It is easy to discern that Taylor's interpretation of confirmation generally corresponded with their emphasis on being "sanctified wholly through his Spirit," as John Wesley put it in his *Plain Account of Christian Perfection*.[15] The similarity in meaning between Taylor's treatise and the Wesleys' writings on holiness is striking. Charles' language for Christian perfection used Taylor's confirmation language of the Holy Spirit in strikingly similar ways. (This discourse is included in Appendix 3, and the reader can judge for themselves about this similarity). Just why they did not mention this discourse on confirmation will be examined in the final chapter, where we will see John Wesley favored the evangelical experience of holiness rather than a focus on this rite.

Citing from the primitive fathers, Jeremy Taylor wrote: "We must pass through water and fire, before we enter into rest; that is, we must first be baptized with water and then with the Holy Spirit. . . . The only way to enter into Christ's kingdom is by these two doors of the 'tabernacle, which God hath pitched, and not man,'—first by baptism, and then by confirmation; first by water, and then by the Spirit."[16]

Jeremy Taylor explained: "In confirmation we receive the Holy Spirit as the earnest of our inheritance, as the seal of our salvation. . . . [Gregory of Nazianzus says:] 'We therefore call it a seal or signature, as being a guard and custody to us, and a sign of the Lord's dominion over us.'"[17] Taylor wrote: "In baptism we are made the sons of God, but we receive the witness and testimony of it in confirmation."[18]

Charles appropriated these exact terms—earnest of our inheritance, seal, signature, and witness—to speak of an evangelical experience of Christian perfection. Particularly, Charles related the witness of the Spirit primarily to Christian perfection.

In describing a woman who had experienced Christian perfection on September 26, 1739, Charles described her experience this way: "The Spirit of God came in with his testimony, and put it beyond the possibility of doubt."[19]

He frequently defined the experience of holiness in terms of "full assurance."[20] On May 21, 1740, Charles said that "forgiveness and the witness of the Spirit are distinct gifts and generally given at different times."[21] If Charles Wesley associated the witness of the Spirit primarily to perfection, he learned this already from the ordinance of confirmation.

In fact, virtually every term and expression used by the Wesley brothers to define holiness as a subsequent moment to justification is contained in the Anglican interpretation of confirmation as seen in Taylor's writings. If Jeremy Taylor made sanctification the core meaning of confirmation, John Wesley also pointed out in a discussion on catechism that the inner meaning of confirmation was "sanctification," and not merely the ritual.[22]

Charles Wesley also referred to confirmation in his writings. It is not surprising that someone asked Charles about his view on the importance of it, considering that he often preached on the "Promise of the Father" and the "descent of the Holy Spirit as the Comforter" on the day of Pentecost. It is also not surprising that Charles' language for Christian perfection bore striking similarity to the language of his Anglican theology of confirmation.

What may be surprising is that the Wesley brothers largely ignored the rite of confirmation in favor of an evangelical, personal experience. That is why Charles said that none of the ordinances of the Church are meaningful "unless you are in Christ a new creature."

Even Jeremy Taylor recognized that the rite of confirmation did not in itself make the confirmand a complete, sanctified Christian believer, but it was the formal offer and beginning of the perfected life in Christ which was to be attained in "its due season."[23] This allowance of a due process of time corresponded with the Wesley brothers' view of both a personal crisis moment of sanctification and a lifelong process of continuing growth and development.

Taylor does not limit the appropriation of "perfection" to the imposition of hands in the rite of confirmation. He writes: "The grace of Christ is not tied to the sacraments," particularly mentioning the ordinance of confirmation.[24] The decisive thing is the "inward unction."[25]

If one substituted "full sanctification" in place of the term, confirmation, one would have almost thought that John Wesley wrote this essay. It also used so many of Charles Wesley's expressions for Christian perfection in his hymns. It is saturated with Pentecost language as descriptive of "perfective" and "sanctifying" grace.[26]

Taylor specifically described the inner meaning of confirmation as signifying: "perfection,"[27] "power from on high,"[28] "sanctification and power,"[29] "divine unction,"[30] "His holy comforts,"[31] "effusion of the Spirit,"[32] "descent of the Holy Spirit,"[33] "seal of the Spirit,"[34] "the gift of the Spirit,"[35] and he repeatedly used the phrase, "baptism of the Holy Spirit,"[36] to speak of the sanctification of believers subsequent to their baptism with water. Taylor makes it clear that "baptism with water is . . . something distinct from it [baptism of the Spirit]."[37] He wrote:

> St. John tells of another baptism which was Christ's peculiar; "He shall baptize you with the Holy Spirit and with fire"; that these words were literally verified upon the apostles in Pentecost . . . who besides the baptism of water distinctly had the baptism of the Spirit in confirmation.[38]

Taylor explained that "sanctification . . . is the proper effect of confirmation."[39] He further noted: "The effect is felt in all the sanctification and changes of the soul."[40] Its purpose was to make "perfect Christians,"[41] whereas those who have not received the baptism with the Spirit are but "babes in Christ"[42] He further wrote: "The apostles themselves (as the holy fathers observe) were timorous in the faith until they were confirmed in Pentecost, but after the reception of the Holy Spirit they waxed valiant in the faith and in all their spiritual combats."[43]

John and Charles Wesley likewise often spoke of "babes in Christ" as a designation of those not yet made "perfect" in love. John Wesley also noted that the weakness of the disciples' faith before Pentecost was "a plain proof that the sanctifying 'Spirit was not' then 'given'."[44]

Taylor said the Samaritans became Christians at their water baptism (Acts 8), but until they received the Spirit through the imposition of hands, they lacked "a τελείωσις something to make them perfect."[45] This perfection was defined as sanctification: "The baptism of water profits us, because it washes away the sins we have formerly committed, if we repent of them; but it does not sanctify the soul."[46]

He further writes: "Without the grace of baptism we shall die in our sins; and without the grace or internal part of confirmation we shall never be able to resist the devil, but shall be taken captive by him at his will."[47]

John Wesley in his *Explanatory Notes on the New Testament* also described the bestowal of the Spirit to the Samaritans as their moment of "sanctification."[48] And so did Charles Wesley.

Charles explained that the Samaritans had their "sins forgiven" through receiving the Word of God from Philip when they were baptized with water, but now through the laying on of hands by Peter in Acts 8:14-15, they were looking for a "farther grace . . . the Spirit of holiness, to seal" them. Using the same language as Taylor to describe confirmation, Charles said this gift of the Spirit to the Samaritans after their repentance and water baptism meant their "souls [were] confirmed," their "hearts by grace established," "rooted fast in love," "filled with the Holy Ghost," and were able to "live that sinless life above."

> 1. Who have the gospel truth believ'd,
> And mercy from the Lord receiv'd,
> And known our sins forgiven,
> We surely need a farther grace,

> We want the Spirit of holiness,
>   To seal us heirs of heaven.
>
> 2. Our souls confirm'd by solemn prayer,
>   Our hearts by grace establish'd are,
> And rooted fast in love;
>   And when the Giver we receive,
> Filled with the Holy Ghost we live
>   That sinless life above.[49]

It is not coincidental that Charles used the specific term, "confirmed," to describe this Samaritan event. His understanding of the imposition of hands (baptism with the Spirit) to denote the reception of holiness corresponded closely with his Anglican theology of confirmation as we will see in his sermon, "Awake, Thou that Sleepth."

Taylor spoke of the gift and reception of the Holy Spirit as a subsequent event in the life of the baptized person: "The necessity of confirmation, or receiving the Holy Spirit after baptism, is imitation of the divine precedent of our blessed Saviour."[50]

Yet Taylor emphasized that the Spirit is present in the life of the baptized person. He spoke of the "Spirit of regeneration in baptism, of renovation in repentance." The Spirit "begins in one [water baptism] and finishes and perfects in another [confirmation]."[51] This is also similar to John Wesley's emphasis that a believer receives the Holy Spirit at the moment of their justification and subsequently are filled with the Spirit in sanctifying grace.

Another emphasis in Taylor's essay is the "witness of the Spirit," that assures believers of their salvation. This assurance comes to those persons who are confirmed through the baptism of the Spirit, the Comforter, who descended on the day of Pentecost.

> By this Spirit we are then sealed; that whereas God hath laid up an inheritance for us in the kingdom of heaven, and in the faith of that we must live and labour, to confirm this faith God hath given us this pledge, the Spirit of God is a witness to us, and tells us by His holy comforts, by the peace of God and the quietness and refreshments of a good conscience, that God is our Father, that we are His sons and daughters, and shall be co-heirs with Jesus in his eternal kingdom. In baptism we are made the sons of God, but we receive the witness and testimony of it in confirmation.[52]

Here it can be seen that Taylor's focus on "the witness of the Spirit" is connected primarily with the sanctifying Spirit. As we will see below, John and Charles Wesley highlighted the "full assurance of faith" and the "seal of the Spirit" as having reference primarily to perfection.[53] If John Wesley's doctrine of the witness of the Spirit was influenced by the Moravian Pietists through Peter Böhler and Christian David, Anglican theology had already prepared the Wesleys to embrace it as seen in the writings of Jeremy Taylor.

Taylor also emphasized that confirmation was the moment when one received the seal of the promise of the Father when the Holy Spirit was sent as a "Comforter."

> This is ὁ Παράκλητος, the Holy Spirit the Comforter, this is He whom Christ promised

and did send in Pentecost, and was afterwards ministered and conveyed by prayer and imposition of hands: and by this Spirit He makes the confessors bold and the martyr valiant, and the tempted strong, and the virgins to persevere, and widows to sing His praises and His glories. And this is that excellency which the church of God called the Lord's seal, and teaches to be imprinted in confirmation.[54]

Taylor defined "the Spirit of comfort" to mean: "Now this Spirit of comfort is the hope and confidence, the certain expectation of partaking, in the inheritance of Jesus; this is the faith and patience of the saints. . . . The Spirit of God 'fills us with joy in believing'."[55] This Spirit of comfort is the result of the baptism of the Spirit who "enkindles charity and the love of God." This baptism of the Spirit means being "born of the Spirit" in contrast to repentance signified in being "born of water." This birth of the Spirit provides "the comforts" of "joy in believing," and possessing "joys unspeakable and full of glory."[56]

Taylor said to:

receive the Holy Spirit . . . gives us a taste of the powers of the world to come, that is, of the great efficacy that is in the article of eternal life, to persuade us to religion and holy living:—then we feel that as the belief of that article dwells upon our understanding, and is incorporated into our wills and choice, so we grow powerful to resist by the strengths of the Spirit, to defy all carnal pleasure, and to suppress and mortify it by the powers of this article: those are "the powers of the world to come."[57]

On May 15, 1740 Charles recorded in his journal: "I exhorted the Society to wait for the promise of the Father. Many cried out in the birthpangs."[58] "The promise of the Father" is used in Charles' hymns for Christian perfection, as we shall see below.

It will come perhaps as a surprise to some who have not carefully examined Charles' writing to learn that he equated the new birth with sanctification, although Charles Wesley scholars like Ernest Rattenbury and John Tyson have pointed this out many years ago. He learned this meaning of the new birth from his Anglican theology, reflected in the writings of Jeremy Taylor and William Law, as it will be shown in the next chapter.

We will also show that John Wesley linked the new birth with Christian perfection until 1760 when he reframed his understanding of the new birth as the moment of justifying faith.

Charles recorded in his journal: "The day of Pentecost, May 25 [1740]. Discoursed on the first pouring out of the Spirit, Acts 2. He gave me utterance. Many felt his descent in an invisible power; and even trembled at his presence. At the Common I again declared *the promise* [Acts 2:37-39] to many thousands."[59]

Charles preached on July 28, 1740, and "spoke searchingly on those words of our Lord: 'Nevertheless, I tell you the truth; it is expedient for you that I go away. For if I go not away, the Comforter will not come.'"[60]

Charles learned from his Anglican theology of confirmation that the coming of Holy Spirit as Comforter was linked to the perfection of the Christian life.

Here is an example in Charles' repertoire of 9,000 hymns, showing that the indwelling comforter bestows holiness and pure love and wholly sanctifies through being saturated in the baptismal flood of the Spirit:

> 5. Our Father, mov'd by Jesu's prayer,
>   Hath sent th' indwelling Comforter,

> The Spirit of holiness,
> > To cleanse in the baptismal flood [baptism of the Spirit],
> Renew our spirits after God,
> > And perfect us in grace.
>
> 6. Thy Spirit which wholly sanctifies,
> > Shall ascertain the heavenly prize,
> Before we hence remove,
> > Seal us the heirs of glorious bliss,
> And plunge in the divine abyss
> > Of pure eternal LOVE.[61]

Taylor believed that the baptism of the Spirit given on the day of Pentecost was repeatable for all subsequent generations: "Christ himself made the baptism of the Spirit to be necessary to the church. He declared the fruits of this baptism, and did particularly relate it to the descent of the Holy Spirit upon the church at and after that glorious Pentecost."[62]

He further writes: "The perpetuity of this holy rite appears, because this great gift of the Holy Spirit was promised to abide with the church forever."[63] Taylor recognized that the mere performance of the rite did not produce sanctifying grace in the life of the justified believer, unless it was met with personal faith.[64]

Likewise John Wesley spoke of the bestowal of the Spirit on the day of Pentecost as being offered to all subsequent generations.[65] And it is also expressed in Charles Wesley hymns. Here is one of many examples:

> Assembled here with one accord,
> > Calmly we wait the promis'd grace,
> The purchase of our dying Lord—
> > Come, Holy Ghost, and fill the place![66]

Taylor also emphasized that the permanent aspect of Pentecost was not the "extraordinary gifts" and manifestations of the Spirit, but rather he believed that the ordinary gifts of the "Holy Spirit remain with the church for ever; sanctification and power, fortitude and hope, faith and love."[67]

This is similar to John Wesley's emphasis in his Pentecost sermon on Acts 4:31, "They were all filled with the Holy Spirit" ("Scriptural Christianity") in which he identified being filled with the Spirit in terms of the fruit of the Spirit and the "fullness of love," not the "extraordinary gifts" of the Spirit.

Even if John and Charles Wesley did not read this comprehensive discourse by Taylor, it shows that the concept of perfection permeated the intellectual and theological background reflected in High Anglican liturgy. It will also be seen in Chapter 4 that the inner meaning of confirmation as defined by Jeremy Taylor corresponded to the meaning of Pentecost as explained in the Pentecost sermon of John Heylyn, which influenced John Wesley.

The idea of a sanctifying baptism with the Spirit as necessary for those who were already believers predated John Wesley.

Notes

1. *Letters III (1756–1765)*, 27:242.
2. Charles Wesley. *Short Hymns on Select Passages of the Holy Scriptures*. (Bristol: Farley, 1762), 1:325.
3. *Hymns and Sacred Poems* (Bristol: Farley, 1942), 159.
4. Jeremy Taylor, "A Discourse of Confirmation," *The Whole Works of the Right Reverend Jeremy Taylor* (London: Longman, 1849), 5:636, 633.
5. Ibid., 5:609-669.
6. Ibid., 5:612.
7. Ibid., 5:618-619.
8. Ibid., 5:619ff.
9. *Susanna Wesley, The Complete Writings,* ed. Charles Wallace Jr. (New York: OUP, 1997), 110-111.
10. Jeremy Taylor, *The Rule and Exercises of Holy Living* (Philadelphia: J. W. Bradley, 1860), 196.
11. Ibid., 110.
12. "A Sermon on 1 Corinthians 7:35," *The Arminian Magazine,* 7 (February 1784): 67.
13. *Journal of John Wesley,* ed. Nehemiah Curnock (New York: 1909), 1:438.
14. *Manuscript Journal,* 1:132-333.
15. John Wesley, "Preface," *Hymns and Sacred Poems* (1740), *Doctrinal and Controversial Treatises II*, eds. Paul Wesley Chilcote and Kenneth J. Collins, vol. 13 of *The Bicentennial Edition of the Works of John Wesley* (Nashville: Abingdon Press, 2013), 191.
16. *Discourse on Confirmation,* 5:624.
17. Ibid., 5:658.
18. Ibid., 5:659.
19. *Manuscript Journal,* 1:206.
20. *Manuscript Journal,* 1:279.
21. *Manuscript Journal,* 1:261. May 21, 1740.
22. *Works* (Jackson edition), 10:117, "A Roman Catechism, Faithfully Drawn Out of the Allowed Writings of the Church of Rome, With a Reply Thereto." John Wesley's objection was the extreme ceremonialism of the Roman Catholic Church, not the inner meaning of confirmation.
23. *Discourse on Confirmation,* 5:658.
24. Ibid., 5:654.
25. Ibid., 5:634, 652, 659, 660.
26. Ibid. 5:616, 642.
27. Ibid., 5:616, 642.
28. Ibid., 5:655.
29. Ibid., 5:636.
30. Ibid., 5:622, 652.
31. Ibid., 5:659.
32. Ibid., 5:635.
33. Ibid., 5:622.
34. Ibid., 5:638, 656, 658.
35. Ibid.
36. Ibid., 5:, 624, 633,
37. Ibid., 5:624.
38. Ibid., 5:624.
39. Ibid., 5:657.
40. Ibid. 5:660.
41. Ibid. 5:654.
42. Ibid., 5:616.
43. Ibid., 5:658.
44. Outler, *Sermons,* 2:454, "The Mystery of Iniquity"
45. *Discourse on Confirmation,* 5:629.
46. Ibid., 5:622.

47. Ibid., 5:628.
48. Wesley, *Explanatory Notes upon the New Testament* (London: The Epworth Press, 1958; originally published January 4, 1754), 471.
49. MS Acts, MARC: MA 1977/555 (Charles Wesley Notebooks Box 1), 148.
50. *Discourse on Confirmation*, 5:622.
51. Ibid., 5:615-616.
52. Ibid., 5:658-659.
53. Cf. Wesley, *Works* (Jackson edition), 11:423-424, 496, "A Plain Account of Christian Perfection."
54. *Discourse on Confirmation*, 5:658-659.
55. Ibid., 5:414.
56. Sermon I. Whitsunday, "Of the Spirit of Grace," *The Whole Works of The Right Reverend Jeremy Taylor* (London: C. and J. Rivington, 1828), 5:412ff.
57. Ibid., 5:412.
58. *Manuscript Journal*, 1:258.
59. *Manuscript Journal*, 1:261.
60. *Manuscript Journal*, 1:275
61. Charles Wesley. *Short Hymns on Select Passages of the Holy Scriptures* (Bristol: Farley, 1762), 2:342-343.
62. *Discourse on Confirmation*, 5:633.
63. Ibid.
64. Ibid., 5:634, 659, 660.
65. John Wesley, *Journal and Diaries,* ed. W. Reginald Ward and Richard Heitzenrater, vols. 18-24 in *The Bicentennial Edition of the Works of John Wesley* (Nashville: Abingdon Press, 2013), 18:241.
66. *Hymns and Sacred Poems* (Bristol: Farley, 1942), 165, "Hymn for the Day of Pentecost."
67. *Discourse on Confirmation*, 5:635-637.

Chapter 3

John and Charles Wesley's Time-Line for their Developing Theology of Pentecost and Sanctification

"Lord, if I on Thee believe,
   The Second Gift [i.e., Christian perfection] impart,
With th' Indwelling Spirit give
   A new, a loving Heart:
If with Love Thy Heart is stor'd,
   If now o'er me Thy Bowels move,
   Help me, Saviour, speak the Word,
And perfect me in Love."[1]
—Charles Wesley

"When my heart is circumcis'd
   Emptied of the hell within,
When my spirit is baptiz'd [with the Holy Spirit]
   Perfectly detach'd from sin,
Fervent then as those above
   Thee I shall entirely love."[2]
—Charles Wesley

"Rejoice, rejoice ye Fallen Race,
   The Day of Pentecost is come!
Expect the Sure-descending Grace,
   Open your Hearts to make him Room.

Assembled here with one Accord,
   Calmly we wait the Promis'd Grace,
The Purchase of our Dying Lord —
   Come, Holy Ghost, and fill the Place!

Wisdom and Strength to Thee belongs,
   Sweetly within our Bosoms move,
Now let us speak with Other Tongues
   The New, Strange Language of Thy [perfect] Love."[3]
—Charles Wesley

John Wesley read William Law's book, *A Practical Treatise upon Christian Perfection*, in December 1726 soon after it was published[4] when he was twenty three years old. His nineteen-year-old younger brother Charles followed his guidance in theology, and so he too read it. They literally consumed it, and it became their often-quoted textbook on holiness.

William Law, "A Parent" of Methodism

In 1728 William Law had recommended to those who were "desirous of perfection they should unite themselves into little societies" and engage in "voluntary poverty, virginity, retirement, and devotion, living upon bare necessities, that some might be relieved by their charities and all be blessed with their prayers, and benefited by their example."[5]

Religious societies were not a new thing to the Wesley brothers. There were numerous Anglican religious societies in the 18th century, and it is likely that Law's recommendation in 1728 incentivized Charles Wesley that very same year to start a society composed of three persons. They were soon labeled by a critic as "a new set of Methodists."[6]

After temporarily serving as his father's curate in Epworth, John returned to Oxford in 1729. He organized Charles' little group under his leadership with Charles' approval, for Charles willingly allowed his brother to assume the primary role of leadership. This little society quickly grow in size. George Whitefield had read William Law's *Treatise on Christian Perfection* and was deeply affected by it and he too joined the Holy Club in 1735 at the invitation of Charles Wesley in their pursuit of Christian perfection.[7]

William Law (1686-1761) lived in the Putney district in London in the home of Edward Gibbons where he consulted privately with those who were sincere in pursuing a holy life. John and Charles Wesley were among those who often consulted with him in his home when they were at Oxford.

William Law once expressed to John Wesley the transparency of their relationship together: "You sought my acquaintance, you came to me as you pleased, and on what occasion you pleased, and to say to me what you pleased." William Law also observed that he had functioned as "a sort of oracle to John Wesley."[8]

John Wesley acknowledged that William Law "convinced me more than ever of the absolute impossibility of being *half a Christian*; and I determined, through his grace (the absolute necessity of which I was deeply sensible of) to be *all-devoted* to God, to give him *all* my soul, my body, and my substance."[9] He came to understand "true religion [is] . . . God's dwelling and reigning in the soul." By religion, John Wesley meant the experience of holiness, that is, loving God with all one's heart, mind, and soul, and not a system of beliefs.[10]

John Wesley admitted in a qualified sense that William Law was a "parent" of Methodism.[11] This is a fair assessment considering that John Wesley derived the term and substance of Christian Perfection primarily from William Law.

Charles Wesley also acknowledged his indebtedness to Law in his diary of October 17, 1736: "While I was talking at Mr. Chicheley's on spiritual religion, his wife observed that I seemed to have much the same way of thinking with Mr. Law. Glad I was and surprised to hear that good man mentioned, and confessed, all I knew of religion was through him."[12] Again notice the term, religion, means holiness of heart (perfect love), and not a system of beliefs."[13]

John Wesley first visited William Law in July, 1732 at Putney.[14] They would have discussed Law's idea of perfection, which was incorporated into John Wesley's sermon delivered at St. Mary's Church (Oxford University) on January 1, 1733, entitled "The Circumcision of Heart."

This sermon was written five years before John Wesley's "heart-warming" Aldersgate experience. This sermon forever defined his understanding of Christian perfection. Even as late as September 1, 1778, John Wesley wrote in his journal that he could not write "a better [sermon] on *The Circumcision of Heart* than I did five and forty years ago."[15] In May 1765, John Wesley said to John Newton that this sermon "contains all that I now teach concerning salvation from *all sin*, and loving God with an *undivided heart* . . . This was then, as it is now, my idea of perfection."[16]

John Wesley's opening sentence in this sermon on "The Circumcision of Heart" referred to William Law,[17] and it employed his categories, including his definition of Christian perfection as (1) loving God with all one's heart, mind and soul and one's neighbor as oneself, (2) purity from all "inbred" "corruption,"[18] (3) being "born again of the Holy Spirit,"[19] (4) having the inner and abiding assurance of the Holy Spirit that one is a child of God,[20] and (5) the only source of happiness.[21] The inclusion of humility along with faith, hope, and love as characteristics of Christian perfection also reveals Law's influence.[22]

John Wesley wrote another sermon based on a frequent motto used by William Law. It was entitled, "The One Thing Needful" (1734). John Wesley said: "To be born again, to be formed anew after the likeness of our Creator" is to have "perfect soundness . . . and our uncleanness done away."[23]

William Law continued to serve as a mentor to the Wesley brothers between 1732 and 1735 until they decided to go to Georgia as missionaries.

The Wesley Brothers Seek to Be Holy by Becoming Georgia Missionaries

On October 14, 1735, the Wesley brothers sailed with General James Oglethorpe as missionaries to Georgia on board the *Simmonds*.[24] They hoped missionary activity would be the means of their own perfection. They had learned from Law there was no personal salvation unless one is involved in saving others.[25] This is why John Wesley said: "My chief motive [for going as a missionary to Georgia] . . . is the hope of saving my own soul. I hope to learn the true sense of the gospel of Christ by preaching it to the heathens."[26]

When Wesley talked about the need to save his own soul, he had not yet developed the understanding of a time-lapse between justifying faith and sanctifying grace. So when John Wesley talked about being "saved" as a motive for being a missionary, he was assuming that to be saved one is, according to Law's definition of Christian perfection, "saved by putting off this old man, and being renewed in holiness and purity of life."[27] This definition of being saved to mean entire sanctification is one that John Wesley later consistently used in his standard sermons[28] and Charles Wesley in his hymns.[29]

Aboard the *Simmons*, William Law's *Treatise on Christian Perfection* served as their textbook, which John and Charles frequently consulted and read to others on the ship.[30] This book emphasized that Christian perfection was achieved through a "resolution to attend only to the *one thing needful*."[31] Consequently the twenty-nine-year-old John Wesley followed William Law's instructions on board the ship for being wholly dedicated to

God through "fresh resolutions"[32] and "full resolutions of devoting himself wholly unto God."[33]

John Wesley's had much confidence in William Law's High Church liturgical doctrines and in his will-mysticism, that is, the idea that he could achieve Christian perfection through a disciplined act of the will, but this confidence was sorely tested in the midst of a life-threatening storm with water surging over the ship. John Wesley was terrified, but he noticed that a group of Moravian immigrants from Herrnhut, Germany on the way to Georgia were calm because they possessed a personal assurance of faith in God and were unafraid to die.[34]

The Wesley brothers arrived in Georgia on February 5, 1736, and two days later John Wesley talked with a Moravian missionary, Augustus Spangenberg, who confronted him with the need to experience personally an assurance of faith in Christ. John Wesley said that he had an opportunity from February 14, 1735, to December 2, 1737, to engage in many conversations with the Moravians two and three times a day. This contact with the Moravians eventually led John Wesley to realize that William Law could no longer serve as his mentor because of Law's lack of an understanding of a personal, evangelical faith.

When John Wesley was returning to England, he again experienced a life-threatening storm. John Wesley was terrified, but resolved that he would begin preaching the doctrine of saving faith to everyone on board the ship.[35] He said: "I was strongly convinced that . . . the gaining a true, living faith was the 'one thing needful' for me."[36]

Here Wesley equated the Moravian understanding of "a true, living faith" with William Law's language of Christian perfection, "the one thing needful." Law italicized this phrase nine times as a reference to Christian perfection in his *Practical Treatise on Christian Perfection*,[37] and John Wesley put it in quotation marks to indicate its specific meaning of Christian perfection.

John Wesley had earlier written a sermon in May, 1734 entitled, "One Thing Needful," which is defined in the same way as William Law defined it: "to love the Lord his God with all his heart," "the recovery of the image of God," "to be made perfectly whole," and "the most entire renovation of our nature."[38] In this sermon, John Wesley said "the one thing needful," is "perfection" and "to love the Lord his God with all his heart, and soul, and mind, and strength."[39] He preached this sermon in Georgia, and Charles also preached it in Boston[40] on September 26, 1736, and other occasions,[41] as it was his custom to preach his brother's sermons.[42]

Charles had earlier returned to England on December 3, 1736 before his brother. He was still in pursuit of the "One Thing Needful,"[43] and spoke to others about the need for "the new birth" (i.e., Christian perfection) and he read to others "Mr. Law's account of redemption."[44] On November 10, 1737, Charles "had much serious conversation with a gentlewoman in the coach concerning the new birth. I read part of Mr. Law. She was deeply struck, melted, conquered."

Another person whom Charles encouraged to seek perfection was Mrs. Delamotte on August 18, 1737. Charles said: "I went to see her. We fell into discourse upon resignation, and she seemed resolved to acquiesce in the will of God."[45] Subsequently she questioned Charles' preaching on the "new birth," but after hearing Charles preach on the "love of God," she burst into tears and "confessed there could be no happiness in anything else."[46]

Although Charles was preaching on Christian perfection and urging others to experience "resignation" and the "new birth" (i.e., Christian perfection)," he himself was unable to experience it.

He took his complaint to William Law on August 31, 1737: "I talked at large upon my state with Mr. Law at Putney. The sum of his advice was, 'Renounce yourself; and be not impatient'."[47] Still not satisfied with Law's advice, he went again several days later to talk with him on September 9, 1737. Charles received the discouraging news from Law that "nothing I can either speak or write will do you any good."[48]

Charles relied emotionally and spiritually upon his brother, and having missed him for more than a year, he was delighted to hear that his brother had returned home. On February 3, 1738, Charles wrote in his journal: "In the afternoon news was brought me at James Hutton's that my brother was come from America. I could not believe, till at night I saw him."[49]

John Wesley made it back to England from Georgia on February 1, 1738. If Charles had not yet attained Christian perfection, neither had his brother. So what had John Wesley learned about himself in the meantime? This will sound very unusual for a missionary to say: "I went to Georgia to convert the Indians, but Oh! who will convert me?"[50] Again, it is important to recognize that the word "convert" was not a reference to justifying faith as distinct from full sanctifying grace because this clear distinction was not yet made in John Wesley's thinking and because John Wesley believed that being a Christian was being a full Christian wholly devoted to God, not a half-Christian, which he said was "an impossibility."[51] John Wesley had already equated Law's idea of Christian perfection with the Moravian idea of a living faith, as Richard Heitzenrater has pointed out.[52]

John Wesley wrote in his journal for February 1, 1738 (on the day of his return to England from Georgia) he had "*a sort* of faith" equivalent to the faith of the disciples of the earthly Jesus who "had not then 'the [Pentecost] faith that overcometh the world'." He then described his quest for Christian perfection when he further explained: "The faith I want is, 'a sure trust and confidence in God,' . . . I want that faith which none can have without knowing that he hath it. . . . For whosoever hath it is 'freed from sin'; 'the whole body of sin is destroyed' in him [i.e., Christian perfection]. He is freed from fear. . . . And he is freed from doubt, 'having the love of God shed abroad in his heart through the Holy Spirit which is given unto him'."[53] Here John Wesley distinguished between "the faith of the disciples of the earthly Jesus" and the full assurance of faith that frees one from all sin "through the Holy Spirit which is given unto him" (Pentecost).

Later John Wesley changed his view about this assessment. In the first edition of his journal, he wrote: "I who went to America to convert others, was never myself converted to God." In the 1774 edition of his journal containing his later reflections, he inserted this parenthetical comment: "(I am not sure of this)."[54] He also changed his view of this early assessment, "I was, on Sunday, the 5th, clearly convinced of unbelief, of the want of that faith whereby alone we are saved." In the 1774 edition, he inserted in parenthesis, "(With the full Christian salvation),"[55] showing that he was expecting at that time to receive Christian perfection. In this early stage of his thinking, he believed one must have attained Christian perfection, or otherwise one was not a Christian. His later parenthetical remarks showed that he had come to see what he was lacking was Christian perfection, and hence he said he had at least the faith of a "servant,"[56] [i.e., justification] and what he was missing was "full Christian salvation."[57]

Another hint of how John Wesley was moving in this direction of a temporal distinction between justifying faith and full sanctifying grace at this time is seen in the first standard sermons, "Salvation by Faith," (preached at Oxford on June 11, 1738). This sermon was first preached just ten days before his Aldersgate conversion on May 14, 1738 at St Ann's Church, Aldersgate, and at Savoy Chapel. He distinguished between salvation by faith that frees believers "from all their sins: from original and actual," on the one hand, from the faith "which the Apostles themselves had while Christ was yet upon earth," on the other hand. John Fletcher would later cite this sermon as a source for his idea of Pentecost and sanctification (as will be discussed later).[58]

The Missing Ingredient in William Law—
The Full Assurance of Faith

A week after his return from Georgia, John Wesley met the Moravian Peter Böhler who had just arrived in England from Herrnhut for a brief stay on his way as missionary to South Carolina and Georgia. John Wesley noted in his diary: "God prepared [Peter Böhler] for me as soon as I came to London."[59] When Böhler told John Wesley that faith is "dominion over sin and constant peace from a sense of forgiveness," he "looked upon it as a new gospel."[60] What further astounded Wesley was the claim that the full assurance of faith could be received "instantaneously." When he turned his attention to the book of Acts, he said "to my utter astonishment, found scarce any instances there of other than instantaneous conversions" of individuals who were in an instant delivered "from sin and misery to righteousness and joy in the Holy Spirit."[61] When John Wesley spoke of "instantaneous conversions," it should be noted that he was talking about Christian perfection because he was seeking for "the full Christian salvation," as he later explained in 1774.

The Wesley brothers replaced the fifty two year-old William Law with the twenty six year-old Peter Böhler as their mentor. Law had not been able to help them to break through the faith-barrier. Interestingly enough, John Wesley introduced Böhler to William Law, but this interview was not productive in bringing the two men together in a common understanding of how salvation is attained.[62]

In a letter to William Law on May 14, 1738, John Wesley complained that "for two years . . . I have been preaching after the model of your two practical treatises" without any success. John Wesley admitted that the only faith that he personally had up to that point was a "speculative, notional, airy shadow, which lives in the head, not in the heart." Compared to the intellectual resolutions of will-mysticism of trying to be holy, John Wesley said to Law: "What is this to the living, justifying faith in the blood of Jesus? The faith that cleanseth from sin, that gives us to have free access to the Father, to rejoice in hope of the glory of God, to have the love of God shed abroad in our hearts by the Holy Spirit which dwelleth in us; and the Spirit itself bearing witness with our spirit, that we are the children of God?"[63]

This letter showed that John Wesley was disappointed that, while William Law had advised him on many occasions and had properly defined Christian perfection, he had failed to help him to know how to attain it as a personal experience.

It should not be thought that John or Charles Wesley simply disowned William Law despite their disappointment with his "few unguarded expressions" and his failure to help them understand the assurance of faith. Even after their conversions, they continued to reference his books over the years. Charles remarked in 1739 that William Law was "the truest guide to happiness with which God has blessed our age and nation."[64] They never abandoned his fundamental notion of the Christian life, and it was he, not the Moravians, who taught them the substance of Christian experience.

Having met Peter Böhler, this letter showed that John Wesley came to believe that "justifying faith" is the same as being "cleansed from sin" (i.e., Christian perfection), entailing freedom from fear and doubt, the full assurance of faith, and being cleansed from all sin in an instant moment of personal faith in contrast to Law's will-mysticism of a protracted, ritualistic, and self-defeating process of perfection.[65]

On the very same day that John Wesley had written to William Law (May 14, 1738), it was noted above that he preached a sermon on "Salvation by Faith" at St. Ann's Church on Aldersgate Street.[66] This was ten days before his Aldersgate experience. This sermon showed that John Wesley linked Law's idea of Christian perfection with the Moravian concept of justification by faith, defining "justification" to mean "salvation from sin" and it frees believers "from all their sins: from original and actual." This sermon, "Salvation by Faith," became the first sermon in his standard sermons. It also equated being "born again of the Spirit" with Christian perfection and being cleansed from all sin so that the believer "desireth the holy and perfect will of God" and does not have "any tendency to an unholy desire."[67]

Charles Wesley had also learned from William Law that Christian perfection constitutes the new birth.[68] On November 30, 1737, Charles said: "Had much serious conversation with a gentlewoman in the coach concerning the new birth. I read part of Mr. Law. She was deeply struck, melted, conquered."[69] Although John Wesley would later nuance the new birth in his mature years to mean justifying faith as distinct from entire sanctification, Charles Wesley always retained the equation of new birth with entire sanctification, as he had learned it from William Law. As an example of this equation, Charles wrote:

> Blessed are the Pure in Heart,
>   Those who never disobey,
> Never from their Lord depart,
>   Never leave his Perfect Way:
> From All Sin *Entirely* freed
>   Here they walk with GOD above,
> Born again, and Saints indeed,
>   Fully perfected in Love.[70]

The evangelical conversions of Charles and John Wesley were initially assumed by them to be their moment of Christian perfection. The immediate self-interpretation of

John Wesley's own personal Aldersgate experience of faith was in terms that he described for the meaning of Christian perfection.[71]

The self-understanding of Charles Wesley's moment of justifying faith as also entailing Christian perfection is confirmed in that he preached his brother's sermon, "Salvation by Faith" on September 3, 1738, which identified justification with entire sanctification.[72] It is also confirmed by the fact that when Charles defined his own evangelical conversion he defined it as the coming of the Holy Spirit to take up his abode in his heart to allow him to experience "the hope of [perfect] love," as will be seen in the next chapter. As John Tyson has also shown, Charles Wesley's "Hymns for Whitsunday" interpreted the Pentecost sending of the Spirit as functionally synonymous with Christian perfection.[73] So when Charles and John Wesley were taught by Peter Böhler that justification is the full assurance of faith, it was only natural that both brothers would filter their idea of Christian perfection through the notion of an instantaneous faith.

Notes

1. John and Charles Wesley, *Hymns and Sacred Poems* (Bristol: Farley, 1742), 220, "A Prayer for Holiness," v. 7.
2. MS Festivals: MARC: DDCW 6/71, 54.
3. *Hymns and Sacred Poems* (Bristol: Farley, 1942), 165, "Hymn for the Day of Pentecost."
4. *The Journal of the Rev. John Wesley*, ed. Nehemiah Curnock (New York: Eaton and Mains, 1909), 1:467n2.
5. William Law, *A Serious Call to a Devout and Holy Life* (Suffolk: Richard Clay and Sons, 1906), 96, 98.
6. Thomas Jackson, *The Life of the Rev. Charles Wesley* (New York: G. Lane & Sandford, 1842), 31.
7. Thomas Jackson, *Memoirs of Charles Wesley* (London: John Mason, 1848), 14.
8. Alexander Whyte, *Characters and Characteristics of William Law, Nonjuror and Mystic* (London: Hodder and Stoughton, 1893), xxvi.
9. John Wesley, "Preface," *Hymns and Sacred Poems* (1740), *Doctrinal and Controversial Treatises II*, eds. Paul Wesley Chilcote and Kenneth J. Collins, *The Bicentennial Edition of the Works of John Wesley* (Nashville: Abingdon Press, 2013), 13:137.
10. Ibid.
11. John Wesley, *Sermons III*, ed. Albert C. Outler, in *The Bicentennial Edition of the Works of John Wesley* (Nashville: Abingdon Press, 1976-), 3:504, "On God's Vineyard."
12. *The Manuscript Journal of the Reverend Charles Wesley, M.A.*, ed. S. T. Kimbrough, Jr and Kenneth G. C. Newport (Nashville: Kingswood Books, 2008) 1:57-58..
13. The Wesley brothers were always consistent in their definition of true religion as holiness of heart and life. In his sermon "On Charity" (1784), John Wesley said that love is "the whole of true religion." "true religion, in the very essence of it, is nothing short of *holy tempers*" which is "gentle, patient love" and "'the one thing needful' (i.e., Christian perfection)." Outler, *Sermons III*, 3:293, 306.
14. "Review of *The English Church in the Nineteen Century (1800–1833)* by John H. Overton, Longmans, 1894," in *The London Quarterly and Holborn Review*, 82 (April, July,, 1894). 352. (Published in London: C. H. Kelly, 1894).
15. *Journals and Diaries VI (1735–38)*, ed. W. Reginald Ward and Richard Heitzenrater, 23:105, September 1, 1778.
16. John Wesley, *Letters III (1756–1765)*. ed. Ted A. Campbell, of *The Bicentennial Edition of the Works of John Wesley* (Nashville: Abingdon Press, 2015), 27:428, "To John Newton, May 14, 1765). Cited hereafter as *Letters III (1756–1765)*.
17. Cf. William Law, *A Serious Call to a Devout and Holy Life* (Suffolk: Richard Clay and Sons, 1906), 98; Outler, *Sermons*, 1:401, "The Circumcision of Heart."
18. William Law, *A Practical Treatise upon Christian Perfection* (London: William and John Innys, 1726), 250; cf. Wesley, "Unless his heart is circumcised . . . of that inbred 'corruption of his nature'." Outler, *Sermons*, 1:409. "The Circumcision of Heart."
19. William Law, *A Serious Call to a Devout and Holy Life*, 112. Outler, *Sermons*, 1:406, "The Circumcision of Heart". Wesley equated "born of God" with Christian perfection.

20. John Wesley said "'circumcision of heart' implies... the testimony of their own spirit with the Spirit which witnesses in their hearts, that they are the children of God." Outler, *Sermons*, 1:406. Similarly Law wrote regarding the definition of Christian perfection and assurance: "But when the temper and taste of our soul is entirely changed, when we are renewed in the spirit of our minds, and are full of a relish and desire of all godliness, of a fear and abhorrence of all evil, then, as St. *John* speaks, *may we know that we are of the truth, and shall assure our hearts before him, then shall we know, that he abideth in us by the Spirit, which he hath given us.*" *A Practical Treatise upon Christian Perfection*, 51, 534.

21. The language of being "happy in God" in early Methodism as a euphemism for Christian perfection can be traced back to William Law's numerous references linking holiness and happiness. Law. *A Practical Treatise upon Christian Perfection*, 11.

22. Outler, *Sermons*, 1:403, "The Circumcision of Heart"

23. Outler, *Sermons*, 4:355, "One Thing Needful"

24. *Journal and Dairies I (1735–1739)*, 18:137, (Tuesday, October, 14, 1735).

25. Law, *A Practical Treatise upon Christian Perfection*, 467-468.

26. *Letters I (1721-1739)*, ed. Frank Baker (Oxford: Clarendon Press, 1980), 25:439, Oct 10, 1735.

27. Law, *Treatise upon Christian Perfection* (1726), 219.

28. "By salvation I mean, not barely... deliverance from hell, or going to heaven, but a present deliverance from sin, a restoration of the soul to its primitive health, its original purity; a recovery of the divine nature; the renewal of our souls after the image of God in righteousness and true holiness, in justice, mercy, and truth. This implies all holy and heavenly tempers, and by consequence all holiness of conversation. Cragg, *Appeal* 9:106, "A Farther Appeal to Men of Reason and Religion, Part I."

29. "Saved from sin, and doubt, and fear, In full confidence divine." Charles Wesley. *Short Hymns on Select Passages of the Holy Scriptures* (Bristol: Farley, 1762), 2:364. Cited hereafter as *Scripture Hymns* (1762).

30. *Journals and Diaries, I (1735–1738, The Bicentennial Edition of the Works of John Wesley*:18:317, (October 30-31 1785).

31. Law, *Practical Treatise on Christian Perfection*, 82.

32. Ibid., 454. Law emphasized that "loving God with all their heart, and with all their soul, and with all their strength, and with all their mind" was achieved through a "resolution to attend only to the one thing needful." Ibid., 82.

33. *A Serious Call to a Devout and Holy Life*, 150. Cf. Geordan Hammond, "Restoring Primitive Christianity: John Wesley and Georgia, 1735-1737," (PhD thesis, Manchester University, 2008), 71-72.

34. *Journals and Diaries I (1735–1738), The Bicentennial Edition of the Works of John Wesley*, 18:143, (Sunday Jan 25, 1735).

35. Ibid., 18:210, (Jan 13, 1738).

36. Ibid., 18:247.

37. William Law, *Practical Treatise upon Christian Perfection*, 82.

38. William Law, *Practical Treatise upon Christian Perfection*, 82.

39. Outler, *Sermons*, "One Thing Needful," 4:355-359.

40. See *Manuscript Journal* for Sept. 26, 1736. Outler, *Sermons*, "Introduction to the Sermon," 4:351.

41. *Manuscript Journal*, 1:88.

42. *The Sermons of Charles Wesley: A Critical Edition with Introduction and Notes*, ed. Kenneth G. C. Newport (OUP Oxford. 2001), 78-81.

43. *Manuscript Journal*, 1:88, 93.

44. *Manuscript Journal* 1:87, 89.

45. *Manuscript Journal*, 1:86.

46. *Manuscript Journal*, 1:94.

47. *Manuscript Journal*, 1:87.

48. *Manuscript Journal*, 1:87.

49. *Manuscript Journal*, 1:96.

50. *Journal and Diaries I (1735–1738), The Bicentennial Edition of the Works of John Wesley*, 18:214, (January 29, 1738).

51. "A Plain Account of Christian Perfection," *Doctrinal and Controversial Treatises II*, ed. Paul Wesley Chilcote and Keeneth J. Collins, in *The Works of John Wesley* (Nashville: Abingdon, 2011), 13:137.

52. Richard Heitzenrater, *Mirror and Memory* (Nashville: Kingswood Books, 1989), 106-149.

53. *Journals and Diaries I (1735–38)*, ed. W. Reginald Ward and Richard Heitzenrater, *Works of John Wesley*, 18:215–216, February 1, 1738.

54. *Journal and Diaries, I (1735–1738)*, 18:214, Feb. 1, 1738.

55. *Journal and Diaries I (1735–1738)*, 18:228. Cf. Henry Moore, *The Life of John Wesley* (New York: Bangs & Emory, 1826), 1:202.

56. *Journals and Diaries I (1735–38)*, 18:215, Feb. 1, 1738.

57. Cf. Henry Moore, *The Life of John Wesley* (New York: Bangs & Emory, 1826), 1:202.

58. E. H. Sugden, *Wesley's Standard Sermons* (London: The Epworth Press, 1921), 1:35–36). See *The Equal Check, Works of the Rev. John Fletcher*, ed. Joseph Benson (London: Conference Office, 1815), 4:259, "Essay on Truth." See also Wesley's special abridged edition of Fletcher's *Essay on Truth* in *The First Part of an Equal Check* (Bristol: W. Pine, 1774), 168.

59. *Journal and Diaries I (1735–1738)*, 18:247.

60. Ibid. 18:248.

61. Ibid., 18:234.

62. Thomas Jackson, *Memoirs of Charles Wesley* (London: John Mason, 1848), 55

63. John Wesley, *Letters I*, 25:540–542, To the Revd. William Law, May 14, 1738.

64. *The Letters of Charles Wesley, A Critical Edition, with Introduction and Notes, Volume I, 1728–1756*, ed. Kenneth G. C. Newport and Gareth Lloyd (Oxford: University Press, 2013). Cited hereafter as *Letters of Charles Wesley*.

65. William Law urged the pursuit of holiness in his concluding chapter: "I exhort the reader to labour after this Christian perfection." He writes: "Here therefore I place my first argument for *Christian perfection*. I exhort thee to labour after it, because there is no choice of anything else for thee to labour after, there is nothing else that the reason of man can exhort thee to." *A Practical Treatise upon Christian Perfection*, 512.

66. E. H. Sugden, *Wesley's Standard Sermons*, 1:36.

67. Outler, *Sermons*, 1:121–124, "Salvation by Faith"

68. Law, *A Practical Treatise on Christian Perfection*. 67.

69. *Manuscript Journal*, 1:95.

70. MS Psalms, MARC: MA 1977/553 (Charles Wesley Notebooks Box 1), 139.

71. *Journals and Diaries I (1735–38)*, *The Bicentennial Edition of the Works of John Wesley*, 18:253, (May 29, 1738).

72. *The Manuscript Journal of the Reverend Charles Wesley, M.A.*, ed. S. T. Kimbrough, Jr and Kenneth G. C. Newport (Nashville: Kingswood Books, 2008), 1:146.

73. John Tyson, *Charles Wesley on Sanctification* (Grand Rapids: Zondervan, 1986), 195.

Chapter 4

John Heylyn's Pentecost Sermon and Charles Wesley's Pentecost Conversion

> "Conscious of the indwelling God,
> We feel thy love diffus'd abroad,
> Thy perfect love reveal'd;
> Come is our day of Pentecost,
> And Father, Son, and Holy Ghost
> His spotless Church hath filled."[1]
> —Charles Wesley

The Holy Spirit was an integral part of John Wesley's theology. Expressions such as, "all holiness," "entire sanctification," "the seal of the Spirit," and "the earnest of the Spirit," were common expressions that he used to describe Christian perfection. As we have seen, his particular use of the phrases "the earnest of his Spirit" and "seal of the Spirit" are found in the Anglican theology of confirmation.

Richard Heitzenrater has pointed out that John Wesley's sermons had an even stronger focus on the Holy Spirit after his Aldersgate experience.[2] Charles Wesley scholar, John Tyson, has shown that Charles Wesley virtually linked Christian perfection with the language of the Holy Spirit.[3] Tyson showed that "the single most important contribution that the Wesleyan hymns made to pneumatology was the hymnal entitled, *Hymns of Petition and Thanksgiving for the Promise of the Father*, which the brothers published jointly in 1746."[4]

Tyson pointed out this collection of hymns on Pentecost had "the chief purpose of describing the coming of the Holy Spirit ('the Promise of the Father') as an event that binds both Father and Son in covenantal promise with those who receive Christ." This triune relationship with humanity was made possible by Pentecost and it means being "filled with God," or Christian perfection. These Pentecost hymns "do not merely recount the story of Pentecost, they re-create the event in the lives of contemporary Christians. The singers of these hymns pray for their own Pentecost,"[5] as Tyson showed.

John Wesley did not derive his emphasis on the Holy Spirit simply from Peter Böhler, but it came from two other sources—a High Anglican source and a German Moravian source. The High Anglican source showed that the substance of their doctrine of holiness was Anglican and that their understanding of it preceded their evangelical conversions. The Moravian source inspired them to understand how holiness could be attained in an instant moment through the full assurance of faith after justification, and this understanding was developed after their evangelical conversions.

We will first consider the High Anglican source showing the connection between Pentecost and sanctification.

John Wesley Heard John Heylyn's Pentecost Sermon on the Same Day As Charles Wesley's Personal Pentecost

Three days before his Aldersgate experience, John Wesley with some friends visited Charles Wesley on Pentecost Sunday, May 21, 1738 who was lying in a sick-bed in the home of a Moravian friend. They "sang a hymn to the Holy Spirit" to Charles.

It is not known which hymn this might have been, but a few weeks later Charles mentioned "a Hymn to the Holy Spirit" in his journal for July 11, 1738 that was already being used even though it had not yet been published.[6] The words of this hymn referred to the Holy Spirit as "Comforter" and being "born of God." Charles (and John) had already learned from William Law to use "born of God" as a reference to Christian perfection. The words of this hymn reflected their pursuit of holiness, or Christian perfection, "the seal," "more than pardon," and "all the plenitude of God."

1. Hear, Holy Spirit, hear,
    My inward Comforter!
Loos'd by thee my stamm'ring tongue
    First essays to praise thee now,
This the new, the joyful song,
    Hear it in thy temple thou!

3. Thee I exult to feel,
    Thou in my heart dost dwell:
There thou bear'st thy witness true,
    Shedd'st the love of God abroad;
I in Christ a creature new,
    I, ev'n I am born of God!

8. Thou art thyself the seal;
    I more than pardon feel,
Peace, unutterable peace,
    Joy that ages ne'er can move,
Faith's assurance, hope's increase,
    All the confidence of love!

9. Pledge of thy promise given,
    My antepast of heaven;
Earnest thou of joys divine,
    Joys divine on me bestowed,
Heaven and Christ, and all is mine,
    All the plenitude of God.

Immediately after singing to Charles, John Wesley left the house and went to hear John Heylyn preach.

John Heylyn was a High Church Anglican, the first rector of St. Mary-le-Strand (1724–59) who became prebendary of Westminster Abbey and was buried in Westminster Abbey (1743–59). He was a much-admired minister and theologian[7] whose writings had already exercised a strong influence on John Wesley when he was in Georgia.[8] John Wesley used Heylyn's devotional writings extensively while he was in Georgia, and he later included them in his recommendations to his preachers. He was also later to use Heylyn's *Theological Lectures* as a source of his *Explanatory Notes upon the New Testament* (1755).[9]

As John Wesley was listening to this Pentecost sermon on that eventful day, Heylyn highlighted what Pentecost meant personally. He noted that "to enlighten, to purify, and to warm, are the properties of fire. Now if we transfer these to the spiritual world, the light of the soul is truth, the purity of the soul is holiness, the warmth or heat of the soul is an active, vigorous ardour to surmount obstacles."[10]

He showed that the Holy Spirit is called "holy" because He is "the hallowing, i. e. sanctifying Spirit."[11] He further explained: "When it is said that the Holy Spirit sanctifies Christians, the meaning is, that he infuses this generous motive, extinguishing the narrow principles of covetousness, pride, and sensuality, and exalting our nature to the noble disinterested purpose of glorifying our Maker."[12]

Heylyn then said that a Christian believer is sanctified through the "baptism with the Spirit," "purging away . . . carnal desires," producing "perfect Purity."

John Fletcher[13] and Thomas Coke,[14] who became John Wesley's right hand assistant and bishop of American Methodism, cited extensively from this sermon as an explanation of the Methodist idea of Pentecost and holiness. Heylyn said:

> To *wash, cleanse, baptize, and sanctify,* are commonly synonymous in Scripture hence the phrase of being baptized with the Holy Spirit, which is elsewhere called being baptized with fire, to signify the universal and intimate purification of the inmost springs of action thereby. With this view the Prophet Malachi [Mal iii.3] compares the Spirit to refiner of gold or silver destroying the dross, and separating all heterogeneous particles from those metals by force of fire, till they are reduced to perfect purity. Thus the Spirit sanctifies the soul by abolishing all sordid inclinations, by purging away the multiplicity of carnal desires, and reducing all the powers of the mind to one simple constant pursuit, viz. that of God's glory. This renders the soul holy, i. e. pure, all of kind, concentered in the end of its creation, even the glory of its Maker.[15]

If there is any doubt that John Wesley was right when he said the Methodist doctrine of holiness was "the religion of the Church of England,"[16] the above definition of Pentecost as the basis of sanctification ought to be convincing. [Heylyn's Pentecost sermon is included in the appendix as an exhibit to show that the distinction between a justified person on the one hand, and a person who is yet to be sanctified from all carnality through the sanctifying baptism with the Spirit is an Anglican doctrine and preceded the writings and preaching of John and Charles Wesley].

In this sermon based on Acts 2:2-3, John Wesley heard Heylyn distinguish between pre-Pentecost and Pentecost believers. Heylyn showed how the sanctifying baptism of the Spirit equipped the disciples with power after Pentecost, transforming them from weak to strong believers in Christ.

This description is similar to the way that John Wesley would later explain the weakness of the disciples prior to Pentecost as being "a plain proof that the sanctifying 'Spirit was not' then 'given,' because 'Jesus was not glorified'."[17]

Heylyn said "to show how the Apostles were thus sanctified" would require him "to relate their history, which is but one continued narrative of their holiness. They were purified from all corrupt principles of action.... They rejoiced that they were accounted worthy to die.... Such was the holiness of the Apostles, was the purity of their hearts, the unity of their desires all meeting in one point, the glory of their Maker."[18]

At the conclusion of the sermon, Heylyn (who already knew John Wesley) asked him to assist in Holy Communion because the curate was ill.

After hearing this sermon, John Wesley recorded in his journal that Heylyn "preach[ed] a truly Christian sermon on 'They were all filled with the Holy Spirit'—and so, said he, may *all you* be."[19] This sermon made quite an impression on John Wesley because he often made a similar comment when he preached on this same text on multiple occasions. (I mentioned this so the reader will be looking for it when we come to those future instances).

Heylyn's sermon on the call to receive the sanctifying baptism with the Spirit could not be more direct. Here is what Heylyn's published sermon on Pentecost said: "The same Holy Spirit, which then descended upon the apostles, does still descend upon all the living members of Christ, according to his gracious promise."[20]

He then offered these instructions on how Christian believers today can be filled with the Spirit:

> It remains only that I add a word or two concerning the disposition by which we must prepare our hearts to receive him [the Holy Spirit]: and this, as our Lord teaches us, is earnest and persevering prayer. We have his direction, *Luke xi. Ask, and it shall be given you; seek, and ye shall find; knock, and it shall be opened unto you.— If a Son shall ask Bread of any of you that is Father, will he give him Stone? how much more shall your heavenly Father give his holy Spirit to them that ask him?* The terms you see are very easy, are highly reasonable: if we do not perform them we shall be without excuse. But if by humble, fervent, incessant prayer we seek from our heavenly Father the Gift of his Spirit, we shall infallibly receive it, we shall be enlightened, purified, and confirmed in all goodness, we shall advance from strength to strength, till we *become meet to be partakers of the inheritance of the saints in light.*[21]

Heylyn's sermon on Pentecost contains virtually everything that John Wesley and Charles Wesley had explained about the connection between Pentecost and sanctification, including the idea that the baptism with the Spirit will sanctify and cleanse one who is already a Christian believer from all impurity if one prays and will receive "the gift of his Spirit."

The main difference is that this Anglican idea of Pentecost and sanctification[22] was nuanced by John Wesley to occur suddenly in a moment of faith—a nuance that he obtained from the Moravians.

Heylyn directed his hearers "to be baptized with the Holy Spirit" through earnest prayer as the disciples were on the day of Pentecost. He said that a Christian believer is sanctified through the "baptism with the Spirit," "purging away ... carnal desires," producing "perfect purity."²³ As noted by John Wesley in his journal, Heylyn encouraged believers today to be filled with the Holy Spirit. He showed that Pentecost was not merely a single past event that marked a new stage in the history of revelation, but it marked the beginning of the very possibility of a personal Pentecost for all subsequent believers. Heylyn said believers only need to do today what the disciples did on the day of Pentecost—wait in prayer.

Charles Wesley's Personal Pentecost

At the same time John Wesley was listening to Heylyn's Pentecost sermon, the bed-ridden Charles Wesley received his own personal Pentecost at the house of a Moravian layman, Mr. Bray.

Charles Wesley had already learned from William Law that Christian perfection was "to "make us like himself, to fill us with his *Spirit*"²⁴ and that the only way we can practice the perfect love of God was through being "full of the Spirit of Christ."²⁵ So when he heard the Moravians talking about an instantaneous moment of justifying faith, it was understandable that the High Churchman Charles Wesley would link the Moravian idea of faith's sudden attainment to his Anglican theology of Christian perfection.

It was not as if Charles Wesley had never repented of his sins previously, which he had done daily as an Anglican priest. What he lacked and what he was searching for was the *full assurance* of his sins forgiven and his "pardon sealed" (i.e., Christian perfection).

His equation of justification by faith and Christian perfection was indicated in Charles' journal for May 14, 1738. He wrote: "Who would believe our Church had been founded on this important article of justification by faith alone? I am astonished I should ever think this a new doctrine; especially while our Articles and Homilies stand unrepealed, and the key of knowledge is not yet taken away." He goes on to explain that "from this time I endeavoured to ground as many of our friends as came in this fundamental truth, salvation by faith alone, not an idle, dead faith, but a faith which works by love, and is necessarily productive of all good works and all holiness."²⁶ Notice the equation of "salvation by faith" with "all holiness."

With the Anglican theology of Pentecost as the basis of sanctification as seen in Heylyn's Pentecost sermon and in the Anglican rite of confirmation as well as in Law's *Practical Treatise on Christian Perfection*, it was understandable why Charles described his expectation of saving faith (from all sin) in reference to Jesus' promise of the Holy Spirit as Comforter:

> At nine my brother and some friends came, and sang an hymn to the Holy Spirit. My comfort and hope were hereby increased. In about half an hour they went: I betook myself to prayer; the substance as follows: "O Jesus, Thou hast said, 'I will come unto you'; Thou hast said, 'I will send the Comforter unto you'; Thou hast said, 'My Father and I will come unto you, and make our abode with you'. Thou art God who canst not lie; I wholly rely upon Thy most true promise: accomplish it in Thy time and manner."²⁷

Immediately after this private prayer, he heard a woman in the house speak, "Arise, and believe." When he heard her words, he said: "I felt a strange . . . palpitation of heart. I said . . . 'I believe, I believe'."²⁸

He described this experience to mean: "I now found myself at peace with God, and rejoiced in hope of loving Christ."[29]

J. Ernest Rattenbury said that May 21, 1738 was Charles' day of justification with only a "hope of loving Christ" perfectly at some point in the future. Rattenbury observed that when Charles spoke of "love" he almost always meant "perfect love,"[30] However, it appears that by "hope" Charles was not merely speaking of the future, but rather he now "rejoiced in hope of loving Christ." So it was not merely a hope to be actualized in the future. In one of his ascension hymns, Charles spoke of the assurance of hope ("In assurance of hope").[31] He also spoke about "holy purifying hope... perfect me in love divine."[32] Likewise John Wesley linked "hope" with "full assurance."[33] So it would appear that Charles really thought he was made perfect in love at this time.

Within weeks after his Pentecost conversion, Charles preached his brother's sermon, "'Salvation by Faith' to a deeply attentive audience" on July 2, 1738. As we already noted, this sermon equated being born of God, justification, and Christian perfection, showing they had not yet developed their understanding of the chronological sequence and theological distinction between justifying and sanctifying faith.

Charles then recorded an event in his journal of a woman who that very evening (July 2, 1738) had an experience similar to his own. She "received the Spirit" and as they "sung the hymn to Christ," she was "full of peace, joy, and love." He wrote:

> In the evening we met, a troop of us, at Mr. Syms's. There was one Mrs. Harper there, who had this day in like manner received the Spirit by the hearing of faith, but feared to confess it. We sung the hymn to Christ. At the words, "Who for me, for me hath died," she burst out into tears and outcries, "I believe, I believe!" and sunk down. She continued, and increased in the assurance of faith; full of peace, and joy, and love.[34]

Here is the "Hymn to Christ" they sang expressing their spiritual status of being "born" of God" and being possessed fully by God:

> O filial deity,
>   Accept my new-born cry!
> See the travail of thy soul,
>   Saviour, and be satisfy'd;
> Take me now, possess me whole,
>   Who for me, for me hast dy'ed![35]

His brother John was still at Herrnhut at this time, and as it will be shown in the next chapter it was not until John's return that they worked out the chronological sequence between justification and sanctification by faith.

It cannot be emphasized too much that the tendency for us today is to interpret the conversion experiences of Charles and John in the light of their later theology. This is a mistake because neither Charles nor John had explicitly worked out a distinction between justification and sanctification at this stage of their thinking. Their search was for Christian perfection, believing that sanctification preceded justification. That is, if they truly loved God with all their heart, then on that basis they would be justified in the eyes of God.

If Charles had earlier learned to pursue Christian perfection (defined as the "new birth") through the writings of and in personal consultations with William Law, we have seen that he had learned from the Moravians that a personal decision of faith is the means of salvation. He had learned from his brother's sermon, "Salvation by Faith," to equate justification with Christian perfection. So there is no indication that Charles understood a clear distinction between justification by faith and sanctification by faith at this time.

That Charles believed he had attained Christian perfection at the moment of his Pentecost-conversion is contained in a conversation that he had with Mrs. Delamotte, whom he had earlier encouraged to receive Christian perfection on August 18, 1737.

Charles explained to Mrs. Delamotte (June 11, 1740): "Three years ago God sent me to call you from the form to the power of godliness. I told you what true religion was, a new birth, a participation of the divine nature." Charles then acknowledged that "the way to this I did not know myself till a year after" which was the time when he met the Moravian Peter Böhler leading to his Pentecost conversion. Charles continued: "Then I showed it to you, preaching Jesus Christ, and faith in his blood . . . . God soon after called you to a living faith by my ministry."[36] In this conversation, Charles equated the new birth, Christian perfection, and a living faith, which he recounted as his own experience of faith on this Whitsunday, May 21, 1738.

Whatever Charles may have thought of his Whitsunday experience at that time, it is clear that he later did not believe he had attained Christian perfection, at least not in a continuing sense. In a hymn written on his birthday (1740 or 1741), he wrote:

> The tyranny of sin is past,
>   And tho' the carnal mind remains,
> My guiltless soul on thee is cast,
>   I neither hug, nor bite my chains,
> Prisoner of hope to thee I turn,
>   And bless the day that I was born.[37]

Rattenbury was probably right to say that Charles' Pentecost-conversion was not an attainment of Christian perfection, if we read back into it the implications of his later reflections, although his intimate friend John Fletcher assumed it was Charles's moment of Christian perfection, as it can been seen in his personal correspondence with Charles.

Rattenbury is also right that if Charles did not experience Christian perfection, his "experience of God did not involve for Charles what he meant by the new birth." Charles believed, said Rattenbury:

> He was adopted into God's family, and in that sense was a child of God, but his carnal mind needed a reconstruction for which he yearned and sought to the end of his life. He did, in a metaphorical sense, employ the term "born of God" at least once to describe the entirely new life into which he entered at his conversion, but almost invariably he uses the term "new birth" for an experience [of Christian perfection] which is to be sought in the future.[38]

Charles' hymns reflected this equation of born of God with Christian perfection, as can be seen multiple times in this work.

Notes

1. MS Acts, MARC: MA 1977/555 (Charles Wesley Notebooks Box 1), 293-294.
2. Heitzenrater, *Mirror and Memory*, 108-109. Cf. Colin W. Williams, *John Wesley's Theology Today, A Study of the Wesleyan Tradition in the Light of Current Theological Dialogue* (Nashville: Abingdon Press, 1960). 102-104.
3. John Tyson, *Charles Wesley on Sanctification: A Biographical and Theological Study* (Grand Rapids, Zondervan, 1986), 195.
4. John Tyson, *Charles Wesley on Sanctification: A Biographical and Theological Study* (Grand Rapids, Zondervan, 1986), 193.
5. Tyson, *Charles Wesley on Sanctification*, 193-194.
6. John and Charles Wesley. *Hymns and Sacred Poems* (London: Strahan, 1739), 111. Cf. *Manuscript Journal*, 1:135 where Charles recorded the use of this hymn as early as July 11, 1738.
7. Jackson, *Memoirs of Charles Wesley*, 64; *Journal of Charles Wesley*, ed. Thomas Jackson (London: John Mason, 1849), 1:146.
8. *Journals and Diaries I (1735-38), The Bicentennial Edition of the Works of John Wesley*, 18:241n15.
9. Ibid., 18:241n15.
10. John Heylyn, "Discourse XV. On Whitsunday," *Theological Lectures at Westminster-Abbey* (London: Printed for J. and R. Tonson and S. Draper in the Strand, 1749), 114.
11. Ibid., 116.
12. Ibid., 118.
13. Fletcher, John Fletcher, "The Doctrine of the New Birth, as it is stated in these sheets, is directly or indirectly maintained by the most spiritual divines, especially in their sacred poems." *The Asbury Theological Journal*. 50.1 (Spring, 1998): 56; cited hereafter as *New Birth*.
14. Thomas Coke, *A Commentary on the New Testament* (London: G. Whitfield, 1803), 2:942-957. Coke actually quoted the entire sermon of John Heylyn without acknowledging his source.
15. Heylyn, *Theological Lectures*, 118.
16. Outler, *Sermons*, 3:585, "On Laying the Foundation of the New Chapel"
17. Outler, *Sermons*, 2:454, "The Mystery of Iniquity"
18. Ibid. 119-120.
19. Ibid., 18:241, (May 19, 1738). Italics are Wesley's.
20. Ibid., 112.
21. Ibid., 121.
22. Cf. *Meaning of Pentecost in Early Methodism*, 341-345.
23. John Heylyn, "Discourse XV. On Whitsunday," *Theological Lectures at Westminster-Abbey* (London: Printed for J. and R. Tonson and S. Draper in the Strand, 1749), 119-120.
24. Law, A *Practical Treatise on Christian Perfection* (1726), 463.
25. Ibid., 520.
26. *Manuscript Journal* 1:104.
27. *The Early Journal of Charles Wesley*, ed. John Telford (London: Charles H. Kelly, 1909), 146.
28. Ibid.,146-147.
29. Ibid., 149.
30. J. Ernest Rattenbury, *The Evangelical Doctrines of Charles Wesley's Hymns* London: Epworth Press, 1941), 280-281.
31. Charles Wesley, *Hymns for Ascension Day* (Bristol: Farley 1746), 7.
32. Charles Wesley, *Hymns and Sacred Poems* (Bristol: Farley, 1749), 1:167.
33. Outler, *Sermons*, 1:423, "The Marks of the New Birth
34. *Manuscript Journal* 1:130-131.
35. *Hymns and Sacred Poems*, 110.
36. *Manuscript Journal*, 1:265-266.
37. *Hymns and Sacred Poems* (1742), 123.
38. Rattenbury, 260.

Chapter 5

John Wesley's Aldersgate Experience and the Influence of Christian David

"My brother coming, we joined in intercession for him. In the midst of prayers, I almost believed the Holy Spirit was coming upon him."
—Charles Wesley

John Wesley, as he was leaving the church after hearing Heylyn preach, was told "the surprising news, that my brother had found rest to his soul."[1]

The very next day, on May 22, 1738, Charles believed that his brother John was about to have his personal Pentecost. Charles said: "My brother coming, we joined in intercession for him. In the midst of prayer, I almost believed the Holy Spirit was coming upon him."[2]

John Wesley's Aldersgate Experience

Three days after Charles' Pentecost, John Wesley on May 24, 1738 "felt his heart strangely warmed" and believed in Christ. Here is how he described what happened in his moment of faith as he listened to someone reading from the preface to Martin Luther's commentary on the book of Romans, while seated in a Moravian society meeting: "I have *constant peace*;—not one uneasy thought. And I have *freedom from sin*;—not one unholy desire [i.e., Christian perfection]."[3] When he was tempted to doubt, he felt reassured that he had a "true heart in full assurance of faith."[4] By "full assurance," John Wesley meant a faith that excludes all fear and doubt and a heart filled with perfect love.

On this very day, Charles recorded in his journal that "towards ten my brother was brought in triumph by a troop of our friends and declared, 'I believe.' We sang the hymn with great joy and parted with prayer."[5] [See front cover portrait by Richard Douglas].

Charles did not explicitly identify "the hymn" that he and his brother sang together with their friends, but earlier in the same day he recited part of a hymn, and this hymn was published the following year entitled "A Hymn for Whitsunday."[6] This may or may not be the same hymn. It showed how focused Charles Wesley was on Pentecost as the basis for Christian perfection. The specific verse that Charles recited in his journal were the words: "Now descend and shake the earth, Wake us into second birth [i.e., Christian perfection]."

1. Granted is the Saviour's prayer,
    Sent the gracious Comforter;
Promise of our parting Lord,
    Jesus to his heav'n restor'd:

2. Christ; who now gone up on high,
    Captive leads captivity,
While his foes from him receive
    Grace, that God with man may live.

3. God, the everlasting God,
    Makes with mortals his abode,
Whom the heavens cannot contain,
    He vouchsafes to dwell in man.

4. Never will he thence depart,
    Inmate of an humble heart;
Carrying on his work within,
    Striving till he cast out sin.

5. There he helps our feeble moans,
    Deepens our imperfect groans;
Intercedes in silence there,
    Sighs th' unutterable prayer.

6. Come, divine and peaceful guest,
    Enter our devoted breast;
Holy Ghost, our hearts inspire,
    Kindle there the gospel-fire.

7. Crown the agonizing strife,
    Principle, and Lord of life;
Life divine in us renew,
    Thou the gift and giver too!

8. Now descend and shake the earth,
    Wake us into second birth [i.e., Christian perfection];
Now thy quick'ning influence give,
    Blow—and these dry bones shall live![7]

This hymn suggested that the Wesley brothers believed that they had received Christian perfection. However, John Wesley's hope in having received entire sanctification was short-lived because two days later he experienced again the old feelings of doubt and fear.

Charles was also struggling to maintain his Pentecost faith at this same time. On May 25, 1738, he felt "a little cast down by feeling some temptation" but was delivered from "fear."⁸ On May 27, 1738, he "felt a motion of anger from a trifling disappointment," but overcame it.⁹ He consulted with Mrs. Bray about his inner conflict who reassured him with her testimony that she too after receiving "faith" struggled to maintain her joy until she finally had victory over doubt and was preserved "in all the triumph of faith."¹⁰ Charles continued to experience "inward trials, but at the same time I experience the superior power of Christ."¹¹

On June 7, 1738, Charles again found reassurance of his faith after reading Matthew 7:1: "Ask, and ye shall receive." He wrote: "I asked some sense of his life in the Sacrament. It was there given me to believe assuredly that God loved me, even when I could have no sense of it."¹² He then recorded in his journal: "Returning home in triumph I found Dr. Byrom and, in defiance of the tempter, simply told him the great things Jesus had done for me and many others. This drew on a full explanation of the doctrine of faith, which he received with wonderful readiness. Toward midnight I slept in peace."¹³

Significantly enough thereafter, Charles recorded few inner struggles, but preached with confidence the faith that he had received on May 21. Not until John came back from Herrnhut did Charles imply that he was "justified but not sanctified," as expressed in *Hymns and Sacred Poems* (1739).¹⁴ We also know from Charles' hymns, journal, and letters to his wife that he said multiple times he had not yet attained.

John Wesley Learned from Christian David to Distinguish between the Pre-Pentecost and Pentecost Experience of the Disciples as a Paradigm for the Distinction between Justification and Sanctification

On June 14, 1738, Charles Wesley (who took his cues from his brother) learned that "my brother was gone with Mr. Ingham and [Johann] Toltschig to Herrnhut. The news surprised, but did not disquiet me." Herrnhut, Saxony, was the Moravian settlement and headquarters that had been established by Count Zinzendorf.¹⁵

John Wesley said the reason why he went for a visit to Herrnhut on June 13, 1738 was hoping that "those holy men . . . would be a means, under God, of so establishing my soul."¹⁶ Having been so disappointed by the short-lived results of faith that he had experienced on Aldersgate Street in a Moravian society meeting, he wanted further instructions on how he could personally be free from inward sin, doubt, and fear, since he felt his Aldersgate experience did not succeed in providing that kind of spiritual freedom.

As we have already seen, William Law taught John Wesley the meaning of Christian perfection, and Peter Böhler had taught him to expect an instantaneous moment of the full assurance of faith. It was now another Moravian who would teach him to see more clearly that sanctifying grace is subsequent in time to justifying faith.

On August 3, 1738, John Wesley met a lay preacher at Herrnhut by the name of Christian David. Throughout the following week, John Wesley said he heard him preach multiple times on the exact issues that he was trying to resolve in his own mind about holiness.¹⁷ John Wesley also held extended private conversations with him.¹⁸

John Wesley recorded a comprehensive report in his journal on the teachings of

Christian David. Christian David explained that the real-time distinction between justifying faith and being cleansed from all sin (full sanctifying grace) is patterned after the disciples' pre-Pentecost and Pentecost experiences.

Christian David said the full assurance of faith comes through "the indwelling of the Spirit." He said the pre-Pentecost disciples of Jesus lacked this full assurance, although they were justified and forgiven before Pentecost. Because of the descent of the Holy Spirit on the day of Pentecost, Christian David said one can, like the disciples, be cleansed from all sin.[19]

The disciples' experience is thus cited as a pattern for all subsequent believers. John Wesley recorded his explanation. "The state the apostles were in from our Lord's death (and indeed for some time before) till the descent of the Holy Spirit at the day of Pentecost" included a degree of faith. Christian David compared "being justified" with the experience of the disciples of the earthly Jesus prior to Pentecost, whereas the coming of the Spirit at Pentecost meant they were "fully assured" and "cleansed from all sin."[20]

He heard Christian David explain the varying degrees of assurance. It was consoling to Wesley to hear him say that those "weak in the faith" may still be believers with some measure of assurance, even though they may not have full assurance. John particularly liked Christian David's threefold distinction among (1) those in bondage, (2) those in an intermediate state of faith, and (3) those with the fullness of faith. John gave a full report of this explanation in his diary:

> Thrice he described the state of those who are "weak in faith", who are justified, but have not yet a new, clean heart; who have received forgiveness through the blood of Christ, but have not received the indwelling of the Holy Spirit. This state he explained once ... when he showed at large from various Scriptures that many are children of God and heirs of the promises long before their hearts are softened by holy *mourning*, before they are *comforted* by the abiding witness of the Spirit ... before they are "pure in heart" from all self and sin. ...
>
> A second time he pointed out this state from those words, "Who shall deliver me from the body of this death? I thank God, Jesus Christ our Lord." "There is therefore now no condemnation to them which are in Christ Jesus." Hence also he at large both proved the existence and showed the nature of that intermediate state which most experience between that bondage which is described in the seventh chapter of the Epistle to the Romans, and the full glorious liberty of the children of God described in the eighth and in many other parts of Scripture.
>
> This he yet again explained from the Scriptures which describe the state the apostles were in from our Lord's death (and indeed for some time before) till the descent of the Holy Spirit at the day of Pentecost. They were then "clean," as Christ himself had borne them witness, "by the word which he had spoken unto them". They then *had faith*. ... Yet they were not properly *converted*; and they were not *delivered from* the spirit of fear; they had not *new hearts*; neither had they received "the gift of the Holy Spirit".[21]

In reporting this conversation between John Wesley and Christian David in his biography, Henry Moore (John Wesley's clerical assistant) took the editorial liberty to qualify the remark of Christian David that though the disciples "had faith" before Pentecost, they had not "[fully] received 'the gift of the Holy Ghost.'" This qualification comes with the insertion of the word "fully" in brackets, indicating there is a difference between receiving the Spirit in justifying faith and fully receiving the Spirit in Christian perfection.[22] As we shall see in Chapters 10 and 13, this distinction between receiving the Spirit in some measure and fully receiving the Spirit was to be emphasized by John Wesley in 1760 and further clarified with Joseph Benson and John Fletcher in 1770. Moore's editorial explanation "[fully]" is a retroactive anticipation of this later clarification by John Wesley.

In a private conversation, Christian David explained to John Wesley that he himself once struggled with feelings of assurance concerning his own salvation, but finally through increasing degrees of assurance he came to experience "the full assurance of faith, or the destruction of the body of sin, and the extinction of all its motions."[23] John Wesley recorded Christian David's testimony about his struggle moving from fear to faith:

> Neither saw I then that the "being justified" is widely different from the having the "full assurance of faith". I remembered not that our Lord told his apostles before his death, "ye are clean"; whereas it was not till many days after it that they were fully assured, by the Holy Spirit then received, of their reconciliation to God through his blood.[24]

Christian David said this full assurance of faith comes through "the indwelling of the Spirit." He said the pre-Pentecost disciples of Jesus lacked this full assurance, although they were justified and forgiven before Pentecost. Because of the descent of the Holy Spirit on the day of Pentecost, one can, like the disciples, be cleansed from all sin.[25] The disciples' experience is thus cited as a pattern for all subsequent believers.

What is noteworthy is the statement: "The state the apostles were in from our Lord's death (and indeed for some time before) till the descent of the Holy Spirit at the day of Pentecost" included a degree of faith. Christian David compared "being justified" with the experience of the disciples of the earthly Jesus prior to Pentecost, whereas the coming of the Spirit at Pentecost meant they were "fully assured" and "cleansed from all sin."[26]

Arvid Gradin was another person at Herrnhut who affirmed John Wesley in his understanding of the full assurance of faith. John Wesley said: "In August, I had a long conversation with Arvid Gravid." He asked Gradin "to give me, in writing a definition of 'the full assurance of faith,' which he did in the following words. . . . 'Repose in the blood of Christ; a firm confidence in God, and persuasion of his favour; the highest tranquility, serenity, and peace of mind, with a deliverance from *every fleshly desire*, and a *cessation of all sin, even inward sins*'."

John Wesley noted about this definition: "This was the first account I ever heard from any living man, of what I had before learned myself from the oracles of God, and had been praying for (with the little company of my friends) and expecting for several years."[27]

This equation between "full assurance of faith" and "a cessation of all sin, even inward sins" corresponded to the Wesley brothers' idea of Christian perfection. This is why they had earlier linked Peter Böhler's idea of justifying faith which was defined as the full assurance of faith with Christian perfection. But now after discussing this subject with the senior members of the Herrnhut community, John had come to recognize a real-time distinction between justifying faith and sanctifying grace and that there were degrees of faith, based on the pattern of the disciples' pre-Pentecost and Pentecost stages of justifying and sanctifying faith.

He also recognized that there was a conflicting view among the Moravians on this subject.[28]

In the Meantime, Charles . . .

In the meantime, Charles was preaching in England while his brother John was getting further instruction about the stages of faith in Herrnhut.

On May 28, 1738, Charles began to compose his first sermon after his conversion, entitled "The Three-Fold State," which he preached on July 16, 1738.[29] These three states were not the same as the stages of faith that his brother was learning in his conversations with Christian David. Charles preached this sermon multiple times in 1738 and 1739.[30]

Charles' sermon distinguished between "the two opposite states of nature and grace, into the former of which our first birth introduced us, into the latter, our second birth in Christ Jesus." The first birth is the "natural" state of "mere sin and death." The second state is someone who has "ineffectual stirrings and endeavours towards the divine life" but is still under the "dominion of sin" that "cannot qualify a man for pardon, or put him into a state of grace and salvation." The third state consists of one who "is born of the Spirit and of God, and doth not commit sin because his seed remaineth in him."[31] The one in the second state is in pursuit of "the One Thing Needful, even a participation of the divine nature, the life of God in the soul of man." Yet, he may be "reproved of sin, but not rescued from it" until he is "justified by faith."[32]

Here Charles has only one state of faith—those who have been "made partakers of the divine nature . . . and all holiness"[33] and has attained Christian perfection—unlike what his brother was learning at Herrnhut about several stages of faith.

This sermon equated justification by faith with Christian perfection. He also equated Christian perfection with the promise of the Spirit of Pentecost as "the legacy of your Lord." He said: "You and I and every baptized person may claim as his heritage forever" this promise: "'I will pray the Father, and he shall give you another Comforter, that he may abide with you forever. I will not leave you comfortless, I will come unto you'."[34] This promise of the Holy Spirit as comforter "belongs only to them that believe with a living, saving, justifying faith, which you [the Second State] have not as yet."[35]

This promise of the Spirit as the Comforter was the language that Charles used to describe his Pentecost-conversion, thus further suggesting that Charles considered his Pentecost-conversion as his moment of Christian perfection.

Another phrase that Charles had used in his description of his Pentecost-conversion was "the hope of loving Christ." Here in his first written post-Pentecost sermon he described one who is born of God (Third State) as one who "finds that he hath laid hold of the hope set before him." He described this hope as not a mere future expectation, but describes the present actuality of the believer who has already laid hold of the hope.[36]

This sermon also used the imagery of the Israelites crossing the Jordan River as illustrative of those who have entered the promised land of rest of Christian perfection,[37] a theme which would appear in the subsequent writings of both John and Charles, where Canaan Land was a symbol of perfect love.

On June 22, 1738, Charles "read my brother's sermon [Salvation by Faith]. God set his seal to the truth of it, by sending his Spirit upon Mr. Searle and a maidservant, purifying their hearts by faith."[38]

When Charles reported in his journal that God had sent the Holy Spirit upon both Mr. Searle and a maidservant, purifying their hearts by faith, he believed that they were made perfect in love.

We can determine what Charles meant about "sending his Spirit" from his hymns where Charles consistently interpreted the sending of the Spirit to mean the bestowal of perfect love instead of justification. In 1763, in his lyrical theological reflection on John 14:20, "At that day ye shall know, that I am in my Father, and you in me, and I in you," Charles Wesley showed that the promise of the Spirit on the day of Pentecost was for the full sanctification of the disciples:

> Conscious of the indwelling God,
>   We feel thy love diffus'd abroad,
> Thy perfect love reveal'd;
>   Come is our day of Pentecost,
> And Father, Son, and Holy Ghost
>   His spotless Church hath filled.[39]

While John was still in Herrnhut, Charles recorded on June 26, 1738 that Mrs. Delamotte "accused my brother with preaching an instantaneous faith." Charles replied: "'We cannot but speak the things which we have seen and heard.' I received it in that manner, as have above thirty others in my presence." Here Charles is referring to his experience of faith on Pentecost Sunday, May 21, 1738, showing that he believed himself to be entirely sanctified.

Charles continued to preach his brother's sermons while John was still in Herrnhut. On September 3, 1738, Charles "preached Salvation by Faith at Westminster Abbey."[40] Not only did Charles preach his brother's sermons, he also accepted his brother's views on the nature of faith. We shall see in the next chapter that Charles began to make a theological as well as a real-time distinction between justifying and sanctifying faith after John's return from Herrnhut.

If John Wesley had heard from Christian David to make a real-time distinction between justifying and sanctifying faith, John and Charles already knew from their Anglican theology that Pentecost was the basis of Christian perfection. What they apparently had not yet come to see clearly was the real-time distinction between justification and sanctification, even though it was implicit in their Anglican theology of confirmation and in the Pentecost sermons of High Anglicans like John Heylyn.

During the interlude following Charles Wesley's evangelical conversion and before his brother's return from Germany, his preaching continued to equate justification by faith with Christian perfection. His journal shows that he engaged in preaching his newfound faith, sharing it with others and recording multiple accounts of others who had come to faith through his preaching.

He often preached his brother's sermon, "Salvation by Faith." As noted already, this sermon showed that he conflated justification by faith with Christian perfection under the influence of the English Moravians.

Charles Wesley's view of the "plan of salvation" would soon change as a result of his brother's visit to Herrnhut when he would come to see salvation occurred in two stages. Charles respected his brother's primary role of leadership, and Charles' theology was largely shaped by John and together they developed the holiness message that would forever shape Methodism. His mother, Susanna, acknowledged John's primary role and would later encourage Charles "to join hand and heart with your brother in vindicating the glory and honour of our ever blessed Redeemer! Proclaim his universal love and free grace to all men."[41]

John's visit to Herrnhut was the turning point in their theology. John Wesley wrote to Charles from Germany on June 28, 1738, informing him that the German Moravians made a distinction between justifying faith and the full or absolute sense of faith. He also told Charles that the Moravians identified being "born of God," not with justifying faith, but with faith in the full and absolute sense which is "often distant in time" from justifying faith.[42]

Although it was implicit in his Anglican theology, this letter to Charles Wesley appears to be the first time that John Wesley became aware of an explicit distinction between the two stages of faith that was soon to become the prominent focus of his theology.

He later wrote another letter to Charles Wesley from Herrnhut on August 4, 1738. This was the day after John's conversations with Christian David concerning the distinction between justifying faith and the full assurance of faith that cleanses one from all sin. John promised Charles in this letter: "An account of the people here you must not expect till we come face to face, when I hope we shall part no more." He signed his letter as "Your most affectionate friend and brother."

We noted in the previous chapter that Charles was "surprised" about his brother leaving England for Herrnhut "but did not disquiet me." The bond between the two brothers was emotionally deep and Charles' reliance upon his brother was strong. Charles shared his brother's views on almost every topic during these early days of the revival.

On September 16, 1738, John Wesley returned to England from Herrnhut. He met with Charles on that same evening. Now that he had come "face to face" with Charles he was able to give him a first-hand report of what he had learned from the leaders of the Herrnhut community. Charles recorded in his journal: "At night my brother returned from Herrnhut. We took sweet counsel together, comparing our experiences."[43]

The next day they continued their conversation as "my brother entertained us at night with the Moravian experiences." Here is when John gave a full explanation of all that he had learned from the German Moravians.

His "Moravian experiences" forever changed their understanding of the order of salvation. From that day forward, their writings embraced a theology that emphasized a chronological distinction between justifying faith and sanctifying grace. Although this distinction was inspired by John's conversations with the German Moravians, it did not exactly correspond with Moravian theology because the Wesley brothers filtered it through their Anglican theological heritage in terms of Christian perfection.

The Wesley brothers specifically distinguished between justifying faith and a subsequent experience of Christian perfection, using the pattern of the disciples' experience before and after Pentecost as the basis of the distinction between justification and sanctification. Although "the Moravian experiences" were the precipitating cause of this new understanding that Christian perfection "was distant in time" (as John Wesley put it) from justification, it was also not an unnatural extension of their own Anglican theology of Pentecost.

On October 14, 1738, a month after John's "Moravian experiences" at Herrnhut, he carefully nuanced the distinction between justification and Christian perfection autobiographically. In his journal for October 14, 1738,[44] he said that he himself was not fully sanctified, but he acknowledged that he had "a measure of faith" and was justified (i.e., "accepted in the Beloved"). He wrote:

> Yet, upon the whole, although I have not yet that joy in the Holy Spirit, nor that love of God shed abroad in my heart, nor the full assurance of faith, nor the (proper) witness of the Spirit with my spirit that I am a child of God, much less am I, in the full and proper sense of the words, in Christ a new creature; I nevertheless trust that I have a measure of faith am "accepted in the Beloved."[45]

Two Weeks later on October 30, 1738, in a letter to his older brother Samuel, John Wesley explained that Christian perfection is to be delivered from all fear and doubt, freed from all sin, and to receive the seal of the Spirit, the indwelling Spirit, and the fullness of faith.

He explained in careful and precise details to his older brother Samuel that he was justified and sins no longer "reigned over me" as a result of his Aldersgate faith-experience but he did not yet "feel" God's "'love shed abroad in their hearts by the Holy Spirit which is given unto them'."[46] And hence he said that he was only a "Christian in that imperfect sense" because he did not have "the indwelling of the Spirit."[47] Here is a portion of that letter:

> By a Christian I mean one who so believes in Christ as that sin hath no more dominion over him. And in this obvious sense of the word I was not a Christian till May the 24 last past. For till then sin had the dominion over me, although I fought with it continually; but since then, from that time to this, it hath not. Such is the free grace of God in Christ. What sins they were which till then reigned over me, and from which by the grace of God I am now free, I am ready to declare on the house-top, if it may be for the glory of God.
>
> If you ask by what means I am made free (though not perfect, neither infallibly sure of my perseverance,) I answer, by faith in Christ; by such a sort or degree of faith as I had not till that day....
>
> Some measure of this faith, which bringeth salvation, or victory over sin, and which implies peace and trust in God through Christ, I now enjoy by his free mercy, though in very deed it is in me but as a grain of mustard-seed: for the πληροφορία της πίστεως "the seal of the Spirit," "the love of God shed abroad in my heart," and producing joy in the Holy Spirit, "joy which no man taketh away," "joy unspeakable and full of glory"—this witness of the Spirit I have not, but I patiently wait for it. I know many who have already received it, more than one or two in the very hour we were praying for it. And having seen and spoken with a cloud of witnesses abroad, as well as in my own country, I cannot doubt but that believers who wait and pray for it will find these scriptures fulfilled in themselves. My hope is that they will be fulfilled in me. I build on Christ, the Rock of Ages, on his sure mercies, described in his Word, and on his promises, all which I know are yea and amen. Those who have not yet received joy in the Holy Spirit, the love of God, and the *plerophory*

of faith, (any or all of which I take to be the witness of the Spirit with our spirit that we are the sons of God,) I believe to be Christians in that imperfect sense wherein I may call myself such; and I exhort them to pray that God would give them also "to rejoice in hope of the glory of God," and to feel his "love shed abroad in their hearts by the Holy Spirit which is given unto them."[48]

Inspired by what John Wesley learned from Christian David, John Wesley explained his own experience to his older brother according to the two stages of faith based on the pattern of the "justifying faith" of the disciples before Pentecost and subsequently the disciples being "cleansed from all sin" as a result of the outpouring of the Spirit on them on the day of Pentecost, granting to them a full and abiding assurance of faith.

If John Wesley felt compelled to give his older brother Samuel a full report of his views based on reports that were streaming back to him about possible fanaticism, Charles also felt compelled seven months later to answer his brother Samuel's concerns about his possible extreme views. In a letter dated May 1, 1739, he noted that John had spoken with "explicitness" about his views to Samuel, but Samuel was unhappy with his response because it lacked sufficient clarity. What particularly was concerning to Samuel was Charles' doctrine of assurance. Charles assured Samuel that his view of assurance was exactly the same as his.

Charles then explained that he believed that there was a possibility for one to have "the full assurance of faith." He said to his brother Samuel: "That there is such a thing as the πληροφορία της πίστεως [I] must allow for I find it in scripture: but that a man cannot be a Christian without it I as absolutely [deny as] you do. I have it not myself, yet I humbly hope that [in the] lowest sense of the word, I am a true Christian. [This then] is my belief, & my doctrine of assurance, how w[idely] distant from what is has been [mis]represented to you!"[49]

Here it is clear that Charles had downsized his interpretation of what had happened to him on his conversion day of May 21, 1738, just as his brother had also explained in his letter to their older brother Samuel. And as we shall see, though Charles did not profess to have the full assurance of faith, he preached it and believed others had received Christian perfection.

NOTES

1. *Journals and Diaries I (1735–38), The Bicentennial Edition of the Works of John Wesley*, 18:253, (May 29, 1738).
2. *Manuscript Journal*, 1:109
3. *Journals and Diaries I (1735–38), The Bicentennial Edition of the Works of John Wesley*, 18:253, (May 29, 1738).
4. Ibid.
5. *Manuscript Journal* 1:111.
6. *Hymns and Sacred Poems (1739)*, 213.
7. *Hymns and Sacred Poems (1739)*, 213-214.
8. *Manuscript Journal* 1:111.
9. *Manuscript Journal* 1:112.
10. *Manuscript Journal* 1:113.
11. *Manuscript Journal* 1:113.
12. *Manuscript Journal* 1:114.
13. *Manuscript Journal* 1:116.
14. *Hymns and Sacred Poems (1739)*, 150.
15. *Manuscript Journal* 1:122.

16. *Journals and Diaries I (1735–38)*, Bicentennial Edition of the Works of John Wesley, 18:254, (June 7 - June 13, 1738).
17. Wesley, August 8, 1738, *Journals and Diaries I (1735–38)*, in *Works of John Wesley* 18:270.
18. Ibid., 18:270, (August 8, 1738).
19. Christian David equated "full assurance" and being "cleansed from all sin." Cf. Ibid, 18:272, (August 10, 1738).
20. The Moravians did not all agree about being "cleansed from all sin." Christian David affirmed this doctrine, but John learned three years after his Aldersgate experience that Peter Böhler rejected it, as he told John Wesley on May 16, 1741. *Journals and Diaries II (1735–38)*, in *The Bicentennial Works of John Wesley*, 19:195.
21. Ibid., 18:270-271 (August 8, 1738).
22. Henry Moore, *The Life of John Wesley* (New York: N. Bangs and J. Emory, 1826), 1:229.
23. *Journals and Diaries I (1735–38)*, 18:274, (August 10, 1738).
24. *Journals and Diaries I (1735–38)*, 18:274, (August 10, 1738).
25. Christian David equated "full assurance" and being "cleansed from all sin." Cf. Ibid, 18:272, (August 10, 1738).
26. Cf. *Journals and Diaries II (1735–38)*, in *Works*, 19:195.
27. *Doctrinal and Controversial Treatises II*, ed. Paul Wesley Chilcote and Kenneth J. Collins, 13:140-141.
28. John Wesley, *A Library of Protestant Thought*, ed. Albert Outler (New York: Oxford University Press, 1964), 372.
29. *Manuscript Journal* 1:112, 137. Cf. *The Sermons of Charles Wesley: A Critical Edition with Introduction and Notes*, ed. Kenneth G. C. Newport (OUP Oxford. 2001),
30. Cf. editor's notations on 131-132.
31. *Sermons of Charles Wesley*, 134.
32. *Sermons of Charles Wesley*, 139-140.
33. *Sermons of Charles Wesley*, 151.
34. *Sermons of Charles Wesley*, 147.
35. *Sermons of Charles Wesley*, 147.
36. *Sermons of Charles Wesley*, 147.
37. *Sermons of Charles Wesley*, 143.
38. *Manuscript Journal*, 1:123.
39. Based on John 14:20. MS John, MARC: MA 1977/573 (Charles Wesley Notebooks Box 3), 293-294.
40. *Manuscript Journal* 1:146.
41. *Susanna Wesley, The Complete Writings*, 190.
42. *Letters I (1721-1739)*, ed. Frank Baker (Oxford: Clarendon Press, 1980), 25:554, June 28, 1738.
43. *Manuscript Journal* 1:147, September 16, 1738.
44. *Journal and Diaries II*, in *The Bicentennial Works of John Wesley*, 19:19, (October 14, 1738).
45. *Journal and Diaries II*, in *The Bicentennial Works of John Wesley*, 19:19, (October 14, 1738).
46. *Letters I (1721-1739)*, 25:575-578, A letter to Samuel Wesley, October 30, 1738.
47. Ibid.
48. *Letters I (1721-1739)*, 25:575-578, A letter to Samuel Wesley, October 30, 1738.
49. *The Letters of Charles Wesley*, 73-74.

Chapter 6

"Holiness *after* Justification"

"Strongly insisted on the necessity of holiness *after* justification."[1]
—Charles Wesley speaking of George Whitefield"s preaching

"Parker frankly told her he did not understand what we meant by talking of holiness after forgiveness—that he has all he can have, and looks for no more."
—Charles Wesley

"The reason why I did not come sooner to Christ was my seeking to be sanctified before I was justified."
—Charles Wesley to William Law

"Exhorted them to get forgiveness *before* they could perform the best part of the law [i.e., Christian perfection]."
—Charles Wesley

The first time sanctifying grace was defined by the Wesleys in an explicit manner as subsequent in time to the moment of justifying faith appeared in *Hymns and Sacred Poems* in 1739. One of the hymns was entitled "Justified *but not* Sanctified."[2] As mentioned previously, John Wesley noted that he and Charles published this book after he had heard from the German Moravians (as Arvid Gradin) about their understanding of the difference between justifying faith and the full assurance of faith and freedom from indwelling sin.

Christian David and Arvid Gradin served as a catalyst for a view that John and Charles Wesley so quickly developed because they were already inclined to believe it because Anglican liturgy linked water baptism to repentance and confirmation to sanctification.

That John Wesley so quickly embraced the distinction between justifying faith and sanctifying grace after hearing of a similar distinction with the Moravians at Herrnhut was most likely because he was emboldened to do so because he knew Anglican liturgy distinguished between repentance of baptism and sanctification of confirmation. If Charles Wesley was so quickly persuaded by his brother on this matter after John's return from Herrnhut, he knew it was consistent with confirmation, and that explains why Charles' expressions for Christian perfection were literally versifying confirmation themes. If the Wesley brothers got their primary idea of Christian perfection from William Law, they apparently derived their multiple expressions to describe it from the theology of confirmation in Jeremy Taylor.

This is not to minimize the importance of their own personal experience in coming to see the distinction. In the preface to *Hymns and Sacred Poems* (1740), the Wesley brothers said: "We know a cloud of witnesses, who have received *in one moment*, either a clear sense of the forgiveness of their sins, or the abiding witness of the Holy Spirit," but they said they did not know "a single instance" where anyone ever received both at the same time—forgiveness of sins and the abiding witness of the Spirit (i.e., "a clean heart").[3]

Immediately following this observation, the Wesley brothers published their first-ever understanding of the order of salvation describing the transition from justification to sanctification:

> Indeed how God *may* work we cannot tell. But the general manner where he *does* work is this.... Those who once trusted in themselves and "see the wrath of God hanging over their heads" will "cry unto the Lord, and he shows he hath taken away their sins." "Knowing they are justified... they have peace with God."

Following the moment of justification, the Wesley brothers said:

> In this peace they remain for days, or weeks, or months, and commonly suppose they shall not know war any more, till some of their old enemies, their bosom sins, or, the sin which did most easily beset them (perhaps anger or desire) assault them again.... Then arises fear... and [they] often doubt.... their sins were forgiven.... Under these clouds... they go *mourning* all the day long.... But it is seldom long before their Lord answers for himself, sending the Holy Spirit, *to comfort* them, to bear witness continually with their spirit, that they are the children of God.[4]

Being aware of "the depths of pride," they "hunger... after a full renewal in his image, in 'righteousness,' and all true holiness. Then God... giveth them a single eye and a clean heart. He stamps upon them his own image and superscription. He createth them anew in Christ Jesus. He cometh unto them with his Son and blessed Spirit, and fixing his abode in their souls, bringeth them into the 'rest which remaineth for the people of God' [i.e., Christian perfection]."[5]

John Wesley also at this time began to make a distinction between being born of God in the lower sense [i.e., justifying faith] and being born of God in the highest sense of Christian perfection. In his journal entry for Thursday, January 25, 1739, he said:

> I baptized John Smith (late an Anabaptist) and four other adults at Islington. Of the adults I have known baptized lately, one only was at that time born again, in the full sense of the word; that is, found a thorough, inward change, by the love of God filling her heart. Most of them were only born again in a lower sense; that is, received the remission of their sins. And some (as it has since too plainly appeared) neither in one sense nor the other.[6]

In John Wesley's sermon, "The Marks of the New Birth," written in 1748, John Wesley used the same definition of new birth as William Law, except that John Wesley emphasized that the new birth happens by faith and was not only an "assent... but a disposition," which God hath wrought in his heart, "a sure trust and confidence in God, that through the merits of Christ his sins are forgiven." The new birth is "an immediate and constant fruit of this faith whereby we are born of God... [with] power over outward sin of every kind; over every evil word and work; for wheresoever the blood of Christ is thus applied, it 'purgeth the conscience from dead works'; — and over inward sin; for it purifieth the heart from every unholy desire and temper."[7]

In 1754 in his *Explanatory Notes on the New Testament* on John 3:3, John Wesley defined "born again" to mean "an entire change of heart," and "inwardly changed from all sinfulness to all holiness." He also described Peter's language (1 Peter 2:23-24) of "being born again" to mean "purity of heart" and "pure from any spot of unholy desire, or inordinate passion" [i.e., Christian perfection]. Six years later in his sermon on "The New Birth" he defines the new birth only as the beginning moment of justifying faith and not full sanctification, although Charles Wesley retained the language of the new birth as equivalent in meaning with the experience of Christian perfection as subsequent to justifying faith, (as already noted with Charles Wesley scholars like Ernest Rattenbury[8] and John Tyson[9]).

John Wesley wrote a letter on February 20, 1739, to George Whitefield (who in earlier days believed in Christian perfection): "The society at Mr. Crouch's does not meet till eight, so that I expound before I go to him near St. James Square, where one woman has been lately filled with the Holy Spirit, and overflows with joy and love"[10]

On Monday, January 1, 1739 John wrote about a New Year's Eve Watch-Night Service. He described that meeting in Pentecost terms:

> Monday, January 1, 1739. Mr. Hall, Kinchin, Ingham, Whitefield, Hutchins, and my brother Charles, were present at our love-feast in Fetter-Lane, with about sixty of our brethren. About three in the morning, as we were continuing instant in prayer, the power of God came mightily upon us, insomuch that many cried out for exceeding joy, and many fell to the ground. As soon as we were recovered a little from that awe and amazement at the presence of his majesty, we broke out with one voice, "We praise thee, O God; we acknowledge thee to be the Lord."[11]

Here is George Whitefield's comment on this Pentecost experience at that Fetter Lane Society Meeting:

> It was a Pentecost season indeed. . . . Sometimes whole nights were spent in prayer. Often have we been filled as with new wine. And often have I seen them overwhelmed with the Divine Presence, and crying out, "Will God, indeed, dwell with men upon earth!—How dreadful is this place!—This is no other than the house of God, and the gate of Heaven!"[12]

On August 10, 1739, Charles took the Moravian layman, John Bray, with him on one of his multiple visits to William Law. Drawing from what he had learned from the Moravian Christian David through his brother John that justification precedes holiness, he frankly told William Law that he had now come to see that one must first be justified by faith before one is sanctified. Charles said: "I told him he was my schoolmaster to bring me to Christ, but the reason why I did not come sooner to him was my seeking to be sanctified before I was justified."[11]

Charles' evangelistic preaching was now largely focusing on these two themes—justification and sanctification.

On August 16, 1739, Charles Wesley sent detailed "accounts" of his evangelistic preaching to his brother John, noting that he was being barred from preaching in the churches because of "their natural aversion to the gospel."[14]

On August 20, 1739, Charles reported "I expounded at eight in the schoolroom, which contains two hundred; and held out the promises from John 16: 'I will send the Comforter,' &c."[15]

We can determine the content of this particular sermon on John 16 because Charles Wesley composed a hymn on this text that was published the same year (1739).

The hymn was based on John 16:24: "Ask, and ye shall receive, that your joy may be full." This hymn is for one who is already justified and is an adopted child of God who cries out "Abba, Father! Hear thy child,[16] Late in Jesus reconciled!"

The prayer is for the Holy Spirit as Comforter to come to one who recently is reconciled to God who will bring fullness of grace, purity of heart, perfect love, the fullness of God, an entire change into the likeness of the nature of Christ, and the permanent and abiding witness of the Spirit.

1. Rise my soul with ardor rise,
   Breathe thy wishes to the skies;
Freely pour out all thy mind,
   Seek, and thou art sure to find;
Ready art thou to receive?
   Readier is thy God to give.

2. Heavenly Father, Lord of all,
   Hear, and show thou hear'st my call;
Let my cries thy throne assail
   Entering now within the veil:
Give the benefits I claim—
   Lord, I ask in Jesu's name!

3. Friend of sinners, King of saints,
   Answer my minutest wants,
All my largest thoughts require,
   Grant me all my heart's desire,
Give me, till my cup run o'er,
   All, and infinitely more.

4. Meek and lowly be my mind,
   Pure my heart, my will resign'd!
Keep me dead to all below,
   Only Christ resolved to know,
Firm and disengaged and free,
   Seeking all my bliss in thee.

5. Suffer me no more to grieve
   Wanting what thou long'st to give,
Show me all thy goodness, Lord,
   Beaming from th' incarnate Word,

Christ, in whom thy glories shine,
  Efflux of the light divine.

6. Since the Son hath made me free,
    Let me taste my liberty,
Thee behold with open face,
    Triumph in thy saving grace,
Thy great will delight to prove,
    Glory in thy perfect love.

7. Since the Son hath bought my peace,
    Mine thou art, as I am his:
Mine the Comforter I see,
    Christ is full of grace for me:

Mine (the purchase of his blood)
    All the plenitude of God.

8. Abba, Father! Hear thy child
    Late in Jesus reconcil'd!
Hear, and all the graces shower,
    All the joy, and peace, and pow'r,
All my Saviour asks above,
    All the life and heaven of love.

9. Lord, I will not let thee go,
    Till THE BLESSING thou bestow:
Hear my advocate divine;
    Lo! To his my suit I join:
Join'd to his it cannot fail—
    Bless me, for I *will* prevail!

10. Stoop from thy eternal throne,
    See, thy promise calls thee down!
High and lofty as thou art,
    Dwell within my worthless heart!
Here a fainting soul revive;
    Here for ever walk and live.

11. Heavenly Adam, life divine,
    Change my nature into thine:
Move and spread throughout my soul,
    Actuate and fill the whole:
Be it I no longer now,
    Living in the flesh, but thou.

12. Holy Ghost, no more delay,
    Come, and in thy temple stay;
Now thy inward witness bear
    Strong and permanent, and clear;
Spring of life, thyself impart,

> Rise eternal in my heart![17]

On September 25, 1739, Charles recorded that he preached on Romans 12, "but I could not press particular duties till they had the foundation, and therefore exhorted them to get forgiveness *before* (italics Charles') they could perform the best part of the law [living sacrifice]."

So he appealed to those who were already justified ("the brethren") to seek Christian perfection: "The *brethren* I besought to present their bodies a living sacrifice, and pointed out the part of Acts 2 of this devotion."[18]

From his poems we know that when he preached "a living sacrifice" he was speaking of Christian perfection, and when he connected it to Acts 2, he was saying that Christian perfection is based on Pentecost. The connection can be seen in how he defined "living sacrifice" with "sinless days [i.e., Christian perfection]"—

> Present thee all our sinless days
> A living sacrifice to God.[19]

He also defined "a living sacrifice" as:

> A living sacrifice, restor'd
>   Entire, devoted to the Lord:[20]

In this sermon, Charles Wesley connected Romans 12 with Acts 2. Charles noted that Romans 12 was a call to those who were already "Brethren" to consecrate themselves as a "living sacrifice."

He explained Acts 2:1, "When the day of Pentecost was fully come," to mean the law of God was written on the heart as "the law of love."

> God who on Sinai's top came down
> The law of fear t' engrave in stone,
> Returns all-gracious from above
> To teach mankind the law of love,
> And by his Spirit's power imparts,
> And writes it on his people's hearts.[21]

He explained Acts 2:2, "Suddenly there came a sound from heaven, as of a rushing mighty wind," to mean that the Holy Spirit "fills, and purifies" "our spirit."

> 2. See in the strong impetuous sign
> Th' almighty power of grace Divine!
> The Wind which on our spirit blows,
> And moves, and pierces, and o'erthrows,
> Refreshes, fills, and purifies,
> And swiftly lifts us to the skies![22]

Charles Wesley explained the day of Pentecost in Acts 2:3: "And there appeared unto them cloven tongues, like as of fire," Charles Wesley said "the burning Spirit" with "fire inflames the heart," "burns up all our [inbred] sin," and "consecrates the soul."

1. Divided tongues of fire
    The burning Spirit express,
Who doth his messengers inspire,
    And gives his word success:
Active as darted flame
    It flies with rapid speed,
As lightning, with resistless aim
    It strikes the sinner dead.[23]

2. That Fire inflames the heart,
    Expands and spreads within,
Severs the pure and drossy part,
    And burns up all our sin;
It consecrates the soul
    A living sacrifice,
And offers up the saint a whole
    Burnt-offering to the skies.[24]

He explained Acts 2:4, "They were all filled with the Holy Spirit, and began to speak with other tongues," to mean to be "filled with the Spirit of holiness":

Fill'd with the Spirit of holiness
    One family is join'd
With all the tongues of earth to praise
    The Saviour of mankind;
Earnest of the whole world, employ'd
    In their own tongues to sing,
In season due, th' incarnate God,
    The saints' eternal King.[25]

On September 26, 1739, Charles recorded in his journal:

Sarah Pearce declares she received the first comfort in hearing Rom. 5 explained. She was then justified but did not draw nigh in full assurance of faith [i.e., Christian perfection] till last night. . . . Every word I spoke came with power. She had the witness of her own spirit or conscience that all the marks I mentioned were in her. And the Spirit of God came in with his testimony, and put it beyond the possibility of doubt. Some of her words were: "I perceive a real change on myself, and expect a greater. I feel a divine attraction in my soul. Was once so afraid of death that I durst not sleep but now I do not fear it at all. I desire nothing upon earth. I dread nothing but sin".

Charles then noted her attainment of Christian perfection: "See here the true assurance of faith!"[26]

On September 28, 1739, Charles Wesley said in his journal: "I met with Sarah Putnam. . . . She informed me that Christ did then break off her yoke, and she felt herself at liberty from sin. . . . Soon after news was brought me that the man I had prayed by beyond Hanham was now in the full triumph of faith."[27] Liberty from sin and full triumph of faith are expressions of Christian perfection.

On October 3, 1739, Sarah Townsend testified that while they were singing on Sunday evening, as Charles put it, "the Spirit in that instant sealing her pardon upon her heart ["pardon sealed" i.e., Christian perfection, as John Tyson has also pointed out].²⁸ She was filled all night with joy unspeakable."²⁹

In their first edition of Hymns and Sacred Poems *(1739), the Wesley brothers frequently showed that Christian perfection was based on Pentecost.* They showed that being "washed in the fountain of blood" was not enough (i.e., justification by faith), but the justified believer desired to be "renewed in perfect love." He was pardoned and yet still unclean in his heart. The first gift was not enough. The justified believer was ransomed as were also the disciples before Pentecost who now must "wait for the promise of the Father, which ye have heard of me, Acts 1:4."

Based on this text, Charles showed that the justified believer longed for perfect love through the Spirit of Pentecost.

"Wait for the promise of the Father,
which ye have heard of me." (Acts 1:4)

1. Saviour of men, how long shall I
Forgotten at thy footstool lie!
Wash'd in the fountain of thy blood,
Yet groaning still to be renew'd;

2. A miracle of grace and sin,
Pardon'd, yet still alas unclean!
Thy righteousness is *counted* mine:
When will it in my nature shine?

3. Darksome I still remain and void,
And painfully unlike my God,
Till thou diffuse a brighter ray,
And turn the glimm'ring into day.

4. Why didst thou the first gift impart,
And sprinkle with thy blood my heart,
But that my sprinkled heart might prove,
The life and liberty of love?

5. Why didst thou bid my terrors cease,
And sweetly fill my soul with peace,
But that my peaceful soul might know
The joys that from believing flow?

6. See then thy ransom'd servant, see,
I hunger, Lord, I thirst for thee!
Feed me with love, thy Spirit give,
I gasp, in him, in thee to live.

7. The promis'd Comforter impart,

> Open the fountain in my heart;
> There let him flow with springing joys,
> And into life eternal rise.
>
> 8. There let him ever, ever dwell,
> The pledge, the witness, and the seal;
> I'll glory then in sin forgiven,
> In Christ my life, my love, my heaven!

Another "Hymn to the Holy Spirit" in the 1739 edition highlighted that the believer "pants for more . . . Till all my hallowed soul be thine: Plunged in the Godhead's deepest sea, And lost in thy immensity." The "all-quickening fire" will provide the "seal of my sins in Christ forgiven, Earnest of love, and pledge of heaven." Charles Wesley used "seal" as another term for Christian perfection.

> Hymn to the Holy Ghost
>
> 1. Come, Holy Ghost, all-quick'ning fire,
>   Come, and in me delight to rest!
> Drawn by the lure of strong desire,
>   O come, and consecrate my breast:
> The temple of my soul prepare,
>   And fix thy sacred presence there!
>
> 2. If now thy influence I feel,
>   If now in thee begin to live;
> Still to my heart thyself reveal,
>   Give me thyself, for ever give.
> A point my good, a drop my store:
>   Eager I ask, and pant for more.
>
> 3. Eager for thee I ask and pant,
>   So strong the principle divine
> Carries me out with sweet constraint,
>   Till all my hallow'd soul be thine:
> Plung'd in the Godhead's deepest sea,
>   And lost in thy immensity.
>
> 4. My peace, my life, my comfort now,
>   My treasure, and my all thou art!
> True witness of my sonship thou,
>   Engraving pardon on my heart:
> Seal of my sins in Christ forgiven,
>   Earnest of love, and pledge of heav'n.
>
> 5. Come then, my God, mark out thy heir,
>   Of heav'n a larger earnest give,
> With clearer light thy witness bear;
>   More sensibly within me live:
> Let all my pow'rs thy entrance feel,
>   And deeper stamp thyself the seal.

The identification of the Pentecost-bestowal of the Spirit with Christian perfection was often affirmed in their hymns, using such phrases as, "The Spirit of Adoption, "baptize me now with fire," "O that the Comforter would come," "Come, Holy Ghost, all Quickening fire," "the indwelling Spirit," etc.

They used multiple expressions for Christian perfection. Charles once said to John Fletcher: "Christian perfection is nothing but the full kingdom in the Holy Spirit."[30] In his journal, Charles said he "rejoiced once more with our brethren at Wednesbury, who . . . walk in the comfort of the Holy Spirit."[31] As noted above, the Holy Spirit as "Comforter" is a term designating Christian perfection.

On April 6, 1740, Charles exhorted a Methodist society "to go on to perfection."[32] Charles' journal and his poetry revealed that the primary focus of his ministry was Christian perfection.

On April 9, 1740, Charles "prayed in faith that some might receive the second gift."[33] John Wesley spoke of the "second blessing," and Charles spoke of the "second gift" as a reference to Christian perfection.

On July 15, 1740 Charles Wesley preached on 2 Peter 1:4 and Acts 2, "pressing the example of the primitive Christian" on experiencing true "religion, a participation of the divine nature."[34]

His lyrical hymns on Acts 2 were that God's love is poured out into the hearts of those who are filled with the Spirit. This hymn began with "Sinners, lift up your hearts." By sinners, Charles includes justified believers because they have inward sin and hence need the "cleansing blood" "to make an end of sin" and "wholly sanctify."

"I will pour out of my Spirit upon all flesh." (Acts 2:17)

1. Sinners, lift up your hearts
    The PROMISE to receive!
Jesus himself imparts,
    He comes in man to live:
The Holy Ghost to man is given;
    Rejoice in God sent down from heaven.

2. Jesus is glorified,
    And gives the Comforter,
His Spirit, to reside
    In all his members here:
The Holy Ghost to man is given;
    Rejoice in God sent down from heaven.

3. To make an end of sin,
    And Satan's works destroy,
He brings his kingdom in,
    Peace, righteousness, and joy:
The Holy Ghost to man is given:
    Rejoice in God sent down from heaven.

4. The cleansing blood t' apply,
   The heavenly life display,
And wholly sanctify,
   And seal us to that day,
The Holy Ghost to man is given:
   Rejoice in God sent down from heaven.

5. Sent down to make us meet
   To see his open face,
And grant us each a seat
   In that thrice happy place,
The Holy Ghost to man is given:
   Rejoice in God sent down from heaven.

6. From heaven He shall once more
   Triumphantly descend,
And all his saints restore
   To joys that never end:
Then, then when all our joys are given,
   Rejoice in God, rejoice in heaven![35]

On July 25, 1740, Charles "began examining each member of the [Bristol] Society. One came crying out, 'I am born of God. I have the indwelling Spirit. I have a new heart,' and she could give no account of her faith, no proof of her pretensions."[36]

Examining those who claim to have been made perfect love was regularly performed by John and Charles Wesley as they supervised the societies. Both could be ruthless in requiring "evidence" for their claims to be perfect in love. As already noted, at this early stage of the revival, John as well as Charles Wesley defined being "born of God" to mean Christian perfection.

On August 6, 1740, Charles reported he was near death with fever. His brother John came from London to Bristol to be with him "when I was just able to stand" and they spent time together "comparing our dangers, temptations, and deliverances." His mother Susanna also responded to this news of his illness and recovery, noting his problem with health issues.[37] Following his recuperation with his brother, Charles Wesley said: "I found myself... more earnestly longing for deliverance and the fullness of Christian salvation."[38]

On September 26, 1740, Charles Wesley wrote that he "was greatly assisted in the evening to preach the Christian perfection—that is, utter dominion over sin; constant peace, and love, and joy in the Holy Spirit; the full assurance of faith, righteousness, and true holiness. I see more and more into the height of our privileges, and that God will give them to me."[39] These expressions were often used synonymously with Christian perfection.

The very next day, Sunday, September 28, Charles Wesley recorded in his journal that "at the Sacrament I received power to believe sin shall not have dominion over me."[40] Here it would seem that Charles Wesley was testifying to Christian perfection in that moment since "sin shall not have dominion over me" was one of his terms for full redemption.

On September 29, 1740, Charles recorded in his journal, "God was wonderfully with our assembly, and opened my eyes to see the promise of holiness or perfection, not in some, but in almost every Scripture."[41] This journal entry reinforced what is evident throughout Charles' journal and poems that his "obsession" is with holiness as the perfect love of God in his heart and life. His own life and ministry, as will be shown even in his correspondence with his wife-to-be, were consumed with his pursuit of Christian perfection.

If Charles preached so passionately about holiness, it was because he so desired to attain it. This passion is evident in his letters to his mother, Susanna Wesley. On October 2, 1740, she wrote to him in response to his letter exhorting her to be to "made partakers of the heavenly gift or of the Holy Spirit." She acknowledged her self-awareness of "sin, both original and actual" and need of this gift. She was, however, perplexed that he said he was not a Christian, showing that Charles (as well as John) in these early days of the revival assumed one was a real Christian only if they had attained Christian perfection. She advised him not to belittle his experience:

> I cannot conceive why you affirm yourself to be not Christian; which is, in effect, to tell Christ to his face that you have nothing to thank him for, since you are not the better for anything he hath yet done or suffered for you. Oh, what great dishonour, what wondrous ingratitude, is this to the ever-blessed Jesus! I think myself far from being so good a Christian as you are, or as I ought to be; but God forbid that I should renounce the little Christianity I have: nay, rather let me grow in grace and in the knowledge of our Lord and Saviour Jesus Christ. Amen.[42]

In a subsequent letter on April 28, 1741, she responded to his exhortation to her to be baptized with the Spirit, saying:

> I don't well understand what you mean by the baptism which remains for us to be baptized with, but suppose by what follows you think we are not yet fully convinced of [inbred] sin. I hope we are in good measure convinced already that we do feelingly know we are poor sinners—but to be fully apprized of the evil of sin in its nature and consequences it is, I humbly conceive, necessary that we have a more full and perfect knowledge of God.[43]

His mother Susanna was referring to Charles' theology of "inbred sin" that needed to be cleansed through the baptism with the Spirit before one attains Christian perfection, as his hymns often mentioned.

On October 10, 1740, Charles mentioned "Mrs. Purnell, who patiently waits for the seal of her pardon [i.e., Christian perfection].[44]

John Tyson cited this poem from Charles Wesley to show that Charles used "sealed pardon" for Christian perfection:

> Now, even now, I yield, I yield
> With all my sins to part;
> Jesus, speak my pardon seal'd,

> And purify my heart,
> Purge this love of sin away,
> Then I into nothing fall.
> Then I see the perfect day,
> And Christ is all in all.[45]

On Sunday May 24, 1741 Charles Wesley recorded that he "preached on Jacob wrestling for the blessing. Many then I believe took hold on his strength and will not let him go till He bless them and tell them his name." He also heard his brother John preach at the mills at Bristol and together they visited the Methodist Society there. Charles noted: "A woman was constrained to testify, 'God this moment assures me that my pardon is sealed [i.e., Christian perfection]'."[46]

NOTES

1. *Manuscript Journal*, 2:643.
2. *Hymns and Sacred Poems* (London: Strahan, 1739), 150. Small capitals and italics are the Wesleys'.
3. *Hymns and Sacred Poems* (1740), ix.
4. *Hymns and Sacred Poems* (1740), x.
5. *Hymns and Sacred Poems* (1740), xi.
6. *Journal and Diaries II (1738-1743)*, 19:32
7. Outler, Sermons, 1:423, 427, 428, "The Marks of the New Birth."
8. J. Ernest Rattenbury, *The Evangelical Doctrines of Charles Wesley's Hymns* (London: Epworth Press, 1941), 303, 308.
9. John Tyson, *Charles Wesley on Sanctification* (Grand Rapids: Zondervan, 1986), 219-220.
10. *George Whitefield's Journals* (Edinburgh, Scotland: The Banner of Truth Trust, 1992), 224.
11. *Journal and Diaries II (1738-1743)*, 19:29.
12. John Gillies, *Memoirs of the Life of George Whitefield* (New Haven: Joseph Barber, 1812), 24 note.
13. *Manuscript Journal* 1:184.
14. *Manuscript Journal*, 1:185.
15. *Manuscript Journal*, 1:185-186.
16. Rattenbury has shown that Charles interprets those who are justified to be "adopted" sons of God, even though they are not "born of God." *Evangelical Doctrines of Charles Wesley*, 260.
17. *Hymns and Sacred Poems* (1739), 219-220.
18. *Manuscript Journal*, 1:205.
19. "Hosea 14," MARC: MA 1977/424 (Charles Wesley Notebooks Box 1).*Hymns for Times of Trouble and Persecution* (1744), v. 5, 131.
20. Charles Wesley, *Short Hymns on Select Passages of the Holy Scriptures* (Bristol: Farley, 1762), 1:131.
21. MS Acts, MARC: MA 1977/555 (Charles Wesley Notebooks Box 1), 15.
22. MS Acts, MARC, accession number MA 1977/555 (Charles Wesley Notebooks Box 1), 16.
23. A sinner included anyone who is not fully sanctified because justified believers have inward sins.
24. MS Acts, MARC, accession number MA 1977/555 (Charles Wesley Notebooks Box 1), 15-16.
25. MS Acts, MARC, accession number MA 1977/555 (Charles Wesley Notebooks Box 1), 16.
26. *Manuscript Journal*, 1:206.
27. *Manuscript Journal*, 1:207.
28. John Tyson, *Charles Wesley on Sanctification*, 101.
29. *Manuscript Journal* 1:210.
30. In a letter to Charles Wesley (July 4, 1774), *The Asbury Theological Journal* 53.1 (Spring 1998): 92. Cf. Benson, *The Life of the Rev. John W. de la Flechere* (London: J. Mason, 1838), 166.
31. *Manuscript Journal* , 2:477, October 14, 1746.
32. *Manuscript Journal* 1:236.
33. *Manuscript Journal* 1:238.
34. *Manuscript Journal* 1:273.

35. MS Acts, MARC: MA 1977/555 (Charles Wesley Notebooks Box 1), 21.
36. *Manuscript Journal* 1:274.
37. *Susanna Wesley The Complete Writings*, ed. Charles Wallace Jr. (Oxford: OUP, 1997), 185. She mentioned "the weakness of your body." Ibid., 190 (Letter, April 28, 1741).
38. *Manuscript Journal* 1:277.
39. *Manuscript Journal* 1:279.
40. *Manuscript Journal* 1:279.
41. *Manuscript Journal* 1:280.
42. *Susanna Wesley The Complete Writings*, 185-186.
43. Ibid.,187-188.
44. *Manuscript Journal* 1:281.
45. Tyson *Charles Wesley on Sanctification*, 101.
46. *Manuscript Journal*, 1: 310.

Chapter 7

"Th' Indwelling Comforter"

> "I want the sanctifying God,
>   Th' indwelling Comforter."
>   —Charles Wesley

> "From all sin *entirely* freed
>   Here they walk with GOD above,
> Born again, and saints indeed,
>   Fully perfected in Love."
>   —Charles Wesley

Charles exhorted a Methodist society on April 6, 1740 "to go on to perfection."[1] Charles' journal and his poetry reveal that a primary focus of his ministry was Christian perfection, as well as being a focus in his hymns.

On April 9, 1740, Charles "prayed in faith that some might receive the second gift."[2]

On May 15, 1740 Charles said: "I exhorted the Society to wait for the Promise of the Father. Many cried out in the birthpangs."[3] The Promise of the Father is often used in Charles' hymns to speak of Christian perfection, just as the new birth is described as Christian perfection.

In a lyrical hymn, "A Prayer for Holiness," he defined Christian perfection in terms of the new birth.

> 4. Gifts, alas! Cannot suffice,
>   And comforts all are vain,
> *While one evil thought can rise,*
>   *I am not born again*:
> Still I am not as my Lord,
>   Thy holy will I do not prove:
> Help me, Saviour, speak the word,
>   And perfect me in love.[4]

Here is another hymn equating being born again with freedom from inbred sin (i.e., Christian perfection).

> But tell us, are we born again?
> Are we redeem'd from inbred sin?[5]

Continuing with his Pentecost preaching, Charles Wesley preached on July 28, 1740, and he "spoke searchingly on those words of our Lord: 'Nevertheless, I tell you the truth; it is expedient for you that I go away. For if I go not away, the Comforter will not come'."[6]

In a poetic commentary on John 16:7, Charles explained what this text means. It describes Jesus ascending to heaven, leaving his disciples discouraged and lonely. The departure of Jesus ascending to heaven was necessary in order to send the Holy Spirit to dwell within them as a Comforter and impart to them "perfect grace" so that "we thine endless love shall feel."

"If I go not away, the Comforter will not come unto you" (John 16:7)

> Son of God, for Thee we languish,
>   Still thine absence we bemoan,
> Overwhelm'd with grief and anguish,
>   Poor, forsaken, and alone:
> Thou art to thine heaven departed;
>   See us thence, with pity see,
> Comfortless and broken-hearted,
>   Drooping, dead for want of Thee.
>
> 2. Once thy blissful love we tasted,
>   Cheer'd by Thee with living bread
> O how short a time it lasted,
>   O how soon the joy is fled!
> Where is now our boasted Saviour,
>   Where our rapture of delight?
> Thou hast, Lord, withdrawn thy favor,
>   Thou art vanish'd from our sight.
>
> 3. Yet Thou hast the cause unfolded,
>   Could we but the truth receive,
> Thou in humbling love hast told it,
>   Needful 'tis for us to grieve:
> Stripped of that *excessive* pleasure,
>   Fondly we the loss deplore,
> 'Till we find again our treasure,
>   Find, and never lose thee more.
>
> 4. That we may Thyself inherit,
>   Us Thou dost a while forsake,
> That we may receive thy Spirit,
>   Thou hast took his comforts back;
> After a short night of mourning
>   We again shall see thy face,
> Triumph in thy full returning,
>   Glory in thy perfect grace.
>
> 5. For thy transient outward presence
>   We thine endless love shall feel,
> Seated in our inmost essence

> Thou shalt by thy Spirit dwell:
> Jesus come; Thyself the Giver
>   Let us for the gift receive,
> Let us live in God forever,
>   God in us forever live![7]

Charles Wesley linked the promise of the Holy Spirit to sanctification often in his hymns, such as this verse:

> I want the sanctifying God,
>   Th' indwelling Comforter[8]

In his poetic commentary on John 14:16, "And I will pray the Father, and he shall give you another Comforter, that he may abide with you forever," he spoke of "thy weakest followers" who are waiting for their "day of Pentecost" when "thy good Spirit descend from high." Then the Holy Spirit will "fill with life, and love, and peace . . . and seal our present and eternal bliss."

> 1. Jesus, thy weakest followers hear,
>   On whom thou kindly hast bestow'd
> A principle of pious fear,
>   An heart to seek our joy in God:
> This smallest seed of love unfeign'd
>   We surely have receiv'd from Thee,
> And tempted with our Lord remain'd,
>   And hoped thine utmost word to see.
>
> 2. While feebly in thy paths we tread,
>   And most imperfectly obey,
> Thy goodness and thy truth we plead,
>   And for the promis'd Blessing pray:
> Our day of Pentecost is nigh,
>   Yet still it is not fully come,
> Till thy good Spirit descend from high
>   To make us his eternal home.
>
> 3. Upon thy faithful mercies stay'd,
>   We hold the general Promise fast
> To us and to our children made,
>   To all, as long as time shall last:
> That Spirit purchas'd by thy blood,
>   That Spirit granted to thy prayer,
> Is daily on thy church bestow'd,
>   The saints abiding Comforter.
>
> 4. Father who always hearest our Friend,
>   And Advocate before thy throne,
> Vouchsafe that Paraclete to send,
>   That Spirit of thy spotless Son;
> Ah, give him in our hearts to dwell,

> To fill with life, and love, and peace,
> To constitute, and fix, and seal
> Our present and eternal bliss.[9]

The identification of the Pentecost-bestowal of the Spirit with Christian perfection is affirmed in their hymns, using such phrases as, "The Spirit of Adoption, "baptize me now with fire," "O that the Comforter would come," "Come, Holy Ghost, all Quickening fire," "the indwelling Spirit," etc.

In his journal, Charles recorded on October 14, 1746 that he "rejoiced once more with our brethren at Wednesbury, who . . . walk in the comfort of the Holy Spirit."[10] As noted above, the Holy Spirit as "comforter" is a term normally designating Christian perfection.

On April 6, 1740, Charles exhorted a Methodist society "to go on to perfection."[11]

On April 9, 1740, Charles "prayed in faith that some might receive the second gift."[12] John Wesley spoke of the "second blessing," and Charles spoke of the "second gift" as a reference to Christian perfection.

On Friday, August 1, 1740, John Wesley recorded in his journal: "I described that 'rest' which 'remaineth for the people of God'." The "rest of faith" was one of the Wesley brothers' texts to preach on Christian perfection, as we shall see in the next chapter.[13]

Notes

1. *Manuscript Journal* 1:236.
2. *Manuscript Journal* 1:238.
3. *Manuscript Journal* 1:258.
4. John and Charles Wesley. *Hymns and Sacred Poems* (Bristol: Farley, 1742), 1:219.
5. John and Charles Wesley. *Hymns and Sacred Poems* (Bristol: Farley, 1742), 2:172–173.
6. *Manuscript Journal*, 1:275.
7. MS John, MARC: MA 1977/573 (Charles Wesley Notebooks Box 3), 326-327.
8. MS Preparation for Death. MARC: MA 1977/578 (Charles Wesley Notebooks Box 3). 5.
9. MS John, MARC: MA 1977/573 (Charles Wesley Notebooks Box 3), 289.
10. *Manuscript Journal* , 2:477.
11. *Manuscript Journal,* 1:236.
12. *Manuscript Journal,* 1:238.
13. *Journal and Diaries II (1738–1743),* 19:163, August 1, 1740.

Chapter 8

The Promised Land

> The Lord his Spirit's seal applies,
> His people all to circumcise,
> And when our sins and us He parts,
> Cuts off the foreskin of our hearts.
> —Charles Wesley

> O that I now, from sin releas'd,
> Thy word might to the utmost prove!
> Enter into the promis'd rest,
> The Canaan of thy perfect love!
> —Charles Wesley

Charles recorded on May 1, 1741 that "our sister Hooper" was "dying in the Lord," but she lacked the sense of God's pure love, and then she received it "while I finished my discourse on Numbers 14."[1]

Numbers 14 is the Promised Land motif. It was used as a type of Christian perfection and was a preaching theme for Charles at Bristol from April 24 through May 1, 1741, with an emphasis on "'let us go up at once and possess it [the Promised Land], for we are well able to overcome it'."

Charles compared "the famous history of the spies who brought up an evil report of the Promised Land" to those who say: "We can never conquer *all* sin; we must sin sometimes."[2] A key element of the idea of Christian perfection is total deliverance from all inner and outer sin if one is filled with love.

On May 4, 1741, Charles asked her, "How are you now? Her answer was, 'full, full of love'."[3]

On May 6, 1741, she again testified to "her fullness of confidence and love." She was nearing the end of her life in complete submission to the will of God. Charles noted that her testimony of full confidence and love was the meaning of "holiness, or absolute resignation, or Christian perfection!"[4]

If "our sister Hooper" received perfect love while Charles was preaching on Numbers 14, she is not the only one in Methodism who heard this interpretation of the "Promised Land" motif. It was a theme with the Wesley brothers for interpreting Christian perfection. Their interpretation was not based on a fanciful flight of the imagination, but based on a "typological correspondence" between the Old and New Testament, similar to that advocated by Gerhard von Rad.[5]

Charles Wesley explained that the Old Testament "concealed" what was later "revealed" in the gospel message of the New Testament. Here is the poem Charles wrote as a comment on Acts 7:8, "He gave him the covenant of circumcision":

> The cov'enant old in types concealed
>   Now in the gospel is reveal'd;
> The gospel-cov'enant has took place,
>   And saves us not by works but grace:
> The Lord his Spirit's seal applies,
>   His people all to circumcise,
> And when our sins and us He parts,
>   Cuts off the foreskin of our hearts.[6]

This Promise Land motif was a common way of defining Christian perfection. I will weave together a variety of biblical passages that they assumed as a basis for the Promised Land imagery.

Fifteen years after Abraham had first believed in God (which Paul defined as Abraham's "justification," Romans 4:2-3), the Lord appeared to Abraham again and said to him: "Walk before me, and be perfect [blameless in love]" (Gen. 17:1).

The Wesley brothers linked the Promised Land motif to Christian perfection because of this requirement of being *perfect* if they were to occupy the land. As a sign of this everlasting covenant, the Lord said to him: "You shall be circumcised in the flesh of your foreskins" (Gen.17:11). Genesis 17:23 says that on "that very day" when God told Abraham to be perfect, "every male among the men of Abraham's house" was circumcised. Hence the connection between being "perfect" and "circumcision."

The removal of the inherited flesh in the rite of circumcision symbolized perfection of love (Gen. 17:1) and purity of heart (Deuteronomy 10:17). Paul was assuming this symbolic meaning of the circumcision of the foreskin when he equated "the carnal" and "the flesh" with the "sin which dwells within me" (Romans 7:13-20), as Rudolf Bultmann has shown.[7] That's why Paul said that a "real Jew" is one who is circumcised inwardly because "real circumcision is a matter of the heart, spiritual and not literal" (Romans 2:28-29). The meaning of circumcision of the heart is perfect love, according to Moses' prophetic expectation (Deuteronomy 30:5-6).

Moses described the land of Canaan as "the abode, the sanctuary" of the Lord, and he had stipulated that the requirement for living in this land was for them to be "a holy nation" (Ex. 19:6). To be a holy nation meant they would love the Lord with all their heart: "Hear, O Israel, the Lord our God is one Lord; and you shall love the Lord your God with all your heart, and with all your soul, and with all your might" (Deuteronomy 6:5-6).

Here is Charles Wesley's interpretation of this passage in Deuteronomy 6:5, showing the true meaning of the "kingdom" is perfect love for God.

> Lord, I believe thy mercy's power
>   Shall every obstacle remove,
> I trust thy promise to restore
>   In me the kingdom of thy love:
> Jesus, thy word cannot be vain;

> Truth, power, and love divine thou art;
> And I shall love my God again,
> With all my mind, soul, strength, and heart.[8]

Charles interpreted the struggles and wars of the Israelites against their enemies in the land of Canaan to be an object lesson and metaphor of the victorious life in Christ. In his comment on Deuteronomy 7:24: "There shall no man be able to stand before thee, until thou have destroyed them," Charles Wesley wrote:

> Jesus, I in thy promise trust,
> No bosom-sin, no darling lust
>   Too strong for me shall prove,
> Till thou their nature hast destroy'd,
> And fill'd my soul's unbounded void
>   With all thy perfect love.[9]

Moses often reiterated that the Lord required perfect love: "What doth the Lord thy God request of thee, but to love him, and to serve the Lord thy God with all thy heart, and with all thy soul, to keep the commandments of the Lord" (Deuteronomy 10:12-13). Here are Charles Wesley's comments on this passage:

> 1. O my most condescending Lord,
>   He humbly stoops to ask my love!
> 'Tis no impracticable word;
>   I may, I will obedient prove,
> His grace accept, his power exert,
>   And serve my God with all my heart.
>
> 2. Full of thy holy love I rise,
>   To worship spiritual and true,
> On eagle's wings my spirit flies,
>   Whatever my Lord commands to do,
> To answer all my Saviour's will,
>   And perfectly his law fulfil.[10]

In his comments on Deuteronomy 10:16, "Circumcise the foreskin of your heart, and be no more stiff-necked," Charles wrote:

> If thou command it, Lord, we may
>   With our transgressions part:
> We do cut off, and cast away
>   The foreskin of our heart;
> Our stiff-neck'd souls we bow to thee,
>   And trusting in thy power,
> We need no more rebellious be,
>   We will rebel no more.[11]

When Moses said to the Israelites "Thou shalt be perfect with the Lord thy God" in Deuteronomy 18:13, this is the same command given to Abraham to be "perfect" in Genesis 17:1. Charles Wesley versified this to mean a perfection of love:

> I shall (when he who saith I shall,
> Hath with himself bestow'd
> Sufficient strength to walk in all
> The righteous ways of God)
> I shall attain my heart's desire,
> And serve like those above,
> Complete in his whole will, entire
> And perfect in his love.[12]

This requirement of perfect love for living in the Promised Land was often repeated by Moses in his instructions as the Israelites prepared to enter the Promised Land (Deuteronomy 7:9,12; 10:12; 11:1,13; 13:3).

Moses told the Israelites that when they came into the land of Canaan, these two events—Exodus and Conquest— were to be a part of the liturgy of their worshiping congregation as they remembered their saving history.

> And you shall make response before the Lord your God. A wandering Aramean was my father; and he went down into Egypt. . . . And the Egyptians treated us harshly. . . . And we cried to the Lord. . . . And the Lord heard our voice. . . . And the Lord brought us out of Egypt. . . . with signs and wonders [Exodus event]; and be brought us into this place [Conquest event] (Deuteronomy 26:5).

The recitation of this liturgy permitted each succeeding generation of Israelites to participate in a personal way with their forefathers in the saving history of God. To show that this liturgy of the congregation was not merely a memory of what had happened to their forefathers, this confession entailed the personal pronouns "treated *us* harshly, and *we* cried to the Lord."

What was true of the experience of their forefathers was also the same experience of each succeeding generation even though the original event occurred many years ago. This means space-time does not consist of merely isolated points, but the God who acted in the past events of salvation history carried the actuality of the same events into the future.

In Deuteronomy 30, Moses predicted that after the Israelites got settled in the land of Canaan they would backslide and their hearts would be turned away from God and they would not love God with all their hearts. As a result, God would drive them into captivity again.

Moses, however, offered them the good news that though they would be driven from the land, they would once again return from their captivity and be restored to the land of Israel.

> And it shall come to pass, when all these things are come upon thee, the blessing and the curse, which I have set before thee, and thou shalt call them to mind among all the nations, whither the LORD thy God hath driven thee, And shalt return unto the LORD thy God, and shalt obey his voice according to all that I command thee this day, thou and thy children, with all thine heart, and with all thy soul; That then the LORD thy God will turn thy captivity, and have compassion upon thee, and will return and gather thee from all the nations, whither the LORD thy God hath scattered thee. If any of thine be driven out unto the outmost parts of heaven, from thence will the LORD thy God gather thee, and

from thence will he fetch thee: And the LORD thy God will bring thee into the land which thy fathers possessed, and thou shalt possess it; and he will do thee good, and multiply thee above thy fathers. And the LORD thy God will circumcise thine heart, and the heart of thy seed, to love the LORD thy God with all thine heart, and with all thy soul, that thou mayest live (Deuteronomy 30:1-6).

In his *Explanatory Notes on the Old Testament* on Deuteronomy 30:6-9, John Wesley said: "This promise principally respects the times of the gospel, and the grace which was to be then imparted to all Israel by Christ."

In his poem on Deuteronomy 30: 6, Charles Wesley wrote:

> 1. On thee, O God, my soul is stay'd,
>   And waits to prove thine utmost will:
> The promise by thy mercy made
>   Thou canst, thou wilt in me fulfil:
> No more I stagger at thy power,
>   Or doubt thy truth, which cannot move:
> Hasten the long-expected hour,
>   And bless me with thy perfect love.
>
> 2. One of the stubborn, harden'd race,
>   Now, Lord, on me the work begin,
> And by the Spirit of thy grace
>   Cut off the foreskin of my sin:
> My stiff-necked heart to circumcise,
>   Thy sanctifying power exert,
> And I shall then attain the prize,
>   And love my God with all my heart.[13]

How shocking it must have been to the Israelites to be told by Moses that the Lord would "uproot them from their land" (Deuteronomy 29:28) because they would not live up to the terms of the covenant made with Abraham to be perfect in heart.

He explained that the reason for their future backsliding was because the rite of physical circumcision was inadequate. What they needed was an inner circumcision (Deuteronomy 30:6).

Although they would be taken into captivity again, Moses said that they would be brought back to Canaan through a new Exodus and they would experience a new Conquest (Deuteronomy 30:6; cf. Jeremiah 31:40). This time they would remain forever in Canaan, never to be driven out again. "Then the Lord will *restore* your fortunes, and have compassion upon you, and he will gather you again (a new Exodus] from all the peoples where the Lord your God has scattered you. . . . And the Lord thy God will bring you into the land [a new Conquest] which your fathers possessed" (Deuteronomy 30:4-5).

Here the Israelites would enjoy the everlasting covenant made with Abraham and delight in the "fruit" of the land and be "abundantly prosperous" (Deuteronomy 30:9). The difference, Moses said, between the old Conquest and the new Conquest was that God would circumcise their hearts so that now they could love God with all their hearts: "And the Lord your God will circumcise your heart and the heart of your offspring, so that you will love the Lord your God with all your heart and with all your soul. that you may live" (Deuteronomy 30:6).

This *restoration* theme became the message of the prophets. The original Exodus and Conquest would be followed up with a new Exodus and Conquest, which would restore the kingdom of Israel. Physical circumcision was no longer of any benefit because it did not empower the Israelites to walk perfectly in heart before God. It needed to be replaced with an inner circumcision. Jeremiah proclaimed: "Circumcise yourself to the Lord, remove the foreskins of your hearts" (Jeremiah 4:4). The Old Testament prophets replaced the language of physical circumcision with the language of inner cleanness.

This cleansing was not something that they were able to do for themselves. Rather, it was to be done by the Spirit of God. John Wesley cited Ezekiel 36 as the prophecy for the coming day of Pentecost when "you shall be clean; from all your filthiness" when "I will put my Spirit within you."[14] Ezekiel prophesied:

> I will take you from the nations [a new Exodus], and gather you from all the countries, and bring you into your own land [a new Conquest]. I will sprinkle clear water upon you, and you shall be clean from all your uncleannesses, and from all your idols I will cleanse you. A new heart I will give you, and a new spirit I will put within you; and I will take out of your flesh the heart of stone and give you a heart of flesh. And I will put my Spirit within you, and cause you to walks in my statutes. . . . You shall be my people, and I will be your God" (Ezekiel 36:24-28).

Ezekiel also described this new Conquest as meaning that Israel would be made holy, not by their own efforts and good works, but by God alone: "Then the nations will know that I the Lord sanctify Israel, when my sanctuary is in the midst of them for evermore" (Ezekiel 37:28).

This future restoration of the fortunes of Israel will occur, Ezekiel said, "when I pour out my Spirit upon the house of Israel" (Ezekiel 39:29). Jeremiah said: "Behold, the days are coming, says the Lord, when I will make a new covenant with the house of Israel, not like the [old] covenant. . . . I will put my law within them, and I will write it upon their hearts" (31:31-34). Joel prophesied that God "will pour out my spirit on all flesh" (Joel 2:28) and that God "will restore the fortunes of Judah" (Joel 3: 1). This means that "my people shall never again be put to shame" (Joel 2:27) because "I am the Lord your God, who dwell in Zion, my holy mountain. And Jerusalem shall be holy" (Joel 3: 17).

Peter proclaimed that Joel's prophecy of the coming of the Spirit during the last days occurred on the day of Pentecost (Acts 2:16-21). His choice of words to describe Jesus' resurrection from the dead was Exodus language: "With mighty works and wonders and signs . . . God raised him up" (Acts 2:22-24). This phrase ("mighty works and wonders and signs") in the Old Testament was always used as an allusion to the original Exodus event (cf. Deuteronomy 6:20-24; 26:5-10; Joshua 24:1 7; Deuteronomy 4:34; 7:19; 11:3; 29:3; Jeremiah 32:20-21; Acts 7:36), and Peter used this phrase as an allusion to Jesus' resurrection.

The phrase "having freed him from death" (Acts 2:24) is also Exodus language. "Loosed" is the root word for "ransom" and is used in the Septuagint for Israel's deliverance from Egypt. It is also used in Revelation 1:5–6 as an allusion to the Exodus and served as a paradigm of Jesus' resurrection from the dead. Jesus' resurrection is thus the new Exodus.

Peter also used Conquest language to describe Jesus' ascension and sending of the Holy Spirit. Jesus went to heaven to sit on the "throne" and was "exalted at the right hand of God" and sent "from the Father the promise of the Holy Spirit" which "be poured out" on us "which you see and hear" (Acts 2:29-32).

Peter's Jewish hearers would have immediately caught the nuances of his choice of words. Peter was saying that the new Exodus was Jesus' resurrection and the new Conquest was Jesus' exaltation and the pouring out of the Spirit upon his people, as the Old Testament prophets had predicted regarding the restored Israel.

Just as there were two events that established Israel as a nation (the Exodus from Egypt and the Conquest of Canaan Land), so there were two events (Easter and Pentecost) that established the New Israel, which is the Church. Easter is the new Exodus and Pentecost is the new Conquest. Participating in these two events through water baptism and the laying on of hands are the sacramental means of Christian initiation.

If John and Charles Wesley interpreted the Exodus event from Egyptian bondage and the crossing over Jordan into the Land of Canann as a foreshadowing of justifying grace and sanctifying grace, it was because this typology was already part of their Anglican tradition, reaching back in time to the writings of the Early Church Fathers (as seen in Taylor's *Discourse on Confirmation,* Appendix 3).

The late Anglican scholar, Alan Richardson, showed that "there can be no doubt that it was upon the historical experiences of the deliverance from Egypt and the establishment in Canaan that the fundamental certainty of all biblical faith was based." He further showed: "But it is uniquely the genius of the Bible that the historical is transmuted by the eschatological, so that the action of God in the past becomes the type or foreshadowing of his action in the future."[15] Richardson then showed these saving events are not just events of the past. Rather, "the salvation that was once-for-all wrought for the whole people is appropriated by each family or each individual as the family or the individual makes response in worship and thanksgiving (Exodus 12:26-27; Deuteronomy 6:20-25; 26:1-11; John 6:53-58; I Cor. 10:16-17; 11:23-26)."[16] Richardson wrote:

> The act of deliverance, so to speak, remains active and potent throughout the continuing history of the people for whom it was wrought; in the biblical view it is not a mere event of the past, but something that is ever and again made present and real in the lives of those who celebrate it in word and sacrament.[17]

Edmond Jacob, the late Old Testament scholar of Strasbourg University, also showed that there were two historical themes which formed the basis of Israel's creed--the Exodus and the Conquest. While the Exodus-Conquest events were the *formative events* for the beginning of the national life of Israel, it can also be seen that they formed a *normative pattern* for the salvation of every Israelite in every new generation. In addition to these two historical themes were two other memories which "were subordinate and whose links were of a sacred rather than an historical nature"—the Sinai and Temple themes. Later the Temple which occupied the center of the Promised Land was fused with the Conquest theme. Jacob writes: "Thus the temple becomes very clearly the object [goal] of the Exodus, and by giving Jerusalem to the Israelites, David only continues the role of Moses, who promised a country to the people."[18]

These two historical events—the Exodus and the Conquest—became for all subsequent time in the history of Israel the pattern for God dealing with his people. For example, the liturgy of Israel extolling the salvation of God (cf. Psalm 68; 77:11-20; 78; 114; 136:10-22) focuses upon these two decisive events. The creed of Deuteronomy 26:5ff is a reliving and personalizing of these two saving events. During their exile and captivity, the prophets envisaged Israel's salvation through a new Exodus and a new Conquest which would restore the Davidic kingdom in the Promised Land.[19]

The Exodus and Conquest were not merely events which formed Israel as a nation in the past. Every individual Israelite throughout the ongoing history of Israel in subsequent years experienced redemption from Egyptian bondage and the sanctifying presence of God in the Land of Canaan through their own participation in the events of Exodus and Conquest by means of reciting the Word of God in the congregation. What happened to the Israelite nation as a whole was to be appropriated personally by every individual in all generations. Jacob wrote:

> At the Passover feast, the departure from Egypt was enacted through the ritual, so clearly that it may be said that at least once a year the Exodus ceased to be a fact of the past and became a living reality, and that never, even after five centuries, did the Israelites consider themselves different from their ancestors who, under Moses' guidance, had experienced the deliverance (cf. Amos 3:2) . . . . The credo of Deuteronomy 26 mentions the entry into Canaan as a second article; the deliverance of the Exodus was only made with a view to the possession of the country.[20]

This Exodus-Conquest pattern was also decisive for the history of Jesus. Old Testament scholar G. E. Wright showed in his book, *God Who Acts*, that the primary means of God revealing God's self was through decisive acts in salvation history. He shows that the Exodus and the Conquest "are as important for the New Testament as for the Old. In Christ is the new Exodus and the new inheritance [the Conquest]."[21]

Karl Barth showed that "the New Testament witnesses, too, counted upon the Christian life only on the basis of these factors [of Easter and Pentecost]."[22] These two events are the focal points of Christian initiation. As we shall see in the final chapter, the new baptismal liturgy captures the significance of these two events—Easter and Pentecost—as the New Tesament counterpart of the Exodus and Conquest events.

When the people asked on the day of Pentecost, "What shall we do?" Peter's response was for them to have their own personal Exodus and Conquest event: "Repent, and be baptized every one of you in the name of Jesus Christ for the forgiveness of your sins [the Exodus event]; and you shall receive the gift of the Holy Spirit [the Conquest event]. For the promise [made by the prophets that the fortunes of Israel would be restored] is to you and to your children and to all who are far off [i.e., the Gentiles]" (Acts 2·38-39; cf. Acts 22:2 1; Ephesians 2:13, 17). Here Peter is saying that the gift of the Spirit makes you a member of the restored kingdom, not physical circumcision.

Luke showed that the original Pentecost event happened suddenly and was not by human effort. The prophets repeatedly said: God will sanctify you (Ezekiel 28:25; 36:23, 37:28, 38:16; 39:27); God will circumcise your heart so that you may love him perfectly (Deuteronomy 30:6); God will bring you back to this place (Jer. 30:3); God will restore your fortunes (Ezekiel 29: 14); God will pour out His Spirit (Ezekiel 39:29).

As the background for understanding the meaning of Pentecost, Luke said that the disciples were expecting the restoration of the new kingdom to occur at any time. After his resurrection, Jesus appeared to the disciples for forty days, "speaking of the kingdom of God" and instructing them "not to depart from Jerusalem, but to wait for the promise of the Father, which, he said, you heard from me, for John baptized with water, but before many days you shall be baptized with the Holy Spirit" (Acts 1:3-5).

The disciples then asked: "Lord, will you at this time *restore* the kingdom to Israel?" (Acts 1:6). This question showed that the disciples believed that the new Conquest was about to happen. Jesus encouraged his disciples to be patient with God's timing, assuring them that this would happen according to what "the Father has fixed by his own authority" (Acts 1 :7). Jesus then told them that they would receive "power."

During his earthly ministry, Jesus had promised his disciples that they would see "the kingdom of God ... come with power" (Mark 9:1) and they would be "clothed with power from on high" (Luke 24:49). This "power from on high" would give them the ability to be faithful citizens of the new kingdom, unlike the weak and fickle loyalty of the ancient Israelites whose hearts were uncircumcised and rebellious toward God. The terrified and timid group of 120 believers were baptized with the Holy Spirit and fire, and suddenly they were "more than conquerors" (to use a favorite phrase of the Wesleys to describe perfection of love).

Beginning with Jerusalem (the center of the old kingdom) this restored kingdom would spread to the ends of the earth (Acts 1:8) through the power of the Spirit until there would be "a grand Pentecost" (as John Wesley put it in his sermon on "The General Spread of the Gospel" when righteousness will cover the earth as waters cover the sea).

Pentecost celebrated the fulfillment of the prophecy of Moses in Deuteronomy 30. Pentecost meant that "the law of God was written on the heart." (Jeremiah 31:33). This was because God's Spirit had been poured out (Ezekiel 36:27).

Pentecost was an infusion of pure love for God and each other as they lived in "one accord" (Acts I: 14) and in fellowship *(koinonia)* together (Acts 2:42). The sign of this new reality was the restoration of spiritual gifts—prophecies, visions, dreams, wonders, and tongues (Acts 2:5-20).

What connected the Old Testament and the New Testament writers was their theology of salvation history, and the goal of this history is for God's people to live in loving fellowship with each other.

To think of the display of power on the day of Pentecost as intending to emphasize primarily supernatural phenomena would contradict the purpose of salvation history. Jesus's condemned the Pharisees who were obsessed with the sensational need for miracles rather than with him (Matt. 12:38-42). The phenomena of miracles were part of the Messianic expectation when in the last days the kingdom would be restored. Miracles were signs that the kingdom had come with the Messiah. Miraculous phenomena are important confirmations of the work of God in any day or age and play a supporting role, but they are not the essence of God's revelation—which is that God is love and God wants this love which the Father has for the Son through the Spirit to be poured out on the Church.

Some scholars use a modern historical-critical method of exegesis to say that because love and sanctification are not explicitly mentioned in Acts 2 shows that Pentecost was only about miraculous gifts and phenomena. This interpretation fails to understand Pentecost in its salvation-historical context. The day of Pentecost was the arrival of the inner meaning of the kingdom of God ("righteousness, peace, and joy in the Holy Spirit," as the Wesleys put it), and the visible miracles served as a confirmation that the new kingdom had arrived.

Rudolf Bultmann, the most prominent and significant New Testament scholar in the 20th century, is right to say that "it is self-evident" with Peter that "the outpouring of the Spirit at Pentecost" means "sanctification by the Spirit" (1 Peter 1:2) because it was "the fulfilment of Joel's prophecy for the end of days." Bultmann showed that Peter and the disciples on the day of Pentecost considered themselves "the sanctified heirs-apparent of the eschatological salvation."[23]

If Peter understood the day of Pentecost to mean "sanctification by the Spirit," his Jewish hearers would have understood exactly the same meaning. They would have understood what Paul said about the giving of the Spirit on the day of Pentecost as the outpouring of divine love (Romans 5:3) and what Peter said happened as their hearts were circumcised by faith, i.e. sanctified (Acts 15:8-9), as will be noted below.

An abstract exegesis fails to get the full story of Acts 2 because it does not include the larger context of salvation history. It has well been said that "a text without a context is a pretext." Also part of the context is the Church, and as we shall see in the last chapter the liturgy of the primitive Church included Pentecost as the seal, or sanctification, of the Spirit. Easter and Pentecost together constituted the two saving moments of intiation into the Church.

In his sermon on "Christian Perfection" (1741), John Wesley cited all twenty eight verses of Charles Wesley's hymn, *"The Promise of Sanctification,"* based on *Ezekiel 36:25*. This hymn was intended to show that the Promised Land of Canaan was a foreshadowing of the coming of the Spirit on the day of Pentecost to enable the New Israel to love God with a pure heart.

> The Promise of Sanctification (Ezekiel 36:25, &c.)[24]
>
> 1. God of all power, and truth, and grace,
>   Which shall from age to age endure;
> Whose word, when heaven and earth shall pass,
>   Remains, and stands for ever sure:
>
> 2. Calmly to thee my soul looks up,
>   And waits thy promises to prove;
> The object of my steadfast hope,
>   The seal of thine eternal love.
>
> 3. That I thy mercy may proclaim,
>   That all mankind thy truth may see,
> Hallow thy great and glorious name,
>   And perfect holiness in me.
>
> 4. Chose from the world, if now I stand
>   Adorn'd in righteousness divine;
> If, brought unto the promis'd land,
>   I justly call the Saviour mine;

5. Perform the work thou hast begun,
     My inmost soul to thee convert:
Love me, for ever love thine own,
     And sprinkle with thy blood my heart.

6. Thy sanctifying Spirit pour,
     To quench my thirst, and wash me clean;
Now, Father, let the gracious shower
     Descend, and make me pure from sin.

7. Purge me from every sinful blot;
     My idols all be cast aside:
Cleanse me from every evil thought,
     From all the filth of self and pride.

8. Give me a new, a perfect heart,
     From doubt, and fear, and sorrow free;
The mind which was in Christ impart,
     And let my spirit cleave to thee.

9. O take this heart of stone away,
     (Thy rule it doth not, cannot own;)
In me no longer let it stay:
     O take away this heart of stone.

10. The hatred of my carnal mind
      Out of my flesh at once remove;
Give me a tender heart, resign'd,
      And pure, and filled with faith and love.

11. Within me thy good Spirit place,
      Spirit of health, and love and power;
Plant in me thy victorious grace,
      And sin shall never enter more.

12. Cause me to walk in Christ my Way,
      And I thy statutes shall fulfill;
In every point thy law obey.
      And perfectly perform thy will.

13. Hast thou not said, who canst not lie,
      That I thy law shall keep and do?
Lord, I believe, tho' men deny;
      They all are false, but thou art true.

14. O that I now, from sin released,
      Thy word might to the utmost prove!
Enter into the promised rest,
      The Canaan of thy perfect love!

15. There let me ever, ever dwell;

By thou my God, and I will be
Thy servant: O set to thy seal!
Give me eternal life in thee.

16. From all remaining filth within
   Let me in Thee salvation have:
From actual, and from inbred sin
   My ransom'd soul persist to save.

17. Wash out my old original stain:
   Tell me no more It cannot be,
Demons or men! The Lamb was slain
   His blood was all pour'd out for me!

18. Sprinkle it, Jesu, on my heart:
   One drop of thy all-cleansing blood
Shall make my sinfulness depart,
   And fill me with the life of God.

19. Father, supply my every need:
   Sustain the life thyself hast given;
Call for the corn, the living bread,
   The manna that comes down from heaven.

20. The gracious fruits of righteousness,
   Thy blessings' unexhausted store,
In me abundantly increase;
   Nor let me ever hunger more.

21. Let me no more in deep complaint
   "My leanness, O my leanness!" cry;
Alone consum'd with pining want,
   Of all my Father's children I!

22. The painful thirst, the fond desire,
   Thy joyous presence shall remove;
While my full soul doth still require
   Thy whole eternity of love.

23. Holy, and true, and righteous Lord,
   I wait to prove thy perfect will;
Be mindful of thy gracious word,
   And stamp me with thy Spirit's seal!

24. Thy faithful mercies let me find,
   In which thou causest me to trust;
Give me the meek and lowly mind,
   And lay my spirit in the dust.

25. Show me how foul my heart hath been,
   When all renew'd by grace I am;
When thou hast emptied me of sin,

> Show me the fullness of my shame.
>
> 26. Open my faith's interior eye,
>   Display thy glory from above;
> And all I am shall sink and die,
>   Lost in astonishment and love.
>
> 27. Confound, o'erpower me with thy grace:
>   I would be by myself abhor'd;
> (All might, all majesty, all praise,
>   All glory be to Christ my Lord!)
>
> 28. Now let me gain perfection's height!
>   Now let me into nothing fall!
> Be less than nothing in thy sight,
>   And feel that Christ is all in all!

Charles Wesley often used the Promised Land motif as a description of Christian perfection. Here is a typical lyric hymn for Number 13:30, "Caleb stilled the people, and said, Let us go up at once, and possess it, for we are well able to overcome it"—

> Is anything too hard for God?
>   Thro' Jesus we can all things do;
> Who Satan and his works destroy'd,
>   Shall make us more than conquerors too:
> Let us at once the land possess,
>   And taste the blessings from above,
> The milk sincere of pardoning grace,
>   The honey of his perfect love.[25]

Here is another lyric hymn that showed that the occupation of the land of Canaan symbolized the realization of perfect love here and now while at the same time symbolizing the rest of heaven. It is based on Number 14:24, "And his seed shall possess it."

> All that in his footsteps tread,
>   And dare their faith confess,
> They are valiant Caleb's seed,
>   And shall the land possess:
> Trusting God to bring *us* in,
>   We shall be perfected in love,
> Enter here the rest from sin,
>   And then the rest above.[26]

Moses prophesied that they would be restored forever in the land because their hearts would be circumcised enabling them to love God with all their hearts. What physical circumcision was unable to accomplish for them, a circumcision of the heart would succeed so that they could live up to the requirement of a perfect love for God. (Deuteronomy 30:1-6).

This theme of spiritual circumcision became a theme of the prophets regarding the

Messianic times. This is why Peter said on the day of Pentecost that the prophecy of Joel had now been fulfilled—when in the last days the Messiah would come to rescue and restore the people of Israel to their land. The restoration on the day of Pentecost was not anything like what was expected because the kingdom was not a restored political kingdom, but the kingdom was a new kingdom of righteousness, peace, and joy in the Holy Spirit when God's full presence was restored inwardly in the hearts of Jesus' followers.

Now, as a result of Pentecost, the new kingdom was begun. Jesus had told his disciples not to be preoccupied with the question when the kingdom would come because that would happen in God's timing. His instruction was "to wait for the promise of the Father … [when] you shall be baptized with the Holy Spirit" (Acts 1:4-5). They would then "receive power" to be "my witnesses."

Using the *filling* language of "pouring," Paul said the love of God filled their hearts on the day of Pentecost (Romans 5:3–5): "God's love has been poured [Pentecost language] into our hearts through the Holy Spirit which has been given to us [Pentecost language]."

Peter reported to the Jerusalem Council that physical circumcision was not able to accomplish God's intent for Israel, and hence a new kind of circumcision was necessary. Peter said what happened to the uncircumcised house of Cornelius in Acts 10 was the same thing that happened to them on the day of Pentecost: "God made no distinction between us and them, but cleansed their hearts by faith" (Acts 15:8-9).

"Cleansing" was the term that the Old Testament prophets substituted for circumcision.[27] Jeremiah proclaimed: "Circumcise yourself to the Lord, remove the foreskins of your hearts" (Jeremiah 4:4). The Wesley brothers often used being "cleansed from all sin" and "circumcision of heart" for Christian perfection.

Charles Wesley linked the promise that Jesus would baptize with the Spirit to circumcision of heart, cleansing from sin, and perfect love:

> By thy first Blood-shedding heal us,
>   Cut us off from every Sin;
> By thy Circumcision seal us,
>   Write thy Law of Love within;
> Let thy Spirit circumcise us:
>   Kindle in our Hearts a Flame,
> By thy Baptism [with the Holy Spirit] baptize us
>   Into all thy glorious Name.[28]

Here is Charles Wesley's commentary on Acts 15:8, 9, "God gave them the Holy Ghost, purifying their hearts by faith."

> God of grace, vouchsafe to me
>   That Spirit of holiness,
> Sighs my heart for purity,
>   And pants for perfect peace;
> Spirit of faith, the blood apply,
>   Which only can my filth remove,
> Fill my soul, and sanctify
>   By Jesu's heavenly love.[29]

Here is another commentary on Acts 15:8, 9:

> By thy Spirit's inspiration
>   Bid my evil thoughts depart,
> All the filth of pride and passion,
>   Purge out of my faithful heart:
> Then I shall with joy embrace thee,
>   Meet to see thy face above,
> Then I worthily shall praise thee,
>   Then I perfectly shall love.[30]

He also gives this commentary on Acts 15:8-9:

> 2. Yet if in me thy Spirit dwell,
>   The Pledge, the Witness, and the Seal,
> My heart shall lose its inbred stain,
>   Holy, and just, and pure remain,
> Free from concupiscence and pride,
>   While God doth in his house reside.[31]

The distinctive mark of physical circumcision was replaced by the Old Testament prophets with the language of "cleanness." Unable to do it themselves, this cleansing was to be done by the Spirit of God. Ezekiel prophesied:

> I will take you from the nations [a new Exodus], and gather you from all the countries, and bring you into your own land [a new Conquest]. I will sprinkle clear water upon you, and you shall be clean from all your uncleannesses, and from all your idols I will cleanse you. A new heart I will give you, and a new spirit I will put within you; and I will take out of your flesh the heart of stone and give you a heart of flesh. And I will put my Spirit within you, and cause you to walks in my statutes. . . . You shall be my people, and I will be your God (Ezekiel 36:24-28).

Ezekiel also described this new Conquest as meaning that Israel would be made holy: "Then the nations will know that I the Lord sanctify Israel, when my sanctuary is in the midst of them for evermore" (Ezekiel 37:28). This future restoration of the fortunes of Israel will occur, Ezekiel says, "when I pour out my Spirit upon the house of Israel" (Ezekiel 39:29). Jeremiah said: "Behold, the days are coming, says the Lord, when I will make a new covenant with the house of Israel, not like the [old] covenant. . . . I will put my law within them, and I will write it upon their hearts" (31:31-34). Joel prophesied that God "will pour out my spirit on all flesh" (Joel 2:28) and that God "will restore the fortunes of Judah" (Joel 3: I). This means that "my people shall never again be put to shame" (Joel 2:27) because "I am the Lord your God, who dwell in Zion, my holy mountain. And Jerusalem shall be holy" (Joel 3: 17).

Citing this future expectation of Joel and the prophets of a new kingdom when the people of God would be filled with the Holy Spirit enabling them to live up to the terms of the covenant made with Abraham, Peter said simply "this is what" happened on the day of Pentecost (Acts 2:16).

As noted above, this is why Peter said to the Jerusalem Council that the day of Pentecost marked the beginning of the new kingdom consisting of those whose hearts had been cleansed by the Holy Spirit. This is why Paul said that on the day of Pentecost God's love was poured into their hearts by faith (Romans 5:5).

Gerhard von Rad has shown that the image of the Promised Land in the Old Testament was not a picture of heaven, but a reality for here and now.[32] There are some remarkable dissimilarities between Canaan and heaven—giants stalking the place, spiritual defeat, starvation, and even exile from it. Surely the Christian life is a life of trial and tribulation, but such trouble does not exist in heaven.

The Hebrew writer encouraged believers "Today . . . to enter into that rest." He said: "Let us therefore strive to enter that rest" (Hebrews 4:7, 11). John Calvin also saw Canaan as a symbol of the Christian life. Calvin's commentary on Hebrews 4:8, shows that the writer thought of Canaan as land of rest to be enjoyed here and now.[33]

The Wesley brothers interpreted the land of Canaan as a symbol of the restored kingdom through the outpouring of the Spirit of Christ upon the church, and at the same time they saw it as "an earnest of eternal inheritance."[34]

The "rest" of Hebrews 4 has both a present and an eschatological meaning in John Wesley[35] and Charles Wesley. Charles' hymns also less frequently referred to the "heavenly rest" and "the Celestial Canaan," preferring to speak of "the earnest of heaven" here and now and "the Canaan of perfect love."

This corresponds to the widely acknowledged distinction in the New Testament between "the already" and "not yet" aspects of the kingdom of God. The kingdom is coming, but it is also already here. What is here is an anticipation of the "not yet," similar to Charles' idea of perfect love as the "antepast" and "earnest" of heaven.

This can be seen in one of his "Hymn to the Holy Ghost" where he speaks of the giving of the Holy Spirit as being "born of God" and as bestowing "all the plentitude of God":

> 9. Pledge of thy promise giv'n,
>   My antepast of heav'n;
> Earnest thou of joys divine,
>   Joys divine on me bestowed,
> Heav'n and Christ, and all is mine,
>   All the plentitude of God.[36]

Here is a hymn where Charles used "hasten" as the meaning of "labor"—to hurry up—in Hebrews 4:11, "Let us hasten to enter that rest," The King James Version translated Joshua 4:10, "and the people hastened and passed over." Charles connected this original idea of hastening into the promised land with the prophetic expectation in Jeremiah 30:8, "In that day I will break this yoke."

> Hasten, Lord, the day of rest
>   From this indwelling sin,
> Vindicate thy church oppressed,
>   And still enslav'd within;
> Burst our bonds, and let us go
>   From every thought of evil freed,
> Pure in heart, and saints below,

And like our sinless head.[37]

Charles Wesley composed a hymn in 1783 based on Hebrew 4:11, "Let us labour to enter into that rest."

> 1. Rest to my soul I gasp to find
>   In Jesus meek and lowly mind,
> In holy joy, and spotless love
>   That foretaste of the rest above!
> But ah, my flesh doth oft complain,
>   Tired with the long, laborious pain,
> And fainting in the vehement strife
>   I quit my hold of endless life.
>
> 2. Jesus, thy feeblest servant fill
>   With power to labour up the hill
> With zeal toward the high prize to press,
>   With violent faith the crown to seize;
> By Thee stir'd up I'll strive again,
>   I'll after full perfection strain
> Instant in prayer's strong agony
>   Till pure in heart, thy face I see.
>
> 3. Then, then my soul with rapid speed
>   Shall labour up to grasp its Head:
> All vigor, all activity
>   I live, not I, but Christ in me;
> Passive, yet swift as light I fly
>   Filled with the Power, who fills the sky,
> And draws me to that glorious throne
>   To rest, with God for ever one![38]

Charles also spoke of the rest of Christian perfection to be "the earnest of *my* heaven!"[39]

Their writings and hymns contain numerous references to the Promised Land as the Land of Rest and the Land of Perfect love. The writer to the Hebrews (4:11) said; "Let us hasten to enter into this rest."

The writer's sense of urgency was to inspire the believer to enjoy the kingdom here and now and to make haste and enter—lest we too fall away from the privileges of the restored kingdom. Charles Wesley wrote:

> 14. O that I now from sin releas'd
>   Thy word might to the utmost prove!
> Enter into the promis'd rest,
>   The Canaan of thy perfect love![40]

Here are two verses from another lengthy hymn on the Promised Land as a symbol of perfect love. The hymn is entitled, "Desiring to Love." He conludes this verse with a "lot" of love. The division of Canaan Land into "lots" (Joshua 14:2) is the typological meaning of the expression "lot of love."

> 7. O that I might at once go up,
> No more on this side Jordan stop,
>   But now the land possess,
> This moment end my legal years,
> Sorrows, and sins, and doubts and fears,
>   An howling wilderness!
>
> 8. Now, O my Joshua, bring me in,
> Cast out my foes; the inbred sin,
>   The carnal mind remove:
> The purchase of thy death divide,
> And O! With all the sanctified
>   Give me a lot of love.[41]

Charles Wesley also saw the Promised Land as an "antedate" of heaven. To "feel our sins forgiven" is another expression for the "second rest" and "perfect Gift."

> 2. Thro' Jesus' righteousness alone
>   We feel our sins forgiven,
> And find eternity begun,
>   And antedate our heaven.
> 3. But shall we rest in Pardning Grace
>   On this side Jordan stop?
> No, Lord, we look to see thy Face,
>   And after Thee wake up.
>
> 4. A glorious Prize is still behind,
>   For those that dare believe,
> And we the Second Rest shall find,
>   The perfect Gift receive.[42]

Charles Wesley also related the Promised Land to the Promise of the Holy Spirit to come on the day of Pentecost:

> 7. Led thro' the howling wilderness
>   If now I view the promis'd land,
> Here let my weary wandrings cease,
>   Divide the waves with thy right-hand,
> Bid me thro' Jordan's stream go on;
> Speak, Father; am I not thy son?
>
> 10. If now the bowels of thy love
>   Yearn over such a worm as me,
> Send down thy Spirit from above,
>   And make me clean, and set me free,
> The promised Comforter send down;
> Speak, Father; am I not thy son?

> 14. I cannot rest 'till pure within;
>   Tho' he hath wash'd away my stains,
> Remov'd the guilt and power of sin,
>   Yet while the carnal mind remains,
> I still must make my ceaseless moan;
> Speak, Father; am I not thy son?[43]

John Wesley cited Charles Wesley's hymn in *A Plain Account of Christian Perfection* that captures the imagery of Canaan Land, Pentecost, and Christian perfection. Its biblical reference is the promise of rest in the Land of Canaan which the Hebrew writer shows is only a prefiguration of the "rest which belongs to the people of God" (Hebrews 4:9). Here is the full hymn:

> "There remaineth therefore a rest to the people of God."
>
> 1. Lord, I believe a rest remains
>   To all thy people known,
> A rest, where pure enjoyment reigns,
>   And thou art lov'd alone.
>
> 2. A rest, where all our soul's desire
>   Is fixed on things above,
> Where doubt, and pain, and fear expire,
>   Cast out by perfect love.
>
> 3. A rest of lasting joy and peace,
>   Where all is calm within:
> 'Tis then from our own works we cease,
>   From pride, and self, and sin.
>
> 4. Our life is hid with Christ in God;
>   The agony is o'er,
> We wrestle not with flesh and blood,
>   We *strive* with sin no more.
>
> 5. Our sp'rit is right, our heart is clean,
>   Our nature is renew'd,
> We cannot now, we cannot sin,
>   For we are born of God.
>
> 6. From ev'ry evil motion freed,
>   (The Son hath made us free)
> On all the powers of hell we tread,
>   In glorious liberty.
>
> 7. Redeem'd, we walk on holy ground,
>   On God we cast our care;
> No lion in that way is found,
>   No rav'nous beast is there!

8. Safe in the way of life, above
   Death, earth, and hell we rise;
We find, when perfected in love,
   Our long-sought paradise.

9. Within that Eden we retire,
   We rest in Jesu's name:
It guards us, as a wall of fire,
   And as a sword of flame.

10. O that I now the rest might know,
    Believe, and enter in!
Now, Saviour, now the power bestow,
    And let me cease from sin.

11. Remove this hardness from my heart,
    This unbelief remove,
To me the rest of faith impart,
    The Sabbath of thy love.

12. I groan from sin to be set free,
    From self to be releas'd;
Take me, O take me into thee
    My everlasting rest.

13. I would be thine, thou know'st I would,
    And have thee all my own,
Thee, O my all-sufficient good,
    I want, and thee alone.

14. Thy name to me, thy nature grant;
    This, only this be given,
Nothing besides my God I want,
    Nothing in earth or heaven.

15. Come, O my Saviour, come away,
    Into my soul descend,
No longer from thy creature stay,
    My author, and my end.

16. The bliss thou hast for me prepar'd
    No longer be delay'd;
Come, my exceeding great reward,
    For whom I first was made.

17. Come, Father, Son, and Holy Ghost,
    And seal me thine abode,
Let all I am in thee be lost,
    Let all I am be God![44]

In Ezekiel 36 is the promise of the new kingdom being established because the old kingdom failed:

> I scattered them among the nations, and they were dispersed through the countries; in accordance with their conduct and their deeds I judged them . . . They profaned my holy name." The prophets then announced that the Lord was about to something new: "It is not for your sake, O house of Israel, that I am about to act, but for the sake of my holy name, which you have profaned among the nations to which you came. And I will vindicate the holiness of my great name, which has been profaned among the nations, . . . and the nations will know that I am the Lord, says the Lord God, when through you I vindicate my holiness before their eyes. For I will take you from the nations, and gather you from all the countries, and bring you into your own land. I will sprinkle clean water upon you, and you shall be clean from all your uncleanness, and from all your idols I will cleanse you. A new heart I will give you, and a new spirit I will put within you; and I will take out of your flesh the heart of stone and give you a heart of flesh. And I will put my spirit within you, and cause you walk in my statutes and be careful to observe my ordinances. You shall dwell in the land which I gave to your fathers; and you shall be my people, and I will be your God. And I will deliver you from all your uncleannesses; and I will summon the grain and make it abundant and lay no famine upon you. I will make the fruit of the tree and the increase of the field abundant, that you may never again suffer the disgrace of famine among the nations Ezekiel 36:19-30).

John Wesley cited this passage as the Old Testament expectation of the coming of the Spirit to fully sanctify believers so that they will be clean and enabled to love God perfectly.[45]

On May 7, 1741, Charles "visited Hannah Cennick, full of love to her savior, crying out 'Liberty, liberty! This is the glorious liberty of God's children!'"[46] The use of the term "liberty" was a term Charles Wesley, like his brother John, used for Christian perfection.

On May 24, 1741, Charles recorded that he had "preached on Jacob wrestling for the blessing."[47] The scene in Genesis 32:24-31 was the basis of his famous poem "Wrestling Jacob." It was printed in *Hymns and Sacred Poems* in 1742. It is an inspiring description of one seeking to experience the perfect love of God. Isaac Watts said of this poem: "That single poem, Wrestling Jacob, is worth all the verses which I have ever written."[48]

Wrestling Jacob

1. Come, O thou traveller unknown,
    Whom still I hold, but cannot see,
My company before is gone,
    And I am left alone with thee,
With thee all night I mean to stay,
    And wrestle till the break of day.
2. I need not tell thee who I am,
    My misery, or sin declare,
Thyself hast called me by my name,
    Look on thy hands, and read it there,
But who, I ask thee, who art thou,
    Tell me thy name, and tell me now?

3. In vain thou strugglest to get free,
   I never will unloose my hold:
Art thou the man that died for me?
   The secret of thy love unfold;
Wrestling I will not let thee go,
   Till I thy name, thy nature know.

4. Wilt thou not yet to me reveal
   Thy new, unutterable name?
Tell me, I still beseech thee, tell,
   To know it now resolv'd I am;
Wrestling I will not let thee go,
   Till I thy name, thy nature know.

5. 'Tis all in vain to hold thy tongue,
   Or touch the hollow of my thigh:
Though every sinew be unstrung,
   Out of my arms thou shalt not fly;
Wrestling I will not let thee go,
   Till I thy name, thy nature know.

6. What tho' my shrinking flesh complain,
   And murmur to contend so long,
I rise superior to my pain,
   When I am weak then I am strong,
And when my all of strength shall fail,
   I shall with the God-man prevail.

7. My strength is gone, my nature dies,
   I sink beneath thy weighty hand,
Faint to revive, and fall to rise;
   I fall, and yet by faith I stand,
I stand, and will not let thee go,
   Till I thy name, thy nature know.

8. Yield to me now—for I am weak;
   But confident in self-despair:
Speak to my heart, in blessings speak,
   Be conquer'd by my instant prayer,
Speak, or thou never hence shalt move,
   And tell me, if thy name is love.

9. 'Tis love, 'tis love! Thou diedst for me,
   I hear thy whisper in my heart.
The morning breaks, the shadows flee:
   Pure UNIVERSAL LOVE thou art,
To me, to all thy bowels move,
   Thy nature, and thy name is love.

10. My prayer hath power with God; the grace

> Unspeakable I now receive,
>   Thro' faith I see thee face to face,
>   I see thee face to face, and live:
> In vain I have not wept, and strove,
>   Thy nature, and thy name is love.
>
> 11. I know thee, Saviour, who thou art,
>   Jesus, the feeble sinner's friend;
> Nor wilt thou with the night depart,
>   But stay, and love me to the end;
> Thy mercies never shall remove,
>   Thy nature, and thy name is love.
>
> 12. The Sun of righteousness on me
>   Hath rose with healing in his wings,
> Withered my nature's strength; from thee
>   My soul its life and succour brings,
> My help is all laid up above;
>   Thy nature, and thy name is love.
>
> 13. Contented now upon my thigh
>   I halt, till life's short journey end;
> All helplessness, all weakness I,
>   On thee alone for strength depend,
> Nor have I power, from thee, to move;
>   Thy nature, and thy name is love.
>
> 14. Lame as I am, I take the prey,
>   Hell, earth, and sin with ease o'ercome;
> I leap for joy, pursue my way,
>   And as a bounding hart fly home,
> Thro' all eternity to prove
>   Thy nature, and thy name is love.[49]

An earlier hymn written within a few weeks of his conversion using the "wrestling" imagery in pursuit of holiness was quoted earlier, based on John 16:24.

> Lord, I will not let thee go,
>   Till THE BLESSING thou bestow.

In "Hymns to the Trinity" (1767), Charles Wesley used this imagery of Wrestling Jacob to speak of perfect love:

> Wrestling on in mighty prayer,
>   Lord, we will not let thee go,
> 'Till thou all thy mind declare,
>   All thy grace on us bestow;
> Peace, the seal of sin forgiven,
>   Joy, and perfect love impart,
>   resent, everlasting heaven,
> All thou hast, and all thou art.[50]

Charles and John both used this imagery in their journals and letters to speak of Christian perfection. In a letter Samuel Lloyd on July 17, 1750, Charles urged him to pursue "the One Thing needful" and a "victorious faith" and to "wrestle for the blessing of the gospel" and urging him that "you may never rest without it."[51]

The imagery of "wrestling Jacob" also became part of a Methodist way of speaking of Christian perfection.[52] Multiple examples could be cited, and the following is one instance that was popularized in John Wesley's biography of John Fletcher, whom he called on the title page, "That Truly Great and Venerable Man."

John Wesley's report comes from Joseph Benson, who was the principal of Trevecca College when John Fletcher was the president. At the conclusion of his lectures, John Fletcher invited students who were . . .

> "athirst for this fullness of the Spirit, follow me into my room." On this, many of us have instantly followed him, and there continued till noon, wrestling like Jacob for the blessing, praying one after another, till we could bear to kneel no longer. This was not done once or twice, but many times.[53]

Benson reported that sometimes on these occasions John Fletcher was "so filled with the love of God that he could contain no more."

John Wesley inserted the imagery of "wrestling like Jacob for the blessing" from Charles' hymn in his account of Fletcher, Benson, and the students at Trevecca who were "athirst for this fullness of the Spirit":

> Give me the enlarg'd desire
> And open, Lord, my soul,
> Thy own fullness to require,
> And comprehend the whole!
> Stretch my faith's capacity
> Wider, and yet wider still:
> Then with all that is in thee
> My ravish'd spirit fill![54]

Another example is contained in a letter which John Wesley quoted from John Manners in one of his journal entries:

> The fire catches all that come near. An old soldier, in his return from Germany to the north of Ireland, fell in one night with these wrestling Jacobs, to his great astonishment. He was justified seventeen years ago, but afterward fell from it for five years. As he was going to Germany, in the beginning of the war, the Lord healed him in Dublin; and in spite of all the distresses of a severe campaign, he walked in the light continually. On his return through London, he was convinced of the necessity of sanctification; and soon after he came hither, his heart was broken in pieces, while he was with a little company who meet daily for prayer. One evening, as they were going away, he stopped them, and begged they would not go till the Lord had blessed him. They kneeled down again, and did not cease wrestling with God, till he had a witness that he was saved from all sin.[55]

More details about the ministry of John Manners with John Wesley in this same time frame is given in the official history of Methodism in Ireland using the expression "wrestling" for "a baptism of the Holy Spirit in sanctifying power" and hoping "to enter that rest which remains to the people of God."[56]

We can see here as early as 1762, the "baptism with the Spirit" was being used for full sanctification within Methodism, which is well before Fletcher would soon popularize the expression in his "Essay on Truth" in *Checks to Antinomianism* in 1774. We know that Fletcher was using this expression in his preaching in the early 1760s when he became vicar of Madeley.[57] He derived this phrase from John Wesley and Charles Wesley. Other preachers such as Joseph Pilmore were also using this expression well before Fletcher wrote on this topic, as seen in Pilmore's diaries.[58]

"The rest of faith" and "wrestling with Jacob" along with Pentecost expressions were common. In the *Arminian Magazine* in 1799 is a report of one who "soon began to cry very earnestly for full sanctification, and Jacob like, wrestle till she prevailed: and then cried out, —Glory be to God, he hath now fully saved me."[59]

NOTES

1. *Manuscript Journal* 1:302.
2. *Manuscript Journal* 1:301.
3. *Manuscript Journal* 1:303.
4. *Manuscript Journal* 1:304.
5. Gerhard von Rad, *The Problem of the Hexateuch, and Other Essays* trans. E. W. Trueman Dicken (London: SCM press Ltd., 1984; Gerhard von Rad, "Typological Interpretation of the Old Testament," in *Essays on Old Testament Hermeneutics*, ed. Claus Westermann. Trans. James Luther Mays (London: SCM Ltd., 1963), 17-39.
6. MS Acts, MARC: MA 1977/555 (Charles Wesley Notebooks Box 1), 111.
7. Cf. Rudolf Bultmann, *Theology of the New Testament* (New York: Charles Scribner's Sons, 1955) 1:233.
8. Charles Wesley. *Short Hymns on Select Passages of the Holy Scriptures* (Bristol: Farley, 1762), 1:91.
9. Ibid., 1:94.
10. *Scripture Hymns* (1762), 1:98-99.
11. Ibid., 1:99.
12. Ibid., 1:100.
13. Ibid., 1:103.
14. Outler, *Sermons*, 3:78, "On Perfection"
15. Alan Richardson, "Salvation, Savior," *The Interpreter's Dictionary of the Bible*, ed. George A. Buttrick (Nashville: Abingdon Press, 1962), R-Z, 170.
16. Ibid. 172
17. Ibid.
18. Edmond Jacob, *Theology of the Old Testament*, trans. Arthur W. Heathcote and Philip J. Allcock (New York: Harper and Brothers, 1958), 192.
19. Ibid., 192-193.
20. Ibid., 191.
21. G. Ernest Wright, *God Who Acts* (London: SCM Press, 1962), 63.
22. Karl Barth, *Church Dogmatics*, trans. G. W. Bromiley (Edinburgh: T. & T. Clark, 1969), IV, Part IV, 30.
23. Rudolf Bultmann, *The Theology of the New Testament,* (New York: Charles Scribner's Sons, 195), 1:155.

24. Outler, *Sermons,* 2:122-124, "Christian Perfection"
25. Charles Wesley. *Short Hymns on Select Passages of the Holy Scriptures.* (1762), 1:170
26. Ibid., 1:75.
27. Gerhard von Rad, *Deuteronomy. A Commentary,* trans. Dorothea Barton (Philadelphia: Westminster Press, 1966), 183-184.
28. Charles Wesley, *Hymns for Our Lord's Resurrection* (London: Strahan, 1746), 10.
29. Charles Wesley. *Short Hymns on Select Passages of the Holy Scriptures*, 2:271.

30. Ibid., 2:271.

31. MS Acts, MARC: MA 1977/555 (Charles Wesley Notebooks Box 1), 555.

32. Gerhard von Rad, *The Problem of The Hexateuch*, trans. E. W. Dicken (London: SCM Press, Ltd., 1984), 95. Cf. Yehezkel Kaufmann, *The Religion of Israel*, trans. and abridged by Moshe Greenberg (Chicago: The University of Chicago Press, 1960), 241.

33. Cf. John Calvin, *Commentaries on the Epistle of Paul the Apostle to the Hebrews,* ed. John Owen (Grand Rapids: Wm. B. Eerdmans, 1948), 98-99. Calvin wrote: "Now this conformation the Apostle teaches us takes place when we rest from our works. It hence at length follows, that man becomes happy by self-denial. For what else is to cease from our works, but to mortify our flesh, when a man renounces himself that he may live to God? For here we must always begin when we speak of a godly and holy life, that man being in a manner dead to himself, should allow God to live in him, that he should abstain from his own works, so as to give place to God to work. We must indeed confess, that then only is our life rightly formed when it becomes subject to God. But through inbred corruption it is never the case, until we rest from our own works; nay, such is the opposition between God's government and our corrupt affections, that he cannot work in us until we rest. But though, the completion of this rest cannot be attained in this life, yet we ought ever to strive for it. Thus believers enter it but on this condition,—that by running they may continually go forward." The editor (although representing the Reformed tradition) disliked Calvin's interpretation of the Canaan rest as symbolic of holiness. Hence he disagreed with Calvin, noting that "many, like *Calvin,* have made remarks of this kind, but they are out of place here; for the rest here mentioned in clearly the rest in heaven." (99n).

34. *Hymns and Sacred Poems* (1740), 134.

35. *Explanatory Notes on the New Testament*, 571.

36. *Hymns and Sacred Poems* (1739), 111.

37. Charles Wesley. *Short Hymns on Select Passages of the Holy Scriptures.*, 2:26.

38. MS Scriptural Hymns, MARC: MA 1977/576 (Charles Wesley Notebooks Box 3). (1783), 92.

39. John and Charles Wesley, *Hymns and Sacred Poems* (London: Straham, 1740), 131-132.

40. John and Charles Wesley. *Hymns and Sacred Poems* (Bristol: Farley, 1742), 45.

41 *Hymns and Sacred Poems* (1742), 245.

42. *The Unpublished Poetry of Charles Wesley.* ed. S T Kimbrough Jr. & Oliver A. Beckerlegge (Nashville: Kingswood Books, 1988-92), 3:157-58.

43. *Hymns and Sacred Poems* (1742), 143-144.

44. *Hymns and Sacred Poems* (1740), 207.

45. Outler, *Sermons*, 2:120-121, "Christian Perfection"

46. *Manuscript Journal* 1:305.

47. *Manuscript Journal* 1:310.

48. *The Methodist Societies, The Minutes of Conference*, 10:646.

49. *Hymns and Sacred Poems* (1742), 115-118.

50. Charles Wesley. *Hymns for the Use of Families* (Bristol: Pine, 1767), 43.

51. *Letters of Charles Wesley*, 300. July 27, 1750.

52. *Charles Wesley: A Reader*, ed. John R. Tyson (Oxford University Press, 1989), 198.

53. Benson, *The Life of the Rev. John W. de la Flechere*, 146.

54. John Wesley, *A Short Account of the Life and Death of the Rev. John Fletcher* (New York: W. C. Robinson, Printer, 1803), 35-36.

55. *Journal and Diaries, IV (1755–1765)*, 21:375, (July 24, 1762).

56. C. H. Crookshank, *History of Methodism in Ireland* (Belfast: R. S. Allen,Son & Allen-University House, 1885),, 2:168.

57. This sermon is found in a bound book of pages in Fletcher's own handwriting in the Fletcher-Tooth Archival Collection in the John Rylands Library of Manchester (Box 18, Misc. Manuscripts). The booklet opens with these comments to the reader: "Reader. Grant these sheets an impartial perusal, they contain an account of the Doctrine of Salvation by Faith alone, as it is preached in Madeley Church. They will (it is hoped) answer the objections that are made against this important doctrine" Cf. *The Works of the Reverend John Fletcher* (New York: W. Waugh and T. Mason, 1833), 4:270, "The Test of a New Creature." Melville Horne believes these were written during the first few years of his ministry. Ibid. 4:18, "Mr. Horne's Preface."

58. *The Journal of Joseph Pilmore* (Philadelphia: Message Publishing Co., for the Historical Society of the Philadelphia Annual Conference of the United Methodist Church, 1969), 46.

59. *The Methodist Magazine*, 22 (December 1799), 585.

Chapter 9

"The Holy Spirit ... in His Sanctifying Graces"

"That we 'must be baptized with the Holy Spirit,' implies this and no more, that we cannot be 'renewed in righteousness and true holiness' any otherwise than by being over-shadowed, quickened, and animated by that blessed Spirit."[1]
—John Wesley to William Law

"Be 'baptized with the Holy Spirit and with fire' ... till the love of God inflame your heart, and consume all your vile affections! ... That the Spirit alone ... inspires all holiness; that by his inspiration men attain perfect love."[2]
—John Wesley in "A Farther Appeal to Men of Reason and Religion"

"The Holy Spirit was not yet given in his sanctifying graces, as he was after Jesus was glorified. ... And 'when the day of Pentecost was fully come', *then first it was*[2] [in the history of salvation], that they who 'waited for the promise of the Father' were made more than conquerors over sin [a common phrase for Christian perfection] by the Holy Spirit given unto them .... That this great salvation from sin [i.e., Christian perfection] was not given till Jesus was glorified, St. Peter also plainly testifies."[3]
—John Wesley's sermon on "Christian Perfection"

"The Comforter, the Holy Spirit, whom the Father will send in my name," entailed "such a large manifestation of the Divine presence and love, that the former [lower degree of love in the disciples prior to Pentecost] in justification is as nothing in comparison of it [Pentecost gift of perfect love]."[4]
—John Wesley, *Explanatory Notes on the New Testament*

After John Wesley came to learn that the German Moravians had a different view of the stages of faith (as noted above) than the English Moravians, he wrote a letter to them at Herrnhut in August 1741, urging them to provide clarification of their views.[5] This difference between the Moravians entailed the distinction between justification and sanctification.

This letter provoked a personal visit of Count Zinzendorf to John Wesley at Gray's Inn Walks in London on September 3, 1741.[6] The topic of their conversation was over the question whether or not entire sanctification occurred after justifying faith. Zinzendorf essentially denied there were any differences among the Moravians; rather, he said John Wesley's letter showed "you abandon the religion we have been professing together in favor of a new one."

John Wesley was puzzled by this. He explained that his concern was that Christian perfection be properly understood as the goal of this life. John Wesley maintained that "the apostles were justified before Christ's death" and "they were more holy after the day of Pentecost" because "they were 'filled with the Holy Spirit'."

Over against this view, Zinzendorf argued that "from the moment of justification he [any believer] . . . is also entirely sanctified."[7] Ironically, John Wesley used the argument of Christian David against Zinzendorf on whose estate the village of Herrnhut was built. Zinzendorf was also the organizer and bishop of the Moravian Church.

John Wesley's point was that the justifying faith of the disciples before Pentecost and the entire sanctification after Pentecost is a pattern for believers for all times. Here is the full text of that debate, translated by John Wesley's assistant and biographer, Henry Moore[8]:

Z. Why have you changed your religion?

W. I do not know that I have changed my religion. Why do you think so? Who has reported this to you?

Z. Plainly, yourself. I see it from your epistle to us. There, having departed from the religion which you professed among us, you have held out a new one.

W. How so? I do not understand you.

Z. Nay, you say there, that Christians are not miserable sinners: This is most false. The best of men are most miserable sinners, even unto death. If any speak otherwise, they are either manifest impostors, or diabolically seduced. Our Brethren, who taught better things, you have opposed: and when they desired peace, you have refused it.

W. I do not yet understand what you aim at.

Z. When you wrote to me from Georgia, I loved you very much. I perceived that you were simple in heart. You wrote again: I saw, that you were still simple in heart, but troubled in your ideas. You came to us: Your ideas were then still more troubled and confused. You returned to England. A little after, I heard that our Brethren were contending with you. I sent Spangenberg to make peace between you. He wrote to me that the Brethren had injured you. I wrote again, that they should not pursue the strife, but desire forgiveness of you. Spangenberg wrote again, that they had desired this, but that you, glorying over them, had refused peace. Now that I am come, I hear the same thing.

W. The matter does not at all turn on this point. Your Brethren, it is true, did not use me well. Afterwards they desired forgiveness. I answered,—that was superfluous, that I had never been offended with them; but I feared, 1. Lest they should teach falsely. 2. Lest they should live wickedly. This is, and was, the only question between us.

Z. Speak more fully [on that question.]

W. I feared lest they should teach falsely; 1. Concerning the end of our faith in this life, to wit, Christian Perfection. 2. Concerning the means of grace, so termed by our church.

Z. I acknowledge no inherent perfection in this life. This is the error of errors. I pursue it through the world with fire and sword. I trample upon it: I devote it to utter destruction. Christ is our sole perfection. Whoever follows inherent perfection, denies Christ.

W. But, I believe, that the Spirit of Christ works this perfection in true Christians.

Z. By no means. All our perfection is in Christ. All Christian Perfection is, Faith in the blood of Christ. Our whole Christian Perfection is imputed, not inherent. We are perfect in Christ: In ourselves we are never perfect.

W. I think we strive about words. Is not every true believer holy?

Z. Highly so. But he is holy in Christ, not in himself.

W. But does he not live holy?

Z. Yes, he lives holy in all things.

W. And has he not a holy heart?

Z. Most certainly.

W. And is he not consequently holy in himself?

Z. No, no. In Christ only. He is not holy in himself: He hath no holiness at all in himself.

W. Hath he not the *love of God*, and his neighbour, in his heart? Yes, and the whole image of God?

Z. He hath. But these constitute legal holiness, not evangelical. Evangelical holiness is Faith.

W. The dispute is altogether about words. You grant that a believer is altogether holy in heart, and life: that he loves God with all his heart and serves him with all his powers. I desire nothing more. I mean nothing else [by the term] Perfection, or Christian Holiness.

Z. But this is not his holiness. He is not more holy if he loves more, or less holy, if he loves less.

W. What! Does not every believer, while he increases in love, increase equally in holiness?

Z. Not at all. In the moment he is justified, he is sanctified wholly. From that time he is neither more nor less holy, even unto death.

W. Is not therefore a father in Christ holier than a new-born babe?

Z. No. Our whole justification, and sanctification, are in the same instant, and he receives neither more nor less.

W. Does not a true believer increase in love to God daily! Is he *perfected in love,* when he is justified?

Z. He is. He never can increase in the love of God. He loves altogether in that moment, as he is sanctified wholly.

W. What therefore does the Apostle Paul mean by, *"We are renewed day by day?"*

Z. I will tell you. Lead, if it should be changed into gold, is gold the first day, and the second day, and the third: And so it is renewed day by day; but it never is more gold than in the first day.

W. I thought that we should grow in grace!

Z. Certainly ; but not in holiness. Whenever anyone is justified, the Father, the Son, and the Holy Spirit, dwell in his heart; and from that moment his heart is as pure as it ever will be. A babe in Christ is as pure in heart as a father in Christ. There is no difference.

W. Were not the Apostles justified before the death of Christ?

Z. They were.

W. But were they not more holy after the day of Pentecost, than before Christ's death?

Z. By no means.

W. Were they not on that day *filled with the Holy Spirit*?

Z. They were. But that gift of the Spirit did not respect their holiness. It was the gift of miracles only.

W. Perhaps I do not comprehend your meaning. Do we not, while we deny ourselves, die more and more to the world, and live to God?

Z. We reject all self-denial. We trample upon it. We do, as believers, whatsoever we will, and nothing more. We laugh at all mortification. No purification precedes perfect love.

W. What you have said I will thoroughly weigh, God being my helper.

Charles Wesley received a letter three days later from his brother John on September 6, 1741 that he had been interviewed by Zinzendorf. Charles Wesley expressed disappointment that Zinzendorf had denied the possibility of perfection: "Who would believe it of Count Zinzendorf, that he should deny all Christian holiness!"[9]

This friendly debate between John Wesley and Zinzendorf illustrated what was pointed out in Chapter 3—that the substance of John Wesley's theology was Anglican, although the Moravians helped him to understand faith as the means of appropriating justifying and sanctifying grace. The Germans Moravians also helped him also to see that the biblical basis for understanding the distinction between the two stages of faith was the experience of the disciples before and after Pentecost, although this distinction was already present in his Anglican theology of confirmation.

In 1741 after the Bishop of London told the Wesleys to preach their idea of Christian perfection to the world,[10] John Wesley wrote a sermon on "Christian Perfection" containing some of the same emphases found in John Heylyn's Pentecost sermon and in the teaching of Christian David. John Wesley said the possibility of being cleansed from all sin and made perfect in love became a possibility for the world only when the Holy Spirit descended on the disciples on the day of Pentecost. Like John Heylyn, John Wesley explained "the wide difference" between a pre-Pentecost and Pentecost experience in terms of sanctifying grace.[11] He writes:

> The Holy Spirit was not yet given in his sanctifying graces, as he was after Jesus was glorified.... And "when the day of Pentecost was fully come", *then first it was*[12] [in the history of salvation], that they who "waited for the promise of the Father" were made more than conquerors over sin [a common phrase for Christian perfection] by the Holy Spirit given unto them.... That this great salvation from sin [a common phrase for Christian perfection] was not given till Jesus was glorified, St. Peter also plainly testifies.[13]

John Wesley further explained that "this great salvation" was not available to David, and hence David is not the "pattern or standard of Christian perfection" because "the Holy Spirit is now given; the great salvation of God is brought unto men, by the revelation of Jesus Christ." This means the "least in the kingdom of God... is greater than he [David]."

Attached to this sermon (as noted in the previous chapter) is the hymn by Charles Wesley, "The Promise of Sanctification," which highlights the instantaneous sanctifying work of the Spirit of Pentecost to occur "now,"[14] insisting that it is not a mere dream or aspiration but a real possibility in this world:

Charles interpreted Acts 2:4: "They were all filled with the Holy Spirit" to mean they were "filled with the Spirit of holiness.[15]

On July 18, 1741, Charles "took sweet counsel with Mr. Jones alone. The seed is sown in his heart and shall bring forth fruit unto perfection."[16]

On July 26, 1741, at Kingswood Charles preached a sermon, "The One Thing Needful." On July 28, 1741, Charles recorded the complaint "of a predestinarian that the plague of perfection reigns at Bristol, and many of the Welsh catch it. O that all mankind were infected with this plague to be healed of every plague."[17]

In 1742, John Wesley' critics understood him to link "the indwelling of the Spirit" with full sanctification, not justification. In "The Principles of a Methodist" (1742), he answered one of his critics by noting: "I desire not a more consistent account of my principles than he has himself given in the following words" that a justified believer "hath not yet, in the full and proper sense, a *new* and *clean heart*, or the *indwelling* of the Spirit." One who was sanctified was described as one who had attained "the last and highest state of *perfection* in this life. For then are the faithful born again in the full and perfect sense. Then have they the indwelling of the Spirit."[18]

In the 1742 edition of *Hymns and Sacred Poems,* Charles Wesley equated hymn Christian perfection with the abiding witness of the Spirit.

> If we do in thee believe,
> Now the second gift impart,
> Now th' abiding witness give,
> Give us now the perfect heart.[19]

On Sunday, April 4, 1742, Charles Wesley preached a sermon before the University of Oxford, "Awake Thou That Sleepest." John Wesley later included it as Sermon 3 in his standard sermons that formed the basis of what the Methodist preachers were to believe and preach.

This sermon linked Christian perfection, "the one thing needful," and born again. This sermon had the same theme in another sermon that he began to compose three days after his coming to faith on May 21, 1738, entitled, "The Three-Fold States" that allowed one true state of faith (see Chapter 3).

He allowed only one state of faith also in this sermon on "Awake Thou That Sleepest." There are only two "states"—one who is asleep spiritually ("state of nature," "unawakened sinner") and one who is fully awake, who has "secured 'the one thing needful," and "hast recovered the image of God, even 'righteousness and true holiness'."[20] He is one who has come to "love the Lord thy God with all thy heart and with all his mind, and with all thy soul, and with all thy strength."[21]

To be "fully awake" is to have received "the Promise of the Father," "the indwelling of the Spirit of God," and "to be a habitation of God through his Spirit." Charles Wesley particularly identified being "fully awake" with "the Spirit of Christ" who "is that great gift of God, which at sundry times, and in divers manners, he hath promised to man, and hath fully bestowed since the time that Christ was gloried. Those promises, before made to the fathers, he hath thus fulfilled: 'I will put my Spirit within you, and cause you to walk in my statues' (Ezekiel 36:27). 'I will pour water upon him that is thirsty, and floods upon the dry ground, I will pour my Spirit upon thy seed, and my blessing upon thine offspring (Isaiah 44:3)'." We have already cited many of Charles Wesley's hymns and sacred poems showing that he linked these Old Testament passages regarding the Pentecost gift of the Spirit with Christian perfection.

We earlier pointed out the link between the Anglican order of confirmation and the Wesley brothers' idea of perfection. In this sermon, Charles explicitly mentioned that being fully awake means being "filled with the Holy Spirit" which he said was contained in the Anglican "Order of Confirmation."

This sermon is like some of John Wesley's early sermons where the distinction is not made between the justifying and sanctifying stages of faith. This distinction between justification and sanctification is not denied in these particular sermons, but it is not explained and hence the two stages seemed to be conflated because they are not explained. For example, John Wesley preached the sermon, "The Almost Christian," at St. Mary's, Oxford, before the University, on July 25, 1741. This sermon presents an either/or alternative. Either one is an altogether Christian (i.e., Christian perfection) or not a Christian at all.

Charles Wesley was John Fletcher's most frequent correspondent, and their friendship was intimate.[22] Their correspondence particularly highlighted the link between Pentecost and Christian perfection. Fletcher once said to Charles Wesley in a humorous way that he should "Awake" out of his sleep (a reference to Charles' sermon on "Awake Thou that Sleepest") and have another day of Pentecost.

These comments to Charles Wesley showed that they assumed that his Pentecost conversion was anticipated to be at least an initial moment in the ongoing process of entire sanctification. This is why Fletcher referred to the repetition of Pentecost in Acts 4.

As J. Ernest Rattenbury has also pointed out,[23] this theme of future Pentecosts was a dominant theme in the sacred poems of Charles Wesley. The reason why Pentecosts were to be repeated in the future is because it was connected to sanctification, not justification.

On January 7, 1743 Charles Wesley noted that one person who was near death was "waiting every moment for full redemption." On January 8, 1743, Charles Wesley noted that another person says "she has already attained," although he thought she probably had not done so.[24]

On May 20, 1743, Charles recorded that "a society of above 300 are seeking full redemption in the all-cleansing blood."[25]

On May 24, 1743, Charles preached near the home of Lady Huntingdon at Castle Donington, Leicestershire on Acts 19:2: "Have ye received the Holy Spirit since ye believed?"[26] Charles Wesley interpreted this question to mean that one can have faith in Jesus as Lord without having received the "power" and "all the fruits, the tempers" of the Holy Spirit, "the Comforter," showing that to enjoy the entire fruit and tempers of the Spirit, or Christian perfection, is different from justification:

"Have ye received the Holy Spirit, since ye believed?"

> I who long have call'd him Lord,
>   And Jesus mine believ'd,
> Have I prov'd the Saviour's word,
>   The Comforter receiv'd?
> Him do I my Leader know,
>   His power throughout my life express,
> All the fruits, the tempers show,
>   The works of righteousness?[27]

This is similar to Charles Wesley's interpretation of Acts 15:8-9, when Peter explained to the Jerusalem Council that what happened to the household of Cornelius is the same thing that happened to them on the day of Pentecost: "God gave them the Holy Spirit, purifying their hearts by faith." This meant that they were entirely sanctified. Charles said they experienced the "Spirit of holiness," "perfect peace," "purity" of heart, and that the purpose of the coming of the Spirit on the day of Pentecost was to "fill my soul and sanctify by Jesu's heavenly love."

> God of grace, vouchsafe to me
>   That Spirit of holiness,
> Sighs my heart for purity,

> And pants for perfect peace;
> Spirit of faith, the blood apply,
>   Which only can my filth remove,
> Fill my soul, and sanctify
>   By Jesu's heavenly love.[28]

In another poem he explained similarly the meaning of Acts 15:8-9, "God gave them the Holy Ghost, purifying their hearts by faith":

> By thy Spirit's inspiration
>   Bid my evil thoughts depart,
> All the filth of pride and passion,
>   Purge out of my faithful heart:
> Then I shall with joy embrace thee,
>   Meet to see thy face above,
> Then I worthily shall praise thee,
>   Then I perfectly shall love.[29]

On June 22, 1743, Charles said that "one asked me if there was any good in confirmation. I answered, 'No, nor in baptism, nor in the Lord's Supper, or any outward thing, unless you are in Christ a new Creature'." Charles did not deny the importance of these "outward things," but showed "by relating my own experience under the law" how a personal faith in Christ is the decisive reality.[30]

Interestingly enough, it was just in the previous month that he had preached on a text which was one of the biblical texts for the rite of confirmation, Acts 19:2, "Have ye received the Holy Spirit since ye believed?" It was only natural that Charles' hearer would connect his message on receiving the Spirit with confirmation.

One year earlier on April 4, 1742 Charles had defined the order of confirmation to mean being "filled with the Spirit," and he linked it to the meaning of being "fully awake," or Christian perfection. Jeremy Taylor in his *Discourse on Confirmation* explained that "in confirmation we receive the Holy Spirit as the earnest of our inheritance, as the seal of our salvation.... We therefore call it a seal or signature, as being a guard and custody to us, and a sign of the Lord's dominion over us." Taylor explained: "In baptism we are made the sons of God, but we receive the witness and testimony of it in confirmation."

This definition of confirmation corresponded with Charles Wesley's definition of Christian perfection, and Taylor also emphasized the element of personal faith in order for confirmation to be effective, except that Charles Wesley put greater emphasis on the meaning of personal faith as nuanced through the Moravian influence.

On August 26, 1743, Charles mentioned someone, who was "denying both justification and sanctification."[31]

On September 11, 1743, Charles recorded that he had "met one of the Tabernacle, thoroughly convinced of the necessity of holiness" with the expectation that "many more shall follow."[32]

On June 23, 1743, Charles reported that someone named Parker "did not understand what we meant by talking of holiness after forgiveness—that he has all he can have, and looks for no more."[33]

Charles Wesley's hymns frequently speak of the need for "holiness" after justification. Here is one sample in "Hymns for Believers" where he said that though he possessed pardon he could not "rest in the first gift, but earnestly covet the best" gift of "perfect love."

> 1. My Jesus, my Lamb,
>   All weakness I am,
> But strength, and salvation are found in thy name.
>
> 2. I come for the grace
>   Thy Father did place
> On thee for myself, and for all the lost race.
>
> 3. Be near to defend,
>   Continue my friend;
> I know thou hast lov'd me; but love to the end.
>
> 4. Our safeguard thou art,
>   And shou'dst thou depart,
> I perish, destroyed by my own evil heart.
>
> 5. But I trust, thou wilt stay
>   'Till I see the glad day,
> When thy blood shall have washed all my evil away.
>
> 6. I have faith in thy blood,
>   It hath brought me to God,
> And I in thine image shall soon be renew'd.
>
> 7. I shall throughly be clean,
>   And all-holy within;
> Thine image can harbour no relics of sin.
>
> 8. Of pardon possessed,
>   Yet can I not rest
> In the first gift, but earnestly covet the best.
>
> 9. The best I shall prove,
>   When perfect in love,
> I serve thee on earth as the angels above.
>
> 10. This, this is the prize,
>   To perfection I rise,
> And walk before God, till I fly to the skies.[34]

In 1744, John Wesley preached before St. Mary's Church at Oxford University on "Scriptural Christianity" on Acts 4:31[35]: "They were all filled with the Holy Spirit."

Following the introduction where Wesley defined the meaning of being filled with the Spirit, Albert Outler pointed out that Part I listed the order or sequence of salvation from "repentance" and "justification" to "full 'renewal of his soul in righteousness and true holiness'," "saved both from passion and pride . . . from every temper which was not in Christ," and finally a witness to the "hope of that 'crown of glory', that 'inheritance incorruptible, undefiled, and that fadeth not away'."

Bishop Ole Borgen rightly listed "Scriptural Christianity" in his bibliography on John Wesley's sermons as a sermon on Christian perfection.[36] The content of this sermon should be compared with John Heylyn's Pentecost Sermon (see appendix) because some of the ideas are strikingly similar.

John Fletcher interpreted this sermon as a sermon on Christian perfection. John Wesley said he agreed with Fletcher's interpretation that this was a sermon on Christian perfection.[37]

John Wesley defined the day of Pentecost in terms of Christian perfection: "Such was Christianity in its rise." They "were all filled with the Holy Spirit . . . 'were of one heart and of one soul' . . . So did the love of him in whom they had believed constrain them to love one another."

Part II is an eschatological section regarding the spread of Christianity from the day of Pentecost when the church was "in one accord" until finally "the tares appear with the wheat" and "the mystery of iniquity" began to work and weaken the church.

Part III foresees the goal of Pentecost realized when "the earth shall be full of the knowledge of the Lord, as the waters cover the sea" and "'filled with peace and joy' . . . united in one body . . . they all 'love as brethren'; they are all of 'one heart, and of one soul' . . . and every man loveth his neighbor as himself."

Part IV is a practical application challenging the administrators, professors, and students to examine where this Pentecost Christianity "now exists." He asked: "Which is the country, the inhabitants whereof are 'all filled with the Spirit'? Are all of 'one heart and of one soul'? . . . Who one and all have the love of God filling their hearts, and constraining them to love their neighbor as themselves?. . . . Why then, let us confess we have never yet seen a Christian country upon earth."

John Wesley then addressed the professors: "Are you 'filled with the Holy Spirit'? Are ye lively portraitures of him whom ye are appointed to represent among men?. . . an heart full of God?" He further asked them: "Are you 'filled with the Holy Spirit'? With all those 'fruits of the Spirit' which your important office so indispensably requires? Is your heart whole with God? Full of love and zeal to set up his kingdom on earth?"

This sermon began with being filled with the Spirit, who was given "to fill them with 'love, joy, peace'" and "to crucify the flesh with its affections and lusts,'" then spreading throughout the world, and finally an eschatological hope of the day when all inhabitants of the world would be filled with the Spirit, concluding with a practical application that Oxford University needs a Pentecost of its own—if only its administrators, professors, and students were filled with the Spirit with a "heart whole with God" and "full of love and zeal to set up the kingdom on earth." He called upon them to be "patterns . . . in charity . . . in purity" reflecting a clean heart possessing all the tempers of Christ and fruits of the Spirit freed from pride.

John Wesley said in this sermon that being filled with the Spirit entailed the "full renewal . . . in righteousness and true holiness." He equated "filled with the Holy Spirit?" with a "heart whole with God? full of love and zeal to set up his kingdom on earth?"

This sermon contained numerous references to "full"—such as "full of God," "full of love," "full renewal," "fully crucified," "full knowledge" "fullness of salvation," It is with good reason John Wesley in his special edition of *An Essay on Truth* in "The First Part of an Equal Check" approved John Fletcher's citation of "Scriptural Christianity" as equating Christian perfection with being "filled with the Spirit."[38]

This sermon was similar to the one he had heard John Heylyn preached on May 21, 1738, which he had called "a truly Christian sermon." In the introduction to this sermon, John Wesley linked the day of Pentecost with subsequent "fresh"[39] infillings of the Spirit in the book of Acts, in contrast to the initial moment of justification which is not "freshly" repeated.

It was typical of Wesley to equate being "filled with the Spirit" and Christian perfection. For example in 1745, Wesley wrote: "It was hereby shown that you were filled with the Holy Spirit and delivered from all unholy tempers; when ye were all 'unblamable and unrebukable, without spot, or wrinkle, or any such things', a chosen generation, a royal priesthood, an holy nation, a peculiar people, showing forth' to all . . . by your active, patient, spotless love of God and man."[40]

One of his correspondents in 1757 mentioned John Wesley's equation: "O that you was filled with the Holy Spirit, with all inward and outward Holiness!" and then expressed her feelings that she wished this for herself.[41]

In Charles Wesley's poetic commentary on Acts 19:6, "The Holy Spirit fell on them, and they spake with tongues, and prophesied," he explained that the miraculous powers "are rarely now received" (though he did not discount them today) but the "indwelling Comforter . . . works his miracles within . . . and wholly sanctifies."[42]

In an essay written in 1745, "Farther Appeal to Men of Reason and Religion," John Wesley defined "the baptism with the Spirit" as the "inward baptism" which had a deeper meaning than "water baptism." He said: "Would to God that ye would . . . 'repent and believe the gospel!' Not repent alone, (for then you know only the baptism of John,) but believe, and be 'baptized with the Holy Spirit and with fire' . . . May the Lord constrain you to cry out, 'How am I straitened till it be accomplished!' even till the love of God inflame your heart, and consume all your vile affections!"

John Wesley then said the baptism with the Spirit means "that we are all to be taught of God, and to be 'led by his Spirit;' that the Spirit alone reveals all truth, and inspires all holiness; that by his inspiration men attain perfect love."[43] As we shall see, whenever John Wesley used the phrase, baptism with the Spirit, it was an equivalent of Christian perfection.

In this same essay, John Wesley said being "filled with the Spirit" means to be "delivered from all unholy tempers" and to have the "spotless love of God and man."

He also said "zealous" meant:

When ye were zealous of every good word and work, and abstained from all appearance of evil; when it was hereby shown that you were filled with the Holy Spirit and delivered from all unholy tempers; when ye were all "unblamable and unrebukable, without spot, or wrinkle, or any such things", "a chosen generation, a royal priesthood, an holy nation, a peculiar people, showing forth" to all Jews, infidels and heretics, by your active, patient, spotless love of God and man.[44]

In every instance in his writings that I have seen when he used the expression, "filled with the Spirit" it was a reference to Christian perfection. I do not know of a single exception. Frank Baker once told me the same thing.

On March 5, 1744, Charles preached on "The One Thing Needful."[45]

On March 18, 1744, Charles "invited much larger company in the evening to draw nigh with a true heart, in full assurance of faith."[46]

On July 23, 1744, Charles recorded: "I breakfasted at Mr. L's, a poor slave of Satan, till, at the sound of the gospel, his chains fell off, and left him waiting for the seal of his pardon."[47]

On February 17, 1745, Charles Wesley recorded in his journal: "Was strengthened by a zealous Quaker, who informed me he had received the Spirit of adoption in hearing me a year ago, and has walked in the light from that time to this."[48]

Charles Wesley made a temporal distinction between justifying faith and the witness of the Spirit. On May 22, 1740, he said: "Forgiveness and the witness of the Spirit are distinct gifts and generally given at different times."[49]

He and his brother John had a discussion about this issue, and John came to agree with Charles. In the annual conference for June 1747, John Wesley said that "no man can be justified and not know it."[50] John Whitehead (Wesley's personal physician, a Methodist preacher, and Wesley's first biographer) reported that shortly after this conference, John Wesley wrote to Charles Wesley in July, retracting this opinion: "I cannot allow, that justifying faith is such an assurance, or necessarily connected therewith."[51]

In this letter to his brother, John Wesley defined "an explicit assurance" as the "proper Christian faith, which purifieth the heart, and overcometh the world [i.e., Christian perfection]," allowing at the same time that one may be justified without having the "proper Christian faith" entailing assurance. One who has justifying faith is not "under the wrath and the curse of God," but this does not necessarily entail "a sense of pardon."[52] Of course, John and Charles both believed that a measure of assurance normally accompanies justifying faith, and both believed that Christian perfection always accompanied a clear sense of one's justification.[53]

The Wesley brothers would also have known from their Anglican order of confirmation that the witness and assurance of one's forgiveness is guaranteed through being filled with the Spirit subsequent in time to justification signified by water baptism, As Jeremy Taylor explained: "In baptism we are made the sons of God, but we receive the witness and testimony of it in confirmation."[54] This reinforces the recognition that the Wesley brothers were more indebted to their Anglican heritage than they were to the Moravians, as noted several times already.

We know from his hymn, "Groaning for the Spirit of Adoption," (published in 1740) Charles Wesley equated the Spirit of Adoption with Christian perfection. Although he did not think that the witness of the Spirit was necessary for justifying faith, he believed the Spirit of Adoption brought an assurance of salvation which was necessary for an authentic experience of Christian perfection.

In this hymn, Charles interpreted the Spirit of Adoption as occurring subsequently in time to "sin forgiven"— "Come, Holy Spirit . . . Come, and baptize me now with fire." This baptism with the Spirit "makes me thy conscious child," "of power, to conquer inbred sin," "attest[s] that I am born again," and "ascertains the kingdom mine."

Groaning for the Spirit of Adoption

1. Father, if thou my Father art,
    Send forth the Spirit of thy Son,
Breathe him into my panting heart,
    And make me know, as I am known:
Make me thy conscious child, that I
    May "Father, Abba, Father" cry.

2. I want the Sp'rit of power within,
    Of love, and of an healthful mind;
Of power, to conquer inbred sin,
    Of love to thee, and all mankind,
Of health, that pain and death defies,
    Most vig'rous, when the body dies.

3. When shall I hear the inward voice,
    Which only faithful souls can hear!
Pardon, and peace, and heavenly joys
    Attend the promis'd Comforter:
He comes! And righteousness divine,
    And Christ, and all with Christ is mine

4. O that the Comforter would come,
    Nor visit, as a transient guest,
But fix in me his constant home,
    And take possession of my breast,
And make my soul his lov'd abode,
    The temple of indwelling God.

5. Come, Holy Ghost, my heart inspire,
    Attest that I am born again!
Come, and baptize me now with fire,
    Or all thy former gifts are vain.
I cannot rest in sin forgiven;
    Where is the earnest of *my* heaven!

6. Where thy indubitable seal
    That ascertains the kingdom mine,
The powerful stamp I long to feel,
    The signature of love divine:
O shed it in my heart abroad,
    Fullness of love,—of heaven—of God![55]

When Charles Wesley said a Quaker had "received the Spirit of adoption" after hearing him preach a year earlier, it is apparent Charles believed he had attained Christian perfection. This is also consistent with Charles Wesley's usual interpretation of the language of the Spirit as equivalent to Christian perfection.

On August 26, 1745 Charles Wesley wrote a letter to Jane Sparrow. He urged her to attain Christian perfection: He wrote to her: "Has my dear friend obeyed the repeated call! Are you crucified to the world, and the world to you? Wholly taken up with the one thing needful [i.e., Christian perfection]? Do you look steadily into the things unseen; eternal? Is the residue of your days entirely devoted to God in serious thankful love?" He then encouraged her to: "O stir yourself up to lay hold of the Lord, and labour more abundantly having obtained mercy. . . . Let me then conjure you my dear friend & sister to break off *entirely* that friendship with the world, which is enmity with God."[56]

On May 29, 1746, Charles reported: "In conference found many of our children in a thriving condition. Not one of those that are justified dreams that he is sanctified at once and wants nothing more."[57] As we have seen, both the Wesley brothers insisted that the attainment of sanctification is also a lifelong process of greater enlargement and further growth, but Charles Wesley emphasized more the process toward the attainment of holiness, whereas John Wesley consistently insisted on the instantaneous moment of holiness.

On July 13, 1746, Charles preached on "the twofold rest of pardon and holiness."[58] This account shows (as already noticed) that the focus of the evangelistic preaching of Charles, as well as John, consisted of these two themes—justification and sanctification.

On August 22, 1746, Charles Wesley preached on the "full assurance of faith."[59] Charles reported on multiple occasions that he preached on this theme. As we have seen, the assurance of faith was part of his Anglican theology as seen in the writings of Jeremy Taylor, but it was the Moravians who guided him and his brother to experience personally the assurance of faith. We noted that Christian David had led them to see that the full assurance of faith was equivalent to Christian perfection.

Charles Wesley wrote a sacred poem specifically intended to explain the meaning of Hebrews 10:19-22: "Having boldness to enter into the holiest by the blood of Jesus, by a new and living way which he hath consecrated for us, through the veil, that is to say, his flesh; and having an high priest over the house of God; let us draw near with a true heart, in full assurance of faith, having our hearts sprinkled from an evil conscience, and our bodies washed with pure water."

In his lyrical method of doing theology, Charles Wesley used Pentecost language to explain that God "pours His Spirit of purity . . . to wholly sanctify, [and] take me sinless to the sky." He explained that Christian perfection is the full assurance of faith, "Saved from sin, and doubt, and fear, In full confidence divine, Each assured, that Christ is mine." Here are all the lyrics of his theological explanation:

> 1. Happy we, who humbly prove
> The true liberty of love,

Thro' the all-atoning blood,
We have free access to God,
Enter the most holy place,
Stand before our Father's face.

2. Boldly we approach the throne
By a living way unknown,
Way of faith which Jesus made,
Thro' the vail of flesh displayed;
Thro' his rent humanity
God our friend in heaven we see.

3. There we see our great high-priest,
Enter'd his triumphant rest,
There he pleads his death below,
There he lives his wounds to show,
Offers up our prayers with his,
Claims for us eternal bliss.

4. Draw we then thro' Jesus near,
Sav'd from sin, and doubt, and fear,
In full confidence divine,
Each assur'd, that Christ is mine,
Mine, O God, thro' Christ thou art,
Mine I have thee in my heart.

5. Upright now my heart and true
Lo, I offer to thy view,
Lightened of its guilty load,
Sprinkled with my Saviour's blood,
Conscious of thy pardoning grace,
Cleansed from all unrighteousness.

6. He that made my conscience clean,
Still preserves from acting sin,
Pours his Spirit of purity,
Every moment waters me;
He shall wholly sanctify,
Take me sinless to the sky.[60]

On September 11, 1746, Charles Wesley recorded that a child "died in the most triumphant manner, being perfected in the short space of nine years."[61] Charles Wesley, as did John Wesley, recorded multiple accounts of those who had been sanctified.

On September 21, 1746, Charles said: "To the bands, I explained the nature of Christian perfection, another name of Christian salvation."[62] Being saved and salvation are terms consistently used by John Wesley, as well as Charles Wesley, for Christian perfection. They did not use distinctions such as being "saved" and being "sanctified. Rather, their terms were being justified and being sanctified.

In 1756, in "An Extract of a Letter to the Reverend Mr. Law," John Wesley said: "That we 'must be baptized with the Holy Spirit,' implies this and no more, that we cannot be 'renewed in righteousness and true holiness' any otherwise than by being over-shadowed, quickened, and animated by that blessed Spirit."[63]

As we have already seen, John Wesley connected the language of "the baptism with the Holy Spirit," not to justifying faith or forgiveness of sins, but to holiness, as seen in "Farther Appeal to Men of Reason and Religion" (1745), even as in his "Principles of a Methodist" (1742) he connected "the indwelling of the Spirit" with perfection, and not justification.

Likewise Charles Wesley consistently interpreted the language of Pentecost primarily with perfection, particularly in his references to "the baptism with the Spirit." Both John and Charles highlighted the "baptism with the Holy Spirit and with fire" as denoting sanctification. Here is one of many hymns by Charles, linking the baptism with the Spirit to Christian perfection (i.e., new birth with Charles), as an interpretation of Acts 11:16: "Ye shall be baptized with the Holy Spirit."

> 3. The pure baptismal Fire
>   Shall me, ev'n me inspire
> I from my own works shall cease,
>   I the Spirit's birth shall know,
> Live the life of holiness,
>   Perfect holiness, below.[64]

Another Pentecost hymn probably written about the same time was based on Charles Wesley's reading of Psalm 21.[65] This hymn linked "holiness" with "that image of God," "perfected in love," "pure unmingled with sin," and "the baptizing fire" (a reference to Jesus baptizing with the Holy Spirit and fire as promised by John the Baptist). Charles Wesley also defined this sanctifying "grace" as being offered to those who are believers waiting for "Thy Spirit receive."

> 1. The soul shall be glad, in Jesus restor'd,
> Anointed and made a King with his Lord;
> His high exaltation with transport receive,
> And in thy salvation triumphantly live.
>
> 2. His hearty request, Thou, Lord, hast bestow'd,
> With holiness blest, That image of God;
> The baptizing fire, The heavenly birth,
> Hath lifted him higher Than kings of the earth.
>
> 3. His head thou hast crowned with gold from above,
> No dross can be found in perfected love;
> The gold—it is pure, unmingled with sin,
> The kingdom is sure of heaven within.
>
> 4. Long life he desir'd, to spend in thy praise;
> And thou hast inspired his soul with thy grace,
> Hast bid the believer Thy Spirit receive,
> And gave him for ever and ever to live.[66]

This hymn is another instance when Charles Wesley linked "perfected in love" with "the heavenly birth," as was done by his mentor, William Law.

Linking the new birth with the sanctifying baptism with the Spirit is also consistent with another much-admired Anglican theologian, Jeremy Taylor who distinguished between being born of water as distinct from being born of the Spirit. In the opening section of "The Discourse of Confirmation," he likens the birth of water to an "embryo" until the new birth is completed with confirmation.[67] The birth of water is to be followed by being born of the Spirit.

If Charles Wesley understood Christian perfection to be the meaning of the new birth, his source was Anglican—unlike the way the new birth is understood in the larger Evangelical movement today.

In 1747 Charles Wesley wrote a Pentecost hymn which was to become one of the most widely sung of Christian hymns of all times. The congregation sang it at the Royal Wedding of Prince William and Kate Middleton on April 29, 2011 in Westminster Abbey, probably unaware that it is the best holiness hymn that Charles Wesley ever wrote, affirming that believers can "suddenly" in an instant moment through the Pentecost gift of the Holy Spirit be empowered to love God perfectly.

> 1. Love Divine, all Loves excelling,
>   Joy of Heaven to Earth come down,
> Fix in us thy humble Dwelling,
>   All thy faithful Mercies crown;
> Jesu, Thou art all Compassion,
>   Pure unbounded Love Thou art,
> Visit us with thy Salvation,
>   Enter every trembling Heart.
>
> 2. Breathe, O breathe thy loving Spirit
>   Into every troubled Breast,
> Let us all in Thee inherit,
>   Let us find that Second Rest:
> Take away our *Power* of Sinning,
>   Alpha and Omega be,
> End of Faith as its Beginning,
>   Set our Hearts at Liberty.
>
> 3. Come, Almighty to deliver,
>   Let us all thy Life receive,
> Suddenly return, and never,
>   Never more thy Temples leave.
> Thee we would be always blessing,
>   Serve Thee as thy Hosts above,
> Pray, and praise Thee without ceasing,
>   Glory in thy perfect Love.
>
> 4. Finish then thy New Creation,
>   Pure and sinless let us be,

> Let us see thy great Salvation,
>   Perfectly restor'd in Thee;
> Chang'd from Glory into Glory,
>   Till in heaven we take our place,
> Till we cast our Crowns before Thee,
>   Lost in Wonder, Love, and Praise![68]

On May 21, 1740, Charles recorded in his journal that a Quaker woman was baptized with water. Using the language of full assurance of faith (i.e., Christian perfection), Charles said: The Spirit infallibly bears witness on this occasion . . . and assuredly knows that she is born of water and of the Spirit."[69]

On October 29, 1747, Charles wrote a letter from Dublin to London addressed to Ebenezer Blackwell, a close friend and business supporter of the Wesley brothers' ministry: "Observe, you will never love Jesus Christ a *little*. When his love is shed abroad in your heart, it will fill the whole capacity thereof, and you will rejoice from that moment to feed his lambs and his sheep, and even to lay down your life for them." He then encouraged Ebenezer: "Our sister must not *rest* in being a servant of God, but strive and wrestle and pray for the Spirit of Adoption; many foretastes of this, I know, she has had; yet still he doth not cry Abba Father in her heart, or bear an abiding witness with her spirit that she is a child of God."[70] The Spirit of Adoption and the abiding witness of the Spirit were phrases used to denote Christian perfection. What is also apparent is the passionate language of Charles as he urged his friends and correspondents to attain Christian perfection.

On August 31, 1748, Charles "invited many sinners at the marsh to Him who has promised them the rest of pardon, holiness, heaven. They seemed to taste the *good* word. One told me after it that from the time I spake to her at the palace she had expected the blessing every moment, and was sure beyond the possibility of a doubt that she should have it. 'I seem,' said she, 'to be laying hold on Christ continually. I am so light, so happy, as I never was before. I waked, two nights ago, in such rapture of joy, that I thought, Surely this is the peace they preach. It has continued ever since. My eyes are opened. I see all things in a new light. I rejoice always'." Charles then concludes: "Is not this the language of faith, the cry of a new-born soul? But prayed over her that the Lord might confirm it."[71]

On March 7, 1748, Charles recorded in his journal: "Spake with eleven of them who had received a clear sense of pardon. Another went to his house justified."[72] "A clear sense of pardon" is equivalent to holiness.

On November 1747, he wrote a letter to his future wife, Sarah Gwynne, encouraging her to "wait all the day (or hours) of your appointed time [on earth], till your change come."[73] As it will be seen below, he regularly in his letters to his wife encouraged her to seek holiness and not to grow discouraged.

On August 1, 1748, Charles wrote to James Erskine; "I pray God for Christ sake give you the fullness of his Spirit."[74]

On August 9, 1748, Charles wrote to his future wife: "Jesus is your Jesus. His Spirit dwells *with* you & shall be *in* you. In Him you shall find all fullness. His love is sufficient for you. His love is heaven, present & eternal."[75]

On August 12, 1748, Charles Wesley wrote again to his future wife in passionate language about his desire for the "baptism" with the Spirit, which is the "one thing needful . . . the pure perfect love of Christ Jesus." This is a truly remarkable "love letter" to one who is not yet his wife.

> I write from the Prophet's Chamber where I am still detained a willing prisoner, to converse with my best beloved friend. I ask you, is your heart cheerful? & answer for you, that it sure is or mine would be in great heaviness. Who is it that so strangely bears our burdens? The creator of all the ends of the earth. He who fainteth not, neither is weary. He who loved us & gave himself for us.
>
> I am enabled to pray for you in every prayer that you may have the abiding witness of his life, that nothing may ever damp your desires or slacken your pursuit of that supreme good, that all sufficient happiness, which is in Jesus. I settle it in your heart that in him all fullness dwells & that one touch, one word, one look from him can fill you with present heaven. Both you & I have still a baptism to be baptized with; & how should we be straightened till it is accomplished! This, this is the one thing needful—not a friend—not health—not life itself, but the pure perfect love of Christ Jesus—O give me love, or else I die!—O give me love, & *let* me die! I am weary of my want of love—weary to death; & would fain throw off this body, that I may love him, who so loved me.
>
> If you do indeed love me for his sake . . . O wrestle with that friend of sinners in my behalf, & let him not go till he bless me with the sense of his love? How shall I feed his lambs unless I love him? How shall I give up all, even those friends who are dearer to me than my own soul? How shall I suffer for one I do not love? O eternal Spirit of love come down into my heart & into my friend's heart & knit us together in the bond of perfectness. Lead us by the waters of comfort. Swallow up our will in thine. Make ready the bride, & then call us up to the marriage supper of the lamb![76]

On August 22, 1748, Charles preached "with divine assistance, 'One Thing Needful.'"[77]

On October 24, 1748, Charles said he "met the select band for the first time. The cloud overshadowed us, and we all said, 'It is good to be here!'" The select band consisted of Methodist leaders who had experienced sanctifying grace.[78]

On January 15, 1749, Charles wrote a lengthy letter to his future wife, Sarah Gwynne, anticipating their wedding day. He admitted that "it is *not fair* for me, in the noon of life, to wish a friend only in the morning of hers, to accompany *me* to paradise. Many happy years may you labour in the vineyard after I am gone to my reward. But many, yea, a thousand years, are only as one day. We shall shortly meet again, to sing that song of Moses & the Lamb."

He told her that he wanted her "to receive all the holiness possible for a creature." He gave her an extensive account of his evangelistic activities, noting that some were seeking Christ as their savior and others were seeking holiness: "The spirit of supplication was with us again among the Women's bands & prayed particularly for a family seeking Christ & for one who wants the abiding witness."

He said he then ministered to a "select band," which was the group of those who professed and were in pursuit of holiness: "My mouth was opened this morning to confirm the souls of the disciples by the precious sanctifying promises. In the select band we prayed for you again in great faith. O never, never doubt, when so many righteous souls bear you on their hearts to the Throne!"

He also reported that he "gave the Sacrament to a dying believer." He said: "I ask her if she *knew* that her sins were forgiven. She answered 'I am perfectly sure of it. I cannot doubt or fear. I am all joy, all love'."

Charles believed that most believers were sanctified briefly before they died. Here is a case of one who died with the full assurance of faith shortly before she died. He concluded his letter with a prayer for both of them to experience the full assurance of faith, or Christian perfection:

> Yet still I humbly hope our gracious Lord will guard us, over and above all outward providence concerning the testimony of his Spirit of love, and supplication. O that it were now! O that might my bosom friend might this moment *assuredly* know it, *delightfully* feel that her sins *are* forgiven! I seem to desire it even more for you than for myself. I am sure I wish your perfection *as much as* my own & can conceive it as greater happiness on this side of heaven than to minister grace to your dearest most precious soul![79]

On April 11, 1749, Charles preached on "The One Thing Needful."[80] This sermon, although written by John, was preached multiple times by Charles. It does not distinguish between justifying faith and full sanctifying grace as occurring at different times. Another one of his earlier sermons was on "The Three-Fold States," which also did not distinguish temporally between justification and sanctification, and he also preached it multiple times as well. John Wesley also preached other sermons, such as "The Witness of the Spirit" (1746) where he did not distinguish between justification and sanctification.[81]

Some Wesley scholars have said that John Wesley was inconsistent in his order of salvation because he did not always distinguish between justification and sanctification.[8] However, John Wesley apparently did not think he was inconsistent simply because he did not always specify these two stages in his preaching. John and Charles Wesley were rather focused on the fullness of the Christian life, while at the same assuming this distinction.

On April 26, 1749, Charles Wesley recorded that someone "had a second blessing [i.e., Christian perfection] among the bands."[83] He also recorded on the next day, he "expounded John 17. There was scarce a soul present that was not broken down."

In his lyrical theology of a specific reference to John 17:23, he defined it as a text on holiness: "I in them, and they in me, that they may be made perfect in one, and that the world may know that thou hast sent me, and hast loved them, as thou hast loved me."

> 1. Jesus, with thy Father come,
> And bring our inward Guide,
> Make our hearts thy humble home,
> And in thine house abide,

> Show us with thy presence filled,
>   Filled with glory from thy throne,
> Wholly sanctified, and seal'd,
>   And perfected in one.[84]

On January 14, 1750, Charles recorded that "a daughter of our brother Grimshaw's was just departed in the Lord, being perfected in a short space."[85]

On Sunday, June 2, 1751, Charles reported he "baptized Sarah and Elizabeth, a Quaker and a Baptist." Afterwards, he said "all were moved by the descent of that Spirit."[86] Here Charles connected water baptism and the subsequent descent of the Spirit as with Jesus' baptism by John the Baptist and the subsequent descent of the Spirit upon him.

On September 29, 1756, Charles said he "explained, 'Being made free from sin, and become the servants of God, ye have your fruit unto holiness, and the end everlasting life' [Rom. 6:22]. I insisted largely on freedom from sin, as the lowest mark of faith, and the necessity of laboring after holiness. The hearers appeared much stirred up."[87]

On October 25, 1756, Charles recorded that George Whitefield preached at one of their societies, affirming the universal call of the gospel to all people and the need for holiness after justification:

> Here [Manchester] I rejoiced to hear of the great good Mr. Whitefield had done in our Societies. He preached as universally as my brother. He warned them everywhere against apostasy, and strongly insisted on the necessity of holiness *after* justification, illustrating it with this comparison: "What good would the King's pardon to a poor malefactor dying of a fever? So, not withstand you have received forgiveness, unless the disease of your nature be healed by holiness, ye can never be saved". . . . In a word: he did his utmost to strengthen our hands, and deserves the thanks of all the churches for his abundant labour of love.[88]

This is a very interesting journal entry because George Whitefield had a strained relationship with John and Charles Wesley over the issue of absolute predestination. When Whitefield was part of the original group of the society at Oxford, he was in agreement with the Wesley brothers over the doctrine of Christian perfection.

Whitefield had been won over to Calvinism in 1739 during his first trip to America. The original Methodists (including Whitefield) "utterly abhorred" Calvinism.[89] The Wesley brothers remained dear friends in spite of their theological differences, and when Whitefield died in 1770, John Wesley preached his memorial sermon at Whitefield's request.

It was thus an inspiring moment for Charles Wesley to hear Whitefield preach on the universal gospel call and the need for "holiness after justification," apparently as a concession to what the Wesley brothers expected him to preach in one of their society meetings.

Fletcher cited from one of Whitefield's pre-Calvinist sermons to show that George Whitefield equated Christian perfection with those "who have received the Holy Spirit in all its sanctifying graces."[90] Apparently Whitefield reached back into his pre-Calvinist days to support the teaching and preaching of Charles Wesley with his people. He could have preached on a different topic, but chose rather to earn the appreciation of his dear friend.

On October 27, 1756, Charles "preached from Rom. 6[:22], 'But now being made free from sin, and become the servants of God, ye have your fruit unto holiness, and the end everlasting life.' The Lord confirmed his word with a double blessing [i.e., second blessing]."[91]

In 1754 John Wesley said in *The Explanatory Notes upon the New Testament* that the disciples before Pentecost were justified and enjoyed a measure of God's love, but as a result of the coming of the Spirit on the day of Pentecost, their love for God would be greatly enlarged.

Based on John 14:23-27, John Wesley noted that it was because the disciples already had a "love" for the earthly Jesus that he would send the Holy Spirit to "make our abode with him."

Jesus' promise that "The Comforter, the Holy Spirit, whom the Father will send in my name," entailed, John Wesley said, "such a large manifestation of the Divine presence and love, that the former [lower degree of love in the experience of the disciples prior to Pentecost] in justification is as nothing in comparison of it [Pentecost gift of perfect love]."[92]

Here John Wesley said the disciples had experienced justification prior to Pentecost and "a large manifestation of . . . love" after Pentecost (even as he argued in his debate with Zinzendorf in Sept 3, 1741 that the disciples were justified before Pentecost and were entirely sanctified on the day of Pentecost).

Continuing his commentary on this high priestly prayer of Jesus to send the Holy Spirit in his *Notes on the New Testament*, John Wesley said that Jesus's prayer in John 17:17 to "sanctify them through thy word" means to "perfect them in holiness."[93]

In his *Explanatory Notes* on Acts 2:17, Wesley said that the day of Pentecost was not intended to be the only day of Pentecost but rather the Spirit was to be poured out "upon all flesh." This is why Wesley said the promise, "Ye shall be baptized with the Holy Spirit," is a promise for "all true believers to the end of the world."[94] This observation corresponds to what John Wesley heard Heylyn say in his Pentecost sermon—"They were all filled with the Holy Spirit'—and so, said he, may *all you* be."

In his *Explanatory Notes* on Acts 2:38, John Wesley defined the bestowal of the Holy Spirit on the day of Pentecost to mean "the constant fruits of faith, even righteousness, and peace, and joy in the Holy Spirit."[95] By the "constant fruits of faith" Wesley elsewhere explained that the Holy Spirit "purifieth the heart from every unholy desire and temper" [i.e., Christian perfection] that "the body of sin might be destroyed."[96] His use of the words "constant fruit," "constant love, joy, and peace," and "constant peace" in his sermons and journal denoted full sanctifying grace.[97]

Here are examples of the use of the word "constant" to denote full sanctification. John Wesley wrote: "I buried the remains of Thomas Salmon, a good and useful man.

What was peculiar in his experience was, he did not know when he was justified; but he did know when he was renewed in love, that work being wrought in a most distinct manner. After this he continued about a year in *constant* [italics mine] love, joy, and peace; then, after an illness of a few days, he cheerfully went to God.[98]

In a letter from one of his preachers about Martha Wood on August 16, 1777, John Wesley recorded this testimony:

> For the first ten years, she was sometimes in transports of joy, carried almost beyond herself. But for these last ten years, she has had the *constant* [italics mine] witness that God has taken up all her heart. "He has filled me," said she, "with perfect love; and perfect love casts out fear. Jesus is mine. God, and heaven, and eternal glory, are mine. My heart, my very soul is lost, yea, swallowed up, in God."[99]

In his journal for March 1787 Monday 19, John Wesley wrote:

> I left Bristol with much satisfaction, expecting to hear of a plentiful harvest there; and in the evening preached at Stroud. The House was unusually filled, both with people and with the power of God. *Tuesday*, 20. We had a large congregation at five. Afterwards I met the select society, many of them enjoying the pure love of God, and *constantly* [italics mine] walking in the light of his countenance.[100]

As noted above, the connection between the baptism with the Spirit on the day of Pentecost with full sanctifying grace is consistent with the same interpretation provided by John Heylyn in his Pentecost sermon. John Wesley acknowledged the substantial influence of John Heylyn's *Theological Lectures* (which contained his Pentecost sermon) for his *Explanatory Notes upon the New Testament*.[101] John Wesley considered himself in agreement with Heylyn's theology.

This interpretation of Acts 2:38 coincides with Adam Clarke's commentary on the book of Acts where he said that the promise of the Spirit means: "by whose refining power the heart is purified."[102] John Wesley also used this text in his extempore preaching, as we shall later see.[103]

In his *Explanatory Notes*, Wesley noted that the Samaritan and Ephesian Pentecostal reception of the Spirit meant their "sanctification." John Fletcher showed that in this passages John Wesley intended by "sanctification" to mean "[full] sanctification."[104] Indeed as it is commonly recognized, when Wesley used the term "sanctification" he used it in the sense of entire sanctification, as already noted.[105]

Two years after he published his *Explanatory Notes on the New Testament*, was when John Wesley said to William Law: "That we 'must be baptized with the Holy Spirit,' implies this and no more, that we cannot be 'renewed in righteousness and true holiness' any otherwise than by being over-shadowed, quickened, and animated by that blessed Spirit."[106]

"To be renewed in the image of God in righteousness, and true holiness" is Wesley's definition of full sanctification.[107] For example, he said about those who had been "justified . . . not to think themselves anything after they had this; but to press forward for the prize of their high calling, even a clean heart, thoroughly renewed after the image of God, in righteousness and true holiness."[108]

As early as 1733, John Wesley in his sermon on "The Circumcision of Heart" said loving God with all one's heart, mind, and soul means "to renew our whole souls in righteousness and true holiness" by "the Spirit of God."[109] In Herrnhut in 1738, he had learned from Christian David to equate to "be cleansed from all sin" with "being renewed day by day in righteousness and all true holiness."[110] On his return to England from his visit to Herrnhut in 1738, John Wesley said he exhorted some Englishmen on board the ship "to pursue inward religion: the renewal of their souls in righteousness and true holiness."[111] In 1740, John Wesley equated "a full renewal in his image, in 'righteousness,' and all true holiness."[112]

His consistent practice was to speak of true holiness as a synonym for Christian perfection—"the full 'renewal of his soul in righteousness and true holiness'," as he described the meaning of "Scriptural Christianity," or being "filled with the Holy Spirit."[113]

As we have already seen, Wesley connected the language of "the baptism with the Holy Spirit," not to justifying faith or forgiveness of sins, but to holiness, even as he had connected "the indwelling of the Spirit" with perfection, and not justification.[114] So John Wesley's definition of the baptism with the Holy Spirit as being "renewed in righteousness and true holiness" was equating the baptism with the Spirit with Christian perfection, and he was emphatically making this equation because he said "it implies this and no more."

For John and Charles Wesley, water baptism was a once-for-all event even as Jesus' died and rose only once. So there was only one Easter day, but there were multiple days of Pentecost, as in Acts 4, 10, 19.

Charles Wesley also linked Pentecost primarily to holiness, not justification. Of course, the Holy Spirit enabled one to become an adopted child of God in justification in the Wesley brothers' theology of Christian initiation, but the fullness of the Christian life is linked with fullness of the Holy Spirit given on the day of Pentecost to the church.

In this regard, sanctification is initiated with justification through the Spirit, but the completion of sanctifying grace comes with the fullness of the Spirit given on the day of Pentecost. We shall see in the next chapter how John and Charles Wesley understood the multiple days of Pentecost.

Notes

1. *The Works of John Wesley,* (Jackson edition), 9:495, "An Extract of a Letter to the Rev. Mr. Law."
2. Cragg, *Appeals,* 11:253, "A Farther Appeal to Men of Reason and Religion, Part II."
3. Outler, *Sermon,* 2:110, "Christian Perfection"(italics mine).
4. *Explanatory Notes on the New Testament,* v. 23, 257.
5. *John Wesley, A Library of Protestant Thought,* 372.
6. Ibid., 367ff.
7. Ibid., 367ff.
8. Henry Moore, *The Life of the Rev. John Wesley* (New York: N. Bangs and J. Emory, 1826), 281-283.
9. *Manuscript Journal* 1:330.
10. John Wesley, "A Plain Account of Christian Perfection," *Doctrinal and Controversial Treatises II* in *Works,* 13:146. *A Plain Account of Christian Perfection* (7th edition, G. Paramore, Printer, 1794), 12.
11. Outler, *Sermons,* in *The Bicentennial Works of John Wesley,* 2:110-111, "Christian Perfection."
12. Italics mine.
13. Outler, *Sermons,* 2:110.

14. "Pleading the Promise of Sanctification," *Hymns and Sacred Poems* (1742), vv. 6, 11, 261-262.
15. MS Acts, MARC: MA 1977/555 (Charles Wesley Notebooks Box 1), 16.,
16. *Manuscript Journal* 1:322.
17. *Manuscript Journal* 2:324,
18. John Wesley, "The Principles of a Methodist" (1742), in *The Methodist Societies: History, Nature, and Design*, ed. Rupert E. Davies, *Wesley, Works*, 9:64-65.
19. *Hymns and Sacred Poems* (1742), 159
20. *Sermons of Charles Wesley*, Sermon 8, Eph. 5:14, 217.
21. *Sermons of Charles Wesley*, Sermon 8, Eph. 5:14, 218.
22. See Peter Forsaith, "The Long Fletcher Incumbency," *Religion, Gender, and Industry: Exploring Church and Methodism in a Local Setting*, ed. Geordan Hammond and Peter S. Forsaith (Eugene, Oregon: Pickwick Publications, 2011), 216-217.
23. Rattenbury, 177. 185-187.
24. *Manuscript Journal* 2:338.
25. *Manuscript Journal* 2:342.
26. *Manuscript Journal* 2:344.
27. MS Acts, MARC: MA 1977/555 (Charles Wesley Notebooks Box 1), 376.,
28. Ibid., 288.
29. Ibid.
30. *Manuscript Journal* 2:354.
31. *Manuscript Journal* 2:371.
32. *Manuscript Journal* 2:372.
33. *Manuscript Journal* 2:354.
34. MS Cheshunt, the Collection of The Cheshunt Foundation, Westminster College, Cambridge, 119-120.
35. John Wesley, in *The Bicentennial Works of John Wesley*, 1:159-180, "Scriptural Christianity."
36. Ole Borgen, "A Bibliography on John Wesley's Sermons on Christian Perfection," Asbury Theological Seminary Course Syllabus for the Theology of John Wesley.
37. John Wesley special abridged edition, "The First Part of an Equal Check," *The Works of John Fletcher* (New York: John Wilson and Daniel Hitt for the Methodist Connection in the United States, 1809), 3:174. See John Wesley's approving asterisk.
38. Ibid.
39. John Wesley, *The Explanatory Notes on the New Testament* (New York: Carlton & Porter, nd) on Acts 4:31, 286.
40. John Wesley, *The Appeals to Men of Reason and Religion and Certain Related Open Letters*, ed. Gerald R. Cragg, *Works of John Wesley*, 11:261, "A Farther Appeal to Men of Reason and Religion, Part II."
41. *Arminian Magazine* (London: J. Paramore, 1782) 5:214.
42. MS Acts, MARC: MA 1977/555 (Charles Wesley Notebooks Box 1), 379.
43. Cragg, *Appeals*, 11:253, "A Farther Appeal to Men of Reason and Religion, Part II."
44. Cragg, *Appeals*, 11:261, "A Farther Appeal to Men of Reason and Religion."
45. *Manuscript Journal* 2:392.
46. *Manuscript Journal* 2:400.
47. *Manuscript Journal* 2:411.
48. *Manuscript Journal* 2:436.
49. *Manuscript Journal* 1:261
50. Cf. John Whitehead's discussion of this issue, *The Life of the Rev. John Wesley* (Auburn: Alden, Beardsley, 1852), 406ff.
51. Whitehead, 417.
52. Whitehead, 417.
53. John Wesley's sermon on "Salvation by Faith" (1738) identified "the Spirit of Adoption" with Christian perfection: "He will save from all their sins; from original and actual, past and present sin" through "the Spirit of adoption, whereby they cry, Abba, Father: the Spirit itself also bearing witness with their spirits, that they are the children of God." The Spirit of Adoption enables one to "love the Lord thy God with all thy heart." Outler, *Sermons*, 1:121-124, "Salvation by Faith."
54. *Discourse on Confirmation*, 5:559. Jeremy Taylor wrote in his *Discourse on Confirmation*: "To conclude

this enquiry. The Holy Spirit is promised to all men.... Confirmation... is the solemnity and rite used in scripture for the conveying of that promise, and the effect is felt in all the sanctifications and changes of the soul.... Hear what the scriptures yet further say in this mystery. 'Now He which confirmeth or stablisheth us with you in Christ, and hath anointed us, is God; who hath also sealed us, and given the earnest of the Spirit in our hearts.'.... By this grace we are adopted and incorporated into Christ; God hath anointed us; that is, He hath given us this unction from above, He hath 'sealed us by His spirit,' made us His own .... He hath given us His spirit to testify to us that He will give us of His glory." *Discourse on Confirmation*, 5:660.

55. *Hymns and Sacred Poems* (1740), 131–132.
56. *Letters of Charles Wesley*, ed. Newport and Gareth Lloyd, August 26, 1745, 120.
57. *Manuscript Journal* 2:460.
58. *Manuscript Journal* 2:466.
59. *Manuscript Journal* 2:474.
60. Charles Wesley. *Short Hymns on Select Passages of the Holy Scriptures*, 2:364.
61. *Manuscript Journal* 2:475.
62. *Manuscript Journal* 2:475.
63. *The Works of John Wesley*, ed. Thomas Jackson, Third Edition (Hendrickson Publishers, Inc., 1984), 9:495, "An Extract of a Letter to the Rev. Mr. Law."
64. MS Acts, MARC: MA 1977/555 (Charles Wesley Notebooks Box 1).
65. This hymn was first published in *The Methodist Magazine* in 1799 with no suggestion of its composition.
66. Published posthumously by Henry Fish, editor in *Poetical Version of the Nearly the Whole of the Psalms of David* by Charles Wesley (London: John Mason and Alexander Heylin, 1854), 38.
67. *Discourse on Confirmation*, 6.
68. Charles Wesley, *Hymns for Those That Seek, And Those That Have, Redemption in the Blood of Christ* (London: Strahan, 1747, 11–12. Italics are Wesley's.
69. *Manuscript Journal* 1:161
70. *Letters of Charles Wesley*, Newport, October 29, 1747, 138.
72. *Manuscript Journal* 2:541.
72. *Manuscript Journal* 2:525.
73. *Letters of Charles Wesley*, Newport, 139.
74. *Letters of Charles Wesley*, Newport, 119.
75. *Letters of Charles Wesley*, Newport, 155–156.
76. *Letters of Charles Wesley*, 1:157, August 12, 1748.
77. *Manuscript Journal* 2:537.
78. *Manuscript Journal* 2:558.
79. *Letters of Charles Wesley*, Newport, 205–210. January 15, 1749.
80. *Manuscript Journal* 2:572.
81. Outler, *Sermons*, 1:267–284, "The Witness of the Spirit"
82. Cf. E. H. Sudgen, *The Standard Sermons of John Wesley*, 2:148.
83. *Manuscript Journal* 2:573.
84. MS John, MARC: MA 1977/573 (Charles Wesley Notebooks Box 3), 369.
85. *Manuscript Journal* 2:587.
86. *Manuscript Journal* 2:607.
87. *Manuscript Journal* 2:627.
88. *Manuscript Journal*, 2:643.
89. *The Arminian Magazine* 1(January 1778): 179. Fletcher, *Works*, 1:590–591n, "An Equal Check;" cf. *Works*, 2:550, 560, "The Last Checks"; cf. Whitefield, *Twenty-Three Sermons on Various Subjects* (London: W. Strahan, 1745), 218–219.
90. Fletcher, *The Last Check*, 6:222–224.
91. *Manuscript Journal*, 2:644.
92. *Explanatory Notes on the New Testament*, 257
93. *Explanatory Notes on the New Testament*, 263.
94. *Explanatory Notes on the New Testament*, 275.
95. *Explanatory Notes on the New Testament*, 280.

96. Outler, *Sermons*, in *The Bicentennial Works of John Wesley*, 1:423, 427, 428, "The Marks of the New Birth."
97. *Journal and Diaries IV*, in *The Bicentennial Works of John Wesley*, 21:351, (Sunday, February 14, 1762). *Journal and Diaries V (1765–1775)*, in *The Bicentennial Works of John Wesley*, 22:462. *Journal and Diaries VII (1787–1791)*, in *The Bicentennial Works of John Wesley* 22:9.
98. *Journal and Diaries IV*, in *The Bicentennial Works of John Wesley*, 21:351, (Sunday, February 14, 1762).
99. *Journal and Diaries V (1765–1775)*, in *The Bicentennial Works of John Wesley*, 22:462
100. *Journal and Diaries VII (1787–1791)*, in *The Bicentennial Works of John Wesley* 22:9.
101. *Explanatory Notes on the New Testament*, 4.
102. Adam Clark, *The New Testament*, "Commentary on the Book of Acts" (New York: Peter Myers, 1835), 3:341.
103. *Journal and Diaries I (1735–1738)*, 18:271.
104. John Fletcher, *The New Birth*, 45.
105. Cf. Harald G. Lindström, *Wesley and Sanctification* (Nashville: Abingdon, 1946), 127.
106. *The Works of John Wesley*, ed. Thomas Jackson, Third Edition (Hendrickson Publishers, Inc., 1984), 9:495, "An Extract of a Letter to the Rev. Mr. Law."
107. Henry Moore, *The Life of John Wesley*, 2:42.
108. *Journal and Diaries II (1738–1743)*, 19:164, August 10, 1740.
109. Outler, *Sermons*, 1:403-404, "The Circumcision of Heart"
110. *Journal and Diaries I (1735–38)*, 19:164, August 10, 1738.
111. *Journal and Diaries II (1738–1743)*, 19:12.
112. *Hymns and Sacred Poems* (1740), xi.
113. Outler, *Sermons I*, 1:162, "Scriptural Christianity"
114. E.g., see "The Principles of a Methodist," in *The Bicentennial Works of John Wesley*, 9:60.

Chapter 10

John Wesley's Day of Pentecost

"Nine were justified in one hour. The next morning I spoke severally with those who believed they were sanctified."
—John Wesley

"Many years ago my brother [Charles] frequently said, 'Your day of Pentecost is not fully come. But I doubt not it will, and you will then hear of persons sanctified as frequently as you do now of persons justified'."
—John Wesley

> "The Holy Ghost that blood applies
> Which purifies believing hearts."
> —Charles Wesley

"God would on *that* day visit my soul, and make it a Pentecost *indeed* to me."
—Elizabeth Bennis (John Wesley's band leader in Ireland)

"There is a day of Pentecost for believers; a time when the Holy Spirit descends abundantly. Happy are they who receive most of this perfect love, and of that establishing grace."
—John Fletcher (sermon in the early 1760s during the holiness revival many years before writing his *Checks to Antinomianism*, showing this terminology was already being used before he standardized it)

"I was baptized as with the Holy Spirit and with fire, and felt that perfect love casteth out fear."
—John Oliver, a Methodist preacher stationed in London, in a letter to John Wesley

John Wesley's journal often reported accounts of those who experienced justification followed later by sanctification.[1] The frequency of these incidents increased significantly after a holiness revival spontaneously developed in 1760. He described the progress of this revival in this way:

> All January 1762 God continued to work mightily, not only in and about London, but in most parts of England and Ireland. February 5th I met at noon, as usual, those who believed they were saved from sin.... Such a season I never saw before! Such a multitude of sinners were converted from the error of their ways, in all parts both of England and Ireland, and so many were filled with pure love. In April I crossed over to Ireland, and in every part of the kingdom, north, west, and south, found cause to bless God for the abundant increase of his work.[2]

On October 28, 1762, John Wesley described this holiness revival in terms of a new Pentecost:

> Many years ago my brother [Charles] frequently said, "Your day of Pentecost is not fully come. But I doubt not it will, and you will then hear of persons sanctified as frequently as you do now of persons justified." Any unprejudiced reader may observe that it was now fully come. And accordingly, we did hear of persons sanctified in London and most other parts of England, and in Dublin and many other parts of Ireland, as frequently as of persons justified, although instances of the latter were far more frequent than they had been for twenty years before.[3]

During this time, John Wesley requested his preachers to send letters of testimony to sanctification to him. John Oliver was one who responded with a detailed account of his experience of sanctification during the "great outpouring of the Spirit in London" in 1762. He said to John Wesley: "I was baptized as with the Holy Spirit and with fire, and felt that perfect love casteth out fear."[4] He reported that "from that day to this, I have not lost my sight of, nor my, affection for, Christian perfection."[5]

This revival of Pentecost among the Methodists was widespread, including Ireland, which can be seen in the following testimony given by one of his women "select band" leaders, Eliza Bennis.[6]

In a letter to one of her friends, she gave an account of her experience of a personal Pentecost of full sanctification during this revival:

> In the year 1762 Mr. Wesley came to this town [Limerick, Ireland], and again revived the doctrine of holiness of heart.... The Lord had greatly revived his work amongst us at this time, and was deepening it in the hearts of his children, he had enable some to testify that the blood of Christ cleanseth from *all* sin, and other were earnestly seeking after it. This made me cry the more mightily to God, lest the showers should pass away and my soul remain unwatered.... I continued earnestly striving... until the 22nd of May 1763, being Whitsunday [Pentecost Sunday].... God would on *that* day visit my soul, and make it a Pentecost *indeed* to me. Under these expectations, I attended the Lord's table, and being on my knees before I went to the altar, I laid my case before the Lord.... In receiving the memorials, my soul was enabled to lay hold on Christ for my complete salvation from *all* sin.... My soul so filled with his love.... My love to God, was now quite of another kind, from that I had ever before experienced; more pure, entire and disinterested, without any mixture of self.... What I now experienced, under the full influence of sanctification, did as far exceed what I felt in a justified state, as what I then experienced did what I felt when I was first seeking redemption".... I *do not,* nor *have not* found since the Whitsunday before mentioned, anything in my heart contrary to pure love.[7]

As we have already noted, John Wesley had introduced Pentecost expressions for Christian perfection after his trip to Herrnhut in 1738, including the phrase, "the baptism with the Spirit." John Wesley now referred to this holiness revival as a Pentecost-like event.

Long before John Fletcher was to popularize these Pentecost expressions in Methodism in his *Checks to Antinomianism,* he had already learned from John and Charles Wesley to use the expression of the "baptism with the Spirit" for Christian perfection. For example, in one of his sermons in the early 1760s after he had become vicar of Madeley, he linked Pentecost and perfect love, showing that this highest stage of grace is attained "when the Holy Spirit descends abundantly." Fletcher wrote:

> There is a day of pentecost for believers; a time when the Holy Spirit descends abundantly. Happy are they who receive most of this perfect love, and of that establishing grace, which may preserve them from such falls and decays as they were before liable to.[8]

In his sermon notes for these early years at Madeley, Fletcher said the "general necessity of the baptism of the Holy Spirit" is that through it one "must be sanctified."[9]

In a letter to Miss Hatton (November 1, 1762), Fletcher made the distinction between justifying faith and being "sealed by the Spirit" (or, "the abiding witness of the Spirit") when "they are fully assured of that justification" (i.e., Christian perfection). Fletcher noted that most persons experience these two events separately, citing the Samaritans (Acts 8) as an example of those who received the seal of the Spirit after their justification.[10] In another letter to Miss Hatton (August 8, 1765), Fletcher also defined Christian perfection in terms of such biblical references as, "Have ye received the Holy Spirit since ye believed?" and "After that ye believed, ye were sealed with the Holy Spirit of promise."[11]

Fletcher would later say (see chapter 12), with John Wesley's approval, that "Christ opened his glorious baptism [of the Spirit] on the day of Pentecost" and that this message was "of late years gloriously revived by Mr. Wesley and the ministers connected with him."[12] This holiness revival in the 1760s was specifically linked to theme of Pentecost and sanctification as expressed in the words of John Wesley, and he said he was hearing of people sanctified as frequently as those who were being justified.

John Wesley noted in his journal that the revival did not occur in some places because "Christian Perfection has been little insisted on; and wherever this is not done, be the preachers ever so eloquent, there is little increase, either in the number or the grace of the hearers."[13]

John Wesley and Charles Wesley never disagreed on the importance of preaching holiness, but they did come to disagree on whether or not the experience of holiness was an instantaneous crisis moment or a process that entailed suffering and tribulation through "gradual holiness."[14] John Wesley worried that Charles Wesley had set the standard of holiness too high, making it impossible for anyone to attain it. Charles Wesley worried that it was too easy with his brother for some to profess holiness without showing evidence of the fruit of the Spirit.

John Wesley said he allowed for both process and crisis, although he gave greater emphasis to the crisis moment.[15] Charles Wesley continued to allow for the "now" of the instantaneous moment, but his emphasis became the progressive realization of holiness.[16]

We have noted that his journal often referred to those who had attained perfection, or the full assurance of faith prior to this holiness revival. Even after his focus became "gradual holiness" as means of counteracting some extreme claims to Christian perfection during the holiness revival, he believed that he knew some who were indeed perfected in love long before their death.

Charles Wesley said to his wife on August 16, 1766 that Mary Bosanquet (later

Fletcher) possessed "pure and perfect love."[17] The esteem that Charles Wesley had for her is expressed to his wife: "You cannot think what general satisfaction it gave the sight of us both in the Foundery – pulpit on Thursday in our habits [clerical garb].[18]

This change in Charles Wesley's understanding of the timing of perfection appeared in 1762 in his *Short Hymns on Select Passages of the Holy Scriptures*. These hymns were published independent of John's editorial corrections. John was not happy with some of these hymns because of Charles' critical comments about those who claimed entire sanctification in an instant moment. Charles Wesley expressed the view that claiming to have achieved perfection may be because one was lacking in humility. One of Charles' close friends, Charles Perronet, advised him against having a negative view of attaining entire sanctification in an instant moment: "Let us take care that while we root up the tares, we root not up the wheat at the same time!"[19]

John Wesley as well as Charles was also concerned about the eruption of fanaticism during the holiness revival from 1762 to 1765 when some were claiming to be "perfect as angels."[20] One of his leading preachers, Thomas Maxfield, allowed his London Societies to be carried away with what John Wesley believed were extreme claims about the gifts of the Spirit. They were professing to have dreams, visions, and impressions, and they called themselves "the witnesses." John Wesley came to believe that their claim to have spiritual gifts was fanciful.[21] He admitted that they were at one time "full of love [entirely sanctified]" and "were favoured with extraordinary revelations and manifestations from God. But by this very thing Satan beguiled them from the simplicity that is in Christ. By insensible degrees they were led to value these extraordinary gifts more than the ordinary grace of God; and I could not convince them that a grain of humble love was better than all these gifts put together."[22] The consequence was that "the frightful stories . . . made all our Preachers in the north afraid even to mutter about perfection."[23]

After unsuccessful attempts to convince Maxfield, and his friend, George Bell, to discontinue these practices, John Wesley in effect dismissed them from the Methodist connection.[24]

If there were shifts in the way Charles Wesley understood holiness in the 1760s, there were shifts in John Wesley's thinking as well. The brothers had previously enjoyed a period of many years of speaking with one voice about Christian perfection. If Charles Wesley developed a stricter standard of holiness and became concerned about the too-easy way some were claiming to be made perfect in love in the 1760s,[25] John Wesley became concerned that the doctrine of justifying faith was being minimized at the expense of elevating the importance of holiness.

To combat this tendency to downplay justification, John Wesley introduced a more carefully nuanced way of speaking of the new birth. To understand the changes that were taking place in his developing idea of the new birth, it may be helpful to review his previous view. He initially linked the new birth to Christian perfection.

Rattenbury has noted that both "Wesleys taught two new births."[26] That is, John had one version of it, and Charles had a different one. John Wesley's sermon on "The Circumcision of Heart" (written in 1733) identified Christian perfection with the new birth,[27] and his first standard sermon, "Salvation by Faith" (1738) speaks of justification and being "born again of the Spirit" in the larger Anglo-Catholic sense derived from William Law combined with his Moravian interpretation of being saved from "actual" and "original" sin.[28] In his sermon on "Christian Perfection" (1741) he made a distinction between "babes in Christ" as being "born again in the lowest sense" as distinguished from "perfect men."[29] He referred to those who are born again in the lowest sense" as being "justified."[30] In "The Principles of a Methodist," (1742), John Wesley defined Christian perfection as "born again in the full and perfect sense."[31] He explained that Christian perfection entails the idea that one has attained "the last and highest state of *perfection* in this life. For then are the faithful born again in the full and perfect sense. Then have they the indwelling of the Spirit."[32]

The Marks of the New Birth (1748) still operated with the idea that the new birth equaled Christian perfection, defining the new birth as, "the Spirit of adoption," "the full assurance of faith" and "loving God with all your heart, with all your mind, and soul, and strength, and in loving your neighbour as yourself," and being "perfect, as you Father which is in heaven is perfect."[33]

According to the Sermon Register, John Wesley's first sermon on the new birth was the morning of May 29, 1743, which was the day that he opened up His West Street Chapel. E. H. Sugden said the Sermon Register shows that John Wesley preached on the new birth more than 50 times from 1747 until 1760.[34]

Outler noted that in 1760 Wesley gave "an updated version of his doctrine of the 'new birth'" as "tensions in the Revival mounted" as "the whole problem of regeneration in relation both to justification and sanctification became more and more urgent."[35] John Wesley placed this sermon on "The New Birth" as Sermon 45 in the Standard Sermons.

This sermon explained that justification by faith is what God does for us in the act of forgiving our sins, whereas the new birth is what God does for us in renewing our fallen nature. Justification and the new birth are distinguished from each other logically, but they occur simultaneously. The new birth is also explained as different from sanctification, although initial sanctification begins with the new birth. John Wesley criticized William Law in this sermon for equating new birth with full sanctification. John Wesley's point is that the new birth happens in a completed instant, as the process of sanctification begins.

On the other hand, Charles Wesley retained the view of William Law who equated the new birth with Christian perfection. Two significant Charles Wesley scholars, J. Ernest Rattenbury[36] and John Tyson,[37] have pointed out that Charles consistently used the concept of being born again with full sanctification. John Tyson pointed out this distinction between John and Charles Wesley: "John placed the new birth at the beginning of the process of sanctification, but Charles located it at the end, at the realization of faith's goal."[38] Likewise, Ernest Rattenbury said that Charles Wesley "almost invariably . . . uses the term 'new birth' for an experience" of Christian perfection.[39] Rattenbury put it this way: "It is only when the carnal mind which remains is destroyed and the mind of Christ substituted, thus bringing about a total reconstruction of character, that Charles speaks of new birth."[40]

In the updated sermon on "The New Birth" in 1760, John Wesley said no "full account and at the same time a clear account of the new birth" had ever been previously written, apparently including his own previous sermons on the new birth. In this sermon, John Wesley highlighted that when one is also "born of the Spirit" one is justified by faith and the life of holiness is begun. This sermon clearly elevated the beginning moments of sanctifying grace in the experience of justified persons.

In 1763, John Wesley published a sermon "On Sin in Believers," which was intended to show that the justified believer still retains "inward sins" even though one has ceased to commit "outward sins." In spite of sin remaining inwardly in the heart of one who is justified, one does not allow it to reign.

If John Wesley's intent was to recognize that justified persons have indwelling sin, he at the same time wanted to stress the high state of grace they had attained. He said: "We allow that the state of a justified person is inexpressibly great and glorious. He is 'born again'.... And he has power both over outward and inward sin, even from the moment he is justified."[41]

John Wesley described one who is justified in the same way that he described one who is entirely sanctified, except the degree is greater.

> A justified person . . . is a child of God, a member of Christ, an heir of the kingdom of heaven. "The peace of God, which passeth all understanding, keepeth his heart and mind in Christ Jesus." His very body is a "temple of the Holy Spirit," and an "habitation of God through the Spirit." He is "created anew in Christ Jesus:" He is *washed*, he is *sanctified*. His heart is purified by faith; he is cleansed "from the corruption that is in the world;" "the love of God is shed abroad in his heart by the Holy Spirit which is given unto him." And so long as he "walketh in love," (which he may always do,) he worships God in spirit and in truth. He keepeth the commandments of God, and doeth those things that are pleasing in his sight; so exercising himself as to "have a conscience void of offence, toward God and toward men:" And he has power both over outward and inward sin, even from the moment he is justified.[42]

This elevated assessment of a justified person is consistent with his previous sermons that sanctification begins at the moment of justification. In 1741 in his sermon on "Christian Perfection, he said: "A Christian is so far perfect as not to commit sin.... This is the glorious privilege of every Christian; yea, though he be but 'a babe in Christ'."[43] In his sermon on "Justification by Faith" (1746), he distinguished between justification as forgiveness and sanctification, noting that the "immediate *fruit* of justification" is sanctification.[44]

This high standard of a justified person was consistent with his Anglican theology as seen in the *Discourse on Confirmation* by Jeremy Taylor. Taylor emphasized that the action of the Spirit in confirmation was a completion and perfection of the activity of the Spirit in water baptism denoting forgiveness of sins. Easter and Pentecost exist in a theological continuum instead of being two separate, isolated events. The Spirit who perfects the believer in confirmation is already active in regeneration as signified in water baptism.

Similarly, John Wesley insisted there is a distinction between justification and sanctification, but not a separation. The difference between the two stages is one of degree. In a letter to Thomas Maxfield on Nov 1, 1762, he said that he disliked that Maxfield was playing down the significance of justification. Thomas Maxfield and his fanatical followers during the early days of the holiness revival were parading themselves as being "perfect as an angel." Here is what John Wesley said to him:

> I dislike your directly or indirectly depreciating justification: saying, a justified person is not "in Christ", is not "born of God", is not "a new creature", has not a "new heart", is not "sanctified", not a "temple of the Holy Spirit"; or that he "cannot please God", or cannot "grow in grace".[45]

In his sermon on "Sin in Believers," John Wesley corrected some of these misconceptions about the distinction between justification and sanctification. He said: "Although even babes in Christ are *sanctified*, yet it is only *in part*. In a degree, according to the measure of their faith, they are *spiritual*; yet in a degree they are *carnal*."

If John Wesley said that a justified person had received "the love of God shed abroad in his heart by the Holy Spirit which is given to him," it was because he was saying that justification and full sanctification were distinct but inseparably connected in a continuum of one complex salvation event. Already the sanctifying grace of the Holy Spirit given on the day of Pentecost was at work in the newly justified person. Hence he said: "Although we are renewed, cleansed, purified, sanctified, the moment we truly believe in Christ, yet we are not then renewed, cleansed, purified altogether." This kind of clarity is not found in his pre-1760 sermons.

In 1767, John Wesley wrote another sermon clarifying the distinction between justification and sanctification. If the sermon on "Sin in Believers" emphasized that the justified believer has "the love of God shed abroad in his heart by the Holy Spirit given to him" and sanctification had thus begun, this sermon on "The Repentance of Believers" emphasized that the justified believer continued to sin with impure thoughts, which he called "inner sins." Although sin does not "reign" it continues to "remain." As one progressed toward Christian perfection, the justified believer needed to repent of these inward sins until at last his heart is entirely pure with the perfect love of God.

If John Wesley held a high view of the regenerated status of justified believers, he also held a pessimistic view of their inner sinfulness. He said the justified person will "find in themselves *inward defects* without number. Defects of every kind: they have not the love, the fear, the confidence they ought to have toward God. They have not the love which is due to their neighbour, to every child of man; no, nor even that which is due to their brethren, to every child of God, whether those that are at a distance from them, or those with whom they are immediately connected. They have no holy temper in the degree they ought; they are defective in everything."

These inward defects thus require justified persons to daily repent of their inner sins. These sins cannot be overcome simply by our good choices, but only by full sanctifying grace.

> Though we watch and pray ever so much, we cannot wholly cleanse either our hearts or hands. Most sure we cannot, till it shall please our Lord to speak to our hearts again, to "speak the second time, 'Be clean.'" And then only "the leprosy is cleansed." Then only the evil root, the carnal mind, is destroyed, and inbred sin subsists no more. But if there be no such second change, if there be no instantaneous deliverance after justification, if there

be none but a gradual work of God (that there is a gradual work none denies) then we must be content, as well as we can, to remain full of sin till death.⁴⁶

This sermon also highlighted that the possibility of attaining full sanctification was made possible because of the "power" of the Holy Spirit "promised" in the Old Testament to cleanse and circumcise the heart to enable one to love God with all their heart—which was fulfilled in the New Testament on the day of Pentecost:

> He has promised it over and over, in the strongest terms. He has given us these "exceeding great and precious promises" both in the Old and the New Testament. So we read in the law, in the most ancient part of the oracles of God, "The Lord thy God will circumcise thy heart, and the heart of thy seed, to love the Lord thy God with all thy heart and all thy soul." So in the Psalms: "He shall redeem Israel (the Israel of God) from all his sins." So in the Prophet: "Then will I sprinkle clean water upon you, and ye shall be clean; from all your filthiness, and from all your idols, will I cleanse you. . . . And I will put my Spirit within you, [. . .] and ye shall keep my judgments and do them. [. . .] I will also save you from all your uncleannesses." So likewise in the New Testament: "Blessed be the Lord God of Israel; for he hath visited and redeemed his people, and hath raised up an horn of salvation for us. . . . To perform [. . .] the oath which he sware to our father Abraham, that he would grant unto us that we, being delivered out of the hands of our enemies, should serve him without fear, in holiness and righteousness before him, all the days of our life."⁴⁷

John Wesley consistently maintained that Christian perfection is a possibility because of the bestowal of the Holy Spirit on the day of Pentecost. If he began to highlight the action of the Holy Spirit in bestowing initial sanctifying grace in justification, it was because he saw with clearer eyes that Easter and Pentecost form a continuum, not a separation. It was the mutuality and reciprocity of these two events that John Wesley held together in dialectical tension as the basis of Christian initiation.

Charles' emphasis had always been on Christian perfection, and he interpreted Pentecost language primarily in reference to Christian perfection. In 1764, he composed this lyrical theological reflection to show that the receiving of the Holy Spirit by the disciples at Ephesus in Acts 19:6 entailed their entire sanctification, not their justification.

"The Holy Spirit fell on them, and they spake with tongues, and prophesied."

1. Gifts extraordinary bestow'd,
    On them that first believed,
Powers miraculous from God
    Are rarely now received:
True and faithful as Thou art,
    We yet thy promis'd Spirit claim:
Every fearful sinner's heart [i.e. inbred sin]
    May still expect the same.

2. Still the Holy Ghost descends
    Th' indwelling Comforter,
All the griefs and troubles ends
    Of those that Christ revere;

> Works his miracles within,
>   Renews their hearts, and tongues, and eyes,
> Makes an utter end of sin
> And wholly sanctifies.[48]

This is not to say that Charles downplayed the significance of justification; nor does it mean that Charles failed to see the activity of the Holy Spirit in justification.[49] It is rather to acknowledge that Charles saw, as important as justification was, that the primary purpose of the coming of the Holy Spirit on day of Pentecost was the bestowal of "the second gift" which brings "utter dominion over sin." For him, receiving the Spirit implied receiving the fullness of the Spirit because he allowed the Spirit was God's agent at work in all stages of one's life.

In his *Short Account of the Death of Mrs. Hannah Richardson* in 1765, he described her justification as leaving her unstable and exposed to doubt and fear. He noted that "the heavenly guest" (the Holy Spirit) came to her originally with a measure of assurance, but he did not abide with her leaving her unstable spiritually because the Holy Spirit is not allowed to remain in a heart that still retains indwelling sin. Hannah Richardson "mourned" over her struggle with "original sin" in her heart after she was justified and she continued to lack the abiding witness of the Spirit until a year later when she experienced that "perfect love hath cast out fear" through "full redemption in the blood of Jesus" and she testified: "*I am sanctified wholly, Spirit, soul, and body.*"[50]

What is so remarkable about this account of Hannah Richardson is the same language is used in the preface to *Hymns and Sacred Poems* (1740) when John and Charles Wesley first laid out their understanding of the subsequent nature of Christian perfection. The focus of the initial explanation for the need of Christian perfection was the lack of an abiding assurance of one's sense of forgiveness and that after their justification "then arises fear, that they shall not endure to the end, and often doubt. . . . their sins were forgiven. . . . Under these clouds . . . they go mourning all the day long. . . . But it is seldom long before their Lord answers for himself, sending the Holy Spirit, to comfort them, to bear witness continually with their spirit, that they are the children of God" [see above, p. 50]. Charles' description of Hannah Richardson matches this first description that they first ever produced on this topic. Charles' hymns consistently linked the abiding witness of the Spirit with Christian perfection, and until that moment one is threatened by fear that their sins have not been forgiven because the Holy Spirit is not "abiding" in a permanent way.

In 1772, in "Hymns in Preparation for Death," Charles composed a prayer to receive the Holy Spirit for sanctification. Two key terms for Christian perfection in his writings were being "saved" from sin and "renewed" in righteousness and true holiness, and he typically linked the indwelling of the Spirit with holiness. Charles wrote:

> 3. Oft have I for thy Spirit pray'd,
> Ten thousand times invok'd his aid,
>   And found his presence near,
> Yet still unsav'd, and unrenew'd
> I want the sanctifying God,
>   Th' indwelling Comforter.[51]

Charles connected the assurance of salvation primarily with Christian perfection. This equation first goes back at least to John Wesley's sermon on "The Circumcision of Heart" (1733) when he said "'circumcision of heart' implies . . . the testimony of their own spirit with the Spirit which witnesses in their hearts, that they are the children of God."[52]

We have already seen that the identification of assurance with Christian perfection was explained most clearly for the first time in the preface to *Hymns and Sacred Poems* in 1740 jointly written by John and Charles.[53] We also noted that Charles said that assurance is distinct from justification and usually followed it by a distance in time.[54]

The following verse is one of numerous instances in Charles' poetry where he equated Christian perfection with assurance. Notice also that he equated "the indwelling Spirit" with Christian perfection.

> 2. I must of my salvation doubt,
> Till I have fully wrought it out,
>   And all my sins are gone:
> Till perfect love hath fear expel'd,
> And by th' indwelling Spirit seal'd,
>   I serve my God alone.[55]

In the *Arminian Magazine* in 1780 is a hymn by Charles (published by John Wesley) to shows that the Holy Spirit works in both justifying faith and Christian perfection. Charles described how the Holy Spirit was with the disciples of the Lord during his earthly existence, and similarly the Holy Spirit is with believers today who "trust" in him who "controls the flesh which lusts within, keeps down the rebel in our souls, and holds us back from sin" until "streaming from above the Father, Son, and Comforter fills all our hearts with love." This hymn described a justified person as the Spirit "dwelleth *with you*" and Christian perfection as the Spirit "shall be *in* you."

> "He dwelleth *with* you, and shall be *in* you." John 14:7

> 1. With us we know He dwells,
>   The Spirit of our Lord,
> For still His counsels He reveals,
>   Interpreting His word:
>   To us the promise made
>   We still thro' Him receive,
> And trust, the Spirit of our Head
>   Shall *in* His members live.

> 2. His present pow'r controls
>   The flesh which lusts within,
> Keeps down the rebel in our souls,
>   And holds us back from sin:
>   He visits us unsought,
>   And freely doth inspire
> Our hearts with every serious thought
>   And every good desire.

>   3. He gives the grace unknown,
>   Helps our infirmity,
>   And groans th' unutterable groan
>   And pleads th' effectual plea:
>   Our God is pleased to hear,
>   And streaming from above
>   The Father, Son, and Comforter
>   Fills all our hearts with love.
>
>   4. Come then, celestial Guest,
>   Into Thy temple come,
>   Take full possession of the breast
>   That pants to be Thy home:
>   Spring up, Thou living Well,
>   Thou Lord of life Divine,
>   And now Thy humble mansion seal
>   Thro' endless ages thine.[56]

His *Select Hymns* was published in 1762, and his *Hymns on the Trinity* in 1767 and they showed his continuing focus on Christian perfection. His frequent reference to justification is followed by a plea for Christian perfection, in such terms as "pardon sealed."

These hymns also showed that Charles' focus on the sanctifying Spirit was Trinitarian. The significance of the coming of the Holy Spirit was because the Holy Spirit "applies the cleansing blood" of Christ.[57] His focus is never simply on the Holy Spirit, but Father and Son.

>   3. To sanctify those
>   By mercy foreknown,
>   The Comforter flows
>   From Father and Son:
>   Renew'd by the Spirit,
>   In holiness pure,
>   The joy we inherit,
>   And make the prize sure.
>
>   4. The merciful God,
>   The hallowing Three
>   Himself hath bestow'd
>   On sinners like me:
>   Our full sanctifier
>   He perfects in one,
>   And raises us higher,
>   And seats on his throne.[58]

In the following hymns to the Trinity, Charles prayed for another Pentecost when "the Holy Ghost . . . purifies believing hearts."

> Hymn XXVII
> 4. Poor and blind, condemn'd and lost,
>   Thy ransom'd creature own;

> Father, send the Holy Ghost,
>   And send in him, thy Son,
> By th' indwelling Comforter
>   Renew me in thy holiness;
> Tri-une God, regard my prayer,
>   And bid me die in peace.[59]

> Hymn XXIX
> The Father freely justifies,
>   The Son his pardoning power asserts,
> The Holy Ghost that blood applies
>   Which purifies believing hearts;
> Yet God who sin forgives alone
> In Persons Three is only One.[60]

> Hymn CVI
> Come Holy Ghost, thou Lord most high,
>   The veil of unbelief remove,
> And in us Abba Father cry,
>   And lead our hearts into his love;
> Our hearts into his patience lead
>   Whose blood hath washed our sins away,
> And perfected like Christ our head,
>   Seal and preserve us to that day.[61]

In the following hymn, Charles Wesley prayed for another day of Pentecost for believers to know the fullness of the Trinity's presence in their lives, highlighting "the Spirit that doth from both proceed" who is the source of "holiness." The multiple instances of Charles' prayer-hymns for new Pentecosts would not be intelligible if he were connecting the day of Pentecost with the initial moment of justifying faith. His hymns consistently link Pentecost with believers expecting to be made perfect in love, not forgiveness of sins.

> "At that day ye shall know, that I am in my Father,
>   and you in me, and I in you." John 14:20.

> 1. Whene'er our day of Pentecost
>   Is fully come, we surely know
> The Father, Son, and Holy Ghost
>   Our God, is manifest below:
> The Son doth in the Father dwell,
>   The Father in his Son imparts
> His Spirit of joy unspeakable,
>   And lives for ever in our hearts.

> 2. Our hearts are then convinc'd indeed
>   That Christ is with the Father One;
> The Spirit that doth from both proceed,
>   Attests the co-eternal Son;
> The Spirit of truth and holiness

> Asserts his own divinity:
> And then the orthodox confess
> One glorious God in Persons Three.[62]

In 1767, Charles in the following verse from "Family Hymns," invited the Trinity through the Holy Spirit sent down by the Trinity to bring the "fullness of peace" and "the whole Godhead impart, and eternally dwell in the sanctified heart."

> 3. Come, Father, and Son,
> With the Comforter down,
> In the fullness of peace,
> The ecstatical earnest of heavenly bliss:
> One ineffable Three
> To my household and me
> The whole Godhead impart,
> And eternally dwell in the sanctified heart.[63]

On May 19, 1765, while in Ireland, John Wesley heard "Mr. S[ampson], one of the curates, preached an excellent sermon on 'Receiving the Holy Spirit'. I afterwards accepted his invitation to dinner, and found a well-natured, sensible man, and one well acquainted with every branch of learning which we had occasion to touch upon."[64]

John Wesley did not provide the content of this sermon, but it would have been consistent with Anglican theology as reflected in the rite of confirmation and in Anglican sermons on Pentecost as preached by John Heylyn. This would have included a focus on the need for baptized persons to be filled with the Spirit in sanctifying grace and was probably based on the text in Acts 19:1.

NOTES

1. John Wesley, "Thoughts upon Methodism" (1786), in "The Methodist Societies: History *Nature*, and Design," in *The Bicentennial Works of John Wesley*, 9:528.

2. "A Short History of the People Called Methodists," *The Methodist Societies, History, Nature, and Design*, 9:476–477.

3. Ibid., 21:392, October 28, 1762.

4. *The Experience of Several Eminent Methodist Preachers in a Series of Letters to John Wesley* (Bernard, Vermont: Joseph Dix, Publisher, 1812), 141.

5. Ibid., 142.

6. See *Christian Correspondence Being a Collection of Letters, written by the late Rev. John Wesley, and several Methodist Preachers, in connection with him to the Late Mrs. Eliza Bennis with her Answers, Chiefly explaining and enforcing the doctrine of sanctification, now first published from the originals* (Philadelphia: B. Graves: 1809), 133.

7. Letter from Eliza Bennis to Mr____. Limerick, October 18, 1765. *Christian Correspondence Being a Collection of Letters, written by the late Rev. John Wesley, and several Methodist Preachers, in connection with him to the Late Mrs. Eliza Bennis with her Answers, Chiefly explaining and enforcing the doctrine of sanctification, now first published from the originals* (Philadelphia: B. Graves: 1809), 321–339.

8. *The Works of the Reverend John Fletcher* (New York: W. Waugh and T. Mason, 1833): 4:270, "The Test of a New Creature." This sermon is found in a bound book of pages in Fletcher's own handwriting in the Fletcher-Tooth Archival Collection in the John Rylands Library of Manchester (Box 18, Misc. Manuscripts). The booklet opens with these comments to the reader: "Reader. Grant these sheets an impartial

perusal, they contain an account of the Doctrine of Salvation by Faith alone, as it is preached in Madeley Church. They will (it is hoped) answer the objections that are made against this important doctrine" Melville Horne believes these were written during the first few years of his ministry, Fletcher, *Works*, 4:18, "Mr. Horne's Preface."

9. *Posthumous Pieces of The Reverend John William de la Flechere*, ed. Melville Horne (Philadelphia: Parry Hall, 1793), 195.

10. Ibid., 100-101.

11. Cited in *The Arminian Magazine* 18 (May 1795): 258, "Mr. Fletcher's Letters (to Miss Hatton, August 8, 1765)."

12. Wesley's special abridged edition of John Fletcher, *The First Part of an Equal Check* (Bristol: W. Pine, 1774), v.

13. *Journal and Diaries (1765–1775)*, 22:23.

14. In his lyrical commentary on Genesis 2:1, "Thus the heavens and the earth were finished," Charles Wesley wrote:

> Who madest thus the earth and skies,
>   A world, a six days' work of thine,
> Thou bidst the new creation rise,
>   Nobler effect of grace divine!
> We might spring up at thy command,
>   For glory in an instant meet;
> But by thy will at last we stand
>   In gradual holiness complete.

Charles Wesley, *Short Hymns on Select Passages of the Holy Scriptures* (Bristol: Farley, 1762) 1:5.

15. Telford, *Letters*, 5:16 (to Charles Wesley, June 27, 1766).

16. J. Crichton Mitchell, *Charles Wesley, the Man with the Dancing Heart* (Kansas City, MO: Beacon Hill Press, 1994), 169; cf. Wesley, *Works* (Jackson) 12:132, Letter to Charles Wesley (February 12, 1767).

17. August 16-19, 1766, Letter to Sally Wesley, transcribed by Gareth Lloyd (MARC:DDCW 7/88.

18. Letter to Sarah Wesley (August 25, 1766), transcribed by Gareth Lloyd < MARC: DDCW 7-27

19. Thomas Jackson, *Life of Charles Wesley*, 597.

20. *Letters III (1756–1765)*, 27:306-307, "Letter to Thomas Maxfield" (Nov. 1, 1762).

21. Cf. for a discussion of this, cf. Tyerman, *Wesley's Designated Successor* (New York: Phillips and Hunt, 1883), 84.

22. Wesley, Works (Jackson) 12:481, (a letter to Miss Bolton, December 5, 1772).

23. *Letters III (1756–1765)*, 27:369, "Letter to Charles Wesley (May 25, 1764),

24. Telford, *Letters,* 4:211, Letter to "A Friend." Though Wesley dealt severely with those leaders who compromised Methodist doctrine, he was tender and compassionate with those weak in the faith or who had fallen by the wayside. Cf. Telford, *Letters* 6:334.

25. In a letter to Dorothy Furly on September 15, 1762, John Wesley explained that the only "perfection I believe and teach" is perfect love, which is "consistent with a thousand nervous disorders" as opposed to the "high-strained perfection" reflected in Charles Wesley's "Short Hymns." *Letters III (1s756–1765)*, 27:302.

26. Rattenbury, 83.

27. Outler, *Sermons*, 1:406, "The Circumcision of Heart.".

28. John Wesley, Sermon 17, "Circumcision of Heart," § 2, in *Works*, 1:124.

29. John Wesley, Sermon 40, "Christian Perfection," in *Works*, 2:105.

30. Ibid., 2:106

31. John Wesley, "The Principles of a Methodist" (1742), in *The Methodist Societies: History, Nature, and Design*, ed. Rupert E. Davies, Wesley, *Works*, 9:64.

32. Davies, *Societies*, 9:64-65,"The Principles of a Methodist.".

33. Outler, Sermons, 1:423, 427, 428, "The Marks of the New Birth."

34. Sugden, *Wesley's Standard Sermons*, 2:226

35. Outler, *Sermons*, 2:186, "The New Birth"

36. J. Ernest Rattenbury, 260-264.

37. John Tyson, *Charles Wesley on Sanctification*, 214-225.

38. John Tyson, *Charles Wesley on Sanctification*, 219.

39. Rattenbury, 260.

40. Rattenbury, 308.
41. Outler, *Sermons,* 1:328, "On Sin in Believers"
42. Ibid.
43. Outler, *Sermon* 2:116-117, "Christian perfection.
44. Outler, *Sermons,* 1:186-187, "Justification by Faith."
45. *Letters III (1756–1765),* ed. Ted A. Campbell, 27: 306-307. Letter to Thomas Maxfield (Nov. 1, 1762)
46. Outler, *Sermons,* 1:346, "Repentance of Believers"
47. Outler, *Sermons,* 1:347-348, "Repentance of Believers"
48. MS Acts, MARC: MA 1977/555 (Charles Wesley Notebooks Box 1), 379.
49. Charles Wesley, *Hymns on the Trinity* (Bristol: Pine, 1767), 40.

>   1. Holy Ghost, regard our prayers,
>   Third of the glorious Three,
>   Send forth faithful labourers
>   To gather souls for thee:
>   Sovereign, everlasting Lord,
>   The harvest is entirely thine,
>   Thine the preachers of the word,
>   The messengers divine.
>   2 Move their hearts, and more stir up
>   Salvation to proclaim,
>   Bold on every mountain-top
>   To shout in Jesus' name,
>   Tidings of great joy to tell,
>   Of peace obtain'd, and sin forgiven;
>   Then, thy word of grace to seal,
>   O God, come down from heaven.

50. Charles Wesley, *A Short Account of the Death of Mrs. Hannah Richardson* (Bristol: Pine, 1765), 4, 8-9.
51. MS Preparation for Death, MARC: MA 1977/578 (Charles Wesley Notebooks Box, 3), 5.
52. Wesley said "'circumcision of heart' implies . . . the testimony of their own spirit with the Spirit which witnesses in their hearts, that they are the children of God." Outler, *Sermons,* 1:406. Similarly Law wrote regarding the definition of Christian perfection and assurance: "But when the Temper and Taste of our Soul is entirely changed, when we are renewed in the Spirit of our Minds, and are full of a Relish and Desire of all Godliness, of a Fear and Abhorrence of all Evil, then, as St. *John* speaks, *may we know that we are of the Truth, and shall assure our Hearts before him, then shall we know, that be abideth in us by the Spirit, which he hath given us.*" *A Treatise upon Christian Perfection,* 51, 534.
53. *Hymns and Sacred Poems,* (London: Strahan, 1740), ix.
54. *Manuscript Journal* 1:261.
55. MS Miscellaneous Hymns, MARC: MA 1977/556 (Charles Wesley Notebooks Box 2), 301.
56. *Arminian Magazine,* 3 (London, May 1780): 282-83.
57. Charles Wesley, *Hymns on the Trinity* (Bristol: Pine, 1767), 69.

>   3. The Spirit testifies of him,
>   And gives us faithfully to call
>   Jesus, the Lord and God supreme,
>   Whose streaming blood hath ransomed all:
>   That blood the Spirit of Christ applies,
>   That blood of God who never dies.

58. *Hymns to the Trinity,* 86.
59. Ibid., 111.
60. Ibid., 113.
61. Ibid., 68.
62. *Hymns to the Trinity,* 42.
63. Charles Wesley, *Hymns for the Use of Families* (Bristol: Pine, 1767), 6.
64. *Journal and Diaries V (1765–1775),* in *The Bicentennial Works of John Wesley,* 22:512.

Chapter 11

Introducing the Reverend John Fletcher, Vicar of Madeley

"Power from on high is what I want still . . . an abiding day of Pentecost."
—John Fletcher

"I believe one that is perfected in love, or filled with the Holy Spirit, may be properly termed a father. This we must press both babes and young men to aspire after —yea, to expect. And why not now?"
—John Wesley

"O, baptize my soul, and make as full an end of the original sin which I have from Adam . . . . Give me thine abiding Spirit, that he may continually shed abroad thy love in my soul . . . . Send thy Holy Spirit of promise to fill me therewith, to sanctify me throughout."
—John Fletcher, *Last Check to Antinomianism*
Edited and Approved by John Wesley and Charles Wesley.[1]

John Fletcher wrote a letter to Lady Huntingdon on February 10, 1769. This letter revealed that the motif of Pentecost and sanctification was about to become a dominant theme for John Fletcher. He was at this point about to become John Wesley's "Vindicator" in the debate with Calvinist Methodists over the question of predestination and holiness. His highly celebrated *Checks to Antinomianism* became the textbook of Methodist doctrine, including America where Bishop Francis Asbury required his preachers to read them in their ministerial course of study.

In January 1773, John Wesley in an extended letter urged Fletcher to become his successor, followed by repeated appeals.[2] Earlier John Wesley had invited Fletcher to take over the leadership of Methodism, and he said he would be willing to serve under Fletcher, if he preferred that role instead of serving as his equal.[3]

Fletcher immigrated to England from Switzerland when he was twenty one years old. John Wesley became his mentor, and he also enjoyed an even closer friendship with Charles Wesley, even becoming the god-father to his daughter Sally.[4] Charles Wesley was John Fletcher's most frequent correspondent for almost twenty five years.[5] Charles Wesley took charge of overseeing Fletcher's writings being published, including correcting the printer's proof copy. They enjoyed a remarkable level of intimacy and transparency in their relationship.

Just as Charles Wesley had taken his theological cues from his brother John in their early days at Oxford, even so John Fletcher relied upon John Wesley as his theological mentor. Fletcher had been trained and brought up in the Calvinist tradition in Geneva, Switzerland, but he was already predisposed against absolute predestination before he came to England, and he embraced the Anglican version of John Wesley's theology.

Fletcher became the successful apologist of John Wesley. It was because of his "clear understanding" of Methodist doctrine that John Wesley chose him to be his successor, even offering to serve under Fletcher's leadership.

Fletcher never agreed to serve as the leader of Methodism, although he was repeatedly urged by the Wesley brothers and the Methodists to do so. He was the vicar of Madeley in Shropshire, England, and preferred to remain there, in part because he felt unworthy of the offer. He also enjoyed a wider range of contacts within the Church of England than just with the Methodists.

King George III appreciated Fletcher's political writings about the American colonists, offering him "a preferment" in the Church of England which he declined, saying that he only wanted "more grace."[6] Fletcher enjoyed a friendly relationship with Lord Dartmouth, who was the British Secretary to the Colonies on the eve of the American Revolution. Peter Forsaith has shown that Fletcher's response to Lord Dartmouth in a letter (September 19, 1774) could indicate that King George might have offered him a position in the United States. In another letter to Lord Dartmouth from Thomas Rankin (a Methodist preacher whom John Wesley sent to supervise the Methodists for five years until the revolution broke out in 1775), Rankin mentioned that Lord Dartmouth said Fletcher would "make an acceptable Bishop for America," though Rankin thought it was necessary to wait until the political struggle in American should first subside.[7] Upon his return to England, Rankin gave Fletcher a comprehensive report of the Methodists in America, with Fletcher responding passionately as if "they had been his own flock."[8]

This evidence makes it interesting to speculate (though not certain) that Fletcher was offered to become the first bishop in America. If he had done so, it is likely a Methodist denomination in America would not have been formed with Wesley's designated successor as the bishop of the English Church in America. Fletcher's intellectual abilities and integrity show him to have been an appropriate choice as a High Churchman and loyal to King George. The depth of Fletcher's inspirational life is reflected in Rankin's account of his meeting with Fletcher after his return from America:

> The different conversations I had with him, his prayers and preaching during the few days which he stayed at Bristol and Brislington, left such an impression on my mind, and were attended with such salutary effects, that for some months afterwards not a cloud intervened between God and my soul, —no, not for one hour. His memory will ever be precious to me while life shall remain; and the union of spirit which I felt with that holy and blessed man will have its consummation in those regions of light, love, and glory, where parting shall be no more.[9]

Having refused to be John Wesley's successor and having declined King George's offer of a "preferment" in the Church, his appointment at Madeley afforded him the occasion to write his famous *Checks to Antinomianism* in defense of John Wesley's theology. John and Charles Wesley both corrected and approved his writings. Fletcher died at the age of fifty five from a highly contagious fever epidemic while ministering to his ill parishioners despite the risks to his own life.

The only biography that John Wesley ever wrote was the life of Fletcher, which was later revised by Joseph Benson, as an example of one who lived the sanctified life. This biography exerted an enormous influence in early British and American Methodism. It was reprinted more than twenty seven times in the 18th century. There were at least 174 different printings of Fletcher's various books in the nineteenth century in America and Britain.[10]

It was everywhere assumed that Fletcher was John Wesley's official interpreter. This perception is typically reflected in a comment by the editors of *The Methodist Magazine* in America in 1831 which jointly placed John Wesley and John Fletcher side by side as the standards of Methodist doctrine: "After the Holy Scriptures, and, in subordination to these, the works of Mr. John Wesley, the writings of John Fletcher are held next in estimation, we believe, by the whole body of Wesleyan Methodists throughout the world."[11]

One of the obvious reasons why Fletcher was considered authoritative was because John Wesley had closely edited and corrected Fletcher's manuscripts before he published them and then gave them his unqualified approval. Some Fletcher scholars think that John Wesley so altered Fletcher's writings that we cannot be sure exactly what are his distinctive views.[12] However, we do have some writings like *The Portrait of St Paul* that John Wesley was not privy to, and these are consistent with the ones that John Wesley edited.

John Wesley said of their relationship that they had "no secrets between us." Wesley noted that Fletcher's intellectual abilities were superior to anyone whom he knew.[13] Wesley admired "the purity of the language, "the strength and clearness of the argument," and "the mildness and sweetness of the spirit" which typified Fletcher's writings.[14]

Fletcher's artful and clear style of writing and his saintly life provided the resources for him to articulate a theology of the Holy Spirit which has done more to influence Methodism than any other writings, next only to John and Charles Wesley. He was loved and highly respected among John Wesley's preachers who affectionately referred to him as "the great and good man, Mr. Fletcher."[15]

One of Fletcher's admirers was Mr. Joshua Gilpin, a scholarly priest of the Church of England. His description of Fletcher's writings and preaching was based on an intimate acquaintance with him. He also edited and translated Fletcher's posthumous and influential work, *A Portrait of St. Paul*. Gilpin wrote:

> Had he aimed at celebrity as a public speaker, furnished as he was with the united powers of learning, genius, and taste, he might have succeeded beyond many, who are engaged in so insignificant a pursuit. But his design was to *convert,* and not to *captivate* his hearers; to secure their eternal interests, and not to obtain their momentary applause. Hence, his *speech and his preaching were not with enticing words of man's wisdom, but in demonstration of the Spirit, and of power.* He spake, as in the presence of God, and taught, as one having divine authority. There was an energy in his preaching, that was irresistible. His subjects, his language, his gestures, the tone of his voice, and the turn of his countenance, all conspired to fix the attention and affect the heart. Without aiming at sublimity, he was truly sublime; and uncommonly eloquent without affecting the orator.[16]

Here is what John Wesley said of him in his memorial sermon:

I was intimately acquainted with him for above thirty years. I conversed with him morning, noon, and night, without the least reserve, during a journey of many hundred miles; and in that time, I never heard him speak one improper word, nor saw him do an improper action. To conclude. Many exemplary men have I known, holy in heart and life, within fourscore years. But one equal to him I have not known—one so inwardly and outwardly devoted to God. So unblamable a character in every respect I have not found either in Europe or America. Nor do I expect to find another such on this side of eternity.

As it is possible we all may be such as he was, let us then endeavour to follow him as he followed Christ![17]

Richard Watson (the first systematic theologian of Methodism) described Fletcher as "a man eminent for genius, eloquence, and theological learning."[18] A recent biographer, George Lawton, has said that it is more appropriate to call Fletcher "a genius in the great company of the saints."[19] Lawton believed that Wesley had greater organizational skills, but Fletcher's "writings reveal him as Wesley's intellectual equal."[20] United Methodist theologian, Albert Outler, compared Fletcher's intellectual abilities as next only to John Wesley's abilities and attainments.[21] Kenneth Kinghorn, the late Professor Emeritus of Church History at Asbury Theological Seminary, in *The Heritage of American Methodism* has noted: "If Fletcher was an inspiring saint, he was also a brilliant theologian."[22]

Fletcher's relationship to Wesley and Methodism in general is symbolized in a monument erected in his honor in the City Road Methodist Chapel in London, which Wesley built in 1777. Here Fletcher is memorialized as a "genius." His monument is located to the right side of the communion table and immediately beneath John Wesley's monument. At the top of Fletcher's monument is a sculpture of the Ark of the Covenant. Highlighting his intellectual accomplishments, on one side is a sculpture of books entitled, "Checks" and "Portrait of St. Paul." On the other side is a scroll with the theme, "With the meekness of wisdom." Located at the bottom is a sculpture of a dove flying above pens and a roll of paper.

The following epitaph was inscribed on the tablet, composed by Richard Watson:[23]

SACRED TO THE MEMORY OF
THE REV. JOHN WILLIAM DE LA FLECHERE,
VICAR OF MADELEY IN SHROPSHIRE;
BORN AT NYON, IN SWITZERLAND, THE XII. OF
SEPTEMBER A.D. MDCCXXIX;
DIED THE XIV. OF AUGUST, MDCCLXXXV.

A man eminent for genius, eloquence, and theological learning;
Still more distinguished for sanctity of manners, and the
virtues of primitive Christianity,
Adorned with "whatsoever things are pure, whatsoever things are lovely,"
And bringing forth "the fruits of the Spirit," in singular richness and maturity.
The measure of every other grace in him was exceeded by his deep and unaffected
humility.
Of enlarged views as to the merit of the atonement,
And of those gracious rights with which it invests all who believe.
He had "boldness to enter into the holiest by the blood of Jesus,"
And, in reverent and transporting contemplations, the habit
of his devout and hallowed spirit,

> There dwelt as beneath the wings of the cherubim,
> Beholding "the glory of God in the face of Jesus Christ,"
> and was "changed into the same image;"
> Teaching, by his own attainments, more than even by his
> writings, the fullness of evangelical promises,
> And with what intimacy of communion man may walk with God.
>
> He was the friend and coadjutor of the Rev. John Wesley,
> Whose Apostolic views of the doctrines of General Redemption,
> Justification by Faith,
> And Christian Perfection, he successfully defended,
> Leaving to future ages an able exposition of "the truth which is
> according to Godliness,"
> And erecting an impregnable rampart against Pharisaic
> and Antinomian error,
> In a series of works, distinguished by the beauty of their style,
> by force of argument,
> And by a gentle and catholic spirit; affording an edifying example
> of "speaking the truth in love,"
> In a long and ardent controversy.
> For twenty-five years, the parish of Madeley was the scene of his
> unexampled pastoral labours;
> And he was there interred amidst the tears and
> lamentations of thousands,
> The testimony of their hearts to his exalted piety, and to his
> unwearied exertions for their salvation;
> But his memory triumphed over death;
> And his saintly example exerts increasing influence in the
> Churches of Christ,
> Through the study of his Writings, and the publication of his Biography.
> In token of their veneration for his Character,
> And in gratitude for the Services rendered by him to the cause of Truth,
> This Monument was erected by the Trustees of this Chapel,
> A.D. MDCCCXXII

Certainly this monument and the commemoration written by Richard Watson tell of the influence of John Fletcher upon the development of Methodist doctrine and practice. This monument and its location directly under John Wesley's monument will always remind us that Methodist history and theology will never be appreciated and understood adequately without reference to John Fletcher.

William Larrabee within sixty years of John Wesley's death referred to John Wesley, Charles Wesley, and John Fletcher as "the great triumvirate of Arminian Methodism" with "each one peculiarly adapted to the work which Providence assigned him to do—John Wesley to travel and superintend the societies, Charles Wesley to make the hymns, and John Fletcher to perfect the doctrines. Each did well his part. Each deserves, perhaps equally, a 'place in the memory' of the great Methodist family."[24]

Methodist historian Abel Stevens in 1864 wrote this assessment of Fletcher's influence:

> No polemical works of a former age are so extensively circulated as these "Checks." They are read more today than they were during the excitement of the controversy. They control the opinions of the largest and most effective body of evangelical clergymen of the earth. They are staples in every Methodist publishing-house. Every Methodist preacher is sup-

posed to read them as an indispensable part of his theological studies, and they are found at all points of the globe whither Methodist preachers have borne the cross. They have been more influential in the denomination than Wesley's own controversial writings on the subject.[25]

In 1882, Luke Tyerman wrote that "Fletcher's 'Checks' are as much read to-day as they were a hundred years ago. The demand for them increases almost every year, both in England and in America; and they are found in every land where Methodism has been founded."[26]

Why his writings are no longer read and studied today is a different story than we can discuss here, except to say that when theological liberalism made its way into the Methodist Episcopal Church in the final years of the 19th century, his writings were removed from the conference of study. He and John Wesley were neglected because it was assumed their ideas were out of date. The significance of John Wesley as a Church reformer and theologian was reawakened in 1935, with the landmark study of G. C. Cell, *The Rediscovery of John Wesley*. However, the rediscovery of John Fletcher has not yet happened. Of course, Charles Wesley's hymns have continued to be sung every week in Sunday services throughout the world, and his lyrical theology is largely responsible for preserving Methodist doctrine in the minds of most people today. That Fletcher has been largely neglected is a loss to a complete understanding of the success of Methodism in the 18th and 19th centuries.

We will now go back and pick up the story of how Fletcher became a central part of the ongoing development of the Methodist understanding of Pentecost and sanctification.

Fletcher's letter to Lady Huntingdon on February 10, 1769 was composed within only a few months after he had accepted her invitation to serve as the first president of Trevecca College, a Methodist Calvinist school, which she had established as a training center for Methodist preachers.

Fletcher said to her: "Power from on high is what I want still." He confessed and was hoping for "an abiding day of Pentecost." He admitted that his "unbelief runs . . . so high that I doubt whether it will come before my dying day."[27] This theme of "Power from on high" and "Pentecost" constitute a repeated theme in his correspondence with Lady Huntingdon.

One of Fletcher's assignments to the students at Trevecca College was to "draw a parallel between John's baptism and Christ's, and prove the superiority of the latter over the former." They were also "to draw up an Address to Jesus for the [bestowing of] the Holy Spirit urging the strongest reasons you can think of and feel to engage him to grant it you."[28] Being filled and baptized with the Spirit was Fletcher's primary preaching and teaching theme.

In his biography of Fletcher, Benson said that Fletcher insisted that "to be filled with the Holy Spirit was a better qualification for the ministry of the Gospel than any classical learning, (although that too be useful in its place)." He often turned "the school-room" into a chapel service. His addresses emotionally and spiritually moved the students profoundly. At the close of a typical service, he would say to his students: "As many of you as are athirst for this fullness of the Spirit, follow me into my room."[29] Benson reported that "many of us have instantly followed him, and there continued for two or three hours, wrestling, like Jacob, for the blessing, praying for one another."[30]

During the early days of his presidency of Trevecca, Fletcher chose Joseph Benson to be the principal of the college. Benson was a classics scholar and one of the most promising young preachers among John Wesley's preachers. Fletcher and Benson were of the opinion that one way of convincing the Calvinist Methodists to accept John Wesley's doctrine of Christian perfection was to explain that it meant being "baptized with the Spirit," a phrase commonly used by the Countess of Huntingdon to mean power to do ministry and to live the Christian life.[31]

The controversy at Trevecca marked the decisive moment when the baptism of the Spirit became a focus in Fletcher's theology. We know considerably more about his developing theology of Pentecost because of the multiple letters that Fletcher wrote to Charles Wesley during this time, for he was corresponding with Charles at the very time that the Trevecca conflict was heating up.

Around December 15, 1770, Joseph Benson sent a letter to John Wesley explaining his and Fletcher's views on the baptism with the Spirit that they were using to explain Christian perfection.[32] Benson was obviously hoping to get his positive evaluation and recommendation. After all, the contents of this essay reflected what they had learned from John and Charles Wesley's use of Pentecost expressions, as shown above.

On December 16, 1770, Fletcher sent a letter to Charles telling him about his manuscript on the baptism with the Spirit.[33] If Benson was seeking John Wesley's approval for using the baptism with the Spirit as a way of explaining Christian perfection, Fletcher likewise had sent a letter to Charles Wesley to explain his early attempt to do the same thing. After all, Methodist preachers were expected to get John and Charles Wesley's approval before they printed anything.

On December 28, 1770, John Wesley responded in a surprising letter to Benson, telling him that the phrase, "receiving the Spirit," is not a proper term for full sanctification because all believers have received the Spirit.[34]

In addition to this letter, a fragment recently discovered from some of John Wesley's personal notes contained comments that strongly disagreed with only linking the phrase, "baptized with the Holy Spirit," with full sanctification. John Wesley noted that the phrase was controversial and used by the Quakers in order to set aside water baptism.[35] There is no indication that these notes were ever sent to Benson, but it is clear that Benson and Fletcher had come to suspect that John Wesley no longer seemed to use the idea of "receiving the Spirit" and "baptism with the Spirit" as equivalent in meaning to Christian perfection.

On January 7, 1771, Fletcher resigned as president of Trevecca College.[36] Shortly before his resignation, Benson had been dismissed because of his views on predestination and holiness. Benson and Fletcher had been unsuccessful in convincing Lady Huntingdon to accept the idea of sanctification as corresponding to her idea of the baptism with the Spirit. Fletcher unsuccessfully requested Lady Huntingdon to allow him to address the students to explain to them that he was leaving the college because of the lack "of freedom in the College since the grand point to be maintained there (the baptism of the Holy Spirit and day of power) hath been given up either in whole or in part."[37]

Not only had the Calvinist Methodists rejected the idea of the baptism with the Spirit as equivalent in meaning to sanctification, Benson and Fletcher were even more perplexed by John Wesley's apparent rejection of it. It seemed to them that John Wesley himself had changed his mind. It is understandable that they would be perplexed because even John Wesley's *Plain Account of Christian Perfection* in 1766 reaffirmed his earlier sermon on "Christian Perfection" (1741) on Pentecost and sanctification.[38] He also said that "a larger measure of the Spirit" had been given on the day of Pentecost in order to make entire sanctification possible.[39] But now in 1770 John Wesley seemed to abandon this idea, or at least so it surely seemed to them because of his brief comments.

On March 16, 1771 (three months after his letter of criticism) John Wesley sent a follow-up letter to Benson. In this letter, John Wesley affirmed the equation between being "filled with the Spirit" and entire sanctification. John Wesley wrote to Benson: "A *babe* in Christ (of whom I know thousands) has the witness *sometimes*. A young man (in St. John's sense) has it continually. I believe one that is *perfected in love*, or *filled with the Holy Spirit*, may be properly termed a father. This we must press both babes and young men to aspire after — yea, to expect. And why not now?"[40]

This follow-up letter showed at least John Wesley continued to affirm "filled with the Spirit" as an equivalent to Christian perfection.

On March 22, 1771 the forty-year old Fletcher expressed his disappointment with John Wesley's criticism to Benson. Fletcher reported to Benson the details about his final visit to Trevecca, and Fletcher specifically explained how Benson's essay on "the baptism with the Holy Spirit" had been ridiculed by the Calvinist Methodists.

Then in defiance of John Wesley, Fletcher concluded with these words of advice to Benson: "Now with respect to Mr. Wesley's letter to you, I would have you ... preach the *seal of the Spirit, the witness of the Spirit*, or as he [John Wesley] *properly* calls it *the Spirit of Adoption: None can have it* (for *a* constancy) but the *baptized [with the Spirit]*; that you know, whether he assents to it or not." These remarks to Benson showed that Fletcher believed that John Wesley previously used these Pentecost expressions for Christian perfection, as Joseph Benson also believed.

The only written criticism from John Wesley was about the use of this particular phrase, "receiving the Spirit." They did not see the hand-scribbled notes (previously discussed) questioning the use of "the baptism with the Spirit." Certainly Charles Wesley's hymns used Pentecost expressions for Christian perfection, but now apparently John Wesley was modifying his interpretation. Fletcher requested Benson to keep this negative part of the letter about disagreeing with John Wesley confidential, except that he would allow Charles Wesley to read it.[41]

Because John Wesley still equated being "filled with the Spirit" with Christian perfection, it is really difficult to know exactly what Benson and Fletcher thought they were hearing from John Wesley because at the same time he was cautioning them about Pentecost expressions, he was at the same time using them in his correspondence to Benson.

It is likely that he was willing for Charles Wesley to know about his dispute because of his intimate friendship with Charles, and he was already in correspondence with Charles about this matter. Also, Fletcher believed that Charles was in agreement with him (see below).

Benson always respected Fletcher's request of confidentiality about this dispute. When Benson quoted this lengthy letter in his biography of Fletcher, he deleted this controversial portion. It has only been discovered in recent years.[42] The confidentiality surrounding this dispute is the reason why no one else knew about it except John Wesley, Charles Wesley, John Fletcher, and Joseph Benson.

We may not know why John Wesley seemed to have changed his mind, if in fact he had modified his views. The difficulty is how to interpret these sketchy comments from John Wesley. In the previous chapter, it was shown that John Wesley began to use Pentecost expressions for both justifying faith and Christian perfection in 1763 and he said the difference between justification and full sanctification was the degree of fullness for the latter. In the period of time before 1760, John Wesley in some of his sermons did not distinguish between justifying faith and sanctification, but rather talked about the full meaning of being a Christian, as in his sermons "The Almost Christian," "The Witness of Our Spirit," and "The Spirit of Bondage and of Adoption," as E. H. Sudgen has pointed out.[43]

He did not always distinguish between the stages of graces in these earlier sermons because his point was to describe the whole Christian life, but it was not because he was embracing Zinzendorfianism.[44] In his sermon on "Sin in Believers" in 1763 John Wesley continued to describe the whole Christian life, but in so doing, he now in a more precise manner showed that the whole Christian life is divided into two stages with Christian perfection being the completion of the process begun with justification. In this way, he wanted to avoid the idea that every justified person was free from "inbred sin," which some of his preachers were saying. At the same time, he did not like the way some of his preachers (like Thomas Maxfield) were "depreciating justification."

If John Wesley had actually changed his mind, the two people who should have known are Fletcher and Benson. By their reaction it seems apparent that something had changed because they were very surprised.

Is it possible that John Wesley really made a decisive and permanent shift in his thinking? Was this only a blip, a temporary departure from his normal understanding? Or was his intent to more clearly explain the relationship between the justified and fully sanctified person in his sermons on "Sin in Believers" and the "The Repentance of Believers" written in 1763 and 1767 respectively? It is clear that Pentecost expressions continued to be used primarily for Christian perfection in John Wesley's subsequent writings, but it seems he wanted to make sure it was understood that some measure of the sanctifying benefits of Pentecost were already being appropriated by justified persons.

So his sermons on "Sin in Believers" (1763) and the "The Repentance of Believers" (1767) insisted that the work of the Spirit who was given on the day of Pentecost already imparted holiness in a lower degree to justified person. So on the one hand, John Wesley could say to Benson that "receiving the Spirit" occurred in justifying faith, but being "filled with the Spirit" occurs in full sanctification.

"Fullness" corresponded to John Wesley's idea of a higher degree as distinct from a lower degree of grace. John Wesley consistently used the expression of being "filled" with the Spirit with Christian perfection, not justifying faith.

This use is also consistent with his leaders. For example, in a letter of November 15, 1775 written to John Wesley by his closest female friend and "band" leader, Elizabeth Ritchie, she said to him: "May you be filled with faith and love and with the Holy Spirit." She obviously was not suggested that John Wesley needed again to be "justified," but rather she was wishing him to "be filled with faith and love." This expression of being "filled with the Spirit" was also consistently used by Charles Wesley for perfection.

Whatever may have been some modifications in John Wesley's theology of Pentecost at this time, the answer will have to be decided on the basis of how John Wesley defined and used Pentecost expressions in his subsequent writings. My examination of the historiography will show that John Wesley continued to affirm the use of the "baptism with the Spirit" and being "filled with the Spirit" to mean Christian perfection.

We will also see how Joseph Benson never shifted his views, but rather we will see in his correspondence with Mary Bosanquet in 1778 he said there was no dispute about the meaning of the baptism with the Spirit among anyone of the Methodists. We will also cite an extended letter to Fletcher in 1781 where Benson expressed this prayer: "Oh! Heavenly love baptize me with thy sacred fire, and let it burn night and day upon the altar of my heart, till night and day with me should cease and the spark should return to its great original!" It is this understanding of the baptism with the Spirit that Benson said everyone accepted, including John Wesley.

From 1742 to 1777, it is clear that Charles Wesley made no changes in his lyrical theology of Pentecost.

We have already pointed out the use of "the indwelling of the Spirit" for Christian perfection that the Wesley brothers had espoused in multiple instances in their writings.[45]

In 1749 Charles compiled his *Hymns and Sacred Poems* independent of his brother's editorial assistance. Here he continues with this same idea of the indwelling Spirit as equivalent to Christian perfection.

> 3. On every soul that thirsts for grace,
>   I will the living water shower,
> I will on all thy gasping race
>   The fullness of my Spirit pour.
>
> 4. The grace shall on thy sons descend,
>   Thro' all succeeding ages flow,
> And all who on my truth depend,
>   Th' indwelling Comforter shall know.[46]

If John Wesley had modified his use of Pentecost expressions in 1763 with his sermon on "Sin in Believers" to allow that all justified persons have "the indwelling Spirit" in some measure, there is no indication that Charles modified his use of the expression of the indwelling Spirit as an equivalent to Christian perfection. His prayer-hymn in 1772 was that:

> Through thy pure indwelling Spirit,
> Perfect holiness to gain.[47]

References to "thy pure indwelling Spirit" appear in Charles' hymns for holiness, although he allowed that a justified person has passing moments of the Spirit's assurance. As noted earlier, Charles reported "the Comforter was as a Guest that tarrieth but a day" in the justified experience of Hannah Richardson. She was "a soul standing up under the intolerable weight of original sin! Troubled on every side; perplexed, but not in despair; persecuted by sin, the world, and the devil, but not forsaken; cast down, but, not destroyed."

Charles encouraged her that "yet a little while, and He [the Holy Spirit] that shall come will come, and will not tarry." In the midst of "this deepest distress . . . the Comforter came. The Lord, her Saviour, came suddenly to his temple."

She said to Charles: "I have power with God, and with man, and have prevailed." With the coming of "the Comforter" she had the full assurance of faith: "I cannot doubt, although I did doubt. I cannot fear now; perfect love hath cast out fear. I have full redemption in the blood of Jesus."

Charles asked her if prior to this experience of the coming of the Holy Spirit in full redemption if she felt she was justified: "I asked, whether that peace which she tasted above a year ago, was the same as she now enjoyed. She answered, 'It was of the same kind, in the lowest or first degree. It surely was justification'."

Charles's account of Hannah Richardson is consistent with his use of Pentecost expressions in his hymns and poems regarding the descent of the Holy Spirit as equivalent in meaning to Christian perfection. The Spirit came in justification but "as a Guest that tarrieth but a day."[48]

In 1767 in his "Trinity Hymns," he affirmed:

> By the indwelling Comforter
> Renew me in thy holiness.[49]

In 1772, he wrote "perfect holiness" is gained "through thy pure indwelling Spirit," while prior to this attainment "pardon" is obtained through Jesus' death:

> 2. Thro' thy death and righteous merit
>   Pardon still I hope t' obtain,
> Thro' thy pure indwelling Spirit
>   Perfect holiness to gain:
> Partner of thy sinless nature,
>   All thy spotless mind to show,
> Fashion'd after my Creator,
>   God as I am known to know.[50]

In 1772, Charles Wesley again sees "the indwelling Spirit" as the basis of Christian perfection:

> 1. I know, and feel it cannot be
> That I the holy God should see,
>   Or stand before his sight,
> Unless I after him awake,
> His nature here on earth partake,
>   And in his love delight.

2. But he my flesh and blood assum'd,
That I, to death eternal doom'd,
   His Spirit might retrieve,
The favour of my Lord regain,
Substantial holiness obtain,
   And in his image live.

3. Come then, great God, thyself reveal,
With ecstasies unspeakable
   Thy pard'ning love impart;
Thy sanctifying blood apply,
To purge my nature's deepest die,
   And purify my heart.

4. My heart, which then to thee I give,
To earthly things no more shall cleave,
   Or seek its rest below,
No more to vile affections yield,
But with the indwelling Spirit fill'd,
   My only Jesus know.

5. Soon as of thee possess'd I am,
The leopard sinks into a lamb,
   And with thy nature blest,
Thy lowly, meek, unspotted mind,
Rest to my hallowed soul I find,
   The true eternal rest.

6. Then, then, mature for my reward,
Fit to behold my glorious Lord
   With all thy white-robed choir,
(My faith and holiness fill'd up)
I reach the sacred mountain's top,
   And in thy sight expire![51]

In his "Hymns for Love" (1777), he prays for the baptism with the Spirit to enable him to love perfectly:

1. God in Christ to whom I pray,
   Thy omnipotence exert,
Take these evil thoughts away,
   Change this poor, polluted heart
By the energy of grace
   By the Spirit of holiness.

2. When my heart is circumcised,
   Emptied of the hell within,
When my spirit is baptis'd [with the Holy Spirit],
   Perfectly detached from sin,
Fervent then as those above
   Thee I shall entirely love.[52]

Notes

1. *Last Check to Antinomianism, Works of John Fletcher*, 6:399.
2. For the entire letter see Tyerman, 1; cf. Patrick Streiff, *Reluctant Saint? A Theological Biography of Fletcher of Madeley*, trans. G. W. S. Knowles (London: Epworth Press, 2001), 217. Thanks to the publication of Fletcher's letters by Peter Forsaith and the biography of Fletcher by Bishop Patrick Streiff, the details of Fletcher's larger significance is now coming to light.
3. *'Unexampled Labours,' Letters of the Revd John Fletcher to leaders in the Evangelical Revival*, ed., with an introduction by Peter Forsaith, with additional notes by Kenneth Loyer (London: Epworth, 2008), 134. Cited hereafter as *'Unexampled Labours'*.
4. *'Unexampled, Labours'*, 88, 252.
5. Cf. *'Unexampled Labours,' Letters of the Revd John Fletcher to leaders in the Evangelical Revival*, 25.
6. Benson, *The Life of the Rev. John W. de la Flechere*, in *Works of John Fletcher*, 1:190; cf. *The Letters of the Rev. John Wesley, A.M.*, ed. John Telford, (London: Epworth Press, 1931), 6:197 (cf. Telford's comments). Cf. Wood, *The Meaning of Pentecost in Early Methodism*, 191.
7. Peter S. Forsaith, "The Long Fletcher Incumbency," *Religion, Gender, and Industry*, edited by Geordan Hammond and Peter S. Forsaith (Eugene, Oregon: Pickwick Publications, 2011), 220.
8. Benson, *The Life of the Rev. John W. de la Flechere*, in *Works of John Fletcher*, 1:310. Cf. *The Meaning of Pentecost in Early Methodism*, 253-54.
9. Ibid.
10. Cf. *The National Union Catalog Pre-1956 Imprints*, 175:232-240. There were also other imprints of this work not listed in *The National Union Catalog*, such J. Kingston, Fletcher's *Appeal to Matter of Fact & Common Sense* (Baltimore: J. Robinson, Printer, 1814).
11. *The Methodist Magazine and Quarterly Review*, 13 (January 1831): 104.
12. Peter Forsaith thinks we cannot be sure what is truly Fletcher's ideas because of John Wesley's editorial pen. That might well be accurate in some instances, but Fletcher once told Charles Wesley that he was the only one who had the unrestricted right to change his manuscript—*"carte blanche to add, or lop off, but to none but you,"* specifically mentioning that his brother John was reading and approving his current manuscript. But John Wesley was not given the permission to change his manuscript without his approval. *'Unexampled, Labours'*, 321. On the other hand, Fletcher once noted that unless John Wesley expressed disapproval of something in his manuscripts, he agreed with it, even the very "words" that he choose. "Fifth Check to Antinomianism," *Works of John Fletcher*, 3:392.
13. Benson, *The Life of the Rev. John W. de la Flechere*, 172.
14. Outler, *Sermons*, 3:617, "The Death of the Rev. Mr. John Fletcher."
15. Cf. Samuel Bradburn, *God Shining Forth from between the Cherubim*: a sermon preached at the opening of the Methodist Chapel, Bridge-Street, Bolton, on Sunday, September 30, 1804, and the opening of the Methodist Chapel in Wrexham, on Tuesday, January 1, 1805, (no publication facts), iv. Wesley's sermon "On Faith," in Outler, *Sermons*, 3:492.
16. Mr. Gilpin, "The Character of Mr. Fletcher, " *The Arminian Magazine* 16 (February 1793): 60.
17. Outler, *Sermons*, 3:627-268, "On the Death of John Fletcher." In a letter to Joseph Benson, November 21, 1776, Fletcher mentioned that John Wesley "invited me to travel with him . . . through Oxfordshire, Northamptonshire, and Norfolk." Luke Tyerman documents this lengthy trip from Shropshire to Norwich and to London. This trip began on November 20, 1776 and lasted for a couple of weeks. This trip was both a preaching tour and health trip intended to help Fletcher recover from his illness of TB. *Wesley's Designated Successor*, 369-373. This reference to having travelled with Fletcher probably is this limited tour. Otherwise, John Wesley and Fletcher spent considerable time together on specific days and occasions throughout their relationship, beginning in London where they first met.
18. Inscribed on the Fletcher monument in Wesley's City Road Methodist Chapel in London.
19. George Lawton, *Shropshire Saint* (London: The Epworth Press, 1960), xiii7
20. Ibid., ix.
21. *John Wesley*, edited by Albert C. Outler (New York: Oxford University Press, 1964), 425.
22. Kinghorn, *The Heritage of American Methodism* (Lexington, Kentucky: Emeth Press, 2009), 18.
23. Thomas Jackson, *The Centenary of Wesleyan Methodism* (New York: T. Mason and G. Lane, 1839), 118-119.

24. William C. Larrabee, *Wesley and his Colaborers*, edited B. F. Tefft (New York: Carlton and Lanahan, 1851), 2:258-159.

25. Abel Stevens, *The History of the Religious Movement of the Eighteenth Century, Called* Methodism (London: George Watson, 1864) 2:55.

26. Tyerman, *Wesley's Designated Successor*, 329-330.

27. *'Unexampled Labours'*, 235.

28. Ibid., 256.

29. *Benson, The Life of the Rev. John W. de la Flechere, Works of the Rev. John Fletcher*, 156.

30. Ibid.

31. A letter published for the first time in Tyerman, *Wesley's Designated Successor,* 182-183. Though Fletcher was concerned about the antinomian tendencies of the Calvinist Methodists, he did not think that the Countess herself was guilty of "the charge of Antinomianism." Cf. letter to Mr. Ireland (March 27, 1774) in *The Letters of the Rev. John* Fletcher, ed. Melville Horne (New York; Lane & Scott, 1849), 260.

32. Randy Maddox and Russell Frazier, "Joseph Benson's Initial Letter to John Wesley concerning Spirit Baptism and Christian Perfection," *The Wesleyan Theological Journal*, 48:2 (Fall 2013): 66, 72.

33. *'Unexampled Labours'*, 258

34. Telford, *Letters* 5:214-215 (to Joseph Benson, December 28, 1770).

35. This fragment is housed in the Manuscript Department of William R. Perkins, Duke University and transcribed by M. Robert Fraser and Frank Baker. M. Robert Fraser. *Strains in the Understanding of Christian Perfection in Early British Methodism*. Ph. D. Thesis, Vanderbilt University, 1988. Photocopy (Ann Arbor, MI: University Microfilm.Inc., 1992), 490-492. Cited by permission from M. Robert Fraser.

36. Cf. John Fletcher's letter to Lady Huntingdon, March 7, 1771 in *Unexampled Labours,* 260-270.

37. *'Unexampled, Labours',* 271, (March 9, 1771).

38. *Plain Account of Christian Perfection, Doctrinal and Controversial Treatises II, Works of John Wesley*, 13:147. A Plain Account of Christian Perfection (7th edition, G. Paramore, Printer, 1794), 13-14.

39. *A Plain Account of Christian Perfection* (7th edition, London: G. Paramore, 1794), 52.

40. Telford, *Letters*, 5:228-229 (to Joseph Benson, March 16, 1771).

41. *Fraser Doctoral Dissertation*, 489. John Wesley defined the language, "seal of the Spirit" and "full assurance of hope" with perfection in his *Plain Account of Christian Perfection* (7th edition, G. Paramore, Printer, 1794), 70-71.

42. The original manuscript is housed in the Manuscript Department of the William R. Perkins Library, Duke University, and it is transcribed by M. Robert Fraser. Cf. *Fraser's Doctoral Dissertation*, 489. Cited with the permission of M. Robert Fraser who discovered this document.

43. Sudgen, 2:148.

44. Wilbur T. Tillett, *Personal Salvation, Studies in Christian Doctrine Pertaining to the Spiritual Life* (Nashville: Publishing House of the M.E. Church, South, 1902), 455.

45. Cf. *Hymns and Sacred Poems* (1742), 220.

46. *Hymns and Sacred Poems* (1749), 1:13.

47. *Preparation for Death, in Several Hymns*. London, 1772., 32.

48. Charles Wesley, *A Short Account of the Death of Mrs. Hannah Richardson* (Bristol: Pine, 1765), 3-11.

49. *Trinity Hymns* (1767), 111.

50. *Preparation for Death, in Several Hymns*. London, 1772, 32.

51. *Preparation for Death, in Several Hymns* (London, 1772), 35-36.

52. MSLove, 1772, 53-54. Charles Wesley defined "the hell within" as inbred sin:

> O snatch me from this Hell within,
> From all the Mire of Inbred Sin,
> From all the Tempter's Power.

[MsPsalms, MS Psalms, MARC: MA 1977/553 (Charles Wesley Notebooks Box 1), 182].

Chapter 12

"New Baptisms are Necessary From Time to Time"

"Undoubtedly the apostles went into the kingdom before the 3000 on the day of Pentecost. If we . . . get in, who knows but perhaps 3 scores . . . may follow us. This is the only way to retrieve the aspersed doctrine of perfection."
—John Fletcher to Charles Wesley

"But new baptisms are necessary from time to time. Compare Acts 2 and Acts 4. The more the magnet rubs the needle the more magnetized it becomes. Why did you not follow the Lord for another Baptism, and by his Spirit dwelling within you, when he once gave you an earnest of that happy day of Pentecost that you have not forgotten?"
—John Fletcher to Charles Wesley

Fletcher's writings intended to make John Wesley consistent on Pentecost and sanctification. It will be seen that Fletcher may have succeeded in this attempt with his proleptic idea of the dynamic interflow of grace throughout salvation history—so that the redemptive benefits of Easter and Pentecost existed retroactively in some measure from the very beginning of salvation history with Abraham.

In the previous chapter, we noted that John Wesley's two sermons, "Sin in Believers" (1763) and "The Repentance of Believers" (1767) had used Pentecost expressions for describing justification, with these same expressions being used also for Christian perfection in a higher degree. Fletcher's *Checks to Antinomianism* intended to explain the interflow of grace in the continuum of salvation history. We will also see that Fletcher's theology was an extension of what he had learned from both Wesley brothers, who had served as his mentors and intimate friends. We will also see that Fletcher brought together the different nuances in their theology—synthesizing their respective views on the crisis and process of sanctification and their respective views on Pentecost expressions for sanctification.

In 1771, Fletcher observed that there was an inconsistency in John Wesley's theology. This observation is found in a document entitled, "An account of John Fletcher's case, with the reasons that have induced him to resign the superintendency of the Countess of Huntingdon's College in Wales." This undated document was labeled, "Letter to Lady Huntingdon." Fletcher explained in this document to Lady Huntingdon that their many conversations on the theme of Pentecost were intended by him to be a bridge for them to come together over John Wesley's doctrine of perfection since she also had often spoken of the need of Pentecostal power for strength to live out the Christian life. Fletcher wrote: "With regard to perfection itself, I believe that when Mr. Wesley is altogether consistent upon that subject, he means absolutely nothing by it but . . . the baptism of the Holy Spirit, the Spirit of adoption."[1]

Fletcher was not introducing a new idea into Methodism. As we have seen, in 1745 in his essay, "Farther Appeal to Men of Reason and Religion," John Wesley distinguished "the baptism with the Spirit" and "water baptism." He equated to be "baptized with the Holy Spirit and with fire" with "perfect love."[2]

It is also important to remember that in "An Extract of a Letter to the Reverend Mr. Law" in 1756, John Wesley said: "That we 'must be baptized with the Holy Spirit,' implies this and no more, that we cannot be 'renewed in righteousness and true holiness' any otherwise than by being over-shadowed, quickened, and animated by that blessed Spirit."[3]

John Wesley had consistently connected the language of "the baptism with the Holy Spirit," not to justifying faith or forgiveness of sins, but to holiness, even as he had connected "the indwelling of the Spirit" with perfection, and not justification, in his "Principles of a Methodist" (1742).

As the debate at Trevecca was coming to a climax leading up to the firing of Joseph Benson and the resignation of John Fletcher over the question of Christian perfection and predestination, Charles Wesley and John Fletcher were engaged in extensive conversation over Fletcher's new writings, especially regarding the meaning of "the baptism with the Spirit."

On Dec. 16, 1770, Fletcher sent a letter to Charles mentioning his exploratory ideas about the baptism with the Spirit. He noted that Mrs. Power (who lived at Mr. Ireland's home) had asked him: "What is that evangelical faith of which you speak that you do not have, and that gift of the Holy Spirit which is the baptism of the true Christian?"[4] Because Mr. Ireland was in a hurry to leave, Fletcher said to Charles: "I do not have time to copy my ideas that I have tossed rapidly onto paper. She will communicate them. I pray you to say to me what you think of them."[5]

Drawing from Charles Wesley's multiple references to future Pentecosts in his hymns, Fletcher then suggested in a good humored way that Charles himself should have another Pentecost as a follow up to his original personal Pentecost:

> But new baptisms are necessary from time to time. Compare Acts 2 and Acts 4. The more the magnet rubs the needle the more magnetized it becomes. Why did you not follow the Lord for another Baptism, and by his Spirit dwelling within you, when he once gave you an earnest of that happy day of Pentecost that you have not forgotten. Well then, Jonah, sleeper, why do you not cry to your God for the Spirit of Resurrection and of life which must enter again in the witnesses who are dead, or sleeping [an allusion to Charles' sermon, "Awake thou, that Sleepeth," which was a summons to perfection].[6]

On August 14, 1774, Fletcher mentioned to Charles about his possible disagreement with his brother John. He observed in this letter that "the difference [between your brother and me] consists, (if there is any) in my thinking, that those who . . . [were] baptized and sealed with the Holy Spirit on the day of Pentecost . . . were in the state of Christian perfection . . . as contradistinguished from the faith of . . . babes, or carnal believers . . . which the apostles had before the day of Pentecost."[7]

This distinction between justification and sanctification based on the distinction between disciples before and after Pentecost was prominent in Charles' hymns. For example, in his versifying Jesus' promise to the disciples that the Holy Spirit is "*with* you" but then shall be "*in* you" (John 14:17), Charles explained: "With us we know he dwells . . . to us the promise made" and today "we still through Him receive, and trust, the Spirit of our Head shall *in* his members live."

The distinction between the Spirit "dwelleth *with* you, and shall be *in* you" is a distinction between justified persons who have "present power" over "the flesh which lusts within" because the Spirit "keeps down the rebel in our souls, and holds us back from sin;" and sanctified persons on the other hand who pray: "Come, then, celestial Guest, into thy temple come, take full possession of the breast," the result being that the Holy Spirit "fills all our hearts with love."[8]

John Wesley published this hymn in *The Arminian Magazine* in 1780, so that Methodists everywhere would understand the difference between a justified person "with whom the Spirit dwells" as with the disciples before Pentecost and the fully sanctified persons "in him the Spirit dwells" like the disciples after Pentecost.

So Charles did not disagree with Fletcher's desire to be more exact than his brother's possible shift in thinking. Fletcher was still not sure that John Wesley had really made any shift in his thinking at this date because he qualified his observation by saying "if there is any" real difference between them. The fact that John Wesley published this hymn for all Methodists to read shows that Fletcher was right to think there probably was no difference between them. We will see later that they did in fact work out their differences.

Fletcher further explained to Charles Wesley in this letter (August 14, 1774) that he was writing an *Essay on Truth* to show that there is a difference between the faith of those who like the apostles were "babes, or carnal believers" before Pentecost and the faith of those who are in "the state of Christian perfection" as a result of being "baptized and sealed with the Holy Spirit on the day of Pentecost."[9]

This treatise was his first attempt to develop this theme in a focused manner, and it was passed back and forth between John Wesley and Fletcher.[10] Both John and Charles Wesley were very much involved in the pre-publication process of critiquing, editing, and approving this work.

The first action of John Wesley, once he had received Fletcher's corrected manuscript on the *Essay on Truth*, was to publish an abridged edition in 1774 so that it would be more widely read. John Wesley worried that Fletcher's tendency to be verbose would limit his readership.[11] Fletcher also asked Charles Wesley to help him in his writings to be "sententious" and "shorter and full."[12]

In John Wesley's special abridged edition of the *Essay on Truth*, he said he had marked the most useful parts of it with an approving asterisk.[13] In the preface, Fletcher stated that he did not intend to "dissent" from the Church of England, but he said that "our church" talked about faith "according to the fullness of the *Christian* dispensation." He intended on the other hand to examine the *"inferior* dispensations" represented by the different degrees of faith as typified in "John the Baptist, Moses, and Noah."

By presenting the progressive order of salvation from the lowest to the highest, he showed that an assurance of faith "was not *fully* opened till Christ opened *his* glorious baptism [of the Spirit] on the day of Pentecost" when "his spiritual kingdom was set up with power in the hearts of his people."

Fletcher said this message was "of late years gloriously revived by Mr. Wesley and the ministers connected with him." John Wesley's approving asterisk appears in front of this paragraph, indicating his approval of the Pentecost expression, "baptism with the Spirit," for Christian perfection and that Methodism had already been preaching this doctrine.[14]

This approving asterisk showed that John Wesley had not really changed his mind in any substantive manner. Fletcher was also not implying something that really was not true when he said that "Mr. Wesley and the ministers connected with him" had "gloriously revived" the preaching that "Christ opened *his* glorious baptism [of the Spirit] on the day of Pentecost." As we have already seen, "the baptism with the Spirit" was used both in John Wesley's writings and Charles Wesley's hymns since John Wesley's visit to Herrnhut.

The following exposition will use John Wesley's special abridged edition to show his agreement with Fletcher.

What specifically did Fletcher mean by the idea of a "glorious baptism [of the Spirit] on the day of Pentecost" that the Methodists had "revived"? Fletcher explained it represented the goal of God's saving history on the day of Pentecost, making it possible for believers to have the full assurance of salvation and to be empowered to love God perfectly.

Fletcher explained that the "everlasting gospel" was present from the beginning of humankind and progressively developed in the history of salvation through "four grand dispensations."[15]

(1) The intuitive faith in God the Father (the Gentile dispensation, Noah) was the first dispensation and it was superseded by . . .

(2) the Jewish dispensation (Moses) with its expectation that the Messiah will come.

(3) This is followed by the dispensation of John the Baptist which "was as singular [to himself] as that of Moses," because just as Moses pointed beyond himself to the leadership of Joshua, so the dispensation of John the Baptist prepared the way for Jesus.[16] The dispensation of John the Baptist proclaimed that the "Messiah is come in the flesh" and this pre-Pentecostal stage typifies "*babes in Christ,*"[17] and "imperfect Christians, who like the apostles before the day of Pentecost, are yet strangers to the great outpouring of the Spirit."[18]

(4) The dispensation of the Spirit is that "the Promise of the Father is fulfilled" and believers are "intimately one with Christ,"[19] through being "baptized with the Holy Spirit."[20] Imperfect Christians are like the "Lord's disciples before the day of Pentecost" who have not been "fully baptized [with the Spirit]."[21] To be "baptized with the Holy Spirit" means to experience "an uncommon degree of sanctifying grace."[22] Being perfected in love was the primary purpose of the baptism with the Spirit, while the mirac-

ulous gifts were "a *temporary appendage*, and by no means an *essential part* of Christ's spiritual baptism."²³ Fletcher also interpreted the three thousand converts on the day of Pentecost to have moved quickly from "faith in the Father, to an explicit faith in the Son" to the dispensation of the Spirit when they were *"filled with the Spirit."*²⁴

If Fletcher's preface to the *Essay on Truth* began with an announcement about the "glorious baptism [of the Spirit] on the day of Pentecost" which had been "revived by Mr. Wesley and the ministers connected with him," John Wesley's abridged edition concluded with the explanation of why "Christ opened the dispensation of his Spirit."

With John Wesley's approving asterisk, Fletcher said the purpose was "that they may be made *perfect in one*" with " 'gladness and singleness of heart, praising God, and having favour with all the people,' by their humble, affectionate, angelical behaviour."²⁵ Fletcher then noted that this promise of the Spirit given on the day of Pentecost was not just for the disciples, but for all those that believe through their word of testimony. His point was that a day of Pentecost is promised to all future justified believers, even as he learned from Charles Wesley's prayer hymns for future Pentecosts.

Fletcher also explained his idea of "the glorious baptism [of the Spirit] on the day of Pentecost" in direct reference to John Wesley's early sermons on "Salvation by Faith" and "Christian Perfection." Specifically, Fletcher showed that Wesley "clearly distinguishes Christian faith properly so called, or faith in Christ glorified" from "the faith of initial Christianity, i.e., 'the faith which the apostles had while our Lord was upon earth'."²⁶

Fletcher then showed that Wesley identified "Christian Perfection" with "the *Christian* dispensation in its fullness" as distinct from the dispensation of the Gentiles, Jews, and John the Baptist.²⁷ Significantly, John Wesley included this explanation in his special edition of the *Essay on Truth*.

Even more significantly, John Wesley promoted with his own approving asterisk Fletcher's idea of the role of his Methodist preachers in proclaiming that the full assurance of "adult Christians" is possible because of Christ's "glorious baptism [of the Spirit] on the day of Pentecost."²⁸ This means, as Fletcher explained, "imperfect Christians" are like "our Lord's disciples before the day of Pentecost" and hence they were not "fully baptized [with the Spirit].... They had not yet been made *perfect in one*."²⁹

Consideration in this treatise was given to correcting what Fletcher perceived to be a misinterpretation of assurance by John Wesley's earlier views, as if a person was still "under the wrath of God" unless they felt an assurance of sins forgiven. Fletcher thus argued, with John Wesley's blessing, that any "God-fearer" (like Cornelius), Jewish believer, or infant Christian (like John the Baptist and the apostles during the earthly life of Jesus) was "justified." John Wesley placed an asterisk in front of paragraphs where Fletcher maintained this point.³⁰

Significantly enough, this was the very same year in the 1774 edition of his journals that Wesley revised his earlier judgment allowing that he himself was justified (or at least he said he had the faith of a servant) before May 24, 1738, apparently having been fully persuaded by Fletcher with whom he had collaborated in the writing of *An Equal Check*.

John Wesley praised the *Essay on Truth* exuberantly in a letter to his closest female friend and band leader, Elizabeth Ritchie (1754-1835), with whom he affectionately corresponded in over fifty letters. He had a special relationship with her. He said that "Betsy Ritchie" was a woman "after my own heart."[31] He first wrote to her on May 8, 1774: "It is not common for me to write to any one first: I only answer those that write to me. But I willingly make an exception with regards to you, for it is not a common concern that I feel for you."[32] She responded on May 17 1774, letting it be known that her feeling for him was mutual. Her opening sentence was: "How shall I express the gratitude I feel to God and you."

She was fifty one years younger than he was, and she signed her letters to him as "your affectionate though unworthy daughter," and he referred to her as "My Dear Betsy." She also referred to him as "my dearest friend."[33] They travelled together in his chaise on occasions where they spent many hours in conversation together and she often read to him. He brought her to his home in London in his final days to care for him.

If anyone would have known John Wesley's view of Fletcher's idea of being baptized with the Spirit, it would certainly have been her. After John Wesley's wife died, speculation was rampant that he would marry her, which caused Joseph Benson to express his strong disapproval of such an idea.[34] Benson himself had once proposed marriage to her, but she turned him down but recommended her friend Karen Thompson, whom Benson then married. Elizabeth Ritchie also attended their wedding. She would later marry Harvey Walklake Mortimer, Esq. in 1801[35] which is about ten years after John Wesley died.

The purpose of including these personal details is to show the continuity of ideas within the matrix of John Wesley's friends and leaders. John Wesley referred to the association of his preachers as his "Connection," by which meant that they agreed with his theology, placing themselves under his supervision. Providing the personal details of the network of women leaders and closest friends in relationship to John Wesley puts his theology in a true-to-life context. Given his Tory sentiments where there is "one king" and "one leader," those in close relationship with John Wesley as their "father in the faith" and leader of the Methodists accepted his ideas and decisions without much freedom to disagree. He was for all practical purposes functioning almost like the "Pope" of Methodism, as his critics charged.

Here is what John Wesley said to Elizabeth Ritchie on January 17, 1775: "Mr. Fletcher has given us a wonderful view of the different dispensations which we are under. I believe that difficult subject was never placed in so clear a light before. It seems God has raised him up for this very thing.... By confining yourself to those who write clearly, your understanding will be opened and strengthened."[36]

Fletcher's idea of "different dispensations" was his way of speaking of the varying degrees of faith, especially pointing out the distinction between the justifying faith of the disciples before Pentecost and the full sanctifying grace of the disciples after Pentecost.

Elizabeth Ritchie replied on January 10, 1775 that she read the *Equal Check to Antinomianism and Phariseeism* noting that she "must acknowledge I never saw the doctrine of dispensation in so clear a light before."

On February 6, 1777, Elizabeth Ritchie said to John Wesley that she had read Fletcher's treatise on Christian perfection: "I have lately read Mr. Fletcher's *Last Check* and felt it as marrow and fatness to my soul. May I run more swiftly the race set before me. I am athirst for the Perfection of my dispensation."

One of the themes in the *Last Check* was for Christ to "baptize with the Holy Spirit" who will "continually shed abroad thy love in my soul." Fletcher always insisted that the purpose of being baptized with the Spirit was to experience the perfect love of Christ. His emphasis was never merely on the Spirit, but on the Spirit of Christ who baptizes with the Holy Spirit; his theology was thoroughly Trinitarian.[37]

In another letter to John Wesley on Dec. 5, 1778, Elizabeth Ritchie said to John Wesley: "I long for the Spirit's fullest Baptism [i.e., baptism of the Holy Spirit], and so see and feel all the promises of God yea and amen that my soul rejoices in hope of that glory which shall be revealed to the believing heart."[38]

It would hardly be expected that she would have used the expression "baptism with the Holy Spirit" for Christian perfection if her mentor and "my dearest friend" for many years would have not agreed with it because John Wesley was careful to instruct her in proper Methodist teaching. Certainly if he "corrected" Benson's idea of "receiving the Spirit" to make sure that he understood that even justified persons have some measure of the Spirit, he would have corrected her expression of the baptism with the Spirit if he thought it was an error. Instead, as it will be shown, this Pentecost reference to the baptism with the Spirit is a frequent expression in her correspondence with her closest friends.

The same month that Fletcher's *Essay on Truth* was completed, John Wesley wrote a letter to one of his prominent Irish "select band" leaders, Elizabeth Bennis, saying that Fletcher had written with more clear understanding on "pardon, [and] holiness" than "scarcely any one has done before or since the Apostles."[39]

John Wesley who was one of the best read intellectuals in his day also called Fletcher "one of the finest writers of the age."[40] In this letter, John Wesley placed John Fletcher in the same category as "my brother and I" noting that Fletcher "has beautifully explained it ["salvation by faith"].[41]

Elizabeth Bennis in her correspondence with John Wesley reported back to him that she was reading Fletcher's *Checks* and found them helpful.[42] She also exchanged several letters with John Fletcher about the pursuit of "complete happiness . . . sure, substantial happiness," raising the question, "How is this happiness to be attained?" She then said "answering this is *your* province."[43] Fletcher briefly replied affirming that "we may reasonably expect that assistance from above which will carry us through our Christian warfare."[44]

Eliza Bennis in a follow-up letter offered her more detailed explanation of the definition of happiness and its attainment, asking for Fletcher's guidance and "inspection . . . that as a friend you would set me right where you think I may be wrong. She then tried to explain the meaning of happiness: "I suppose that *true happiness* consists wholly in *union* and *communion* with *him*, is a hidden life, a spiritual blessing, such as the world cannot see—except by the fruits, but is wholly transacted between God and the soul; and is that kingdom of heaven which the Lord says is within . . . consisting of righteousness and peace and joy in the Holy Spirit."⁴⁵ This "real happiness . . . is wholly spiritual, and we by nature wholly carnal" and hence "natural reason alone" can neither "direct our choice, or enable us to gain this great end . . . until enlightened by the Spirit of God."

She then employed Fletcher's emphasis upon Pentecost as the source of happiness that will deliver one from inward corruption instantaneously:

> Our blessed savior knowing the ignorance of the human heart, promised his disciples to send them the Holy Spirit, the comforter: to teach them all these things, and to remain with them, as his gift to his church, to the end of the world; not to the apostles only, for St. Peter informs us, that "the promise was to them, and to their children, and to *all that are afar off*, even as many as the Lord our God shall call." (Acts 2 & 39). Blessed be God for the extent of this blessed promise; then it is free for me, for my friend [John Fletcher], for all; surely then is the will of our God that we should be happy; let us not refuse our own mercies, or delay our happiness, by trying to overcome our corruption by little and little; be assured my dear friend there is a shorter way, a more speedy remedy; the Lord is able and willing to destroy them all at a stroke: a *word*, a *touch*, a *look*, will do, when the soul is *willing* to be made whole in God's own way: O may we be made willing in this day of his power, to receive, all his goodness waits to give.⁴⁶

Elizabeth Bennis then asked John Fletcher to "set me right, where you may differ from me," asking for his "advice" as to whether or not she understood correctly how true happiness (i.e., Christian perfection) can be attained.⁴⁷

In a biography of John Summerfield (1770-1824), an Irish Methodist preacher who also preached in Limerick,⁴⁸ we see that Fletcher's influence was continuing to be significant even after Eliza Bennis was deceased.⁴⁹ Summerfield was said to have "a new and deep baptism of the Holy Spirit" and "was so overpowered with the love of Jesus."⁵⁰ Summerfield valued highly Fletcher who was referred to as "the celebrated Fletcher"⁵¹ and whose "truly spiritual writings" were valued over others.⁵² He was himself converted "under the preaching of the Rev. Joseph Benson, at that time stationed at Manchester."⁵³ Considering the influence of Fletcher and Benson, it is not surprising that the expression, "baptism with the Spirit," was used by Summerfield's experience of entire sanctification.⁵⁴

It was also recorded in *The History of Methodism in Ireland* that when John Wesley was visiting the Methodist society in Dublin: "On Sunday, May 9th, during the Society meeting, she [Mrs. King] received a baptism of the Holy Spirit in sanctifying power. The blessing then realized she appears never to have lost, nor even to have doubted the possession of."⁵⁵

The official history of Methodism in Ireland often spoke of entire sanctification using the expression, "the baptism with the Spirit." For example, in August, 1791, it was reported that Mr. Ouseley "received such a baptism of the Holy Spirit, in sanctifying fullness, as made him unspeakably happy in the love of Christ."⁵⁶

For John Wesley to say about Fletcher that God had "raised him up for this very thing" and no one "since the Apostles" had explained holiness better than he is the highest recommendation and approval that could have ever been offered to anyone.

That John Wesley said Fletcher's writings were without parallel among writers since the days of the Apostles, and that he personally marked specific texts with his approving asterisk, including the language of the baptism of the Spirit for Christian perfection, is remarkable considering John Wesley had only a few years earlier seemed to question the connection of the baptism with the Spirit with perfection—except that he approved it with the understanding that the Holy Spirit was given in justification but given in greater measure in Christian perfection.

NOTES

1. A lengthy document label "A Letter to Lady Huntingdon." A letter published for the first time in Tyerman, *Wesley's Designated Successor*, (London: Hodder and Stoughton, 1882), 182-183. Though Fletcher was concerned about the antinomian tendencies of the Calvinist Methodists, he did not think that the Countess herself was guilty of the charge of Antinomianism. Cf. letter to Mr. Ireland (March 27, 1774) in *The Letters of the Rev. John Fletcher*, ed. Melville Horne (New York; Lane & Scott, 1849), 260.

2. Cragg, *Appeals*, 11:253, "A Farther Appeal to Men of Reason and Religion, Part II."

3. *The Works of John Wesley*, ed. Thomas Jackson (London: Wesleyan Conference Office, 1872): 9:495, "Extract of a Letter to the Rev. Mr. Law" (January 6, 1756).

4. *'Unexampled Labours'*, 258.

5. Ibid.

6. Ibid.

7. Ibid., 320 (August 14, 1774).

8. *Arminian Magazine*, 3 (London, May1780): 282-83.

9. *'Unexampled Labours*, 320.

10. *The Letters of the Rev. John Wesley, A.M.*, ed. John Telford (London: Epworth Press, 1931), (to John Fletcher, Feb. 26, 1774), 6:75. *The Works of John Wesley, Journal and Diaries*, (1765-75), ed. W. Reginald Ward (Journal) and Richard Heitzenrater (Diaries), (Nashville: Abingdon Press, 1990), 22:400 (March 21, 1774).

11. Cf. Telford, *Letters*, 6:175 (a letter to John Fletcher 18, 1775).

12. *Unexampled Labours*, (Letter to Charles Wesley, May 21, 1775), 321.

13. Wesley's special abridged edition of John Fletcher, *The First Part of an Equal Check* (Bristol: W. Pine, 1774), vi.

14. Wesley's special abridged edition of John Fletcher, *An Equal Check*, v.

15. Ibid., 112.

16. *The Works of the Rev. John Fletcher*, ed. Joseph Benson, 6:182.

17. Fletcher, *An Equal Check* (Wesley's special edition), 115

18. Ibid., 122

19. Ibid., 115

20. Ibid., 179.

21. Ibid., 177n.

22. Ibid., 180

23. Ibid., 180.

24. Ibid., 180.

25. Ibid., 181

26. Ibid., 174.

27. Ibid., 175.

28. Ibid., v.

29. Ibid.. 177.

30. Ibid.,155. 156. Cf. 108.

31. *Works of John Wesley* (Jackson edition), 16:310, Letter to Adam Clarke

32. Agnes Bulmer, *Memoir of Mrs. Elizabeth Mortimer* (New York: Mason and Lane, 1836), 47

33. Ibid., 125

34. See Page A. Thomas, "John Wesley: Spiritual Advisor To Young Women As He Speaks Through His Letters," on NNU Online Wesley page.

35. *Memoir of Mrs. Elizabeth Mortimer*, 181.

36. Telford, *Letters* 6:136-137. Letter to Elizabeth Ritchie (January 17, 1775).

37. *Last Check to Antinomianism, Works of John Fletcher*, 6:399.

38. Elizabeth Ritchie Correspondence in the Frank Baker Collection, David M. Rubenstein Book and Manuscript Library.

39. John Wesley's letter to Elizabeth Bennis, May 2, 1774. *Christian Correspondence Being a Collection of Bennis Letters, written by the late Rev. John Wesley, and several Methodist Preachers, in connection with him to the Late Mrs. Eliza Bennis with her Answers, Chiefly explaining and enforcing the doctrine of sanctification, now First published from the Originals* (Philadelphia: B. Graves: 1809). Cited hereafter as *A Collection of Bennis Letters*. Cf. Telford, *Letters*, 6:79-80. Letter to Mrs. Bennis (May 2, 1774), 106

40. Letter to Elizabeth Bennis, March 1, 1774. *A Collection of Bennis Letters*, 101-102.

41. Letter to Elizabeth Bennis, March 1, 1774. *A Collection of Bennis Letters*, 101-102.

42. Letter to John Wesley, April 12, 1774. *A Collection of Bennis Letters*, 104.

43. Letter from Elizabeth Bennis to John Fletcher, April 19, 1783. *A Collection of Bennis Letters*, 262-263.

44. Letter from John Fletcher to Elizabeth Bennis, May 12, 1783. *A Collection of Bennis Letters*, 263.

45. Letter from Elizabeth Bennis to John Fletcher, May 26, 1783 *A Collection of Bennis Letters*, 266

46. Letter from Elizabeth Bennis to John Fletcher, May 26, 1783. *A Collection of Bennis Letters*, 266-268

47. Letter from Elizabeth Bennis to John Fletcher, May 26, 1783. *A Collection of Bennis letters*, 268.

48. John Holland, *Memoirs of the Life and Ministry of the Rev. John Summerfield* (New York: McElrath & Bangs, 1830), 168. Cited hereafter as *Life of Summerfield*. I found a copy of this biography with the name "Clara Bennis" engraved on the front cover, indicating that she not only owned it but treasured it. I did not know what, if any, relation Clara Bennis had to Elizabeth Bennis. But possibly it shows the esteem he had with the Bennis family in Limerick before he came to America.

49. *Life of Summerfield*, 168.

50. Ibid., 82-83.

51. Ibid., 163.

52. Ibid, 85, 248.

53. Ibid.,16.

54. Ibid., 82.

55. C. H. Crookshank, *History of Methodism in Ireland* (Belfast: R. S. Allen, Son & Allen-University House, 1885), 1:163.

56. Ibid. 2:446

CHAPTER 13

"I DO NOT PERCEIVE . . . THAT THERE IS ANY DIFFERENCE BETWEEN US"

"It seems our views of Christian Perfection are a little different, though not opposite. It is certain every babe in Christ has received the Holy Spirit, and the Spirit witnesses with his spirit that he is a child of God. But he has not obtained Christian perfection."
—John Wesley to John Fletcher, March 22, 1775

"I have now received all your [revised] papers, and here and there made some small corrections. I do not perceive that you have granted too much [to babes in Christ by allowing that they too have received the Spirit], or that there is any difference between us."
—John Wesley to John Fletcher, August 18, 1775

Fletcher was assigning his Trevecca students to write an essay on the baptism with the Holy Spirit in November 1770 at the same time he was in conversation with Charles Wesley about his developing understanding of this topic.[1]

Written Correspondence of Charles Wesley and John Fletcher

Fletcher was more personally intimate with Charles than John. This difference in their relationship is seen in Fletcher's letters. He greeted John as "Reverend and dear Sir," but with Charles his letters began with, "My very dear friend." Charles also spoke affectionately of Fletcher as "my friend" and in a letter to John and Mary Fletcher, he signed his letter as "My beloved friends, your faithful brother Charles Wesley."[2] Their intimate friendship explains why Fletcher served as the godfather of Charles' daughter (as already noted).[3]

Fletcher once said to Charles: "I correspond with no one regularly but you—Your brother . . . and my mother have one letter from me in six months."[4] Those letters to Charles revealed Fletcher's inner thoughts about everything, from the state of his spiritual life, to reports of ill will and problems within his parish, and to what we call chit-chat.[5]

These letters also revealed Fletcher's reliance on Charles' theological advice. They also show that Charles supervised the printing of Fletcher's manuscripts, including proof reading the press copy.[6]

These letters also reveal that Fletcher relied on John Wesley for editing and correcting his manuscripts, as well as Fletcher expecting to receive his "imprimatur."[7] Realizing his tendency to be too lengthy, John Wesley reassured Fletcher "not to cramp myself, as he would abridge if necessary."[8] In a letter addressed to John and Charles, Dec. 26, 1771, Fletcher wrote: "I am quite satisfied with your alterations. I make no doubt but you correct and alter for God."[9]

Unfortunately Fletcher destroyed all of his personal correspondence in 1777 when he thought he might be dying, His reason for doing so was to protect his correspondents, and he did not want his "loose papers" and letters from his friends to be taken by strangers.[10] Consequently, Charles' letters to Fletcher and other correspondents mostly do not exist. Nonetheless, it is easy to discern that Charles Wesley and Fletcher were in agreement.

Fletcher's letters to Charles show his theology of Pentecost and sanctification was an extension and expansion of what John Wesley had learned from Christian David and what John Wesley had incorporated into his early sermons and what Charles Wesley had incorporated into his hymns.

He said to Charles, what he had already told the Countess of Huntingdon, that he believed "the dispensation of the Holy Spirit . . . to be the grand characteristic of Christian perfection" and "that by maintaining . . . the doctrine of Christian perfection, and connected with the . . . accomplishment of the promise of the Father, we can make the doctrine more intelligible to and defensible against all opposing friends."[11]

On November 24, 1771 Fletcher said to Charles that he was writing his *Third Check to Antinomianism* and his *Last Check to Antinomianism.* The *Last Check* explained in detail Fletcher's theology of Pentecost and perfection.

Fletcher said to Charles Wesley his manuscript would show that they "perfectly agree" on the Pentecost basis of Christian perfection and he wanted Charles to give him a critical response:

> I am busy about my *Third* and *Last Check* which I trust will be the most useful. I want sadly both your prayers and advice. I shall introduce *my,* why not *your* doctrine of the Holy Spirit, and make it one with your brothers perfection. He holds the truth, but this will be an improvement upon it, if I am not mistaken. In some of your *pentecost hymns* you paint my light wonderfully. If *you do not recant* then we shall perfectly agree [a humorous reference to a Calvinist who recanted his writings when Fletcher drew from them to disprove absolute predestination].[12]

As mentioned in the previous chapter, Fletcher said to Charles that he was not sure whether or not John Wesley would altogether agree with him "that those who . . . [were] baptized and sealed with the Holy Spirit on the day of Pentecost . . . were in the state of Christian perfection. . . . as contradistinguished from the faith of . . . babes, or carnal believers . . . which the apostles had before the day of pentecost."[13] Fletcher would soon get a response from John Wesley about this.

Fletcher assumed that one did not experientially appropriate the Pentecost dispensation if one was not perfected in love. He often confessed to Charles that Pentecost was an event that was yet to occur for him in the future. Fletcher's typical self-assessment was: "I am quite clear that I shall die only a disciple of John unless I receive the baptism [of the Spirit] you have so well described—What you saw in Hannah Richardson."[14] She was someone whom Charles led to experience entire sanctification in 1765 and who testified: "*I am sanctified wholly, Spirit, soul, and body.*"[15]

It is apparent that Charles was sympathetic to Fletcher's idea of a future Pentecost because he spoke of it as though they were together engaged in an ongoing conversation about it: "We await a day of Pentecost, but we do not pray enough to obtain it."[16]

Charles' hymns emphasized that believers "should look for and expect new Pentecosts," as J. Ernest Rattenbury has shown.[17] For example, Rattenbury cited Charles Wesley's passionate prayer to the Holy Spirit:

> Refining fire, go through my heart,
>   Illuminate my soul,
> Scatter Thy life through every part,
>   And sanctify the whole. [18]

As we shall see below, John Fletcher reported that his Anglican congregation frequently sang this song in their quest for full sanctification. It can be equally certain that it was sung throughout Methodist congregations, as it still is today.

Rattenbury cited other hymns that spoke of "the Holy Spirit to man is given" to "wholly sanctify."[19]

Another topic that often appeared in Fletcher's correspondence with Charles is whether Christian perfection is instantaneous or gradual. Fletcher preferred a synthesis of John's and Charles' differing interpretation of whether entire sanctification is gradual or instantaneous. He suggested to Charles that "in general when my views of things seems clearer I think that those in a gradual rising to the top of John [the Baptist's] ... dispensation, and that when we . . . are gradually risen to that top, and are fit for the baptism of Christ, it is an instant conferred."

He then encouraged Charles Wesley to join him "after the example of the Apostles" who "retired from the world, to wrestle . . . 10 or 30 days in an upper room . . . with *much* fasting and *hard* prayer." Here then is how the process and instantaneous moment of entire sanctification come together—praying and waiting until the Holy Spirit descends in sanctification in an instant.

He confessed to Charles that "we must . . . be reawakened, and a death must pass upon us which you have admirably described in your hymns. But now you must stand to *them*, and I to the *checks practically.*"[20]

Fletcher then pressed Charles to recognize the need to experience personally their own theology of perfection: "I think at this time we are perhaps less called to recommend perfection to others in *words*, than heartily pursue it in *deeds* ourselves. The world will generally cry out to use *Physician heal thyself*, and laugh at us for our pains, unless we are . . . benefited by our doctrine. . . . Shall we only talk about it, or write hymns and checks?"

Fletcher proposed to Charles that he should convene "*a conference of prayer* and mutual exhortation" for this purpose of encouraging the experience of perfection. "I, and thousand more, look at you and your brother, just as some of my flock look at me. If it is not for him, say they, it is not for me. Thus they give it up."[21]

Fletcher realized his own responsibility in this matter as one of the promoters of the Methodist doctrine of perfection. "What can I say? I . . . remain confounded, and . . . conscious I am guilty of the pharisaic absurdity of saying and not doing, of tying perceptive . . . burdens upon the shoulders of others which I touch more with my pen or tongue than with my hand and shoulders. I hope God has not yet sworn . . . that I shall die in the wilderness for my past cowardice, disobedience, hypocrisy."

He then urged Charles Wesley: "Come, let me have the benefit of your example. . . . Undoubtedly the apostles went into the kingdom before the 3000 on the day of Pentecost. If we . . . get in, who knows but perhaps 3 scores . . . may follow us. This is the only way to retrieve the aspersed doctrine of perfection. Our works will preach, and back our words with . . . influence."[22]

Two years later on January 16, 1773 when Fletcher was completing the writing of *The Last Check*, he brought up again this subject with Charles as he continued to resolve this question of whether or not Christian perfection is gradual or instantaneous.

> I have but one doubt. Perfection is nothing but the unshaken kingdom of God peace righteousness and joy in the Holy Spirit or by the baptism of the Holy Spirit. Now Quere. Is this baptism instantaneous as it was on the day of Pentecost, or will it come as a dew gradually. Nothing can set me clear herein but my own experience. And suppose I was clear by my own experience, would this be a sufficient reason to fix it as a rule for all believers?
>
> If I consult reason, it seems to me . . . that perfection is nothing but the acts of holiness faith, love, prayer, praise, and joy so frequently repeated as to be turned into easy . . . delightful habits. If I consult scripture I rather think it is nothing but the Spirit dwelling in a believer in consequence of an instantaneous baptism. I should be glad to be fully . . . taught of God in this point, not only not to set any one upon a false scent, but to seek the blessing properly myself; because if the instantaneous baptism is absolutely necessary, it is absurd to repeat fruitless acts in order to form a habit which the Holy Spirit . . . alone can instantaneously infuse: and on the other hand if I may so gradually improve my talent as to attain the perfect habit of holiness it is enthusiasm to look for its being immediately infused.[23]

Fletcher's concept of perfection was most fully developed and explained in *The Last Check*. It was finished in March 1775, but it was begun at least by November 24, 1771, having been interrupted by other pressing matters,[24] although Charles had encouraged Fletcher to give priority to its completion.[25]

John Wesley's Critical Suggestion

At some point in early 1775, Fletcher gave John Wesley a copy of the manuscript for his editorial review. John returned it to Fletcher on March 22, 1775, noting their views were "a little different, though not opposite" on the meaning of "receiving the Holy Spirit."[26]

> It seems our views of Christian Perfection are a little different, though not opposite. It is certain every babe in Christ has received the Holy Spirit, and the Spirit witnesses with his spirit that he is a child of God. [Notice here that John Wesley linked "received the Holy Spirit" and "the Spirit witnesses with his spirit," which confirms the issue of assurance

was the way Benson and Fletcher understood the caution about using the expression, "receiving the Spirit"]. But he has not obtained Christian perfection. Perhaps you have not considered St. John's threefold distinction of Christian believers: little children, young men, and fathers. All of these had received the Holy Spirit [that is, they had received the witness of the Spirit]; but only the fathers were perfected in love.[27]

John Wesley had told Benson in 1771 that the connection between "receiving the Spirit" and Christian perfection was "Mr. Fletcher's late discovery," and that it was divisive and would be rejected among the Methodists. But now in 1775, having read Fletcher's manuscripts and having understand more fully his ideas, John softened his criticism to say their views were "a little different." Yet John wanted Fletcher now to affirm that "babes in Christ" (i.e., "little children") have the Spirit in some measure. As Patrick Streiff put it, John Wesley wanted Fletcher to allow that "'babes in Christ' had received the Holy Spirit, though not yet in such full measure as 'fathers in Christ'."[28]

This shows that John Wesley's real concern was that justified persons should be thought of as having some measure of the Spirit and that he was not rejecting the idea of the fullness of Pentecost as equivalent in meaning to Christian perfection.

John expected Fletcher to make an adjustment in his thinking, and Fletcher complied by making the requested revisions in his manuscript. However, Fletcher had learned to speak of Christian perfection using the language of receiving the Spirit from John Wesley, and particularly from Charles Wesley's hymns, ever since John Wesley's conversations with Christian David. In reality, it was John Wesley who had modified and clarified his views and he was now asking his most significant leader to make the same adjustment, and he complied.

In this manuscript, *The Last Check*, in 1775 Fletcher had prominently featured "the baptism with the Holy Spirit" as the means for being made perfect in love. For example, Fletcher wrote: "O, baptize my soul, and make as full an end of the original sin which I have from Adam.... Give me thine abiding Spirit, that he may *continually* [italics mine] shed abroad thy love in my soul.... Send thy Holy Spirit of promise to fill me therewith, to sanctify me throughout."

Notice that Fletcher qualified his sentence about the love of God being shed abroad in one's heart with the word "continually" as a reference to Christian perfection, allowing that some measure of the love of God is shed abroad in the heart of all justified persons. As we shall see, this qualification satisfied John Wesley.

Fletcher Re-sends His Manuscript to Charles

After receiving John Wesley's recommended correction, Fletcher revised the manuscript and then sent it to Charles on May 21, 1775 for his evaluation. In a passionate plea, he asked Charles to ensure that his *Last Check* is theologically sound:

> I throw myself at your feet to put my manuscript upon Perfection [Last Check to Antinomianism] into your hands, and I implore your convictions for Christ's sake, and for the sake of truth and souls. I give you *carte blanche to add, or lop off, but to none but you.* Your brother saw it as he went to Ireland, and I believe approved of it in general: I hope you see it improved, as I have made many alterations, I trust, for the better. I have not skill to make

my book *shorter* and *full* [another of John Wesley's recommendations]. God has given you the gift to be sententious: my . . . way is the reverse of yours, correct it.

I shall set about the Application, as soon as possible. Give me your directions, corrections, reproofs.[29]

In another letter from Fletcher to Charles (August 8, 1775), we know that Fletcher gave his final revisions to his brother John: "I have *sent to* . . . him [John Wesley] *the four addresses* which conclude my Essay on perfection. So he has seen the whole."[30]

John Wesley Approves—No "difference between us"

John Wesley responded to Fletcher on August 18, 1775, giving his approval to Fletcher's revised manuscript, *The Last Check*: "I have now received all your papers, and here and there made some small corrections." John goes on to say, "I do not perceive that you have granted too much [to babes in Christ by allowing that they too have received the Spirit], or that there is any difference between us."[31]

John Wesley expressed no disagreement to Fletcher's multiple references to the baptism with the Holy Spirit and holiness in this manuscript. Not only was John Wesley pleased with Fletcher's acceptance of his suggested correction, but in this same letter he encouraged Fletcher to travel with him whenever he was not writing in preparation for the time when Fletcher could become his successor.

Two years later in 1777, John Fletcher showed how he and John Wesley agreed on the meaning of the receiving the Spirit.

> The apostle says to the Ephesians, *After that ye believed in him* [Christ] *ye were sealed with that Holy Spirit of promise* Eph. 1.13. Mr. Wesley in his note on that verse, observes (1) That the Ephesians were there sealed "*probably some time after their first* believing;" (2) That this sealing Spirit is "promised to all the children of God;" whence it follows, that people may be believers and children of God in the inferior sense of these words, *before* they are sealed with the Holy Spirit, and have received the Promise of the Father: And (3) That "this sealing seems to imply a *full impression* of the image of God on their souls; and a full assurance of receiving all the promises, whether relating to time or eternity." Accordingly Mr. Wesley does not scruple to intimate in his Note on Act viii.15, that the *believers* of Samaria, who *had been baptized in the name of the Lord Jesus* had not yet *received the Holy Spirit* either "*in his miraculous gifts or his [full]* sanctifying graces:"—those full and ripe ~~perfect~~ graces, which distinguish the ~~perfect believer~~ the believers, who have been baptized with the Holy Spirit from those who have not. For in the language of the Scriptures the *giving*—the *pouring out*—the *shedding forth*—and the *baptism of the Holy Spirit*, are phrases of the same import. And *to receive the Holy Spirit* —to *be sealed with the Spirit of promise*—to *be baptized with the Holy Spirit* —and to have the *Holy Spirit falling upon one*—and to *be endued with [Pentecostal] power from on high*, are expressions, which convey the same meaning.[32]

Fletcher distinguished between those "who have the Holy Spirit according to the ante-Pentecostal measure of it, and those who *are* endued with it according to its Pentecostal measure." This does not mean "all baptized [justified] persons have this abundant measure of the Spirit but only those who come up to the standard of spiritual Christianity."[33]

This difference between some measure of the Spirit being granted in justification and the full measure of the Spirit, or the full baptism with the Spirit, in sanctification is apparently what satisfied John Wesley's concern.

It was mentioned in Chapter 5 that Henry Moore qualified the words of Christian David to John Wesley in 1738 about the disciples having justifying faith prior to Pentecost though they had not "[fully] received 'the gift of the Holy Spirit.'"[34] As we then noted, Christian David's explanation about the difference between the justifying faith of the disciples before Pentecost and their sanctifying experience on the day of Pentecost was a decisive moment in the Wesley brothers' clarity of understanding about the order of salvation. In the 1760s when the holiness revival occurred and in conversation with Benson and Fletcher in the 1770's, Wesley clarified the difference of degrees of receiving the Spirit in justifying and sanctifying faith. This clarification was the occasion for Moore to qualify the original words of Christian David with "[fully]."

The Last Check contains more references to John Wesley's writings and to Charles' hymns than any of his previous writings[35] to show that he was in agreement with them. This was important because Christian perfection was the central tenet of Methodism. If John Wesley was particularly concerned to edit Fletcher's writings to insure that his ideas reinforced his own views, it was equally important that Fletcher receive both John and Charles' imprimatur.

Among John's many words of commendation about Fletcher's writings on holiness, he said that Fletcher had written with more clear understanding on the theme of "pardon and holiness" than "scarcely any one has done before since the Apostles."[36] Charles said to Fletcher on October 11, 1783: "You had from the beginning my Imprimatur."[37] Charles had specifically given his approval to Fletcher's *Essay on Truth*, but his only concern was that Fletcher's idea of dispensations of salvation might encourage some to remain in a lower stage of faith. Fletcher reassured Charles that he would obviate that possible misunderstanding.[38]

When John Wesley expressed disagreement with Fletcher's ideas about perfection, it was always when Fletcher's writings were still in manuscript form. John never criticized any of Fletcher's published writings, which John Wesley and Charles published after their editorial corrections had been made.

Charles Wesley had great affection for Fletcher and his affirmation of "gospel truths." Once when Fletcher was very ill, Charles wrote a hymn on June 30, 1776 in his honor which was sung by the London and Bristol Methodist congregations.[41] Fletcher survived that particular illness, and later Charles sent the hymn to his wife during another illness shortly before Fletcher's death in 1785.[42]

> Jesus, Thy feeble servant see,
> Sick is the man beloved by Thee:
>   Thy name to magnify.
> To spread Thy gospel truths again.
> His precious soul in life detain,
>   Nor suffer him to die.

> The fervent prayer Thou oft hast heard,
> Thy mighty arm in mercy bared;
>   Thy wonder-working power
> Appear'd in all Thy people's sight,
> And stopped the spirit in its flight,
>   Or bade the grave restore.
>
> In faith we ask a fresh reprieve;
> Frequent in deaths he yet shall live,
>   If Thou pronounce the word;
> Shall spend for Thee his strength renew'd,
> Witness of the all-cleansing blood,
>   Forerunner of his Lord.
>
> The Spirit which rais'd Thee from the dead,
> Be in its quickning virtue shed,
>   His mortal flesh to raise,
> To consecrate Thy human shrine,
> And fill with energy Divine
>   Thy minister of grace.
>
> Body and soul at once revive,
> The prayer of faith in which we strive,
>   So shall we all proclaim,
> According to Thy gracious will,
> Omnipotent the sick to heal,
>   In every age the same.[43]

NOTES

1. "Letter to the Students," November 1770, enclosed with letter to Selina, Countess of Huntingdon," November 1770. *'Unexampled Labours'*, 256.

2. *The Journal of the Rev. Charles Wesley, M.A.* ed. Thomas Jackson (Grand Rapids: Baker, 1980), 2:234; Letter to John and Mary Fletcher, June 21, 1785. Transcribed by Gareth Lloyd. MARC: DDCW 1/75.

3. *'Unexampled, Labours'*, 88, 252.

4. Ibid. 164.

5. Ibid., 136.

6. Ibid., 281.

7. Ibid., 305.

8. Ibid., 286.

9. Ibid., 290.

10. Ibid., 341.

11. *'Unexampled, Labours'*, 319. Letter of (August 14, 1774).

12. *'Unexampled, Labours'*, 287-288. Cf. Patrick Streiff, *Reluctant Saint*, 184. Words that have been stricken out are part of Fletcher's original manuscript.

13. Ibid., 320 (August 14, 1774).

14. Ibid., 288.

15. Ibid., 288. Cf. Charles Wesley, *A Short Account of the Death of Mrs. Hannah Richardson* (Bristol: Pine, 1765), 4, 8-9. Hannah Richardson struggled with "original sin" in her heart after she was justified and she lacked the abiding witness of the Spirit, but a year later she discovered that "perfect love hath cast out fear"

through "full redemption in the blood of Jesus" and testified: "I am sanctified wholly, Sprit, soul, and body." Charles Wesley, *A Short Account of the Death of Mrs. Hannah Richardson* (Bristol: Pine, 1765), 4, 8-9.

16. Ibid., 173.

17. J. Ernest Rattenbury, *The Evangelical Doctrines of Charles Wesley's Hymns* (London: Epworth Press, 1941), 185.

18. HSP 1740, 157; cf. Rattenbury, *The Evangelical Doctrines of Charles Wesley's Hymns,* 187.

19. John and Charles Wesley. *Hymns of Petition and Thanksgiving for the Promise of Father* (Bristol: Farley, 1746), 6; cf. Rattenbury, *The Evangelical Doctrines of Charles Wesley's Hymns,* 176.

20. 'Unexampled, Labours', 290. (January 1772).

21. Ibid., 291

22. Ibid.

23. Ibid., 302-303.

24. Patrick Streiff, *Reluctant Saint? A Theological Biography of Fletcher of Madeley,* trans. G. W. S. Knowles (London: Epworth Press, 2001), 183.

25. Henry Moore, *The Life of the Rev. John Wesley* (London: John Kershaw, 1825), 2:260.

26. Telford, *Letters,* 6:146, (to John Fletcher, March 22, 1775).

27. Telford, *Letters,* 6:146, (to John Fletcher, March 22, 1775).

28. Patrick Streiff, *Reluctant Saint? A Theological Biography of Fletcher of Madeley* (London: Epworth, 2001), 184.

29. 'Unexampled, Labours', 321.

30. Ibid., 330.

31. Telford, *Letters,* 6:174-175, (to John Fletcher, August 18, 1775).

32. Fletcher, *The New Birth,* 45.

33. Fletcher, *The New Birth,* 54.

34. Henry Moore, *The Life of John Wesley,* 1:229

35. Streiff, 184.

36. Telford, *Letters,* 6:79-80. Letter to Mrs. Bennis (May 2, 1774).

37. A letter loosely contained in and bound up in a large volume (or folio) in John Rylands Library, entitled, *Letters Relating to the Wesley Family,* stored in JRULM MAW F1 Box 18. The immediate context of the approval of Fletcher's writings given by Charles Wesley was related to a pamphlet that Fletcher wrote on "Three National Grievances," but Charles expands on the extent of approval to include Fletcher's writings from the beginning.

38. Joseph Benson, *The Life of the Rev. John Fletcher* (1804), in Fletcher, *Works of John Fletcher,* ed. Joseph Benson (London: Richard Edwards, 1806), 1:180-181, (a letter to Charles Wesley, January 1775).

39. 'Unexampled Labours,' 319.

40. Ibid., 320.

41. Thomas Jackson, *Life of Charles Wesley* (London, Mason, 1941), 2:306.

42. Frank Baker, *Charles Wesley As Revealed by His Letters* (London: Epworth Press, 1948), 146.

43. MS Hymns, MARC: MA 1977/556 (Charles Wesley Notebooks Box 2), 187.. Cf. Luke Tyerman, *Wesley's Designated Successor,* 362.

Chapter 14

A Consensus between John Wesley and John Fletcher

"I preached on, 'they were all filled with the Holy Spirit;' and showed in what sense this belongs to us and our children."
—John Wesley

"My friend [John Wesley] . . . chiefly rests the doctrine of Christian perfection on being baptized and filled with the Spirit. . . . This is Mr. Wesley's sentiment."
—John Fletcher

". . . that baptism of the Holy Spirit which the apostles received at the day of Pentecost, and which in a lower degree is given to all believers."
—John Wesley

"The Lord hath promised to circumcise our heart, so that we shall love him with all our heart. . . . God may, and that he often does, instantaneously so baptize a soul with the Holy Spirit, and with fire, as to purify it from all dross, and refine it like gold, so that it is renewed in love, in pure and perfect love."
—Joseph Benson and published by John Wesley in *The Arminian Magazine*

John Wesley not only permitted but approved Fletcher's use of the "baptism with the Spirit," which was only a refinement of John Wesley's own view. There was only praise and recommendation for his published writings. The only possible suggestion that Fletcher did not follow was John Wesley's caution about being too lengthy.[1]

Some have cited John Wesley's letter to Joseph Benson about their views being "a little different" as a final statement, as if this proved that John Wesley rejected the link between Pentecost and sanctification.

These same scholars have failed to mention John Wesley said this disagreement between them was resolved. They also ignore that John Wesley himself embraced Fletcher's treatise on Christian perfection—after he clarified that the Holy Spirit was given to all believers according to their stage of faith development.

We noted that it was typical of him to link being "filled with the Spirit" and Christian perfection. For example in 1745, John Wesley wrote:

> It was hereby shown that you were filled with the Holy Spirit and delivered from all unholy tempers; when ye were all "unblameable and unrebukeable, without spot, or wrinkle, or

any such things, a chosen generation, a royal priesthood, an holy nation, a peculiar people, showing forth" to all . . . by your active, patient, spotless love of God and man."[2]

As we will see in another chapter, John Wesley frequently preached on the subject of being "filled with the Spirit" and on "the baptism with the Spirit."

Fletcher's Preferred Expression

Fletcher's preference for the expression "baptism with the Spirit" can be seen in a letter to Mary Bosanquet in 1778. Fletcher explained that the difference between him and John Wesley was a difference of emphasis, not a difference in theology.

Here is what Fletcher said to Mary Bosanquet in 1778: "If you ask me what I think to be truth with respect to Christian perfection, I reply my sentiments are exposed to the world in my Essay on 'Christian Perfection' [*The Last Check*] and in my Essay on 'Truth' [in the *Equal Check*] where I lay the stress on the doctrine on the great *promise of the Father*, and on the *Christian fullness of the Spirit*."

He then says: "You will find my views of this matter in Mr. Wesley's sermons" on Christian Perfection [1741] and on Scriptural Christianity [1744]. Both of these early sermons by Wesley highlighted Pentecost and sanctification.

Fletcher then mentioned to her: "I would distinguish more exactly between the believers baptized with the Pentecostal power of the Holy Spirit, and the believer who, like the Apostles after our Lord's Ascension, is not yet filled with that power."

He observed that when he preached on this theme at Trevecca, it was called "Mr. Wesley's *whim*," and when "I preached it to our brethren, some have called it Lady Huntingdon's *whim*; and others have looked upon it as a *new thing*." This controversy, Fletcher wrote, "is the strongest proof that this capital Gospel doctrine is as much under a cloud now as the doctrine of justification by faith was at the time of the Reformation."[3]

He then told her that he had recently completed an *Essay on the New Birth*,[4] and told her where she could find the manuscript in London. He had written this essay after the *Last Check* had been published and a just prior to a three-year visit to his home country in Switzerland in 1777.[5]

This essay disclosed that John Wesley agreed with him on the use of the language of the baptism with the Holy Spirit. Fletcher reported "that Mr. Wesley rests the perfection of Christianity on the Pentecostal dispensation of the Spirit, and teaches, that, imperfect believers need only '*wait for the promise of the Father*,' till '*the Holy Spirit* is given unto them' according to the fullness of that grand promise."

He said: "My friend [John Wesley] . . . chiefly rests the doctrine of Christian perfection on being *baptized and filled with the Spirit*," noting that "this is Mr. Wesley's sentiment."[6]

Of course we have John Wesley's own statement that there was no longer any disagreement between them after Fletcher had accepted John Wesley's suggested correction.

Do we have any further evidence that Fletcher was genuinely expressing "Mr. Wesley's sentiment"? The answer is Yes. After his treatise on perfection (*The Last Check*) was published, John Wesley wrote to John Fletcher on June 1, 1776: "The generality of believers in *our* Church (yea, and in the Church of Corinth, Ephesus, and the rest, even in the Apostolic age) are certainly no more than babes in Christ; not young men, and much less fathers. But we have some [fathers], and we should certainly pray and expect that our Pentecost may fully come."[7]

Comparing this letter to John Wesley's earlier letter about a slight difference between them, both letters referred to three categories of believers—"babes in Christ," "young men" and "fathers"—and each category of believers had "received the Spirit," although only "fathers" were perfected in love, John Wesley said.

If John Wesley reported that there was no difference between them on August 18, 1775 because Fletcher incorporated John Wesley's correction, here in this letter ten months later (June 1, 1776) Wesley specifically mentioned again the categories of "babes in Christ," "young men," and "fathers," but this letter showed that John Wesley accepted Fletcher's idea that Pentecost belonged uniquely to the category of "fathers" or those who had been perfected in love.

In one of Fletcher's letters to Charles Wesley in 1776, Fletcher expressed the hope of seeing "an outpouring of the Spirit, inwardly and outwardly" which will establish "a Pentecost Christian Church." He noted that "if it is not to be seen at this time upon earth, I am willing to go and see that glorious wonder in heaven."[8]

This concept of a coming Pentecost church was a frequent theme in Fletcher's writings, and he believed that just as everyone on the day of Pentecost were fully sanctified, so he believed there would be a worldwide Pentecost church.

John Wesley had the idea of the one hundred twenty in the Upper Room on the day of Pentecost as being filled with the Spirit,[9] but it was Fletcher's observation that all three thousand hearers experienced a quick transition to perfect love as explained in his *Essay on Truth*.

This idea of everyone on the day of Pentecost, including the three thousand hearers, were entirely sanctified became a theme of John Wesley's sermons thereafter, such as "The Mystery of Iniquity" and "The General Deliverance of the Gospel." Coinciding with Fletcher's idea, John Wesley argued that just as on the day of Pentecost when all believers were entirely sanctified, then in the millennium there would be a Pentecost-church when "righteousness will cover the earth as waters cover the sea."

John Wesley's critics in his day believed that Fletcher's writings were written with John Wesley's *Imprimatur*. Richard Hill, who was one of Fletcher's primary controversialists, noted that "Mr. Wesley revised, corrected, and gave his own *imprimatur* to all Mr. Fletcher's *checks*, throughout which, Mr. John is the *Alpha* and the *Omega*."[10] Fletcher believed that John Wesley also approved the actual wording of his manuscripts unless he changed it.[11] It is also apparent that Fletcher influenced John Wesley's ideas as well, especially in his attempt to make John Wesley consistent.

In his memorial sermon for John Fletcher, John Wesley said in regard to Fletcher's "excellent *Checks to Antinomianism* . . . one knows not which to admire most, the purity of the language . . . , the strength and clearness of the argument, or the mildness and sweetness of the spirit which breathes through the whole." John Wesley noted that reading Fletcher's writings was enough to be convinced of his ideas and apparently his writings on Pentecost and sanctification was also convincing to Him.[12]

John Wesley also said: "I was intimately acquainted with him for above thirty years. I conversed with him morning, noon, and night, without the least reserve, during a journey of many hundred miles. . . . One equal to him I have not known. . . . Nor do I expect to find another such on this side of eternity."[13] We know that Fletcher and John Wesley spent much time together over the years, preaching together, and consulting together. We also know of only one lengthy trip that they toured together.[14]

It is common to find the phrase, "Mr. Wesley and I," in Fletcher's writings to indicate that he was in agreement with his mentor.[15] Fletcher, as much as John Wesley, wanted everyone to see their close association and sameness of purpose as leaders of the Methodist movement. John Wesley intentionally and self-consciously affirmed this link between himself and Fletcher.

This approval can be seen in a manuscript in Fletcher's handwriting which is located in the John Ryland Library. It shows that it was Fletcher's practice to strike through Wesley's name, as for example "~~Mr. Wesley and~~ I."[16] This kept Fletcher from feeling presumptuous about making this equation, and it allowed Wesley the choice to restore his own name before he gave the manuscript to the printers. So the equation of "Mr. Wesley and I" was as much John Wesley's statement as it was Fletcher

In his biography of Fletcher written soon after his death, John Wesley reported that Fletcher's "favourite subject" in conversations among his friends was being "filled with the Spirit."

> When he was able to converse, his favourite subject was, *the promise of the Father, the gift of the Holy Spirit*, including that rich peculiar blessing of union with the Father and the Son, mentioned in that prayer of our Lord which is recorded in the seventeenth chapter of St. John. Many were the sparks of living fire which occasionally darted forth from him on this beloved theme. "We must not be content," said he, "to be only cleansed from sin; we must be filled with the Spirit." One asking him what was to be experienced in the full accomplishment of the promise? "O," said he, "what shall I say! All the sweetness of the drawings of the Father; all the love of the Son; all the rich effusions of peace and joy in the Holy Spirit; more than ever can be expressed are comprehended here! To attain it the Spirit maketh intercession in the soul, like a God wrestling with a God!"[17]

Fletcher emphasized Pentecost and sanctification everywhere he preached without a word of censure from John Wesley—whether he was preaching at John Wesley's annual conference or travelling with him. As noted above, Wesley mentioned that he had travelled with Fletcher on occasions. On the day before Fletcher left Madeley with John Wesley on a trip to London in 1776 by way of Oxfordshire, Northamptonshire, and Norfolk, Fletcher wrote a letter to some Methodist friends at Hull and York on November 12, 1776, where he had been invited to come to preach. He said:

> If I have any desire to live at any time, God is my witness, that it is principally to be a witness in word and deed, of the dispensation of *power from on high*; and to point out that kingdom which does not consist in word, but in *power*, even in *righteousness, peace, and joy by the Holy Spirit*, the *Spirit of power*. I am writing an Essay upon that important part of the Christian doctrine, and hope that it will be a mite in the treasury of truth, which the Lord has opened for the use of his people.[18]

This letter was quoted in *The Methodist Magazine* in 1801, which illustrates that Fletcher's "favourite subject" continued to receive attention.

John Wesley's Later Sermons on Pentecost and Sanctification

John Wesley later sermons showed that he continued with his earlier understanding of Pentecost and sanctification, except with greater clarity. In his "Preface" to *The Arminian Magazine* for January, 1781, Wesley said he intended "to write, with God's assistance, a few more plain, practical discourses, on those which I judge to be the most necessary of the subjects I have not yet treated of." The decisiveness of Pentecost for sanctification was one of those subjects that he made even clearer in these later sermons.

A sermon "On Zeal" was one of those sermons in the 1781 issue of The Arminian Magazine. It was entitled, "Sermon on Galatians iv.18," affirming Pentecost and sanctification. He wrote: "In a Christian Believer, *Love*, sits upon the throne, which is erected in the inmost soul; namely, love of God and man, which fills the whole heart, and reigns without a rival.... This is that Religion which our Lord has established upon earth, ever since the descent of the Holy Spirit on day of Pentecost.... Love enthroned in the heart."[19] He preached this sermon on May 6, 1781.[20]

Love is "the queen of all graces, the highest perfection in earth or heaven, the very image of the invisible God."[21] Having shown that Pentecost is the foundation for the possibility of sanctifying grace, he concludes this sermon with an invitation to his readers to open their hearts to a greater expansion of love in their hearts.

In this same 1781 volume of The Arminian Magazine, John Wesley published an article by Joseph Benson, "Thoughts on Christian Perfection." If John Wesley earlier said that he did not agree with the language of the baptism of the Spirit being used exclusively for speaking of Christian perfection when Benson was principal at Trevecca College, this essay showed that he now had no reservations about Benson's use of it.

If Fletcher told Benson at Trevecca College that only those who have been baptized with the Spirit have the full sanctifying assurance of faith whether or not John Wesley was willing to "assent to it," this essay shows that John Wesley now assented to it.

We also know from this essay that Benson did not change his mind about the language of the baptism with the Holy Spirit since he left Trevecca, and also because he said he was still committed to it.[22]

This 1781 essay by Benson was approved for publication by John Wesley. It was addressed to those who already profess entire sanctification. Benson expressed concern about "the many instances of misconduct in the professors of Christian Perfection" who "have fallen" because of pride, unwatchfulness, lukewarmness and indolence. Christian perfection is "an extirpation of all sin," but "the whole deliverance from sin, depends on the constant indwelling of the Holy Spirit." The main thing, Benson said, is that while "the Lord hath promised to *circumcise our heart*, so that we shall love him *with all our heart* ... those who love Him *perfectly*, may love him *more perfectly* still. Thus will the flame of holy desire be kept alive in their soul."

Benson then affirmed the importance of being baptized with the Spirit:

Once more [as a reminder to his readers about how they may be kept from backsliding by always pressing forward]: Allowing, what (I think) neither Reason nor Scripture forbids us to allow, that God *may*, and that he often *does*, *instantaneously* so baptize a soul with the Holy Spirit, and with fire, as to purify it from all dross, and refine it like gold, so that it is *renewed in love*, in *pure* and *perfect love*, as it never was before; yet ought not those who have experienced this, to be repeatedly told, 1. That there is a further, and still further renewal to be experienced *day by day*.²³

This advice is reminiscent of what John Fletcher had said six years earlier in his *Last Check*:

Should you ask, how many baptisms, or effusions of the sanctifying Spirit are necessary to cleanse a believer from all sin, and to kindle his soul into perfect love; I reply, that the effect of a sanctifying truth depending upon the ardour of the faith with which that truth is embraced, and upon the power of the Spirit with which it is applied, I should betray a want of modesty if I brought the operations of the Holy Spirit, and the energy of faith, under a rule which is not expressly laid down in the Scriptures. . . . If one powerful baptism of the Spirit "seal you unto the day of redemption, and cleanse you from all [moral] filthiness," so much the better. If two or more be necessary, the Lord can repeat them.²⁴

Fletcher had also said: "Many consider that *perfect love, which casteth out fear,* as instantaneous: all grace is so; but what is given in a moment, is enlarged and established by diligence and fidelity. That which is instantaneous in its descent, is perfective in its increase."²⁵

Benson and Fletcher were acknowledging that entire sanctification may and often does happen *instantaneously*, but the believer must continue to rely upon "*this* power from on high for further growth. No matter how holy a believer is, Benson reminded them there must be continual growth. Benson concluded with an exhortation for "professors of Christian perfection" to be increasingly "full of zeal."²⁶

Benson's reference to "full of zeal" is precisely the topic of Wesley's sermon in this same volume of *The Arminian Magazine* (noted above) in which John Wesley had affirmed that "love enthroned in the heart" which "fills the heart" was made possible by the descent of the Holy Spirit on the day of Pentecost.

Benson's focus on a dynamic understanding of the Spirit-filled life as a lifelong process is why Fletcher had talked about "deeper baptisms," "daily baptisms," "many baptisms," and "fuller baptisms" (phrases also often found in the testimonies recorded in the literature of the early Methodists).

Of course, John Wesley did not believe that God "*often . . . instantaneously*" justified and fully sanctified an unbeliever at the same moment. In *Plain Account of Christian Perfection,* John Wesley wrote: "Neither dare we affirm, as some have done, that *all this salvation* is given *at once*. . . . We do not know a single instance, in any place, of a person's receiving, *in one and the same moment*, remission of sins, the abiding witness of the Spirit, and a new, clean heart."²⁷ So this essay on "Thought of Christian Perfection" was addressed to those who were already justified to encourage them to be diligent in living a life of holiness.

In the same year (June 22, 1781) Benson (and John Wesley) defined the baptism with the Spirit as the means of full sanctification, Fletcher wrote to Thomas Coke's future wife, Miss Loxdale: "The other Comforter in his fullness, or the *Pentecostal gift of the Holy Spirit*" gives "great grace, and *abundant life*; it destroys self, it fills with *power from on high, perfects in one*, it *perfects in love*."²⁸ John Wesley also published this letter in the *Arminian Magazine*.²⁹

Two days after writing this letter to Miss Loxdale, Fletcher sent a letter to John Wesley giving him a report of her spiritual progress. John Wesley published this letter in The Arminian Magazine in 1782: "As to Miss L[oxdale], I believe her to be a simple, holy follower of the Lord. Nothing throws *unscriptural* Mysticism down like holding out the promise of the Father, and the fullness of the Spirit, to be received *now*, by faith in the two Promisers, the *Father* and the *Son*. Ah! what is the *penal* fire of the Mystics, to the *burning love of the Spirit*, revealing the glorious power of the *Father* and the *Son*, according to John xiv.26, and filling us with all the fullness of God?" ³⁰

In the same 1782 issue, John Wesley quoted a testimony from the diary of Mr. G.C. This Methodist disciple of John Wesley prayed for a personal "descent of the Holy Spirit on the Apostles" to "rest upon me" that he might be "purified . . . from inbred sin" and obtain "the fullness of love."³¹ John Wesley remarked: "I do not remember ever to have met with a more remarkable account than is contained" in this testimony.³²

In May-June 1783, John Wesley preached a sermon on "The Mystery of Iniquity." As John Heylyn had done in his sermon, John Wesley noted the "weakness" of the disciples prior to Pentecost:

> How exceeding small was the number of those whose souls were healed by the Son of God himself! "When Peter stood up in the midst of them, the number of names were about a hundred and twenty" (Acts 1:15.) And even these were but imperfectly healed; the chief of them being a little before so weak in faith that, though they did not, like Peter, forswear their Master, yet 'they all forsook him and fled". ³³

John Wesley then explained the reason why the disciples were not perfectly healed by Jesus himself prior to Pentecost was because the Spirit had not yet come to make them holy. Wesley cited this weakness of the disciples prior to Pentecost as "a plain proof that the sanctifying 'Spirit was not' then 'given,' because 'Jesus was not glorified'" ³⁴ and hence the disciples "were but imperfectly healed."

John Wesley's point is easily understood. It was not until the Pentecost outpouring of the Holy Spirit that the disciples of Jesus were fully sanctified.

As a result of being filled with the Holy Spirit, their hearts were perfectly healed with the pure love of God. John Wesley further said:

> It was then [after the coming of "the sanctifying Spirit" who was not previously given because "Jesus was not glorified"], when he had "ascended up on high, and led captivity captive," that "the promise of the Father" was fulfilled, which they had heard from him. It was then he began to work like himself, showing that "all power was given to him in heaven and earth." "When the day of Pentecost was fully come, suddenly there came a sound from heaven, as of a rushing mighty wind, and there appeared tongues as of fire; and they were all filled with the Holy Spirit." In consequence of this, three thousand souls received "medicine to heal their sickness," were restored to the favour and the image of God, under one sermon of St. Peter's.³⁵

John Wesley showed that the members of this Pentecost Church "were of one heart, and of one soul . . . while their hearts so overflowed with love."[36] They were filled with "*righteousness . . . peace . . .* and *joy* unspeakable and full of glory."[37] The prophecy of Moses was that the new kingdom would be "a chosen generation, a royal priesthood, a holy nation, a peculiar people."

These descriptions were typically linked with Christian perfection.[38] John Wesley noted that Peter cited these description as a reference to "the first Christian Church, which commenced at the day of Pentecost."[39] What made the difference between the disciples before and after Pentecost? John Wesley said it was the "Promise of the Father" to bestow the "sanctifying Spirit" upon his disciples.[40]

John Wesley noted that "here was the dawn of the proper gospel day. Here was a proper Christian church."[41] Here was the planting of a Church in the earth where every believer was filled with "*righteousness*, gratitude to God and good-will to man, attended with a *peace*, that surpassed all understanding, and with *joy* unspeakable and full of glory."

But John Wesley noted "how soon did *the mystery of iniquity* work again" and the early Christians as seen in Ananias and Sapphira began to lose their perfect spiritual health and pollute the purity of the gospel.[42] Wesley explicitly connects "perfection" and 'Pentecost." He said:

> We have been apt to imagine that the primitive Church was all excellence and perfection! Answerable to that strong description which St. *Peter* cites from *Moses*: "Ye are a chosen generation, a royal priesthood, a holy nation, a peculiar people." And such, without all doubt, the first Christian church which commenced at the day of Pentecost, was. But how soon did the fine gold become dim? How soon was the wine mixed with water![43]

Here John Wesley defined Pentecost as the basis of Christian "excellence." He concluded his sermon on "The Mystery of Iniquity" this way:

> And we have not farther ground for thankfulness, yea, and strong consolation, in the blessed hope which God hath given us that the time is at hand when righteousness shall be as universal, as unrighteousness is now? Allowing that "the whole creation now groaneth together", under the sin of man; our comfort is, it will not always groan: God will arise and maintain his own cause. And the whole creation shall then be delivered both from moral and natural corruption. Sin, and its consequence pain, shall be no more; holiness and happiness will cover the earth. Then shall the ends of the world see the salvation of our God. And the whole race of mankind shall know and love and serve God, and reign with him for ever and ever![44]

This coming Pentecost will be a globalization of holiness unlike the first Pentecost which has been replicated only in the lives of a few people. For John Wesley, Pentecost means the full restoration of fallen humanity to the full image of God in Jesus Christ through the power of the Holy Spirit. Pentecost means the ancient Israelite promise of living in the kingdom of Israel with a circumcised heart of perfect love becoming a reality as the kingdom is internalized within the believer through the indwelling sanctifying Spirit.

These sanctified believers are the members of the true Pentecost Church which began on that day when the Holy Spirit descended upon the congregation of believers. This

Pentecost "kingdom within" will expand globally so that all the world will know the God of Abraham, Moses, and Jesus. Then will be fulfilled God's promise to Abraham that all the world would be blessed through his seed.

Here in this sermon John Wesley self-consciously embraced the idea that a personalized Pentecost is the basis of Christian perfection. What is also noticeable is that Fletcher's emphasis on the coming worldwide Pentecostal display of the Spirit in the millennium became a theme in John Wesley's later sermons,[45] although Fletcher and John Wesley did not speculate about any details or dates surrounding the expectation of a millennium.

In the sermon on "The Mystery of Iniquity," John Wesley said there has never been a true Christian Church, except for a very brief time following the day of Pentecost. He believed not even the Protestant Reformation was a revival of true religion because it involved almost exclusively a reformation of rites and doctrines.[46]

He noted that there have been a few individuals who were "real Christians" throughout the history of Christianity possessing inward and outward holiness, but Wesley prophesied that a new Pentecost Church would be re-established in the earth and the whole world would be a global reflection of the original Pentecost. He writes: "The time is at hand when righteousness shall be as universal as unrighteousness is now."[47] John Wesley thus believed the Methodist revival in his day was the first sign of a new Pentecost when true holiness would be restored in the earth.

Three months later, on June 3, 1781 (Pentecost Sunday), John Wesley wrote in his journal: "I preached on, 'they were all filled with the Holy Spirit;' and showed in what sense this belongs to us and our children."[48] The expression, "to us and our children," is a paraphrase of Acts 2:39 where Peter says the Pentecost gift of the Spirit is "to you and your children," and is a similar comment he wrote in his journal after he heard John Heylyn's Pentecost sermon.

Two months after John Wesley had preached this Pentecost sermon, Fletcher preached on the same Pentecost theme at the Leeds Conference at 5:00 in the morning to two thousand people with John Wesley's full commendation.[49] On Wednesday, August 8, 1781, John Wesley wrote: "I desired Mr. Fletcher to preach. I do not wonder he should be so popular; not only because he preaches with all his might, but because the power of God attends both his preaching and prayer."[50]

A letter written by one of John Wesley's preachers, John Pescod, to his wife while he was still at the conference reported that Fletcher preached on "the promise of the Holy Spirit, whom our Lord told His disciples He would send after His ascension. The dispensation of the Spirit is to renew us after the image of God."[51]

Considering John Wesley's insistence on unity of doctrine among Methodists, Fletcher's sermon would surely have been consistent with his sermon preached two months earlier on being "filled with the Spirit," especially considering the fact that Fletcher was perceived as one of the leaders of the Methodist movement along with John and Charles Wesley and also he was the hoped-for successor to John Wesley.

Wesley published two sermons in 1783 in the Arminian Magazine which highlighted the meaning of Pentecost, entitled "The Mystery of Iniquity" and "The General Spread of the Gospel." In his sermon on "The General Spread of the Gospel," he says that the kingdom of God is now being realized in the world in an unprecedented fashion through the holiness preaching of Methodism. He recited the Old Testament promise concerning the restoration of the kingdom of Israel: "I will put my laws in their minds, and write them in their hearts: And I will be to them a God, and they shall be to me a people." This promise of the restored kingdom of God, Wesley showed here, referred to "the experimental knowledge and love of God, of inward and outward holiness."[52]

The initial fulfilment of this Old Testament promise came on the day of Pentecost when the disciples were "filled with the Holy Spirit." Their lives were characterized by "gladness and singleness of heart," and being "all of one heart and of one soul." Pentecost was the fulfilment of the promise that God would circumcise the hearts of his people.[53] Wesley identified the Methodist revival as "only the beginning of a far greater work; the dawn of 'the latter day glory,'"[54] which will lead to "the grand 'Pentecost'"[55] which will spread to the whole world so that "all the inhabitants of the earth" will "receive those glorious promises made to the Christian Church."[56]

Wesley identified the earliest beginning of this "grand Pentecost" with his group of Oxford Methodists. He predicted ("prophesied") that this reign of Christ in his kingdom on the earth will occur because of "the grand stumbling-block being thus happily removed out of the way, namely, the lives of the Christians." As a result of Christians being filled with the Holy Spirit and reflecting the image of Christ by their love for God and for each other, their witness will catch the attention of everyone because "their words will be clothed with divine energy, attended with the demonstration of the Spirit and of power" and those who "fear God will soon take knowledge of the Spirit whereby the Christians speak."[57]

This "grand 'Pentecost'" means the final fulfilment of the first Pentecost. It means the kingdom of God, first contained in God's promise to Abraham that his children will form an everlasting kingdom, is becoming an actuality. It is a kingdom of the heart, of "righteousness, peace, and joy in the Holy Spirit."[58] What Wesley describes here is not a reference to heaven,[59] but to a time on this earth when the Pentecostal outpouring of the Holy Spirit will perfect all believers in God's love.

The connection between Pentecost and Christian perfection is made throughout this sermon. John Wesley did not use the term, "Christian perfection," in this sermon, but he actually used that terminology rarely. He also rarely used the term, "entire sanctification." These were technical terms to describe his theology more formally. More often John Wesley used the metaphors and common expressions of Scripture in speaking of full sanctification. He listed several common phrases for Christian perfection in this sermon such as being "holy as He that hath called them is holy," being "filled with righteousness, and peace, and joy in the Holy Spirit," "that mind in them which was also in Christ Jesus" and "walk as Christ also walked." He further describes it as "the loving knowledge of God, producing uniform, uninterrupted holiness and happiness." Wesley wrote:

> Let us observe what God has done already. Between fifty and sixty years ago God raised up a few young men in the University of Oxford, to testify those grand truths which were then little attended to: — That without holiness no man shall see the Lord; That this holiness is the work of God, who worketh in us both to will and to do; That he doeth it of

his own good pleasure, merely for the merits of Christ; That this holiness is the mind that was in Christ; enabling us to walk as he also walked; That no man can be thus sanctified till he is justified; and, That we are justified by faith alone. These great truths they declared on all occasions in private and in public; having no design but to promote the glory of God, and no desire but to save souls from death. . . . From Oxford, where it first appeared, the little leaven spread wider and wider. More and more saw the truth as it is in Jesus, and received it in the love thereof. More and more found "redemption through the blood of Jesus, even the forgiveness of sins." They were born again of his Spirit, and filled with righteousness, and peace, and joy in the Holy Spirit. It afterwards spread to every part of the land, and a little one became a thousand. It then spread into north Britain and Ireland, and, a few years after, into New York, Pennsylvania, and many other provinces in America, even as high as Newfoundland and Nova Scotia. So that although at first this "grain of mustard seed" was "the least of all the seeds;" yet, in a few years, it grew into a "large tree, and put forth great branches."[60]

John Wesley linked Pentecost and "uninterrupted Holiness," "Inward and Outward holiness," and "holiness and happiness." These themes are as self-consciously developed in Wesley as in Fletcher. He particularly equated Christian perfection with "universal holiness" which he linked to the Spirit given at Pentecost.

John Wesley defined "universal holiness" with perfection throughout his writings. For example, in his sermon "On Perfection," he says: "Perfection is another name for universal holiness: Inward and outward righteousness: Holiness of life, arising from holiness of heart."[61]

In "The General Spread of the Gospel," Wesley plainly said the giving of the Holy Spirit on the day of Pentecost is the basis for "universal holiness."

John Wesley concluded his sermon on "The General Spread of the Gospel" with this prophesy:

> All unprejudiced persons may see with their eyes that he is already renewing the face of the earth. And we have strong reason to hope that the work he hath begun, he will carry on unto the day of the Lord Jesus, that he will never intermit this blessed work of his Spirit until he has fulfilled all his promises: until he hath put a period to sin and misery, and infirmity, and death; and re-established universal holiness and happiness, caused all the inhabitants of the earth to sing together, "Hallelujah! The Lord God omnipotent reigneth!" "Blessing, and glory, and wisdom, and honour, and power, and might be unto our God for ever and ever!"[62]

John Wesley was in Ireland from April 11 until May 8, 1783, and this sermon on "The General Spread of the Gospel" was written in Dublin, April 22, 1783,[63] just a few days before the annual conference in Ireland, which began on April 29, 1783. Undoubtedly, this was one of his conference sermons. We know that a similar theme was the basis of one of his conference sermons at Bristol just four months later when he preached on "the baptism with the Holy Spirit."

The Dublin conference convened just a few months before John and Mary Fletcher came to Dublin in August, where they stayed until October, 1783. They had come at the written invitation of the Irish Methodists which was hand-delivered to them at Madeley by Thomas Coke.[64]

A dramatic revival occurred in Dublin as a result of the preaching of John Fletcher and the "exhortations" of his new wife, Mary Fletcher. Henry Moore was appointed to the Dublin Circuit three years after the Fletchers' visit, and he reported that this revival more than doubled the size of the Methodists in Ireland.[65]

The "indwelling power and fullness of the Holy Spirit" was Fletcher's preaching theme during this revival, as reported by one of John Wesley's young preachers who attended these meetings.[66] Moore reported that a typical sermon during this revival was on the text in Acts 26:28, "Almost thou persuadest me to be a Christian." In this sermon Fletcher described the various stages of grace from repentance to becoming a full Christian through "the inspiration of the Holy Spirit" to love God perfectly.

His preaching, Henry Moore said, was with such "earnestness and power that astonished the congregation, some of whom seemed to doubt if he were not more than human."[67] Even Charles Wesley wrote Fletcher from London, asking him for the details of the Dublin revival.[68]

This revival inspired by the Fletchers would have appeared to the Irish Methodists as a preliminary confirmation of John Wesley's prophecy in *The General Spread of the Gospel* that "a grand Pentecost" patterned after the first Pentecost in Jerusalem would occur in the world and that righteousness would cover the earth as waters cover the sea. This new Pentecost would mean that "all will be filled with the Holy Spirit" in order that the whole of humanity would be restored to the image of God in Christ.[69]

This expectation of the millennium fit well with Fletcher's thinking as well. The coming millennium would be a restoration of the original Pentecost, a time when the whole world would be integrated into the kingdom of God. Fletcher wrote: "And St. John describes this glorious sanctuary, where he said, 'I saw no temple in the new Jerusalem, for the Lord God Almighty and the Lamb,' or Jehovah and the Divine Mediator, in whom he manifests himself, are 'the temple of it,' Rev. xxi, 22."

This final event of salvation would be a fulfilment of the prophecy of John the Baptist: "I indeed baptize you with water, but he shall baptize you with the Holy Spirit."[70] Hence John Wesley's conference sermon certainly helped to prepare the Irish Methodists for the "Pentecost" preaching of the Fletchers.

This idea of a coming grand Pentecost in the millennium was also used by Mary Fletcher in her exhortations. She noted that it was common in Methodism to preach on this theme, but she also emphasized that a Pentecost-like event, "baptism of the Spirit," must first be appropriated by believers today.[71]

A year after the Leeds Conference in 1784 when John Wesley had given his blessing to the forming of a Methodist denomination in America, he wrote a sermon, entitled "Of the Church," based on Ephesians 4:1-6, "One Lord, One Faith, One Baptism." [Sept. 28, 1785]. It was published in The Arminian Magazine *in 1786.*[72] *This sermon reflected his agreement with Fletcher's concept of "the baptism with the Holy Spirit," that while the Holy Spirit is given in a lower degree to all justified believers, the full baptism with the Holy Spirit is given to believers perfected in love.*

This is why Wesley said: "Some indeed have been inclined to interpret this [water baptism] in a figurative sense, as if it referred to that baptism of the Holy Spirit which the apostles received at the day of Pentecost, and which in a lower degree *[italics mine] is given to all believers."*[73]

John Wesley's comments agreed with Fletcher's statement that the disciples only "received the Holy Spirit" in part "until they were endued with power from on high." Before Pentecost, the disciples "were not *fully baptized* [italics mine]. The comforter, that visited them, did not properly dwell in them."[74] This phrase, "a lower degree," is common in John Wesley's writings to define justified believers not yet perfected in love.[75]

It had been ten years since Fletcher's treatise on Christian perfection (*The Last Check*) had been published and promoted by John Wesley, and the Pentecost paradigm had now become widely accepted.

We also know that John Wesley on occasions quoted from Fletcher's treatise on Christian perfection (*The Last Check*) in his extempore preaching as he travelled about from place to place. One such instance was recorded in a letter from Miss R to Mrs. P, November 5, 1789, which was two years before John Wesley's death: "I often think of an expression of Mr. Wesley's from the pulpit last winter. . . . 'If we had more of what Mr. Fletcher calls *perfect faith,* we should have more lively hopes and more active love'."[76]

Fletcher defined "perfect faith" in *The Last Check* to mean Christian perfection and is attained through being "baptized with the Spirit." The mutual citing of each other's writings so favorably showed that among these early Methodists John Wesley and Fletcher were in agreement, especially on this primary distinctive belief of Methodism.

We shall see in the next chapter that John Wesley also preached on "They were baptized with the Holy Spirit," and it is probable that he would have referred to Fletcher in this sermon because, as John Wesley noted in his biography, being filled with the Spirit was Fletcher's preferred subject. Fletcher was highly popular with Methodists who eagerly wanted him to be Wesley's successor.[77]

If John Fletcher preached with John Wesley as they travelled together, Fletcher's wife Mary also preached[78] with John Wesley at designated locations after her husband's death.[79] She and her dear friend Sarah Crosby (even before her) were the first women Methodist preachers, and Mary Bosanquet mentioned in her diaries about preaching on a "horseblock" in the streets.[80]

In one of her messages perhaps even when she was preaching ("expounding") with Wesley, she alluded to John Wesley's later sermon on "The General Spread of the Gospel" (1783) about a "grand Pentecost" when believers would be enabled to love God perfectly with all their heart through spiritual circumcision (Deuteronomy 30:6).[81] She said: "We often talk of the time when *righteousness is to overspread the earth*, but this millennium must overspread our own hearts, if we would see the face of God with joy." She then exhorted her hearers to have a personal Pentecost and to enter into the "spiritual Canaan [of perfect love], that *baptism of the Spirit*, to which every believer is expressly called."[82]

On April 28, 1784, John Wesley preached a sermon on "The Wisdom of God's Counsels." The Pentecost theme is continued in this sermon. He used Fletcher's dispensational distinctions beginning with "Noah, from Noah to Moses, and from Moses to Christ."[83]

The dispensation of Christ was incomplete until the higher dispensation of the Holy Spirit was begun on the day of Pentecost. This superior dispensation of the Holy Spirit could not occur until Jesus was glorified. God "laid the foundation of his Church" with the dispensation of his Son, but the Church "hardly appeared till the day of Pentecost. And it was then a glorious Church; all the members thereof being 'filled with the Holy

Spirit,' being 'of one heart and of one mind, and continuing steadfastly in the Apostles' doctrine, and in fellowship'."[84]

John Wesley said his purpose in this sermon was not to dwell on the earliest days of the Church, except to point out that so soon after the days of the Apostles the Church fell from its Pentecost purity. He believed that only a few lights, such as Montanus, preserved the message of holiness — until the Methodist movement began to preach that it was possible to "attain the whole image of God."[85] Here again John Wesley connected Pentecost and perfection.

In his sermon, "On God's Vineyard," (Oct. 17, 1787) John Wesley again cited Pentecost as the pattern which the Methodists are following. The Methodists are described as those who know the difference between justification and sanctification and emphasize both equally.

Unlike Martin Luther who understood well the doctrine of justification by faith and yet possessed a flawed concept of sanctification, he said the Methodists have promoted forgiveness of sins and inward holiness received by faith alone. This "new thing" called Methodism is a restoration of the first Pentecost.[86] Wesley writes: "I believe this is a thing wholly without precedent. I find no other instance of it, in any age of the Church, from the day of Pentecost to this day."[87]

In his sermon "On Faith" (April 9, 1788), John Wesley self-consciously used Fletcher's model of the different categories of faith.[88] John Wesley so much liked Fletcher's doctrine of dispensations that he wrote this sermon based in part on Fletcher's interpretation of his own thought.

In the beginning of his sermon, he highlighted Fletcher's fourfold dispensations: (1) *Noah* (pious Gentiles), (2) *Moses* (sincere Jewish believers), (3) *John the Baptist* (who believed Jesus to be the Son of God), and (4) *the Christian dispensation* that began on the day of Pentecost. John Wesley's sermon is based on Hebrews 11, which was one of the texts that Fletcher used, showing how the climax of grace comes with "adult sons" of God who are perfected in love and have received "the Spirit of Adoption."[89] Wesley thus noted that by the full Christian dispensation "Mr. Fletcher means one that has received the Spirit of adoption."[90]

Praising and accepting Fletcher's doctrine of four dispensations, John Wesley's intent was not to redefine or simply restate it, but to develop this concept in a "similar" way, "to point out the several sorts of faith" and "to draw some practical inferences" from it.[91]

Drawing from Fletcher's basic categories, John Wesley developed the following "sorts of faith": (1) the materialist, as "the lowest sort of faith," (2) the deist "who believes there is a God, distinct from matter, but does not believe the Bible," (3) "the faith of *heathens*" and "that of Moslems" who are preferred over the deists because they are denied sufficient "light" to believe properly, (4) Jews, (5) Roman Catholics, and (6) "the faith of the *Protestants* . . . embraces only those truths necessary to salvation which are clearly revealed in the oracles of God." Yet the faith of the Protestants will not "avail any more before God than the faith of a Mahometan or a heathen, yea of a deist or materialist." Even "the devil and his angels . . . are convinced that every title of Holy Scripture is true."

What then "is the faith which is properly saving?" It is to "fear God and work righteousness" (Stage 7). John Wesley has two descriptions of this stage of faith—it is one who is in an "infant stage" and who "is at present only a *servant* of God, not properly a *son*."

One in this stage of faith does not entail "the wrath of God" since one is like an "infant," [i.e., justifying faith?]. This stage of faith may lack the assurance of sins forgiven, but "unless the servants of God halt by the way, they will receive the adoption of sons." Nonetheless, a servant is "accepted by God," denoting justification.

The highest stage of faith (Stage 8) is to "receive the adoption of sons."[92] John Wesley identified this highest stage as "the most excellent way."[93] He further described it as "walking in the glorious liberty [a common term for entire sanctification] of the children of God."[94]

John Wesley concluded his sermon with a reminder that one who has received the highest stage of faith, "the Spirit of adoption," must continually "go on to perfection" and not stop growing in grace which is "impossible" because one will "either rise or fall" in their faith walk.[95]

In regard to those whose faith is like the faith of John the Baptist, "Mr. Fletcher well describes them." John Wesley observed that the dispensation of John the Baptist "was peculiar to himself."[96] This is a reference to Fletcher's comment that "the case of John the Baptist was as singular as that of Moses," because just as Moses pointed beyond himself to the leadership of Joshua, so the dispensation of John the Baptist prepared the way for Jesus.[97]

John Wesley's practical application of this model was to encourage believers to continue to grow in grace until they had attained "the Spirit of Adoption": "Press on till you receive the Spirit of adoption. Rest not till that Spirit clearly witnesses with your spirit that you are a child of God."[98]

In his earlier writings and in the hymns of Charles Wesley, "the Spirit of adoption" referred to Christian perfection, as earlier noted. Fletcher also showed that George Whitefield was using John Wesley idea of "the Spirit of adoption" as a testimony of his own experience of Christian perfection before he converted to Calvinism.[99]

We also noted in his sermon in 1760 "On Sin in Believers" John Wesley began using expressions like "the indwelling of the Spirit" for all justified persons. His point was that the Holy Spirit is given to all believers in "a lower degree." We also noticed earlier that John Wesley once said to Fletcher that "young men" had the "full assurance of faith" even though they were not perfected in love.

Albert Outler has noted that this sermon "On Faith" represents John Wesley's "concluding comment on the whole idea of degrees of faith (each valid in its degree)" and it is a "retraction of his earlier harsh judgments against '*lower degrees of faith.*' "[100]

Richard Heitzenrater has pointed out the "rather remarkable development" in Wesley's thinking when he affirmed that one with "the faith of a servant" is accepted by God.[101] Heitzenrater believes this new understanding "seems to emerge from a maturing pastoral sensitivity as well as a more sophisticated theological perspective."[102]

This sermon showed the decisive influence of John Fletcher upon his thought. The occasion for John Wesley to write this sermon was an interview that he had with Melville Horne who was John Fletcher's successor as vicar of Madeley *in absentia* so that Mary Fletcher could be the actual "pastor" of the Church.

Horne had put the question to John Wesley whether or not he believed that assurance was a necessary part of justifying faith. John Wesley told Horne: "When fifty years ago, my Brother Charles and I, in the simplicity of our hearts, told the good people of England, that unless they knew their sins forgiven, they were under the wrath and curse of God, I marvel, Melville, they did not *stone us.*"[103] John Wesley repeated this same observation in this sermon.[104]

After the interview Horne said that he again read Fletcher's *Essay on Truth*, and he learned what "I had not before clearly noticed, that Mr. Fletcher and Mr. Wesley had at least, in the year 1774 . . . explicitly and publicly rejected the damnatory clause [that one who does not have the witness of the Spirit is damned]."[105] He noticed that Wesley had placed an asterisk in one of the sections where Fletcher rejected the idea that one must have the witness of the Spirit as proof that one was justified by faith.[106]

1774 was the year that John Wesley noted in the new edition of his journal that he no longer agreed with the harsh assessment of his spiritual state prior to his Aldersgate experience, as earlier discussed, This change was made most likely under the influence of Fletcher's *Essay on Truth*. Horne knew both John Wesley and Fletcher very well and believed that they spoke with one voice.[107]

In a short essay (July 13, 1788), John Wesley put together his "Thoughts upon a Late Phenomenon." Here John Wesley linked "all holiness" with being "filled with the Holy Spirit." As noted earlier, Fletcher and John Wesley believed that on the day of Pentecost the disciples and all the new converts were justified and fully sanctified. He writes:

> A glorious work of God began upon the earth on the day of the descent of the Holy Spirit, on the day of Pentecost; which *so swiftly* increased that in a very short time, in Jerusalem alone, thousands of sinners were brought from darkness to light, and from the power of Satan to God. Those were effectually changed from all vice to all holiness; indeed, being 'all filled with the Holy Spirit [. . .], they were all of one heart and one mind'. And their life was suitable thereto.[108]

John Wesley noted that soon the "mystery of iniquity" worked against the "mystery of godliness" and the result was that "iniquity had overspread the Christian church." This process of wickedness "did not come to its height till the fatal time when Constantine called himself a Christian." Since then, there have been those few holy believers who have not fallen under the yoke of evil. However, they often withdrew into the desert or formed a religious body separated from any contact with the mainstream of ordinary life. "So their light no longer shone among men, among those that needed them most."[109]

John Wesley then recounted the emergence of the Methodist movement and called it "an utterly new phenomenon"[110] because its members refused to withdraw into the desert or form a separate Church. Their unique calling was to recover the power of the original Pentecost[111] when sinners were immediately transformed from "all vice to all holiness" and they were perfectly bonded together in love through being "filled with the Holy Spirit."[112]

Pentecost Expressions and The Mystical Temperaments of Charles Wesley and John Fletcher

John Wesley said his brother Charles had no equals among hymn-writers, placing him in the same category as "Spenser, Shakespeare, or Milton" and that he was "born a poet." Recognizing that his *Collection of Hymns for the People Called Methodists* in 1780 were mostly written by Charles Wesley, he said no one else had produced "a little body of experimental and practical divinity" with "so full account of scriptural Christianity . . . for perfecting holiness in the fear of God."[113] It has often been observed that Charles Wesley's success as a hymn-writer was also indebted to John Wesley in part because of his editorial selection of the best verses of Charles Wesley's poetry.

As shown in previous chapters, Charles Wesley was also highly indebted to his brother's theological mentoring, for it was largely John Wesley's theology that Charles Wesley versified. Likewise it was John Wesley's theology that Fletcher theologized. Charles Wesley and Fletcher brought out the feeling and mystical nuances of John Wesley's theology, especially in their use of Pentecost expressions.

John Wesley also considered Fletcher to be a witness of Christian perfection which is why he wrote a biography of him.[114] The Methodist preachers genuinely admired and felt strong affection for Fletcher as a "saint." Samuel Bradburn, a Methodist preacher, said being in Fletcher's presence was like being in the presence of Jesus Christ, and when he found himself in difficult moments, he would pray: "God of Mr. Fletcher, bless me!"[115] Henry Moore reported that the Methodist preachers "pressed Mr. Wesley" to try to persuade Fletcher to be his successor because of their affection for him.[116]

It was rumored that Voltaire said that, if ever he came to be a Christian it would be through two lives, that of Christ himself and that of Fletcher of Madeley.[117]

Fletcher attended his last Methodist conference at Leeds in 1784[118] before his death the following year. Fletcher preached twice during this conference. The impact of his preaching powerfully moved everyone, according to the reports of Joseph Benson and Henry Moore.[119] John Wesley's assistant, Henry Moore, was scheduled to preach the morning after Fletcher. His affection and respect for Fletcher is reflected in the following entry in his journal:

> I went on the Monday morning to the chapel at the hour appointed, when, to my dismay, who should be in the pulpit, with his hand leaning upon his staff, but the venerable Mr. Fletcher himself. At the sight of this . . . my first impression was to run away altogether: a moment's reflection changed my purpose into a feeling of submission to my appointed duty, accompanied by an indescribable fear of performing it. I ascended the pulpit and gave out the hymn; while I did so my knees smote one against the other: I knelt down to pray, and indeed lifted my heart with my voice, that I might be endued with power and wisdom from on high: my soul was calmed with the holy exercise, and when I arose from my knees, the bondage of my spirit was broken; I took my text, and continued the service, fully set free from that fear which has torment,—and strengthened in my resolution ever to obey the voice of duty.[120]

If Fletcher refused to be John Wesley's personally designated successor, it may have been due in part to his mystical temperament. He once said to John Wesley that the very thought of replacing him "would make me take my horse, and gallop away."[121]

If Fletcher and Charles Wesley preferred the energy of Pentecost expressions, such as the "baptism with the Spirit," it was also more compatible with their mystical personalities and passionate temperaments. If John Fletcher said to Charles Wesley that his hymns on Pentecost showed that they "perfectly agree," a computer count of the multiple times that Charles Wesley used the expression, "baptize with the Spirit" for Christian perfection is remarkably high.

In a "Hymn for Believers," Charles wrote:

> 4. Thou seest my heart's desire,
> I would thy cross partake;
> I long to be baptized with fire,
> And die for thy dear sake;
> I long to rise with thee,
> And soar to things above,
> And spend a blest eternity
> In praise of dying love.[122]

In his commentary verse on Luke 3:16, "He shall baptize you with the Holy Ghost and with fire," Charles Wesley wrote:

> 1. Holy, hallowing Spirit, come,
> Cleanse my life's impurity,
> All my nature's filth consume,
> Make an end of sin in me,
> Spread the pure, baptismal flame,
> Plunge me deep in Jesus name.[123]

John Wesley worried about his brother's and Fletcher's tendency toward mysticism with its self-denying notion of humility, and he believed that they would have been more forthcoming in their leadership roles if they had been less inclined toward it.

John Wesley said Fletcher had "hid his candle under a bushel" because he chose to remain located at Madeley rather than travelling with him. In his memorial sermon for Fletcher, John Wesley said: "I can never believe it was the will of God that such a burning and shining light should be *hid under a bushel* [at Madeley]. No; instead of being confined to a country village, it ought to have shone in every corner of our land."[124]

Notes

1. Telford, *Letters*, 6:175 (a letter to John Fletcher, August 18, 1775).
2. Cragg, *Appeals*, 11:261, "A Farther Appeal to Men of Reason and Religion"
3. Fletcher's letter to Mary Bosanquet, written from Marseilles, March 7, 1778, cited and transcribed by Luke Tyerman, *Wesley's Designated Successor*, 411–412.
4. Published for the first time in *The Asbury Theological Journal*. 50.1 (Spring, 1998):35–56.
5. For a fuller discussion of this essay and its influence with others who had a private copy of it, including

Thomas Coke, cf. *The Meaning of Pentecost in Early Methodism* (Lanham, MD: Scarecrow Press, 2002), 263-264.

6. *The Doctrine of the New Birth*, 46-47.

7. Telford, *Letters* 6:221 (to John Fletcher, June 1, 1776). Cf. Harold Lindström, *Wesley and Sanctification*, 135.

8. *The Arminian Magazine* 18 (December, 1795): 614-615.

9. Outler, Sermon, "Christian Perfection," 2:110.

10. Richard Hill, *Logica Wesleiensis, or, The Farrago Double Distilled with an Heroic Poem in Praise of Mr. John Wesley* (London: Printed for E. and C. Dilly, in the Poultry; J. Matthews, near Hungerford-market, in the Strand; and W. Harris, No. 70, in St. Paul's Church-yard, 1773), 53.

11. Cf. *Fifth Check, Works of John Fletcher*, 3:392.

12. Outler, *Sermons*, 3:617, "On the Death of John Fletcher."

13. Outler, *Sermons*, 3:627-268, "On the Death of John Fletcher."

14. In a letter to Joseph Benson, November 21, 1776, Fletcher mentioned that John Wesley "invited me to travel with him . . . through Oxfordshire, Northamptonshire, and Norfolk." Luke Tyerman documents this lengthy trip from Shropshire to Norwich and to London. This trip began on November 20, 1776 and lasted for a couple of weeks. This trip was both a preaching tour and health trip intended to help Fletcher recover from his illness with TB. *Wesley's Designated Successor*, 369-373. This reference to having travelled with Fletcher probably is a reference to this tour. Otherwise, John Wesley and Fletcher spent considerable time together on specific days and occasions throughout their relationship, beginning in London where they first met. Elizabeth Ritchie in her journal, June 26th, 1784 mentioned that John Wesley and John Fletcher preached together on occasions: "On Saturday we came to Leeds, where my spirit was much refreshed by the sight of my dear old friends, Mr. and Mrs. Fletcher. Mr. Fletcher preached on Sunday morning, and Mr. Wesley in the evening: they were both solemn and animating occasions."

15. Fletcher, *Works*, 1:238, 296, "Fourth Check to Antinomianism."

16. As an example of this practice, Fletcher wrote in his widely circulated manuscript, entitled "The Doctrine of the New Birth, as it is stated in these sheets, is directly or indirectly maintained by the most spiritual divines, especially in their sacred poems": "From the preceding extract I conclude, that, if Macarius, who lived near 1300 years ago, so clear preached the baptism and dispensation of the Holy Spirit, Mr. John Wesley and I cannot reasonably be charged with *novelty* for doing the same thing." Fletcher, *New Birth*.

17. John Wesley, *A Short Account of the Life and Death of the Rev. John Fletcher, Vicar of Madeley* (New York: Ezekiel Cooper and John Wilson, 1803), 51-52. Cf. Joseph Benson, *The Life of The Rev. John William de la Flechere, Works of John Fletcher*, 214.

18. Cf. *The Methodist Magazine* (London edition), 24 (January, 1801): 43.

19. *Arminian Magazine* (1781), 4:467, 1781.

20. Outler, *Sermons* 3:313-314, "On Zeal"

21. Outler, *Sermons*, 3:313-314, 321, "On Zeal"

22. James MacDonald, *Memoirs of the Rev. Joseph Benson* (New York: Bangs and T. Mason, for the Methodist Episcopal Church, 1823), 52.

23. Benson, "Thoughts on Perfection," *The Arminian Magazine* 4 (January, 1778):553.

24. *Last Checks, Works of the Rev. John Fletcher*, 6:360.

25. "Fragments," *Last Checks, Works of the Rev. John Fletcher*, 8:431.

26. "Thoughts on Perfection," *The Arminian Magazine* 4 (January, 1778): 549-553.

27. John Wesley, *Doctrinal and Controversial Treatises II*, eds. Paul Wesley Chilcote and Kenneth J. Collins, The Bicentennial Edition of *The Works of John Wesley*, 13:152-153. The only exception to those who might have been fully justified and fully sanctified at the same moment were the three thousand on the day of Pentecost who quickly moved from the dispensations of the Father, to the Son, and to the Holy Spirit. *A Plain Account of Christian Perfection* (7th edition, London. G. Paramore, Printer, 1794). Cf. Fletcher, *The First Part of an Equal Check*, abridged by John Wesley to enlarge the reading audience (Bristol: W. Pine Printer, 1774), 179-181.

28. Cited in *The Methodist Magazine, being a continuation of The Arminian Magazine*, volume XXXIV or the eighth volume of the new series (London: Conference Office, City-Road, 1811), 312.

29. Ibid.

30. This letter was written to Miss Loxdale on June 24, 1781, and published in *The Arminian Magazine* 5 (January, 1782): 49.

31. John Wesley, "An Extract from the Journal of Mr. G. C.," *The Arminian Magazine*, 6 (May 1783): 244-245.
32. John Wesley, "An Extract from Journal of Mr. G.C," *The Arminian Magazine* 5 (June 1782): 298.
33. Outler, *Sermons*, 2:454, "The Mystery of Iniquity"
34. Ibid.
35. Ibid., 2:454, "The Mystery of Iniquity"
36. Ibid., 2:455, "The Mystery of Iniquity"
37. Ibid., *2:455,* "The Mystery of Iniquity"
38. Cf. Ibid., 2:461, "The Mystery of Iniquity"
39. Ibid., *2:461,* "The Mystery of Iniquity"
40. Ibid., 2:454, "The Mystery of Iniquity"
41. Ibid., 2:454-455, "The Mystery of Iniquity"
42. Ibid., 2:455-456, "The Mystery of Iniquity"
43. Ibid., 2:461, "The Mystery of Iniquity."
44. Ibid., 2:470, "The Mystery of Iniquity."
45. *The Arminian Magazine* 6 (August 1783): 403.
46. Outler, *Sermons*, 2:465, "The Mystery of Iniquity."
47. Ibid., 2:470, "The Mystery of Iniquity."
48. Wesley, June 3, 1781, *Journals and Diaries VI (1776–86)*, in *Works of John Wesley*, 23:206.
49. John F. Hurst, *The History of Methodism* (New York: Eaton and Mains, 1902), 2:948.
50. John Wesley, August 8, 1781, *Journals and Diaries VII (1776–1786)*, 23:218.
51. *The Wesleyan Methodist Magazine* 8 (August 1829): 528.
52. Outler, *Sermons*, 2:494, "The General Spread of the Gospel."
53. Ibid., 2:498, "The General Spread of the Gospel."
54. Ibid., 2:493, "The General Spread of the Gospel."
55. Ibid., 2:494, "The General Spread of the Gospel."
56. Ibid., 2:498, "The General Spread of the Gospel."
57. Ibid., 2:495, "The General Spread of the Gospel."
58. Ibid., 2:491, "The General Spread of the Gospel."
59. Newport shows that Wesley's view of the millennium in this sermon is not the premillennialism of Charles Wesley's earlier writings. Newport, "Premillennialism in the Early Writings of Charles Wesley," *The Wesleyan Theological Journal* 32.1 (Spring 1997), 105. Newport defines premillennialism as the "belief in the literal, visible and apocalyptic appearance of Jesus prior to the inauguration of the millennium described in Revelation 20" (Ibid., 85). Fletcher's letters to Charles Wesley would indicate that they both had largely abandoned a strict premillennialism. For example, in a letter to Charles Wesley (May 11, 1776), cited in *The Arminian Magazine* 18 (December, 1795): 614-615, Fletcher noted that they were waiting for a Pentecost-Church to be established on the earth, and he does not mention or imply the idea of the visible return of Christ to set up a millennium.
60. Outler, *Sermons*, 2:491, "The General Spread of the Gospel"
61. Ibid., 3:75, "On Perfection."
62. Ibid.*s*, 2:499, "The General Spread of the Gospel"
63. *The Arminian Magazine* 6 (August 1783): 403; Outler, *Sermons,* 2:485.
64. Moore, *The Life of Mary Fletcher,* 141.
65. Ibid., 146.
66. Thomas Rutherford, "Preface" to *Christian Perfection, Being an Extract from the Rev. John Fletcher's Treatise on That Subject* (New York: T. Mason and G. Lane, 1837 edition), 4-7. Cf. Moore, *Life of Mrs*. Fletcher, 144ff.
67. Moore, *The Life of Mrs. Mary* Fletcher, 146n.
68. A letter loosely contained in and bound up in a large volume (or folio) in John Rylands Library, entitled, *Letters Relating to the Wesley Family*, stored in JRULM MAW F1 Box 18.
69. John Wesley, "A Sermon on Isaiah ix.11," [later renamed, "The General Spread of the Gospel"], *The Arminian Magazine,* 6 (June, 1783): 398.
70. Fletcher, *Works* 3:523-526, "Socinianism Unscriptural."
71. Moore, *The Life of Mrs. Mary* Fletcher, 398.
72. Outler, *Sermons*, 3:45, "Of the Church."
73. "Low degree" is used frequently by Wesley to indicate a justified believer who is not entirely sanctified.

John Wesley said those who are justified or a "babe in Christ" have "the love of God" in their heart "in a low degree." Cf. Outler, *Sermons*, 3:175, "On Patience"

74. Fletcher, *The First Part of An Equal Check*, Wesley's abridged edition (New York: John Wilson and Daniel Hitt, 1809, Second American Edition), 171. Cf. Ibid., 169.

75. Outler, *Sermons* 3:177, "On Patience."

76. *The Arminian Magazine*, 20 (January, 1797), 49.

77. Henry Moore, *The Life of the Rev. John Wesley*, 2:261.

78. Cf. Henry Moore's comments about "her preaching" in Moore, *The Life of Mrs. Mary Fletcher* (New York: Mason and Lane, 184), 386.

79. John Wesley, March 8, 10, and 12, 1787, *Journals and Diaries VII (1787-1791)*, ed. W. Reginald Ward and Richard Heitzenrater, *The Bicentennial Edition of the Works of John Wesley* (Nashville: Abingdon Press, 2003), 24:7-8.

80. *The Life of Mrs. Mary Fletcher*, 115. Cf. Paul W. Chilcote, *She Offered Them Christ: The Legacy of Women Preachers in Early Methodism* (Nashville: Abingdon Press, 1993), 62-106.

81. Wesley, Sermon 63, "The General Spread of the Gospel," §§ 20-25, in Outler, *Sermons II*, 494-498.

82. *Life of Mrs. Mary Fletcher*, 398.

83. Outler, *Sermons*, 2:554, "The Wisdom of God's Counsel"

84. Ibid.

85. Ibid., 2:555

86. Ibid.s, 3:514, "On God's Vineyard"

87. Ibid., 3:514, "On God's Vineyard"

88. Ibid., 3:492, "On Faith"

89. Fletcher, *An Equal Check* (Wesley's special edition), 147-151, "Essay on Truth,"

90. Outler, *Sermons* 3:493, "On Faith"

91. Ibid., 3:492-493, "On Faith"

92. Ibid., 3:497. 498, "On Faith"

93. Ibid., 3:498, "On Faith"

94. Ibid., 3:500, "On Faith"

95. Ibid., 3:501, "On Faith"

96. Ibid., 3:495, "On Faith"

97. Fletcher thus observes this about the unique relevance of John the Baptist: "But John was beheaded before Christ glorified opened his peculiar kingdom. Thus John saw the kingdom of heaven: he was not far from it. But yet he did not enter into it." Fletcher, *Works*, 2:526, "The Last Check."

98. Outler, *Sermons*, 3:498, "On Faith"

99. Benson, *Works of John Fletcher*, 6:222-224.

100. Outler, *Sermons*, 3:491.

101. Heitzenrater, *Mirror and Memory*, 144.

102. Ibid.

103. Melville Horne, *An Investigation of the Definition of Justifying Faith* (London: Longman, Hurst, Rees, and Orme, 1809), 2-3. Cf. "We believe a man may be a real Christian without being 'assured of his salvation'." Wesley, *Letters*, "Letter to Dr. Green" (April 2, 1761), 4:144.

104. Outler, *Sermons*, 3:497, "On Faith"

105. Melville Horne, *An investigation on the Definition of Justifying Faith*, 3.

106. Ibid., 3, 50-51.

107. Ibid., 50.

108. Davies, *Societies*, 9:534, "Thoughts upon a Late Phenomenon." At least in regard to the first Christian believers on the day of Pentecost, Wesley (and Fletcher) agreed with Zinzendorf that those justified were fully sanctified.

109. Ibid., 9:535.

110. Ibid, 9:536.

111. Ibid., 9:534.

112. Ibid., 9:534.

113. *A Collection of Hymns for the Use of the People Called Methodists* (London: John Mason, 1780), 4.

114. Outler, *Sermons*, 3:627-628, "On the Death of John Fletcher"

115. Cited by *Tyerman, Wesley's Designated Successor*, 267-268

116. Henry Moore, *The Life of the Rev. John Wesley*, 2:261.
117. http://madeleylocalhistory.org/people/fletcher.html.
118. Tyerman, *Wesley's Designated Successor*, 541–542.
119. Ibid., 543. Cf. Mrs. Richard Smith, *The Life of Rev. Henry Moore*, 337–340.
120. Mrs. Richard Smith, *The Life of Rev. Henry Moore*, 340.
121. John Fletcher's letter to John Wesley on January 9, 1776, contained in the "Fletcher Volume" (103) of the Fletcher-Tooth Archival Collection in the John Rylands Library of Manchester University.
122. *Hymns and Sacred Poems* (1749), 210.
123. MA 1977/575 (Charles Wesley Notebooks Box 3), 44.
124. Wesley, *Works* (Jackson) 11:302, "A Short Account of the Life and Death of the Reverend John Fletcher."

Chapter 15

John Wesley's Many Sermons on "Baptized with the Holy Spirit"

"He shall baptize you with the Holy Spirit and with fire—He shall fill you with the Holy Spirit, inflaming your hearts with that fire of love, which many waters cannot quench. And this was done, even with a visible appearance as of fire, on the day of Pentecost."
—John Wesley in *Explanatory Notes on the New Testament* (Matthew 3:11-12)

"Ye shall be baptized with the Holy Spirit."
—John Wesley (a sermon to the Bristol Conference, 1783)

"You perhaps remember the account I gave you of the select prayer-meeting . . . for those only who had either attained, or were groaning after, full redemption. I thought that, as we were *all with one accord in the same place*, we had reason to expect *a glorious descent of the purifying flame*. It was even so. Soon five or six were able to testify that God had cleansed their souls from all sin."
—Adam Clarke to John Wesley (1789)

"I breathe for nothing but more of the pure nature of God; and even now am constrained to cry out, 'O for more of that inward fiery baptism of the Holy Spirit, which alone makes one spirit with the Lord, and causes true Christians to be of one heart and of one mind!'"
—J. W. Salmon to John Wesley (1782)

"Hold fast what you have . . . till he baptizes you with the Holy Spirit and with fire."
—A Letter of John Fletcher, published by John Wesley in *The Arminian Magazine* in the last issue that he managed as editor (January 1791)

Adam Clarke was one of John Wesley's younger preachers whose scholarly brilliance and leadership among the Methodists were highly respected. He was to become a president of the Conference three times, 1806, 1814, and 1822.[1]
John Wesley's last written words on holiness were addressed to Adam Clarke about three months before his death.

> To retain the grace of God is much more than to gain it; hardly one in three does this. And this should be strongly and explicitly urged on all who have tasted of perfect love. If any can prove that any of our local preacher or leaders, either directly or indirectly, speak

against it, let him be a local preacher or leader no longer. I doubt whether he should continue in the Society.[2]

Clarke was gifted in ancient languages. His knowledge of Hebrew and Greek was exceptional, and his *Commentaries on the Old and New Testaments* represented impressive scholarship. His help in deciphering the Rosetta Stone was significant. He was appointed in 1808 by a committee of the House of Commons to examine the public records and codify the various documents scattered through the British Isles.[3] His services to the British government earned him a great reputation and brought honor to the Methodist movement. Maldywn Edwards says that "Adam Clarke was the greatest name in Methodism in the generation which succeeded Wesley." He further believed that Clarke "was not only the greatest scholar in Methodism, but amongst the greatest of his age."[4]

When he was 22 years of age, Clarke was received into full connection as a Methodist preacher at the Bristol Conference on August 6, 1783.[5] This occurred at the same time that the Fletchers were preaching the famous revival in Clarke's birthplace of Ireland.[6] Fletcher was 53, Coke 36, and John Wesley was 80 years old.

In his annual conference sermon in 1781 at Leeds, Fletcher had highlighted the dispensation of the Spirit, the baptism with the Holy Spirit.[7]

Then, in 1783 when he was being brought into full connection with the annual conference, Clarke heard John Wesley preach on "the baptism with the Holy Spirit" at the Bristol conference. This happened when he was attending the Bristol conference early in the morning on August 3, 1783.

He first heard "Mr. Bradburn preach on Christian perfection, from 1 John iv.19."

Then at 10:00 a.m. he heard John Wesley preach on the text from Acts. 1:5, "Ye shall be baptized with the Holy Spirit."[8] John Wesley also recorded (with emphasis) in his diary that he had preached on "Acts 1:5!" on this date.[9] Afterwards, Thomas Coke assisted John Wesley in Holy Communion. We also know that Thomas Coke used the expression, "baptism with the Holy Spirit," as an equivalent to Christian perfection (see below).

Again later on during the day, he heard John Wesley preach on the text, "Let us go on to perfection," (Heb. 6:1).[10] John Wesley also recorded in his diary that he had preached on "Heb. 6:1!"[11]

Clarke apparently did not hear John Wesley's conference sermon on the previous Tuesday when he preached to "the leaders" on Acts 2:4: "They were all filled with the Holy Spirit"[12] since he did not mention it.

Then again on Wednesday his conference sermon was on Acts 2:4.[13] On other occasions when he preached on this text, we have observed that he explained this call to be filled with the Spirit "is to you and your children," an exhortation he had heard from John Heylyn's Pentecost sermon on May 21, 1738 when Heylyn appealed to his hearers to pray for "the sanctifying baptism with the Spirit" in order to attain "perfect purity."

So these two sermons on Tuesday and Wednesday on being "filled with the Holy Spirit" preceded his Sunday sermon on being "baptized with the Spirit," which Adam Clarke heard.

On September 10, 1783 in Buxton, John Wesley recorded in his diary that he again preached on Acts 1:5, "Ye shall be baptized with the Holy Spirit."[14]

On October 25, 1783, Clarke noted in his journal that when John Wesley came into his district of Norwich, he again heard Wesley preach a sermon on the text, "They were all baptized with the Holy Spirit."[15] As confirmation of Adam Clarke's journal, John Wesley also recorded in his diary that he had preached on "Acts 1:5" on that day.[16]

Within the space of less than three months, Clarke heard John Wesley preach two sermons on the baptism with the Holy Spirit, and these instances are confirmed in John Wesley's diary.

In addition, John Wesley also used Acts 1:5 in a sermon he preached on September 10, 1783,[17] and so there are three instances in this short space of time when John Wesley preached on the baptism with the Spirit.

In addition to these three sermons on the "baptism with the Spirit" (Acts 1:5), John had also preached two sermons on "they were all filled with the Holy Spirit." This means five sermons on this theme were preached all within this same brief period of less than three months.

By this time, Fletcher's *Checks* had widely popularized the Wesley brothers' expression of the "baptism with the Holy Spirit" as an equivalent for Christian perfection.

We do not have the contents of these sermons that John Wesley preached on the baptism with the Holy Spirit, partly because John Wesley's "later preaching was primarily extempore."[18] However, we know his later published sermons highlighted Pentecost and sanctification; we know that he said to William Law that to be "baptized with the Holy Spirit" meant only to be renewed in righteousness and true holiness; we know he said in "Farther Appeal to Men of Reason and Religion" that "the baptism with the Spirit" is the means "men attain perfect love;" we know he said in *his Explanatory Notes on the New Testament* on John 14:23-27 that the coming day of Pentecost meant an effusion of love that will exceed their pre-Pentecost state of "justification;" we know he said in his commentary on Acts 1:5 that the baptism of the Spirit is the privilege of "all true believers to the end of the world," and was not limited to the original day of Pentecost; we know he interpreted the enduring meaning of Pentecost to mean the "constant fruits of faith, even righteousness, and peace, and joy in the Holy Spirit" (i.e. Christian perfection].

We also know that John Wesley equated being "baptized with the Spirit" and being "filled with the Spirit" and that he defined these expressions in terms of Pentecost, meaning that the disciples' hearts were filled with love. He explained in Matthew 3:1-12 that the baptism of fire of love was intended for those who were already "his" people (i.e. justified). John Wesley explained this connection of being baptized and being filled with the Spirit with being "inflamed with the fire of love" promised to those who were already his followers in his *Explanatory Notes on the New Testament*:

> Matthew 3:11: "He shall baptize you with the Holy Spirit and with fire—He shall fill you with the Holy Spirit, inflaming your hearts with that fire of love, which many waters cannot quench. And this was done, even with a visible appearance as of fire, on the day of Pentecost. 3:12. Whose fan—That is, the word of the Gospel. His floor—That is, his [people].

If John Wesley preached on Acts 1:5, we know (based on his *Notes on the New Testament* on Matthew 3:11-12) that he equated it with being filled with the Spirit and being "inflamed with the fire of love (i.e. Christian perfection)."

We also know exactly how Adam Clarke interpreted Acts 1:5 in his commentary on the book of Acts:

> John baptized with water, which was a sign of penitence, in reference to the remission of sin; but Christ baptizes with the Holy Spirit, for the destruction of sin [i. e., entire sanctification].[19]

It can be gathered that these extempore sermons corresponded with his recent sermons that were appearing in *The Arminian Magazine* where he made Pentecost the basis of sanctification. We also can gather that his preaching corresponded with Fletcher's sermon delivered in his conference sermon in 1781. We can also gather his sermons on Pentecost corresponded with Fletcher's treatise on Christian perfection (*The Last Check*) because John Wesley said after Fletcher had made his recommended changes about "receiving the Holy Spirit" that there was no difference between them. We also pointed out that John Fletcher said John Wesley based his "doctrine of Christian perfection on being *baptized and filled with the Spirit*," with an emphasis that "this is Mr. Wesley's sentiment."[20]

Since we know Clarke's meaning, this would be the same meaning John Wesley gave it. After all, that is consistent with John Wesley's own early use of it as he had learned from Christian David and John Heylyn.

Thomas Coke was the secretary of this 1783 Bristol Conference when Adam Clarke was brought into full connection. We also know that Coke linked the baptism with the Holy Spirit and Christian perfection in his sermons and letters.[21]

This 1783 Bristol Conference commissioned "Dr. Coke to visit the Societies throughout England" to make sure that all the preaching houses were promoting "the Conference Plan [that is, the Methodist distinctive beliefs]."[22]

We can assume, if Coke were given the responsibility of enforcing the distinctive beliefs of Methodism, then the baptism with the Holy Spirit as the means of attaining it was considered to be Methodist doctrine. Not only did Coke himself use the expression of the baptism with the Spirit for Christian perfection, he said that it was John Fletcher's writings, especially his "Essay on Truth,"[23] which was "the blessed means of bring me among that despised people called Methodists."[24] Coke would have first encountered this expression "baptism with the Holy Spirit" in this essay. He referred to his friendship with Fletcher "as one of the greatest external privileges" of his life.[25] He also reported that Fletcher's writings were approved by John Wesley himself and that they were received into the British Conference as authoritative, as already noted.[26]

If John Wesley preached a sermon on the baptism with the Holy Spirit at the conference, there is no reason to think it was not consistent with the interpretation which Thomas Coke gave to it, as well as Adam Clarke.

Thomas Coke had signed Clarke's copy of "The Large Minutes." These minutes were put into manual form and given to everyone brought into full connection with the Conference. Coke wrote on the reverse side of the title page: "To Adam Clarke: As long as you freely consent to, and earnestly endeavor to walk by, these Rules, we shall rejoice to acknowledge you as a fellow-laborer."[27]

Significantly, "The Large Minutes" contained the specific instructions of what Methodist preachers were obligated to believe. The standard of doctrine enforced upon every Methodist preacher in that manual included the writings of John Fletcher. If Wesley's sermon on the baptism with the Holy Spirit at the Bristol Conference differed from Fletcher's interpretation, it would have occasioned controversy and confusion. It would also have been unusual for Clarke to have embraced this Pentecost expression himself unless it was similarly explained in John Wesley's own preaching at this conference when he became a Methodist preacher.

Fletcher died within two years of Clarke's entrance into full Methodist connection. Nevertheless, Clarke developed a profound sense of respect for Fletcher's writings.[28] He recommended in his *Christian Theology* that preachers should particularly read John Wesley and Fletcher, and he placed Fletcher's writings right alongside Wesley's writings as the basis for Methodist doctrine.[29]

Clarke also described Fletcher as a "truly apostolic man."[30] Quoting from an anonymous source, he cited in agreement what someone had said of Fletcher: "I must pronounce him the first polemical writer this or any other age has produced: a man, mighty in the Scriptures, and full of the unction of God."[31]

It is easy enough to determine what John Wesley's sermon on the baptism with the Spirit meant through paying attention to what Adam Clarke understood by the baptism with the Spirit. Though Clarke's primary term for holiness was being "cleansed from all sin," he identified Pentecost as the basis for full sanctification.[32]

Clarke showed that Pentecost was the fulfilment of the "Promise of the Father" to establish the kingdom within the hearts of his people, so that "they may perfectly love thee and worthily magnify thy name," a citation from the Anglican collect for the Communion Service.[33]

Clarke further showed that the descent of the Holy Spirit on the day of Pentecost meant that the "supernatural light and power [was] *constantly resident* in them." This emphasis upon the *constant* and *abiding* testimony of the Holy Spirit was a common phrase to mean Christian perfection, as Clarke showed.[34] We noted earlier in his *Explanatory Notes upon the New Testament* that John Wesley also interpreted the "Promise of the Spirit" in Acts 2:28 to mean "the constant fruits of faith, even righteousness, and peace, and joy in the Holy Spirit," which is offered to all people in all subsequent generations.

Clarke further described the day of Pentecost to mean that the Holy Spirit "shall fill you with the fullness of God."[35] He further pointed out that the concept of "the baptism with the Holy Spirit" used the emblem of "fire" to mean that the Spirit will "penetrate every part, and assimilate the whole to the image of God."[36]

The Pentecost expression, "Promise of the Father," a favorite term of Fletcher to describe Christian perfection, is found in Clarke's writings as well. In a letter to Mary Cooke (who became his wife), he wrote on January 23, 1787: "You cannot be too much in earnest for full salvation, therefore continue pleading the 'Promise of the Father,' for it is yea and amen to you, the blessing is as free as the air you breathe,—the willingness of God to fulfil his promise to you infinitely exceeds my description and your conception."[37]

In Acts 2:38, Peter said on the day of Pentecost: "Repent, and be baptized every one of you in the name of Jesus Christ, for the remission of sins; and ye shall receive the gift of the Holy Spirit." Clarke commented on this passage: "Receive the baptism, *in reference to the removal of sins*, and ye shall receive the Holy Spirit, by whose agency alone the efficacy of the blood of the covenant is applied, and by whose refining power the heart is purified."

Acts 6:3 required as one of the qualifications for being a deacon that they be "full of the Holy Spirit." Clarke explained that this meant being "saved into the spirit of the Gospel dispensation; and made partakers of that Holy Spirit by which the soul is sanctified, and endued with those graces which constitute the mind that was in Christ."[38]

On July 15, 1789, Clarke wrote to John Wesley the following letter to report on the work as it was progressing in Jersey. Notice that Christian perfection is described as a personal Pentecost-like experience.

> My Reverend Father in Christ,—In my last I gave you a short account of the prosperity of the work of God among us, and the prospect we had of an increase. Since that time the Lord has indeed wrought wonderfully. You perhaps remember the account I gave you of the select prayer-meeting I had just then established for those only who had either attained, or were groaning after, full redemption. I thought that, as we were all with *one accord in the same place* [italics mine to indicate the Pentecostal setting], we had reason to expect *a glorious descent of the purifying flame* [italics mine to indicate the use of Pentecost language]. It was even so. Soon five or six were able to testify that God had cleansed their souls from all sin.[39]

In his *Christian Theology* where he defined the meaning of sanctification, he again located the possibility of perfect love in Pentecost. He said:

> What then is this complete sanctification? It is . . . washing the soul of a true believer from the remains of sin . . . making one who is already a child of God more holy. . . . Arise, then, and be baptized with a greater effusion of the Holy Spirit, and wash away thy sin [notice the singular noun is used to refer to indwelling sin], calling on the name of the Lord."[40]

Here Clarke used both "baptism" and "effusion" to speak of entire sanctification—terms used interchangeably among the early Methodists. If Adam Clarke heard John Wesley preach sermons on the baptism with the Spirit, his preaching would certainly have been consistent with John Wesley.

Clarke's report of John Wesley preaching on being "baptized with the Spirit" was not the only times he preached on this subject. We can determine from his diaries that John Wesley preached on "baptized with the Spirit" and "filled with the Spirit" on multiple occasions.

In addition to these instances that we have already mentioned, here are other occasions listed in his manuscript dairies.

On June 5, 1777, John Wesley preached on Acts 2:4, "They were all filled with the Holy Spirit," citing Elizabeth Ritchie as a model of it.[41]

On June 3, 1781, John Wesley preached on Acts 2:4 at Castleton, highlighting "in what sense this belongs to us and to our children." Apparently the contemporary application of being "filled with the Spirit" was an important part of his message, calling his hearers today to be filled with the Spirit.

This was the same year that Fletcher preached at John Wesley's annual conference on the baptism with the Spirit.[42] This was the same year that John Wesley published Benson's essay equating being "baptized with the Spirit" and "perfect love."[43] And this same focus on the "sanctifying baptism of the Holy Spirit" was a theme in Heylyn's sermon, which John Wesley heard with great approval on the day of Charles Wesley's Pentecost moment of personal faith.

On March 16, 1782, J. W. Salmon, one of the Methodist preachers, wrote a letter to John Wesley "out of the abundance of my heart" about the baptism with the Spirit:

> The Lord is deepening his blessed work in my soul; and I breathe for nothing but more of the pure nature of God; and even now am constrained to cry out, "O for more of that inward fiery baptism of the Holy Spirit, which alone makes one spirit with the Lord, and causes true Christians to be of one heart and of one mind!"

John Wesley later published this letter in *The Arminian Magazine* shortly before he died in 1790.[44] This letter (published by John Wesley) confirms that his preaching on the baptism with the Spirit was about Christian perfection, and as Gareth Lloyd has pointed out, John Wesley "exercised close editorial oversight" over *The Arminian Magazine*.[45]

And if Adam Clarke and his other preachers were using the baptism with the Spirit as an equivalent to Christian perfection, that surely was John Wesley's understanding as well in his extempore preaching on being baptized with the Spirit, especially since he and Charles were the first to use the baptism with the Spirit as equivalent in meaning to Christian perfection.

On June 8, 1783, John Wesley preached on Acts 2:1-4 at the City Road Chapel in London.[46]

On May 30, 1784, he preached on Acts 2:4 at Newcastle.[47]

On June 29, 1784, he preached on Acts 4:31, "They were all filled with the Holy Spirit," at Owston.[48] John Wesley had preached on this text which became one of his standard sermons, "Scriptural Christianity," where he equated being filled with the Spirit with the fruit of the Spirit and full of love. As mentioned previously, John Fletcher quoted from this sermon on "Scriptural Christianity" (based on Acts 4:31) to show that Pentecost is the basis of full sanctification, and John Wesley showed his approval with an asterisk placed in front of this comment in his special abridged edition of Fletcher's *Essay on Truth*.[49]

On May 15, 1785, he preached on Acts 2:4 at Dublin.[50]

On June 15, 1785, he again preached on Acts 2:4 at Derryanvil, Ireland. This was the year that John Fletcher died, and John Wesley immediately began writing his biography.

In this biography, John Wesley noted that Fletcher's "favourite subject" was "being cleansed from all sin" through being "filled with the Spirit."[51] This was also the same year that John Wesley said "the baptism with the Holy Spirit" is given to all believers "in a lower degree" with the implication that the fullest meaning of "the baptism with the Spirit" is Christian perfection (cf. sermon "On the Church."

We know from Crookshank's history of Methodism in Ireland that the expression "baptism with the Spirit" was widely used there. In 1790, a revival broke out and a leader of the society "pleaded with God for a rich baptism of His Spirit, and the prayer was answered."[52] In 1791, one of the members "received a wonderful baptism of the Spirit in sanctifying power."[53] In 1804 when Thomas Coke was president of the conference in Ireland, the members of the conference "resolved to seek a renewed baptism of the Holy Spirit."[54]

Adam Clarke, another Irishman, said: "to be sanctified wholly ... requires ... nothing but a fullness of the Spirit."[55] He cited the "Pentecostal church" when the believers were of "one heart and one soul" to show that they were then sanctified.[56]

On April 5, 1786 John Wesley preached on Acts 2:4 at Bullocksmithy (Manchester).[57]

On June 4, 1786, John Wesley preached on Acts 2:4 at Ballast Hills,[58] and the very next day at Ballast Hills on June 5, 1786, he preached on Acts 19:2, "Have ye received the Holy Spirit since ye believed?"[59]

As it will be recalled from previous discussion, John Wesley cautioned Joseph Benson about using this topic of "receiving the Holy Spirit" for Christian perfection. Apparently John Wesley wanted to ensure that if it is used, it should also be recognized that all believers have some measure of the Spirit. He resolved this issue with Fletcher with a distinction being made between receiving the Spirit according to one's stage of grace—with the full reception of the Spirit denoting Christian perfection.

We know that John Wesley previously used this very expression of "receiving the Spirit" for Christian perfection. For example, in his comments on Acts 19:2 in *Explanatory Notes on the New Testament*, John Wesley identified receiving the Spirit to mean: "The extraordinary gifts of the Spirit, as well as his sanctifying graces."[60] He did not link it to justification, but sanctification. This interpretation was also consistent with the Anglican rite of confirmation and with his brother Charles.

As we shall see, Joseph Benson in his commentary on this passage also gave it the same interpretation. So did Charles Wesley interpret this same passage in Acts 19:2, 6— "Still the Holy Spirit descends ... Makes an utter end of sin, and wholly sanctifies."[61]

John Fletcher interpreted this passage to mean the believers at Ephesus "received the abundant measure of the Spirit, which was [also] bestowed on the disciples at the day of Pentecost."[62] This emphasis on "abundance" corresponded with John Wesley's caution to allow some measure of the Spirit is given to all justified persons.

On May 27, 1787, John Wesley preached on Acts 2:4 at Clones.[63] He recorded in his journal that "God did indeed send a gracious rain upon their souls, so that many rejoiced with joy unspeakable [often used by John Wesley to mean Christian perfection]."[64]

On May 11, 1788, he preached on Acts 2:4 at Whitehaven, noting that "his power was eminently present in the congregation."[65]

The very next day on May 12, 1788 he preached on Acts 2:4 at Cockermouth. He noted: "Several ministers were there, and so was the power of God in an uncommon degree. All that were under the roof seemed to be moved more or less. And so they were in the morning, Tuesday 13, when I besought them to 'present themselves a living sacrifice to God'."[66] Here John Wesley connected "living sacrifice [i.e., Christian perfection]" with being "baptized with the Spirit."

On May 31, 1789, John Wesley preached on Acts 2:4 at Londonderry. This was two years before he died. His journal and diaries showed him preaching multiple times on being filled and baptized with the Spirit, and his preaching theme on being filled and baptized with the Spirit continued on in Londonderry. Crookshank reported that in Londonderry in August 1818 was when he "received such a baptism of the Holy Spirit in sanctifying fullness, as made him unspeakably happy in the love of Christ."[67]

If John Wesley preached on the baptism with the Spirit, we have seen that Charles Wesley's hymns are replete with references to the connection between Pentecost and sanctification. Any of Charles' hymns on the baptism with the Spirit could have been sung at John Wesley's Annual Conferences, especially when John Wesley and John Fletcher preached on this topic.

It would have been most appropriate for the preachers to have sung the following hymn by Charles Wesley on this very text from which John Wesley had preached, "'John truly baptized with water; but ye shall be baptized with the Holy Spirit" (Acts 1:5).

This hymn included an explanation of the two different baptisms—one with water and the other with the Holy Spirit. "The mystical sign" of water baptism can be administered "only once" because Jesus died and rose only once, but the Spirit can be received "as oft as in Christ we believe." The purpose of water baptism is to "cleanse our original guilt" of sin, but the Holy Spirit is the Living Water that "overflows" us and "imparts the love shed abroad in our purified hearts."

"John truly baptized with water; but ye shall
be baptized with the Holy Ghost" (Acts 1:5).

The mystical sign
Which our Lord did enjoin
Only once we receive;
But the Spirit, as oft as in Christ we believe:

He offers the Grace
To baptize our whole race,
The water to cleanse
Our original filth, and our actual offense.

2. In all places and times
He blots out our crimes,
His Spirit bestows;
And with water of life the believer overflows:

> The Earnest we feel,
> The Witness and Seal,
> The joy He imparts
> And the love shed abroad in our purified hearts.[68]

In his lyrical commentary on Matthew 3:11, "He shall baptize you with the Holy Spirit and with fire," Charles penned these words, highlighting the baptism with the Spirit fills one's soul with love:

> 1. Pure, baptismal Fire Divine,
>   All thy heavenly powers exert,
> In my deepest darkness shine,
>   Spread thy warmth throughout my heart;
> Come, Seraphic Spirit, come,
>   Comforter thro' Jesus given,
> All my earthly dross consume,
>   Fill my soul with love from heaven.
>
> 2. Love in me intensely burn,
>   Love mine inmost essence seize,
> All into thy nature turn,
>   All into thy holiness;
> Spark of thy celestial flame,
>   Then my soul shall upward move,
> Trembling on with steady aim
>   Seek, and join its Source above.[69]

So numerous are Charles Wesley's hymns on the baptism with the Spirit that anyone of them could have been sung at the Annual Conference, especially when the preaching theme was normally on Christian perfection.

In the final months of his life, John Wesley continued to be active in his ministry, including editing and publishing *The Arminian Magazine*. He included two personal notations in the 1791 January issue, showing that he continued to edit and oversee its publication. This is the last issue where we have his direct input showing his involvement prior to his death on March 2, 1791.

In this issue, John Wesley included a letter written by John Fletcher to a person seeking his spiritual counsel. Fletcher observed: "You got out of Egypt with gladness, and now you seem entangled in the wilderness!" He advised her to "hold fast what you have, and to be thankful for it till the Lord come with more: till he baptizes you with the Holy Spirit and with fire" and "till the Lord comes to his temple, to make his abode there."[70]

This showed that one of John Wesley's final pastoral acts before his death was to inspire his readers of *The Arminian Magazine* not to remain contented with justification or deliverance from the bondage of Egypt, but to expect the "baptism with the Spirit" or the abiding witness of the Spirit in sanctifying grace and to enter the Canaan of perfect love.

It was only fitting that John Wesley should have published this letter from John Fletcher when two months later his widow, Mary (Bosanquet) Fletcher, would be attending his funeral. She had been like a daughter to him. She had preached (or "exhorted") with him at designated points in the open air after her husband's death in 1785. In one of her sermons (as already noted), she mentioned his expectation that there would be a Grand Pentecost when righteousness would cover the earth as waters cover the sea, but she exhorted her hearers now to enter "the Canaan" of perfect love through "the baptism with the Holy Spirit" if "we would see this millennium."

By publishing this letter of his once "designated successor" who was encouraging a believer to get out of the "wilderness" and move into the Canaan of perfect love, John Wesley was encouraging the need for preaching on being "baptized with the Holy Spirit" as the means of attaining Christian perfection.

This shows that John Wesley and John Fletcher were in agreement on being "filled and baptized with the Spirit" as Fletcher had noted in 1776 (see page 172 above).

The many sermons of John Wesley on being "baptized with the Spirit" in the final years of his evangelistic ministry as shown in this chapter corresponded exactly with Fletcher's interpretation, as this letter demonstrated.

Notes

1. Hurst, *History of Methodism*, 3:1260.
2. Telford, *Letters* 8:249, To Adam Clarke, (November 26, 1790).
3. Maldywn L. Edwards, *Adam Clarke* (London: The Epworth Press, 1942), 34.
4. Ibid., 45.
5. *Life of Adam Clarke* (autobiography), 1:103.
6. Moore, *Life of Mary Fletcher*, 145-147; Thomas Coke and Henry Moore, *The Life of the Rev. John Wesley* (London: Paramore, 1792), 4ff.
7. *The Wesleyan Methodist Magazine* 8 (August 1829): 528.
8. *Life of Adam Clarke* (autobiography), 1:110.
9. *Journal and Diaries VI (1776–1786)*, 23:457.
10. *Life of Adam Clarke* (autobiography), 1:110.
11. *Journal and Diaries VI (1776–1786)*, 23:457.
12. *Journal and Diaries VI (1776–1786)*, 23:456.
13. *Journal and Diaries VI (1776–1786)*, 23:456.
14. *Journal and Diaries VI (1776–1786)*, 23:461.
15. Ibid., 171. In his autobiography, Clarke said for "most of these sermons" that Wesley preached during October 1783 he had "preserved either the *skeletons*, or the leading thoughts." *The Life of Adam Clarke* (autobiography), 1:110. I have been unable to locate this information among Adam Clarke's archival collections at Duke University Library or the John Rylands University Library.
16. *Journal and Diaries VI (1776–1786)*, 23:466.
17. *Journal and Diaries VI (1776–1786)*, 23:461.
18. Outler, *Sermons* 4:525, "Appendix C" by Richard Heitzenrater.
19. Adam Clarke, *Commentary* (New York: Abingdon-Cokesbury Press, n.d.), 5:683.
20. *The Doctrine of the New Birth*, 46-47.
21. Thomas Coke, *Funeral Sermon, Preached in Spitafields-Chapel, London, on Sunday, Oct. 26, 1794 on the Death of Mrs. Hester Ann Rogers* (Birmingham: J. Belcher, 1975), 18. Cf. *The Life and Correspondence of Mrs. Hester Ann Rogers*, 300; Coke, *A Commentary on the New Testament* (London: G. Whitfield, 1803), 2:942-957. Letter to Thomas Morrell (July 6, 1789).109; Letter to William Holmes (October 12, 1790), 126.
22. *Minutes of the Methodist Conferences* (London: Mason, 1862), 1:167, (conference met at Bristol, Tuesday, July 29, 1783).
23. Copied from the original letter in the Wesleyan Mission House collection, Bishopsgate Street, London, by Luke Tyerman, *Wesley's Designated Successor*, 331.
24. Cited by John Vickers, *Thomas Coke, Apostle of Methodism* (London: Epworth Press, 1965), 23. Cf. Warren A. Candler, *Life of Thomas Coke* (Nashville: Publishing House M.E. Church, South, 1923), 11.

25. Vickers, *Thomas Coke, The Apostle of Methodism*, 23.

26. Thomas Coke, *A Series of Letters Addressed to the Methodist Connection* (London: A. Paris, Printer, 1810), 97, 190. Cf. He quoted approvingly of Fletcher's use of the "baptism with the Spirit. Cf. 108, 148-151.

27. Etheridge, *The Life of the Rev. Adam Clarke*, 84.

28. In a letter written for "junior preachers" Clarke recommended as part of their "plan of study" to read Fletcher's works because they show "that is it the privilege of every believing soul to be cleansed from all sin in this life." Clarke, *Detached Pieces*, 191.

29. Adam Clarke, *Christian Theology* (Salem, OH: Schmul Publishers, 1967) 33.

30. Adam Clarke and J. B. B. Clarke, *An Account of the Religious and Literary Life of Adam Clarke* (New York: T. Mason and G. Lane, 1837), 1:200.

31. Ibid., 200-201. Cf. Clarke, *Detached Pieces* 3:404, 410, for his appreciation for Fletcher's writings.

32. Adam Clarke, *Commentary on the Book of Acts*, 5:683.

33. Ibid., 683.

34. Ibid., 628. Cf. Adam Clarke, *Entire Sanctification* (Baltimore: Armstrong and Berry, 1838), 140.

35. *Commentary on the Book of Acts*, 5:625.

36. Ibid., 53, 531.

37. *Life of Adam Clarke* (autobiography), 1:162-163.

38. Clarke, *Commentary on the Book of Acts* 5:723.

39. J. W. Etheridge, *The Life of the Rev. Adam Clarke* (New York: Carlton & Porter, 1859), 130.

40. Adam Clarke, *Christian Theology*, 206.

41. *Journal and Diaries VI (1776–1786)*, 23:54.

42. *The Wesleyan Methodist Magazine* 8 (August 1829): 528.

43. Benson, "Thoughts on Perfection," *The Arminian Magazine* 4 (January, 1778):553.

44. "Letter from Mr. J. W. Salmon to John Wesley," *The Arminian Magazine* Volume XIII (May 1790): 272-273.

45. Gareth Lloyd, *Charles Wesley and the Struggle for Methodist Identity*, 235.

46. *Journal and Diaries VI (1776–1786)*, 23:270, 451.

47. *Journal and Diaries VI (1776–1786)*, 23:314, 488.

48. *Journal and Diaries VI (1776–1786)*, 23:491.

49. Wesley' special edition of *Essay on Truth*, 174–175.

59. *Journal and Diaries VI (1776–1786)*, 23:523.

51. John Wesley, *A Short Account of the Life of John Fletcher*, 187.

52. C. H. Crookshank, *History of Methodism in Ireland* (London: T. Woolmer, 1886), 2:27.

53. Crookshank, 2:41.

54. Crookshank, 2:252.

55. Adam Clarke, *Entire Sanctification*, 112.

56. Ibid., 111.

57. *Journal and Diaries VI (1776–1786)*, 23:556.

58. *Journal and Diaries VI (1776–1786)*, 23:562.

59. *Journal and Diaries VI (1776–1786)*, 23:562.

60. Wesley, *Explanatory Notes upon the New Testament*, 329.

61. MS Acts, MARC: MA 1977/555 (Charles Wesley Notebooks Box 1), 379.

62. Fletcher, *The New Birth*, 54.

63. *Journal and Diaries VII (1787–1791)*, 24:210.

64. *Journal and Diaries VII (1787–1791)*, 24:30.

65. *Journal and Diaries VII (1787–1791)*, 24:82.

66. *Journal and Diaries VII (1787–1791)*, 24:82.

67. Crookshank, 2:446.

68. MS Acts, MARC: MA 1977/555 (Charles Wesley Notebooks Box 1), 3-4.

69. MS MA, MARC:1977/577 (Charles Wesley Notebooks Box 3).

70. "A Letter from the Rev. Mr. Fletcher to C.B." *The Arminian Magazine* 14 (London, January 1791): 48-49.

Chapter 16

John Wesley's Inner Circle and Other Prominent Leaders

"I long for the Spirit's fullest Baptism, and so see and feel all the promises of God yea and amen that my soul rejoices in hope of that glory which shall be revealed to the believing heart"
—Elizabeth Ritchie to John Wesley

"I know a much deeper baptism of the Holy Spirit is my Lord's will concerning me . . . [for] perfect love."
—Elizabeth Ritchie to Mary Fletcher

I have been led to pray in faith for a universal and pentecostal outpouring of His divine fullness; and it surely will descend."
—Hester Ann Rogers to John Wesley

". . . that great outpouring of the Spirit" producing "pure love" of "many of our brethren and sisters in London."
—John Wesley to Hester Ann Rogers

"I explained and applied, 'They were all filled with the Holy Spirit'."
—John Wesley

John Wesley's closest associates would be expected to embrace and represent his theology as their spiritual father. If they used Pentecost expressions for sanctification, it is because they perceived these expressions to reflect his interpretation.

The historiography shows John Fletcher derived his use of these Pentecost expressions from the writings of John and Charles Wesley. If John Wesley's inner circle of friends and adherents used the expression, baptism with the Holy Spirit, it was because they perceived this language to be the way that John Wesley used it as well. If they were inspired in particular by Fletcher's preferred use of it, it is because they considered him to be John Wesley's official interpreter.

In *A Series of Letters Addressed to the Methodist Connection* (1810), Thomas Coke engaged in an extended discussion of Fletcher's theology, endorsing it and arguing that it "coincides" with John Wesley's view.[1]

Coke particularly noted that Fletcher's *Checks* were "acknowledged and disseminated by John Wesley" and officially "recognized by the [British] Methodist Conference."[2]

Francis Asbury and Thomas Coke placed the writings of Fletcher alongside John Wesley's in the original book of disciple for American Methodism as the authoritative source of Methodist doctrine.[3]

The following discussion contains a sampling of the historiography of early Methodism, and it will show that the basis of sanctification in Pentecost was embraced in early Methodism. What this historiography reveals is that John Wesley's closest friends and leaders understood him to affirm that full sanctification entails being filled and baptized with the Spirit.

Joseph Benson

It is fitting to start with Joseph Benson who had written a defense of John Wesley's idea of sanctification in an essay entitled, "The Baptism with the Holy Spirit," when he and Fletcher were together at Trevecca College in 1770.

Richard Treffry, one of John Wesley's preachers, described Benson's Trevecca essay in this way: "He had previously published a pamphlet on the baptism of the Holy Spirit, in which he declared his belief in the infinite efficiency of the eternal Spirit to eradicate the principle of innate depravity, and cleanse the soul from the last remains of sin in this life."[4]

Benson never altered his idea of Pentecost and sanctification even after John Wesley reminded him that justified persons also have "received the Spirit." That is because he and Fletcher believed the phrase "receiving the Spirit" was used interchangeable with being "filled with the Spirit" and they both also allowed the Spirit was given to the justified person in some measure.

We know Benson never did change his mind because he said so. Benson observed on December 4, 1777: "About six years ago, when at Oxford [at the same time with Fletcher at Trevecca], my convictions, desires, were the same that they are now; and then, as now, I longed for the baptism of the Holy Spirit."[5] These comments are contained in *The Memoirs of Joseph Benson* by James MacDonald, who became Benson's assistant editor of *The Arminian Magazine*.[6] He reported many instances in the *Memoirs of Joseph Benson* where Benson continued his use of the expression, the baptism with the Spirit, as equivalent to Christian perfection.[7]

In a letter May 21, 1776 to Walter Churchey, Benson worried that John Wesley and John Fletcher were being too occupied with political matters regarding the struggle between the American colonies and Britain, spending their time writing in defense of King George "which detain them from more valuable and important work." Benson said: "But, the principal thing to be thought, talked, and wrote about, is the *baptism of the Spirit*, or the *inward kingdom of God*. Oh! my friend, this is but little known among us! May we seek it with our whole hearts and recommend it to the complaining or Laodicean church everywhere."[8]

On January 1, 1776, Benson read Fletcher's recent work on Christian perfection and he found the book to be very encouraging to him.[9] Benson remained in closed contact with Fletcher until his death.

In September 1776, Fletcher told Benson he was finishing "my Essay on the Dispensation of the Spirit, which is the thing I want most to see your thoughts upon."[10] Fletcher gave this essay the title, "An Essay on the Doctrine of the New Birth." This essay included a section entitled, "The Language of the Father's Dispensation."[11] This essay is in his own handwriting and was written in early 1776.[12]

On December 4, 1777, Fletcher took a tour to his homeland in Switzerland for several years.[13] While he was gone, this essay on the new birth was circulated among some of his friends especially Mary Bosanquet, Joseph Benson, and Thomas Coke.[14]

In a critique of this essay in a letter (1778) to Mary Bosanquet who was Fletcher's future wife,[15] Benson said that he and everyone among them fully endorsed the expression of "the baptism—the gift—the fullness—the indwelling—of the Spirit" for Christian perfection that had been used in this essay.

> The object Mr. Fletcher has in view throughout the whole piece is the baptism – the gift – the fullness – the indwelling – of the Spirit – to set up and establish the kingdom of God in our hearts righteousness, peace and joy in the Holy Spirit, and this to render us Christians indeed professing the privileges of our glorious dispensation. Now who of us will speak a word against this? Who of us will not, rather as we have ability and opportunity bear our testimony to it? About this there can be no disputation."[16]

However, Benson worried that Fletcher had elevated the status of those who were in a pre-Christian state of the Gentile dispensation and those who had fallen back into such a condition. Fletcher had expressed this view in the section of the manuscript, entitled, "The Language of the Father's Dispensation," referring to them as "children of God" who have "comfort" according "to their dispensation.[17]

Benson said to Mary Bosanquet:

> I am afraid if these papers are published in their present form, they will not only have a tendency to puzzle or perplex the minds of those who have been ~~taught~~ accustomed to hear (from the pulpit or the press) a different kind of language, but also to produce worse effects!! I fear what he says of the dispensation of the Father and of being accepted according to that dispensation if we only fear God and work righteousness will have a tendency to make many rest without faith working by love which only availeth in Christ.

Benson further worried that Fletcher's energy of expression concerning "those miraculous gifts bestowed so plentifully on the day of Pentecost will tend to raise the expectation of earnest faithful souls too high and of consequence when after long striving their expectations are not answered will strip them of all their confidence, plunge them into doubt or despondency if not into infidelity or sin."

Benson said this observation grew out of his own experience when he was with Fletcher at Trevecca. He said because of his disappointed expectations, "I was even tempted to doubt the being of a God," though he said he was soon delivered from this temptation.

He acknowledged: "When first I was exceeding eager and diligent in the pursuit of these things, I watched. I prayed. I fasted. I strove. I wrestled, I did comparatively nothing else for a near a year . . . , thinking I was not born of God, had not received the Holy Spirit [i.e., Christian perfection]."

He said for four or five years later he was "often comforted but often distressed, often delivered, but often also enthralled." After "about 3 years ago I was brought more into the way of faith . . . and the Lord established me" with "a peace that passeth all understanding and a love that casteth our fear." With his abiding confidence he said "I look indeed to be *more* filled with faith and the holy Spirit, to be filled even with all the fullness of God," He said he was now no longer "anxious" about have "received the Spirit" and "born again" which he equated with the "precious promises" that "Christ Jesus will sanctify me wholly."

Benson then asked Mary Bosanquet to send his lengthy letter to Fletcher along with the manuscript and requested that when Fletcher returned from Switzerland he would like to have an opportunity to discuss the manuscript with him about his concerns.[18]

Mary Bosanquet followed up with Benson's worries in her own written correspondence with Fletcher. Fletcher responded on August 30, 1778 to her letter: "I had thought of what you name, respecting a *less plan* of the doctrine of the New Birth . . . I shall be glad of an opportunity of consulting with you about that sketch."[19]

In 1781, Mary Bosanquet told Benson that Fletcher had returned to England. Benson immediately wrote Fletcher. He began his letter expressing his respect for Fletcher: "No difference of place can ever erase your memory from my mind . . . while I breathe to respect you above all men upon earth." He showed that he continued to be inspired by Fletcher's example of seeking the baptism with the Spirit: "Heavenly love baptize me with thy sacred fire . . . till . . . the spark should return to its great original!"

He reminded Fletcher that when they were at Trevecca together, he completely agreed with his emphasis on "the *promise of the Father,* the great gospel blessing, the baptism of the Holy Spirit." He then noted that "if I have anything to blame in my *then* views of things . . . is first that I formed too *gross* an idea of the gift of the Holy Spirit and expected something too marvelous and extraordinary."

He told Fletcher that a second correction was he did not appreciate at that time the act of simple faith in receiving this "unbounded love of God in Christ Jesus" and "fullness of the Spirit." He now reported to Fletcher that he was "established in the belief of this great truth . . . and I bear my testimony to it from day to day."

Here is my entire transcription of this lengthy letter, June 12, 1781, contained in the Manchester Archives Research Center of John Rylands University Library:

Reverend and Dear Sir,

It gave me great pleasure to hear of your safe arrival in England, after so long an absence, and that your health was considerably better than when you went abroad; and more especially as I understand from Miss. Bosanquet that you have some thoughts of visiting Yorkshire, where (I am in June) thousands will be glad to see you and none more so than myself, who once had the honour of being your intimate friend, and whose one motive for troubling you at this time is a desire to renew that friendship, formerly so beneficial to my soul. Mr. Fletcher, no length of time, no difference of place can ever erase your memory from my mind, nor should it, while I breathe to respect you above all the men upon earth, and that for one only reason, because the Lord Jesus Christ has in a great measure drawn his likeness upon you. I love truth and love, piety, and virtue wherever I see them, and where I discern these divine qualities exhibited in the most lively characters; there my esteem rises the highest and my affection glows with the greatest warmth. And oh! if the faint picture of goodness, the distant resemblance of beauty touches my heart and inflames my soul; should not the original good, the grand archetype of perfection and source of blessedness, inspire me with a love stronger than death and kindle a fire which should consume me in its flames and melt me down into the same ever living, ever-working element! Oh! Heavenly love, baptize me with thy sacred fire, and let it burn night and day upon the altar of my heart, till night and day with me should cease and the spark should return to its great original! Dear Sir, pray for me!

Being at Cross-Hall a week ago I had the happiness of hearing Miss Bosanquet read a letter from you, which I found exceeding edifying and which brought former times fresh to my remembrance, wherein we took sweet counsel together and spent comfortable hours upon our knees, in supplications and prayer for the promise of the Father, the great gospel blessing, the baptism of the Holy Spirit. If I have anything to blame in my then views of things and manner of proceeding more particularly than another it is first that I formed too gross an idea of the gift of the Holy Spirit and expected something too marvelous and extraordinary and second that I did not do sufficient honour to faith nor cast myself with a proper confidence on the unbounded love of God in Christ Jesus. I did not simply believe in Christ that I might be justified by the faith of Christ, nor of consequence had I a settled conviction that I was justified from all things. Though I cannot look back with complacency upon the more than three years I have spent since I parted with you in the stable belonging to the preacher's house in Bristol, being conscious of much infirmity and sin, yet have I cause to praise the Lord he has taught me many blessed lessons during this time, and has indeed in many respects done great for me. In particular I have learned both to live and to preach the way of faith perfectly, and find in proportion as I do this the Lord blesses me of a truth. As I find no doctrine so blessed to my own soul as "salvation by grace through faith," so I find none so constantly owned of God. This I am persuaded is never preached in vain. It is so agreeable to the justice and love of God, does such honour to the death and mediation of Christ and is so suited to the guilt and weakness of fallen men that it never fails to be followed with a particular blessing: and in particular the blessing of blessings—the fullness of the Spirit (as well as the first fruits thereof) is promised to this alone in John 7.37 and I am persuaded when we exhort persuade people to live by faith in the Son of God, to look to him, to trust _____ [torn page], to hang upon him, to cleave to him, we _____ [torn page] the most effective way to help them to the _____ [page smeared] enjoyment of this indwelling source of truth and love[,] holiness and comfort. I bless God I am established in the belief of this great truth that since the glorification of Christ we are called to be a habitation of God through the Spirit. And I bear my testimony to it from day to day: but I find it answers no end if I do not also say "If any man thirst let him come unto Christ and drink. . . ." But let me recollect to whom I am writing: Oh! what should I give for 2 hours conversation with you! I entreat you come this way. At Miss Bosanquet desire two years ago, I wrote some remarks on your treatise on the New Birth. I designed them for your inspection and with you could see them. But I have many things to say before you, and things of very great importance.

If you have thought it worth your while to enquire about such an insignificant creature, you have perhaps heard that I have I changed my condition since I saw you. I never undertook anything in which I had so much cause to adore the leadings of providence and adore the condescending love of God. He has given me a partner every way suitable, and has blessed our union with a love, and since we came together has given us numerous proofs of his care.

But will you favour me with a line? Shall I have the honour of receiving a free and faithful letter from you? Do note though I am conscious, my not improving duly your advice and intimacy in time past, might justly deprive me of that help for the future—

I am, with much respect, Your servant in Christ,
Joseph Benson[20]

The essay on the new birth was never finished probably because of his busy life style after getting married to Mary Bosanquet and his health issues and early death. This unfinished essay was first published in 1998 in the *Asbury Theological Journal*.[21]

In a letter to Sarah Thompson on August 11, 1779, Benson continued to press the importance of the baptism with the Spirit with his future wife:

> Permit me to advise and entreat you not to rest satisfied in your present state: you are undoubtedly called to enjoy greater and better things even to live and walk in the Spirit, experiencing his witness and bringing forth his fruits day by day. Now be you fully persuaded of this: settle in your very heart, that you are called to be an habitation of God thro' the Spirit; and be satisfied also God alone can put you in possession of this blessing.... Be instant in prayer for this one thing that he would lift up the light of his countenance upon you and *baptize you with the Spirit* [italics mine] of his grace.[22]

In 1781 (as noted previously), John Wesley published an essay in *The Arminian Magazine* by Benson on "Thoughts on Perfection," in which Benson noted that "God *may*, and that he often *does*, *instantaneously* so baptize a soul with the Holy Spirit, and with fire, as to purify it from all dross, and refine it like gold, so that it is *renewed in love*, in *pure* and *perfect love*, as it never was before."[23]

One year later in 1782 after John Wesley published this essay, Benson published *Two Sermons on Sanctification*, where he connected the fullness of the Spirit with perfection. Benson writes: "So that, in order to our, *full*, *perfect*, and *entire* sanctification, we must *be filled with the Spirit*."[24] He invited his hearers to receive "the fullness of that Spirit which is the one source of our sanctification.... The Spirit of truth, holiness, and comfort will take up his abode in us, and enlighten, sanctify, and save us."[25]

This emphasis on Pentecost and sanctification is evidenced throughout Benson's "Two Sermons on Sanctification." These two sermons were written with John Wesley's approval.[26]

On October 4, 1782, when Joseph Benson was spending time in prayer, He wrote in his journal: "O how I longed to live to his glory, and to be filled with his Spirit!"[27]

Benson used "receive the Holy Spirit" for entire sanctification is his commentary on Acts 19:2, where Benson explained the question, "Have ye received the Holy Spirit since ye believed?" to mean whether or not they had received "the sanctifying graces of the Holy Spirit." Benson then observes: "Many are deceived in this matter, and think they have received the Holy Spirit, when really they have not.... We should therefore strictly examine ourselves on this subject; and inquire whether *we* have received the Holy Spirit since *we* believed?"[28]

This connection of "receiving the Spirit" with Christian perfection would be consistent with Fletcher who believed that the normal use of this expression in the New Testament was interchangeable with being "filled with the Spirit." So "receiving the Spirit" means receiving the fullness of the Spirit, while at the same time allowing that the Spirit regenerates the justified person.

In 1787, Benson preached a sermon entitled "The Nature and Design of the Gospel of Christ."[29] He showed that the gospel of Christ "offers us a free, full, and universal pardon, but "this leads me to speak of another principal blessing . . . the ministration of the Spirit [i.e., "dispensation of the Spirit"]." He explained: "Christ offers *to baptize us with the Holy Spirit and with fire, to live in us that we may live also, to quicken us and raise up and make us fit together with himself in heavenly places.*" This means "such abundance of spiritual life that we possess that it shall overflow." This means "the Holy Spirit has stripped sin of its disguise. . . . Holiness is now unmasked and blooming in all its beauty, kindles in our hearts the most fervent love to, and inflames our souls with the warmest desires after, an object so incomparably excellent and worthy of our highest regard. . . . Considering his *great and precious promises*, which are all given to us, that we *may be made partakers of the divine nature*, we rejoice in hope of possessing to our entire and endless satisfaction this holiness so amiable in our eyes." This "ministration of the Spirit" is "our entire sanctification."[30]

Benson also showed that the "extraordinary gifts" of the Holy Spirit were given to some but the permanent benefit of the descent of the Spirit on the day of Pentecost is sanctifying grace.[31] In his commentary on Acts 11:24, he defined being "full of the Holy Spirit and faith" meant to be "largely endowed with the sanctifying graces" of the Spirit.[32] Likewise with Paul when he was "filled with the Spirit" in Acts 9:17.[33]

His intimate friendship with Fletcher served as the basis for his being asked by Mary Fletcher and the British Conference in 1801 to write a larger account of the life of John Fletcher than had been given by John Wesley in 1786,[34] which was reprinted seventeen times in America.

In 1804 in an appendix, he vigorously defended Fletcher's idea of the "fullness of the Spirit" and the connection between Pentecost and sanctification, saying that Fletcher "expected a Pentecost" that entailed the idea of being "sanctified wholly."[35] This biography showed that Benson never wavered in his loyalty and respect for Fletcher.

Benson was not just reporting on past history when he described Fletcher and their relationship together, showing that he continued to advocate for Fletcher's theology. He said: "The reader will pardon me, if he thinks I exceed. My heart kindles while I write." Benson thus described Fletcher: "He was revered; he was loved; he was almost adored. . . . Here I saw a descendent of fallen Adam, so fully raised above the ruins of the fall, that though by the body he was tied down to earth, yet was his whole *conversation in heaven:* yet was his *life*, from day to day, *hid with Christ in God.* Prayer, praise, love, and zeal, all ardent, elevated above what one would think attainable in this state of frailty, were the element in which he continually lived. . . . His full heart would not suffer him to be silent. He *must* speak" and the students were soon "all in tears, and every heart catched fire from the flame that burned in his soul." Benson reported that his addresses at the college would be "generally terminated in this. Being convinced that to the *filled with the Holy Spirit* was a better qualification for the ministry of the Gospel than any classical learning . . ., he used to frequently say, 'As many of you as are athirst for this fullness of the Spirit, follow me into my room.' On this, many of us have instantly followed him."[36] Reflecting his current state of mind in 1802, Benson said: "I was then much athirst" for "the baptism of the Holy Spirit."[37]

When Benson was the editor of *The Arminian Magazine* (1803-1821), he published a sermon in 1817 by a well-known Jesuit preacher (Louis Bourdaloue, 1632-1704), "Sermon for the Feast of Pentecost." His text, "They were all filled with the Holy Spirit—Acts ii.4."[38]

Remarkably, this sermon corresponded with Fletcher's and Benson's idea about the connection between Pentecost and holiness. This text was a basis for the Roman Catholic rite of confirmation, which symbolized the idea of a personal Pentecost subsequent to one's water baptism.

The appropriateness of this sermon in *The Arminian Magazine* was that Fletcher had already shown the close connection between John Wesley's doctrine of Christian perfection and the rite of confirmation.[39]

Significantly, this Roman Catholic preacher, Bourdaloue, said nothing about the ritual of confirmation, but his emphasis was upon "the interior baptism of the Holy Spirit"[41] and "how to enter into the full meaning of . . . the baptism of the Holy Spirit."[42] Citing from the Early Church Father Chrysostom, he showed that "as fire has a power infinitely more active, more penetrating, and more purifying than water; so by the coming of the Holy Spirit, the hearts of men were to be purified in a manner much more perfect than they had been by the first baptism of Jesus Christ." He further wrote:

> After the baptism of Jesus Christ, the apostles, though initiated into the faith by that ordinance, still remained very imperfect. According to the report, the gospel makes of them, they were still ambitious, interested, jealous; dissensions were still seen among them, and they fell into weaknesses, from which the elementary baptism of the Son of God, had not preserved them. But scarcely have they received the Holy Spirit, than they become men wholly spiritual, men detached from the world, men superior to every selfish interest; men not only holy, but of a consummate holiness; men empty of themselves, and full of God in one word, men perfect and irreprehensible."[43]

Bourdaloue said this baptism of the Spirit is not for those who "are carnal."[44] but rather it is through "the Holy Spirit our hearts are filled with love."[45] In conclusion, he prayed: "Grant, Lord, the same precious gift to my dear auditors. Give thy benediction to my word, or rather, to thy word. Pour out upon all this assembly the plenitude of thy Spirit. And thou, O Spirit of my God, principle of every grace, author of all holiness, come and enlighten and fortify us, and seal thy believing family unto the day of eternal redemption."[46]

Benson's decision to publish this Jesuit sermon was apparently intended to show the broad ecumenical basis of the Methodist belief in Pentecost and sanctification.

In a collection of his sermons (1827-1828), Benson maintained that Pentecost is the basis of Christian perfection. Benson said that the gospel "perfects our sanctification . . . and the Holy Spirit, promised in all his fullness, imparting this great blessing, that is, a purgation from sin," and "not resting till we [are] 'an habitation of God through the Spirit;' and till we 'dwell in God, and God in us.'"[47] Benson's emphasis is: "Perfect holiness is the effect of the fullness of the Spirit."[48] Being "full of faith and the Holy Spirit" means to be "perfected in holiness" and "wholly sanctified."[49]

Another remarkable achievement of Benson was to edit and publish John Fletcher's complete works in 1806. In the "preface" to this edition, Benson shows the same kind of respect for Fletcher that he had when they were together at Trevecca. In an astonishing way, Benson placed Fletcher's writings only in second place of importance to the Bible ahead of John Wesley: "No writings that we have known, save those of the Divine Oracles, appear to us more adapted to answer the great ends of Christianity, vis. To bring lost sinners to God, and build them up in faith and holiness."[50] Benson said the General Conference "ordered the present Edition to be prepared for the press, and offered to the public as soon as convenient."[51]

Benson wrote a commentary on the various books of the Bible between 1811 and 1818. In his New Testament commentary on Acts 2, Benson explained that "the incorporation of the Christian Church"[52] occurred on the day of Pentecost when the one hundred twenty believers in the Upper Room were "united in their desire and expectation of the baptism of the Holy Spirit, *the power from on high,* which Christ had promised them; and in praying earnestly and importunately for it whenever they met together."[53] When they were filled with the Holy Spirit, "this whole company [of one hundred and twenty believers] were abundantly replenished with both the gifts and graces of the Holy Spirit. . . . They were filled with the *graces* of the Spirit, and were more than ever under its sanctifying influences; were now holy, and heavenly, and spiritual; more weaned from this world, and better acquainted with the other. They were more filled with the comforts of the Spirit, rejoiced more than ever in the love of Christ, and the hope of heaven, and in it all their griefs and fears were swallowed up."[54]

He defined baptism with water as a symbol of "repentance" and being "justified,"[55] but the baptism with the Spirit denoted sanctifying grace, as a universal benefit of Pentecost, although some (though not everyone) also received "extraordinary gifts of the Spirit" for preaching and spreading the gospel.[56]

Jabez Bunting (president of the British Methodist Conference) said that Benson's "opinions were the same, on all great doctrinal questions, with those which are well known as characterizing the living ministry and printed works of Mr. Wesley and Mr. Fletcher."[57] The use of "Mr. Wesley and I" are often found in *The Checks* and reflected John Wesley's approval.[58] Likewise throughout the history of early Methodism, references to "Mr. Wesley and Mr. Fletcher" are frequent without the slightest suggestion that Fletcher's view of Pentecost and sanctification was incompatible with John Wesley.

Darcy, Lady Maxwell

Lady Maxwell belonged to the nobility of Scotland and was known for her philanthropy, contributing regularly from her wealth to help poor children and widows, and those who were sick. She was born around 1742. She became closely acquainted with John Wesley whom she first heard preach on June 16, 1764 in Edinburgh. Thereafter they corresponded and she joined the Methodist society and became devoted to the cause of Methodism.[59] In 1770 she established a school for the poor in Edinburgh.[60] John Wesley mentioned his visits to her home in his journal for April 31, 1781, noting she engaged him in her ministry to the poor while he was there.

John Wesley wrote a letter to Lady Maxwell on February 8, 1772, recommending that she read John Fletcher. This letter showed his unqualified approval of Fletcher's role as his authorized interpreter of Methodist doctrine.

He mentioned to Lady Maxwell his deep appreciation for Fletcher's lifting the burden from his own shoulder of having to defend himself. In this respect, Wesley observed how easy it is to "lose our love in that rough field (controversy), than to find truth. This consideration has made me exceedingly thankful to God for giving me respite from polemical labours."

He further noted how deeply thankful he was that Fletcher had "both the power and will to answer them that trouble me; so that I may not always be forced to hold my weapons in one hand, while I am building with the other. I rejoice, likewise, not only in the abilities, but in the temper, of Mr. Fletcher. He writes as he lives: I cannot say that I know such another Clergyman in England or Ireland. He is all fire, but it is the fire of love."[61]

Lady Maxwell was friends with Elizabeth Ritchie and Mary (Bosanquet) Fletcher. She also became a close friend of Joseph Benson, often corresponding with him.[62]

In a letter to Joseph Benson in 1774, after he had recently been assigned to Edinburgh where she lived, she expressed a prayer for them: "He who dwells on high would baptize us all afresh with the Holy Spirit, as with fire!" She also used the imagery from Charles Wesley's widely known hymn on "The Wrestling Jacob" to speak of waiting in prayer for its attainment:

> O how little do the greater number of us know of this divine temper! or of conformity to our living Head in general! What mere dwarfs are we in the ways of God, swimming upon the surface of religion, when it is our privilege to sink into all the depths of humble love, and rise into all the life of God, all the heights of Christian confidence! O that He who dwells on high would baptize us all afresh with the Holy Spirit, as with fire! Then surely we should arise and shake ourselves from the dust, and give no rest to our eyes, nor slumber to our eyelids, till possessed of every blessing Christ has purchased for us. Let us, Jacob-like, wrestle with the Lord in faithful prayer, and we shall soon enjoy all the sweets of entire devotion, as far as humanity will permit."[63]

Her memoirs reveal how deeply committed she was to John Wesley's teaching on sanctification, connecting it with being filled with the Holy Spirit. Her pursuit in life was for sanctification: "My God still continues to teach me the useful lesson of living by faith, particularly as to sanctification; but it is a difficult lesson. In all I come short. Help me, holy Father, to press on with renewed vigour; increase my faith; fill, yea, fill with faith and with the Holy Spirit."[64]

Elizabeth Ritchie

We mentioned her earlier, but it is also important to include Elizabeth Ritchie in this current discussion. As noticed already, John Wesley and Elizabeth Ritchie became each other's best friend.

Her *Memoirs* show that Wesley was active right up to the end of his life, attending to the business of the conference and preaching. She was with him in his dying moments, and he specifically requested her to pray for him as he was dying.[65] She expressed her affection for her spiritual father after his death in these words: "I loved him with a grateful and affectionate regard, as given by God to be my guide, my spiritual father, and my dearest friend; and was truly thankful to be assured that those attentions were made comforts to him [in his dying moments]."[66]

The purpose of pointing out the friendship between them is to show that as her mentor with a father-like friendship, her views were deeply shaped by his views. To indicate the depth of feeling that Elizabeth Ritchie and John Wesley shared together, here is one of multiple letters showing their feelings as friends for each other. She wrote to John Wesley on September 4, 1777: "My Lord united my heart unto you. I should be ungrateful to the highest degree if I did not love you as well or better than ever, never will the truly spiritual union that I feel with you lessen except I should live less near to God."[67]

This letter referred to her close friendship with Mary Bosanquet. She also referred to John Fletcher in this letter: "Pray tell me in your next [letter] how Mr. Fletcher does. I hope God will spare him and you yet many years, and at last give us all to meet on Sion's peaceful shore."[68]

She on occasions went with him in his chaise to his preaching and visitation locations. When she was only twenty five years old, he made her a leader of a Methodist class in November, 1775.[69] She often read to him.[70] She remained single for as long as he lived devoting herself to his ministry.

Her network of intimate friends showed that the idea of the baptism with the Spirit was a common expression among John Wesley's inner circle. If John Wesley disagreed with her views about the baptism with the Spirit, it is certain she would not have used this expression for Christian perfection, especially in his correspondence with him. She likely heard this expression first from him. The following samples from her writings show her use of this expression.

John Wesley was the first person to tell her to read John Fletcher's idea of the various dispensations in salvation history, culminating in Christian perfection through the baptism with the Spirit. He described Fletcher's explanation as "wonderful" and being the best explanation ever given since the days of the apostles. He advised her in this letter of January 17, 1775 to restrict her reading to books like Fletcher's so her "understanding would be opened and strengthened."

Elizabeth Ritchie was closely connected in ministry with a number of John Wesley's inner circle, including Mary Bosanquet, Hester Ann Rogers (Roe), and Joseph Benson—all of whom often used this Pentecost expression. Here is what her friend and biographer said: "Mr. Fletcher she regarded with peculiar veneration, and ever cherished an unabated and affectionate esteem for his inestimable wife."[71]

On January 28, 1780, Elizabeth Ritchie attended the wedding of Joseph Benson and Miss Thompson.[72] She also attending the wedding of John and Mary Fletcher on November 12, 1781.[73] Hester Ann Roger recorded John Fletcher's testimony given at their wedding. Here is part of his testimony that explains how these early Methodists understood Fletcher's idea of dispensations. This report was often cited in Methodist literature and was contained in Hester Ann Roger's published diary which became one of the most widely read pieces of devotional literature in American Methodism.

> Leeds, Aug. 24, 1781.—That dear man of God, Mr. Fletcher, came with Miss Bosanquet (now Mrs. Fletcher,) to dine at Mr. Smith's in Park-Row; and also to meet the select society. After dinner I took an opportunity to beg he would explain an expression he once used to Miss Loxdale [later the wife of Thomas Coke] in a letter, viz. "That on all who are renewed

in love, God bestows the gift of prophecy." He called for the Bible: then read, and sweetly explained the second chapter of the Acts, observing: To "prophesy" in the sense he meant, was to magnify God with the new heart of love and the new tongue of praise, as they did, who on the day of Pentecost were filled with the Holy Spirit! And he insisted that believers are now called to make the same confession: seeing, we may all prove the same baptismal fire, showing, that the day of Pentecost was only the opening of the dispensation of the Holy Spirit, the great promise of the Father! and that "the latter-day glory," which he believed was near at hand, should far exceed the first effusion of the Spirit. And, therefore, seeing they then bore witness to the grace of our Lord, so should we; and, like them, spread the flame of love. Then, after singing a hymn, he cried,—"O to be filled with the Holy Spirit! I want to be filled! O my friends, let us wrestle for a more abundant outpouring of the Spirit!" To me he said, "Come, my sister, will you covenant with me this day, to pray for the fullness of the Spirit? Will you be a witness for Jesus?"—I answered, with flowing tears,—"In the strength of Jesus I will." He cried, "Glory, glory, glory be to God! Lord, strengthen thy handmaid to keep this covenant, even unto death." He then said, "My dear brethren and sisters, God is here: I feel him in this place."[74]

If John Wesley told Elizabeth Ritchie that Fletcher's interpretation of the various dispensations is the best ever provided in church history, his testimony explained it with energy of expression that contributed to making the link between Pentecost and sanctification a common Methodist belief.

The correspondence of Elizabeth Ritchie with Mary Fletcher showed their friendship was deep. Mary (Bosanquet) Fletcher had also been like a daughter to John Wesley. John Wesley heartily approved of her marriage to John Fletcher. After Fletcher died, John Wesley took Elizabeth Ritchie with him to Madeley to visit Mary Fletcher in March, 1786.[75]

Elizabeth Ritchie frequently corresponded with Mary Fletcher,[76] as well as with John Wesley. The following are my transcribed excerpts from her writings using the expression, the baptism with the Spirit. The references to John Fletcher showed that she considered him second only to John Wesley as the two voices of doctrinal authority.

On January 10, 1775, Elizabeth Ritchie wrote to John Wesley, "I have been reading Mr. Fletcher's equal Check lately, and must acknowledge I never saw the doctrine of the dispensations in so clear a light before."[77] This letter was in response to John Wesley's request that she read it to learn about his doctrine of dispensations.

On January 15, 1775, Elizabeth Ritchie wrote to Mary Bosaquent (before she became Mary Fletcher): "My whole soul is on stretch for perfect holiness, for I see not only a salvation from sin, but all the fullness of God, is my blessed privilege. This I am pressed hard after, Lord make me still more athirst, for all thou has to give. I believe I do grow in grace, but I long to do it more abundantly. I see all my business is to glorify my God, and this alone do I desire to live for, through the help of my God I will more than ever be. . . . I feel my soul sweetly penetrated with the Love of God." She goes on to say: "I trust my Dear Friend [Mary Bosanquet] is making swift progresses in the divine Life . . . . May you ever abide in Jesus, may your whole soul be filled with His Perfect Love . . . . My kind Love to all your Dear Family. May you all be filled with Holy Spirit, and made altogether like your Lord."[78]

On October 29, 1776, she wrote to Mary Bosanquet: "We have lately heard that dear man of God Mr. Fletcher is better and talks of coming into Yorkshire for the recovery of his health, pray is it so, we shall all be truly glad to see him, and except my Dear Father [Mr. Wesley] I know not who would be a more welcome guest amongst our Societies."[79]

February 18, 1777, she again asked John Wesley: "Pray how does Mr. Fletcher yet?"[80]

In a letter to John Wesley on November 15, 1775, Elizabeth Ritchie closed it: "May you be filled with faith and love and with the Holy Spirit." Nov. 15, 1775.[81]

February 6, 1777, Elizabeth Ritchie said to John Wesley: "I have lately read Mr. Fletcher's *Last Check* and felt it as marrow and fatness to my soul. May I run more swiftly the race set before me. I am athirst for the Perfection of my dispensation."[82] *The Last Check* was Fletcher's primary treatise on Christian perfection where he frequently explained it in terms of being baptized with the Spirit.

August 1, 1777, Elizabeth Ritchie said to John Wesley: "I am truly thankful to hear Mr. Fletcher is better, and pray that the Lord may sanctify his intended journey. I trust he will long be spared to tread in the steps of my ever Dear and much Loved Father [John Wesley]." These comments illustrated the respect for Fletcher and the hope that he would become John Wesley's successor.[83]

In a letter to John Wesley on Dec. 5, 1778, Elizabeth Ritchie said to John Wesley: "I long for the Spirit's fullest Baptism [of the Holy Spirit], and so see and feel all the promises of God yea and amen that my soul rejoices in hope of that glory which shall be revealed to the believing heart." This letter to John Wesley illustrated that he agreed with this Pentecost expression.[84]

In a letter on November 21, 1779 to Mary Bosanquet, Elizabeth Ritchie wrote: "Before we go home [to heaven] our souls may enjoy much more of God than we yet do, how strangely do they talk who say 'when the heart is purified by faith how can people get any farther,' they know not the need such feel to go forward, but blessed be God we do, and such a glorious prospect does faith behold as quite exhilarates the soul, and sets all the springs of desire in motion, toward the attainment of what (Dear Mr. Fletcher calls) the perfection of our dispensation. How ardently my soul thirsts but you my dear friend know by happy experience. How the divine principle within 'carries one out with sweet constraint, after all the fullness of this love'."[85] This letter also showed that the doctrine of dispensations was understood to be primarily about the attainment of Christian perfection.

When Elizabeth Ritchie was once seriously ill for a period of time, John Wesley went to see her on May 9, 1777. He wrote in his journal: "After preaching in the evening at Leeds, I pushed on to Otley. Here I found E. Ritchie weaker and happier than ever: I spent half an hour with her."

John Wesley went again to see her on June 5, 1777. He inserted in his journal notes:

"About noon I came to Otley, and found E. R. just alive; but all alive to God. In the evening it seemed as if the departing saint had dropped her mantle upon the congregation,—such an awe rested upon them while I explained and applied, 'They were all filled with the Holy Spirit'."[86]

Notice that John Wesley said he "explained and applied" the meaning—"They were all filled with the Holy Spirit." This is an instance similar to what he would say later on June 3, 1781, when he preached on being "filled with the Holy Spirit." The idea of applying this text to his hearers is also like what he reported about John Heylyn's "truly Christian sermon" on Pentecost on being "filled with the Holy Spirit" with an invitation "may *all you* be, if it is not your own fault." This illustrated that Heylyn's Pentecost sermon had a continuing impact on him.

It is worth noting on his visit to see the bedridden Elizabeth Ritchie that John Wesley connected her life with his sermon on being "filled with the Holy Spirit." He said it was as if "the departing saint had dropped her mantle upon the congregation." The content of her letters to him over the years were literally saturated with her pursuit of Christian perfection. Expressions such as filled and baptized with the Spirit were used to describe her spiritual desire for being made in the image of Christ. If John Wesley used her as an example of being filled with the Spirit, this is because he believed she was a model of Christian perfection.

Elizabeth Ritchie in her journal, June 26th, 1784 mentioned that John Wesley and John Fletcher preached together on occasions: "On Saturday we came to Leeds, where my spirit was much refreshed by the sight of my dear old friends, Mr. and Mrs. Fletcher. Mr. Fletcher preached on Sunday morning, and Mr. Wesley in the evening: they were both solemn and animating occasions."[87]

On September 28, 1785, Elizabeth Ritchie said to Mary Fletcher in a letter: "I want myself, and others to drink deeper into the Spirit's fullness."[88]

In a letter to Mary Fletcher in 1787, Elizabeth Ritchie said she was praying for a "deeper baptism with the Holy Spirit," as her heart cried out for perfect love. She then cited one of Charles Wesley hymns on the pursuit of perfect love. This showed that Elizabeth Ritchie believed that Fletcher's idea on the baptism with the Spirit corresponded to Charles Wesley's hymns on Christian perfection. She wrote:

Blessed be my Lord! He keeps me in perfect peace, and I generally feel sweet recollection of spirit, but I know a much deeper baptism of the Holy Spirit is my Lord's will concerning me, and am waiting on my Lord for more divine power to use the grace already given, my heart often cries:

> On me that mighty faith bestow
>   Which cannot ask in vain,
> Which holds, and will not let thee go,
>   Till I my suit obtain;
> Till thou into my soul inspire
>   The perfect love unknown,
> And tell mine infinite desire,
>   'Whatever thou wilt, be done!'

Help me my dear friend to reach a higher link of the blessed chain on which my faith has hold, and let me still be animated by the experience of Christ you feel.[89]

Elizabeth Ritchie wrote a letter to Mary Fletcher on October 1, 1788 from City Road, London (the location of Wesley's residence and chapel). She reported that a sermon by Henry Moore (John Wesley's clerical assistant) inspired her to cry out: "Fill me with the Holy Spirit of promise. Let the holy flame burn brighter, let my views of Thee, and of what Thou has prepared for those that love Thee, be clearer, let me be lost and swallowed up in Thee, my God, my All."

This letter also showed that Methodists were continuing to be inspired by John Fletcher who had already died. Here is part of my transcription of the letter:

> I feel a constant cleaving unto Jesus. He keeps me deeply sensible of my entire helplessness; but He is my strength, and with a sweet childlike simplicity my spirit depends on Him for all things, and feels He is my Saviour, Husband, Brother, Friend. I believe I am at this place in my Lord's will, and though it seems to require more simplicity to be childlike amongst the people, than among any other I was ever with, yet I bless the Lord "as my day, so is my strength." Here are many precious souls who experience the whole truth as it is in Jesus and walk in blessed liberty; but here are many more who either do not see the privilege of being wholly the Lord's, or are very easy about the present experience of the deep things of God. I have felt much freedom at the classes, and the people are very kind to me for my Masters sake. I am in great hopes much good will be done as really the Lord has been taking very great pains with His people lately. From the conversation of many they seem determined to take Mr. Moore's advice which he gave us last Sunday, viz: "To seek for a particular revival in their own souls in order to secure a general one." I long for one in my own soul and blessed be God feel the Living Waters rising in my heart, but as I receive my thirst after more increases and my soul cries "come Lord Jesus, fill me with the Holy Spirit of promise. Let the holy flame burn brighter, let my views of Thee, and of what Thou has prepared for those that love Thee, be clearer, let me be lost and swallowed up in Thee, my God, my All."

She continued in this letter to report:

> A very precious old woman was called home lately. . . . She had been a Leader many years and was in the Society from its first forming. For some time before her death she was like a worn out veteran unfit for activity, in her Masters' service but by suffering His will, which she did with such patience and resignation as brought glory to our gracious Lord. A little before her death she thought, your very dear translated friend [i.e., John Fletcher] came and held out his hand to her, from which she concluded she would soon be in glory saying, "she had seen Mr. Fletcher ready to welcome her into the Port, and she would soon reach the shore." It was either in a vision or a dream I know not which.[90]

In a letter on June 13, 1794, Elizabeth Ritchie wrote to Mary Fletcher: "I am thankful to hear of dear Sally's zeal for the glory of our common Lord. May she see abundant fruit, and feel that full baptism of the Holy Spirit in her own soul and will loose every bond and let her into all the privileges of the gospel."[91]

In a letter to Mary Holland, March 2, 1824, Elizabeth Ritchie Mortimer (now married) said: "Our adorable Redeemer has opened a way of constant access for us, into a fullness of Gospel blessings: let us avail ourselves of it, by coming in faith and prayer for a fuller baptism of the Holy Spirit."[92]

James and Hester Ann Rogers

James Rogers was one of John Wesley's inner circle of preachers. His wife Hester Ann Rogers was present at the time of John Wesley's death.[93] John Wesley often corresponded with Hester Ann Rogers, and she was one of his most cherished friends. She and her husband lived with John Wesley in his home at City Road, London, for two years before his death as Elizabeth Ritchie had also done.[94]

Hester Ann Rogers was seeking Christian perfection toward the end of 1775. One of John Wesley's preachers, "Dr. Wright," recommended her to read "Mr. Wesley's Plain Account, and Father Thoughts on Christian Perfection, and Mr. Fletcher's Polemical Essay, especially his Address in the end of it, to imperfect believers."

On February 22, 1776, she said: "Lord, cried I, make this the moment of my full salvation! Baptize me now with the Holy Spirit, and the fire of pure love. . . . Let me perfectly love thee."[95]

In letters to her correspondents, she described John Wesley's life in Pentecostal terms, as a man "so full of the Spirit of his Master,—so full of God."[96]

She once wrote to John Wesley (June 15, 1782): "Oh, my dear sir, I never dwelt so much in God as I have done of late. My whole soul has been swallowed up in communion with the eternal Trinity, and peculiarly within this last fortnight, with the Holy Spirit. I have been led to pray in faith for a universal and Pentecostal outpouring of His divine fullness; and it surely will descend." She then reported that many were sanctified in "a prayer meeting" that she had conducted.[97]

In a letter to her on April 10, 1781, John Wesley also spoke of "that great outpouring of the Spirit" producing "pure love" of "many of our brethren and sisters in London."[98] In a letter on June 25, 1782, John Wesley said "It is certain there has been, for these forty years, such an outpouring of the Spirit."[99]

We noted above that in her diary on August 24, 1781, Fletcher spoke to her in a "select society" on the connection between the millennium and Pentecost. The diary of Hester Ann Rogers helped to make this a topic of interest and frequent discussion among John Wesley's leaders. Her account of that particular meeting was widely circulated among the Methodists.

James Rogers enjoyed John Wesley's full confidence. When he had been a preacher for only five years, he was moved from Edinburgh to Cornwall during the 1777 conference. He was not happy about the five hundred mile transition to Cornwall that he was required to make, but this afforded him an opportunity to meet with Fletcher, which he said more than compensated him for his move. He wrote about this encounter with Fletcher in August, 1777, which highlighted the "descent of the Holy Spirit" as the "privilege of all New Testament believers":

> In the year 1777 I was appointed to [leave Edinburgh, and] labour in the east of Cornwall. A journey of about five hundred miles was no small fatigue in my then weak state of body; but the Lord was with me. I looked upon it as His doing; therefore set out in His name, and found sweet communion with Him in the way.

I had long desired to converse with that great and good man, Mr. Fletcher; and now an opportunity offered itself. Stopping at Bristol for a few days to rest myself and horse, I heard of his being at Mr. Ireland's, about three miles off, in a poor state of health, and with two of my brethren took a ride to see him. When we came there he was returning from a ride, which he was advised by his physician to take every day. Dismounting from his horse, he came to us with arms spread open, and eyes lifted up to heaven. His apostolic appearance, with the whole of his deportment, amazingly affected us.

The first words he spoke, while yet standing in the stable by his horse, were a part of the sixteenth chapter of St. John's Gospel, most of which he repeated. And while he pointed out the descent of the Holy Spirit, as the great promise of the Father, and the privilege of all New Testament believers, in a manner I had never heard before, my soul was dissolved into tenderness, and became as melting wax before the fire.

After discussing some of the details of the Calvinist controversy with Fletcher, Rogers described a remarkable event:

After a little farther conversation upon the universal love of God in Christ Jesus, we were about to take our leave, when Mr. Ireland sent his footman into the yard with a bottle of red wine, and some slices of bread upon a waiter. We all uncovered our heads, while Mr. Fletcher craved a blessing upon the same; which he had no sooner done, than he handed first the bread to each, and then, lifting up his eyes to heaven, pronounced these words, "The body of our Lord Jesus Christ, which was given for thee, preserve thy body and soul unto everlasting life." Afterwards, handing the wine, he repeated in like manner: "The blood of our Lord Jesus Christ," &c. But such a sacrament I never had before. A sense of the divine presence rested upon us all; and we were melted into floods of tears. His worthy friend, Mr. Ireland, grieved to see him exhaust his little strength by so much speaking, took him by the arm, and almost forced him into the house; while he kept looking wishfully, and speaking to us, as long as we could see him. We then mounted our horses, and rode away. That hour more than repaid me for my whole journey from Edinburgh to Cornwall.[100]

Once again we see Fletcher's influence upon the leading Methodist preachers. Fletcher in this meeting with Rogers mentioned "the descent of the Holy Spirit" and "the great promise of the Father," followed by a fresh-air celebration of the Lord's Supper—which served as a primary means of sanctifying grace in his ministry.

When Hester Ann Rogers became John Wesley's housekeeper[101] in the final days of his life, she was already a well-known promoter of John Wesley's doctrine of holiness, particularly using "the baptism of the Holy Spirit" to define her own experience.[102] She and husband were close friends of Fletcher. She died at the age of 39 in childbirth,[103] and Thomas Coke preached her funeral in 1795.

In his funeral sermon for Hester Ann Rogers, Thomas Coke said: "On the morning of February 22, 1776, when at prayer . . . she thought: "Shall I now ask *small blessings* only of my God? Lord, make this the moment of my *full salvation!* Baptize me *now* with the Holy Spirit, and the fire of pure love. Now, cleanse the thoughts of my heart, and let me *perfectly* love thee."[104]

The expression "baptize you with the Holy Spirit and Fire" occurs in the letters of Thomas Coke as well in his other writings.[105]

The devotional literature of early Methodism consisted of the biography of Fletcher by John Wesley and Benson, Moore's biography of Mary Bosanquet Fletcher, and *The Life and Correspondence of Mrs. Hester Ann Rogers*.[106] It is thus understandable that the 'baptism with the Holy Spirit" became a widely used phrase for Christian perfection.

Mary Bosanquet Fletcher's biography (including her personal diaries) was reprinted fifteen times in America. The autobiography of Hester Ann Rogers was published forty five times in the nineteenth century, with the first being published in Bristol, England in 1796, and in New York in 1804. It was re-printed in 1806 (two times) in New York, in 1811 in New York and in 1811 in Baltimore, and also in the following years in America: 1814, 1815, 1818 (two times), 1820 (two times), 1830, 1831, 1832, 1837, 1839, 1841, 1842, 1846, 1850 (two times), 1851, 1852, 1853 (three times), 1854, 1855, 1856, 1861, 1882, and 1893.[107] The frequent publication of this autobiography by the Methodist Episcopal Church illustrated how deeply ingrained was the idea of Pentecost and sanctification in the theology of American Methodism. Nathan Bangs in his *History of the Methodist Episcopal Church* noted that only a few titles were available for these early Methodists to read,[108] and the ones that were available reflected this theme

William Bramwell

If the *Memoirs of the Life and Ministry of William Bramwell* is any indication, then the subject of the "baptism of the Spirit" was common among John Wesley's preachers. He became one of John Wesley's preachers in 1787, and he used Pentecost expressions, such as "the baptism of the Holy Spirit" and being "filled with the Spirit," and he promoted entire sanctification, encouraging his hearers to give public testimony to this experience.[109]

James Sigston included Fletcher's testimony of being baptized with the Spirit (recorded by Hester Ann Rogers) in his biography of his close friend, William Bramwell. Sigston quoted Fletcher's testimony in order to show that Bramwell was one who admired Fletcher and whose life and preaching was patterned after Fletcher's.[110] The publication of the diaries of Hester Ann Rogers and the biography of Bramwell showed that the expectation of a new day of Pentecost was widespread among early Methodists.

John Pawson

John Pawson was John Wesley's successor at City Road Church, London.[111] Pawson was greatly impressed with Fletcher, and he embraced Fletcher's idea of Pentecost and sanctification. He admired Fletcher's preaching effectiveness, noticing that more people came to hear Fletcher than John Wesley. He also noticed that he had read an early draft of Fletcher's *Equal Check* (which contained Fletcher's first fully developed idea of Pentecost and sanctification). He observed: "I think he will set that doctrine [of perfection] in so Scriptural a light, as to stop the mouths of gainsayers."[112]

In *A Serious and Affectionate Address to the Junior Preachers in the Methodist Connection* (September 25, 1798), he asked: "Are we not called of God to preach a full, free, present, and complete salvation . . . and being filled with the Spirit, we may be blameless and harmless. . . . This appears to me the more necessary, because there are many that believe and preach justification by faith, who seem little acquainted with the nature of sanctification."[113]

Adam Clarke, in his eulogy of Pawson described him, as "a man of irreproachable integrity, of unspotted life" whom "God honoured" with "the baptism of the Holy Spirit, and with such a victory and triumph over sin, death, and the grave, as would have been glorious even in apostolic times."[114]

Henry Moore and Mary Fletcher

In 1817 when Benson published the Pentecost sermon by Bourdaloue in *The Arminian Magazine*, linking the "baptism with the Spirit" with "men perfect and irreprehensible" and "filled with love," Henry Moore edited and published the *Life of Mary Fletcher*, which contained the same emphasis.

In his preface, Moore recounted that John Wesley was the founder of Methodism who led a group of Oxford students in search of holiness. He asked, "But did they spend their strength for naught? Were they disappointed of their hope? Were not a holy people raised up? Let the life of Mrs. Fletcher speak."[115]

His biography of Mary Fletcher emphasized that the key to being a holy people is through the baptism with the Spirit. Typical of this idea of Pentecost and sanctification is her diary entry for December 4, 1794: "This is *the baptism of the Spirit* which hath purified my heart from all sin!"[116]

Moore was one of the closest and most trusted friends of John Wesley, spending entire days with him as his clerical assistant and traveling with him extensively.[117] No one knew Methodism better than he did, and no one knew John Wesley's views about his preachers than he did.

Moore said this about her husband, John Fletcher, in his preface: "That great man, *whose praise is in all the Churches*; whose admirable writings will live while piety and learning are honoured in the earth; and which have forced even those who did not know his piety, or affected to lament that such talents should be so connected, to acknowledge his great superiority."[118]

Henry Moore and Thomas Rutherford

One of John Wesley's well-educated preachers was Thomas Rutherford. He was the brother-in-law of Henry Moore who was commissioned to write the eulogy of Rutherford for the Conference's *Minutes* after his death in 1806.[119]

Rutherford said that he had a desire for a long time to meet Fletcher, but then in August, 1783, he got acquainted with him when he came to Dublin with his wife:

> I had an opportunity of being in company with him almost every day, morning, noon, and night; and of hearing him preach five or six times a week for nearly two months; which have ever viewed as a signal instance of the divine condescension and goodness towards an unworthy creature.—At the recollection of those days, (for they were days of the Son of Man!) my heart overflows with gratitude to the Giver of every good and perfect gift.[120]

He reported that Fletcher's preaching theme was on "Pentecost," "the promise of the Spirit," and "the indwelling power and fullness of the Holy Spirit." He also noted: "He was the most devoted, the most heavenly, the most Christlike man I ever saw."[121]

Moore reported that Rutherford recorded in his diary (March 15, 1776) of having been baptized with the Spirit, utilizing John Wesley's idea of Canaan land as a symbol of perfect love and the fullness of the sanctifying Spirit given on the day of Pentecost:

My present state may, I think, properly be called, a panting for a greater fullness of the life and spirit of Jesus. I live in sight of the land of perfect love. It is indeed a good and a pleasant land—a land of light and life, and peace and power; of holy rest, and sweet communion with the Father, Son, and Holy Spirit. And yet, alas, I cannot enter! How long, O Lord, how long shall I wander to and fro, comparatively in the wilderness? Help me, O help me, to go up and possess it! Bid me wash and be clean. Plunge me in the swelling Jordan of thy most precious blood! Baptize, O baptize me with the fullness of thy sanctifying Spirit![122]

In a letter addressed to the Methodist preachers who had gathered for their Annual Conference in London in 1806, Rutherford encouraged them "to apply to Him in good earnest for power from on high; the baptism and continual anointing of the Holy Spirit. Mr. Wesley justly observes" that "every preacher of the gospel" should recognize that "the Spirit of the Lord God is upon me."

Notice here that Rutherford connected Fletcher's idea of the baptism with the Spirit with John Wesley's exhortation, confirming that in the minds of the preachers there was no difference between Fletcher and John Wesley.[123]

Rutherford is known primarily for his work in abridging Fletcher's *Last Check*, under the title, *Christian Perfection, An Extract from John Fletcher*. It was published in Philadelphia in 1796, and it was immediately reprinted in the same year. John Wesley had once encouraged Fletcher not to make *The Last Check* too long because it would come into "fewer hands,"[124] and it was for this reason that Rutherford abridged it—so that more people would be encouraged to read it.[125]

It was also printed as a pocket-size book for convenience. Rutherford's "preface" indicates that Fletcher was considered to be the unquestioned authority on John Wesley's doctrinal system. He noted that "Christian perfection, according to the account which both Mr. Wesley and Mr. Fletcher have given of it" is what "the Methodists believe and teach."[126] His reason for making this extract was because Fletcher offered "a clear, distinct, and Scriptural point of view."

The opening part of this extract defined the meaning of Christian perfection, as "the pure love of God, shed abroad in the heart of established believers by the Holy Spirit, which is abundantly given them under the fullness of the Christian dispensation."[127] It connected Fletcher's emphasis on Pentecost and perfection with extensive citations from John Wesley's *A Plain Account of Christian Perfection*. A dominant motif in this abridged edition is that Pentecost or "the baptism of the Holy Spirit" is the means for attaining Christian perfection.[128]

Henry Moore

Thomas Rutherford, in a letter to Henry Moore, reminded him of what he had once said to him about too many Christians still living as if Pentecost had not happened: "For some years past I have seen much I could not approve of among us as Christians, and brethren, and have thought a hundred times of an expression you mentioned to me of Mr. Fletcher's that 'he thought the generality of Christians are not in a spiritual state, superior to that of the disciples, before the day of Pentecost'."[129] This observation showed that it was common for John Wesley's inner circle to compare the difference between justified and sanctified believers to the justified state of the disciples before Pentecost and their sanctification after Pentecost. It will be recalled that John Wesley first used this distinction as a result of his visit to Herrnhut in 1738.

When Henry Moore was near death, he was asked: "How many of your old friends are gone before you into glory?" With "animation," he replied: "I have known some among the best in the world: the Wesleys, Mr. And Mrs. Fletcher, and many others of the very salt of the earth, but less distinguished in their sphere of usefulness; I shall see them all again, and with power, and riches, and wisdom, and strength, and honor, and glory, and blessing."[130] Typically, the early Methodists placed Fletcher in the same category as the Wesley brothers as one of their leaders and models.

Adam Clarke and Mary Cooper—a Case Study of the Pentecost Preaching of the Early Methodists

Adam Clarke expressed a consensus of understanding when he said that "Christ baptizes with the Holy Spirit, for the destruction of sin."[131]

In a pastoral letter (Feb. 18, 1814) to a dying member, Clarke reminded him that Jesus had died "to purify you unto himself." He encouraged him to "be a partaker of his holiness. Claim every promise of God as your own." He concluded with this exhortation: "May he baptize you with the fullest baptism of his Spirit!"[132]

Clarke edited and published the *Memoirs of the Mrs. Mary Cooper* in 1814. She was the daughter of a wealthy family and "her understanding was sound, her mind carefully cultivated" and her "piety deep and rational," according to Clarke.[133]

Though she was not a preacher, her memoirs were used to promote the message of the Methodists, and they show how a new convert to Methodism soon appropriated the idea of Pentecost and sanctification. In 1809, she began to attend Methodist meetings where the first preachers that she heard were Adam Clarke and Thomas Coke, and soon thereafter she heard Henry Moore and Joseph Benson preach.[134] She considered Henry Moore and his wife, Ann Young Moore, to be her "best advisers."[135]

She noted that the sermons of Clarke and Coke "made a deep impression on my mind," with their emphasis upon "the connection of religion and reason" and "the inhabitation of the Spirit of God."[136] She was especially attracted to the Methodist doctrine of holiness. She wrote:

> My mind is now, I think, made up as to the scriptural nature and holy tendency of the doctrines Mr. Wesley embraced and enforced. I have been happy in the investigation; and am most firmly persuaded that his view of Christian perfection is at once the privilege and the happiness of the Christian. . . . This blessing is only bestowed on those who believe, and who earnestly pray and wait for this full redemption. Although I am not yet the happy possessor of it, I am greatly encouraged by that promise, Psalm cxiv.12. 'He will fulfil the desire of them that fear Him."[137]

She rediscovered the meaningfulness of Holy Communion by attending a Methodist chapel, and she realized its importance as a means of sanctifying grace and enabling her to love God with all heart.[138]

While receiving this sacrament she was led to pray for "the gift of the Holy Spirit" to sanctify her: "Do I not ask with importunity for the gift of Thy Spirit to enable me to perform my resolutions, to overcome every sin, and to seek for entire sanctification?"[139]

On December 29, 1809, she came to a point of accepting "the indwelling of the Spirit." She wrote in her diary: "In tender mercy He has heard my prayer: I feel convinced that *sin* must be a strange work to the believer; it is incompatible with the indwelling of the Spirit of God: I long to feel deeper the Spirit's influence; I want to be filled with that holy love. . . . O may I more fully comprehend the large extent of that salvation Christ came to bestow, even a deliverance from the power of all sin."[140]

The Spirit's "indwelling" and "baptism" became the focus of her developing spiritual life. On January 24, 1810, she wrote: "I wish more powerfully to feel the necessity of constantly seeking the influence of the Holy Spirit, to renovate my nature, to baptize me afresh. . . . If He has been, and is manifested to my soul, sin will be destroyed."[141]

On April 30, 1811, she prayed for "the constant indwelling of the Holy Spirit" as the fulfilment of her desire to be united with Christ.[142] She used another popular metaphor in Methodism for holiness when she described this union with Christ in terms of the abiding witness of the Spirit: "This can be found only when the Spirit takes up His abode in the heart."[143]

She further stated: "When the Comforter takes up His *abode* in my heart, then all will be subdued to my Heavenly King."[144] Another term that she used for holiness was "happy in God." This appeared on back of an admission ticket that Henry Moore had given her to attend a Methodist society. She wrote: "Happy in God, and in possession of the peace which passeth understanding."[145]

Though only a newcomer to Methodism, the connection between Pentecost and entire sanctification is set forth in her diaries: She wrote On August 24, 1810:

> It is His will that, justified freely by His death, we should be sanctified in body, soul and spirit, by the influence of the Holy Spirit, the Comforter, "the Gift of the Father," which he promised should abundantly descend after His resurrection.[146]

Mary Cooper became ill and depressed shortly before she gave birth to a son. Adam Clarke explained that her depression resulted from her illness, not from spiritual decline. However, she was unable to understand this situation.[147] In this state of confusion, she wrote this prayer in her diary on March 11, 1812:

> O Lord, I will renew my dedication to Thy service. Baptize me afresh with Thy Holy Spirit, and sanctify *bodily affliction*. O may it be the *one* desire of my soul, to gain more and more of the Divine image, and to be increasing in holiness and meetness for the eternal world![148]

She died on June 22, 1812, at the age of 26, from complications arising from childbirth. After less than three years of being a Methodist, her diaries reveal the theology she had learned from these early Methodist preachers, especially Adam Clarke, Thomas Coke, and Henry Moore. Because Clarke reported that he heard John Wesley preach on "the baptism with the Holy Spirit" on different occasions,[149] one can gather that John Wesley is the one who had inclined Clarke to think in these terms.

Richard Treffry

Richard Treffry (1771-1842) was admitted into full connection in British Methodism the year after John Wesley died (1792).[150] He was a frequent spokesman for Christian perfection, linking it with the baptism with the Holy Spirit.

The Methodist Magazine contained a sermon by Richard Treffry on Christian perfection, which referred to Fletcher's view that even though one may be fully sanctified through a gradual process, "there is a precise moment when the work is completed."[151]

The Methodist Magazine and Quarterly Review also published another sermon by Treffry, "An Address to the Young Ministers," which was originally delivered August 6, 1834 at the City Road Chapel, London.[152] He urged them to be "seeking deeper baptisms, and larger effusions, of the Holy Spirit" because otherwise "sin may be pardoned and subdued, but it is not wholly extirpated."[153] He reminded them of their obligation "to preach the doctrines of Methodism," which included calling everyone to experience full sanctification. Using Fletcher's categories, he said:

> And, in order to encourage your hearers to come to the fountain opened for sin and for uncleanness, and to avail themselves of all the benefits of redemption, never forget in all your ministrations the doctrine of a Divine influence; that God will give His Holy Spirit to them that ask Him; that Christianity is a dispensation of the Spirit; the promise of the gift of the Holy Spirit being given to us, and to our children, and to all that are afar off, even as many as the Lord our God shall call.[154]

Treffry published the memoirs of his son who died at the age of 33,[155] and these memoirs show that the "baptism of the Spirit" was a common theme. In a letter to his mother on November 28, 1837, his son wrote: "But I want more abundant light, a more copious baptism of the Holy Spirit, and a more perfect conformity to the divine image."[156] In a letter to Henry Davies on November 30, 1837, Richard Treffry, Jr., wrote: "Best of all, my mind is kept calm and happy, waiting for a more perfect manifestation of the love of God before I go hence, and daily crying for a renewed baptism of the Holy Spirit."

Richard Watson (1781-1833)

Richard Watson was the first systematic theologian of Methodism. This is because his *Theological Institutes* formalized Methodist doctrine into a textbook of distinct topics and explained their connection with logical precision. He became a preacher at the Conference of 1797 at the early age of 16 and was appointed to a circuit.[157] Though an Englishman, his writings were influential in America and became part of the conference course of study for ministers until 1876.[158]

In 1830, Richard Watson wrote: "The Entire sanctification of the soul from sin is held forth, both as necessary to qualify us for heaven, and as the result of that *baptism of the Spirit* which we receive in answer to prayer, and through faith in Christ."[159]

In a letter to his dying father, Watson encouraged him to: "Proceed to obtain the full sanctification of your nature. It is not death, but grace, that must destroy our sin, and make us meet for heaven. Have faith in the promise of the Father to send the Holy Spirit in all the power he exerted in the day of Pentecost, to burn up the very root of corruption, and fill you in a moment with all the love and power of God, making you one with Christ, and an entirely new creature."[160]

In his preaching, Watson called his hearers to experience the "baptism of fire" which effects within the believer "an unquenchable love" and "purity." He showed that this Pentecostal event was not just for the disciples, but every believer can "now" experience "a constant, though secret, Pentecost."[161] He exhorted his hearers: "Christ now baptizes with the Holy Spirit and with fire."[162] This personalized Pentecost today means that one can have "purged from the heart of man all its stains of sin."[163]

Watson expressed the unanimous view among Methodists everywhere that John Wesley and Fletcher were seen as having the same interpretation: "If the doctrine of Christian perfection, as taught by Mr. Wesley and Mr. Fletcher, be true, as we all believe it is, I fear we do not give that prominence to it in our preaching which we ought to do: and that some of us do not seek to realize it in our own experience, as it is our privilege and duty."[164]

Notes

1. Thomas Coke, *A Series of Letters Addressed to the Methodist Connection* (London: A. Paris, 1810), 72, 97, 147-157.

2. Ibid., 190.

3. Thomas Coke and Francis Asbury, *The Doctrines and Discipline of the Methodist Episcopal Church in America, with explanatory notes*, 10th ed. (Philadelphia: Tuckniss, 1798), iv. Original date of publication was Nov. 16, 1792 in Baltimore by Thomas Coke and Francis Asbury, 59.

4. *Memoirs of the Rev. Joseph Benson*, by Richard Treffry (New York: Carlton and Phillips, 1853), 31. His primary biographer, George MacDonald, first published Benson's *Memoirs*, and was intimately acquainted with him. *Memoirs of the Rev. Joseph Benson*, by George MacDonald (Bangs & Mason, 1823), iii.

5. *Memoirs of the Rev. Joseph Benson*, by James Macdonald (New York: Bangs and T. Mason, 1823), 52.

6. John Lenton, *John Wesley's Preachers* (Eugene, Oregon: Wipf & Stock, 2009), 117.

7. *Memoirs of the Rev. Joseph Benson,* 13, 19, 38, 52.

8. MARC: PLP 775. Cf. also *John Wesley's Designated Successor,* 358.

9. *Memoirs of Joseph Benson*, 42.

10. Benson, "Life of the Rev. John Fletcher," *Works of John Fletcher*, 1:205.

11. The full title of this essay was, "The Doctrine of the New Birth, as it is stated in these sheets, is directly or indirectly maintained by the most spiritual divines, especially in their sacred poems." It was overlooked by subsequent historians (including Luke Tyerman and J. F. Hurst), which I located, March 1997, in a box of miscellaneous materials written by Fletcher. This essay is contained in the Fletcher-Tooth Archival Collection as part of the Methodist Archives in the John Rylands Library of Manchester University, England, and it is now published in *The Asbury Theological Journal.* 50.1 (Spring, 1998):35-64). Another section of this essay was entitled "The Language of the Father's Dispensation," which continued the discussion on "the capital doctrine of the new birth." Cf. *The Asbury Theological Journal.* 50.1 (Spring, 1998): 65-78.

12. Ibid.

13. Wesley noted in his Journal for Wednesday, December 3, 1777: "I visited as many of the sick as I could in the north-east part of the town; and spent the evening at Newington, with Mr. Fletcher, almost miraculously recovering from his consumption: and on Thursday, 4, he set out with Mr. Ireland for the south of France." Wesley, *Works* (Jackson), 4:113, (Wednesday, December 3, 1777).

14. Cf. *Meaning of Pentecost in Early Methodist, Rediscovering John Fletcher as John Wesley's Vindicator and Designated Successor,* 127-134, 240.

15. In this letter, Benson noted that he had corresponded with Mary Bosanquet (Fletcher's future wife) "two years ago."

16. Cf. the full transcription of the letter in "An Interpretation of the United Methodist Liturgy of Christian Baptism: 'By Water and the Spirit,' in the Matrix of John Wesley, John Fletcher, and Joseph Benson," *The Wesleyan Theological Journal,* 50.2 (Fall 2015): 156-185.

17. "The Language of the Father's Dispensation," *The Asbury Theological Journal.* 50.1 (Spring, 1998): 66-67.

18. "An Interpretation of the United Methodist Liturgy of Christian Baptism: 'By Water and the Spirit,' in the Matrix of John Wesley, John Fletcher, and Joseph Benson," *The Wesleyan Theological Journal*, 50.2 (Fall 2015): 156-185.

19. Tyerman, *Wesley's Designated Successor* 449-450.

20. Letter from Joseph Benson to John Fletcher, June 12, 1781, MARC: PLP 7-8- 9 (MAMF1 6.6.10).

21. John Fletcher, "An Essay on the Doctrine of the New Birth," *The Asbury Theological Journal*, Volume 53, Number 1 (Spring 1998): 35-78.
22. *A Methodist Courtship, Love Letters of Joseph Benson & Sarah Thompson 1779–1780*, ed. Margaret M. , 12.
23. Thoughts on Perfection," *The Arminian Magazine* 4 (October 1781): 553.
24. Benson, *Two Sermons on Sanctification* (Leeds, 1782), 29.
25. Ibid., 36.
26. *The Works of the Rev. John Wesley*, (London: Thomas Cordeux, 1813), 16:294-295, Letter to Joseph Benson (February 22, 1782).
27. James MacDonald, *Memoirs of Joseph Benson*, 110.
28. Joseph Benson, *The New Testament of our Lord and Saviour Jesus Christ with Critical, Explanatory, and Practical Notes* (New York: Carlton and Phillips, 1854), 805.
29. Joseph Benson, *Two Sermons on the Nature and Design of the Gospel of Christ* (Hull: G. Prince, n.d.), 9-14.
30. Joseph Benson, *Two Sermons on the Nature and Design of the Gospel of Christ* (Hull: G. Prince, n.d.), 9-14.
31. Ibid.
32. Ibid., 758.
33. Ibid., 743.
34. *Memoirs of Reverend Joseph Benson*, ed. James Macdonald, 291.
35. Benson, The Life of the Rev. John William de la Flechere, in Works, 1:435-436.
36. Benson, *The Life of the Rev. John William de la Flechere*, in Works, 1:155-156.
37. Ibid. 1:163, 165.
38. Louis Bourdaloue, "Sermon for the Feast of Pentecost," trans. John Keeling, *The Methodist Magazine*, a continuation of *The Arminian Magazine* (40), 13 (London, 1817), 409-418, 491-500.
39. Cf. L. Wood, *Meaning of Pentecost in Early Methodism*, 337-385, for a fuller discussion of Fletcher's idea of the connection between confirmation and Christian perfection.
40. Ibid.
41. Louis Bourdaloue, *The Arminian Magazine*, 495.
42. Ibid., 491.
43. Ibid. 492.
44. Ibid., 496.
45. Ibid., 497.
46. Ibid., 500.
47. Benson, *Sermons, and Plans of Sermons* (Baltimore: Armstong & Plaskitt, 1828), 7:30-31.
48. Ibid., 7:82.
49. Ibid., 6:135-136.
50. "Preface," to *The Works of the Rev. John Fletcher*, ed. Joseph Benson (London: Richard Edwards, 1806), v.
51. Ibid., viii.
52. Joseph Benson, *The New Testament of our Lord and Saviour Jesus Christ*, 685.
53. Ibid., 686.
54. Ibid.,
55. Ibid. 693.
56. Ibid.
57. *The Methodist Magazine* (New York edition), 5 (July, 1822): 250-251.
58. Cf. *Meaning of Pentecost in Early Methodism*, 75-79.
59. Wesley, *Works* (Jackson edition), 16:187-188, "Letter to Lady Maxwell," (September 22, 1764).
60. Cf. John Lancaster, *Life of Lady Maxwell* (New York, Mason and Lane, 1840).
61. Wesley, *Works* (Jackson) 12:349, Letter to Lady Maxwell (February 8, 1772).
62. James MacDonald, *Memoirs of Joseph Benson* (New York: Bangs & Mason, 1823), 36-42.
63. Ibid., 37-38.
64. John Lancaster, *The Life of Darcy, Lady Maxwell* (New York: Mason and Lane, 1840), 321.
65. *Memoir of Mrs. Elizabeth Mortimer*, 126.
66. *Memoir of Mrs. Elizabeth Mortimer*, 124-125.
67. Elizabeth Ritchie Correspondence in the Frank Baker Collection, David M. Rubenstein Book and Manuscript Library.
68. Elizabeth Ritchie Correspondence in the Frank Baker Collection, David M. Rubenstein Book and Manuscript Library.

69. *Memoir of Mrs. Elizabeth Mortimer*, 59.
70. *Memoir of Mrs. Elizabeth Mortimer*, 123–125.
71. *Memoir of Mrs. Elizabeth Mortimer*, 98
72. Ibid., 84.
73. Ibid.
74. *Life and Correspondence of Mrs. Hester Ann Rogers*, 340–347.
75. *Memoir of Mrs. Elizabeth Mortimer*, 105.
76. *Memoir of Mrs. Elizabeth Mortimer*, 99.
77. "Elizabeth Ritchie Correspondence in the Frank Baker Collection in the David M. Rubenstein Rare Book & Manuscript Library, Duke University.
78. January 15, 1775. MARC: MAM F1 6/6/1
79. Elizabeth Ritchie Correspondence in the Frank Baker Collection, David M. Rubenstein Book and Manuscript Library.
80. Elizabeth Ritchie Correspondence in the Frank Baker Collection, David M. Rubenstein Book and Manuscript Library.
81. Elizabeth Ritchie Correspondence in the Frank Baker Collection, David M. Rubenstein Book and Manuscript Library.
82. Elizabeth Ritchie Correspondence in the Frank Baker Collection, David M. Rubenstein Book and Manuscript Library.
83. Elizabeth Ritchie Correspondence in the Frank Baker Collection, David M. Rubenstein Book and Manuscript Library.
84. Elizabeth Ritchie Correspondence in the Frank Baker Collection, David M. Rubenstein Book and Manuscript Library.
85. Elizabeth Ritchie Correspondence in the Frank Baker Collection, David M. Rubenstein Book and Manuscript Library.
86. *Memoir of Mrs. Elizabeth Mortimer*, 77–78.
87. *Memoir of Mrs. Elizabeth Mortimer*, 100.
88. MARC: MAM F1 6/6/6
89. MARC: MAMF1 6.6.10
90. MARC: MAM F1 6/6/16
91. MARC: MAM F1 6.7.1
92. *Memoir of Mrs. Elizabeth Mortimer*, 246.
93. *Life and Correspondence of Mrs. Hester Ann Rogers*, 305.
94. Ibid., 2:916; cf. Mrs. Richard Smith, *The Life of the Rev. Henry Moore*, 125.
95. *Life and Correspondence of Mrs. Hester Ann Rogers*, 62.
96. Ibid., 199, 225.
97. Ibid., 212.
98. Ibid. 265.
99. Ibid., 269.
100. *The Lives of Early Methodist Preachers,* ed. Thomas Jackson, 4 (London: Wesleyan Conference Office, 1872): 301–302.
101. *The Life and Correspondence of Hester Ann Rogers*, 305. Abel Stevens, *The History of the Religious Movement of the Eighteenth Century, called Methodism* 3:101.
102. *Life and Correspondence of Mrs. Hester Ann Rogers*, with an introduction by Thomas O. Summers (Nashville: Publishing House of the Methodist Episcopal Church, South, 1870), 62.
103. *The Life and Correspondence of Mrs. Hester Ann Rogers*, 318
104. Thomas Coke, *Funeral Sermon, Preached in Spitafields-Chapel, London, on Sunday, Oct. 26, 1794 on the Death of Mrs. Hester Ann Rogers* (Birmingham: J. Belcher, 1975), 18. Cf. *The Life and Correspondence of Mrs. Hester Ann Rogers*, 300.
105. *The Letters of Thomas Coke*, ed. John A. Vickers (Nashville: Kingswood Books, 2013), Letter to Thomas Morrell (July 6, 1789).109; Letter to William Holmes (October 12, 1790), 126.
106. *Life and Correspondence of Mrs. Hester Ann Rogers*, with an introduction by Thomas O. Summers (Nashville: Publishing House of the Methodist Episcopal Church, South, 1870), 62.
107. *The National Union Catalog, Pre-1956 Imprints*, 501:180–183.
108. Bangs, *A History of the Methodist Episcopal Church*, 2:318–319.

109. James Sigston, *Memoir of the Life and Ministry of William Bramwell* (New York: Phillips & Hunt), 36-44, 102, 120, 235, 287-288.
110. James Sigston, *Memoir of the Life and Ministry of William Bramwell*, 38-44, 98.
111. Cf. Ward and Heitzenrater, *Journals and Diaries I*, 18:304. Cf. Mrs. Richard Smith, *The Life of Rev. Henry Moore*, 180-181.
112. A letter to "My Very Dear Friend," written from Bristol, September 28, 1772. Cited by Tyerman, *Wesley's Designated Successor*, 242-243.
113. This sermon gives no facts of publication, but it is located in the B. L. Fisher Library Archives of Asbury Theological Seminary.
114. *The Lives of Early Methodist Preachers*, ed. Thomas Jackson, 4 (London: The Wesleyan Conference Office, 1872): 88108. Cf. Clarke, *Detached Pieces* (London: Thomas Tegg, 1841), 3:388.
115. Henry Moore, "Preface," *Life of Mrs. Mary Fletcher*, 5
116. Henry Moore, *Life of Mrs. Mary Fletcher*, 125; cf. 176, 235, 251, 270, 280, 293, 317, 355.
117. Mrs. Richard Smith, *The Life of Henry Moore* (London: Simpkin, Marshall and Company, 1944), 82
118. Ibid., 7.
119. Mrs. Richard Smith, *The Life of the Rev. Henry Moore*, 82, 144, 216.
120. *An Account of the Lord's dealings with the Rev. Thomas Rutherford / the greater part written by himself, the remainder supplied from authentic documents. With the review of his character / by his friend, Henry Moore*, Section III (Baltimore, R. J. Matchett, 1801), 161-162. http://www.wikitree.com/photo.php/a/ab/Rutherford-459-6.pdfby.
121. The editor's "Preface" to *Christian Perfection, Being an Extract from the Rev. John Fletcher's Treatise on That Subject* (New York: T. Mason and G. Lane, 1937 edition), 5.
122. *An Account of the Lord's dealings with the Rev. Thomas Rutherford*, 139-140.
123. Ibid.
124. Telford, *Letters*, 6:175 (a letter to John Fletcher, August 18, 1775).
125. The editor's "Preface" to *Christian Perfection, Being an Extract from the Rev. John Fletcher's Treatise on That Subject*. 7
126. *Christian Perfection, Being an Extract from the Rev. John Fletcher's Treatise on That Subject*, 3.
127. Ibid., 10
128. Cf. ibid., 25 *et passim*.
129. *Life of Henry Moore*, 194.
130. Ibid., 345.
131. Adam Clarke, *Clarke's Commentary* (New York: Abingdon-Cokesbury Press, n.d.), 5:683.
132. Clarke, *Detached Pieces* 3:470-471.
133. *Memoirs of the Late Eminent Mrs. Mary Cooper of London*, ed. Adam Clarke (Halifax: Nicholson and Sons, 1814), 5.
134. Ibid., 52ff., 97, 115.
135. Mrs. Richard Smith, *The Life of Rev. Henry Moore*, 244.
136. *Memoirs of the Late Eminent Mrs. Mary Cooper of London*, 53.
137. Ibid., 85.
138. Ibid., 91-92.
139. Ibid., 93.
140. Ibid., 100.
141. Ibid. 105.
142. Ibid., 171.
143. Ibid., 178.
144. Ibid., 192.
145. Ibid., 114.
146. Ibid., 132.
147. Ibid., 214f.
148. Ibid., 223.
149. *An Account of the Infancy, Religious, and Literary Life of Adam Clarke* (autobiography), edited J. B. B. Clarke (New York: B. Waugh and T. Mason, 1833), 1:110.
150. Cf. Richard Treffry, *A Treatise on Christian Perfection* (Boston: McDonald, Gill, & Co., 1888), 5. Cf. John Fletcher Hurst, *History of Methodism* 3:1325.

151. *The Methodist Magazine* (New York edition), 5 (April 1822): 125.

152. *The Methodist Magazine and Quarterly Review* 18 (July, 1835): 284ff.

153. *The Methodist Magazine and Quarterly Review* 27 (July, 1835): 287-288, 296.

154. Ibid., 296.

155. *Memoirs of the Rev. Richard Treffry, Junior*, ed. Richard Treffry, Senior (London: John Mason, 1839), 264.

156. Ibid., 239.

157. Thomas Jackson, "Memoirs of The Life and Writings of the Rev. Richard Watson," *The Works of the Rev. Richard Watson*, (London: John Mason, 1857), 1:39.

158. Chiles, 33-34.

159. "Conversations for the Young," *The Works of the Rev. Richard Watson* (London: John Mason, 1857), 6:263. Italics mine.

160. Thomas Jackson, "Memoirs of The Life and Writings of the Rev. Richard Watson," *The Works of the Rev. Richard Watson* 1:402.

161. Watson, "Hope the Anchor of the Soul," *The Works of the Rev. Richard Watson* (London: John Mason, 1857), 4:327.

162. Ibid.

163. Ibid.

164. Thomas Jackson, "Memoirs of The Life and Writings of the Rev. Richard Watson," *The Works of the Rev. Richard Watson* 1:402.

CHAPTER 17

A Sampling of the Expression of the Baptism with the Spirit in Methodist History

> "In speaking or writing of holiness... follow the well-sustained views, and even the phraseology employed in the writings of Wesley and Fletcher, which are not superseded by the more recent writers on this subject. Avoid both new theories, new expressions, and new measures on this subject, and adhere closely to the ancient landmarks."[1]
> —The Bishops' Pastoral Address to the General Conference of the Methodist Episcopal Church in 1852

When the Methodist Episcopal Church was established in American in 1784, John Wesley and Fletcher were cited as joint authorities on Methodist doctrine.

The 1784 Christmas Conference at Baltimore and Bishop Francis Asbury

In *The Doctrines and Discipline of the Methodist Episcopal Church* in America, with explanatory notes, Thomas Coke and Francis Asbury wrote:

> We would likewise declare our real sentiments on the scripture doctrine of election and reprobation; on the infallible, unconditional perseverance of all who ever have believed, or ever shall; and on the doctrine of Christian perfection. Far from wishing you to be ignorant of any of our doctrines, or any part of our discipline, we desire you to read, mark, learn, and inwardly digest the whole.[2]

Asbury and Coke told the preachers not to try to write further explanations of these doctrines, but to preach what they had learned from John Wesley and Fletcher: "A few good writers in one church are quite sufficient, especially in ours, which has already been honored with a Wesley and a Fletcher."[3]

Bishop Asbury introduced Fletcher's writings as textbook reading for his preachers,[4] and he was responsible for the first American edition of Fletcher's works. They remained part of the conference course of study until they were removed in 1880,⁵ as theological liberalism swept throughout Methodism.

As a young man Bishop Asbury knew and heard Fletcher preach even before he knew John Wesley.⁶ In a letter (December 31, 1801) to the Methodist book agent, Ezekiel Cooper, Asbury instructed him to publish the writings of Fletcher and John Wesley even placing Fletcher's name before Wesley's.⁷

John Wesley had begun to publish the complete *Works of John William Fletcher* in 1788, which was not completed until 1795. This 1788-1795 British edition was being published at the same time in America. The first and second volumes of the "First American Edition" of Fletcher's works were published in 1791 by Joseph Crukshank in Philadelphia; Crukshank published the third volume in 1792; Parry Hall published the fourth volume in 1793; and Henry Tuckniss published volume five in 1794 and volume six in 1796. All of these were printed in Philadelphia.⁸

The Last Check (Philadelphia, 1796) was reprinted in the same year as Rutherford's abridged edition entitled *Christian Perfection, An Extract from John Fletcher*, for the Methodist Episcopal Church. Rutherford's edition had eight reprints for the Methodist Episcopal Church between 1837 and 1875, and was widely cited by Methodist writers throughout the nineteenth century.

Interestingly enough, there were thirteen imprints of Fletcher's various writings in America, including five reprints of his complete *Works*, from 1796 before John Wesley's complete *Works* were first published in 1826.⁹ Fletcher's *Checks to Antinomianism* were reprinted for the Methodist Episcopal Church eight different times in the nineteenth century. His complete *Works* were reprinted twenty two times throughout the nineteenth century with the last edition being in 1883.¹⁰

As earlier noted, *The Life of John Fletcher* was first written by John Wesley, and then it was rewritten by Joseph Benson in 1804 at the request of the British General Conference. It was subsequently published twenty seven times, with the 1898 edition being the last one. Seventeen of those editions were for The Methodist Episcopal Church, and ten editions were for British Methodism.¹¹ Fletcher's *The Portrait of St. Paul* was published after his death, and it was reprinted nine times, mostly in New York for the Methodist Episcopal Church. There were at least 174 different printings of Fletcher's various books in the nineteenth century.¹²

This remarkably large number of reprints of his writings shows that his doctrinal views formed the thinking of Methodism from its inception. Abel Stevens, a nineteenth-century Methodist historian, claimed that Fletcher's writings "control the opinions of the largest and most effective body of evangelical clergymen of the earth . . . They have been more influential in the denomination than Wesley's own controversial writings on the subject [Antinomianism]." ¹³

In "An Address of the Editors," published in *The* [American] *Methodist Magazine* in 1823,¹⁴ Fletcher's writings are referenced as the authoritative doctrinal standard. In 1828, an editorial comment in *The Christian Advocate* noted: "I consider Mr. Wesley and Mr. Fletcher as standing foremost, perhaps, in the Christian world, as faithful interpreters of the mind and will of God to man, as revealed in the Scriptures of truth" and added a further comment about Fletcher's Checks: "Oh what, an invaluable work!" This editorial particularly cited from Fletcher's treatise on Christian Perfection to refute critics.[15]

An extensive review in *The Methodist Magazine and Quarterly Review* of Fletcher's *Portrait of St. Paul* was given in 1831. It affirmed Fletcher's role in establishing Methodist doctrine: "After the Holy Scriptures, and, in subordination to these, the works of Mr. John Wesley, the writings of John Fletcher are held next in estimation, we believe, by the whole body of Wesleyan Methodists throughout the world."[16]

Portrait of St. Paul represented Fletcher's most mature thoughts, highlighting the baptism with the Holy Spirit, and this emphasis was noted in the review. This review also believed that Fletcher's writings were appreciated throughout Methodism.[17] Typical of this attitude toward Fletcher is an early twentieth century Methodist bishop and author who referred to Fletcher as "the thought of Wesley voiced by Fletcher."[18]

Some Samplings of Pentecost and Sanctification in British and American Methodist Publications

It would have been clear to any reader of *The Arminian Magazine* that Fletcher's emphasis on Pentecost and sanctification was official Methodist doctrine because of the numerous publications of his letters and writings contained in it. When John Wesley was still alive, he included numerous letters and excerpts from Fletcher's writings in *The Arminian Magazine*, including Fletcher's use of "baptism with the Holy Spirit and fire"[19] and "fullness of the Spirit"[20] to denote Christian perfection.

Fletcher's life and writings are mentioned in every annual volume of the British edition of *The Arminian Magazine* for one hundred years until 1878 (except for three volumes),[21] including its continuation *in The Methodist Magazine* and *The Wesleyan-Methodist Magazine*. Fletcher's name also appeared in the American edition of *The Arminian Magazine*, *The Methodist Magazine*, and *The Methodist Quarterly Review* with the same regularity.

In 1790 Francis Asbury published the second volume of the American issue of *The Arminian Magazine* promoting Fletcher as "our almost inimitable friend" and providing an extract from John Wesley's account of his life and death.[22]

This extract from John Wesley's biography began with this biblical quotation from Acts 5:38, 39, as a particular reference to Fletcher: "If this counsel or this work be of men, it will come to naught: But if it be of GOD, ye cannot overthrow it; lest haply ye be found even to fight against GOD."[23]

This extract from John Wesley's biography also included his personal comment:

> No man in England has had so long an acquaintance with Mr. Fletcher as myself. Our acquaintance began almost as soon as his arrival in London, about the year 1752, before he entered into holy orders, or (I believe) had any such intention. And it continued uninterrupted between thirty and forty years, even 'till it pleased GOD to take him to himself. Nor was ours a slight or ordinary acquaintance; but we were of one heart and of one soul. We had no secrets between us for many years; we did not purposely hide any thing from each other. From time to time he consulted me, and I him, on the most important occasions. And he constantly professed, not only much esteem but (what I valued far more) much affection.... I therefore think myself obliged by the strongest ties, to pay this small tribute to his memory.[24]

With Francis Asbury's promotion of Fletcher as "our almost inimitable friend" and John Wesley's unqualified approval of Fletcher as his intimate friend and associate in ministry, it was only normal that those who read the magazine would consider Fletcher as their guide to doctrinal beliefs.

As a reader of this issue of *The Arminian Magazine* continued to read John Wesley's biography of Fletcher, John Wesley would soon inform them that Fletcher's "favourite subject was, *The promise of the Father, the gift of the Holy Spirit.* . . . 'We must not be content,' said he, 'to be only cleansed from sin: we must be filled with the Spirit'."[25]

In 1793, *The Arminian Magazine* published a letter of Fletcher addressed to his congregation at Madeley (1777):

> If I your poor unworthy shepherd am smitten, be not scattered; but rather be more closely gathered unto Christ, and keep near each other in faith and love, till you all receive our second Comforter and Advocate, in the glory of his fullness. You know I mean the Holy Spirit, the third Person in our Covenant God. *He is with you*, but if you plead *the promise of the Father, which,* says Christ, *you have heard of me, he will be in you.* He will fill your souls with his light, love, and glory, according to that verse which we have so often sung together,
>
> "Refining fire go through my heart,
> Illuminate my soul,
> Scatter thy life through every part,
> And sanctify the whole."
>
> This indwelling of the Comforter, perfects the mystery of sanctification in the believer's soul. This is the highest blessing of the Christian Covenant on earth. Rejoicing in the God our Creator, in God our Redeemer, let us look for the full comfort of God our Sanctifier. So shall we live and die in the faith, going on from faith to faith, from strength to strength, from comfort to comfort, till Christ is all in all,—to us all.[26]

In 1797 in *The Arminian Magazine* there is a testimony of one who was seeking Christian perfection. She testified in terms of "being cleansed from the remains of sin" and "waiting for the fuller baptism with his Spirit."[27]

In 1798, *The Arminian Magazine* published a letter of John Fletcher to his congregation at Madeley, written in 1783: "O for a deeper Baptism of the Spirit! I want that promise *more fully* accomplished, 'I and my Father will come, and will make our abode with you'."[28]

The following entry was listed in the index of *The Arminian Magazine* under the category: "From Mr. Fletcher, on the baptism of the Spirit." This focus of his letter on the baptism with the Spirit was thus the reason for publishing this letter in *The Arminian Magazine*.

The Arminian Magazine (1809) published the *Memoirs of Mr. Evans* who recorded in his diary for September 2: "I had to baptize almost fifty persons, more than half of whom were advanced above the years of childhood, and two of them very old men. I have cause to believe that many of them were earnestly seeking to be baptized with the Holy Spirit."[29]

The Arminian Magazine (1817) carried the memoirs of Miss Bunting, who "was very conversant with the writings of the Rev. Mr. Wesley, and Mr. Fletcher."[30] As she was dying, she said to her mother: "O mother, I am going to heaven, I wish you were going with me; but you will not be long after me. I shall see Mr. Wesley. Mr. Fletcher, St. Paul, Abraham, Isaac, and Jacob, and all the Prophets, and Martyrs." " Yes," added Mrs. M. "and Jesus the Mediator."[31]

The Wesleyan-Methodist Magazine gave this report about Mrs. Ludlam on March 24, 1821: "It pleased God to bless her with a peculiar baptism of the Holy Spirit, and to fill her with joy and love."[32] In the same issue was a report of Mrs. Lydia who died on July 13, 1821: "From the time of her conversion, she manifested great tenderness of conscience, and anxiously desired the entire sanctification of her nature. She read the works of Wesley, Fletcher, and others, upon that subject, and often conversed respecting it with experienced Christians : and about five years before her death, she obtained a fuller baptism of the Spirit, which enabled her to love the Lord her GOD with all her heart."[33]

In 1807, Elijah Sabin published two sermons on *Christian Perfection, Displayed and the Objections Obviated*. He was admitted into the Conference in 1801 of the Methodist Episcopal Church. He said Christian perfection is "not only implies a cleansing . . ., but the being *filled* with the pure and perfect love of God." He cites Acts 2:4, "And they were all *filled* with the Holy Spirit," along with Acts 4:8, 31, as well as Ephesians 5:18. He said: "A variety of others might be quoted, but these are sufficient to prove, to every unprejudiced mind, that God will so fill the souls of believers with his Holy Spirit as that all sin shall be destroyed." [34]

The Methodist Magazine in 1809 contained the testimony of Peter Haslam: "Yesterday the Lord was very graciously present with us at our Love feast. Many bore a very clear testimony respecting entire sanctification. If I am convicted of evil, it is by that heart piercing law, 'Thou shall not covet.' The desire of certain things even now possesses me. . . . Nothing less than a glorious baptism of thy Spirit can save me: O let that baptism now descend!"[35]

On August 10, 1818, Wilbur Fisk experienced "perfect love" through the "baptism of the Holy Spirit" through listening to a sermon preached by Timothy Merritt on "Christian perfection" at a campmeeting on Cape Cod. [36] Fisk was one of the educational leaders and was the first president of Wesleyan University. Fisk highlighted in his preaching and writing that full sanctification means purification from sin through being filled with the Spirit of God.[37]

We know from the written diary of Joseph Pilmore that he (who with Richard Boardman were the first British missionaries to America) preached on the baptism of the Holy Spirit in 1770. He had been a close friend of John Fletcher with whom they had many conversations together when Fletcher regularly traveled from Madeley to Trevecca.[38] But well before John Fletcher had written his "Essay on Truth" and his treatise on Christian perfection, Pilmore was preaching on the baptism with the Spirit in North America.

On June 3, 1770, Pilmore wrote: "In the evening, I declared to a very large and attentive audience, 'He shall Baptize you with the Holy Spirit and with fire' (Matt 3:11) and had good reason to believe God fulfilled the promise to many of the hearers by the comforts of his heavenly love [i.e., perfect love]."[39] This shows this expression was being used by Methodists before Fletcher popularized it.

Pilmore wrote frequently about the importance of Christian perfection in his diaries, and we know that this theme was prominent in the preaching of his close friend and preaching partner, Captain Webb.

We do not have many written sermons to indicate to us the details of the preaching of many of John Wesley's preachers, but we do have the gist of the way that Captain Webb preached on this subject, thanks to Henry Moore. In his reminiscences about the older preachers he gave the following report at a social gathering. He noted that Webb's manner of speaking in metaphors was not always so sophisticated. Moore's anecdote about Webb's preaching showed that it was common to talk about the difference between the disciples' experience of being justified before Pentecost and fully sanctified after Pentecost.

> Captain Webb was a red-hot preacher. He took some text about the Holy Spirit out of one of the epistles and went on to this effect: "The words of the text were written by the apostles after the act of justification had passed on them. But you see, my friends, this was not enough for them. They must receive the Holy Spirit after this. So must you. You must be sanctified. But you are not. You are only Christians in part. You have not received the Holy Spirit. I know it. I can feel your spirits hanging about me like so much dead flesh."[40]

Nathan Bangs, the first official historian of American Methodism, provided several reports on the early American Methodist preachers as being baptized with the Spirit. Bangs noted that in 1799 that the "baptism with the Spirit" was a particular focus of Methodist preachers. Bangs said that "the doctrine . . . of *sanctification, or holiness of heart and life* . . . was pressed upon them as their *present* privilege. . . . It was this *baptism of the Holy Spirit* which fired and filled the hearts of God's ministers at that time."[41] Bangs described a great revival that swept through Maryland, Delaware, Pennsylvania, Vermont, Connecticut, and New Hampshire, and stated "that most of the preachers had received a new baptism of the Holy Spirit—like that which had been showered upon Calvin Wooster, and others in Canada, the preceding year [1799]; and wherever they went they carried the holy fire with them, and God wrought wonders by their instrumentality."[42]

In the first volume of *The Methodist Magazine* (New York), a report of "A Short Account of Cow-Harbour Camp-Meeting" in Long Island, New York for August 11, 1818, was given, explaining that many were converted and others "were groaning for full redemption in the blood of the Lamb. While engaged in this exercise, some of the preachers were baptized afresh with the *Holy Spirit and fire*; and their cup run over with love to God, and to the souls of men.[43]

The second volume of the *Methodist Magazine* (1819) in the United States carried this entry from the "Memoir of Mr. William Appleton": "Feb. 1, 1812 Sheffield. I am this day waiting for a double baptism of the Holy Spirit. . . . My soul is more than ever dead to the world."[44] In this same volume, it was reported that "the Methodist ministers have the greatest encouragement to enter upon this work. They have seen the proof of this doctrine in all the Scriptures, especially through the medium of the incomparable writings of Messrs. Wesley and Fletcher. This doctrine every Methodist minister professes to believe."[45]

In 1822, Mrs. Law of Yorkshire, England, testified to having "received a richer baptism of the Holy Spirit" and "her dedication to God . . . was more complete and constant"[46] She also in her experience "realized the truth of the words of the beloved disciple, 'There is no fear in love; but perfect love casteth out fear;' and believing it to be her privilege to be cleansed from all unrighteousness . . . and soon, to her unspeakable joy, that the Spirit of God entirely sanctified her nature."[47]

The Wesleyan-Methodist Magazine for August 1824 reported the testimony of George Clark who sought "complete deliverance from 'the carnal mind.' While he was earnestly pleading with the Lord, he received a deeper baptism of the sanctifying Spirit; and from that time to the closing scene of life, he walked in the full light of God's countenance."[48]

In the January issue of 1824 of *The Wesleyan-Methodist Magazine*, an extract of a letter, dated April 19, 1824 was included: "Preachers, Class-Leaders, and Members, have received a fresh baptism of heavenly love and zeal; many are athirst for the fullness of his sanctifying grace; and some have received that perfect love which casteth out fear."[49]

In the *Wesleyan-Methodist Magazine* (1849), a biographical account was given of Mrs. Brockelsby, noting that "after eighteen years after her conversion . . . she received a richer baptism of spiritual life and power and was enabled humbly but firmly to testify that Christ had all her heart, and that his precious blood had cleansed her from all sin. This perfect love she never lost: it remained with her though life." She acquainted herself with Methodist doctrine through consulting both Wesley and Fletcher. "Profiting as she did by what is sometimes called 'Methodist doctrine,' as preached from the pulpit, in her hours of retirement she made herself familiar with the principal works in which it is contained. With Mr. Wesley's Sermons, Notes, Appeals, and Journal, with Mr. Fletcher's works, and with the chief Wesleyan Biographies, she was well acquainted."[50]

In the *Wesleyan-Methodist Magazine* for 1852, the testimony of James Blackett was published. "Shortly after" he had "obtained the pardoning mercy and love of God," "he saw and felt that there still existed within him the remains of the carnal heart, and that he needed a richer and fuller baptism from on high. He earnestly sought the blessing of perfect love. . . . He was enabled by faith to cast his soul upon Christ for the full salvation . . . and obtained unutterable rest in God. Sin was all destroyed. His soul was filled with holy love."[51] This occurred on November 10, 1798.

In 1832, a book of sermons "by different ministers of the Methodist Episcopal Church" including Wilbur Fisk, Nathan Bangs, and Richard Watson contained a sermon by Aaron Lummus who affirmed that "on the day of Pentecost, the disciples . . . were *all filled with the Holy Spirit*, Acts ii.4. They were therefore emptied of sin, were wholly sanctified."[52]

The editor (George Peck) of *The Methodist Quarterly Review* in 1841 carried an extensive discussion of the current status of the doctrine of Christian perfection in the Methodist Episcopal Church. He wrote: "The true Methodist ground [of entire sanctification] was so clearly stated, and so ably defended, and the whole subject so thoroughly investigated, by Messrs. Wesley and Fletcher, that but little has been done by subsequent writers of the same views but to repeat what they, in the same language, or in substance, had written."[53]

He made the point that "as ministers in the Methodist Episcopal Church, we have fully set our seal to the doctrine of Wesley and Fletcher upon this point."[54] Particular attention is called to the meaning of the baptism with the Spirit. "But it [Christian perfection] is especially indicated as the work of the Holy Spirit by being denominated the *baptism of the Holy Spirit, sanctification of the Spirit &c., &c.* The view of our authors [Wesley and Fletcher] is, that the work is *effected and sustained by the direct agency of the Spirit of God upon the soul.*"[55]

A worry about the neglect of the doctrine is expressed in 1849 by Jesse T. Peck, a prominent Methodist minister and author. He wrote: "I fear attention has not been called so distinctly and forcibly to the doctrine of holiness as it should have been. Sermons have too generally stopped short of it."[56] He also noted that some had not heard the doctrine preached for so long that they do not recognize it as Methodist belief. "Why do those charge its faithful advocates with preaching a new and strange doctrine in the church, though it is taught in the very style of the Scriptures—in the very language of Wesley and Fletcher?"[57] Peck defined the message of entire sanctification as "a soul filled with the Holy Spirit."[58]

Traditional Wesleyan Theology Rejected toward the End of the 19th Century

The Wesleyan doctrine of entire sanctification was uniformly embraced throughout its history until the middle of the 19th century as theological Liberalism began weaving itself into the institutions of higher learning.

When D. D. Whedon became the fifth editor of *The Methodist Quarterly Review* (1856 to 1884)[59] he rejected John Wesley's idea of Christian perfection and denied the idea of a "second blessing."[60]

Other prominent Methodists like James Mudge talked about growth, and denied that one could be free from inbred sin.[61] Mudge did not believe in the possibility of full sanctification, and he rejected Pentecost as its basis.[62]

As a basis for his interpretation, he cited John Wesley's letter of caution to Joseph Benson against defining Christian perfection in terms of "receiving the Spirit.[63] Mudge failed to see this comment from John Wesley to Benson in the larger context of John Wesley's affirmation of Pentecost and sanctification and his approval of Fletcher's *Essay on Truth* and *Last Check*. So Mudge assumed that John Wesley linked Pentecost only to justifying faith.

Mudge's revisionism of traditional Wesleyan theology brought Daniel Steele out of retirement to answer him after having been a professor of theology of Boston University for many years. Steele was also the founding president of Syracuse University and a prolific writer. He was well trained in classical studies and possessed a thorough grasp of the writings of John Wesley and John Fletcher, as well as being knowledgeable of the history of theology in general. Steele's deep lament is summarized in words of great regret.

> I am not a pessimist nor a friend of pessimism; I am not a prophet nor the son of a prophet; yet something like the burden of a prophet is laid upon me, constraining me to cry aloud to the [Methodist Episcopal] Church of my father and mother—the Church in which I had my first and my second birth—the Church which nurtured me in her schools,

and commissioned me to preach in her pulpits and to teach in her universities—a church to which I owe a debt too large for me to pay. It is exceedingly painful to note in this Church the first and the second indication of spiritual decay. The first has long grieved me; it is the neglect of those vital truths which nourish a stalwart spiritual life. The silence of the pulpit these many years respecting the full heritage of the believer, which is nothing less than is expressed in the words of Dr. McClintock, "The holiness of the human soul, heart, mind and will," has been broken at last by the voice of a son of the Church in the open and loud repudiation of that doctrine which is "the inmost essence" and "elemental thought" of Methodism. This is the second token of spiritual decay, the second milestone on the downward road to spiritual death. The fact that this voice sounds out through the very trumpet which was made for the heralding of the glorious evangel of Christian perfection greatly aggravates my sorrow. Yet I am not surprised. The Church that incorporates in itself so large a segment of worldliness will sooner or later reject every doctrine hostile to a love of the world.[64]

Steele's observation about "the silence of the pulpit these many years respecting the full heritage of the believer" was one of the reasons for the rise of the Wesleyan-Holiness tradition. The expression, "the baptism with the Holy Spirit," came to be nuanced with a stronger emphasis on the sudden moment of entire sanctification in the American Holiness Movement at the end of the 19th Century. This happened just as theological Liberalism was embraced by the leadership of the Methodist Episcopal Church, and the distinctive Wesleyan doctrinal beliefs were being marginalized.[65]

The patron saint of the holiness movement was Phoebe Palmer.[66] Her leadership and international influence emerged as she became the editor of *Guide to Holiness*. Her precursor was James Merritt, a prominent Methodist minister in New England and a staff member of the Methodist Publishing Concern.

Merritt started a publication to promote the cause of holiness, entitled, *Guide to Christian Perfection*, in 1839.[67] Stemming from the influence of Merritt and Palmer was the phenomenal growth of the American Holiness Movement that is well documented and explained in *The Holiness Revival of the Nineteenth Century* by Melvin E. Dieter.[68] "Pentecostal sanctification," as Martin Wells Knapp (one of the prominent leaders of the Wesleyan-Holiness movement) termed it,[69] was not only a common interpretation in the Wesleyan-Holiness movement, but it became the preferred mode of speaking of holiness.[70]

Eventually under attack by the leadership of the Methodist Episcopal Church in the second half of the 19th century, the holiness tradition organized itself against the uprising of theological Liberalism and often separated itself into holiness denominations, although many leaders remained within the Methodist Episcopal Church.

Daniel Steele was the most scholarly and the most representative of the best thinking among holiness advocates. As a child, Steele had learned from his mother about instantaneous sanctification through the baptism with the Spirit. In his first publication (*Love Enthroned*, 1875), he defined entire sanctification as being attained through the baptism with the Spirit, and he cited extensively from John Fletcher.[71] In a sermon before the Boston University School of Theology, May 30, 1871, he defined entire sanctification in reference to Fletcher's concept of the baptism with the Spirit, insisting (unlike Fletcher) that "it must be instantaneous."[72] This testimony came six months after his personal experience of holiness.

There is no indication that he ever had any hesitancy about using the language of the baptism with the Spirit, although he recognized that John Wesley did not often use this specific phrase in his published writings, and he recognized that the fullness of the Spirit may have different meanings, ranging from ecstatic fullness, prophetic fullness, to ethical fullness.[73] Everywhere in his writings and from his childhood he linked the baptism and fullness of the Spirit with entire sanctification. He specifically embraced Fletcher's soteriological doctrine of dispensations, while rejecting the eschatological dispensationalism of the Plymouth Brethren and John Darby.[74]

Steele assumed that John Wesley and Fletcher were in agreement and were the primary authorities of Methodist beliefs. Steele's father-in-law was Amos Binney, whose widely-read *Theological Compend of Christian Doctrine* also embraced Pentecost and sanctification in 1839.[75] The idea has been suggested that Steele added the theology of Pentecostal and sanctification later in his career and changed his language to include "the baptism with the Spirit," but that report is not factual,[76] although prior to his own experience of holiness he preferred the idea of progressive sanctification.

Unlike Fletcher, the organized holiness movement sometimes considered full sanctification "as a terminal point with disappointing results," as one of its prominent leaders, the late Hollis Abbott, complained.[77] J. Paul Taylor, a deceased bishop of the Free Methodist Church and a prominent spokesperson for the organized holiness movement, also noted that "the church has suffered incalculable loss because so many of her members have regarded the Canaan rest as the terminus of a journey, instead of the opening of a new realm challenging to endless exploration."[78]

The next chapter will propose another way of "spreading Scriptural holiness across these lands," as John Wesley envisaged the reason for the rise of Methodism. This new way may contribute to a more holistic message of Christian perfection linked to the liturgy of the church and less to the individualistic experience sometimes associated with the camp meeting tradition.

Notes

1. "The Bishops' Pastoral Address to the General Conference of the Methodist Episcopal Church in 1852, *Journal of the General Conference of the Methodist Episcopal Church Held in Boston, MASS, 1852* (New-York: Carlton & Phillips, 1852), 160.

2. Thomas Coke and Francis Asbury, *The Doctrines and Discipline of the Methodist Episcopal Church in America, with explanatory notes*, 10th ed. (Philadelphia: Tuckniss, 1798), iv. Original date of publication was Nov. 16, 1792 in Baltimore by Thomas Coke and Francis Asbury, 59.

3. Thomas Coke and Francis Asbury, *The Doctrines and Discipline of the Methodist Episcopal Church in America*, 59.

4. *Autobiography of Dan Young*, ed. W. Strickland (New York: Carlton and Porter, 1860), 213–214, 164–165, 212ff., 14, 35.

5. Robert E. Chiles, *Theological Transition in American Methodism* (New York: University Press of America, 1983), 40.

6. *Journal and Letters of Francis Asbury*, ed. J. M. Potter, Elmer T. Clark, and J. S. Payton, (Nashville: Abingdon Press, 1958),1:124 (July 24, 1774).

7. Ibid., 1:232.

8. I am indebted to Melvin E. Dieter for this information. He personally own this "First American Edition."

9. Cf. *The National Union Catalog, Pre-1956 Imprints*, 175:232–240.

10. Cf. *The National Union Catalog Pre-1956 Imprints*, 175:232–240.

11. Cf. *The National Union Catalog Pre-1956 Imprints*, 47:250-253.
12. Cf. *The National Union Catalog Pre-1956 Imprints*, 175:232-240. There were also other imprints of this work not listed in *The National Union Catalog*, such J. Kingston, Fletcher's *Appeal to Matter of Fact & Common Sense* (Baltimore: J. Robinson, Printer, 1814).
13. Abel Stevens, *The History of the Religious Movement of the Eighteenth Century, Called* Methodism (London: George Watson, 1864) 2:55. Cf. John Fletcher Hurst, *John Wesley the Methodist* (New York; The Methodist Book Concern, 1903), 204-205.
14. *The Methodist Magazine*, 6 (January – February 1823): 9, 65.
15. *Christian Advocate and Journal*, 2.29 (New York, July 11, 1828): 73.
16. *The Methodist Magazine and Quarterly Review* 13 (January 1831): 104.
17. *Journal of Rev. Francis Asbury* (New York: Eaton & Mains, 1821), 110-111.
18. Neely, *The Doctrinal Standards of Methodism* (New York: Fleming H. Revell Company, 1918), 86.
19. *The Arminian Magazine* 14 (January, 1791), 49.
20. *The Arminian Magazine* 5 (January, 1782); 43, 49.
21. 1778, 1784, 1787 are the only years when Fletcher was not referenced in *The Arminian Magazine*, and most assuredly Fletcher continued to be cited well beyond 1878, although I have not confirmed that fact.
22. *The Arminian Magazine* 2 (New York, January, 1790), iv.
23. Ibid., 27.
24. Ibid., 36-37.
25. Ibid., 187.
26. *The Arminian Magazine* 16 (London, June, 1793): 486.
27. *The Arminian Magazine* (March 1797):144-145
28. *The Methodist Magazine*, volume 1, a continuation of *The Arminian Magazine*, volume 21, (London edition), (November 1798): 597.
29. "Memoir of Mr. Evans," *The Methodist Magazine Being a Continuation of The Arminian Magazine* 32 (London, 1809), 229.
30. *The Arminian Magazine*, (London, January, 1817), 50.
31. Ibid., 52.
32. "Obituary," *The Wesleyan-Methodist Magazine*, 45 (London: March, 1822), 202.
33. "Obituary," *The Wesleyan-Methodist Magazine* (London: March 1822), 203-204.
34. Elijah R. Sabin, *Christian Perfection Displayed and the Objections Obviated: Being the Substance of Two Discourses delivered at Warwick, Rhode Island, September 13, 1807* (Providence, RI: Jones and Wheeler, 1807), 14-15.
35. *The Methodist Magazine*, 32 (London, March 1809). 97.
36. Joseph Holdich, *The Life of Wilbur Fisk* (New York: Harper and Brothers, 1842), 72.
37. Ibid., 87.
38. Benson, *The Life of the Rev. John W. de la Flechere*. Eleventh Edition. London: J. Mason, 1838, 170.
39. *The Journal of Joseph Pilmore* (Philadelphia: Message Publishing Co., for the Historical Society of the Philadelphia Annual Conference of the United Methodist Church, 1969), 46.
40. Cf. J. F. Hurst, *History of Methodism* (New York: Eaton and Mains, 1902), 3:1252.
41. Nathan Bangs, *A History of the Methodist Episcopal Church* (New York: G. Lane and C. B. Tippett, 1845), 2:75.
42. Ibid., 2:101.
43. *The Methodist Magazine*, 1 (September, New York, 1818), 358.
44. *The Methodist Magazine*, 2 (New York, October, 1819). 372.
45. *The Methodist Magazine*, 2 (New York, September, 1819), 344, Signed as "a Preacher" in letter to the editors.
46. George Coles, *Heroines of Methodism; Pen and Ink Sketches of the Mothers and Daughters of the Church*, (New York: Phillips & Hunt, 1883), 281.
47. Ibid., 282.
48. *The Wesleyan-Methodist Magazine*, 3 (May 1824), 566.
49. *The Wesleyan-Methodist Magazine*, 3 (January 1824), 331.
50. *The Wesleyan-Methodist Magazine*, 5 (November 1849), 1121-1122.
51. *The Wesleyan-Methodist Magazine* . 8 (February, 1852), 106.
52. *Twenty Eight Sermons on Doctrinal and Practical Subjects*, contributed by different ministers of the Methodist Episcopal Church (Boston: C. C. Strong, 1832), 317.

53. *The Methodist Magazine and Quarterly Review* 23 (January, 1841): 123-124.
54. Ibid., 139.
55. Ibid., 151.
56. Cf. *Guide to Christian Perfection* 15 (June 1849): 135.
57. Ibid., 136
58. Ibid., 135.
59. *The Encyclopedia of World Methodism*, ed. Nolan B. Harmon (Nashville: The United Methodist Publishing House, 1974) 1:1591.
60. Whedon, "Christian Perfection and the Higher Life," *Methodist Quarterly Review* (October 1878): 695. Cf. Mudge, *The Perfect Life in Experience and Doctrine* (Cincinnati : Jennings and Graham, 1911), 296. Cf. Myung Soo Park, "Concepts of Holiness in American Evangelicalism: 1835-1915," (Ph. D. Dissertation, Boston University, 1992), 91.
61. Cf. Mudge, *The Perfect Life*, 296; Peters, *Christian Perfection and American Methodism*, 151.
62. *Growth in Holiness*, 259.
63. *Growth in Holiness*, 256-257.
64. Steele, *A Defense of Christian Perfection or A Criticism of Dr. James Mudge's "Growth in Holiness Toward Perfection"* (New York: Hunt and Eaton, 1896), 120-121.
65. Cf. John Leland Peters, *Christian Perfection and American Methodism* (Grand Rapids: Francis Asbury Press, 1985). Cf. J. A. Wood, *Perfect Love* (Noblesville, IN: Newby Book Room, 1967), 274).
66. *Phoebe Palmer*, ed. Thomas Oden (Paulist Press, 1988). Cf. Dayton, *Theological Roots of Pentecostalism*, 87.
67. Melvin E. Dieter, *The Holiness Revival of the Nineteenth Century*, second edition (Lanham, MD: 1996), 42.
68. Ibid.
69. Wallace Thornton, *When the Fire Fell* (Lexington: Emeth Press, 2014), 44n162.
70. The term "Pentecostal" was frequently used in titles published by the organized holiness movement. For example, an extract from Fletcher's writings appeared under the title, *Pentecostal Flashlights from the Life of John Fletcher*, ed. W. L. Philipps, (Cincinnati: Published by Mrs. M. W. Knapp of God's Bible School, 1902). On the opposite side of its title page was a list of other recommended booklets on holiness. Out of thirty listed titles, nine of them had the language of Pentecost in their titles. [see Wallace thornton, When the Fire Fell, 60ff.].
71. *Love Enthroned. Essays on Evangelical Perfection* (New York: Philipps and Hunt, 1875, 1880), especially 94, 141ff.
72. Daniel Steele, "The Qualities of a Successful Ministry," *Half Hours with St. Paul* (Boston: The Christian Witness Co., 1895), p291, 294.
73. *A Defense of Christian Perfection or A Criticism of Dr. James Mudge's "Growth in Holiness Toward Perfection"* (New York: Hunt and Eaton, 1896), Chapter 29.
74. Steele, *Antinomianism Revived, or the Theology of the So-Called Plymouth Brethren* (Boston : McDonald, Gill & co., 1887).
75. Binney, *A Theological Compend of Christian Doctrine* (Nashville, Tenn:Southern Methodist Publishing House, 1870, c1840), 83.
76. Cf. the reference to this idea by Wallace Thornton, *When the Fire Fell*, 81n84.
77. *The Word and the Doctrine*, ed. Kenneth E. Geiger (Kansas City, MO: Beacon Hill Press, 1965), 301.
78. Ibid.

CHAPTER 18

A Proposal for Today— Christian Perfection as the Rite of Confirmation *Felt*

> "It is proposed ... Mr. Wesley ... would draw up a petition and present to the Archbishop of Canterbury ... that the important office of confirmation shall be performed with the utmost solemnity by Mr. Wesley."
> —A Letter from John Fletcher to John Wesley on August 1, 1775, proposing that Methodism in "Great Britain, Ireland, and America be formed into a general society—a daughter church of our holy mother, the Church of England," becoming "the *methodist*-church of England."[1]

> "One asked me if there was any good in confirmation. I answered, 'No, nor in baptism, nor in the Lord's Supper, or any outward thing, unless you are in Christ a new Creature'."
> —Charles Wesley

An examination of the historiography of Methodism in the previous chapters has shown that John Wesley's idea of two moments of salvation—justifying faith and full sanctifying grace—arose out of a similar distinction between the justified state of the disciples before Pentecost and the fully sanctified disciples after Pentecost.

This idea of two stages was not an innovation with John Wesley. We have already noted in Chapter Two that the idea of two stages of Christian initiation in the earliest days of the Christian community was an essential part of the baptismal liturgy based on Easter and Pentecost. New data shows this to be the practice of the earliest Christians even before the New Testament writings themselves.

John Wesley's primary source for giving shape to his understanding of a two-stage interpretation of salvation was Christian David in 1738. He also cited one of the lesser known Early Church Fathers in support of it, pseudo-Macarius, whom he quoted to show that inward sin still remains in the justified person.[2] John Wesley translated and published his own abridged version of *The Spiritual Homilies of St. Macarius the Egyptian* and placed it in the first volume of his *Christian Library*. Fletcher used this abridged edition to show that this Early Church Father connected the baptism with the Holy Spirit, circumcision of the heart, and perfection.[3]

In 1776, Fletcher said: "Mr. Wesley and I" agree with pseudo-Macarius: "From the preceding extract I conclude, that, if Macarius, who lived near 1300 years ago, so clear preached the baptism and dispensation of the Holy Spirit, Mr. John Wesley and I cannot reasonably be charged with *novelty* for doing the same thing."[4]

There was, however, a bit of *novelty* in their understanding of Christian perfection. John Wesley and Charles Wesley introduced the idea of the sudden attainment of justification and Christian perfection through faith, although as we have noted Charles eventually came to highlight the element of process for Christian perfection. We previously cited examples from their journals of those who were first justified and then later sanctified. Fletcher attempted a synthesis of both process and sudden attainment, as seen in Fletcher's letters of correspondence with Charles Wesley and in his main book on Christian perfection (*The Last Check to Antinomianism*).

An unintended implication of emphasizing a personal decision of justifying and sanctifying faith could result in a privatized and individualistic experience isolated from the larger community of faith. John Wesley was much aware of this tendency. This is why he said there is "no holiness but social holiness."[5] For John Wesley "social holiness" entailed an accountability group that methodically met together as a community of believers. This is why he established "bands" and "select societies" where the holy life could be cultivated and promoted.

John Fletcher said that in the book of Acts the attainment of Christian perfection always entailed "social prayer" by meeting together as a worshiping body of believers when the Holy Spirit was poured out in sanctifying grace (Acts 2, 8, 10, 19). He copied two verses from Charles Wesley to show the social means of sanctifying grace:

> In Christ when brethren join,
>   And follow after peace,
> The fellowship divine
>   He promises to bless,
> His chiefest graces to bestow
> Where two or three are met below.
>
> Where unity takes place,
>   The joys of heaven we prove;
> This is the gospel grace,
>   The unction from above,
> The Spirit on all believers shed,.
> Descending swift from Christ their head.[6]

Fletcher said this fullness of love did not come to one who was isolated from the community of faith. If "thou art alone" and like "a solitary bird which sitteth on the house-top," one "lookest in vain" for the hope of Christian perfection.[7] Rather, the fullness of love comes in answer to prayer within the worshiping community: "*Baptize me with the Holy Spirit and with fire*: help my unbelief: confirm and increase my faith, with regard to this important baptism. Lord, I have need to be thus baptized of thee, and I am straitened till this baptism is accomplished."[8] Fletcher believed that in such prayer: "So sure will the God of hope and love, soon fill you with all joy and peace, that ye may abound in pure love, as well as in confirmed hope *through the power of the Holy Spirit.*"[9]

John Fletcher's Idea of Confirmation as the Rite of Christian Perfection

Like John and Charles Wesley, John Fletcher was an "Evangelical High Churchman"[10] who honored the liturgical practices and polity of the Church of England. He specifically cited the liturgy of confirmation as a proper way to understand the personal call to the Spirit-filled life.

He said: "Our church-catechism brings to my remembrance the office of confirmation." Citing the biblical texts for the rite of confirmation in Acts, he said the purpose of confirmation "was . . . originally intended to lead young believers to the fullness of the Christian dispensation, agreeably to what we read Acts viii. 12, &c. Peter and John went from Jerusalem to Samaria to lay their hands on the believers who had not yet been baptized with the Holy Spirit, and to *pray, that they might receive him: For as yet he was fallen upon none of them: only they were baptized by Philip in the name of the Lord Jesus.*" Fletcher then asked: "*When the Son of man cometh, shall he find faith upon the earth?* I fear, but little of the faith peculiar to his *full* dispensation."[11]

Fletcher believed the reason for a lack of Spirit-filled living was that "most professors seem satisfied with John's baptism." His hope was for "the Lord [to] raise us apostolic pastors to pray in the demonstration of the Spirit and of power" who would themselves pray sincerely from the liturgy of confirmation in the Book of Common Prayer: "'Strengthen thy servants, O Lord, with the Holy Spirit, the Comforter; and daily increase in them thy manifold gifts of grace; the Spirit of wisdom and understanding; the Spirit of counsel and spiritual strength; the Spirit of knowledge and true godliness; and fill them with the Spirit of thy holy fear now and forever'." Anyone "in whom that prayer is not *now* answered" does not "live under the dispensation of Christianity perfected?"[12]

Fletcher reminded those Anglican ministers who doubted the Methodist teaching on Christian perfection that the Bishop "at your confirmation . . . bound upon you your solemn obligations to *keep God's holy will and commandments,* so as utterly *to abolish the whole body of sin.*" The purpose of confirmation was to transition the baptized person into a life with "perfectly purified" hearts[13]—by which is only meant a heart filled with the love of Christ and purity of intent and does not mean a life of perfect performance.

Fletcher proposed to John Wesley some suggestions for establishing a Methodist Church. He was the first to use the term, "Methodist Church," in a letter to Charles Wesley (September 4, 1759).[14] In another letter to John Wesley (August 1, 1775), Fletcher proposed that Methodism in "Great Britain, Ireland, and America be formed into a general society—a daughter church of our holy mother, the Church of England," becoming "the *methodist*-church of England."[15]

J. F. Hurst noted that "this remarkable letter in which Fletcher's startling proposals are stated was discovered a century later in the cellars of the Methodist Book Room in London." He observes that Wesley had undoubtedly kept this letter because it was too important to be destroyed, and yet he refrained from publishing it because its contents were too advanced for being made public at that time. Hurst noted that none would have trouble believing that Fletcher was a "saint," but few would have imagined him to have "the administrative insight and ability" that this letter revealed.[16]

Among other things Fletcher suggested: "It is proposed ... Mr. Wesley ... would draw up a petition and present to the Archbishop of Canterbury ... that the important office of confirmation shall be performed with the utmost solemnity by Mr. Wesley."[17] John Wesley briefly acknowledged Fletcher's proposals in a letter of August 18, 1775, mentioning also Fletcher's plea that Methodist preachers should be better trained theologically.[18]

In Fletcher's "Essay on the Doctrine of the New Birth," he distinguished between "being born again of water" and "being born again of the Spirit, or baptized with the Spirit."[19] Being born of water refers to repentance and justification; being born of the Spirit refers to perfection of love (sanctification). To be "born again of the Spirit" was the meaning of the rite of confirmation.

In a fragment containing his private personal notes located in the John Rylands Library, Fletcher observed that an Augustinian confusion shadowed parts of the liturgy in the Church of England, not unlike what Jeremy Taylor argued in his rebuttal of the Puritan idea of confirmation (as seen below):

> I wish our church [of England] had carefully maintained in her offices, the capital distinction between the baptism of repentance, and that of the Spirit: But candor obliges me to confess that a degree of the confusion which St. Augustine and others brought into the doctrines of the gospel, remains yet in some parts of her liturgy. Thus, as soon as a child is baptized *with water,* she says: "We yield thee hearty thanks, most merciful Father, that it hath pleased thee to regenerate this infant *with thy Holy Spirit.*" This looks like confounding the baptism of *water,* with the baptism of the *Spirit.* I humbly wish this mistake were rectified. Nay, our Church indirectly rectifies it herself, in a part of the office of confirmation, in which the Bishop solemnly prays, that the baptized person may be "strengthened with the Holy Spirit, the Comforter." But she does it more directly in the Baptism of adults. For, *after* they have been baptized *with water,* and *after* she has thanked God, *"that they are regenerate,"* she prays, *"Give thy Holy Spirit to these persons."* Till our being born again of the Spirit is properly distinguished from our being *born again of water;* and till this distinction is enforced by men *endued with power from on high,* I despair to see the *kingdom of God come with power* in the churches of Christ. In the meantime it becomes every babe in Christ deeply to repent, and humbly to say with John the Baptist, Lord, thou *baptizes with the Spirit,* and *I have need to be baptized of thee.* [20]

As we shall see below, Fletcher's distinction between being "born of water" and "born of the Spirit" anticipated the changes in the newly revised baptismal liturgy that has now been incorporated into the liturgy of all mainline denominations.

The Two Gestures of Baptism in The Primitive Church— Water and Laying on of hands

Christian baptism originally consisted of two distinct gestures—water and the laying on of hands. Those in the primitive church who had been trained in Church beliefs (the catechumens) were baptized in a river symbolizing their participation in Jesus' death-resurrection (Easter), and then immediately afterwards they were escorted into a church house where they had hands laid on them for being "baptized with the Spirit" (Pentecost).²¹ So the larger meaning of Christian baptism included the two gestures of water and the laying of hand (or chrismation in the Eastern Orthodox Church). These gestures indicated the two events of Easter and Pentecost were distinct from each other but inseparably related.

Dom Gregory Dix, an Anglo-Catholic Benedictine and liturgical scholar, showed there was new evidence in patristic studies that predated the New Testament writings themselves revealing the actual liturgical practice of the earliest Christians in apostolic times.²² The New Testament writings recorded the basis for the distinction between water baptism and confirmation in Acts 8:15, 19:2, and Hebrews 6:2.

He also pointed out that the baptism with the Holy Spirit was the New Testament counterpart to the Jewish practice of circumcision, noting that Jewish proselyte baptism included both the symbols of circumcision and water.²³ John Fletcher also pointed out this same correlation between Jewish proselyte baptism and the New Testament view of baptism, noting that water baptism corresponded to the meaning of justifying faith while circumcision corresponded to the meaning of Christian perfection.²⁴

Gregory Dix traced the history of the rite of confirmation through the Early Church Fathers, showing that Christian baptism entailed a duality of water and the laying on of hands until the beginning of the fifth century. This is the century when the two gestures of water and the laying on of hands became separated from each other in time and formed separate rituals. This separation reduced the meaning of Christian baptism to water baptism, and it led to the downgrading of the baptism with the Spirit (the laying on of hands), making it appear to be superfluous.

Dix believed it was a mistake that the laying on of hands was called confirmation instead of a "sealing." He noted that the giving of the Spirit was more than just a confirming of the life begun in the sacrament of water baptism. It was its perfection, its sealing, its inward appropriation in the full sense. The fact that the laying on of hands was eventually downgraded to the status of being called a confirmation weakened the original meaning of the giving of the Spirit as a "deification" (i.e., being made God-like, sealed or imprinted with the Spirit, sanctification).

Instead of a "sealing," the imposition of hands was a "confirming." Instead of sanctification, it was a strengthening. Dix has noted the importance of this shift:

> The change of term has its own significance. A document which needs "sealing" is not valid until the seal has been affixed. The "confirmation" of a document, though it may add to its authority, implies that it was already operative before it was "confirmed." This is precisely the change of emphasis which was now taking place in the West.²⁵

When Christian baptism was reduced only to water baptism, it led to a loss of the full meaning of Christian initiation: "Baptism into the death and resurrection of Christ and the Pentecostal Baptism of the Spirit are not one thing, but two." He said they are "inseparably connected but not one and the same." He argued for the parallel between the events of salvation history on the one hand, and the stages of Christian development in the personal lives of believers today, on the other hand. And he insisted that the baptism with the Spirit in perfecting grace is subsequent to water baptism in forgiveness of sins. Dix said:

First, it seems difficult to exaggerate the importance of the fact that for the Christian as for the Church, baptism into the death and resurrection of Christ and the Pentecostal Baptism of the Spirit are not one thing but two, both of them necessary and inseparably connected, but not the same. It is *after* our Lord's own Baptism in the Jordan—inseparably connected henceforward in his own mind with the coming passion and resurrection—it is immediately after, but after this that the Messianic Spirit descends upon Him. It is after Jesus is "glorified" in death, and resurrection—soon after, but after—that the Spirit is given, first to the Apostles and then to the Church corporately as associated with them. These are two moments in a single salvation into eternity, inseparably connected but not one and the same. The gift of the Spirit is not for those who receive Him a mere *consequence* of a previous salvation by the Son. Rather is it the Spirit who actually *operates* the salvation of each Christian, though the Spirit is shed forth only upon those already united to the crucified and risen Christ by faith and regenerated and incorporated into him. Such, I take it, is the fundamental meaning of the striking duality of the primitive liturgy of Initiation. Baptism into the death and resurrection of Christ being followed by the Sealing unto the day of Redemption—"the laver of regeneration and renewing of the Holy Spirit."[26]

Emerging Ideas of Confirmation— Ratifying, Strengthening, or Sanctifying?

The loss of the larger meaning of Christian baptism in the Fifth Century led in the thirteenth century to confirmation being called into question by Bonaventura (1221-1274) and then by John Wycliffe (1320-1384) in the fourteenth century.[27] In the sixteenth century, the Continental Reformers rejected the idea of confirmation as a subsequent experience of the Spirit beyond justification.

In the Roman Catholic and Greek Orthodox traditions, confirmation always entailed the granting of the Spirit (baptism with the Spirit). With the Protestant reformers (Luther and Calvin) confirmation was changed as a ratification of baptism for those who had been baptized as infant, but it no longer meant granting the Spirit through the laying on of hands.

Martin Luther's idea of confirmation as a reaffirmation of baptism was to be preceded by catechism. Catechism is a term used by him to denote a formal method of teaching the basics of Christian beliefs, specifically focusing on four topics—the Ten Commandments, the Apostles' Creed, the Lord's Prayer, and the sacraments. Luther wrote a *Large Catechism* for pastors in order to help them educate their congregation, and he wrote a *Small Catechism* for children in the form of questions and answers that can be memorized in preparation for confirmation. Although there have always been manuals of Christian doctrine throughout the history of the church, Luther specifically used this term to highlight the importance of doctrinal teaching. Subsequently, many catechisms appeared in various denominations, including a *Catechism of the Council of Trent* for Roman Catholics, and each of them followed Luther's format of explaining doctrine in reference to these four topics in preparation for confirmation.

The English reformer Thomas Cranmer held to a mediating view of confirmation between the Continental reformers and the Roman Catholic Church. He did not consider confirmation to be a "sacrament," but an "ordinance." *The Book of Common Prayer* (which he largely authored) included confirmation as receiving an "increase in thy Holy Spirit" and be "strength[ed] . . . with the Holy Spirit."[28] It also incorporated Luther's idea of catechism as preparation for confirmation, but it went beyond Luther by linking confirmation to a special reception of the Spirit based on the pericopae in Acts 8:15, 19:2, and Hebrews 6:2. These biblical references were considered to be special occasions used by the Apostles for further strengthening the faith of believers in that first-century context,[29] but he said they were not intended to establish a permanent rite of initiation into the church. Baptism is thus the only sacrament of Christian initiation when one is "baptized with water and the Holy Spirit."[30]

Cranmer retained the rite of confirmation as an ordinance to serve as an occasion for confirmands to publically affirm their own faith "with their own mouth and consent."[31] In response to the question, "What is the efficacy" of confirmation, Cranmer replied: "The bishop, in the name of the church, doth invocate the Holy Spirit to give strength and constancy, with other spiritual gifts, unto the person confirmed."[32] Cranmer rejected the Roman Catholic idea of confirmation as the perfection and completion of baptism, and the marking with the sign of the cross was the gesture used only in baptism to signify Christian sealing.

The Anglican ritual of confirmation was suspended during the Commonwealth Period of English history from 1642-1660 when the Puritans wanted to "purify" the church of what was perceived to be leftover remains of Roman Catholicism, and they did away with the Book of Common Prayer. During this period it was illegal to use the Book of Common Prayer and the rite of confirmation was disallowed.

Ironically, a moderate Puritan theologian and preacher by the name of Richard Baxter called for the restoration of confirmation in 1658. He explained his reason for its restoration in a book entitled, *Confirmation and Restauration: The Necessary Means of Reformation and Reconciliation.*[33]

He defined the rite of confirmation as "corroborative grace" and an "increase in grace."[34] He cited the usual texts in Acts (8, 10, 19) as biblical evidence that believers are to be confirmed subsequent to baptism.[35] He believed that "the eminent gift of the Holy Spirit [was] promised to them that had already the grace of *faith, and repentance, and love of Christ*, wrought in them by the Holy Spirit."[36] Confirmation means "to seal them up to the day of redemption, and be the earnest of the inheritance." This special reception of the Spirit signified in confirmation meant "a clearer knowledge of Christ . . . a fuller measure of love . . . in joy and peace, and sweet consolation . . . in establishment, and corroboration, and firmer resolution for Christ, and everlasting life."[37]

He said the difference between baptism and confirmation is that the Holy Spirit is promised as a *"fundamental right"* in baptism, and confirmation is the "seal." He said :"It's one thing to give the Holy Spirit" as a "Fundamental Right, and another thing to give the graces of the Spirit; and it's one thing to seal and increase the initial, special grace of the Spirit, and another thing to invest in a stablishing degree."[38]

Following Baxter's call for the restoration of confirmation, it was restored after the restoration of the monarchy in 1660, and a new edition of the Book of Common Prayer was issued in 1662 in consultation with the Puritans.

Jeremy Taylor—
A High Church Interpretation of Confirmation

As noted in the second chapter, Jeremy Taylor (1613-67) published a *Discourse on Confir-*

mation (1763) the following year after the Book of Common Prayer had been reintroduced. He wrote this discourse largely against the non-conforming clergy (the dissenters, or puritans).³⁹

This Caroline theologian interpreted confirmation in *The Book of Common Prayer* as the fullness of the Spirit being poured out on one who was already a believer by virtue of their infant baptism. Confirmation further denoted receiving perfecting, sanctifying grace. He defined confirmation as completing and perfecting the grace that was begun in water baptism. His exposition of the meaning of Pentecost was remarkably similar to the idea of Christian perfection espoused by the Wesley brothers.

Taylor cited the Early Church Father, Clement of Alexandria, to show that one must be born of water in baptism and born of the Spirit in confirmation in order to be "a perfect Christian."⁴⁰ He cited another Early Church Father Cyprian to show "they may be fully sanctified, and becomes sons of God, if they be born with both the sacraments [of water baptism and confirmation]."⁴¹ Taylor said: "Justifying and sanctifying grace is the proper entitative [i.e., real] product" of water baptism (Easter) and confirmation (Pentecost). Taylor said Jesus's words to Nicodemus that one must be born of water and of the Spirit shows there is "a double baptism" and that "we must pass through water and fire, before we enter into rest. . . . We must first be baptized with water, and then with the Holy Spirit, who first descended in fire" and "the only way to enter into Christ's kingdom is by these two doors of the tabernacle."⁴²

Taylor's High Anglican views went beyond Cranmer's idea of strengthening. Taylor believed they are two distinctive stages of Christian initiation and someone is not a completed Christian until they have both baptized with water and confirmed with the laying on of hands.

The difference between "strengthening" and "perfecting" is the difference between Fletcher's friend, Lady Huntingdon (the Calvinist Methodist leader) and her idea of the baptism with the Spirit as a strengthening and Fletcher's idea of the baptism with the Spirit as Christian perfection. We pointed out earlier that Fletcher had tried unsuccessfully to use the baptism with the Spirit as an opportunity to get Lady Huntingdon to see her idea was practically equivalent to John Wesley's idea of perfection.

Jeremy Taylor's view of confirmation is consistent with Heylyn's Pentecost sermon which Fletcher cited in support of his interpretation of Pentecost and sanctification, as noted in previous discussions. John Heylyn also considered confirmation as well as baptism to be the two "initiating doctrines" of the Christian life.⁴³

Fletcher brought together two disparate notions of confirmation when he defined it in Thomas Cranmer's terms of a "strengthening" and in Jeremy Taylor's terms as a "perfection" of Christian baptism in sanctifying grace. If Heylyn embraced both baptism and confirmation as the two "initiating doctrines" of the Christian life, his sermon on Pentecost only spoke of the personal appropriation of Pentecost. He called upon believers to wait in prayer and expect to be filled or baptized with the Spirit in a personal way.⁴⁴

John Wesley's View of Confirmation

John Wesley was never inspired to develop the connection between confirmation and Christian perfection. I would guess that his indifference toward confirmation was one of the lingering influences of his Puritan heritage unwittingly passed on to him from his father, which is ironic because he always insisted that he was a High Churchman in his theology and practice. His father's influence can be especially seen in his view of baptism.

Baptism as "Washing away the Guilt of Original Sin" and "Circumcision of Heart"

In 1756, John Wesley adapted his father's "A Treatise on Baptism," as his own treatise. Nothing is mentioned in this treatise about confirmation. Baptism is defined as one's full incorporation into the church, signifying the forgiveness of sins, circumcision of heart, and seal of the Spirit.

It also included the controversial notion of infant baptism as "washing away the guilt of original sin."[45] New Testament scholars have shown this idea of guilt being passed from Adam to the present day is impossible from an exegetical standpoint. Augustine wrongly translated Romans 5:12 with the wording "in whom all sinned." Instead it should be translated "since all have sinned," as Joel B. Green has shown.[46]

This Augustinian notion is impossible today in the light of evolutionary biology. We now know on the basis of chromosomal mapping and fossil evidence that there emerged in East Africa over 100,000 years ago a unique species of intelligent humans with a capacity for abstract and symbolic thought.[47] Unlike previous species, modern humans emerged with a fully developed capacity for self-awareness and an ability to engage in relationship with other self-aware people. This emergence of the human mind enabled humans to have a self-aware knowledge, including that they were made in the moral and spiritual image of God and that they had moral and social responsibility to each other. Among other things, they engaged in divine worship with rules for living together. They also discovered that they were born with a tendency to break the moral rules in self-serving ways.

There was no first female and male, but thousands of modern humans appearing spontaneously at about the same time. The literal idea of a single pair as the original humans in Genesis is "a poetic and powerful allegory,"[48] but Genesis was not intended to be a historical report of the scientific origin of modern humans. The idea of original sin as if all humans are responsible for, and participated in, the sin of an original pair is im-possible to maintain scientifically and exegetically. To be sure, everyone is born with a propensity to sin from birth, but there is no inherent guilt associated with this tendency because no one is responsibility for this inborn propensity.

What would have been John Wesley's response to the new scientific data of human origins? Would he have changed his mind about the idea of the guilt of original sin being washed away in baptism? We know that John Wesley wrote extensively on the relationship between the science of his day and theology, allowing that the findings of science can help us to interpret the Scriptures in places where specific passages may not be intending to speak literally and thus science can give us an "accurate understanding of several passages of Scripture."[49] His own understanding of original sin would have had to be modified in the light of these developments. The idea of the guilt of original sin had no place in the primitive Christian community or with the Early Greek Church Fathers; it emerged with Augustine and needs to be jettisoned.

Some of John Wesley's Methodist Leaders Appreciated Confirmation

Although John Wesley largely ignored confirmation, some of his Methodists appreciated it as a significant means of grace. It was an important means of grace in Fletcher's theology. It had personally meant much to his wife, Mary Bosanquet Fletcher, who had been confirmed at St. Paul's Cathedral, where Susanna Wesley herself had been confirmed.[50] At the age of thirteen, Mary Fletcher reported confirmation to be "a very rousing ordinance" for her. She noted that "for some months after, every time I approached the Lord's table, I had a very peculiar sense of his presence."[51] With her responsibility as one of John Wesley's women leaders, Mary Fletcher exhorted others "to *perfect holiness n the fear of the Lord*" as "you have already promised . . . [in] confirmation."[50]

Confirmation had been a meaningful experience for other Methodists as well. Hester Ann (Roe) Rogers who was almost as well-known as Mary Fletcher and was present with John Wesley at the time of his death (as previously noted).[53] She found confirmation to be a meaningful experience. She was so overwhelmed with this rite that she almost fainted before the bishop.[54]

Adam Clarke found confirmation to be a lifelong meaningful experience to him.[55] In a letter to Mrs. Wilkinson (June 1830), Clarke defended and promoted the rite of confirmation as signifying a "perpetual covenant to give themselves wholly to God, that they may have a thorough "death unto sin" (i.e., entire sanctification).[56]

John Wesley was confirmed, but apparently it was not a meaningful experience for him.[57]

Confirmation Deleted

In 1784, John Wesley modified the Anglican Book of Common Prayer for the benefit of the new Methodist Episcopal Church in America and he called it, *The Sunday Service*. Without any explanation he simply deleted confirmation. He also deleted the catechism in preparation for confirmation.

It could be assumed that John Wesley quietly deleted the rite of confirmation from *The Sunday Service* because there appeared to be no command from Jesus to confirm after baptism (although we now know that "confirmation" was included within the original idea of Christian baptism). Why did he also delete the catechism from *The Sunday Service*? Was it deleted because it had served as preparation for confirmation in the Book of Common Prayer that he had deleted in *The Sunday Service*?

When John Wesley served as a missionary parish priest in Georgia, he wrote catechisms for those who were to be confirmed. There was no single catechism used in the Church of England, and parish priests often developed their own instructional lessons. The catechisms that John Wesley wrote as a parish priest have not survived, except we do have his abridgment of the *Westminster Shorter Catechism*. Whether or not this abridged catechism was ever used in early British Methodism is not known, but it was included in Wesley's *Christian Library*, which was a series of cheap paperback books that Wesley abridged for the instructional benefit of Methodist. Significantly, Wesley altered the *Westminster Shorter Catechism* for his *Christian Library* in those places that contradicted the distinctive beliefs of Methodism. Particularly, he deleted references to absolute predestination and its denial of the possibility of being made perfect in love.

An Implicit Catechism

These twin themes—the universal offer of grace and the possibility of being made perfect in love in this life—constitute the core of an implicit Wesleyan catechism. One can cite many sources that Wesley had established as a means of educating his Methodist followers—including *The Christian Library*, his annual conferencing with his preachers, *The Large Minutes*, his sermons, his *Notes on the New Testament*, Fletcher's *Checks*, *The Arminian Magazine*, his numerous treatises and essays, such as *A Plain Account of Christian Perfection*. One of the most significant sources of doctrine for Methodists was Charles Wesley's hymns. John Wesley highlighted hymns as a source for understanding doctrine in his hymn book, *A Collection of Hymns for the Use of the People Called Methodists*.

A primary means of catechism for early Methodists was the class meetings, made up of 12 to 15 persons. The purpose was not to find out if a person had memorized a series of questions and answers on religious beliefs, but the question was primarily, "How is it with your soul?" Wesley noted in his sermon, "The Mystery of Iniquity," that the Protestant Reformation was primarily a reformation of rites and doctrine, but he said the Methodist revival constituted a true reformation of heart and life.

An implicit distinctive Wesley catechism entailed an examination of one's spiritual life—to see whether or not one is embodying the life of Jesus through the sanctifying power of the Holy Spirit. Scripture, the sacraments, worship, prayer, and the Apostle Creed were essential means of grace.

John Wesley considered it necessary for Methodists to embrace a proper doctrinal understanding and that is why he adapted the Anglican *Articles of Religion* for American Methodism. As Thomas Coke and Francis Asbury said, the purpose of including the *Articles of Religion* was to show that American Methodism believed what all the "reformed" churches believed,[58] but this first Book of Discipline written by Coke and Asbury also showed beyond these articles of belief that Methodists adhered to the first book of discipline, *The Large Minutes*,[59] which set up John Wesley's *Sermons* and *Notes on the New Testament* as the basis of Methodist doctrine.

Beyond the doctrinal beliefs, "a real Christian" is one who is catechized inwardly through the Spirit in justifying and full sanctifying grace. Being held accountable within the Christian community ("class meetings") for this inward catechism is the hallmark of a Wesleyan catechism.

However, the deletion of catechism and the rite of confirmation would surely have disappointed Fletcher. If he had still been living at the time that Wesley revised The Book of Common Prayer, it would be interesting to speculate if John Wesley would have included it, especially since John Wesley said in the preface to his biography of Fletcher that he normally consulted with Fletcher on matters of supreme importance to Methodism. Even more significant, it would have been interesting to see if John Wesley, as Fletcher had proposed, could have prevailed upon the archbishop to allow him to function as a bishop and to confirm Methodists and to incorporate "the growing body of the Methodists in Great Britain, Ireland and America . . . into a general society—a daughter church of our holy mother, the Church of England."⁶⁰ In which case, the rite of confirmation would have been retained for Methodism.

Apparently John Wesley never read John Fletcher's unpublished but selectively-circulated "Essay on the Doctrine of the New Birth," explaining that perfection was the inner meaning of confirmation. If Wesley had read it, what might have been his assessment? The tone of the essay showed that Fletcher fully believed that John Wesley would have agreed with him. John Wesley (and Joseph Benson) specifically noted that Fletcher's arguments and writings were very persuasive (as previously reported). If John Wesley had read it, then perhaps the rite of confirmation might have been included in *The Sunday Service*.

Perhaps the reason for John Wesley omitting confirmation was his insistence upon a personal, non-ceremonial experience of sanctifying grace, and this view also may have reflected John Wesley's growing Low Church liturgical views. John Wesley once expressed his dislike of the Roman Catholic sacerdotalism associated with confirmation, though his critique did not disagree with the rite of confirmation itself. He also understood that confirmation symbolized the meaning of full sanctification, which he also did not disagree with. This can be seen in his critique of a Roman Catholic catechism, which Wesley interpreted this way:

> In consecration of the chrism, the Bishop blows upon it, to signify the descent of the Holy Spirit for the sanctification of it . . . and that it hath [thus] a power of sanctification as the instrument of God . . . so the Bishop prays in the consecration of it, that God "in bestowing spiritual grace upon this ointment, would pour out the fullness of sanctification, and that it may be to all that are to be anointed with it, for the adoption of sons by the Holy Spirit."⁶¹

This Roman Catholic catechism made a connection between a personal Pentecost-like experience and full sanctification: "Pour out [a reference to the Pentecostal outpouring of the Holy Spirit] the fullness of sanctification." Wesley objected to the sacerdotal nature of the rite, emphasizing rather the personal, evangelical experience. In keeping with his Anglicanism, he recognized it as an ordinance, not as a sacrament.⁶²

Elsewhere Wesley publicly noted in a reply to his Anglican critics that he promoted confirmation, along with other Church practices, with "scrupulous exactness" as a loyal priest of the Church of England.⁶³ Considering that the rite of confirmation was "a necessary qualification for participating in Holy Communion,"⁶⁴ it was irregular that John Wesley ignored his Church's teaching on the importance of this ordinance.⁶⁵

Just how did John Wesley understand the meaning of confirmation? Being a High Anglican, his sympathies (like John Fletcher) would have been with the Jeremy Taylor who understood confirmation as signifying the sanctification, sealing and perfection of one who was baptized with water.

Some proposed revisions for Book of Common Prayer in 1689 included this prayer of confirmation: "Confirm and settle the godly Resolutions They have now made. Sanctify *them throughout* [italics mine] that they may become the Temples of the Holy Spirit."⁶⁶ However, the proposed revisions were never voted on because of the Glorious Revolution in 1688 with toleration for differing points of view becoming the new "norm."

This proposed revision would have gone beyond Cranmer's view of confirmation as a "strengthening" of the Christian life. This revision would have included: "An Exhortation to be read the Lord's Day before a confirmation . . . not to rest with the renewing of your vows, but to carry them on to full perfection."[67] By becoming "the Temples of the Living God . . . He may dwell in you by his Holy Spirit," thus "perfecting holiness in the fear of God."[68]

One of the biblical passages for the rite of confirmation was Acts 19:2; "Have ye received the Holy Spirit since ye believed?" (KJV). Of course, this passage could have been translated, "Did you receive the Holy Spirit when you believed?" However, even this translation shows that "believing" does not always involve "receiving the Holy Spirit." The King James Version, as the authorized version of the Church of England, used the translation, "Have ye received . . . since ye believed?" This translation supported the Anglican theology of confirmation.

John Wesley translated this verse the same as the King James Version in his *Explanatory Notes upon the New Testament*. If Wesley thought that Paul intended to say that these disciples should have received the Spirit at the time of their initial conversion, he could have used the alternate rendering which equated "receiving the Spirit" and "believing." Such variations from the King James Version he promised to make in his "Preface" to *The Explanatory Notes upon the New Testament* when he deemed it necessary, and he often did.[69]

Significantly, John Wesley here used the same translation as the King James Version, and he gave the reception of the Spirit the same meaning as Jeremy Taylor for the rite of confirmation— "the extraordinary gifts of the Spirit, as well as His sanctifying graces."[70]

Fletcher said John Wesley interpreted this passage to mean that the Ephesian disciples were fully sanctified through the bestowal of the Spirit.[71] In a parallel passage in Acts 8:15 regarding the Samaritans (which is also used as a basis for confirmation), Fletcher said John Wesley interpreted their reception of the Spirit as their full sanctification.[72] As cited in a previous chapter, Charles Wesley interpreted this passage (Acts 8:15) in his sacred poems to mean Christian perfection.

Nathan Bangs on Confirmation

The first serious American Methodist theologian, Nathan Bangs,[73] would surely have approved the newly revised baptismal liturgy (to be discussed below). He came to his conclusion on this issue through his independent study of the Early Church Fathers.

As one of Bishop Asbury's young scholar/preachers, he was accosted by a Church of England minister in 1804, who claimed that the Methodists were not properly constituted as a true Church. This accusation led him to write a book in 1837, entitled, *An Original Church of Christ: or, A Scriptural Vindication of the Orders and Powers of the Ministry of the Methodist Episcopal Church*.

One issue that he sought to clarify was the meaning of confirmation. He strenuously objected to the idea that confirmation was a separate rite from baptism. On this point he insisted that the Protestant Episcopal Church had departed from the New Testament and the Early Church Fathers. Significantly, he believed that the rite of the laying on of hands was included within the larger meaning of Christian baptism, but it was "unscriptural" to withhold this part of baptism until a much later time.

He insisted that baptism was only "half performed" without the laying on of hands signifying the bestowal of the Spirit.[74] He argued that the laying on of hands was practiced during the first three hundreds of Church history, beginning with apostolic times as seen in the Book of Acts, noting that it "was considered as an essential appendage of the baptismal rite, so much so that the latter was considered incomplete without it."[75]

Bangs further argued against the idea that baptism, including both the symbols of water and the laying on of hands, actually "cleanses and purges the soul from sin." Rather, it is "a divinely appointed means of grace, which, when rightly administered, is accompanied, as all duties are, with God's blessing." So it "should be considered only as a means, in the use of which we are to look for the 'inward and spiritual grace,' prefigured by this outward rite, which is wrought in the soul by the Spirit of God."[76]

While Bangs agreed with John Wesley's decision to eliminate confirmation as a rite separated from baptism, he argued that it should be a part of the baptismal liturgy itself. Though he was strongly influenced by Fletcher's writings and supported his emphasis on the baptism with the Holy Spirit, he does not explicitly draw from Fletcher's various suggestions about the importance of the rite of the laying on of hands. And he apparently did not have access to Fletcher's unpublished essay on the new birth.

Despite his interpretation that the imposition of hands should be included in Christian baptism, it never became a part of Methodist liturgy until recently. If Fletcher's theology of confirmation had been noticed by Bangs, perhaps he could have influenced American Methodism to revise John Wesley's *Sunday Service* to include it as an aspect of the baptismal liturgy.

Early Twentieth-Century Ecumenical Liturgical Studies

Significant developments in the understanding of the rite of confirmation began to take place in the Twentieth Century around 1911 with the emergence of the modern liturgical renewal movement.[77] This movement saw its task to recover the liturgical practices of Christian antiquity.[78] Benedictine scholars formed the primary leadership of this international and ecumenical movement.[79]

Gregory Dix helped to make confirmation an issue of major importance.[80] His study on the Eucharist in *The Shape of the Liturgy* was problematic and not so helpful even though it helped to inspire further critical studies,[81] but his contributions to the liturgy of baptism were significant.

Of particular significance was his contribution in recovering the fragments of a document written by Hippolytus of Rome around 215 A. D., entitled *The Apostolic Tradition*. This work revealed the nature of Christian worship beginning with the earliest days of the New Testament period.[82]

This document showed that Christian baptism consisted of two events. First, the catechumens went down into the river to be baptized with water, and then they came up to the house church where there was a ceremony of "laying on of hands" to bestow the Spirit. Although the time lapse between the administration of water and the laying on of hands was only minutes for the catechumens, it showed that there was a decisive and distinct difference in meaning between the two events. The Samaritans in Acts 8 were baptized with water and then three days later they received the Holy Spirit with the laying of hands. The three-day time lapse was reduced to just minutes between water baptism and the laying on of hands in *The Apostolic Tradition*.

Dix was a major influence in the rediscovery of these fragments and putting them together into a reconstructed text.[83] He correctly predicted that this reconstructed document would "bring about considerable changes in many currently accepted conceptions of primitive Church Order."[84] Dix's critical edition of this document appeared in 1937.

The results of his scholarship on confirmation were summarized in a public lecture at Oxford University on January 22, 1946, subsequently published under the title, *The Theology of Confirmation in Relation to Baptism*. Dix's lecture, along with the new materials that had become available for critical study, inaugurated a heated debate within the Anglican tradition, most notably between Dix and G. W.H. Lampe.

Lampe represented the Calvinist interpretation that Confirmation involved a maturity rite signifying the completion of catechesis, not the "sealing of the Spirit." Lampe not only disputed with Dix, but also argued against the Early Church Fathers because they made a distinction between water baptism and the baptism with the Spirit. Lampe noted that this distinction explained why the Early Church Fathers gave the doctrine of sanctification a greater emphasis than justification, which was a point that Lampe regretted because it allegedly undermined the doctrine of free grace.[85]

Lampe also believed that the pneumatological focus of the post-apostolic writers "began to prepare the way for Baptism itself to be evacuated of much of its meaning and treated as a preparatory ceremony, a prelude to the true 'baptism of the Spirit,' whose outward ceremony was either chrismation or the imposition of hands."[86]

Lampe interpreted this pneumatological shift in theology as a kind of magical view of grace. In this regard, he severely criticized Dix for defining the rite of confirmation as the "sealing" and "baptism with the Spirit" as that event which made the believer ready for eternal salvation.[87] To be sure, Dix insisted that baptism with water and baptism with the Spirit constituted "*a single rite of Baptism*," even though it was a complex event.[88]

Lampe believed that Dix made remission of sins, adoption, or regeneration impossible in baptism, if the indwelling of the Spirit comes later in confirmation.[89] This criticism failed to take into account that Dix believed that regeneration in water baptism was through "the Spirit who actually *operates* the salvation of each Christian,"[90] but the indwelling, or sealing, of the Spirit in its fullness is what confirmation signifies. In this sense, there is no "separation" between Jesus and the Spirit, but a continuum of grace in one's progressive stages of faith.

There was also a renewed interest in the so-called Macarius the Egyptian in the twentieth century liturgical movement. In 1891, A. J. Mason wrote a book on *The Relation of Confirmation to Baptism*.[91] Then, in 1921, he published *The Fifty Spiritual Homilies of St. Macarius the Egyptian*, which defined the seal of the Spirit as a subsequent moment beyond water baptism in the theology of the Early Church Fathers, thus indirectly showing that the rite of the laying on of hands was practiced from the beginning of Christian history because the baptism with the Spirit was preached as a need for believers.

Then, with the recovery of the fragments of *The Apostolic Tradition*, it was clear that both water baptism and the laying on of hands formed the twofold meaning of the baptismal liturgy from the time of the apostles. This means that initiation into Christ is a two-stage development. Dix believed that "these two aspects are not opposed to one another; they are different aspects of the same redemption."[92]

The really significant historical finding came when it was seen that *The Apostolic Tradition* not only contained the view of the Early Church Fathers in the Second and Third Centuries, but it revealed *the practice of baptism from the time of the primitive church*. In other words, *The Apostolic Tradition* contained the truly apostolic practice.

Jesus' own baptism was a pattern of this twofold understanding. Jesus was baptized with water in the Jordan River and subsequently the Spirit descended upon him as a dove, and a voice from heaven announced him to be God's Son. Hence Paul's remarks about the "Spirit of Adoption" (Romans 8:15) should be understood to mean that one is fully initiated into the Christian life as God's "son" when they have experienced their own Easter and Pentecost. When Paul said, "By one Spirit we have all been baptized in Christ" (I Cor. 12:13), this apparently includes both water baptism and Spirit baptism. A rediscovery of the sermons of Pseudo-Macarius indirectly and implicitly helped to reinforce this twofold understanding as well.

Recent Ecumenical Liturgical Developments

Recent ecumenical developments appeared in the so-called Lima Text prepared by the Faith and Order Commission of the World Council of Churches at the Lima Conference in 1982. Christian baptism underwent a significant liturgical change with the inclusion of both gestures— baptism with water (signifying Jesus' death-resurrection) and the laying on of hands (signifying the Pentecost gift of the Spirit).

This recommended pneumatological addition was incorporated into all major Protestant denominational books of worship. Previously, the liturgy of baptism only included the rite of water baptism in Protestantism. Now the bestowal of the Holy Spirit of Pentecost was restored in the liturgy of Christian baptism (as in the earliest days of Christian baptism).[93]

Most mainline denominations (although not Methodism) have always had some practice of confirmation. As noted above, there were three different interpretations of confirmation—the sealing of the Spirit in sanctifying grace, the bestowal of the Spirit to strengthen and increase one's faithful living, and a reaffirmation of baptism through catechism. These three different versions were not necessarily mutually exclusive.

Significantly enough, what has now emerged within the last quarter of the twentieth century is a general consensus that Christian baptism is a complex event involving the two symbols of baptism with water on the one hand and chrismation or the laying on of hands on the other hand. Virtually all the liturgies of the major American denominations have been rewritten to incorporate this new understanding. Lutheran liturgiologist, Frank C. Senn, writes: "In the last quarter of the twentieth century, a massive ecumenical consensus has emerged concerning the forms and content of Christian liturgy in the Roman Catholic and Reformation churches as a result of the impact of the modern liturgical movement."[94]

Senn further writes: "It has been said that if the covers were removed from the major worship books of the late twentieth century, it would be difficult to tell which book belongs to which church body."[95]

The Faith and Order movement (representing all the major Church traditions, including Eastern Orthodox, Roman Catholic, Lutheran, Anglican, Reformed, Methodist, Presbyterians, Disciples of Christ, Mennonite, Brethren, Baptist, Adventist, and Pentecostal) began developing a collaborative investigation concerning the meaning of baptism, eucharist, and ministry since its first conference at Lausanne in 1927.

Gerard Austin summarized the history and results of the ecumenical discussions relating particularly to confirmation. He showed that the high points of the newly emerging consensus on confirmation occurred at the Faith and Order Commission at the Lima Conference in 1982. He pointed out that in previous years, a christological interpretation predominated in the meaning of Christian baptism. Now the pneumatological dimension has been added to comply with the World Council statement: "It would seem appropriate that baptism with water should be followed by the laying-on of hands or chrismation to express dedication and the gift of the Holy Spirit in baptism."

This Lima Conference reflected an ecumenical consensus that was "a result of biblical and patristic studies, together with the liturgical revival and the need for common witness." The Lima Text also noted "that theologians of such widely different traditions should be able to speak so harmoniously about baptism, eucharist and ministry is unprecedented in the modern ecumenical movement."[96]

Systematic Theologians and Church Liturgy

Since the days of Thomas Cranmer, the Anglican tradition made liturgy the foundation of its doctrinal beliefs. As the supreme commentary on the Bible, the Book of Common Prayer was a book of doctrine as well as a book of liturgy and prayer. At the heart of his reform, Cranmer intended to restore the Church of England to primitive Christianity, and that is why the English reformers focused on the liturgical practices of the primitive church, whereas the Continental reformers focused on systematic, doctrinal formulations based on abstract biblical exegesis. The English reformers considered worship as the proper context for doing theology. Hence the prayer book and homilies were the sources of doctrine.

John Wesley and Charles Wesley quoted the Book of Common Prayer as support of their beliefs, insisting that they were loyal Anglicans and adhered to its doctrines and liturgy. In a letter to the *"To the Editor of Lloyd's Evening Post,"* John Wesley said he espoused "the Bible, with the Liturgy, and Homilies of our Church; and do not espouse any other principles but what are consonant to the Book of Common Prayer."[97]

John Wesley said of the Book of Common Prayer: "I believe there is no Liturgy in the world, either in ancient or modern language, which breathes more of a solid, scriptural, rational piety, than the Common Prayer of the Church of England."[98]

Because of the priority of Church liturgy over abstract theology, it is not surprising that the liturgical movement has influenced the constructive work of some systematic theologians. Two contemporary theologians in particular are noteworthy—Karl Barth and Wolfhart Pannenberg.

Karl Barth

The willingness of systematic theologians to pay attention to the liturgical movement has contributed to an overhaul in the theology of Christian initiation, especially in reference to the meaning of Pentecost. Ironically, this new reorientation in thinking about Christian initiation has come primarily from the Reformed and the Lutheran traditions.

Shortly before his death in 1967, Karl Barth expressed his most mature thoughts on the meaning of Christian initiation, which was published in his *Church Dogmatics*, under the title, *Baptism as the Foundation of the Christian Life*. Barth was particularly inspired by the discussion of baptism at the Second Vatican Council (1962-1965). He recalled that he "made a journey to Rome to hear and see for myself various matters relating to it."[99] He stated that he had read most of the literature on baptism that had been written since his retirement, but he found it inadequate.[100]

One noticeable influence of the liturgical renewal movement can be seen in Barth's distinction between baptism with water and baptism with the Spirit.[101] So striking was this contrast that even his editors highlighted this new development in Barth's thinking in the opening paragraph of their preface to *Church Dogmatics*, volume 4, calling it "a sharp distinction."[102] Barth maintained that baptism with the Spirit signified the perfection of the Christian life that is progressively realized in this life and only finally actualized in heaven.

This precise distinction between baptism with water and baptism with the Spirit represented a shift away from Barth's earlier work on baptism, *The Teaching of the Church regarding Baptism* (1948, English Translation).[103] He issued a caution, advising his readers not to take his earlier work as his final statement on baptism. Since Barth considered infant baptism an "irregular" practice, though valid, he had become more sympathetic to the "semi-sacrament" status of confirmation, and he particularly criticized Calvin's severe attack on it.[104] It should be noted that Barth's consideration of Christian initiation was based on his exegesis of the New Testament, while extra-biblical evidence, such as *The Apostolic Tradition of St. Hippolytus*, was not mentioned although he said he had read all of the current literature on this issue.

Barth has shown exegetically that baptism with water and baptism with the Spirit were two events with a distinct meaning of their own. Baptism with water symbolized the beginning of the Christian life in regeneration and was the rite of Easter, whereas baptism with the Spirit (Pentecost) symbolized the perfection and sanctification of the Christian life. Barth exegetically and theologically intended to show that Pentecost was the confirmation of Easter, even as the baptism with the Spirit was the goal of baptism with water.

Barth believed that the several instances of being filled with the Spirit in Acts (Acts 8:15; 10:45; 18:25; 19:2) were an ongoing experience for those who were already believers. This indicated the continuing work of sanctification in the life of believers. In this respect, Barth distinguished Easter and Pentecost as the two decisive events of salvation history which alone are basis for the formation of the Christian life.[105]

Just as these two events are distinct in time and yet related through time, so believers successively experience their own Easter and Pentecost. One's Christian walk proceeds through a personal participation in the event of Easter (Jesus' resurrected life), symbolized through baptism with water, to the ongoing fellowship of the Holy Spirit given at Pentecost.[106] Despite Barth's imputation theory of righteousness,[107] he also emphasized the ongoing dialectical approximation-appropriation of the Spirit's sanctifying fullness.

Karl Barth's exposition of Christian initiation in terms of baptism with water and baptism with the Spirit generated a series of books by others in the Reformed tradition. Interestingly enough, he confessed that he had previously developed an inadequate theology of the Holy Spirit, and shortly before his death he invited others (suggesting a possible former student) to supply this defect.[108]

Dale Bruner and James D. G. Dunn

There were two Reformed scholars who wrote full-length books on the doctrine of the Holy Spirit, addressing in particular the alleged distinction between the baptism with water and baptism with the Holy Spirit (primarily in opposition to Pentecostalism). They were Frederick Dale Bruner[109] and James D. G. Dunn.[110] Dunn ironically transferred his membership from the Church of Scotland to British Methodism, even though he rejected John Wesley's idea of Christian perfection.

Both authors disagreed with Barth's distinction between baptism with water and baptism with the Holy Spirit. They were also motivated, in part, to refute the Wesleyan and Pentecostal theology with its sharp distinction experientially and theologically between these dual meanings of baptism.[111]

They also argued against the liturgical and sacramental distinction between water baptism and the baptism with the Spirit, which Barth had allowed. If Bruner and Dunn had allowed the priority of the primitive liturgy over their own abstract theological and exegetical reconstructions, their attitude toward Barth would likely have been quite different. If they had respected the primitive liturgy of Christian baptism with its distinction between water baptism and the laying on of hands, they would have interpreted the Pentecost passages differently in Acts 8 and Acts 19. We now know that this primitive liturgy preceded the actual writings of the New Testament and was practiced from the beginning of the Christian church. We can now see that Paul's expressions, such as, "sealed with the Spirit" and "the earnest of our inheritance," are references to this practice of the laying on of hands in Christian baptism. Luke was Paul's companion in the book of Acts as he traveled about in his evangelistic ministry, and Luke's account of the laying on of hands provided the historical basis for the liturgy of Christian baptism that was practiced from the very beginning. Instead of the book of Acts being simply "history" with the idea that theology should be done from Paul's writings, we can now see that just the opposite is true. Paul's writings should be interpreted in the light of the liturgy that emerged from the earliest practice of Christian initation in the book of Acts. This priority of liturgy as the guide for theological reflection was the occasion for Barth's new understanding of the expression of being "baptized with the Spirit."

Because Dunn did not embrace this priority of liturgy, he disallowed the theological distinction that Barth had defended—that water baptism represented the beginning of the Christian life in justification while the baptism with the Spirit represented a larger meaning beyond justification to the sanctification and perfection of the Christian life. Likewise Dunn rejected the Pentecostal twofold concept of Christian initiation: "The Pentecostal has followed the Catholic in his separation of Spirit-baptism, from the event of conversion-initiation (represented in water-baptism), and has made the gift of the Spirit an experience which follows after conversion."[112]

Jürgen Moltmann

Another response to Barth's changing views on baptism is given by Jürgen Moltmann. He intended to move beyond Barth's earlier trinitarian christology to a trinitarian pneumatology. A major ecumenical influence in his thinking has been the Eastern Orthodox tradition. While Moltmann does not largely discuss the Orthodox view of baptism, its concept lies in the background of his appropriation of their pneumatological theology. Moltmann noted that the Orthodox Church makes a "distinction between baptismal and paschal dying and rising in Christ which unites us with Christ, and chrismation as the pentecostal sealing with the gift of the Holy Spirit."[113]

Moltmann has observed that Protestant thinking in the tradition of Luther and Calvin has never developed an adequate doctrine of the Holy Spirit.[114] Unlike Bruner and Dunn, Moltmann offers a favorable interpretation both of the Wesleyan and the Pentecostal traditions because of their mutually-related emphasis on the Holy Spirit.

Moltmann particularly affirmed John Wesley's view that "believers are wholly interpenetrated by the Holy Spirit and arrive at the state of Christian perfection, the *theosis*. This would be perfect love."[115] He likewise affirmed the Pentecostal emphasis on the gifts of the Spirit for the purposes of the church, including glossolalia. Significantly, Moltmann's appropriation of Joachim of Fiore's concept of the trinitarian dispensations with its emphasis on the age of the Spirit has similar (despite the differences) to Fletcher's theology of dispensations.

Moltmann can be given some credit for the heightened interest in developing a more biblically based theology of the Trinity in overcoming the monarchical tendencies of the Western view of the Trinity. Moltmann's *Trinity and the Kingdom of God* (1980) has been a major reason why the doctrine has become a major, if not dominant, theme in contemporary theology, and it is influencing particularly Wesleyan and Pentecostal scholarship.

Wolfhart Pannenberg

Another contemporary systematic theologian who incorporated a pneumatological understanding of Christian initiation was Wolfhart Pannenberg (a Lutheran). Just as *The Apostolic Tradition of St. Hippolytus* was influential with the Anglicans, so it was with the Lutherans.[116] As a result, Pannenberg came to accept confirmation as the sealing of the Spirit, catechism, and a reaffirmation of water baptism.[117] More specifically, Pannenberg interpreted the gift of the Spirit through the imposition of hands as empowering one to begin the process of "death to the old nature."

Pannenberg even came close to accepting confirmation as a sacrament since it shared "in the sacramental status of baptism," noting that "Luther was not aware of the original relationship of anointing and the laying on of hands to the baptismal act." If he had been, he would have had "a different view of confirmation's sacramental status." Pannenberg connected the two aspects of Christian baptism to mean:

> The death of the old nature that is anticipated in baptism has to be worked out daily in Christian life in the process of an appropriation of baptism. The practice of infant baptism makes it obligatory that this personal appropriation of baptism in individual faith and confession should also be declared publicly in the congregation, as happens in confirma-

tion. The very form of the liturgical action expresses already that we cannot have here merely an act on the part of the human recipients of baptism. Instead the baptized need "confirmation" by the Holy Spirit, who is given already at baptism if they are to be capable of this independent faith and confession. In this regard the Protestant understanding of confirmation can be in accord with the Roman Catholic theology of confirmation.[118]

We noted above the differing nuances of confirmation as ratifying, strengthening, and sanctifying. Pannenberg came to see through his involvement with the Liturgical Renewal Movement that the newly rediscovered data suggests there is merit to all three views.

If it is true that Luther would have changed his mind about the rite of confirmation with access to the early patristic sources that are available today, what would John Wesley do today?

United Methodist Church Book of Worship in 1992

What would have been John Wesley's response to the new data showing that the larger meaning of Christian baptism included both water baptism and the laying on of hands? His designated successor, John Fletcher, intuitively appropriated its significance that was based on exegetical and theological reasons without the benefit of this new data

We can only imagine that John Wesley would have approved it as it was done at the 1996 General Conference of the United Methodist Church which officially adopted the report of the Baptism Study Commission, "By Water and the Spirit—A United Methodist Understanding of Baptism."

One of the goals embodied in this document was to restore "the Wesleyan blend of sacramental and evangelical aspects" of Christian baptism. Another goal was to restore the laying on of hands in Christian baptism that John Wesley discarded.

The United Methodist bishops in their response to the Lima Text noted that American Methodism had no rite of confirmation from its beginning, and that "the very word itself came into our usage fairly recently but without definition."[119] They remained uncertain about its meaning. At the same time, the bishops noted with regret that its baptismal liturgy made no mention "of the giving of the Holy Spirit in baptism, confirmation or in one's indefinable experience."[120]

The reforms recommended by the World Council of Churches made their way into the rite of initiation of the United Methodist Church in 1976 with the publication of *A Service of Baptism, Confirmation, and Renewal*. Its baptism liturgy now included both the act of water baptism (signifying Jesus' death-resurrection) and the laying on of hands (signifying the descent of the Spirit).

After the application of water the minister lays his hands on the head of the person and says: "The power of the Holy Spirit work within you, that being born through water and the Spirit you may be a faithful witness of Jesus Christ. Amen."

Significantly, Charles Wesley's and Fletcher's definition of the birth of the Spirit as Christian Perfection corresponded with the new baptismal liturgy of the United Methodist Church that "we are incorporated into God's mighty acts of salvation and given new birth through water and the Spirit."

This reform later appeared in *The United Methodist Hymnal* in 1989 and the *United Methodist Book of Worship* in 1992. The alternate words for the laying on of hands uses the expression, "sealing": "You are sealed by the Holy Spirit in baptism and marked as Christ's own forever." This wording seems more fitting and corresponds more closely to the usage of the primitive Church, as Gregory Dix has shown. It also more pointedly captures the meaning of sanctification as being stamped with the image of God, a distinctive teaching of Methodism.

The United Methodist Church also retained a special service which it called confirmation when the confirmand makes a public profession of faith when they have the reached the age of accountability normally after completing the sixth grade in school. Prior to this service of confirmation there is a special time of preparation for developing a self-understanding of the doctrines of the Christian faith and spiritual disciplines necessary for the life of discipleship. Such persons are already full members of the church as a result of having been baptized as infants, but this service entails a personal reaffirmation of their faith.

The gesture of water in Christian baptism cannot be repeated because water means that one has participated in Jesus' death/resurrection. Because Jesus died and rose from the dead only once, water can only be administered once. On the other hand, the laying on of hands in Christian baptism can be repeated because the Holy Spirit was poured out on multiple occasions in the book of Acts.

The United Methodist Book of Discipline says: "Confirmation is a dynamic action of the Holy Spirit that can be repeated."[121] In confirmation the outpouring of the Holy Spirit is invoked to provide the one being confirmed with the power to live an effective Christian life. The ritual action in confirmation is the laying on of hands as the sign of God's continuing gift of the grace of Pentecost.

In his lyrical commentary, Charles Wesley described Acts 8:17, "Then laid they their hands on them, and they received the Holy Spirit," to mean the same as the Anglican rite of confirmation as interpreted by Jeremy Taylor—that the one already baptized with water is to be sanctified through the laying on hands for the bestowal of the Spirit of Pentecost.

> The laying on of hands implies,
>   That God asserts his lawful claim,
> Possession takes, and sanctifies
>   The men baptiz'd into his name;
> Subjecting them to his commands,
>   Uniting to himself, He still
> Keeps them in his own gracious hands,
>   To serve the counsels of his will.[122]

Baptized with Water and the Spirit in John Wesley's *Sunday Service*

If John Wesley omitted the rite of confirmation from *The Sunday Service* in American Methodism, he did not omit the reference to the bestowal of the Spirit in baptism. From the Book of Common Prayer, he retained the expression "that he may be baptized with water and the Holy Spirit."[123] However, the baptismal liturgy in *The Sunday Service* did not include the laying on of hands as the means of bestowing the Spirit.

We previously pointed out that in his private, scribbled notes John Wesley complained that Joseph Benson's essay on the baptism with the Spirit should have been linked to water baptism. John Wesley wrote: "I never yet baptized a real Penitent who was not then baptized with the H. Spirit. See our Catechism [on] One Baptism."[124]

Since John Wesley retained the Anglican wording in the liturgy in *The Sunday Service*, that one is baptized with water and baptized with the Spirit in baptism, does this mean that he rejected the expression, "the baptism with the Spirit," for Christian perfection?

A similar question must also be asked about the expression "circumcision of the heart." In his *Treatise on Baptism* in 1757, John Wesley said that in baptism one's heart is circumcised.[125] Does this mean that he rejected the expression "circumcision of heart" for Christian perfection? The answer to both questions is No. He assumed a distinction between the promise of salvation in baptism and the fulfillment of that promise in personal faith.

For John Wesley, justifying faith and full sanctifying grace occurred as distinct events in time through acts of personal faith separate from baptism, but the acts of justifying and sanctifying faith are inseparably related. "Cleansing from all sin" is a metaphor for Christian perfection and is the equivalent of the expressions, "circumcision of heart" and "baptized with fire and the Holy Spirit." This cleansing begins with justifying faith and is completed in full sanctifying grace. Thus the larger meaning of "circumcision of heart" and the larger meaning of "baptized with the Spirit" is Christian perfection.

John Wesley's distinction between "sanctification begun" and "finished holiness"[126] can be seen in Paul's letter addressed "to the Church of God which is at Corinth, to those sanctified in Christ Jesus, called to be saints." To be "in Christ Jesus" is a prepositional phrase that Paul often used to denote the Church, and he said they were "the Church of God at Corinth." Paul further said to them: "You were washed, you were sanctified, you were justified in the name of the Lord Jesus Christ and in the Spirit of God" (1 Cor. 6:11).

Christian initiation for these Corinthian entailed a ritual action of being born of water and of the Spirit in baptism. This means the gestures of water baptism and the laying on of hands were performed on these Corinthians in Christian baptism following their catechism. We can confidently say this because of the new data recovered after many years of patristic studies by the ecumenical liturgical renewal movement.

John Wesley believed that all Christians are formally baptized with water and baptized with the Spirit in the initiatory rite of Christian baptism, but he insisted that this initiatory event must also be accompanied by a future act of personal faith in Christ. He understood this personal faith to include justifying faith and sanctifying grace as distinct moments in time.

He mentioned in his sermon "On the Church" that the baptism with the Spirit was given "in a lower degree" to all believers, but he also understood the baptism with the Spirit to mean that one "is renewed in righteousness and true holiness," as he once said to William Law. The full baptism with the Spirit (which his diaries show he often preached on) through personal faith is what he and the early Methodists understood to be Christian perfection.

Though the Corinthians were baptized and were "sanctified in Christ Jesus" at the moment of their baptism, Paul could "not address you as spiritual [i.e., not fully endowed with the Holy Spirit, as Rudolf Bultmann has shown]."[127] They were "as babes in

Christ," and "still in the flesh" (1 Cor. 3:1-3). The righteousness imparted to them in baptism had not been fully imparted to them.

In 1763 in his sermon, "Sin in Believers," John Wesley cited the experience of the Corinthians to show that one could be "renewed, cleansed, purified, sanctified, the moment we truly believe in Christ, yet we are not then renewed, cleansed, purified altogether."[128] John Wesley did not say anything about their baptism, but rather under the influence of the Moravians many years earlier he had come to a "low church" view of personal faith without the necessity of baptism for "being in Christ." Of course, John Wesley affirmed the necessity of baptism as commanded by Jesus, and he took issue frequently with the Quakers over its importance.

As noticed previously, a new nuance emerged in his sermon "On Sin Believers" in 1763 because he used the same expressions for justification as for Christian perfection, with the only difference being the higher degree of attainment in those fully sanctified. In many of his early standard sermons, John Wesley did not always distinguish between justifying and full sanctifying grace, but simply described the ideal Christian life.

Charles Wesley in his sacred poems made a distinction between justification and the indwelling of the Spirit (perfect love) as his brother John had once done without calling attention the "lower degree" of the Spirit being given in justification. If John Wesley had come to use the same expressions for both justifying and full sanctifying faith with a difference in degree only, Charles Wesley did not follow his lead on this carefully-measured nuanced distinction, although it was implicit.

To be sure, Charles Wesley allowed the action of the Spirit in the life of the justified believer, but his emphasis was upon the full realization of the Spirit in perfect love in his hymns and poems. So for all practical purposes he used the language of the Spirit for Christian perfection, as did John Fletcher's writings and Methodist writers such as Elizabeth Ritchie and Hester Ann Rogers. John Wesley agreed with his inner circle of leaders on this matter, but he more carefully nuanced how the Spirit was at work in a justified person and more completely in a sanctified persons. His concern was that "babes in Christ" be appreciated as real Christians.

In his sermon "On Sin in Believers," John Wesley identified the expressions, "the indwelling of the Spirit" and "the love God shed abroad in our hearts by the Holy Spirit," with justification, not merely with Christian perfection. The only difference between justification and Christian perfection was one of degree. His said the Corinthians were "*spiritual* men" but they "were not *altogether* spiritual." That is, justified persons have some measure of the Spirit, but not the fullness of the Spirit.

John Wesley further developed this same emphasis is his sermon, "The Repentance of Believers," (1767) where he said to be entirely sanctified was to be "entirely changed" and "wholly transformed." John Wesley's point was to show that full sanctification was the completion of the process begun with justification and not merely two different things.

John Wesley cited the example of the Thessalonian Christians in his sermon "On Perfection" (1784) who were justified but needed to be wholly sanctified.[129] John Wesley's observation about the Thessalonians having been partially sanctified is reflected in Paul having a favorable assessment of "the Church of the Thessalonians" when he said he was "remembering . . . your work of faith and labor of love and steadfastness of hope" (1 Thessalonians 1:3). Timothy also brought Paul a good report of their faith, but Paul also recognized something was "lacking is your faith" (1 Thessalonians 3:10), even though they had been baptized with a good testimony of their faithfulness.

Paul's prayer for them was: "May the Lord make you increase and abound in love . . . so that he may establish your hearts unblamable in holiness" (1 Thessalonians. 3:12-13). He also noted that "this is the will of God, your sanctification" (1 Thessalonians 4:3) so that they will live righteously. His concluding prayer was: "And may the God of peace himself sanctify you wholly," assuring them that "he who calls you is faithful, and he will do it" (1 Thessalonians 5:23). These Thessalonians, like the Corinthians, were members of the Church and hence had received Christian baptism of water and of the Spirit, but they had not yet personally appropriated its full inner meaning.

Paul said in a second letter to the Thessalonians that they were called to "sanctification by the Spirit" (1 Thessalonians 2:13). Sanctifying grace was associated with the gift of the Holy Spirit to the Church on the day of Pentecost. This sanctification was symbolized by the laying on of hands in baptism, although it would be appropriated in due time. John the Baptist implied this entire inner purification when he said that Jesus would "baptize with fire and the Holy Spirit."

To summarize, Jeremy Taylor's *Discourse on Confirmation* and the Whitsunday sermon of John Heylyn showed that the full purification of the heart is through the baptism with the Spirit. In his typical optimistic view of the possibilities of sanctifying grace, John Wesley expected a "grand Pentecost" when the whole world would be "covered with righteousness as waters cover the sea." Charles Wesley's hymns frequently connected the baptism with the Spirit and the fullness of the Spirit with Christian perfection. John Fletcher more pointedly highlighted the association of the full meaning of the baptism with the Spirit to Christian perfection. Largely through Fletcher's writings, the baptism with the Spirit became a common expression for Christian perfection in early Methodism. Gregory Dix in his participation in the 20th century liturgical renewal movement highlighted that the baptism with the Spirit is the sealing and sanctification of the Christian life, although Jeremy Taylor and Dix acknowledged that the inner truth of full sanctification is appropriated in the course of one's life and not just in the formal rite of confirmation. Because of the Lima text, there is now one umbrella of Christian initiation for all denominations, showing that water baptism and Spirit baptism together are liturgically and experientially the foundation of the Christian life.

Pentecost Moments Today

If John Wesley omitted confirmation from *The Sunday Service*, we have seen his omission corrected today. So there are now at least two "Pentecosts" in the liturgy of the United Methodist Church—baptism and confirmation. (1) The first "Pentecost" occurs in infant baptism. After the minister has completed the gesture of administering water, he lays his hands on the infant, saying "The power of the Holy Spirit work within you, that being born through water and the Spirit you may be a faithful witness of Jesus Christ. (2) The second "Pentecost" occurs in the rite of confirmation when the minister lays hands on the confirmand who is now of age, having been properly catechized, and can personally understand and express his faith in Christ.

The United Methodist Church also promotes further confirmation events or "Pentecosts" whenever a person senses the need for it. This recognition for deeper levels of commitment is similar to what Fletcher often said about "deeper baptisms with the Spirit."[130] It could be said that there is a need for multiple moments of a "second blessing" (John Wesley) or a "second gift" (Charles Wesley) throughout one's life.

So when does a person become a Christian—in baptism or through personal acts of faith? John Wesley allowed that an infant is "born again" in baptism, but he also believed there is also a need for personal acts of faith throughout the course of one's Christian life. The Wesley brothers spent their lives calling faithful members of the church to "go on to perfection."

It should be emphasized that the only perfection that John Wesley believed in was a "perfecting perfection," not a static "perfected perfection." As Outler put it, John Wesley's idea of perfection corresponded to the tradition of the Early Greek Fathers' idea of *teleosis* (becoming perfect) in a dynamic sense of constant improvement, not *perfectus* (static or completed perfection) in the Latin tradition.[131] John Fletcher explained it as "imperfect perfection" because as a perfection of intent one needed also to be brought daily into more conformity with right performance. He said Christian perfection means one is "not legally *but* evangelically *perfect*."[132] This Greek-Latin distinction is imperative if one is to appreciate the High Anglican emphasis on confirmation as "perfecting grace" and John Wesley's emphasis on Christian perfection.

We pointed out above that Richard Baxter made a distinction between water baptism as a *"fundamental right"* of receiving the Holy Spirit and confirmation as the "seal" of that right. Extending this idea, it can be said that all persons have in baptism/confirmation received the forgiving and sanctifying grace of God with the promise of the full potential to be realized in future acts of personal faith.

"Adhering Closely to the Ancient Landmarks"

The Wesleyan tradition has always had a love-hate relationship with its doctrine of Christian perfection. By the middle of the 19th century, The Methodist Episcopal Church was struggling with how to understand and to preach it, and a spirit of discontent about the traditional idea of holiness led to revisionist ways of thinking.[133]

A caution about revisionism was given in the "Bishops' Pastoral Address to the General Conference of the Methodist Episcopal Church in 1852" at Boston, Massachusetts. The bishops offered this advice:

> In speaking or writing of holiness . . . follow the well-sustained views, and even the phraseology employed in the writings of Wesley and Fletcher, which are not superseded by the more recent writers on this subject. Avoid both new theories, new expressions, and new measures on this subect, and adhere closely to the ancient landmarks."[134]

This pastoral call is still relevant, and the doctrine of holiness needs to be explained in understandable and meaningful terms that will connect with today's world.

One of the challenges of promoting the Spirit-filled life is avoiding a privatized and elitist notion of being a Christian. The Charles Wesley scholar, J. Ernest Rattenbury, believed that Charles Wesley's idea of the gift of the Spirit was "almost entirely individualistic."[135] Perhaps it is understandable that someone would read him in that way, but to expect a personal infilling of the Spirit does not have to mean that it is "individualistic." Charles Wesley's Pentecost hymns also were never intended to be sung in solitary "individualistic" withdrawal from the worshiping community.

John Wesley's revival movement with its preaching on justifying and sanctifying grace also tended toward turning Christian experience into an individualistic religious experience, except that he always insisted on his Methodist people participating in the worship service of the Church of England. His purpose in giving the American Methodists *The Sunday Service* as a book of worship was to insure that as a revival movement they would also be a worshiping community.

John Wesley's parachurch Methodist societies were arranged into smaller groups of bands and select societies in order to avoid an individualistic and narrow conception of holiness, and he would not allow his Methodist societies to conduct their meetings during Anglican services because he insisted on the importance of the liturgy of the Church of England in worship, especially Holy Communion, as a means of grace. Yet, John Wesley insisted on the importance of "gospel preaching" and revival meetings to call people to personal faith in justifying and sanctifying grace.

As pointed out in the first chapter, in 1790, John Wesley said that "full sanctification . . . is the grand depositum" which God has lodged with the people called Methodists; and for the sake of propagating this chiefly he appears to have raised us up."[136] One of the primary means of propagating holiness was the revival movement. One of the primary themes of the revival movement was Pentecost and sanctification. John Wesley expected a "grand Pentecost" that would embrace the whole world in his sermon, "The General Spread of the Gospel." Charles Wesley urged the expectation of a personal Pentecost as seen in many of his hymns. John Fletcher's writings drew from John and Charles Wesley's writings and from personal conversations with them, and he intensified the call to a personal Pentecost in his *Essay on Truth, The Last Check to Antinomianism,* and *The Portrait of St. Paul.* Fletcher helped to make the Pentecost paradigm a common way of preaching on holiness. John Wesley's inner circle of leaders, like Elizabeth Ritchie, Mary Bosanquet Fletcher, Hester Ann Rogers, Joseph Benson, and Adam Clarke, also spoke of the importance of being baptized with the Spirit as a means of attaining Christian perfection.

Although the Pentecost motif was often used in Methodism, it should not be interpreted to imply that one could be a justified person literally in a pre-Pentecost sense. If one has been baptized with water and received the laying on of hands in Christian baptism, this means all Christians are now experiencing the justifying and sanctifying grace of God in some measure. So today there are no pre-Pentecost Christian believers in a literal sense.

The qualifying term that Fletcher used to describe justified believers who were not yet made perfect love was "like"—"Like the Apostles . . . not yet filled with that power."[137] Fletcher's point was just as the disciples before Pentecost were justified and then made perfect in love after Pentecost, this is a pattern for today to see the distinction between justification and sanctification. This does not mean that anyone today can be literally a pre-Pentecost follower of Jesus. Anyone who has been initiated into the church through baptism is already receiving the beginning action of the Spirit in sanctifying grace through acts of personal faith.

It is one thing to be baptized with water and the Spirit in Christian baptism, but another thing to actualize the saving potentialities of baptism. It is one thing to be justified by faith in Jesus Christ through repentance and to begin receiving the sanctifying baptism of the Spirit. It is another step to actualize the full potential of the sanctifying baptism of the Spirit in a personal way. Justification and Christian perfection exist in a continuum of grace; they are distinct but not separated. John Wesley also insisted that no matter how much one loves Christ, he is still to go on to further perfection because love can always increase and abound more and more.

In response to some critics who thought Fletcher believed in a literal repetition of the day of Pentecost, Joseph Benson insisted that his dear friend and confidant was only insisting on having a personal experience of the fullness of God's love as an extension of the original day of Pentecost; but he was not expecting a literal day of Pentecost with all the phenomena of wind and fire and speaking in tongues.[138] However, it is important to note that John Wesley believed that one of the reasons why the exercise of spiritual gifts was hardly known in the church today was because of a lack of a dynamic faith in Christ.[139]

Fletcher avoided excessive religious individualism because as a High Anglican churchman he interpreted personal faith in the context of worship and the liturgy, including the liturgy of confirmation. That is why Fletcher (as noticed above) highlighted the worship setting of those who were filled with the Spirit in the book of Acts, noting that "social prayer is closely connected with faith in the capital promise of the sanctifying Spirit: and therefore I earnestly recommend that mean of grace . . . as being eminently conducive to the attaining of Christian perfection."

Fletcher also did not divorce the Spirit from Christ as some of his contemporary ecstatic movements had done, but rather he emphasized that Christ was the one who would baptize with the Spirit. Fletcher exhorts: "Christ is ready; and he is all you want. He is waiting for you: he is at the door! Let your inmost soul cry out."

To show his agreement with his mentors, he quoted Charles Wesley's hymn which John Wesley also included in his sermon, "The Scripture Way of Salvation":

> Come quickly in, thou heav'nly guest,
>   Nor ever hence remove,
> But sup with us, and let the feast
>   Be everlasting love.[140]

Confirmation Service for Today

The new baptismal liturgy is a pastoral opportunity for discerning pastors to promote the life of the Spirit in sanctifying grace and perfect love. I propose that confirmation should become an opportunity to instruct confirmands in the Wesleyan understanding of Christian perfection as part of its catechism.

Jeremy Taylor's *Discourse on Confirmation* shows that John and Charles Wesley's doctrine of Christian perfection was "the rite of confirmation *felt*." This discourse is included here in Appendix 3. If the laying on of hands in the new baptismal liturgy is explained in the way that Jeremy Taylor explained the Anglican rite of confirmation (which is the way John and Charles Wesley understood it), this could lead to a deeper and greater appreciation of what it means to be initiated into the life of the Spirit.

I propose that on the week before Confirmation Sunday the minister preach a sermon on one of the passages in the Book of Acts related to the theme of the laying on of hands, explaining what it means to be filled with the Spirit.

Attached also in Appendix 1 and Appendix 2 are two sermons with a helpful interpretation of the meaning of the laying on of hands—one by the English High Church scholar/preacher John Heylyn and another by the American Episcopal scholar/preacher Phillips Brooks. I have never read better sermons on the gift of the Holy Spirit than these two historic sermons. Nor have I have heard a better explanation of "Christian perfection" than contained in these two sermons, although the term is not used.

I am not suggesting that ministers should use the technical expressions of theology in catechism and sermons on confirmation. I am suggesting that confirmands become aware of the personal meaning of the gift of loving God with all one's hearts and one's neighbor as oneself through being filled with the Spirit. To be confirmed with the laying on of hands is to be anointed with the Spirit to live out one's life in perfect love for God and others.

E. Stanley Jones, the world famous Methodist Missionary whose name is officially attached to schools like Candler School of Theology and Asbury Theological Seminary, preached a model sermon on "The Gift of the Holy Spirit: The Birthright of All Christians" at a U.S. Ashram in August 1960. In this sermon, he testified to his personal experience of being baptized with the Spirit, inspired by the classic devotional book on Christian perfection, *The Christian Secret of a Happy Life* by Hannah Whitehall Smith.

This sermon by Jones is included in the 2008 book, *Living upon the Way: Selected Sermons of E. Stanley Jones on Self-Surrender and Conversion*. Here is the YouTube website where the sermon can be heard: https://www.youtube.com/watch?v=nMzGoVdfooQ

Many persons will most likely in their Christian journey have a spiritual desire to make "a reaffirmation of their faith," as recommended by the Book of Discipline. If Charles Wesley did not believe that baptism and confirmation were of any value "unless you are in Christ a new Creature," he believed in the importance of baptism and confirmation. He also believed it was important for everyone to personally pursue the reality of justifying and full sanctifying grace.[141] Charles Wesley travelled across the British Isles for many years on horseback calling his hearers to be justified and sanctified through personal faith and not to rely only on the ordinances of the Church.

If taken seriously, the recent liturgical renewal movement could lead to a spiritual renewal movement within the Wesleyan tradition if the laying on of hands were to become a part of its understanding for inspiring a life of perfect love.

As the United Methodist General Board of Discipleship has recommended, "confirmation can and should be repeated whenever a person has made a new, deeper, clearer commitment."[142]

Charles Wesley's hymn on Acts 1:5, "John truly baptized with water; but ye shall be baptized with the Holy Spirit" contained the same sentiment when he said that water baptism can only be applied once, but the baptism with the Spirit as often as needed:

> The mystical sign
>   Which our Lord did enjoin
> Only once we receive;
>   But the Spirit, as oft as in Christ we believe.[143]

Conducting further confirmation services for all who may have already been confirmed would be a testimonial to others in the congregation and inspire them to live a Spirit-filled life. There is nothing embarrassing or offensive about asking others if they would like for God to enable them to love Him with all their heart, mind, and soul and to request that members of the congregation to support them in this spiritual pursuit. What could be more uplifting than to receive a fresh baptism of holy love that will inspire a sense of intimacy with Christ and accelerate the processs of washing away the negative emotions of distrust, fear, doubt, jealousy, and fill one with faith, hope, and love, and the fruit of the Spirit.

Charles Wesley's hymn, "Jesus , Thine All Victorious Love," is a prayer for the descent of the Spirit of Pentecost to baptize the believer today with love. This would be an a fitting hymn to sing during a confirmation service. Here are the entire twelve verses:

1. My God! I know, I feel thee mine,
    And will not quit my claim,
Till all I have be lost in thine,
    And all renew'd I am.

2. I hold thee with a trembling hand,
    I will not let thee go,
Till stedfastly by faith I stand,
    And all thy goodness know.

3. When shall I see the welcome hour
    That plants my God in me!
Spirit of health, and life, and power,
    And perfect liberty!

4. Jesu, thy all-victorious love
    Shed in my heart abroad;
Then shall my feet no longer rove
    Rooted and fixed in God.

5. Love only can the conquest win,
    The strength of sin subdue,
(Mine own unconquerable sin)
    And form my soul anew.

6. Love can bow down the stubborn neck,
    The stone to flesh convert,
Soften, and melt, and pierce, and break
    An adamantine heart.

7. O! That in me the sacred fire
    Might now begin to glow,
Burn up the dross of base desire,
    And make the mountains flow!

8. O that it now from heaven might fall,
    And all my sins consume!

Come, Holy Ghost, for thee I call,
  Spirit of burning come!

9. Refining fire, go through my heart,
  Illuminate my soul,
Scatter thy life through every part,
  And sanctify the whole.

10. Sorrow and self shall then expire,
  While enter'd into rest,
I only live my God to admire,
  My God forever blest.

11. No longer then my heart shall mourn,
  While purified by grace,
I only for his glory burn,
  And always see his face.

12. My stedfast soul, from falling free,
  Can now no longer move;
Jesus is all the world to me,
  And all my heart is love.[144]

NOTES

1. A letter from Fletcher to Wesley (August 1, 1775), *The Asbury Theological Journal*, 53.1 (Spring 1998): 93-96.
2. Outler, *Sermons*, 2:159, "The Scripture Way of Salvation"
3. Ibid., 40. Fletcher used the edition of Macarius in Wesley's *Christian Library*. Cf. *Pseudo-Macarius, The First Spiritual Homilies and the Great Letter*, trans, edited and with an introduction by George A. Maloney, S.J., Preface by Kallistos Ware (New York: Paulist Press, 1992): "The people of God, being very special, receive the sign of circumcision inwardly in their heart. For the heavenly knife cuts away the excess portion of the mind, that is, the impure uncircumcision of sin. With them was a baptism sanctifying the flesh, but with us there is a baptism of the Holy Spirit and fire. For John preached this: 'He shall baptize you in the Holy Spirit and fire' (Mt. 3:11)." (Ibid., 232).
4. Ibid., 42. It shows that it was Fletcher's practice to strike through Wesley's name, as for example "~~Mr. Wesley and~~ I."
5. *Hymns and Sacred Poems* (1739) (London: Strahan, 1739), viii
6. *The Last Check*, 6:399.
7. *The Last Check*, 6:386.
8. *The Last Check*, 6:399.
9. *The Last Check*, 6:391.
10. George Lawton, *Shropshire Saint* (London: The Epworth Press, 1960), 28.
11. "Essay on Truth," in *Equal Check to Antinomianism*, 4:267-268.
12. *An Essay on Truth*, 4:267–268.
13. *The Last Check*, 6:334.
14. Cf. *'Unexampled, Labours,'* 77.
15. A letter from Fletcher to Wesley (August 1, 1775), *The Asbury Theological Journal*, 53.1 (Spring 1998): 93-96. I located this letter doing research at John Rylands University Library of Manchester. It was published in its entirety in *The Asbury Theological Journal* 53.1 (Spring 1998), 93-96. It is now transcribed in *'Unexampled, Labours,'* 325-330.
16. Hurst, *History of Methodism* 2:928.
17. *The Asbury Theological Journal* 53.1 (Spring, 1998), 93-96.

18. Telford, *Letters*, 6:174, (to John Fletcher, August 18, 1775).

19. John Fletcher, "An Essay on the Doctrine of the New Birth," *The Asbury Theological Journal*, Volume 53, Number 1 (Spring 1998): 37.

20. Fletcher-Tooth Archival Collection of the John Rylands University Library of Manchester University and Methodist Archives and Research Center. PLP 7/12/38, PLP 7/12/35. Fletcher mentioned that he intended to retain these until he was finished with them.

21. Gregory Dix, *The Theology of Confirmation in Relation to Baptism* (Westminster: Dacre Press, 1946).

22. Ibid., 11-12.

23. Dix, *Confirmation, Or Laying on of Hands?* (London: S.P.C.K., 1936), 10

24. Fletcher, *The New Birth*, 35-36.

25. Dix, *The Theology of Confirmation in Relation to Baptism*, 25.

26. Ibid. 36-37.

27. Cf. Dix, *The Theology of Confirmation in relation to Baptism*, 30-31.

28. Book of Common Prayer (1662), 169

29. *Miscellaneous Writings and Letters of Thomas Cranmer*, ed. John Edmund Cox (Cambridge: The University Press, 1846), 79-80. Cf. *Confirmation: History, Doctrine, and Practice*, ed. Kendig Brubaker Cully (Greenwich, Conn, 1962), 21-23.

30. Book of Common Prayer (1662), 161.

31. The Book of Common Prayer, order of confirmation (1662), 169

32. *Miscellaneous Writings and Letters of Thomas Cranmer*, ed. John Edmund Cox, 79-80. Cf. *Confirmation: History, Doctrine, and Practice*, ed. Kendig Brubaker Cully (Greenwich, Conn, 1962), 80.

33. Richard Baxter, *Confirmation and Restauration: The Necessary Means of Reformation and Reconciliation* (London: Nevil Simmons Bookseller, 1658).

34. Baxter, 120

35. Baxter, 27-31, 128.

36. Baxter 107.

37. Baxter 107.

38. Baxter, 113.

39. "Discourse on Confirmation," *The Whole Works of the Right Rev. Jeremy Taylor*, 5:610.

40. Discourse on Confirmation, 5:624, 639,

41. Discourse on Confirmation, 5:624.

42. Discourse on Confirmation, 5:624.

43. Heylyn, "Of the Origin and Progress of Virtues," *Theological Lectures*, 179.

44. Heylyn, "On Whitsunday," *Theological Lectures*, 121.

45. *Works of John Wesley* (Jackson edition), 10:227, "Treatise on Baptism." For a helpful discussion showing that John Wesley came to reject the idea that humans are deserving of condemnation because they are born with an inherited tendency to evil, see Kenneth J. Collins, *The Theology of John Wesley* (Nashville: Abingdon Press, 2007), 64-73. Collins said: "Wesley had every confidence that the atoning work of Christ . . . is more than sufficient to cover the Adamic guilt that in some sense is mediated even to infants" (ibid, 62). Although John Wesley moderated and qualified his interpretation of the guilt of infants in Adam's original sin, this is a notion that needs to be altogether abandoned.

46. Joel B. Green, "Adam, What Have You Done?" *Evolution and the Fall*, ed. William T. Cavanaugh & James K. A. Smith (Grand Rapids: Wm. B. Eerdmans, 2017), 108-109.

47. Cf. Darrel R. Falk, "The Scientific Story," *Evolution and the Fall*, ed. William T. Cavanaugh & James K. A. Smith (Grand Rapids: Wm. B. Eerdmans, 2017), 12-13. Cf. Agustin Fuentes, *The Creative Spark: How Imagination Made Humans Exceptional* (Penguin Books, 2017).

48. Francis Collins, *The Language of God: A Scientist Presents Evidence for Belief* (New York: Free Press, 2007), 2007.

49. *Works of John Wesley* (Jackson edition), 10:483, "Address to the Clergy"

50. John Fletcher Hurst, *John Wesley the Methodist* (New York; The Methodist Book Concern, 1903), 23.

51. Moore, *The Life of Mrs. Mary Fletcher*, 19.

52. Moore, *The Life of Mrs. Mary Fletcher*, 61.

53. Hurst, *History of Methodism* 2:916.

54. *The Life and Correspondence of Hester Ann Rogers*, 23-24. Cf. Hurst, *History of Methodism*, 2:914.

55. *Life of Adam Clarke* (autobiography), 1:90.

56. *Life of Adam Clarke* (autobiography), 3:118.
57. Albert C. Outler, *The Wesleyan Theological Heritage*, 123, 147.
58. Thomas Coke and Francis Asbury, *The Doctrines and Discipline of the Methodist Episcopal Church in America, with explanatory notes*, 10th ed. (Philadelphia: Tuckniss, 1798), iv. Original date of publication was Nov. 16, 1792 in Baltimore by Thomas Coke and Francis Asbury, 59.
59. Cf. Nathan Bangs, *A History of the Methodist Episcopal Church* (New York: Lane & Tippett, 1845), 1:175.
60. Fletcher's letter to Wesley (August 1, 1775), *The Asbury Theological Journal*, 53.1 (Spring 1998): 94.
61. *Works* (Jackson), 10:117, "A Roman Catechism, Faithfully Drawn Out of the Allowed Writings of the Church of Rome, With a Reply Thereto."
62. Wesley, *Works* (Jackson) 10:116-117, "A Roman Catechism." Cf. James Parker, *An Introduction to the History of the Successive Revisions of the The Book of Common Prayer* (Oxford: Parker and Co., 1877), cclx.
63. Cragg, *Appeals*, 11:79, "An Earnest Appeal to Men of Reason and Religion."
64. *The Church of England c.1689-c.1833*, 183.
65. Frank Baker has noted that John Wesley began administering the Lord's Supper to those who had only been baptized when he was in Georgia, since confirmation was not possible there without a bishop. And this seems to have remained Wesley's actual practice throughout his life. *John Wesley and the Church of England*, 157.
66. *Book of Common Prayer, Copy of the Alterations in the Book of Common Prayer prepared by the Royal Commissioners for the Revision of the Liturgy in 1689,"* Extracted from the Original Volume in the custody of the Archbishop of Canterbury at Lambeth Palace, and accompanied by Explanatory Documents (ordered, by The House of Commons, to be printed 2 June 1854), 69. A special commission (consisting of Bishop William Lloyd, Edward Stillingfleet, Symon Patrick, and John Tillotson) was appointed in 1688 to make some minor revisions to the 1662 edition of the Book of Common Prayer, but political changes brought about because of the Glorious Revolution of William of Orange overshadowed the necessity for these revisions and were thus dropped. Cf. http://justus.anglican.org/resources/bcp/1689/BCP_1689.htm.
67. *Copy of the Alterations in the Book of Common Prayer 1689*, 67.
68. *Copy of the Alterations in the Book of Common Prayer 1689*, 68.
69. Wesley, *Explanatory Notes upon the New Testament* (London: The Epworth Press, 1958; originally published January 4, 1754), 6.
70. Ibid., 471.
71. Fletcher, *New Birth*, 54.
72. Ibid., 45.
73. Cf. Thomas A. Langford, *Practical Divinity* (Nashville: Abingdon Press, 1983), who calls Nathan Bangs the first significant Methodist theologian.
74. Nathan Bangs, *An Original Church of Christ: or, A Scriptural Vindication of the Orders and Powers of the Ministry* (New York; T. Mason and G. Lane, 1837), 322, 325.
75. Ibid., 320.
76. Ibid., 323.
77. Frank C. Senn, *Christian liturgy: Catholic and Evangelical* (Minneapolis, Minn: Fortress Press, 1997), 612- 613.
78. Senn writes: "The study of ancient sources aroused an interest in the retrieval of ancient liturgical practises, such as the celebration of the mass facing the people across the altar-table, the offertory procession of the faithful, the epiclesis in the eucharistic prayer, the rites of the Holy Week, the communal and initiatory character of baptism, and the public and communal celebration of the Divine Office." (Senn, 610-611).
79. Senn, 613. Dix's *Shape of the Liturgy* has been heavily criticized for its lack of sources regarding the eucharist in particular. http://www.episcopalnet.org/TRACTS /HowEpiscopaliansDeceived.html.
80. Cf. Aidan Kavanagh, *The Shape of Baptism: The Rite of Christian Initiation* (New York: Pueblo Publishing Company, 1978), 87.
81. A new edition of *The Shape of the Liturgy* was published in 2005 with a new introduction by *Dr. Simon Jones* of *Merton College, Oxford*, which gives an up-to-date assessment of *Dix's* scholarship and its influence upon liturgical revision. http://www. episcopalnet.org/TRACTS/HowEpiscopaliansDeceived.html.

A new edition of *The Shape of the Liturgy* was published in 2005 with a new introduction by *Dr. Simon Jones* of *Merton College, Oxford*, which gives an up-to-date assessment of *Dix's* scholarship and its influence upon liturgical revision.

82. *The Treatise on the Apostolic Tradition of St. Hippolytus of Rome, Bishop and Martyr*, edited Gregory Dix and reissued with corrections, preface and bibliography by Henry Chadwick (London: S.P.C.K., 1968), xi.

83. Ibid., a-p.

84. Ibid., ix.

85. G. W. H. Lampe, *The Seal of the Spirit*, 2nd ed (London: SPCK, 1967), 150-158.

86. Lampe, *The Seal of the Spirit*, 150.

87. Dix, *The Theology of Confirmation in relation to Baptism*, 42.

88. Ibid., 16.

89. *The Seal of the Spirit*, 317.

90. Dix, *The Theology of Confirmation in relation to Baptism*, 36-37.

91. Dix, *The Theology of Confirmation in Relation to Baptism*, 8.

92. Ibid., 42.

93. See Frank C. Senn, *Christian Liturgy: Catholic and Evangelical* (Minneapolis, Minn. : Fortress Press, 1997.

94. Senn, 637.

95. Senn, 645.

96. Cf. Austin, *Anointing with the Spirit, The Rite of Confirmation* (New York: Pueblo Publishing Company, 1985), 92.

97. *Works of John Wesley* (Jackson edition), 4:81, "Letter to the Editor of the *Lloyd Evening* Post (Dec. 20, 1760).

98. John Wesley, *The Sunday Service of the Methodists* (London: J. Kershaw, 1825), A2.

99. *Church Dogmatics*, ed. G. W. Bromiley, T. F. Torrance, trans. G. W. Bromiley (Edinburgh: T. & T. Clark, 1969, 4.4:viii.

100. Ibid., x, 102, 106, 128. Barth interpreted water baptism as a human decision symbolizing repentance, forgiveness of sins and conversion. Only the history of salvation in Jesus Christ is sacramental.

101. Ibid., 35, 102.

102. *Church Dogmatics*, ed. G. W. Bromiley, T. F. Torrance, trans. G. W. Bromiley (Edinburgh: T. & T. Clark, 1969, IV, 4, v.

103. The editors, G. W. Bromiley and T. F. Torrance noted this new emphasis in Barth: "A sharp distinction is drawn between *baptism with the Spirit* which refers to the objective ground of the Christian life in the decisive act of God in changing and renewing our human nature in Jesus Christ, and *baptism with water*, which refers to the subjective aspect of man's initiation into the Christian life performed in the Church in response to the faithfulness of God." *Church Dogmatics*, 4.4.v.

104. Ibid., 188.

105. *Church Dogmatics*, 4:4, 30.

106. Ibid., 34, 38, 41-46.

107. Ibid., 34-35, 78.

108. Karl Barth, *The Theology of Schleiermacher*, ed. Dietrich Ritschl, trans. Geoffrey W. Bromiley (Grand Rapids: Wm. B. Eerdmans, 1982), 276-279.

109. Frederick Dale Bruner, *A Theology of the Holy Spirit* (Grand Rapids, MI: William B. Eerdmans, 1970).

110. James D. G. Dunn, *Baptism in the Holy Spirit* (Philadelphia: The Westminster Press, 1970).

111. In his introduction to *The Baptism in the Holy Spirit*, Dunn traces the idea of an experience of the Holy Spirit subsequent to conversion-intiation from John Wesley and some of the early Puritans (as Thomas Goodwin) through John Fletcher, the nineteenth century Holiness movement, culminating in twentieth century Pentecostalism. His study is intended to counteract this theology, including "the sacramentalists" who distinguish between two moments of Christian initiation (pp. 1-7).

112. Dunn, *Baptism in the Holy Spirit*, 226.

113. The Orthodox tradition believes that the Lima text needs to clarify further the importance of chrismation. Cf. *Baptism, Eucharist & Ministry 1982–1990, Report on the Process and Responses*, Faith and Order Paper No. 149 (Geneva; WCC Publications), 49.

114. Moltmann, *The Spirit of Life*, trans. Margaret Kohl (Minneapolis: Fortress Press, 1992), 164; *The Trinity and the Kingdom*, 207.

115. Moltmann, *The Spirit of Life*, 165.

116. Cf. Senn, 641.

117. *Systematic Theology* (Grand Rapids: Wm. B. Eerdmans, 2009), 3:269.

118. Ibid.

119. *Churches Respond to BEM: Official Response to the "Baptism, Eucharist and Ministry" Text*, ed. Max Thurian, 6 vols. (Geneva: W.C.C., 1986-88), 2:181-182.

120. *Churches Respond to BEM: Official Response to the "Baptism, Eucharist and Ministry" Text*, ed. Max Thurian, 6 vols. (Geneva: W.C.C., 1986-88), 2:182; cf. Wainwright, *Methodists in Dialog*, 210ff.

121. *Follow Me: Handbook for Pastors, Parents, and Congregations*, an official resource for the United Methodist Church prepared by the General Board of Discipleship (Nashville: United Methodist Publishing House, 1993), 27.

122. MS Acts, MARC: MA 1977/555 (Charles Wesley Notebooks Box 1), 149

123. John Wesley, *Sunday Service of the Methodists in North America* (London: 1784), 139.

124. See Laurence W. Wood, *The Meaning of Pentecost in Early Methodism* (Lanham, MD: Scarecrow Press, 2002), 35.

125. *Works of John Wesley* (Jackson edition), 10:229, "Treatise on Baptism"

126. Cf. Fletcher, *Works*, 1:13, "First Check to Antinomianism."

127. Rudolf Bultmann, *The Theology of the New Testament*, trans. Kendrick Grobel (New York: Charles Scribner & Son, 1951): 2:158.

128. Outler, *Sermons*, 1:325-333, "Sin in Believers"

129. Outler, *Sermons*, 3:82, "On Perfection"

130. *The Methodist Magazine*, volume 1, a continuation of *The Arminian Magazine*, volume 21, (London edition), (November 1798): 597.

131. Albert Outler, *The Wesleyan Theological Heritage*, ed Thomas C. Oden & Leicester R. Longden (Grand Rapids: Zondervan, 1991), 51.

132. Fletcher, *The Last Check*, 6:134-135.

133. For a larger discussion see, *The Meaning of Pentecost in Early Methodism*, 313-336.

134. "The Bishops' Pastoral Address to the General Conference of the Methodist Episcopal Church in 1852, *Journal of the General Conference of the Methodist Episcopal Church Held in Boston, MASS, 1852* (New-York, Carlton & Phillips, 1852), 160.

135. *The Evangelical Doctrines of Charles Wesley's Hymns*, 186.

136. *Works of John Wesley* (Jackson edition), 8:238. "Letter to Robert Carr Brackenbury, Esq., of Raithby, Lincolnshire" (September 15, 1790).

137. Fletcher's letter to Mary Bosanquet, March 7, 1778, cited by Tyerman, *Wesley's Designated Successor*, 411-412.

138. Benson, *The Life of the Rev. John W. de la Flechere*, 392.

139. Outler, *Sermons*, 3:263-264, "The More Excellent Way."

140. Charles Wesley, *Hymns on God's Everlasting Love* (London: Strahan, 1742), 25. John Fletcher, *Last Check to Antinomianism*, in *The Works of John Fletcher*, ed. Joseph Benson (London: Richard Edwards, 1806): 6:385.

141. *Manuscript Journal*, 2:354.

142. *Follow Me: Handbook for Pastors, Parents, and Congregations*, an official resource for the United Methodist Church prepared by the General Board of Discipleship (Nashville: United Methodist Publishing House, 1993), 27.

143. MS Acts, MARC: MA 1977/555 (Charles Wesley Notebooks Box 1), 2.

144. *Hymns and Sacred Poems* (1740), 156. It would be worth going back to compare this hymn with the words and ideas of the Wesley brothers' first-ever explanation of the uniqueness of sanctification as distinct from forgiveness of sins contained in the preface to *Sacred Hymns and Poems* (1740). [See Chapter 6, pp. 49-50].

Appendix 1

"A Sermon on Whitsunday" By John Heylyn

John Heylyn was the first rector of St. Mary-le-Strand (1724–59) who became prebendary of Westminster Abbey (1743–59) and was buried in Westminster Abbey, August 1759. John Wesley used Heylyn's devotional writings while he was in Georgia, and he later included them in his recommendations to his preachers. He used Heylyn's *Theological Lectures* as a source of his *Explanatory Notes upon the New Testament* (1754–1755).[1]

This "Sermon on Whitsunday"[2] influenced John Wesley, as well as other early Methodist leaders, in their understanding of Pentecost and sanctification. This is the sermon that John Wesley heard Heylyn preach after visiting his brother Charles on Pentecost Sunday, May 21, 1738. While John Wesley was listening to this sermon, his bed-ridden brother Charles experienced his own personal Pentecost. John Wesley noted in his journal after hearing this sermon that Heylyn "preach[ed] a truly Christian sermon on 'They were all filled with the Holy Spirit'—and so, said he, may *all you* be." John Wesley would later preach multiple sermons on being "filled with the Spirit," concluding with the same exhortation to his hearers. Themes from this Whitsunday sermon are echoed in John Wesley's own sermons. John Wesley also preached multiple sermons on being "baptized with the Holy Spirit." Heylyn's sermon was a call for believers today to be filled and baptized with the Spirit in order to be "sanctified" and to receive "perfect purity." Notice the language of confirmation in being "confirmed in all goodness" at the conclusion.

Imagine yourself sitting in a Church of England worship service in London (perhaps St Paul's Cathedral or Westminster Abbey where he often preached) listening to this sermon by John Heylyn as John Wesley would have heard it on the same day and exact time of his brother's Pentecost experience. Remember also John Wesley's great admiration of John Heylyn's theological works.

1. *Journals and Diaries I (1735–38), The Bicentennial Edition of the Works of John Wesley*, 18:241n15.
2. "Discourse XV. On Whitsunday," *Select Discourses on the Principal Points of Revealed Religion*, contained in *Theological Lectures* by John Heylyn, A Prebendary of Westminster and Rector of St. Mary-le-Strand (London: Printed for J. and R. Tonson and S. Draper in the Strand, 1749), 111-121.

A Sermon on Whitsunday

"Suddenly there came a sound from heaven as of a rushing mighty wind, and it filled all the house where they were sitting; and there appeared unto them cloven tongues like as of fire, and it sat upon each of them" (Acts 2:2-3).

It has been the pious wisdom of the Church to set apart certain days for the solemn commemoration of its principal mysteries, and for the honour of those blessed saints and martyrs who were most instrumental in its establishment. The occasion of the present festival [Pentecost Sunday] is the miraculous effusion of the Holy Spirit upon the apostles, whereby they were qualified for the conversion of mankind, and the Christian Church was completely settled and established: so that the Church does now keep its own festival, celebrate, as it were, its own nativity: and all the Saints Days in the calendar shine but with borrowed rays from this day's glory; for all those virtues and excellencies which have made their names so precious in the Christian World, were as at this time poured forth upon them. To this it is we owe the sanctity of their lives, the purity of their doctrines, the power of their miracles, and all the glorious acts of their martyrdom.

All the other mysteries of the gospel prepare the way for this, which is the end of the Incarnation, the fruit of the death of Christ, and the full accomplishment of all his designs. He had in deed already formed the Body of his Church while he was here on Earth conversing with and instructing his disciples, but by this last act, the descent of the Holy Spirit, he infused a soul into that his mystical Body, he endowed it with a vigorous principle of life, and action, a heart that would always correspond and sympathize with him its Head.

And this indeed seems peculiar to this festival season, that whereas the subjects of other Holy Days are actually past and concluded, so as to require only our devout remembrance and acknowledgement; the occasion of this still subsists, and ever will subsist in the Church. The same Holy Spirit, which then descended upon the apostles, does still descend upon all the living members of Christ, according to his gracious promise in the last words of St. Matthew's Gospel, almost the last words which he spoke upon Earth. *Lo I am with you alway, even unto the end of the world.*

This promise is fulfilled in the mission of the Holy Spirit. Christ is now present in his Church by his Spirit, which as it formerly descended upon the apostles, so it ever shall descend upon all his true disciples *unto the end of the world.* The sacred fountain still stands open, and nothing is retrenched from the bounteous efflux of divine grace, but only the outward prodigies which attended it at the beginning of its course. Now indeed it flows on, as some peaceful river, through opened channels, with silent stream and marking its way only by the riches it spreads in the parts it passes through: But the season we celebrate was the time of its eruption, if I may so speak, when it rapidly issued forth from the divine source to replenish the apostles, who were the conduits prepared to receive and convey it forward to the latest generations. At that time, as was usual upon such extraordinary occasions, it manifested itself even outwardly, by sensible representations, expressive of its energy and the effects it produces in the spirits of men. These sensible representations appeared in the two active elements *air* and *fire*, which kindle and keep up the life of nature.

For when the apostles were assembled *on the Day of Pentecost*, i. e. the day whereon the Law was given to the Jews: *suddenly there came a sound from heaven, as of a rushing mighty wind: and it filled all the house where they were siting. And there appeared to them cloven tongues like as of fire; and it sat upon each of them.* For *cloven tongues like as of fire*, according to our version; I think the sense of the original is *separated* or *distinct flames*. Lambent flames; for *tongue of fire* is a Hebraism for a *flame*, as may be seen in Isaiah. So that here was double prodigy, *a sound was heard from heaven, as of an impetuous wind filling the house; and several distinct flames were seen, one of which* resided over each of the apostles. Now these are two proper emblems or symbolical representations: and in order to judge of their significance we are to observe that there is such an analogy and intimate connection between the material and the spiritual worlds, that not only the names of things visible serve to denote things invisible, and are the only names we have for them, which plainly argues a notorious analogy upon which such use of the names is grounded; but also some extraordinary transactions in the higher order pass on and impress themselves upon the lower, so as to affect outward nature in a similar manner, such I mean as somehow answers to what is then accomplished in the supernatural state. Thus, for instance, a few weeks before this descent of the Holy Spirit, while our Lord was hanging on the cross, the sun was eclipsed; and when he expired, outward nature was convulsed with an earthquake. And she sympathized again, yet to different purpose, in a second earthquake at his resurrection. And now, when his Spirit with the plenitude of divine power was descending upon his apostles, a sound from heaven was heard as of an impetuous *wind*, and distinct *flames* were seen over the heads of the apostles.

It will be proper here, as far as our scanty knowledge will permit, to trace out the analogy wherein these two symbols are grounded.

Concerning the first, it has been observed that among those parts of the material world which are invisible, and whose existence we discover only by their effects, there is scarce anything more subtile, more active, and of greater efficacy than *wind*, i. e. air in motion, or *spirit*, which is the same thing according to the primary sense of the word. Hence in the common use of most languages the name of wind or spirit serves to express those things, which being not discernible to us by reason of the subtility or fineness of their substance, are yet conceived to be moved with great agility, and endued with great force. So naturalists, when they speak of that which is most abstruse, most agile, and most operative in any liquor or other body, call it *spirit*. And for the same reason our souls are called spirits, for the subtility of their nature and those vital powers wherewith they actuate our bodies.

In regard to our capacity and manner of conceiving things, the holy Scriptures have used this term *Spirit* to express even the adorable and incomprehensible deity, signifying his most simple nature and most powerful energy; his most simple *Nature*, I say, which cannot possibly be the object of any of our Senses; and his most powerful *energy*, which pervades and actuates all things.

This name Spirit, as it is common to the whole Godhead, so it is peculiarly applied to the third Person of the ever-blessed Trinity, styled by way of eminence *The Holy Spirit*, and the operations of God towards men are in an especial manner ascribed to him.

Now in all languages commonly known, the operation of a superior mind upon an inferior to raise and invigorate it, is expressed by the metaphor of inspiration, i. e. breathing into: and the general consent of mankind in the use of this metaphor demonstrates its fitness and propriety. And therefore when the infinite Mind vouchsafed to communicate itself with such plenitude and force to the minds of his chosen servants assembled on the Day of Pentecost, this sound from heaven of a mighty rushing wind, or torrent of mysterious *air*, was a proper symbol to indicate its *descent*: as the other miraculous appearance by the element of *fire* was proper to represent the *effects* which it produces.

To *enlighten*, to *purify*, and to *warm*, are the properties of fire. Now if we transfer these to the spiritual world, the light of the soul is *truth*, the purity of the soul is *holiness*, the warmth or heat of the soul is an active, vigorous *ardour* to surmount obstacles, and zealously prosecute the end proposed. The Holy Spirit produces these three effects, and accordingly the Scriptures describe Him as Spirit of *truth*, of *holiness*, and of *power*. As a *Spirit of truth* he enlightens the minds of the faithful, and *leads them into all truth* fit for them to know: as a *Spirit of holiness*, by an intimate union with their hearts, he reforms them and makes them holy; as a *Spirit of power* he gives them vigour to resist temptation, strength to bear their crosses, and full ability to work out their salvation. We shall take these three properties of the Holy Spirit, for three heads to be treated separately.

First he is a *Spirit of truth*, and so our Lord styled him when he foretold his descent upon the apostles, *I have many things to say unto you, but ye cannot bear them now. Howbeit, when he, the Spirit of truth is come, he will guide you into all truth.* Men may teach us diverse truths, but to teach all truth is the distinguishing prerogative of the Spirit of God. There are truths, and those too of the utmost importance, which *flesh and blood* have not, *cannot reveal*: truths which *the world cannot receive* which even the apostles themselves could not *bear*, much less relish, approve, and practice before they had received the Holy Spirit. *Ye cannot bear them now*, said Christ in the passage last quoted, they shock corrupt nature, and our passions recoil at the mention of them. For, besides the mysteries of our holy Religion *the deep things of God*, which cannot be duly apprehended but by minds enlightened by the Spirit of God: besides these, I say, there are many moral truths, whereof we cannot be fully and effectually persuaded but by the immediate operation of the Holy Spirit: such are those in the beginning of our Lord's Sermon on the Mount, *That the poor in spirit, the meek, those that mourn and are persecuted, are blessed above other men. That it is better to pull out our eyes and cut off our hands than use either in the commission of sin. That our enemies are amiable, and that the most provoking Injury ought not only to be forgiven, but requited with benevolence.* These, and others that might be named, are certain and saving truths: but no mortal man can convince us of them, mean with full, lasting, operative conviction, such as shall determine our practical judgment, and become the habitual rule of our conduct. All demonstrations of reason and arts of persuasion are vain to this end: and it is in vain that we ourselves endeavour to reason ourselves into these truths. The Holy Spirit only can work this effectual conviction in our minds, and we must seek this conviction from him by prayer and opening our minds to his operations, or we shall perish in our errors. The same power only that made our minds, can reform them. That Holy Spirit of God, which at the first creation brooded over the rude chaos, and produced this orderly world out of darkness and confusion, must also preside in our minds to make the new creation of virtue, to bring forth light out of our darkness, truth out of our errors. St. Paul alludes to this, where he says, *God who commanded the Light to shine out of darkness, hath shined in our hearts to give the light of the knowledge of the glory of God.*

Such are the advantages we now celebrate, such are the privileges to which we are admitted, if we do not *love darkness more than light because our deeds are evil* and we resolve to continue in them. God's school now stands open to all, his Spirit condescends to be our master, our teacher, and will infallibly lead us into all saving truth, if we devoutly resign ourselves to his direction.

We cannot have plainer proof of this than in the history of the day [of Pentecost]. Consider the apostles, see how wondrous change was wrought in them by the illumination of this Holy Spirit. Observe what they were *before*, what *after* his Descent; and learn from thence what inestimable advantages we are entitled to by Christianity.

Three long years had the apostles been in the School of Christ, and had tired even his patience with their gross stupidity and incapacity to apprehend his spiritual doctrine. Though they had made some progress in the ways of truth by leaving their little all to follow him: though they daily heard his precepts, and saw his practice, that living comment upon his doctrine: yet nothing could rectify their false notions, nothing could wean their vain desires of secular grandeur and magnificence. When our Lord informed them of the necessity of sufferings, the benefits of poverty, the blessedness of persecution, 'twas all riddle to them. *They understood none of these things; these sayings were hid from them, neither knew they the things that were spoken.* Even after the resurrection of Christ the cloud was still upon their minds, and they were yet hankering after an immediate possession of worldly grandeur and dominion. *Lord,* say they, *wilt thou at this time restore again the kingdom to Israel?* Christ no longer opposed their carnal prejudices, but refered them to the Holy Spirit for full information and conviction.

According to the promise of Christ the Holy Spirit came. Immediately all darkness, error, and mistake fled before him. They understood, they believed, they taught, they practiced, they were ready to lay down their lives for those truths, which before they could not receive, they could not bear, nor endure. The cross of Christ was no longer an offence to them, but their boast and their glory and they rejoiced, that they themselves were *counted worthy* to partake of it, and to *suffer shame for his name.*

Such and so effectual were the fruits of the Spirit enlightening the minds of the apostles as a Spirit of *truth*. We are in the next place to consider Him as Spirit of *holiness*. He is not only by way of eminence the *Holy* Spirit, but also the hallowing, i. e. *sanctifying* Spirit, from whence all holiness in the creatures is derived. It would be endless to mention the places of Scripture where this property is ascribed to him. I am more concerned how may explain to you the precise meaning of the word *holiness*, which is to be considered in two respects, first, as it is proper to God alone, and secondly, as it is the duty of creature. According to the first sense we say in the Communion Service. *Thou only art holy*: as *Thou only art the Lord*. This holiness peculiar to the deity, consists in the singularity of his nature, even that surpassing transcendent excellence, which leaves all creatures at an infinite distance beneath his majesty.

It is a common error in men's notion of God, that they conceive of him as *one Being among many*: greater indeed, and higher, and better than all the rest, but yet *as one among others*, one that may be named with them, and however superior, yet not absolutely distinct from the rest. This is a wrong conception, for God is not only *Unus*, but *Unicus*. He is One alone, the First without any second or like. But this is a Subject which no speculations can do justice to, and which should naturally sink the mind into the profoundest devotion. Suffice it then to say, that this sublime exaltation and infinite distance of the Creator from the creatures, constitutes his *holiness*. The Hebrew word signifies *separation*, and when applied to God, imports that unconceivable elevation whereby he is distinguished, and stands alone in his universe. Thus we read; *There is none holy as the Lord: for there is none besides Thee*. There is none beside him, He is whole genus by himself, and this surpassing, singular excellence, which excludes all possible comparison, constitutes his *holiness*, and the exercise of it tends solely to the promoting his own glory. He is *glorious in* (rather *by*) *holiness,* says the Psalmist and the angels incessantly celebrate him by this title *Holy, Holy, Holy Lord God of Hosts Heaven and Earth are full of thy Glory*. The holiness of God is founded, as was said, in the *supremacy of his nature*; and it is perpetually exercised in maintaining that supremacy, in treating himself worthily, exerting all his attributes, and directing all his acts, to one certain point, which is his glory, the exaltation of his nature, the effulgency of his excellence. The reason why God does all things for his own glory is, because that is the end most worthy of God, his supreme excellence requires it of him as due to himself by the eternal laws of Righteousness: truth and justice make this necessary in the deity. The glory of God therefore being the end most worthy of God, and all his acts centering therein, all his acts are holy, i. e. pure from all allay of inferior motives, from everything that does not inflexibly promote that end.

Such is the holiness of God. The creatures too are holy, when they prosecute the same end that God does, the end for which he created them, i. e. *the Glory of God*. We call things or persons holy when they are separated from common use and dedicated to the service of God, devoted to his glory to apply them to any other end is to profane them. All the laws of God are boundaries set to fence in the way that leads to God's glory, and we never transgress those laws, but we at the same time deviate from it. And therefore St Paul defines sin to be *a falling short of the glory of God. All have sinned, and come short of the glory of God*. Holiness on the contrary aims all our actions aright, making the glory of God our scope and design. In a word, every action directed to that end is an holy action, and leads us on towards the participation of the divine glory which we had regard to in performing it, and when it is said that the Holy Spirit sanctifies Christians, the meaning is, that he infuses this generous motive, extinguishing the narrow principles of covetousness, pride, and sensuality, and exalting our nature to the noble disinterested purpose of glorifying our Maker.

Those corrupt motives of covetousness, sensuality, and pride cleave intimately to our souls in the present depraved state, rendering all actions that proceed from them, *unholy* and the Spirit of God does then sanctify us when it disengages us from those corrupt motives. To *wash, cleanse, baptize*, and *sanctify*, are commonly synonymous in Scripture; hence the phrase of *being baptized with the Holy Spirit*, which is elsewhere called being *baptized -with Fire*, to signify the universal and intimate purification of the inmost springs of action thereby. With this view the Prophet Malachi compares the Spirit *to a refiner of gold or silver* destroying the dross, and separating all heterogeneous particles from those metals by force of fire, till they are reduced to a perfect purity. Thus the Spirit sanctifies the soul by abolishing all sordid inclinations, by purging away the multiplicity of carnal desires, and reducing all the powers of the mind to one simple constant pursuit, viz. that of God's glory. This renders the soul holy, i. e. pure, all of kind, concentered in the end of its creation, even the glory of its Maker.

To show how the apostles were thus sanctified, were to relate their history, which is but one continued narrative of their holiness. They were purified from all corrupt principles of action, I mean not absolutely and in that supreme degree which is peculiar to heaven, but yet in an eminent and extraordinary manner. The love of *riches* moved them not: for they had all the treasures of the faithful laid at their feet, without any other concern than for the right distribution of them in charity. The love of *ease and pleasure* moved them not: for their life was spent in incessant labours; they traversed the face of the Earth, doing good, and suffering evil in all the parts they visited. *The love of glory and applause* moved them not, for they gladly suffered reproach in their Master's cause and when divine honours were offered to two of them at Lystra, they rent their clothes, and expressed greater concern for the misplaced reverence of the multitude, than for all the ill usage they had ever met with. And lastly, the *love of life itself* moved them not, when the glory of God required them to resign it. They rejoiced that they were accounted worthy to die in so great and good cause. They went cheerfully to death, although the wit and malice of their persecutors had so circumstanced it with horrid variety of tortures, that only the *manner* of dying was the punishment, and death itself the deliverance.

Such was the holiness of the apostles; 'twas the purity of their hearts, the unity of their desires all meeting in one point, the glory of their Maker.

This *one thing* only they desired: this *one thing* only they pursued: they pursued it through poverty, infamy, and distress; through numberless toils and torments. Death in vain came athwart their passage, they leaped the gulf, and were received into glory, that glory for which they had been so zealous.

If we would arrive where they are ascended, we must follow their steps; we must *be holy, as they were holy*, i. e. we must absolutely prefer the glory of God to all other considerations; for heaven stands open to none but saints and *without holiness no Man shall fee the Lord*.

That we may not be disheartened in so arduous work, I propose the greatest encouragements when I add in the third place, that this *Spirit of holiness* is also Spirit *of power*, inspiring zeal, magnanimity, and fortitude sufficient to surmount all difficulties that occur in the arduous paths of duty. And of this also the apostles were very remarkable instances.

Our Lord having had along experience of their natural weakness and pusillanimity, when he appeared to them after his resurrection, commanded them to live retired, and *wait for the promise of the Father. But (said he) ye shall receive power, after that the Holy Spirit is come upon you, and then ye shall be witnesses unto me both in Jerusalem, and in all Judea, and in Samaria, and unto the utter most part of the earth*. And his prediction was gloriously accomplished as soon as the Holy Spirit came. The zeal which inflamed their hearts found ready channel into their tongues; their tongues were as tongues of fire, communicating their sacred ardour to the hearts of all that heard them.

That conceit of the ancients who represented their famous orator as brandishing flames of lightning with thunderbolt, was never so nearly verified as in the apostles; they flashed conviction into the minds of their hearers, and bore down all opposition of reluctant passion or prejudice with a force and energy most irresistible. They made those very Jews who had lately condemned our Lord, and with bloody cries solicited Pilate for his crucifixion, now condemn themselves with bitter remorse and compunction. It is said, *they were pricked in the heart, and said unto Peter and the rest of the apostles, men and brethren, What shall we do?* Three thousand were thus converted at one Sermon, which, considering the natural weakness of the preachers, with the rooted prejudices, and noted obstinacy of the audience, we may account one of the greatest miracles of our religion.

The apostles *bear witness of Christ*, not before his friends, or even persons indifferent, but those that murdered him. Those apostles, who had deserted him shamefully at his being first seized, so far were they from *bearing witness for* him at his trial. Peter in particular, who trembling before a servant-maid had three times renounced him with oaths; *now standing up with the eleven, lift up his voice and said Ye men of Judea, and all ye that dwell at Jerusalem, be this known unto you, and hearken to my words.* You see he makes no timorous apology, he uses none of the little arts to gain benevolence; but conscious of the divine authority wherewith he stood invested, he charges his hearers with all the enormity of their crime. *Ye have killed* (said he) *the Lord of life*: He tells them, that the person, whom *they had with wicked hands crucified and slain*, was the Messiah: and he proves him to be so, *by bearing testimony of his resurrection: him God hath raised up from the dead whereof we are witnesses.* And he backs his own evidence with irrefragable arguments from Scripture, which he at the same time explained with such force and perspicuity as extorted assent from the most obdurate. Is this the illiterate fisherman? Is this the carnal disciple who presumed to rebuke his Lord, when He first mentioned the Cross to him? Is this the fugitive, apostate, abjuring Peter?

But *with God all Things are possible*: Peter had now received the Holy Spirit *the Spirit of power,* whose property it is to strengthen us with might in the inward man, to create a. new heart, and renew right Spirit within us.

And thus I have endeavoured to represent this Holy Spirit in his operations of truth, holiness, and power.

It remains only that I add a word or two concerning the disposition by which we must prepare our hearts to receive him: and this, as our Lord teaches us, is earnest and persevering prayer. We have his direction, *Luke xi. Ask, and it shall be given you; seek, and ye shall find; knock, and it shall be opened unto you.* —*If Son shall ask bread of any of you that is a Father, will he give him stone? how much more shall your heavenly Father give his Holy Spirit to them that ask him?* The terms you see are very easy, are highly reasonable: if we do not perform them we shall be without excuse. But if by humble, fervent, incessant prayer we seek from our heavenly Father the gift of his Spirit, we shall infallibly receive it, we shall be enlightened, purified, and confirmed in all goodness, we shall advance from strength to strength, till we *become meet to be partakers of the inheritance of the saints in light.*

Appendix 2

"A Sermon on Whitsunday" By Phillips Brooks

Phillips Brooks is known as one of the greatest American preachers of all times. He was rector of Trinity Episcopal Church in Boston from 1869 until 1891. If Trinity Church is famous as a masterpiece of architectural design, Brooks' sermons are famous as masterpieces of literary excellence and spirituality. "A Whitsunday Sermon" is as aesthetically beautiful as it is spiritually inspiring. This Pentecost sermon expresses the meaning of "receiving the Holy Spirit" in elevating terms that will inspire one's heart and motivate one to rise above mundane living into the spiritually-rich atmosphere of *love* and *joy* and *nearness to God*.

This sermon on being "filled with *God*" will serve a model for ministers to enjoin confirmands to understood the meaning of "receiving the Holy Spirit" through the laying on of hands and will challenge them to live a Christ-like life of sincerity and humility. The closing invitation is also a model for ministers on how to inspire confirmands and others in the congregation to "come to Christ's Communion Table and celebrate our union with Him and with one another, putting all fear and selfishness aside, and praying Him to show us there how rich a thing it is to believe in Him and how sweet a thing it is to serve Him by His Holy Spirit."

[This sermon is selected from Phillips Brooks, "A Whitsunday Sermon," in *Candle of the Lord and Other Sermons* (New York: E. P. Dutton and Company, 1881). 217-231. A recent republication of some of the sermons of Phillips Brooks has been released entitled, *The Consolation of God, Great Sermons of Phillips Brooks*, ed. Ellen Wilbur (Grand Rapids: Wm. B. Eerdmans, 2003)].

A Whitsunday Sermon

"And they said unto him: We have not so much as heard whether there be any Holy Spirit" (Acts 19:2).

It is always strange to us to find other people entirely ignorant of what makes the whole interest of our own life. We can hardly understand how it is possible that men should live along year after year, it may be generation after generation, knowing nothing about what really makes life for us. If we did not have this or that resource we should die, we should not care to live. Here is a man who has it not, and yet his life seems to be worth a great deal to him. He goes on bright and contented. Apply this to your love of reading. What would it be to you if every book were shut? What would you do if all communication with great minds through literature were broken off, if all the stimulus which comes to your own mind were stopped? And yet there are plenty of these men whom you meet every day who never open a book! Or take the exercise of charity. You would find little pleasure in life perhaps if you were shut in on yourself and could do nothing for anybody else. At least there are people of whom that is true. To find someone whom you can help, and have him near you so that you can help him, is as necessary to you as your food and drink. But there are people enough who seem to thrive abundantly without one act of charity. No self-sacrifice breaks the smooth level of their selfish days. They live without that which is your very life. So of a multitude of things. To one man it is incredible that life can be worth having without wealth; another cannot understand how men can live without amusement; and another, with his social nature, looks at his friend who lives in solitude, and wonders 'how and why he lives at all.

But nowhere is all this so clear as in the matter of religion. One who is really living a religious life, one who is really trying to serve God, who is loving God and believes with all his heart that God loves him, who finds all through his daily life the thick-sown signs that he is not alone, that Christ is helping him and saving him, how strange and almost impossible it is for him to conceive of a life that has nothing of all that in it. How desolate it seems! How tame it looks! One man's days are full of "joy in the Holy Spirit." He is always looking up for inspiration and always receiving it. When he wants comfort there is the Comforter close beside him, nay, deep within him. And then he opens the gate into some brother's life and learns how he is living, and finds that there is nothing at all there of what is so dear to himself. That brother "has not so much as heard whether there be any Holy Spirit." This was just the position in which St. Paul found himself at Ephesus. He had been a Christian now for many years. It was far back in the past, the time when Jesus had appeared to him at mid-day and made him His disciple. He had felt the powerful aid of the Holy Spirit in many a difficult moment of his life. All that he did and said was in the confidence and by the help of this unseen Friend who was nearer to him than any of his closest earthly · friends. And now he came to Ephesus where there were some people who called themselves Christians, and looking for their sympathy and fellow-feeling he inquired, "Have ye received the Holy Spirit since ye believed?" And they said unto him, "We have not so much as beard if there be any Holy Spirit." What was everything to him, they knew nothing at all about. No wonder that his soul yearned over them and he stayed with them and taught them. We can picture his joy as gradually they became sharers in his happiness. What greater joy can any man desire than to bring any other man who has known nothing of it into the knowledge and the power of the Holy Spirit?

This is our subject for Whitsunday morning. What is it to know and not to know "whether there be any Holy Spirit"? Are there not many men among us who, if Paul asked them the old question, would have to give the old Ephesian answer? "Have you received the Holy Spirit, my friend?" Be honest, and must you not answer as they answered, "Indeed I have not so much as heard whether there be any Holy Spirit. The name indeed has sounded in my ears; but as a real person I have not got any true idea of His existence? "Indeed the element of personal experience is so involved with all our knowledge of the Holy Spirit, that for any man to say "Yes, I know Him," is a vastly profounder acknowledgment than the statement of any other knowledge. That is the reason why it is often so vague and hesitating; but just for the same reason there comes a time when a man certain of his experience can say "Yes, I have received, I do know the Holy Spirit" with a certainty and distinctness with which he cannot lay claim to the knowledge of any other thing or person.

In order to understand our question let us turn to this story of the Ephesians. They were Christian believers. They are called "disciples." They had been baptized after the baptism of John. They believed Christian truth and they accepted Christian duty. They had a knowledge of, a faith in Christ, but they had no knowledge of the Holy Spirit. The perception of a present God who should fill out belief in truth with personal apprehension, and who should make duty delightful by personal love, this they had not reached; no one had told them of it.

It was a strange condition. It is not easy to reconcile it with many of our Christian notions, but yet it is a condition which represents the state of many people whom we know, who seem to have just what they had and to be lacking in just what they wanted. I suppose a man-and it is not all a supposition, the specimens are all around us- who believes the Christian truths. That there is a God who made and governs everything, that this God has revealed Himself in Jesus Christ, that He has lived and taught among men, and that at last He died for men in all the torture of the cross, and rose out of the grave in all the inherent power of His immortality,- this they believe. And all that God requires, all that Christ commanded, they accept. The duties of a good life, purity, honesty, resignation, self-denial, all of these they acknowledge. They try to do these duties. Their lives are often wonderful with the severe and lofty standards that they set themselves. They work heroically to fulfil the Master's will. Do we not know such men? They often puzzle us. The aim of all their life is high. Perhaps as I describe them you know that you are such a man yourself. You know that Christ is the great Master. His truth and His commandments you receive. But all the time you know that something is lacking,—a vividness, a life, a spring, a hopefulness and courage which you hear of other people having, which you sometimes see suggested in the things you do, which you seem to be often just upon the verge of, but which after all you do not get, and for the lack of which you are forever conscious of a certain dryness in your belief and a certain shallowness in your duty. What is it that you lack? This lack which, if I speak to your consciousness at all, you recognize, this something which you want, I take to be precisely the Holy Spirit. I do not know any other way in which He can become so real to a true, earnest man, as in the realization of just this want.

Let us separate the two departments to which I have referred, and speak more particularly, first of Belief and then of Duty. We have all been familiar all our lives with the distinction between head-belief and heart-belief. We have been taught, sometimes in such a way that it puzzles us, sometimes in such a way that it was confirmed by all our deepest experience, that simply to know, even with the most unquestioning conviction, that certain things were true, was not really having faith in those things. We go up to the very limit of the belief that can come either by traditional acceptance or by the conviction which argument produces, and there we stand. We cannot advance one step farther. We seem to have exhausted all the power that is in us. But we are sure that out beyond there is a region which, though we cannot enter it, is real, and is the true completion of the region through which we have already travelled.

How familiar this is in our dealings with our friends! I meet a man whom I have heard of long. Every authority in which I trust has told me that man is wise and good. I come to know him well, and for myself I see the evidence of his wisdom and goodness. He proves it to me by the things he does. I no more doubt it than I doubt the sun. I say that I believe in him and I do believe in him; but all the time I am aware that out beyond the limit of this belief which I have reached and on which I stand, there is a whole new country, the region of another sort of belief in him into which I have not entered, where if I could enter for an hour everything would be different and new. I may be helpless. I may not be able to drag my feet across the border. I may stand as if chained by magic on this line which separates the head's belief from the heart's confidence and trust; but, powerless as I may be to enter it, I know that all this other world is there, with the mists hanging over it and hiding it, but real and certain still, the land of personal friendship and communion.

And just the same is true of truths. I know that some great truth is true; our human immortality, let us say. Every one whom I trust has told me so. Those whose words are to me like gospel have assured me of it. 1 may even hear and believe that voice that speaks out of eternity itself. I may put full trust in the word of Christ which tells me that the dead are not dead but are living still. And my reason may be all convinced. I may be persuaded by every natural argument that the soul does not perish in its separation from the body, but goes on in its unbroken life. All this I steadfastly believe. But what then? Here I stand upon this clear sharp line. I am immortal. I say it over to myself and know that it is true. But still I am not satisfied. This certainty of immortality is nothing to me but a mere conviction. I get nothing out of it. It does not flow up into my duties and experiences. I am not stronger for it. I have not taken hold of it, nor has it taken hold of me. And, until this comes to pass, I feel a sense of incompleteness. I know in all my surest moments that there is an assurance which I have not reached. I know when my feet are planted the firmest on the outmost line of rational conviction that there is beyond that line a region of spiritual confidence which I have not entered.

Here then are the two kinds of belief in persons and in truths. What is the difference between them? The first is clear, definite, and strong. I know that he whom I believe in, be it man or God, is true and good. I know that the truth that I accept is certain and impregnable. But there is something hard, dry, literal, about my faith. I can write it all down and say all that I know about it in letters inscribed upon a book. I may contend for it vigorously, but I do not feed upon it. The other belief has in it just what this belief lacks. It has spirit. I cannot write it down in letters. My heart is full of it and it takes me right into the heart of the Being or the truth that I believe in.

Surely this difference is very clear. Surely we all know well enough that struggle after the heart and spirit of what our minds have accepted, which lets us understand it all. How often we have felt that disheartening certainty that we are holding tight the shells, the mere outside of our richest beliefs, and not getting at their soul and life. Sometimes have we not contended earnestly for our faith and told some unbeliever that he was losing precious truth because he did not hold it, and then gone off from our discussion saying to ourselves gloomily, "Yes, it is all true, but still, if he held it only on the outside as I do, would he be so much richer after all?" How often do we seem to ourselves to be like starving men, holding fruits that we know are rich and nutritious within, but cased in iron rinds which no pressure of ours is strong enough to break.

We are then very often where these Ephesians were. What came to them and saved them was the Holy Spirit. What must come to us and save us is the same Holy Spirit. There they were holding certain truths about God and Jesus, holding them drearily and coldly, with no life and spirit in their faith. Paul came to them and said, "These truths are true, but they are divine truths. You can really see them only as you are sharers in divinity yourself, and look at them with eyes enlightened by the intelligence of God. God must come into you and change yon. His Spirit must come into you and occupy you ; and then, looking with His Spirit, yon shall see the spirit of the truths you look at; full of the Holy Spirit, the spirit, the heart, the soul of these great verities shall open itself in all its holiness to you. You shall see Jesus. Yon shall lay hold on immortality not on the outside but on the inside, in the very heart and spirit. Is not this intelligible, my dear friends? If Raphael could enter into you as you stand before his picture, would you not see deeper than you do now? Would not the Raphael in the picture come out from depths which you have never fathomed? If a child can be filled with the father's spirit, will not the spirit of the household, the intention, the purpose of it all, come out from the hard skeleton of its structure to meet the new spiritual apprehension? And so if you can be filled with *God*, will not the soul of God's truth of every sort, as you stand face to face with it, open to you deeper and deeper depths, changing your belief into a more and more profound and spiritual thing?

This was what Paul prayed for and this was what came to those Ephesians. God the Holy Spirit came into them and then their old belief opened into a different belief; then they really believed. Do you ask what we mean by that? Do you insist on knowing in exact statement how God entered into these people? Ah, if you ask that, you must ask in vain. If you insist upon not receiving God until you know how His life comes to your life, you must go on godless forever. You must know more than you do know, more than any man knows, of what man is and what God is and what are the mysterious channels that run from one life into the other, before you can tell how God flows into man and fills him with Himself. Tell me, if you can the real nature of your friend's influence, the inflow of his life on yours that makes you full of him. Only one thing I think we can know about this filling of man by God, this communication of the Holy Spirit, that it is natural and not unnatural, that it is a restoral of communication, that it is a reenthronement of God where He belongs, that the prayer which invokes the Holy Spirit is the breaking down of an artificial barrier, and the letting in of the flood of divine life to flow where it belongs, in channels that were made for it. If we know this, then· the occupation of man's life by God is simply a final fact. It is just like the occupation of the body by the soul No man can tell how it is; but that it is, is testified by every form of human strength and beauty in which our eyes delight.

Pause then a moment and think what Whitsunday was, the first Whitsunday. We read the story of the miracle. We hear the rushing of the mighty wind and see the cloven tongues of fire quivering above the heads of the apostles. Perhaps we cannot understand it. It seems natural enough that when Jesus is born the sky should open and the angels sing; that when .Jesus dies the skies should darken and the rocks should break. The great events were worthy of those miracles, or greater. But here at Pentecost what was there to call out such prodigies? If what we have said is true, was there not certainly enough? It was the coming back of God into man. It was the promise in these typical men of how near God would be to every man henceforth. It was the manifestation of the God Inspirer as distinct from and yet one with the God Creator and the God Redeemer. It was primarily the entrance of God into man and so, in consequence, the entrance of its spirit and full meaning into every truth that man could know: It was the blossom-day of humanity, full of the promise of unmeasured fruit.

And what that first Whitsunday was to all the world, one certain day becomes to any man, the day when the Holy Spirit comes to him. God enters into him and he sees all things with God's vision. Truths which were dead spring into life and are as real to him as they are to God. He is filled with the Spirit and straightway he believes; not as he used to, coldly holding the outsides of things. He has looked right into their hearts. His belief in Jesus is all afire with love. His belief in immortality is eager with anticipation. Can any day in all his life compare with that day? If it were to break forth into flames of fire and tremble with sudden and mysterious wind, would it seem strange to him the day when he first knew how near God was, and how true truth was, and how deep Christ was? O have we known that day? O, careless, easy, cold believers! if one should come and ask you, "Have you received the Holy Spirit since you believed?" dare you, could you, answer him, " Yes"?

Let us take now a few moments to consider the other part of the Holy Spirit's influence, the way in which, when He enters into a soul, He not merely gives clearness to truth, but gives delight and enthusiastic impulse to duty. These Ephesians had not merely believed much Christian truth, they had been trying also to do what was right.; they had accepted the Christian law so far as they knew it. We can think of them as very patient, persevering workers, struggling to do everything that they were told they ought to do. Now what did Paul do for them here when he brought them the knowledge of the Holy Spirit 1 I think the answer will be found in that verse of the Savior's in which He described what the Holy Spirit's work should be. "He shall take of mine and shall show it unto you," Jesus had said. The work of the Spirit was to make Jesus vividly real to men. What he did then for any poor Ephesian man or woman who was toiling away in obedience to the law of Christianity, was to make Christ real to the toiling soul behind and in the law. He took the laborer there in Ephesus who only knew that it was a law of Christianity that he ought to help his brethren, and. made it as personal a thing, as really the wish of Christ that he should help his brethren, as it had been to the twelve disciples when they were living under Christ's eye, while he was with them in Judea or while they were distributing the bread and fish at his command to the hungry men by the sea of Galilee. This was the change which the Holy Spirit made in Duty. He filled it with Christ, so that every laborer had the strength, the courage, the incitement to fidelity which comes from working for one whom the worker knows and loves.

And very often when our tasks are pressing on us is not this the change we need? Your Christian duties, the prayers you pray, the self-denials that you practice, the charities you give—what is the matter with them? The temptations you resist, the good word that you speak to some brother, the way you teach your class, the way you condemn some prevailing sin,- what is the matter with them all? What is the reason why they are so dull and tame? Why are they not strong enthusiastic work? The reason must be that there is no clear person for whom you do these things. You serve yourself, and how clear you are to yourself; and so, what life there is in every act of your own service; but you serve Christ and how dim He has grown! And so, how listlessly the hands move at His labor! Now if the Holy Spirit can indeed bring Him clearly to you, is not the Holy Spirit what you need? And this is just exactly what He does. I find a Christian who has really "received the Holy Spirit," and what is it that strikes and delights me in him? It is the intense and intimate reality of Christ. Christ is evidently to him the clearest person in the universe. He talks to Christ. He dreads to offend Christ. He delights to please Christ. His whole life is light and elastic with this buoyant desire of doing everything for Jesus, just as Jesus would wish it done. So simple, but so powerful! So childlike, but so heroic! Duty has been transfigured. The weariness, the drudgery, the whole task-nature, has been taken away. Love has poured like a new life-blood along the dry veins, and the soul that used to toil and groan and struggle goes now singing along its way, "The life that I now live in the flesh, I live by the faith of the Son of God who loved me and gave Himself for me."

O my dear friends, have you received the Holy Spirit since you believed? Since you began to do your duty has any revelation come to you of Him who is the Lord of duty? Have you caught any sight of Christ, and begun to know what it is to do it all for Him? Has the love with which He lived and died for you been so brought home to you that you are longing only to thank Him by a grateful and obedient life? Have you so made Him yours that He has made you His? If so, the life of heaven has begun for you. Only to know Him more and more forever and so to grow into completer and completer service, there is your eternity already marked out before you. It stretches out and is lost beyond where you can see; but it all stretches in the one direction in which your face is set; deepening knowledge, bringing deeper love, forever opening into more and more faithful service. Go on into the richest developments of that life, led by the power of the Holy Spirit.

Both in belief and in duty then, this is the work of the Holy Spirit; to make belief profound by showing us the hearts of the things that we believe in; and to make duty delightful by setting us to doing it for Christ. O, in this world of shallow believers and weary, dreary workers, how we need that Holy Spirit! Remember, we may go our way, ignoring all the time the very forces that we need to help us do our work. The forces still may help us. The Holy Spirit may help us, will surely help us, just as far as He can, even if we do not know His name or ever call upon Him. But there is so much more that He might do for us if we would only open our hearts and ask Him to come into them. · Remember, He is God, and God is love. And no man ever asks God to come into his heart and holds his heart open to God, without God's entering. Children, on this Whitsunday pray the dear God, the blessed Holy Spirit, to come and live in your heart and show you Jesus, and make you love to do what is right for His sake. Old men, aspire to taste already here what is to be the life and joy of your eternity. Men and women in the thick of life, do not go helpless when there is such help at hand; do not go on by yourselves, struggling for truth and toiling at your work, when the Holy Spirit is waiting to show you Christ, and to give you in Him the profoundness of faith and the delightfulness of duty.

Let us come to Christ's Communion Table and celebrate our union with Him and with one another, putting all fear and selfishness aside, and praying Him to show us there how rich a thing it is to believe in Him and how sweet a thing it is to serve Him by His Holy Spirit.

This is a facsimile of Jeremy Taylor's "Discourse on Confirmation"
[*Whole Works of Jeremy Taylor* (London: Henry G. Bohn, 1851) 3:6-31].
This discourse was written in 1663 after the monarchy had been restored with the restoration of the Book of Common Prayer and the restoration of the rite of confirmation after having been rejected during the Commonwealth Period of the Puritans. This view of confirmation was the shared view of High Church clergymen, including John and Charles Wesley's understanding of its meaning. John Wesley said he observed it with "scrupulous exactness." (see Chapter 18).

DISCOURSE OF CONFIRMATION

THE INTRODUCTION

NEXT to the incarnation of the Son of God, and the whole economy of our redemption wrought by him in an admirable order and conjugation of glorious mercies, the greatest thing that ever God did to the world, is the giving to us the Holy Ghost: and possibly this is the consummation and perfection of the other. For in the work of redemption Christ indeed made a new world; we are wholly a new creation, and we must be so: and therefore when St. John began the narrative of the gospel, he began in a manner and style very like to Moses in his history of the first creation; "In the beginning was the Word," &c. "All things were made by him; and without him was not any thing made that was made." But as in the creation the matter was first, (there were indeed heavens, and earth, and waters; but all this was rude and "without form," till "the Spirit of God moved upon the face of the waters,") so it is in the new creation. We are a new mass, redeemed with the blood of Christ, rescued from an evil portion, and made candidates of heaven and immortality; but we are but an embryo in the regeneration, until the Spirit of God enlivens us and moves again upon the waters: and then every subsequent motion and operation is from the Spirit of God. "We cannot say that Jesus is the Lord, but by the Holy Ghost." By him we live, in him we walk, by his aids we pray, by his emotions we desire: we breathe, and sigh, and groan, by him: he "helps us in all our infirmities," and he gives us all our strengths; he reveals mysteries to us, and teaches us all our duties; he stirs us up to holy desires, and he actuates those desires; he "makes us to will and to do of his good pleasure."

For the Spirit of God is that in our spiritual life, that a man's soul is in his natural: without it we are but a dead and lifeless trunk. But then, as man's soul, in proportion to the several operations of life, obtains several appellatives (it is vegetative and nutritive, sensitive and intellective, according as it operates); so is the Spirit of God. He is the Spirit of regeneration in baptism, of renovation in repentance; the Spirit of love, and the Spirit of holy fear; the Searcher of the hearts, and the Spirit of discerning; the Spirit of wisdom, and the Spirit of prayer. In one mystery he illuminates, and in another he feeds us: he begins in one, and finishes and perfects in another. It is the same Spirit working divers operations. For he is all this now reckoned, and he is every thing else that is the principle of good unto us; he is the beginning and the progression, the consummation and perfection, of us all: and yet every work of his is perfect in its kind, and in order to his own designation; and from the beginning to the end is perfection all the way. Justifying and sanctifying grace is the proper entitative product in all; but it hath divers appellatives and connotations in the several rites: and yet even then also, because of the identity of the principle, the similitude and general consonancy in the effect, the same appellative is given, and the same effect imputed to more than one; and yet none of them can be omitted, when the great Master of the family hath blessed it, and given it institution. Thus St. Dionysius calls baptism τὴν ἱερὰν τῆς θεογονίας τελείωσιν, "the perfection of the divine birth;" and yet the baptized person must receive other mysteries, which are more signally perfective: ἡ τοῦ μύρου χρίσις τελειωτική· confirmation is yet more perfective, and is properly "the perfection of baptism."

By baptism we are heirs, and are adopted to the inheritance of sons, admitted to the covenant of repentance, and engaged to live a good life; yet this is but the solemnity of the covenant, which must pass into after-acts by other influences of the same divine principle. Until we receive the spirit of obsignation or confirmation, we are but babes in Christ, in the meanest sense, infants that can do nothing, that cannot speak, that cannot resist any violence, exposed to every rudeness, and perishing by every temptation.

But therefore, as God at first appointed us a ministry of a new birth; so also hath he given to his church the consequent ministry of a new strength. The Spirit moved a little upon the waters of baptism, and gave us the principles of life; but in confirmation he makes us able to move ourselves. In the first he is the Spirit of life; but in this he is the Spirit of strength and motion. "Baptisma est nativitas, unguentum verò est nobis actionis instar e motûs," said Cabasilas.—"In baptism we are entitled to the inheritance: but because we are in our infancy and minority, the Father gives unto his son a tutor, a guardian and a teacher in confirmation,' said Rupertus:[a] that as we are baptized into the death and resurrection of Christ; so in confirmatio

[a] De Divin. Offic. lib. 5, c. 17.

THE INTRODUCTION.

we may be renewed in the inner man, and strengthened in all our holy vows and purposes, by the Holy Ghost ministered according to God's ordinance.

The holy right of confirmation is a divine ordinance, and it produces divine effects, and is ministered by divine persons, that is, by those whom God hath sanctified and separated to this ministration. At first all that were baptized, were also confirmed; and ever since, all good people that have understood it, have been very zealous for it; and time was in England, even since the first beginnings of the Reformation, when confirmation had been less carefully ministered for about six years, when the people had their first opportunities of it restored, they ran to it in so great numbers, that churches and churchyards would not hold them; insomuch that I have read[b] that the bishop of Chester was forced to impose hands on the people in the fields, and was so oppressed with multitudes, that he had almost been trod to death by the people, and had died with the throng, if he had not been rescued by the civil power.

But men have too much neglected all the ministries of grace, and this most especially, and have not given themselves to a right understanding of it, and so neglected it yet more. But because the prejudice, which these parts of the christian church have suffered for want of it, is very great, (as will appear by enumeration of the many and great blessings consequent to it,) I am not without hope, that it may be a service acceptable to God, and a useful ministry to the souls of my charges, if by instructing them that know not, and exhorting them that know, I set forward the practice of this holy rite, and give reasons why the people ought to love it and to desire it, and how they are to understand and practise it, and consequently, with what duteous affections they are to relate to those persons, whom God hath in so special and signal manner made to be, for their good and eternal benefit, the ministers of the Spirit and salvation.

St. Bernard in the life of St. Malachias, my predecessor in the see of Down and Connor, reports that it was the care of that good prelate to renew the rite of confirmation in his diocess, where it had been long neglected and gone into desuetude. It being too much our case in Ireland, I find the same necessity, and am obliged to the same procedure, for the same reason, and in pursuance of so excellent an example: "Hoc enim est evangelizare Christum, (said St. Austin,[c]) non tantùm docere quæ sunt dicenda de Christo, sed etiam quæ observanda ei, qui accedit ad compagem corporis Christi;" "For this is to preach the gospel, not only to teach those things which are to be said of Christ, but those also which are to be observed by every one who desires to be confederated into the society of the body of Christ," which is his church: that is, not only the doctrines of good life, but the mysteries of godliness, and the

1. The Divine original, warranty, and in of the holy rite of confirmation.
2. That this rite was to be a perpetual a ceasing ministration.
3. That it was actually continued and pr all the succeeding ages of the purest and churches.
4. That this rite was appropriate to the of bishops.
5. That prayer and imposition of the hands did make the whole ritual; and thou things were added, yet they were not nece any thing of the institution.
6. That many great graces and blessi consequent to the worthy reception and d tration of it.
7. I shall add something of the manne paration to it, and reception of it.

SECTION I.

Of the Divine Original, Warranty, and tion, of the holy Rite of Confirmatic

In the church of Rome, they have d confirmation to be a sacrament, "proprii properly and really; and yet their doct some of them at least, been "paulò iniqui little unequal and unjust" to their proposi somuch that from themselves we have greatest opposition in this article. Bonac Henriquez allow the proposition, but mak crament to be so unnecessary, that a littl may justify the omission and almost neg And Loemilius and Daniel à Jesu, and the English Jesuits, have, to serve some their own family and order, disputed it al contempt, that by representing it as unn they might do all the ministries ecclesi England without the assistance of bishops periors, whom they therefore love not, bec are so. But the theological faculty of P condemned their doctrine as temerarious, an ing of heresy; and in the latter schools proved rather the doctrine of Gamachæu Kellison, and Bellarmine, who indeed do f doctrine of the most eminent persons in th school, Richard of Armagh, Scotus, Hugo and Gerson the learned chancellor of Pa following the old Roman order, Amalariu binus, do all teach confirmation to be of g pious use, of Divine original, and to many necessary, according to the doctrine of the S and the primitive church.

is not of very great use and holiness: and as a man is never the less tied to repentance, though it be no sacrament; so neither is he ever the less obliged to receive confirmation, though it be (as it ought) acknowledged to be of a use and nature inferior to the two sacraments of divine, direct, and immediate institution. It is certain that the fathers, in a large, symbolical, and general sense, call it "a sacrament;" but mean not the same thing by that word when they apply it to confirmation, as they do when they apply it to baptism and the Lord's supper. That it is an excellent and Divine ordinance to purposes spiritual, that it comes from God, and ministers in our way to God, that is all we are concerned to inquire after: and this I shall endeavour to prove not only against the Jesuits, but against all opponents of what side soever.

My first argument from Scripture is what I learn from Optatus and St. Cyril. Optatus writing against the Donatists hath these words: " Christ descended into the water,—not that in him, who is God, was any thing that could be made clearer, but that the water was to precede the future unction, for the initiating and ordaining and fulfilling the mysteries of baptism. He was washed, when he was in the hands of John; then followed the order of the mystery, and the Father finished what the Son did ask, and what the Holy Ghost declared: the heavens were opened, God the Father anointed him, the spiritual unction presently descended in the likeness of a dove, and sat upon his head, and was spread all over him, and he was called 'the Christ,' when he was 'the anointed of the Father.' To whom also, lest imposition of hands should seem to be wanting, the voice of God was heard from the cloud, saying, 'This is my Son in whom I am well pleased, hear ye him.'"—That which Optatus says is this; that, upon and in Christ's person, baptism, confirmation, and ordination, were consecrated and first appointed. He was baptized by St. John; he was confirmed by the Holy Spirit, and anointed with spiritual unction in order to that great work of obedience to his Father's will; and he was consecrated by the voice of God from heaven. In all things Christ is the head, and the first-fruits; and in these things was the fountain of the sacraments and spiritual grace, and the great exemplar of the economy of the church. For Christ was "nullius pœnitentiæ debitor:" baptism of repentance was not necessary to him, who never sinned; but so it became him to fulfil all righteousness, and to be a pattern to us all. But we have need of these things, though he had not; and in the same way in which salvation was wrought by him for himself and for us all, in the same way he intended ᵉ we should walk. He was baptized, because his Father appointed it so: we must be baptized, because Christ hath appointed it, and we have need of it too. He was consecrated to be the great prophet and the great priest, because "no man takes on him this honour, but he that was called of God, as was Aaron:" and all they who are to minister in his prophetical office under him, must be consecrated and solemnly set apart for that ministration, and after his glorious example. He was anointed with a spiritual unction from above after his baptism; for "after Jesus was baptized," he ascended up from the waters, and then the Holy Ghost descended upon him. It is true, he received the fulness of the Spirit; but we receive him by measure ; but " of his fulness we all receive, grace for grace:" that is, all that he received in order to his great work, all that in kind, one for another, grace for grace, we are to receive according to our measures and our necessities. And as all these he received by external ministrations, so must we: God the Father appointed his way, and he, by his example first, hath appointed the same to us; that we also may follow him in the regeneration, and work out our salvation by the same graces in the like solemnities. For if he needed them for himself, then we need them much more. If he did not need them for himself, he needed them for us, and for our example, that we might follow his steps, who, by receiving these exterior solemnities and inward graces, became "the author and finisher of our salvation," and the great example of his church.—I shall not need to make use of the fancy of the Murcosians and Colobarsians, who turning all mysteries into numbers, reckoned the numeral letters of περιστερὰ, and made them coincident to the α and ω; but they intended to say, that Christ, receiving the holy dove after his baptism, became all in all to us, the beginning and the perfection of our salvation; here he was confirmed, and received the ω to his α, the consummation to his initiation, the completion of his baptism and of his headship in the gospel. But that which I shall rather add, is what St. Cyril ᶠ from hence argues: "When he truly was baptized in the river of Jordan, he ascended out of the waters, and the Holy Ghost substantially descended upon him, like resting upon like. And to you also in like manner, after ye have ascended from the waters of baptism, the unction is given which bears the image or similitude of him by whom Christ was anointed—that as Christ after baptism and the coming of the Holy Spirit upon him, went forth to battle (in the wilderness) and overcame the adversary ; so ye also, after holy baptism and the mystical unction, (or confirmation,) being vested with the armour of the Holy Spirit, are enabled to stand against the opposite powers."
—Here then is the first great ground of our solemn receiving the Holy Spirit, or the unction from above after baptism, which we understand and represent by the word confirmation, denoting the principal effect of this unction, spiritual strength. Christ, who is the head of the church, entered this way upon his duty and work : and he who was the first of all the church, the head and great example, is the measure of all the rest; for we can go to heaven no way but in that way in which he went before us.

There are some, who from this story would infer

ᵉ 1 John ii. 8.

ᶠ Cateches. 3. Πνεύματος ἁγίου οὐσιώδης ἐπιφοίτησις αὐτῷ ἐγίνετο.

SECT. I.   OF THE HOLY RITE OF CONFIRMATION.

the descent of the Holy Ghost after Christ's baptism not to signify, that confirmation was to be a distinct rite from baptism, but a part of it,—yet such a part as gives fulness and consummation to it. St. Jerome, Chrysostom, Euthymius, and Theophylact, go not so far, but would have us by this to understand that the Holy Ghost is given to them that are baptized. But reason and the context are both against it. 1. Because the Holy Ghost was not given by John's baptism; that was reserved to be one of Christ's glories; who also, when by his disciples he baptized many, did not give them the Holy Ghost: and when he commanded his apostles to baptize all nations, did not at that time so much as promise the Holy Ghost: he was promised distinctly and given by another ministration. 2. The descent of the Holy Spirit was a distinct ministry from the baptism: it was not only after Jesus ascended from the waters of baptism; but there was something intervening, and by a new office or ministration: for there was prayer joined in the ministry. So St. Luke observes; "while Jesus was praying, the heavens were opened," and the Holy Spirit descended: for so Jesus was pleased to consign the whole office and ritual of confirmation. Prayer for invocating the Holy Spirit, and giving him by personal application; which as the Father did immediately, so the bishops do by imposition of hands. 3. St. Austin observes that the apparition of the Holy Spirit like a dove was the visible or ritual part; and the voice of God was the word to make it to be sacramental; "accedit verbum ad elementum, et fit sacramentum:"[g] for so the ministration was not only performed on Christ, but consigned to the church by similitude and exemplar institution. I shall only add, that the force of this argument is established to us by more of the fathers. St. Hilary upon this place hath these words:[h] "The Father's voice was heard, that from those things which were consummated in Christ, we might know, that, after the baptism of water, the Holy Spirit from the gates of heaven flies unto us; and that we are to be anointed with the unction of a celestial glory, and be made the sons of God by the adoption of the voice of God; the truth by the very effects of things, prefigured unto us the similitude of a sacrament."—So St. Chrysostom:[i] "In the beginnings always appear the sensible visions of spiritual things for their sakes, who cannot receive the understanding of an incorporeal nature; that if afterwards they be not so done, (that is, after the same visible manner,) they may be believed by those things which were already done.—But more plain is that of Theophylact:[k] "The Lord had not need of the descent of the Holy Spirit, but he did all things for our sakes; and himself is become the first-fruits of all things, which we afterwards were to receive, that he might become the first-fruits among many brethren." The consequent is this, which I express in the words of St. Austin, affirming, "Christi in baptismo columbam unctionem nostram præfigurasse," "The dove in Christ's baptism did represent and prefigure our unction from above," that is, the descent of the Holy Ghost upon us in the rite of confirmation. Christ was baptized, and so must we. But after baptism he had a new ministration for the reception of the Holy Ghost: and because this was done for our sakes, we also must follow that example. And this being done immediately before his entrance into the wilderness to be tempted of the devil, it plainly describes to us the order of this ministry, and the blessing designed to us: after we are baptized, we need to be strengthened and confirmed "propter pugnam spiritualem;" we are to fight against the flesh, the world, and the devil, and therefore must receive the ministration of the Holy Spirit of God: which is the design and proper work of confirmation. For (they are the words of the excellent author of the imperfect work upon St. Matthew, imputed to St. Chrysostom)[l] "The baptism of water profits us, because it washes away the sins we have formerly committed, if we repent of them. But it does not sanctify the soul, nor precedes the concupiscences of the heart and our evil thoughts, nor drives them back, nor represses our carnal desires. But he therefore who is (only) so baptized, that he does not also receive the Holy Spirit, is baptized in his body, and his sins are pardoned; but in his mind he is yet but a catechumen: for so it is written, 'He that hath not the Spirit of Christ, is none of his:' and therefore afterward out of his flesh will germinate worse sins, because he hath not received the Holy Spirit conserving him, (in his baptismal grace,) but the house of his body is empty; wherefore that wicked spirit finding it swept with the doctrines of faith, as with besoms, enters in, and in a sevenfold manner dwells there." Which words, besides that they well explicate this mystery, do also declare the necessity of confirmation, or receiving the Holy Ghost after baptism, in imitation of the Divine precedent of our blessed Saviour.

2. After the example of Christ, my next argument is from his words spoken to Nicodemus in explication of the prime mysteries evangelical: "Unless a man be born of water and of the Holy Spirit, he shall not enter into the kingdom of God."[m] These words are the great argument, which the church uses for the indispensable necessity of baptism; and having in them so great effort, and not being rightly understood, they have suffered many convulsions (shall I call them?) or interpretations. Some serve their own hypothesis by saying that water is the symbol, and the Spirit is the baptismal grace: others, that it is a ἓν διὰ δυοῖν, one is only meant, though here be two signatures. But others conclude, that water is only necessary, but the Spirit is superadded as being afterwards to supervene and move upon these waters: and others yet affirm, that by water is only meant a spiritual ablution, or the effect produced by the Spirit; and still they have entangled the words so that they have been made useless to the christian church, and the meaning too many other things makes nothing to be

---

[g] Tract. 80. in Joan.   [h] S. Hilar. can. 4. in fine.   [l] Homil. 4.   [m] John iii. 5.
[i] In Matthæum.   [k] Ibid.

understood. But truth is easy, intelligible, and clear, and without objection, and is plainly this:

Unless a man be baptized into Christ, and confirmed by the Spirit of Christ, he cannot enter into the kingdom of Christ; that is, he is not perfectly adopted into the christian religion, or fitted for the christian warfare. And if this plain and natural sense be admitted, the place is not only easy and intelligible, but consonant to the whole design of Christ and analogy of the New Testament.

For, first, Our blessed Saviour was catechising of Nicodemus, and teaching him the first rudiments of the gospel, and like a wise master-builder, first lays the foundation, " the doctrine of baptism and laying on of hands:" which afterwards St. Paul put into the christian catechism, as I shall show in the sequel. Now these also are the first principles of the christian religion taught by Christ himself, and things which at least to the doctors might have been so well known, that our blessed Saviour upbraids the not knowing them as a shame to Nicodemus. St. Chrysostom and Theophylact, Euthymius and Rupertus, affirm, that this generation by water and the Holy Spirit might have been understood by the Old Testament, in which Nicodemus was so well skilled. Certain it is, the doctrine of baptism was well enough known to the Jews, and the ἐπιφοίτησις τοῦ Πνεύματος τοῦ Θεοῦ, " the illumination and irradiations of the Spirit of God" was not new to them, who believed the visions and dreams, the daughter of a voice, and the influences from heaven upon the sons of the prophets: and therefore although Christ intended to teach him more than what he had distinct notice of, yet the things themselves had foundation in the law and the prophets: but although they were high mysteries, and scarce discerned by them who either were ignorant or incurious of such things; yet to the christians they were the very rudiments of their religion, and are best expounded by observation of what St. Paul placed in the very foundation. But,

2. Baptism is the first mystery, that is certain; but that this of " being born of the Spirit " is also the next, is plain in the very order of the words: and that it does mean a mystery distinct from baptism, will be easily assented to by them who consider, that although Christ baptized and made many disciples by the ministry of his apostles, yet they who were so baptized into Christ's religion, did not receive this baptism of the Spirit till after Christ's ascension.

3. The baptism of water was not peculiar to John the Baptist, for it was also of Christ, and ministered by his command; it was common to both; and therefore the baptism of water is the less principal here. Something distinct from it is here intended. Now if we add to these words, that St. John tells of another baptism which was Christ's peculiar, " He shall baptize you with the Holy Ghost and with fire;" that these words were literally verified upon the apostles in Pentecost, and afterwards upon all the baptized in spiritual effect, (who, besides the baptism of water, distinctly had the baptism of the Spirit in confirmation,) it will follow, that of necessity this must be the meaning and the verification of these words of our blessed Saviour to Nicodemus, which must mean a double baptism: "Transibimus per aquam et ignem, antequam veniemus in refrigerium," " We must pass through water and fire, before we enter into rest;" that is, we must first be baptized with water, and then with the Holy Ghost, who first descended in fire; that is, the only way to enter into Christ's kingdom is by these two doors of the tabernacle, which God hath pitched, and not man,—first by baptism, and then by confirmation; first by water, and then by the Spirit.

The primitive church had this notion so fully amongst them, that the author of the Apostolical Constitutions, attributed to St. Clement,[n] who was St. Paul's scholar, affirms, That a man is made a perfect christian (meaning ritually and sacramentally, and by all exterior solemnity) by the water of baptism and confirmation of the bishop; and from these words of Christ now alleged, derives the use and institution of the rite of confirmation. The same sense of these words is given to us by St. Cyprian,[o] who intending to prove the insufficiency of one without the other, says, " Tunc enim plenè sanctificari et esse Dei filii possunt, si sacramento utroque nascantur, cùm scriptum sit, ' Nisi quis natus fuerit ex aquâ et Spiritu, non potest intrare in regnum Dei,'" " Then they may be fully sanctified, and become the sons of God, if they be born with both the sacraments, or rites; for it is written, ' Unless a man be born of water and the Spirit, he cannot enter into the kingdom of God.' "—The same also is the commentary of[p] Eusebius Emissenus; and St. Austin[q] tells, that although some understand these words only of baptism, and others of the Spirit only, viz. in confirmation; yet others (and certainly much better) understand " utrumque sacramentum," " both the mysteries," of confirmation as well as baptism. Amalarius Fortunatus[r] brings this very text to reprove them that neglect the episcopal imposition of hands: "Concerning them who by negligence lose the bishop's presence, and receive not the imposition of his hands, it is to be considered, lest in justice they be condemned, in which they exercise justice negligently, because they ought to make haste to the imposition of hands: because Christ said, ' Unless a man be born again of water and the Spirit, he cannot enter into the kingdom of God:' and as he said this, so also he said, ' Unless your righteousness exceed the righteousness of the scribes and Pharisees, ye shall not enter into the kingdom of heaven.'"

To this I foresee two objections may be made. 1. That Christ did not institute confirmation in this place, because confirmation being for the gift of the Holy Ghost, who was to come upon none of the apostles till Jesus was glorified, these words seem too early for the consigning an effect that was to be so long after, and a rite that could not be practised till many intermedial events should happen. So

---

[n] S. Clem. Ep. 4. Constit. Apost.
[o] Ad Stephanum.
[p] Homil. in Dominic. prim. post. Ascens.
[q] Epist. 108. ad Seleucianum.
[r] Lib. c. 27.

SECT. I. — OF THE HOLY RITE OF CONFIRMATION.

said the evangelist;[s] "the Holy Ghost was come upon none of them, because Jesus was not yet glorified;" intimating that this great effect was to be in after-time: and it is not likely that the ceremony should be ordained before the effect itself was ordered and provided for; that the solemnity should be appointed before provisions were made for the mystery; and that the outward, which was wholly for the inward, should be instituted, before the inward and principal had its abode amongst us.

To this I answer, 1. That it is no unusual thing; for Christ gave the sacrament of his body before his body was given; the memorial of his death was instituted before his death. 2. Confirmation might here as well be instituted as baptism; and by the same reason that the church from these words concludes the necessity of one, she may also infer the designation of the other; for the effect of baptism was at that time no more produced than that of confirmation. Christ had not yet purchased to himself a church, he had not wrought remission of sins to all that believe on him; the death of Christ was not yet past, into which death the christian church was to be baptized. 3. These words are so an institution of confirmation, as the sixth chapter of St. John is of the blessed eucharist: it was "designativa," not "ordinativa," it was in design, not in present command; here it was preached, but not reducible to practice till its proper season. 4. It was like the words of Christ to St. Peter; "When thou art converted, confirm thy brethren." Here the command was given, but that confirmation of his brethren was to be performed in a time relative to a succeeding accident. 5. It is certain that long before the event, and grace was given, Christ did speak of the Spirit of confirmation, that Spirit which was to descend in Pentecost, which all they were to receive who should believe on him, which whosoever did receive, "out of his belly should flow rivers of living waters," as is to be read in that place of St. John[t] now quoted. 6. This predesignation of the Holy Spirit of confirmation was presently followed by some antepast and "donariola," or "little givings" of the Spirit; for our blessed Saviour gave the Holy Ghost three several times. First, ἀμυδρῶς, "obscurely," and by intimation and secret virtue, then when he sent them to heal the sick, and anoint them with oil in the name of the Lord. Secondly, ἐκτυπωτέρως, "more expressly" and signally after the resurrection, when he took his leave of them, and said, "Receive ye the Holy Ghost:" and this was to give them a power of ministering remission of sins, and therefore related to baptism and the ministries of repentance. But, thirdly, he gave it τελειοτέρως, "more perfectly;" and this was the Spirit of confirmation; for he was not at all until now, οὔπω γὰρ ἦν Πνεῦμα ἅγιον, says the text: "the Holy Ghost was not yet:" so almost all the Greek copies, printed and manuscript; and so St. Chrysostom, Athanasius, Cyril, Ammonius in the Catena of the Greeks, Leontius, Theophylact, Euthymius, and all the Greek fathers read it; so St. Jerome[u] and St. Austin[x] among the Latins, and some Latin translations, read it. Our translations read it, "the Holy Ghost was not yet given," was not ἐν αὐτοῖς, "in them," as some few Greek copies read it: but the meaning is alike, confirmation was not yet actual,—the Holy Spirit, viz. of confirmation, was not yet come upon the church; but it follows not but he was long before promised, designed and appointed, spoken of and declared. The first of these collations had the ceremony of chrism or anointing joined with it, which the church in process of time transferred into her use and ministry: yet it is the last only that Christ passed into an ordinance for ever; it is this only which is the sacramental consummation of our regeneration in Christ; for in this the Holy Spirit is not only ἐνεργείᾳ παρὸν, "present by his power," but present οὐσιωδῶς, ὡς ἄν εἴποι τις συγγινόμενόν τε καὶ πολιτευόμενον, as St. Gregory Nazianzen expresses it, to dwell with us, to converse with us, and to abide for ever; οὗ ἐξέχεε ἐφ' ἡμᾶς πλουσίως· so St. Paul describes this Spirit of confirmation, the Spirit "which he hath poured forth upon us richly or plentifully," that is, in great measures, and to the full consummation of the first mysteries of our regeneration. Now because Christ is the great fountain of this blessing to us, and he it was who sent his Father's Spirit upon the church, himself best knew his own intentions, and the great blessings he intended to communicate to his church; and therefore it was most agreeable that from his sermons we should learn his purposes, and his blessing, and our duty. Here Christ declared "rem sacramenti," the spiritual grace," which he would afterwards impart to his church by exterior ministry, in this as in all other graces, mysteries, and rituals evangelical: "Nisi quis, 'unless a man' be born both of water and the Spirit, he cannot enter into the kingdom of God."

But the next objection is yet more material. 2. For if this be the meaning of our blessed Saviour, then confirmation is as necessary as baptism, and without it ordinarily no man can be saved. The solution of this will answer a case of conscience, concerning the necessity of confirmation; and in what degree of duty and diligence we are bound to take care that we receive this holy rite. I answer therefore, that "entering into the kingdom of God," is being admitted into the christian church and warfare, to become sons of God, and soldiers of Jesus Christ. And though this be the outward door, and the first entrance into life, and consequently the king's highway, and the ordinary means of salvation; yet we are to distinguish the external ceremony from the internal mystery: the "Nisi quis" is for this, not for that; and yet that also is the ordinary way. "Unless a man be baptized," that is, unless he be indeed regenerate, he cannot be saved: and yet baptism, or the outward washing, is the solemnity and ceremony of its ordinary ministration; and he that neglects this, when it may be had, is not indeed regenerate; he is not renewed in the spirit of his mind, because he neglects God's way, and therefore can as little be saved as he who, having received the external sacrament, puts a bar to the intromis-

---

[s] John vii. 39.   [t] Chap. vii. 38.   [u] Qu. 9. ad Heditiam.   [x] In Joan. tract. 22.

sion of the inward grace. Both cannot always be had; but when they can, although they are not equally valuable in the nature of the thing, yet they are made equally necessary by the Divine commandment. And in this there is a great, but general mistake, in the doctrine of the schools, disputing concerning what sacraments are necessary "necessitate medii," that is, as "necessary means," and what are necessary by the necessity of precept, or Divine commandment. For although a less reason will excuse from the actual susception of some than of others, and a less diligence for the obtaining of one will serve than in obtaining of another, and a supply in one is easier obtained than in another; yet no sacrament hath in it any other necessity than what is made merely by the Divine commandment. But the grace of every sacrament, or rite, or mystery, which is of Divine ordinance, is necessary indispensably, so as without it no man can be saved. And this difference is highly remarkable in the words of Christ recorded by St. Mark;[y] "He that believeth and is baptized, shall be saved: but he that believeth not, shall be damned." Baptism itself, as to the external part, is not necessary "necessitate medii," or indispensably; but baptismal faith for the remission of sins in persons capable, that indeed is necessary: for Christ does not say that the want of baptism damns as the want of faith does; and yet both baptism and faith are the ordinary way of salvation, and both necessary; baptism because it is so by the Divine commandment, and faith as a necessary means of salvation, in the very economy and dispensation of the gospel. Thus it is also in the other sacrament; "Unless we eat the flesh of the Son of man, and drink his blood, we have no life in us:"[z] and yet God forbid that every man that is not communicated should die eternally. But it means plainly, that without receiving Christ, as he is by God's intention intended we should receive him in the communion, we have no life in us. Plainly thus, without the internal grace we cannot live; and the external ministry is the usual and appointed means of conveying to us the internal: and therefore although without the external it is possible to be saved, when it is impossible to be had; yet with the wilful neglect of it we cannot. Thus therefore we are to understand the words of Christ declaring the necessity of both these ceremonies: they are both necessary, because they are the means of spiritual advantages and graces, and both minister to the proper ends of their appointment, and both derive from a Divine original: but the ritual or ceremonial part in rare emergencies is dispensable; but the grace is indispensable. Without the grace of baptism we shall die in our sins; and without the grace or internal part of confirmation we shall never be able to resist the devil, but shall be taken captive by him at his will. Now the external or ritual part is the means, the season, and opportunity, of this grace; and therefore is at no hand to be neglected, lest we be accounted despisers of the grace, and tempters of God to ways and provisions extraordinary. For although when without our fault we receive not the sacramental part, God can and will supply it to us out of his own stores, because no man can perish without his own fault; and God can permit to himself what he pleases, as being Lord of the grace and of the sacrament: yet to us he hath given a law and a rule; and that is the way of his church, in which all christians ought to walk. In short, the use of it is greatly profitable; the neglect is inexcusable; but the contempt is damnable. "Tenentur non negligere, si pateat opportunitas," said the bishops in a synod at Paris: "If there be an opportunity, it must not be neglected."—"Obligantur suscipere, aut saltem non contemnere," said the synod at Sens: "They are bound to receive it, or at least not to despise it."—Now he despises it, that refuses it when he is invited to it, or when it is offered, or that neglects it without cause. For "causelessly" and "contemptuously" are all one. But these answers were made by gentle casuists: he only values the grace that desires it, that longs for it, that makes use of all the means of grace, that seeks out for the means, that refuses no labour, that goes after them as the merchant goes after gain: and therefore the old "ordo Romanus"[a] admonishes more strictly; "Omnino præcavendum esse, ut hoc sacramentum confirmationis non negligatur, quia tunc omne baptisma legitimum Christianitatis nomine confirmatur:" "We must by all means take heed, that the rite of confirmation be not neglected, because, in that, every true baptism is ratified and confirmed."—Which words are also to the same purpose made use of by Albinus Flaccus.[b] No man can tell to what degrees of diligence and labour, to what sufferings or journeyings, he is obliged for the procuring of this ministry: there must be "debita sollicitudo," a real, providential, zealous care to be where it is to be had, is the duty of every christian according to his own circumstances; but they who will not receive it unless it be brought to their doors, may live in such places and in such times, where they shall be sure to miss it, and pay the price of their neglect of so great a ministry of salvation. "Turpissima est jactura, quæ per negligentiam fit," "He is a fool that loses his good by carelessness:"[c] but no man is zealous for his soul, but he who not only omits no opportunity of doing it advantage when it is ready for him, but makes and seeks and contrives opportunities. "Si non necessitate, sed incuriâ et voluntate remanserit," as St. Clement's expression is; If a man wants it by necessity, it may, by the overflowings of the Divine grace, be supplied; but not so if negligence or choice cause the omission.

3. Our way being made plain, we may proceed to other places of Scripture to prove the Divine original of confirmation. It was a plant of our heavenly Father's planting, it was a branch of the vine, and how it springs from the root Christ Jesus we have seen; it is yet more visible as it was dressed and cultivated by the apostles. Now as soon as the apostles had received the Holy Spirit, they preached and

---

[y] xvi. 16.   [z] John vi. 53.
[a] In Offic. Sab. Pasch. post orat. quæ dicitur data confirm.
[b] De Offic. Divin. in Sabb. S. Pasch.
[c] Seneca.

baptized, and the inferior ministers did the same, and St. Philip particularly did so at Samaria, the converts of which place received all the fruits of baptism; but christians though they were, they wanted a τελείωσις, "something to make them perfect." The other part of the narrative I shall set down in the words of St. Luke:[d] "Now when the apostles which were at Jerusalem heard that Samaria had received the word of God, they sent unto them Peter and John; who, when they were come down, prayed for them that they might receive the Holy Ghost: for as yet he was fallen upon none of them, only they were baptized in the name of the Lord Jesus. Then laid they their hands on them, and they received the Holy Ghost." If it had not been necessary to have added a new solemnity and ministration, it is not to be supposed the apostles Peter and John would have gone from Jerusalem to impose hands on the baptized at Samaria. "Id quod deerat à Petro et Joanne factum est, ut, oratione pro eis habitâ et manu impositâ, invocaretur et infunderetur super eos Spiritus Sanctus," said St. Cyprian:[e] "It was not necessary that they should be baptized again, only that which was wanting was performed by Peter and John, that by prayer and imposition of hands the Holy Ghost should be invocated and poured upon them."—The same also is, from this place, affirmed by Pope Innocentius the First,[f] St. Jerome,[g] and many others: and in the Acts of the Apostles we find another instance of the celebration of this ritual and mystery, for it is signally expressed of the baptized christians at Ephesus, that St. Paul first baptized them, and then laid his hands on them, and they received the Holy Ghost. And these testimonies are the great warranty for this holy rite. "Quod nunc in confirmandis neophytis manûs impositio tribuit singulis, hoc tunc Spiritûs Sancti descensio in credentium populo donavit universa," said Eucherius Lugdunensis, in his homily of Pentecost: "The same thing that is done now in imposition of hands on single persons, is no other than that which was done upon all believers in the descent of the Holy Ghost;" it is the same ministry, and all deriving from the same authority.

Confirmation or imposition of hands for the collation of the Holy Spirit, we see, was actually practised by the apostles, and that even before and after they preached the gospel to the gentiles; and therefore Amalarius, who entered not much into the secret of it, reckons this ritual as derived from the apostles, "per consuetudinem," "by catholic custom;" which although it is not perfectly spoken as to the whole αὐθεντία or "authority" of it, yet he places it in the apostles, and is a witness of the catholic succeeding custom and practice of the church of God. Which thing also Zanchius observing, though he followed the sentiment of Amalarius, and seemed to understand no more of it, yet says well; "Interim" (says he) " exempla apostolorum et veteris ecclesiæ vellem pluris æstimari:" "I wish that the example of the apostles and the primitive church were of more value amongst christians.—It were very well indeed they were so; but there is more in it than mere example. These examples of such solemnities productive of such spiritual effects are, as St. Cyprian calls them, "apostolica magisteria," "the apostles are our masters" in them, and have given rules and precedents for the church to follow. This is a christian law, and "written, as all Scriptures are, for our instruction." But this I shall expressly prove in the next paragraph.

4. We have seen the original from Christ, the practice and exercise of it in the apostles and the first converts in christianity: that which I shall now remark is, that this is established and passed into a christian doctrine. The warranty for what I say, are the words of St. Paul,[h] where the holy rite of confirmation, so called from the effect of this ministration, and expressed by the ritual part of it, "imposition of hands," is reckoned a fundamental point, θεμέλιος ἐπιθέσεως χειρῶν· "Not laying again the foundation of repentance from dead works, and of faith towards God, of the doctrine of baptisms, and of laying on of hands, of resurrection from the dead, and eternal judgment." Here are six fundamental points of St. Paul's catechism, which he laid as the foundation or the beginning of the institution of the christian church; and amongst these, imposition of hands is reckoned as a part of the foundation, and therefore they who deny it, dig up foundations. Now that this "imposition of hands" is that, which the apostles used in confirming the baptized, and invocating the Holy Ghost upon them, remains to be proved.

For it is true that imposition of hands signifies all christian rites except baptism and the Lord's supper; not the sacraments, but all the sacramentals of the church: it signifies confirmation, ordination, absolution, visitation of the sick, blessing single persons, (as Christ did the children brought to him,) and blessing marriages; all these were usually ministered by imposition of hands. Now the three last are not pretended to be any part of this foundation; neither reason, authority, nor the nature of the thing, suffers any such pretension: the question then is between the first three.

First, "Absolution of penitents" cannot be meant here, not only because we never read that the apostles did use that ceremony in their ablutions; but because the apostle, speaking of the foundation in which baptism is, and is reckoned one of the principal parts in the foundation, there needed no absolution but baptismal, for they and we believing "one baptism for the remission of sins;"[i] this is all the absolution that can be at first and in the foundation. The other was "secunda post naufragium tabula," it came in after, when men had made a shipwreck of their good conscience, and were, as St. Peter says, λήθην λαβόντες τοῦ καθαρισμοῦ τῶν πάλαι αὐτῶν ἁμαρτιῶν, "forgetful of the former cleansing and purification and washing of their old sins."[k]

Secondly, It cannot be meant of "ordination;"

---

[d] Acts viii. 14—17.   [e] Ad Jubaian.   [h] Heb. vi. 1, 2   [i] Symbol. Nicæn. et Constantinop.
[f] Epist. l. c. 3.   [g] Adv. Luciferian.   [k] 2 Pet. i. 9.

and this is also evident. 1. Because the apostle says he would thenceforth leave to speak of the foundation, and "go on to perfection," that is, to higher mysteries. Now in rituals, of which he speaks, there is none higher than ordination. 2. The apostle saying he would speak no more of imposition of hands, goes presently to discourse of the mysteriousness of the evangelical priesthood, and the honour of that vocation; by which it is evident he spake nothing of ordination in the catechism or narrative of fundamentals. 3. This also appears from the context, not only because " laying on of hands" is immediately set after "baptism," but also because in the very next words of his discourse he does enumerate and apportion to baptism and confirmation their proper and proportioned effects: to baptism, illumination, according to the perpetual style of the church of God, calling baptism $\phi\omega\tau\iota\sigma\mu\grave{o}\nu$, "an enlightening;" and to confirmation he reckons "tasting the heavenly gift," and "being made partakers of the Holy Ghost," by the thing signified declaring the sign, and by the mystery the rite. Upon these words St. Chrysostom discoursing, says, "that all these are fundamental articles; that is, that we ought to repent from dead works, to be baptized into the faith of Christ, and be made worthy of the gift of the Spirit, who is given by imposition of hands, and we are to be taught the mysteries of the resurrection and eternal judgment. This catechism (says he) is perfect: so that if any man have faith in God, and being baptized is also confirmed, and so tastes the heavenly gift, and partakes of the Holy Ghost, and by hope of the resurrection tastes of the good things of the world to come,—if he falls away from this state, and turns apostate from this whole dispensation, digging down and turning up these foundations, he shall never be built again, he can never be baptized again, and never be confirmed any more; God will not begin again, and go over with him again, he cannot be made a christian twice: if he remains upon these foundations, though he sins, he may be renewed $\delta\iota\grave{a}$ $\mu\epsilon\tau\acute{a}\nu o\iota a\nu$, 'by repentance,' and by a resuscitation of the Spirit, if he have not wholly quenched him; but if he renounce the whole covenant, disown and cancel these foundations, he is desperate, he can never be renewed $\epsilon\grave{\iota}\varsigma$ $\mu\epsilon\tau\acute{a}\nu o\iota a\nu$, to the title and economy of repentance." This is the full explication of this excellent place, and any other ways it cannot reasonably be explicated: but therefore into this place any notice of ordination cannot come, no sense, no mystery, can be made of it or drawn from it; but by the interposition of confirmation the whole context is clear, rational, and intelligible.

This then is that imposition of hands, of which the apostle speaks. "Unus hic locus abunde testatur," &c. saith Calvin: "This one place doth abundantly witness that the original of this rite or ceremony was from the apostles:" $o\tilde{\upsilon}\tau\omega$ $\gamma\grave{a}\rho$ $\tau\grave{o}$ $\Pi\nu\epsilon\tilde{\upsilon}\mu a$ $\dot{\epsilon}\lambda\acute{a}\mu\beta a\nu o\nu$, saith St. Chrysostom;[1] "for by this rite of imposition of hands they received the Holy Ghost."—For though the Spirit of God was given extra-regularly, and at all times, as God was pleased to do great things; yet this imposition of hands was $\delta\iota a\kappa o\nu\acute{\iota}a$ $\Pi\nu\epsilon\acute{\upsilon}\mu a\tau o\varsigma$, this was " the ministry of the Spirit." For so we receive Christ, when we hear and obey his word: we eat Christ by faith, and we live by his Spirit; and yet the blessed eucharist is $\delta\iota a\kappa o\nu\acute{\iota}a$ $\sigma\acute{\omega}\mu a\tau o\varsigma$ $\kappa a\grave{\iota}$ $a\tilde{\iota}\mu a\tau o\varsigma$, " the ministry of the body and blood of Christ." Now as the Lord's supper is appointed ritually to convey Christ's body and blood to us; so is confirmation ordained ritually to give unto us the Spirit of God. And though, by accident and by the overflowings of the Spirit, it may come to pass, that a man does receive perfective graces alone, and without ministries external: yet such a man without a miracle is not a perfect christian " ex statuum vitæ dispositione;" but in the ordinary ways and appointment of God, and until he receive this imposition of hands, and be confirmed, is to be accounted an imperfect christian. But of this afterwards.

I shall observe one thing more out of this testimony of St. Paul. He calls it " the doctrine of baptisms and laying on of hands:" by which it does not only appear to be a lasting ministry, because no part of the christian doctrine could change or be abolished; but hence also it appears to be of Divine institution. For if it were not, St. Paul had been guilty of that which our blessed Saviour reproves in the scribes and Pharisees, and should have " taught for doctrines the commandments of men." Which because it cannot be supposed, it must follow, that this doctrine of confirmation or imposition of hands is apostolical and Divine. The argument is clear, and not easy to be reproved.

SECTION II.

The Rite of Confirmation is a perpetual and neverceasing Ministry.

Yea, but what is this to us? It belonged to the days of wonder and extraordinary: the Holy Ghost breathed upon the apostles and apostolical men; but then he breathed his last: " recedente gratiâ, recessit disciplina;" when the grace departed, we had no further use of the ceremony. In answer to this I shall $\psi\iota\lambda a\tilde{\iota}\varsigma$ $\dot{\epsilon}\pi\iota\nuo\acute{\iota}a\iota\varsigma$, by divers particulars evince plainly, that this ministry of confirmation was not temporary and relative only to the acts of the apostles, but was to descend to the church for ever. This indeed is done already in the preceding section; in which it is clearly manifested that Christ himself[m] made the baptism of the Spirit to be necessary to the church. He declared the fruits of this baptism, and did particularly relate it to the descent of the Holy Spirit upon the church at and after that glorious Pentecost. He sanctified it, and commended it by his example; just as in order to baptism he sanctified the flood Jordan, and all other waters, to the mystical washing away of sin, viz. by his great example, and fulfilling this righteousness

---

[1] In hunc locum.

[m] John iii. 5.

also. This doctrine the apostles first found in their own persons and experience, and practised to all their converts after baptism by a solemn and external rite; and all this passed into an evangelical doctrine, the whole mystery being signified by the external rite in the words of the apostle, as before it was by Christ expressing only the internal; so that there needs no more strength to this argument. But that there may be wanting no moments to this truth, which the Holy Scripture affords, I shall add more weight to it: and,

1. The perpetuity of this holy rite appears, because this great gift of the Holy Ghost was promised "to abide with the church for ever." And when the Jews heard the apostles speak with tongues at the first and miraculous descent of the Spirit in Pentecost, to take off the strangeness of the wonder and the envy of the power, St. Peter[a] at that very time tells them plainly, "Repent and be baptized every one of you,—and ye shall receive the gift of the Holy Ghost:" ἕκαστος ὑμῶν· not the meanest person amongst you all but shall receive this great thing which ye observe us to have received; and not only you, but your children too; not your children of this generation only, "sed nati natorum, et qui nascentur ab illis," but your children for ever: "for the promise is to you, and to your children, and to all that are afar off, even to as many as the Lord our God shall call." Now then let it be considered,

1. This gift is by promise; by a promise not made to the apostles alone, but to all; to all for ever.

2. Consider here at the very first, as there is a "verbum," "a word" of promise, so there is "sacramentum" too (I use the word, as I have already premonished, in a large sense only, and according to the style of the primitive church): it is a rite partly moral, partly ceremonial; the first is prayer, and the other is laying on of the hands; and to an effect that is but transient and extraordinary, and of a little abode, it is not easy to be supposed that such a solemnity should be appointed. I say, "such a solemnity;" that is, it is not imaginable that a solemn rite annexed to a perpetual promise should be transient and temporary, for by the nature of relatives they must be of equal abode. The promise is of a thing for ever; the ceremony or rite was annexed to the promise, and therefore this also must be for ever.

3. This is attested by St. Paul, who reduces this argument to this mystery, saying, "In whom after that ye believed, 'signati estis Spiritu Sancto promissionis,' 'ye were sealed by that Holy Spirit of promise.'" He spake it to the Ephesians,[o] who well understood his meaning by remembering what was done to themselves by the apostles but awhile before,[p] who, after they had baptized them, did lay their hands upon them, and so they were sealed, and so they received the Holy Spirit of promise; for here the very matter of fact is the clearest commentary on St. Paul's words: the Spirit which was promised to all christians, they then received, when they were consigned, or had the ritual seal of confirmation by imposition of hands. One thing I shall remark here, and that is, that this and some other words of Scripture relating to the sacraments or other rituals of religion, do principally mean the internal grace, and our consignation is by a secret power, and the work is within; but it does not therefore follow, that the external rite is not also intended; for the rite is so wholly for the mystery, and the outward for the inward, and yet by the outward God so usually and regularly gives the inward, that as no man is to rely upon the external ministry, as if the "opus operatum" would do the whole duty; so no man is to neglect the external, because the internal is the more principal. The mistake in this particular hath caused great contempt of the sacraments and rituals of the church, and is the ground of the Socinian errors in these questions.

But, 4. What hinders any man from a quick consent at the first representation of these plain reasonings and authorities? Is it because there were extraordinary effects accompanying this ministration, and because now there are not, that we will suppose the whole economy must cease? If this be it, and indeed this is all that can be supposed in opposition to it, it is infinitely vain.

1. Because these extraordinary effects did continue even after the death of all the apostles. St. Irenæus[q] says they did continue even to his time, even the greatest instance of miraculous power: "Et in fraternitate, sæpissime propter aliquid necessarium, eâ quæ est in quoquo loco, universâ ecclesiâ postulante per jejunium et supplicationem multam reversus est spiritus," &c. When God saw it necessary, and the church prayed and fasted much, they did miraculous things, even of reducing the spirit to a dead man.

2. In the days of the apostles the Holy Spirit did produce miraculous effects, but neither always, nor at all, in all men: "Are all workers of miracles? do all speak with tongues? do all interpret? can all heal?"[r] No, "the Spirit bloweth where he listeth," and as he listeth; he gives gifts to all, but to some after this manner, and to some after that.

3. These gifts were not necessary at all times any more than to all persons; but the promise did belong to all, and was made to all, and was performed to all. In the days of the apostles there was an effusion of the Spirit of God, it ran over, it was for themselves and others, it wet the very ground they trod upon, and made it fruitful; but it was not to all in like manner, but there was also then, and since then, a diffusion of the Spirit, "tanquam in pleno." St. Stephen was full of the Holy Ghost, "he was full of faith and power:"[s] the Holy Ghost was given to him to fulfil his faith principally; the working miracles was but collateral and incident. But there is also an infusion of the Holy Ghost, and that is to all, and that is for ever: "the manifestation of the Spirit is given to every man to profit

---

[a] Acts ii. 38, 39.   [o] Ephes. i. 13.   [r] 1 Cor. xii. 29.   [s] Acts vi. 8.
[p] Acts xix. 6.   [q] Lib. 2, cap. 57.

withal," saith the apostle.[t] And therefore if the grace be given to all, there is no reason that the ritual ministration of that grace should cease, upon pretence that the Spirit is not given extraordinarily.

4. These extraordinary gifts were indeed at first necessary: "In the beginnings always appear the sensible visions of spiritual things for their sakes, who cannot receive the understanding of an incorporeal nature; that if afterward they be not so done, they may be believed by those things which were already done," said St. Chrysostom[u] in the place before quoted; that is, these visible appearances were given at first by reason of the imperfection of the state of the church, but the greater gifts were to abide for ever: and therefore it is observable that St. Paul says that the gift of tongues is one of the least and most useless things; a mere sign, and not so much as a sign to believers, but to infidels and unbelievers; and before this he greatly prefers the gift of prophesying or preaching, which yet, all christians know, does abide with the church for ever.

To every ordinary and perpetual ministry at first there were extraordinary effects and miraculous consignations. We find great parts of nations converted at one sermon. Three thousand converts came in at once preaching of St. Peter, and five thousand at another sermon: and persons were miraculously cured by the prayer of the bishop in his visitation of a sick christian; and devils cast out in the conversion of a sinner; and blindness cured at the baptism of St. Paul; and Æneas was healed of a palsy at the same time he was cured of his infidelity; and Eutychus was restored to life at the preaching of St. Paul. And yet that now we see no such extraordinaries, it follows not that the visitation of the sick, and preaching sermons, and absolving penitents, are not ordinary and perpetual ministrations: and therefore to fancy that invocation of the Holy Spirit and imposition of hands is to cease when the extraordinary and temporary contingencies of it are gone, is too trifling a fancy to be put in balance against so sacred an institution relying upon so many scriptures.

6. With this objection some vain persons would have troubled the church in St. Austin's time; but he considered it with much indignation, writing against the Donatists. His words are these:[x] "At the first times the Holy Spirit fell upon the believers, and they spake with tongues which they had not learned, according as the Spirit gave them utterance. They were signs fitted for the season; for so the Holy Ghost ought to have signified in all tongues, because the gospel of God was to run through all the nations and languages of the world; so it was signified, and so it passed through. But is it therefore expected that they upon whom there is imposition of hands that they might receive the Holy Ghost, that they should speak with tongues? Or when we lay hands on infants, does every one of you attend to hear them speak with tongues? And when he sees that they do not speak with tongues, is any of you of so perverse a heart as to say, they have not received the Holy Ghost; for if they had received him, they would speak with tongues, as it was done at first? But if by these miracles there is not now given any testimony of the presence of the Holy Spirit, how doth any one know that he hath received the Holy Ghost? 'Interroget cor suum, Si diliget fratrem, manet Spiritus Dei in illo.'" It is true, the gift of tongues doth not remain, but all the greater gifts of the Holy Spirit remain with the church for ever; sanctification and power, fortitude and hope, faith and love. Let every man search his heart, and see if he belongs to God; whether the "love of God be not spread in his heart by the Spirit of God:" let him see if he be not patient in troubles, comforted in his afflictions, bold to confess the faith of Christ crucified, zealous of good works. These are the miracles of grace, and the mighty powers of the Spirit, according to that saying of Christ,[y] "These signs shall follow them that believe: In my name shall they cast out devils, they shall speak with new tongues, they shall tread on serpents, they shall drink poison, and it shall not hurt them; and they shall lay their hands on the sick, and they shall recover." That which we call the miraculous part, is the less power; but to cast out the devil of lust, to throw down the pride of Lucifer, to tread on the great dragon, and to triumph over our spiritual enemies, to cure a diseased soul, to be unharmed by the poison of temptation, of evil examples and evil company: these are the true signs that shall follow them, that truly and rightly believe on the name of the Lord Jesus; this is "to live in the Spirit," and "to walk in the Spirit;" this is more than to receive the Spirit to a power of miracles and supernatural products in a natural matter: for this is from a supernatural principle to receive supernatural aids to a supernatural end in the diviner spirit of a man; and this being more miraculous than the other, it ought not to be pretended that the discontinuance of extraordinary miracles should cause the discontinuance of an ordinary ministration; and this is that which I was to prove.

7. To which it is not amiss to add this observation, that Simon Magus offered to buy this power of the apostles, that he also, by laying on of hands, might thus minister the Spirit. Now he began this sin in the christian church, and it is too frequent at this day; but if all this power be gone, then nothing of that sin can remain; if the subject-matter be removed, then the appendant crime cannot abide, and there can be no simony, so much as by participation; and whatever is or can be done in this kind, is no more of this crime than drunkenness is of adultery; it relates to it, or may be introductive of it, or be something like it. But certainly since the church is not so happy as to be entirely free from the crime of simony, it will be hard to say that the power (the buying of which was the principle of this sin, and

---

[t] 1 Cor. xii. 7.
[u] In Matthæum.

[x] Tract. 6. in Canonicam Joan. circa med. et lib. 3. contr. Donatist. c. 6.
[y] Mark xvi. 17.

therefore the rule of all the rest) should be removed, and the house stand without a foundation, the relative without the correspondent, the accessary without the principal, and the accident without the subject. This is impossible, and therefore it remains that still there abides in the church this power, that, by imposition of the hands of fit persons, the Holy Ghost is ministered. But this will be further cleared in the next section.

SECTION III.

The Holy Rite of Imposition of Hands for the giving the Holy Spirit, or Confirmation, was actually continued and practised by all the succeeding Ages of the purest and primitive Church.

NEXT to the plain words of Scripture, the traditive interpretation and practice of the church of God is the best argument in the world for rituals and mystical ministrations; for the tradition is universal, and all the way acknowledged to be derived from Scripture. And although in rituals the tradition itself, if it be universal and primitive, as this is, were alone sufficient, and is so esteemed in the baptism of infants, in the priests' consecrating the holy eucharist, in public liturgies, in absolution of penitents, the Lord's day, communicating of women, and the like; yet this rite of confirmation being all that, and evidently derived from the practice apostolical, and so often recorded in the New Testament, both in the ritual and mysterious part, both in the ceremony and spiritual effect, is a point of as great certainty as it is of usefulness and holy designation.

Theophilus Antiochenus lived not long after the death of St. John,[a] and he derives the name of christian, which was first given to the disciples in his city, from this chrism or spiritual unction, this confirmation of baptized persons; Ἡμεῖς τούτου εἵνεκεν καλούμεθα Χριστιανοί, ὅτι χριόμεθα ἔλαιον Θεοῦ, "We are therefore called christians, because we are anointed with the unction of God." These words will be best understood by the subsequent testimonies, by which it will appear that confirmation (for reasons hereafter mentioned) was for many ages called chrism or unction. But he adds the usefulness of it: "For who is there that enters into the world, or that enters into contention or athletic combats, but is anointed with oil?" By which words he intimates the unction anciently used in baptism, and in confirmation both: for in the first we have our new birth; in the second we are prepared for spiritual combat.

Tertullian[a] having spoken of the rites of baptism, proceeds; " Dehinc" (saith he) " manus imponitur, per benedictionem advocans et invitans Spiritum Sanctum. Tunc ille Sanctissimus Spiritus super emundata et benedicta corpora libens à Patre descendit:"[b] " After baptism the hand is imposed, by blessing, calling, and inviting, the Holy Spirit.

Then that most Holy Spirit willingly descends from the Father upon the bodies that are cleansed and blessed;" that is, first baptized, then confirmed. And again;[c] " Caro signatur, ut anima muniatur. Caro manûs impositione adumbratur, ut anima Spiritu illuminetur;" " The flesh is consigned, or sealed," (that also is one of the known primitive words for confirmation,) " that the soul may be guarded or defended: and the body is overshadowed by the imposition of hands, that the soul may be enlightened by the Holy Ghost." Nay, further yet, if any man objects that baptism is sufficient, he answers,[d] " It is true, it is sufficient to them that are to die presently; but it is not enough for them that are still to live and to fight against their spiritual enemies. For in baptism we do not receive the Holy Ghost" (for although the apostles had been baptized, yet the Holy Ghost was come upon none of them until Jesus was glorified); " sed in aquâ emundati, sub angelo Spiritui Sancto præparamur;" " but being cleansed by baptismal water, we are disposed for the Holy Spirit, under the hand of the angel of the church," under the bishop's hand. And a little after he expostulates the article: " Non licebit Deo in suo organo per manus sanctas sublimitatem modulari spiritalem?" " Is it not lawful for God, by an instrument of his own, under holy hands to accord the heights and sublimity of the Spirit?" for indeed this is the Divine order: and therefore Tertullian reckoning the happiness and excellency of the church of Rome at that time, says,[e] " She believes in God, she signs with water, she clothes with the Spirit," (viz. in confirmation,) " she feeds with the eucharist, she exhorts to martyrdom; and against this order or institution she receives no man."

St. Cyprian,[f] in his epistle [g] to Jubaianus, having urged that of the apostles going to Samaria to impose hands on those whom St. Philip had baptized, adds, " quod nunc quoque apud nos geritur, ut qui in ecclesia baptizantur, per præpositos ecclesiæ offerantur, et per nostram orationem ac manûs impositionem Spiritum Sanctum consequantur, et signaculo Dominico consummentur:" " which custom is also descended to us, that they who are baptized might be brought by the rulers of the church, and by our prayer and the imposition of hands, (said the martyr bishop,) may obtain the Holy Ghost, and be consummated with the Lord's signature." And again:[h] " Ungi necesse est eum qui baptizatus est," &c. " Et super eos qui in ecclesia baptizati erant, et ecclesiasticum et legitimum baptismum consecuti fuerant, oratione pro iis habitâ, et manu impositâ, invocaretur et infunderetur, Spiritus Sanctus:" " It is necessary that every one who is baptized, should receive the unction, that he may be Christ's anointed one, and may have in him the grace of Christ. They who have received lawful and ecclesiastical baptism, it is not necessary they should be baptized again; but that which is wanting must be supplied, viz. that prayer being made for them, and hands imposed, the Holy Ghost be invocated and poured upon them."

[a] A. D. 170.   [a] A. D. 200.   [b] De Baptism, c. 6
[c] De Resur. Carn. cap. 8.   [d] Ubi suprà de Bapt.
[e] De Præscript. cap. 36.   [f] A. D. 250.
[g] Epist. 73.   [h] Epist. 70, 73.

St. Clement[l] of Alexandria, a man of venerable antiquity and admirable learning, tells[k] that a certain young man was by St. John delivered to the care of a bishop, who having baptized him, " postea verò sigillo Domini, tanquam[l] perfectâ tutâque ejus custodiâ, eum obsignavit;" "afterward he sealed him with the Lord's signature" (the church-word for confirmation) " as with a safe and perfect guard."

Origen[m] in his seventh homily upon Ezekiel, expounding certain mystical words of the prophet, saith, " Oleum est quo vir sanctus ungitur, oleum Christi, oleum sanctæ doctrinæ. Cùm ergò aliquis accepit hoc oleum quo ungitur sanctus, id est, Scripturam Sanctam instituentem quomodo oporteat baptizari, in nomine Patris, et Filii, et Spiritûs Sancti, et pauca commutans unxerit quempiam, et quodammodo dixerit, Jam non es catechumenus, consecutus es lavacrum secundæ generationis; talis homo accipit oleum Dei," &c. " The unction of Christ, of holy doctrine, is the oil by which the holy man is anointed, having been instructed in the Scriptures, and taught how to be baptized; then changing a few things he says to him, Now you are no longer a catechumen, now you are regenerated in baptism: such a man receives the unction of God," viz. he then is to be confirmed.

St. Dionysius, commonly called the Areopagite, in his excellent book of Ecclesiastical Hierarchy,[n] speaks most fully of the holy rite of confirmation or chrism. Having described at large the office and manner of baptizing the catechumens, the trine immersion, the vesting them in white garments, he adds, " Then they bring them again to the bishop, and he consigns him" (who had been so baptized) θεουργικωτάτῳ μύρῳ, " with the most divinely-operating unction," and then gives him the most holy eucharist. And afterwards he says,[o] "But even to him who is consecrated in the most holy mystery of regeneration, τοῦ μύρου τελειωτικὴ χρίσις, the perfective unction of chrism, gives to him the advent of the Holy Spirit." And this right of confirmation, then called chrism, from the spiritual unction then effected, and consigned also and signified by the ceremony of anointing externally, which was then the ceremony of the church, he calls it τὴν ἱερὰν τῆς θεογενεσίας τελείωσιν, "the holy consummation of our baptismal regeneration;" meaning, that without this, there is something wanting to the baptized persons.

And this appears fully in that famous censure of Novatus[p] by Cornelius bishop of Rome, reported by[q] Eusebius. Novatus had been baptized in his bed, being very sick and like to die: " but when he recovered, he did not receive those other things, which by the rule of the church he ought to have received; ' neque Domini sigillo ab episcopo consignatus est,' ' he was not consigned with the Lord's signature by the hands of the bishop,' he was not confirmed: ' quo non impetrato, quomodo Spiritum Sanctum obtinuisse putandus est?' ' which having not obtained, how can he be supposed to have received the Holy Spirit?'" The same also is something more fully related by Nicephorus,[r] but wholly to the same purpose.

Melchiades,[s] in his epistle to the bishops of Spain, argues excellently about the necessity and usefulness of the holy rite of confirmation. " What does the mystery of confirmation profit me after the mystery of baptism? Certainly we did not receive all in our baptism, if, after that lavatory, we want something of another kind. Let your charity attend. As the military order requires that when the general enters a soldier into his list, he does not only mark him, but furnishes him with arms for the battle; so in him that is baptized, this blessing is his ammunition. You have given (Christ) a soldier, give him also weapons. And what will it profit him, if a father gives a great estate to his son, if he does not take care to provide a tutor for him? Therefore the Holy Spirit is the guardian of our regeneration in Christ, he is the comforter and he is the defender.

I have already[t] alleged the plain testimonies of Optatus and St. Cyril in the first section. I add to them the words of St. Gregory Nazianzen[u] speaking of confirmation or the christian signature; " Hoc et viventi tibi maximum est tutamentum: ovis enim quæ sigillo insignita est, non facilè patet insidiis; quæ verò signata non est, facilè à furibus capitur:" " This signature is your greatest guard while you live: for a sheep, when it is marked with the master's sign, is not so soon stolen by thieves; but easily, if she be not."—The same manner of speaking is also used by St. Basil, who was himself together with Eubulus confirmed by Bishop Maximinus: " Quomodo curam geret tanquam ad se pertinentis angelus? Quomodo eripiat ex hostibus, si non agnoverit signaculum?" " How shall the angel know what sheep belong unto his charge? How shall he snatch them from the enemy, if he does not see their mark and signature?"—Theodoret[x] also and Theophylact speak the like words: and, so far as I can perceive, these and the like sayings are most made use of by the schoolmen to be their warranty for an indelible character imprinted in confirmation. I do not interest myself in the question, but only recite the doctrine of these fathers in behalf of the practice and usefulness of confirmation.

I shall not need to transcribe hither those clear testimonies, which are cited from the epistles of St. Clement, Urban the First, Fabianus, and Cornelius; the sum of them is in those plainest words of Urban the First: " Omnes fideles per manûs impositionem episcoporum, Spiritum Sanctum post baptismum accipere debent;" " All faithful people ought to receive the Holy Spirit by imposition of the bishop's hands after baptism." Much more to the same purpose is to be read, collected by Gratian " de Consecrat. dist. 4. Presbyt. et de Consecrat. dist. 5. Omnes Fideles, et ibid. Spiritus Sanctus."

St. Jerome[y] brings in a Luciferian asking, "why

---

[l] A. D. 200.
[l] Τὸ τέλειον φυλακτήριον.
[n] De Eccles. Hier. c. 2.
[p] A. D. 260.
[k] Apud Euseb. lib. 3. c. 17.
[m] A. D. 210.
[o] Et cap. 4.
[q] Lib. 6. Hist. Eccles. c. 43.
[r] Lib. 6. cap. 3.
[t] A. D. 370.
[x] In cap. 1. ad Ephes.
[y] Dial. adv. Lucifer.
[s] A. D. 320.
[u] Adhort. ad S. Lavacrum.

he that is baptized in the church, does not receive the Holy Ghost, but by imposition of the bishop's hands?" The answer is, "Hanc observationem ex Scripturæ auctoritate ad sacerdotii honorem descendere," "This observation for the honour of the priesthood did descend from the authority of the Scriptures;" adding withal, "it was for the prevention of schisms, and that the safety of the church did depend upon it. 'Exigis ubi scriptum est?' 'If you ask where it is written,' it is answered, 'In Actis Apostolorum,' 'It is written in the Acts of the Apostles.' But if there were no authority of Scripture for it, 'totius orbis in hanc partem consensus instar præcepti obtineret,' 'the consent of the whole christian world in this article ought to prevail as a commandment.'" But here is a two-fold cord, Scripture and universal tradition; or rather Scripture expounded by a universal traditive interpretation. The same observation is made from Scripture by St. Chrysostom:[a] the words are very like those now recited from St. Jerome's Dialogue, and therefore need not to be repeated.

St. Ambrose[a] calls confirmation "spirituale signaculum quod post fontem superest, ut perfectio fiat," "a spiritual seal remaining after baptism, that perfection be had."—Œcumenius calls it τελειότητα, "perfection."—"Lavacro peccata purgantur, chrismate Spiritus Sanctus superfunditur; utraque verò ista manu et ore antistitis impetramus," said Pacianus[b] bishop of Barcinona: "In baptism our sins are cleansed, in confirmation the Holy Spirit is poured upon us; and both these we obtain by the hands and mouth of the bishop." And again: "Vestræ plebi unde Spiritus, quam non consignat unctus sacerdos?"[c] The same with that of Cornelius in the case of Novatus before cited.

I shall add no more, lest I overset the article, and make it suspicious by too laborious a defence: only after these numerous testimonies of the fathers, I think it may be useful to represent, that this holy rite of confirmation hath been decreed by many councils.

The council[d] of Eliberis, celebrated in the time of Pope Sylvester the First, decreed, that whosoever is baptized in his sickness, if he recover, "ad episcopum eum perducat, ut per manûs impositionem perfici possit;" "let him be brought to the bishop, that he may be perfected by the imposition of hands." To the same purpose is the seventy-seventh canon: "Episcopus eos per benedictionem perficere debebit," "The bishop must perfect those, whom the minister baptized by his benediction."

The council of Laodicea[e] decreed ὅτι δεῖ τοὺς φωτιζομένους κατὰ τὸ βάπτισμα χρίεσθαι χρίσματι ἐπουρανίῳ, καὶ μετόχους εἶναι τῆς βασιλείας τοῦ Χριστοῦ· "all that are baptized, must be anointed with the celestial unction, and (so) be partakers of the kingdom of Christ." All that are so, that is, are confirmed; for this celestial unction is done by holy prayers and the invocation of the Holy Spirit: so Zonaras upon this canon: all such who have this unction shall reign with Christ, unless by their wickedness they preclude their own possessions. This canon was put into the code of the catholic church, and makes the one hundred and fifty-second canon.

The council of Orleans affirms expressly, that he who is baptized cannot be a christian, (meaning according to the usual style of the church, a full and perfect christian,) "nisi confirmatione episcopali fuerit chrismatus," "unless he have the unction of episcopal confirmation."[f]

But when the church had long disputed concerning the rebaptizing of heretics, and made canons for and against it, according as the heretics were, and all agreed that if the first baptism had been once good, it could never be repeated; yet they thought it fit that such persons should be confirmed by the bishop, all supposing confirmation to be the perfection and consummation of the less perfect baptism. Thus the first council of Arles[g] decreed concerning the Arians, that if they had been baptized in the name of the Father, Son, and Holy Ghost, they should not be rebaptized. "Manus tantùm eis imponatur, ut accipiant Spiritum Sanctum;" that is, "Let them be confirmed, let there be imposition of hands, that they may receive the Holy Ghost." The same is decreed by the second council of Arles[h] in the case of the Bonasiaci. But I also find it in a greater record, in the general council[i] of Constantinople; where heretics are commanded upon their conversion to be received, "secundùm constitutum officium;" there was "an office appointed" for it; and it is in the Greek Euchologion, "sigillatos, primò scilicet unctos unguento chrismatis," &c. "et signantes eos dicimus, sigillum doni Spiritûs Sancti." It is the form of confirmation used to this day in the Greek church.

So many fathers testifying the practice of the church, and teaching this doctrine, and so many more fathers as were assembled in six councils, all giving witness to this holy rite, and that in pursuance also of Scripture, are too great a cloud of witnesses to be despised by any man that calls himself a christian.

SECTION IV.

The Bishops were always and the only Ministers of Confirmation.

SAINT CHRYSOSTOM[k] asking the reason why the Samaritans, who were baptized by Philip, could not from him and by his ministry receive the Holy Ghost, answers, "Perhaps this was done for the honour of the apostles," to distinguish the supereminent dignity which they bore in the church from all inferior ministrations: but this answer not satisfying, he adds, "Hoc donum non habebat, erat enim ex sep-

---

[a] Homil. 18. in Act.
[b] In Heb. vi.
[d] Can. 38.
[a] Lib. 3. de Sacram. c. 2.
[c] Lib. 3. contr. Novat.
[e] Can. eod.
[f] Habetur apud Gratian. de Consecrat. dist. 5. cap. Jejun.
[g] Cap. 8.
[h] Can. 17.
[i] Can. 7.
[k] Homil. 18. in Acta.

tem illis, id quod magìs videtur dicendum. Unde, meâ sententiâ, hic Philippus unus ex septem erat, secundus à Stephano; ideo et baptizans Spiritum Sanctum non dabat, neque enim facultatem habebat, hoc enim donum solorum apostolorum erat:" "This gift they had not, who baptized the Samaritans, which thing is rather to be said than the other: for Philip was one of the seven, and in my opinion next to St. Stephen; therefore though he baptized, yet he gave not the Holy Ghost; for he had no power so to do, for this gift was proper only to the apostles." "Nam virtutem quidem acceperant (diaconi) faciendi signa, non autem dandi aliis Spiritum Sanctum; igitur hoc erat in apostolis singulare, unde et præcipuos, et non alios, videmus hoc facere." "The ministers that baptized had a power of doing signs and working miracles, but not of giving the Holy Spirit; therefore this gift was peculiar to the apostles, whence it comes to pass that we see the[m] chiefs in the church, and no other, to do this."

St. Dionysius says,[n] Χρεία τοῦ ἀρχιερέως ἔσται, "There is need of a bishop to confirm the baptized," αὐτὴ γὰρ ἦν ἡ ἀρχαία συνήθεια, "for this was the ancient custom of the church;" and "this was wont to be done by the bishops, for conservation of unity in the church of Christ," said St. Ambrose;[o] "a solis episcopis," " by bishops only," said St. Austin;—for "the bishops succeeded in the place and ordinary office of the apostles," said St. Jerome. And therefore in his dialogue against the Luciferians it is said, "that this observation for the honour of the priesthood did descend, that the bishops only might by imposition of hands confer the Holy Ghost; that it comes from Scripture, that it is written in the Acts of the Apostles, that it is done for the prevention of schisms; that the safety of the church depends upon it."

But the words of Pope Innocentius I. in his first epistle and third chapter, and published in the first tome of the councils, are very full to this particular. "De consignandis infantibus, manifestum est non ab alio quàm ab episcopo fieri licere: nam presbyteri, licèt sint sacerdotes, pontificatûs tamen apicem non habent: hæc autem pontificibus solis deberi, ut vel consignent, vel Paracletum Spiritum tradant, non solùm consuetudo ecclesiastica demonstrat, verùm et illa lectio Actuum Apostolorum, quæ asserit Petrum et Johannem esse directos, qui jam baptizatis traderent Spiritum Sanctum:" "Concerning confirmation of infants, it is manifest, it is not lawful to be done by any other than by the bishop; for although the presbyters be priests, yet they have not the summity of episcopacy: but that these things are only due to bishops, is not only demonstrated by the custom of the church, but by that of the Acts of the Apostles, where Peter and John were sent to minister the Holy Ghost to them that were baptized."—Optatus[p] proves Macarius to be no bishop, because he was not conversant in the episcopal office, and imposed hands on none that were baptized. "Hoc unum à majoribus fit, id est, à summis pontificibus, quod à minoribus perfici non potest," said P. Melchiades:[q] "This (of confirmation) is only done by the greater ministers, that is, by the bishops, and cannot be done by the lesser."—This was the constant practice and doctrine of the primitive church, and derived from the practice and tradition of the apostles,[r] and recorded in their Acts written by St. Luke. For this is our great rule in this case, what they did in rituals and consigned to posterity is our example and our warranty: we see it done thus, and by these men, and by no others, and no otherwise, and we have no other authority, and we have no reason to go another way. The ἄνδρες ἡγούμενοι in St. Luke, the κορυφαῖοι in St. Chrysostom, the πρόεδρος in Philo, and the πρεσβύτερος, "the chief governor," in ecclesiasticals, his office is τὰ μὴ γνώριμα ἐν τοῖς βίβλοις ἀναδιδάσκειν, "to teach such things as are not set down in books;" their practice is a sermon, their example in these things must be our rule, or else we must walk irregularly, and have no rule but chance and humour, empire and usurpation; and therefore much rather, when it is recorded in holy writ, must this observation be esteemed sacred and inviolable.

But how if a bishop be not to be had or not ready? St. Ambrose[s] is pretended to have answered, "Apud Ægyptum presbyteri consignant, si præsens non sit episcopus," "A presbyter may consign, if the bishop be not present;" and Amalarius[t] affirms, "Sylvestrum Papam, prævidentem quantum periculosum iter arriperet qui sine confirmatione maneret, quantum potuit subvenisse, et propter absentiam episcoporum, necessitate addidisse, ut à presbytero ungerentur," "that Pope Sylvester, foreseeing how dangerous a journey he takes who abides without confirmation, brought remedy as far as he could, and commanded that in the absence of bishops they should be anointed by the priest:" and therefore it is by some supposed that "factum valet, fieri non debuit," "the thing ought not to be done but in the proper and appointed way;" but when it is done, it is valid; just as in the case of baptism by a layman or woman. Nay, though some canons say it is "actio irrita," "the act is null," yet for this there is a salvo pretended; for sometimes an action is said to be "irrita" in law, which yet nevertheless is of secret and permanent value, and ought not to be done again. Thus if a priest be promoted by simony, it is said "sacerdos non est, sed inanitur tantùm dicitur," "he is but vainly called a priest, for he is no priest."[u] So Sixtus II. said, "that if a bishop ordain in another's diocess, the ordination is void;" and in the law it is said, "that if a bishop be consecrated without his clergy and the congregation, the consecration is null:" and yet these later

---

[m] Τοὺς κορυφαίους. [n] Cap. 5. Eccles. Hier.
[o] In Heb. vi. q. 44. in N. T. [p] Contra Parmen. lib. 7.
[q] Epist. ad Episc. Hispan.
[r] Voluit Deus dona illa admiranda non contingere baptizatis nisi per manus apostolorum, ut auctoritatem testibus suis conciliaret quàm maximam; quod ipsum simul ad retinendam ecclesiæ unitatem pertinebat: Grotius.—Videtur ergò fuisse peculiare apostolorum munus dare Spiritum Sanctum: Isidor.—Clarius in 8. Actuum Apostolorum.
[s] In Eph. iv. [t] De Offic. Eccles. cap. 27
[u] 1. Qu. 1. cap. Qui vult. 1. et 2 Epist. 2. de Episc. Ordinante. 1. qu. 2. c. In multis. Clement. de Elect. cap. In plerisque.

and fiercer constitutions do not determine concerning the natural event of things, but of the legal and canonical approbation.

To these things I answer, that St. Ambrose's saying that "in Egypt, the presbyters consign in the bishops' absence," does not prove that they ever did confirm or impose hands on the baptized for the ministry of the Holy Spirit; because that very passage being related by St. Austin,[x] the more general word of "consign" is rendered by the plainer and more particular "consecrant," "they consecrate," meaning the blessed eucharist; which was not permitted primitively to a simple priest to do in the bishop's absence without leave; only in Egypt it seems they had a general leave, and the bishop's absence was an interpretative consent. But besides this, "consignant" is best interpreted by the practice of the church, of which I shall presently give an account; they might, in the absence of the bishop, consign with oil upon the top of the head, but not in the forehead; much less impose hands, or confirm, or minister the Holy Spirit: for the case was this.

It was very early in the church, that, to represent the grace which was ministered in confirmation, the unction from above, they used oil and balsam; and so constantly used this in their confirmations, that from the ceremony it had the appellation; "sacramentum chrismatis," St. Austin[y] calls it;—ἐν μύρῳ τελείωσις, so Dionysius. Now because at the baptism of the adult christians, and (by imitation of that) of infants, confirmation and baptism were usually ministered at the same time; the unction was not only used to persons newly baptized, but another unction was added as a ceremony in baptism itself, and was used immediately before baptism; and the oil was put on the top of the head, and three times was the party signed. So it was then, as we find in the Ecclesiastical Hierarchy. But besides this unction with oil in baptismal preparations, and pouring oil into the baptismal water, we find another unction after the baptism was finished. For they bring the baptized person "again to the bishop, (saith St. Dionysius,)[a] who, signing the man with hallowed chrism, gives him the holy eucharist." This they called χρίσιν τελειωτικὴν, "the perfective or consummating unction;" this was that which was used when the bishop confirmed the baptized person: "for to him who is initiated by the most holy initiation of the Divine generation, (that is, to him who hath been baptized, said Pachimeres, the paraphrast of Dionysius,) the perfective unction of chrism gives the gift of the Holy Ghost."—This is that which the Laodicean[a] council calls χρίεσθαι μετὰ τὸ βάπτισμα, "to be anointed after baptism." Both these unctions were intimated by Theophilus Antiochenus: Τίς δὲ ἄνθρωπος εἰσελθὼν εἰς τόνδε τὸν βίον, ἢ ἀθλῶν, οὐ χρίεται ἐλαίῳ; "Every man that is born into the world, and every man that is a champion, is anointed with oil:" that to baptism, this alluding to confirmation.

Now this chrism was frequently ministered immediately after baptism, in the cities where the bishop was present: but in villages and little towns where the bishop was not present, it could not be; but bishops were forced at their opportunities to go abroad and perfect what was wanting, as it was in the example of Peter and John to the Samaritans. "Non quidem abnuo hanc esse ecclesiarum consuetudinem, ut ad eos qui longè in minoribus urbibus per presbyteros et diaconos baptizati sunt, episcopus ad invocationem Sancti Spiritûs manum impositurus excurrat:" "It is the custom of the church, that when persons are in lesser cities baptized by priests and deacons, the bishop uses to travel far, that he may lay hands on them for the invocation of the Holy Spirit."[b] But because this could not always be done, and because many baptized persons died before such an opportunity could be had; the church took up a custom, that the bishop should consecrate the chrism, and send it to the villages and little cities distant from the metropolis, and that the priests should anoint the baptized with it. But still they kept this part of it sacred and peculiar to the bishop:
1. That no chrism should be used but what the bishop consecrated; 2. That the priests should anoint the head of the baptized, but at no hand the forehead, for that was still reserved for the bishop to do when he confirmed them. And this is evident in the epistle of Pope Innocentius the First, above quoted. "Nam presbyteris, seu extra episcopum seu præsente episcopo baptizant, chrismate baptizatos ungere licet, sed quod ab episcopo fuerit consecratum; non tamen frontem ex eodem oleo signare, quod solis debetur episcopis, cùm tradunt Spiritum Paracletum." Now this the bishops did, not only to satisfy the desire of the baptized, but by this ceremony to excite the "votum confirmationis," that they who could not actually be confirmed, might at least have it "in voto" "in desire," and in ecclesiastical representation. This, as some think, was first introduced by Pope Sylvester: and this is the consignation which the priests of Egypt used in the absence of the bishop; and this became afterwards the practice in other churches.

But this was no part of the holy rite of confirmation, but a ceremony annexed to it ordinarily; from thence transmitted to baptism, first by imitation, afterwards by way of supply and in defect of the opportunities of confirmation episcopal. And therefore we find in the first Arausican council,[c] in the time of Leo the First and Theodosius junior, it was decreed, "that in baptism every one should receive chrism: 'de eo autem qui in baptismate, quâcunque necessitate faciente, chrismatus non fuerit, in confirmatione sacerdos commonebitur:' 'if the baptized by any intervening accident or necessity was not anointed the bishop should be advertised of it in confirmation;'" meaning, that then it must be done. For the chrism was but a ceremony annexed, no part of either rite essential to it; but yet they thought it necessary, by reason of some opinions then prevailing in the church. But here the rites themselves are clearly distinguished; and this of

---

[x] Qu. V. et N. T. qu. 101.
[y] Lib. 2. contr. Liter. Petiliani. c. 104.

[a] Eccles. Hier. cap. 2.
[b] S. Hieron. adv. Luciferianos. ante Med.
[c] Can. 48.
[c] Cap. 1

confirmation was never permitted to mere presbyters. Innocentius the Third, a great canonist and of great authority, gives a full evidence in this particular: " Per frontis chrismationem manûs impositio designatur, quia per eam Spiritus Sanctus per augmentum datur et robor. Unde cùm cæteras unctiones simplex sacerdos vel presbyter valeat exhibere, hanc non nisi summus sacerdos vel presbyter valeat exhibere, id est, episcopus conferre:" "By anointing of the forehead the imposition of hands is designed, because by that the Holy Ghost is given for increase and strength; therefore when a single priest may give the other unctions, yet this cannot be done but by the chief priest, that is, the bishop."—And therefore to the question, What shall be done if a bishop may not be had? the same Innocentius answers, "It is safer and without danger wholly to omit it, than to have it rashly and without authority ministered by any other; 'cùm umbra quædam ostendatur in opere, veritas autem non subeat in effectu;' 'for it is a mere shadow without truth or real effect,' when any one else does it but the person whom God hath appointed to this ministration." And no approved man of the church did ever say the contrary, till Richard, primate of Armagh, commenced a new opinion, from whence, Thomas of Walden says, that Wickliffe borrowed his doctrine to trouble the church in this particular.

What the doctrine of the ancient church was in the purest times, I have already, I hope, sufficiently declared; what it was afterwards, when the ceremony of chrism was as much remarked as the rite to which it ministered, we find fully declared by Rabanus Maurus:[d] "Signatur baptizatus cum chrismate per sacerdotem in capitis summitate, per Pontificem verò in fronte; ut priori unctione significetur Spiritûs Sancti super ipsum descensio ad habitationem Deo consecrandum; in secundâ quoque, ut ejus Spiritûs Sancti septiformis gratia, cum omni plenitudine sanctitatis et scientiæ et virtutis, venire in hominem declaretur: tunc enim ipse Spiritus Sanctus post mundata et benedicta corpora atque animas liberè à Patre descendit, ut unâ cum suâ visitatione sanctificaret et illustraret; et nunc in hominem ad hoc venit, ut signaculum fidei, quod in fronte suscepit, faciat cum donis cœlestibus repletum, et suâ gratiâ confortatum, intrepidè et audacter coram regibus et potestatibus hujus seculi portare, ac nomen Christi liberâ voce prædicare:" "In baptism the baptized was anointed on the top of the head, in confirmation on the forehead: by that was signified that the Holy Ghost was preparing a habitation for himself; by this was declared the descent of the Holy Spirit, with his seven-fold gifts, with all fulness of knowledge and spiritual understanding." These things were signified by the appendant ceremony; but the rights were ever distinguished, and did not only signify and declare, but effect, these graces by the ministry of prayer and imposition of hands.

The ceremony of the church instituted and used as she pleased, and gave in what circumstances they would choose; and new propositions entered,

[d] De Instit. Cleric. lib. 1. c. 30.

and customs changed, and deputations were made; and the bishops, in whom by Christ was placed the fulness of ecclesiastical power, concredited to the bishops and deacons so much as their occasions and necessities permitted: and because in those ages and places where the external ceremony was regarded, it may be, more than the inward mystery or the rite of Divine appointment, they were apt to believe that the chrism or exterior unction, delegated to the priest's ministry after the episcopal consecration of it, might supply the want of episcopal confirmation; it came to pass that new opinions were entertained, and the regulars, the friars and the Jesuits, who were always too little friends to the episcopal power, from which they would fain have been wholly exempted, publicly taught (in England especially) that chrism ministered by them with leave from the pope did do all that which ordinarily was to be done in episcopal confirmation. For, as Tertullian complained in his time, "Quibus fuit propositum aliter docendi, eos necessitas coegit aliter disponendi instrumenta doctrinæ;" "They who had purposes of teaching new doctrines, were constrained otherwise to dispose of the instruments and rituals appertaining to their doctrines." These men, to serve ends, destroyed the article, and overthrew the ancient discipline and unity of the primitive church. But they were justly censured by the theological faculty at Paris, and the censure well defended by Hallier, one of the doctors of the Sorbonne; whither I refer the reader that is curious in little things.

But for the main: it was ever called "confirmatio episcopalis, et impositio manuum episcoporum;" which our English word well expresses, and perfectly retains the use; we know it by the common name of "bishopping of children." I shall no further insist upon it, only I shall observe that there is a vain distinction brought into the schools and glosses of the canon law, of a minister ordinary, and extraordinary; all allowing that the bishop is appointed the ordinary minister of confirmation, but they would fain innovate, and pretend, that in some cases others may be ministers extraordinary. This device is of infinite danger to the destruction of the whole sacred order of the ministry, and disparks the enclosures, and lays all in common, and makes men supreme controllers of the orders of God, and relies upon a false principle; for in true divinity, and by the economy of the Spirit of God, there can be no minister of any Divine ordinance but he that is of Divine appointment, there can be none but the ordinary minister. I do not say that God is tied to this way; he cannot be tied but by himself: and therefore Christ gave a special commission to Ananias to baptize and to confirm St. Paul, and he gave the Spirit to Cornelius even before he was baptized, and he ordained St. Paul to be an apostle without the ministry of man. But this I say, that though God can make ministers extraordinary, yet man cannot; and they that go about to do so, usurp the power of Christ, and snatch from his hand what he never intended to part with. The apostles admitted others into a part of their care and of their power; but when they intended to employ them in any ministry, they gave them so much of their order as would enable them; but a person of lower order could never be deputed minister of actions appropriate to the higher: which is the case of confirmation, by the practice and tradition of the apostles, and by the universal practice and doctrine of the primitive catholic church, by which bishops only, the successors of the apostles, were alone the ministers of confirmation: and therefore if any man else usurp it, let them answer it; they do hurt indeed to themselves, but no benefit to others, to whom they minister shadows instead of substances.

SECTION V.

The whole Procedure or Ritual of Confirmation is by Prayer and Imposition of Hands.

THE heart and the eye are lift up to God to bring blessings from him, and so is the hand too; but this also falls upon the people, and rests there, to apply the descending blessing to the proper and prepared suscipient. God governed the people of Israel by the hand of Moses and Aaron:

——— et calidæ fecére silentia turbæ
Majestate manûs:

and both under Moses and under Christ, whenever the president of religion did bless the people, he lifted up his hand over the congregation; and when he blessed a single person he laid his hand upon him. This was the rite used by Jacob and the patriarchs, by kings and prophets, by all the eminently religious in the synagogue, and by Christ himself when he blessed the children which were brought to him, and by the apostles when they blessed and confirmed the baptized converts; and whom else can the church follow? The apostles did so to the christians of Samaria, to them of Ephesus; and St. Paul describes this whole mystery by the ritual part of it, calling it " the foundation of the imposition of hands."[e] It is the solemnity of blessing, and the solemnity and application of paternal prayer. Τίνι γὰρ ἐπιτίθησι χεῖρα; τίνα δὲ εὐλογήσει; said Clement[f] of Alexandria; "Upon whom shall he lay his hands? whom shall he bless?"— "Quid enim aliud est impositio manuum, nisi oratio super hominem?" said St. Austin; "The bishop's laying his hands on the people, what is it but the solemnity of prayer for them?" that is, a prayer made by those sacred persons who by Christ are appointed to pray for them, and to bless in his name: and so indeed are all the ministries of the church, baptism, consecration of the blessed eucharist, absolution, ordination, visitation of the sick; they are all "in genere orationis," they are nothing but solemn and appointed "prayer" by an intrusted and a gracious person, specificated by a proper order to the end of the blessing then designed. And therefore, when St. James commanded that the sick persons should "send for the elders of the church," he adds, "and let them pray over them:" that is, lay their hands on the sick, and pray for them; that is praying over them: it is "adumbratio dextræ," (as Tertullian calls it,) "the right hand of him that ministers, overshadows" the person, for whom the solemn prayer is to be made.

This is the office of the rulers of the church; for they in the Divine eutaxy are made your superiors: they are indeed "your servants for Jesus's sake," but they "are over you in the Lord," and therefore are from the Lord appointed to bless the people; for "without contradiction," saith the apostle, "the less is blessed of the greater;"[g] that is, God hath appointed the superiors in religion to be the great ministers of prayer, he hath made them the gracious persons, them he will hear, those he hath commanded to convey your needs to God, and God's blessings to you, and to ask a blessing is to desire them to pray for you; them, I say, "whom God most respecteth for their piety and zeal that way, or else regardeth for that their place and calling bind them above others to do this duty, such as are natural and spiritual fathers."[h]

It is easy for profane persons to deride these things, as they do all religion which is not conveyed to them by sense or natural demonstrations: but the economy of the Spirit and "the things of God are spiritually discerned."—" The Spirit bloweth where it listeth, and no man knows whence it comes, and whither it goes;" and the operations are discerned by faith, and received by love and by obedience. "Date mihi christianum, et intelligit quod dico;" "None but true christians understand and feel these things." But of this we are sure, that in all the times of Moses's law, while the synagogue was standing, and in all the days of christianity, so long as men loved religion, and walked in the Spirit, and minded the affairs of their souls, to have the prayers and the blessing of the fathers of the synagogue and the fathers of the church, was esteemed no small part of their religion, and so they went to heaven. But that which I intend to say is this, that prayer and imposition of hands were the whole procedure in the christian rites: and because this ministry was most signally performed by this ceremony, and was also by St. Paul called and noted by the name of the ceremony, "imposition of hands;" this name was retained in the christian church, and this manner of ministering confirmation was all that was in the commandment or institution.

But because, in confirmation, we receive the unction from above, that is, then we are most signally "made kings and priests unto God, to offer up spiritual sacrifices," and to enable us to "seek the kingdom of God and the righteousness of it," and that the giving of the Holy Spirit is in Scripture called "the unction from above;" the church of God in early ages made use of this allegory, and passed it into an external ceremony and representation of the mystery, to signify the inward grace.

[e] Heb. vi. 2. [f] Pædag. lib. 3. c. 11. [g] Heb. vii. 7. [h] Hooker, Eccl. Pol. lib. 5. sect. 66.

> Post inscripta oleo frontis signacula, per quæ
> Unguentum regale datum est, et chrisma perenne.[1]

"We are consigned on the forehead with oil, and a royal unction and an eternal chrism are given to us:" so Prudentius[k] gives testimony of the ministry of confirmation in his time. Τοῦτο φυλάξατε ἄσπιλον· πάντων γάρ ἐστι τοῦτο διδακτικὸν, καθὼς ἀρτίως ἠκούσατε τοῦ μακαρίου Ἰωάννου λέγοντος καὶ πολλὰ περὶ τούτου χρίσματος φιλοσοφοῦντος, said St. Cyril: "Preserve this unction pure and spotless: for it teaches you all things, as you have heard the blessed St. John speaking and philosophizing many things of this holy chrism."[l] Upon this account the holy fathers used to bless and consecrate oil and balsam, that, by an external signature, they might signify the inward unction effected in confirmation. Μύρον τοῦτο οὐκ ἔστι ψιλὸν, οὐδ᾽ ὡς ἄν τις εἴποι κοινὸν κατ᾽ ἐπίκλησιν, ἀλλὰ Χριστοῦ χάρισμα, καὶ Πνεύματος ἁγίου παρουσία, τῆς αὐτῆς θεότητος ἐνεργητικὸν γινόμενον, "This chrism is not simple or common when it is blessed, but the gift of Christ, and the presence of his Holy Spirit, as it were effecting the Divinity itself;" the body is indeed anointed with visible ointment, but is also sanctified by the holy and quickening Spirit: so St. Cyril. I find in him and in some late synods[m] other pretty significations and allusions made by this ceremony of chrisms. "Nos autem pro igne visibili, qui die Pentecostes super apostolos apparuit, oleum sanctum, materiam nempe ignis ex apostolorum traditione, ad confirmandum adhibemus:" "This using of oil was instead of the baptism with fire, which Christ baptized his apostles with in Pentecost; and oil, being the most proper matter of fire, is therefore used in confirmation."

That this was the ancient ceremony is without doubt, and that the church had power to do so hath no question, and I add, it was not unreasonable; for if ever the Scripture expresses the mysteriousness of a grace conferred by an exterior ministry, (as this is, by imposition of hands,) and represents it besides in the expression and analogy of any sensible thing, that expression drawn into a ceremony will not improperly signify the grace, since the Holy Ghost did choose that for his own expression and representment. In baptism we are said to be "buried with Christ." The church does according to the analogy of that expression, when she immerges the catechumen in the font; for then she represents the same thing which the Holy Ghost would have to be represented in that sacrament: the church did but the same thing when she used chrism in this ministration. This I speak in justification of that ancient practice: but because there was no command for it, λόγος γεγραμμένος οὐκ ἔστι, said St. Basil;[n] "concerning chrism there is no written word," that is, of the ceremony there is not; he said it not of the whole rite of confirmation; therefore though to this we are all bound,—yet as to the anointing, the church is at liberty, and hath with sufficient authority omitted it in our ministrations.

In the liturgy of King Edward the Sixth, the bishops used the sign of the cross upon the foreheads of them that were to be confirmed. I do not find it since forbidden, or revoked by any expression or intimation, saving only that it is omitted in our later offices: and therefore it may seem to be permitted to the discretion of the bishops, but yet not to be used unless where it may be for edification, and where it may be by the consent of the church, at least by interpretation; concerning which I have nothing else to interpose, but that neither this, nor any thing else which is not of the nature and institution of the rite, ought to be done by private authority, nor ever at all but according to the apostle's rule, εὐσχημόνως καὶ κατὰ τάξιν, "whatsoever is decent, and whatsoever is according to order," that is to be done, and nothing else; for prayer and imposition of hands for the invocating and giving the Holy Spirit, are all that are in the foundation and institution.

SECTION VI.

Many great Graces and Blessings are consequent to the worthy Reception and due Ministry of Confirmation.

IT is of itself enough, when it is fully understood, what is said in the Acts of the Apostles at the first ministration of this rite; "they received the Holy Ghost;" that is, according to the expression of our blessed Saviour himself to the apostles, when he commanded them in Jerusalem to expect the verification of his glorious promise, "they were endued with virtue from on high;" that is, with strength to perform their duty: which although it is not to be understood exclusively to the other rites and ministries of the church of Divine appointment, yet it is properly and most signally true, and as it were in some sense appropriate to this. For, as Aquinas[o] well discourses, the grace of Christ is not tied to the sacraments; but even this spiritual strength and virtue from on high can be had without confirmation: as without baptism remission of sins may be had; and yet we believe one baptism for the remission of sins; and one confirmation for the obtaining this virtue from on high, this strength of the Spirit. But it is so appropriate to it by promise and peculiarity of ministration, that as, without the desire of baptism, our sins are not pardoned, so without at least the desire of confirmation, we cannot receive this virtue from on high, which is appointed to descend in the ministry of the Spirit. It is true, the ministry of the holy eucharist is greatly effective to this

---

[l] Prudent. in ψυχομαχίᾳ.
[l] Catech. Mystag. 3.
[k] A. D. 400.
[m] Synodus Bituricensis, apud Bochel. lib. 1. decret. Eccl. Gal. lit. 5.

[n] Lib. de Spir. S. cap. 17.
[o] Part. 3. qu. 72. art. 6. ad prim.

purpose; and therefore in the ages of martyrs the bishops were careful to give the people the holy communion frequently. "Ut quos tutos esse contra adversarium volebant, munimento Dominicæ saturitatis armarent," as St. Cyprian[p] with his colleagues wrote to Cornelius; "that those whom they would have to be safe against the contentions of their adversaries, they should arm them with the guards and defences of the Lord's fulness." But it is to be remembered that the Lord's supper is for the more perfect christians, and it is for the increase of the graces received formerly, and therefore it is for remission of sins, and yet is no prejudice to the necessity of baptism, whose proper work is remission of sins; and therefore neither does it make confirmation unnecessary: for it renews the work of both the precedent rites, and repairs the breaches, and adds new energy, and proceeds in the same dispensations, and is renewed often, whereas the others are but once.

Excellent therefore are the words of John Gerson,[q] the famous chancellor of Paris, to this purpose: "It may be said that in one way of speaking confirmation is necessary, and in another it is not. Confirmation is not necessary, as baptism and repentance, for without these salvation cannot be had. This necessity is absolute; but there is a conditional necessity. Thus if a man would not become weak, it is necessary that he eat his meat well. And so confirmation is necessary, that the spiritual life and the health, gotten in baptism, may be preserved in strength against our spiritual enemies. For this is given for strength. Hence is that saying of Hugo de St. Victore; "What does it profit that thou art raised up by baptism, if thou art not able to stand by confirmation?" Not that baptism is not of value unto salvation without confirmation; but because he who is not confirmed, will easily fall, and too readily perish." The Spirit of God comes which way he pleases, but we are tied to use his own economy, and expect the blessings appointed by his own ministries: and because to prayer is promised we shall receive whatever we ask, we may as well omit the receiving the holy eucharist, pretending that prayer alone will procure the blessings expected in the other,—as well, I say, as omit confirmation, because we hope to be strengthened and receive virtue from on high by the use of the supper of the Lord. Let us use all the ministries of grace in their season; for "we know not which shall prosper, this or that, or whether they shall be both alike good:" this only we know, that the ministries which God appoints, are the proper seasons and opportunities of grace.

This power from on high, which is the proper blessing of confirmation, was expressed, not only in speaking with tongues and doing miracles,—for much of this they had before they received the Holy Ghost,—but it was effected in spiritual and internal strengths; they were not only enabled for the service of the church, but were endued with courage, and wisdom, and christian fortitude, and boldness, to confess the faith of Christ crucified, and unity of heart and mind, singleness of heart, and joy in God; when it was for the edification of the church, miracles were done in confirmations; and St. Bernard, in the life of Malachias, tells that St. Malchus, bishop of Lismore in Ireland, confirmed a lunatic child, and at the same time cured him: but such things as these are extra-regular and contingent. This which we speak of, is a regular ministry, and must have a regular effect.

St. Austin said that the Holy Spirit in confirmation was given "ad dilatanda ecclesiæ primordia," "for the propagating christianity in the beginnings of the church."—St. Jerome says, it was "propter honorem sacerdotii," "for the honour of the priesthood."—St. Ambrose says, it was "ad confirmationem unitatis in ecclesiâ Christi;" "for the confirmation of unity in the church of Christ."—And they all say true: but the first was by the miraculous consignations, which did accompany this ministry; and the other two were by reason that the mysteries were τὰ προτελεσθέντα ὑπὸ τοῦ ἐπισκόπου, they were appropriated to the ministry of the bishop, who is "caput unitatis," "the head," the last resort, the firmament "of unity" in the church. These effects were regular indeed, but they were incident and accidental: there are effects yet more proper, and of greater excellency.

Now if we will understand in general what excellent fruits are consequent to this dispensation, we may best receive the notice of them from the fountain itself, our blessed Saviour. "He that believes, out of his belly (as the Scripture saith)[r] shall flow rivers of living waters. But this he spake of the Spirit, which they that believe on him should receive."—This is evidently spoken of the Spirit, which came down in Pentecost, which was promised to all that should believe in Christ, and which the apostles ministered by imposition of hands, the Holy Ghost himself being the expositor; and it can signify no less, but that a spring of life should be put into the heart of the confirmed, to water the plants of God; that they should become "trees," not only "planted by the water-side" (for so it was in David's time, and in all the ministry of the Old Testament); but having "a river of living water" within them, to make them "fruitful of good works," and "bringing their fruit in due season, fruits worthy of amendment of life."

1. But the principal thing is this: confirmation is the consummation and perfection, the corroboration and strength, of baptism and baptismal grace; for in baptism we undertake to do our duty, but in confirmation we receive strength to do it; in baptism others promise for us, in confirmation we undertake for ourselves, we ease our godfathers and godmothers of their burden, and take it upon our shoulders, together with the advantage of the prayers of the bishop and all the church made then in our behalf; in baptism we give up our names to Christ, but in confirmation we put our seal to the profession, and God puts his seal to the promise. It is very remarkable what St. Paul says of the beginnings of our being christians, ὁ τῆς ἀρχῆς τοῦ

[p] Epist. 54.   [q] In Opusc. Aur. de Confirmat.   [r] John vii. 38.

Χριστοῦ λόγος, "the word of the beginning of Christ:"[a] Christ begins with us, he gives us his word and admits us, and we by others' hands are brought in, τύπος διδαχῆς εἰς ὃν παρεδόθητε, it is the "form of doctrine, unto which ye were delivered." Cajetan observes right, that this is a new and emphatical way of speaking: we are wholly immerged in our fundamentals; other things are delivered to us, but we are delivered up unto these. This is done in baptism and catechism; and what was the event of it? "Being then made free from sin, ye became the servants of righteousness."[t] Your baptism was for the remission of sins there, and then ye were made free from that bondage: and what then? why then in the next place, when ye came to consummate this procedure, when the baptized was confirmed, then he became a servant of righteousness, that is, then the Holy Ghost descended upon you, and enabled you to walk in the Spirit; then the seed of God was first thrown into your hearts by a celestial influence. "Spiritus Sanctus in baptisterio plenitudinem tribuit ad innocentiam, sed in confirmatione augmentum præstat ad gratiam," said Eusebius Emissenus:[s] "In baptism we are made innocent, in confirmation we receive the increase of the Spirit of grace;" in that we are regenerated unto life, in this we are strengthened unto battle. "Dono sapientiæ illuminamur, ædificamur, erudimur, instruimur, confirmamur, ut illam Sancti Spiritûs vocem audire possimus, intellectum tibi dabo, et instruam te in hac vitâ quâ gradieris," said P. Melchiades;[x] "We are enlightened by the gift of wisdom, we are built up, taught, instructed, and confirmed; so that we may hear that voice of the Holy Spirit, I will give unto thee an understanding heart, and teach thee in the way wherein thou shalt walk:" for so,

Signari populos effuso pignore sancto,
Mirandæ virtutis opus———;[y]

"It is a work of great and wonderful power, when the holy pledge of God is poured forth upon the people."—This is that power from on high, which first descended in Pentecost, and afterward was ministered by prayer and imposition of the apostolical and episcopal hands, and comes after the other gift of remission of sins. "Vides quòd non simpliciter hoc fit, sed multâ opus est virtute, ut detur Spiritus Sanctus. Non enim idem est assequi remissionem peccatorum, et accipere virtutem illam," said St. Chrysostom;[z] "You see that this is not easily done, but there is need of much power from on high to give the Holy Spirit; for it is not all one to obtain remission of sins, and to have received this virtue or power from above."—"Quamvis enim continuò, transituris sufficiant regenerationis beneficia, victuris tamen necessaria sunt confirmationis auxilia," said Melchiades: "Although to them that die presently, the benefits of regeneration (baptismal) are sufficient, yet to them that live, the auxiliaries of confirmation are necessary."—For, according to the saying of St. Leo, in his epistle to Nicetas the bishop of Aquileia, commanding that heretics returning to the church should be confirmed with invocation of the Holy Spirit and imposition of hands, "they have only received the form of baptism 'sine sanctificationis virtute,' 'without the virtue of sanctification:'" meaning, that this is the proper effect of confirmation. For, in short, "although the newly-listed soldiers in human warfare are enrolled in the number of them that are to fight, yet they are not brought to battle till they be more trained and exercised. So although by baptism every one is ascribed into the catalogue of believers, yet he receives more strength and grace for the sustaining and overcoming the temptations of the flesh, the world, and the devil, only by imposition of the bishop's hands:"—They are words which I borrowed from a late synod at Rheims.—That is the first remark of blessing, in confirmation we receive strength to do all that which was for us undertaken in baptism: for the apostles themselves (as the holy fathers observe) were timorous in the faith until they were confirmed in Pentecost; but after the reception of the Holy Ghost they waxed valiant in the faith, and in all their spiritual combats.

2. In confirmation we receive the Holy Ghost as the earnest of our inheritance, as the seal of our salvation: Καλοῦμεν σφραγίδα, ὡς συντήρησιν καὶ τῆς δεσποτείας σημείωσιν, saith Gregory Nazianzen; "We therefore call it a seal or signature, as being a guard and custody to us, and a sign of the Lord's dominion over us."—The confirmed person is πρόβατον ἐσφραγισμένον, "a sheep that is marked,"—which thieves do not so easily steal and carry away. To the same purpose are those words of Theodoret:[a] Ἀνάμνησον σεαυτὸν τῆς ἱερᾶς μυσταγωγίας, ἐν ᾗ οἱ τελούμενοι, μετὰ τὴν ἄρνησιν τοῦ τυράννου, καὶ τὴν τοῦ βασιλέως ὁμολογίαν, οἱονεὶ σφραγῖδά τινα βασιλικὴν δέχονται τοῦ Πνευματικοῦ μύρου τὸ χρῖσμα, ὡς ἐν τύπῳ τῷ μύρῳ τὴν ἀόρατον τοῦ ἁγίου Πνεύματος χάριν ὑποδεχόμενοι. "Remember that holy mystagogy, in which they who were initiated, after renouncing that tyrant," (the devil and all his works,) "and the confession of the true King," (Jesus Christ,) "have received the chrism of spiritual unction like a royal signature, by that unction, as in a shadow, perceiving the invisible grace of the most Holy Spirit."—That is, in confirmation we are sealed for the service of God and unto the day of redemption; then it is that the seal of God is had by us, "the Lord knoweth who are his."—"Quomodo verò dices, Dei sum, si notas non produxeris?" said St. Basil;[b] "How can any man say, I am God's sheep, unless he produce the marks?"—Signati estis Spiritu promissionis per sanctissimum divinum Spiritum, Domini grex effecti sumus," said Theophylact: "When we are thus sealed by the most holy and divine Spirit of promise, then we are truly of the Lord's flock, and marked with his seal:" that is,

---

[s] Rom. vi. 17.   [t] Ver. 18.
[u] Serm. de Pentecoste.
[x] Habetur apud Gratian. de Consecrat. dist. 5. c. Spiritus S.

[y] Tertul. advers. Marcion. lib. 1. Car c. 3.
[z] Homil. 18. in Acta.
[a] Comment. in Cantic. c. i. ii.
[b] In adhort. ad Baptis.

when we are rightly confirmed, then he descends into our souls; and though he does not operate, it may be, presently, but as the reasonable soul works in its due time, and by the order of nature, by opportunities and new fermentations and actualities; so does the Spirit of God: when he is brought into use, when he is prayed for with love and assiduity, when he is caressed tenderly, when he is used lovingly, when we obey his motions readily, when we delight in his words greatly,—then we find it true, that the soul had a new life put into her, a principle of perpetual actions: but the tree planted by the water-side does not presently bear fruit, but "in its due season." By this Spirit we are then sealed; that whereas God hath laid up an inheritance for us in the kingdom of heaven, and in the faith of that we must live and labour, to confirm this faith God hath given us this pledge, the Spirit of God is a witness to us, and tells us by his holy comforts, by the peace of God, and the quietness and refreshments of a good conscience, that God is our Father, that we are his sons and daughters, and shall be coheirs with Jesus in his eternal kingdom. In baptism we are made the sons of God, but we receive the witness and testimony of it in confirmation. This is ὁ Παράκλητος, the Holy Ghost, "the Comforter," this is he whom Christ promised and did send in Pentecost, and was afterward ministered and conveyed by prayer and imposition of hands: and by this Spirit he makes the confessors bold, and the martyrs valiant, and the tempted strong, and the virgins to persevere, and widows to sing his praises and his glories. And this is that excellency which the church of God called "the Lord's seal," and teaches to be imprinted in confirmation: τὸ τέλειον φυλακτήριον, τὴν σφραγῖδα τοῦ Κυρίου, "a perfect phylactery" or guard, even "the Lord's seal;" so Eusebius calls it.

I will not be so curious as to enter into a discourse of the philosophy of this: but I shall say, that they who are curious in the secrets of nature, and observe external signatures in stones, plants, fruits, and shells, of which naturalists make many observations and observe strange effects, and the more internal signatures in minerals and living bodies, of which chemists discourse strange secrets, may easily, if they please, consider that it is infinitely credible, that in higher essences, even in spirits, there may be signatures proportionable, wrought more immediately and to greater purposes by a Divine hand. I only point at this, and so pass it over as, it may be, not fit for every man's consideration.

And now if any man shall say, we see no such things as you talk of, and find the confirmed people the same after as before, no better and no wiser, not richer in gifts, not more adorned with graces, nothing more zealous for Christ's kingdom, not more comforted with hope, or established by faith, or built up with charity; they neither speak better, nor live better: what then? Does it therefore follow that the Holy Ghost is not given in confirmation? Nothing less. For is not Christ given us in the sacrament of the Lord's supper? Do not we receive his body and his blood? Are we not made all one with Christ, and he with us? And yet it is too true, that when we arise from that holy feast, thousands there are that find no change. But there are in this two things to be considered.

One is, that the changes which are wrought upon our souls are not, after the manner of nature, visible, and sensible, and with observation. "The kingdom of God cometh not with observation:" for it is within you, and is only discerned spiritually, and produces its effects by the method of heaven, and is first apprehended by faith, and is endeared by charity, and at last is understood by holy and kind experiences. And in this there is no more objection against confirmation than against baptism, or the Lord's supper, or any other ministry evangelical.

The other thing is this: if we do not find the effects of the Spirit in confirmation, it is our faults. For he is received by moral instruments, and is intended only as a help to our endeavours, to our labours and our prayers, to our contentions and our mortifications, to our faith and to our hope, to our patience and to our charity. "Non adjuvari dicitur, qui nihil facit," "He that does nothing, cannot be said to be helped." Unless we in these instances do our part of the work, it will be no wonder if we lose his part of the co-operation and supervening blessing. He that comes under the bishop's hands to receive the gift of the Holy Ghost, will come with holy desires and a longing soul, with an open hand and a prepared heart; he will purify the house of the Spirit for the entertainment of so Divine a guest; he will receive him with humility, and follow him with obedience, and delight him with purities: and he that does thus, let him make the objection if he can, and tell me, does he "say that Jesus is the Lord?" He cannot say this "but by the Holy Ghost."—Does he love his brother? If he does, then "the Spirit of God abides in him."—Is Jesus Christ formed in him? Does he live by the laws of the Spirit? Does he obey his commands? Does he attend his motions? Hath he no earnest desires to serve God? If he have not, then in vain hath he received either baptism or confirmation. But if he have, it is certain that of himself he cannot do these things: he "cannot of himself think a good thought." Does he therefore think well? That is from the Holy Spirit of God.

To conclude this inquiry: " the Holy Ghost is promised to all men to profit withal;"[c] that is plain in Scripture. Confirmation, or prayer and imposition of the bishop's hand, is the solemnity and rite used in Scripture for the conveying of that promise, and the effect is felt in all the sanctifications and changes of the soul; and he that denies these things hath not faith, nor the true notices of religion, or the Spirit of christianity. Hear what the Scriptures yet further say in this mystery: "Now he which confirmeth or stablisheth us with you in Christ, and hath anointed us, is God: who hath also sealed us, and given the earnest of the Spirit in our hearts."[d] Here is a description of the whole mysterious part of this rite. God is the author of the grace: the

[c] 1 Cor. xii. 7.   [d] 2 Cor. i. 21, 22.

apostles and all christians are the suscipients, and receive this grace; by this grace we are adopted and incorporated into Christ: God hath anointed us; that is, he hath given us this unction from above, "he hath sealed us by his Spirit," made us his own, bored our ears through, made us free by his perpetual service, and hath done all these things in token of a greater; he hath given us his Spirit to testify to us that he will give us of his glory. These words of St. Paul, besides that they evidently contain in them the spiritual part of this ritual, are also expounded of the rite and sacramental itself by St. Chrysostom, Theodoret, and Theophylact, that I may name no more. For in this mystery, "Christos nos efficit, et misericordiam Dei nobis annunciat per Spiritum Sanctum," said St. John Damascen;[e] "he makes us his anointed ones, and by the Holy Spirit he declares his eternal mercy towards us."—"Nolite tangere Christos meos," "Touch not mine anointed ones."—For when we have this signature of the Lord upon us, the devils cannot come near to hurt us, unless we consent to their temptations, and drive the Holy Spirit of the Lord from us.

SECTION VII.

Of Preparation to Confirmation, and the Circumstances of receiving it.

If confirmation have such gracious effects, why do we confirm little children, whom in all reason we cannot suppose to be capable and receptive of such graces? It will be no answer to this, if we say, that this very question is asked concerning the baptism of infants, to which as great effects are consequent, even pardon of all our sins, and the new birth and regeneration of the soul unto Christ: for in these things the soul is wholly passive, and nothing is required of the suscipient but that he put in no bar against the grace; which because infants cannot do, they are capable of baptism; but it follows not, that therefore they are capable of confirmation, because this does suppose them such as to need new assistances, and is a new profession, and a personal undertaking, and therefore requires personal abilities, and cannot be done by others, as in the case of baptism. The aids given in confirmation are in order to our contention and our danger, our temptation and spiritual warfare; and therefore it will not seem equally reasonable to confirm children as to baptize them.

To this I answer, that, in the primitive church, confirmation was usually administered at the same time with baptism: for we find many records, that when the office of baptism was finished, and the baptized person divested of the white robe, the person was carried again to the bishop to be confirmed, as I have already shown out of[f] Dionysius and divers others. The reasons why anciently they were ministered immediately after one another is, not only because the most of them that were baptized, were of years to choose their religion, and did so, and therefore were capable of all that could be consequent to baptism, or annexed to it, or ministered with it, and therefore were also at the same time communicated as well as confirmed;—but also because the solemn baptisms were at solemn times of the year, at Easter only and Whitsuntide, and only in the cathedral or bishop's church in the chief city; whither when the catechumens came, and had the opportunity of the bishop's presence, they took the advantage "ut sacramento utroque renascantur," as St. Cyprian's expression is, "that they might be regenerated by both the mysteries," and they also had the third added, viz. the holy eucharist.

This simultaneous ministration hath occasioned some few of late to mistake confirmation for a part of baptism, but no distinct rite, or of distinct effect, save only that it gave ornament and complement or perfection to the other. But this is infinitely confuted by the very first ministry of confirmation in the world: for there was a great interval between St. Philip's baptizing and the apostle's confirming the Samaritans; where also the difference is made wider by the distinction of the minister; a deacon did one, none but an apostle and his successor a bishop could do the other: and this being of so universal a practice and doctrine in the primitive church, it is a great wonder that any learned men could suffer an error in so apparent a case. It is also clear in two other great remarks of the practice of the primitive church. The one is of them who were baptized in their sickness, the οἱ ἐν νόσῳ παραλαμβάνοντες, καὶ εἶτα ἀναστάντες, when they recovered they were commanded to address themselves to the bishop to be confirmed; which appears in the thirty-eighth canon of the council of Eliberis, and the forty-sixth canon of the council of Laodicea, which I have before cited upon other occasions: the other is, that of heretics returning to the church, who were confirmed not only long after baptism, but after their apostasy and their conversion.

For although episcopal confirmation was the enlargement of baptismal grace, and commonly administered the same day, yet it was done by interposition of distinct ceremonies, and not immediately in time. Honorius Augustodunensis[g] tells that when the baptized on the eighth day had laid aside their mitres, or proper habit used in baptism, then they were usually confirmed, or consigned with chrism in the forehead by the bishop. And when children were baptized irregularly, or besides the ordinary way, in villages and places distant from the bishop, confirmation was deferred, said Durandus. And it is certain, that this affair did not last long without variety: sometimes they ministered both together; sometimes at greater, sometimes

---

[e] Lib. 4. de Fide, cap. 10.
[f] Cap. 4. part 3. de Eccles. Hier. Melchiad. Epist. ad Episc. Hispan. Ordo Rom. cap. de Die Sabbati S. Pasch. Alcuin. de Divin Offic. c. 19.
[g] Vide Cassandrum Schol. ad Hym. Eccl.

at lesser distances; and it was left indifferent in the church to do the one or the other, or the third, according to the opportunity and the discretion of the bishop.

But afterward in the middle and descending ages it grew to be a question, not whether it were lawful or not, but which were better, to confirm infants, or to stay to their childhood or to their riper years. Aquinas, Bonaventure, and some others, say, it is best that they be confirmed in their infancy, "quia dolus non est, nec obicem ponunt," "they are then without craft, and cannot hinder" the descent of the Holy Ghost upon them. And indeed it is most agreeable with the primitive practice, that if they were baptized in infancy, they should then also be confirmed; according to that of the famous epistle of Melchiades to the bishops of Spain: "Ità conjuncta sunt hæc duo sacramenta, ut ab invicem, nisi morte præveniente, non possint separari, et unum sine altero ritè perfici non potest." Where although he expressly affirms the rites to be two, yet unless it be in cases of necessity, they are not to be severed, and one without the other is not perfect; which, in the sense formerly mentioned, is true, and so to be understood,—that to him who is baptized and is not confirmed, something very considerable is wanting, and therefore they ought to be joined, though not immediately, yet εὐχρόνως, according to reasonable occasions and accidental causes. But in this there must needs be a liberty in the church, not only for the former reasons, but also because the apostles themselves were not confirmed till after they had received the sacrament of the Lord's supper.

Others therefore say, that to confirm them of riper years is with more edification. The confession of faith is more voluntary, the election is wiser, the submission to Christ's discipline is more acceptable, and they have more need, and can make better use of their strength then derived by the Holy Spirit of God upon them: and to this purpose it is commanded in the canon law, that they who are confirmed should be "perfectæ ætatis," "of full age;" upon which the gloss[h] says, "Perfectam vocat fortè duodecim annorum;" "Twelve years old was a full age, because, at those years, they might then be admitted to the lower services in the church."—But the reason intimated and implied by the canon is, because of the preparation to it; "they must come fasting, and they must make public confession of their faith."—And indeed that they should do so is matter of great edification, as also are the advantages of choice, and other preparatory abilities and dispositions above mentioned. They are matter of edification, I say, when they are done; but then the delaying of them so long before they be done, and the wanting the aids of the Holy Ghost conveyed in that ministry, are very prejudicial, and are not matter of edification.

But therefore there is a third way, which the church of England and Ireland follows, and that is, that after infancy, but yet before they understand too much of sin, and when they can competently understand the fundamentals of religion, then it is good to bring them to be confirmed, that the Spirit of God may prevent their youthful sins, and Christ by his word and by his Spirit may enter and take possession at the same time. And thus it was in the church of England long since provided and commanded by the laws of King Edgar,[i] cap. 15. "ut nullus ab episcopo confirmari diu nimiùm detrectârit," "that none should too long put off his being confirmed by the bishop;" that is, as is best expounded by the perpetual practice almost ever since, as soon as ever, by catechism and competent instruction, they were prepared, it should not be deferred. If it have been omitted, (as of late years it hath been too much,) as we do in baptism, so in this also, it may be taken at any age, even after they have received the Lord's supper; as I observed before in the practice and example of the apostles themselves, which in this is an abundant warrant: but still the sooner the better: I mean, after that reason begins to dawn: but ever it must be taken care of, that the parents and godfathers, the ministers and masters, see that the children be catechised and well instructed in the fundamentals of their religion.

For this is the necessary preparation to the most advantageous reception of this holy ministry. "In ecclesiis potissimùm Latinis non nisi adultiore ætate pueros admitti videmus, vel hanc certè ob causam, ut parentibus, susceptoribus et ecclesiarum præfectis occasio detur pueros de fide, quam in baptismo professi sunt, diligentiùs instituendi et admonendi," said the excellent Cassander.[k] In the Latin churches they admit children of some ripeness of age, that they may be more diligently taught and instructed in the faith. And to this sense agree St. Austin,[l] Walafridus Strabo, Ruardus Lovaniensis, and Mr. Calvin.

For this was ever the practice of the primitive church, to be infinitely careful of catechising those who came and desired to be admitted to this holy rite; they used exorcisms or catechisms to prepare them to baptism and confirmation. I said exorcisms or catechisms, for they were the same thing; if the notion be new, yet I the more willingly declare it, not only to free the primitive church from the suspicion of superstition in using charms or exorcisms, (according to the modern sense of the word,) or casting of the devil out of innocent children, but also to remonstrate the perpetual practice of catechising children in the eldest and best times of the church. Thus the Greek scholiast upon Harmenopulus renders the word ἐφορκιστὰς by κατηχητὰς, the primitive "exorcist" was the "catechist:" and Balsamon upon the twenty-sixth canon of the council of Laodicea says, that to exorcise is nothing but to catechise the unbelievers, Τινὲς ἐπεχείρουν ἐξορκίζειν, τουτέστι κατηχεῖν ἀπίστους, "Some undertook to exorcise, that is, (says he,) to catechise the unbelievers:" and St. Cyril, in his preface to his catechisms, speaking to the "illuminati," "Festinent (says he) pedes tui ad catecheses audiendas; exorcismos studiosè suscipe," &c. "Let your feet run hastily to hear the catechisms, studiously receive the exorcisms, although thou beest already inspired

---

[h] De Consecrat. dist. 5. c. ut Jejuni.
[i] A. D. 967.

[k] Consultationis, cap. 9.
[l] Serm. 116. in Ramis Palmarum.—De lib. Ecclesiast. c. 26.

and exorcised; that is, although you have been already instructed in the mysteries, yet still proceed: for without exorcisms, (or catechisms,) the soul cannot go forward, since they are divine, and gathered out of the Scriptures." And the reason why these were called exorcisms he adds; "Because when the exorcists or catechists by the Spirit of God produce fear in your hearts, and do enkindle the spirit as in a furnace, the devil flies away, and salvation and hope of life eternal do succeed:" according to that of the evangelist [m] concerning Christ; "They were astonished at his doctrine, for his word was with power:" and that of St. Luke [n] concerning Paul and Barnabas; "The deputy, when he saw what was done, was astonished at the doctrine of the Lord." It is the Lord's doctrine that hath the power to cast out devils and work miracles; catechisms are the best exorcisms. "Let us therefore, brethren, abide in hope, and persevere in catechisings, (saith St. Cyril,) although they be long, and produced with many words or discourses."— The same also we find in St. Gregory Nazianzen,[o] and St. Austin.[p]

The use that I make of this notion, is principally to be an exhortation to all of the clergy, that they take great care to catechise all their people, to bring up children in the nurture and admonition of the Lord, to prepare a holy seed for the service of God, to cultivate the young plants and to dress the old ones, to take care that those who are men in the world, be not mere babes and uninstructed in Christ, and that they who are children in age, may be wise unto salvation: for by this means we shall rescue them from early temptations, when being so prepared they are so assisted by a divine ministry; we shall weaken the devil's power, by which he too often and too much prevails upon uninstructed and unconfirmed youth. For μύρον τῆς βεβαίωσις ὁμολογίας, "confirmation is the firmament of our profession;" but we profess nothing till we be catechised. Catechisings are our best preachings, and by them we shall give the best accounts of our charges, while in the behalf of Christ we make disciples, and take prepossession of infant understandings, and by his holy rite, by prayer and imposition of hands, we minister the Holy Spirit to them, and so prevent and disable the artifices of the devil; "for we are not ignorant of his devices," how he enters as soon as he can, and taking advantage of their ignorance and their passion, seats himself so strongly in their hearts and heads.

Turpius ejicitur quam non admittitur hostis;

"It is harder to cast the devil out than to keep him out." Hence it is that the youth are so corrupted in their manners, so devilish in their natures, so cursed in their conversation, so disobedient to parents, so wholly given to vanity and idleness; they learn to swear before they can pray, and to lie as soon as they can speak. It is not my sense alone, but was long since observed by Gerson [q] and Gulielmus Parisiensis, "Propter cessationem confirmationis tepiditas grandior est in fidelibus, et fidei defensione;" there is a coldness and deadness in religion, and it proceeds from the neglect of confirmation rightly ministered, and after due preparations and dispositions. A little thing will fill a child's head: teach them to say their prayers, tell them the stories of the life and death of Christ, cause them to love the holy Jesus with their first love, make them afraid of a sin; let the principles which God hath planted in their very creation, the natural principles of justice and truth, of honesty and thankfulness, of simplicity and obedience, be brought into act, and habit, and confirmation, by the holy sermons of the Gospel. If the guides of souls would have their people holy, let them teach holiness to their children, and then they will (at least) have a new generation unto God, better than this wherein we now live. They who are most zealous in this particular, will with most comfort reap the fruit of their labours, and the blessings of their ministry; and by the numbers which every curate presents to his bishop fitted for confirmation, he will in proportion render an account of his stewardship with some visible felicity. And let it be remembered, that in the last rubric of the office of confirmation in our liturgy it is made into a law, that "none should be admitted to the holy communion, until such time as he could say the catechism, and be confirmed:" which was also a law and custom in the primitive church, as appears in St. Dionysius's Ecclesiastical Hierarchy, and the matter of fact is notorious. Among the Helvetians, they are forbidden to contract marriages, before they are well instructed in the catechism: and in a late synod at Bourges, the curates are commanded to threaten all that are not confirmed, that they shall never receive the Lord's supper, nor be married. And in effect the same is of force in our church: for the married persons being to receive the sacrament at their marriage, and none are to receive but those that are confirmed, the same law obtains with us as with the Helvetians or the "synodus Bituricensis."

There is another little inquiry which I am not willing to omit; but the answer will not be long, because there is not much to be said on either side. Some inquire whether the holy rite of confirmation can be ministered any more than once. St. Austin [r] seems to be of opinion that it may be repeated: "Quid enim aliud est impositio manuum nisi oratio super hominem?" "Confirmation is a solemn prayer over a man;"—and if so, why it may not be reiterated can have nothing in the nature of the thing; and the Greeks do it frequently, but they have no warranty from the Scripture, nor from any of their own ancient doctors. Indeed when any did return from heresy, they confined them, as I have proved out of the first and second council of Arles, the council of Laodicea, and the second council of Seville: but upon a closer intuition of the thing, I find they did so only to such, who did not allow of confirmation in their sects, such as the Novatians and the Donatists. "Novatiani pœnitentiam à suo conventu arcent penitus, et iis qui ab ipsis tinguntur,

---

[m] Luke iv. 32. [n] Acts xiii. 12.
[o] Orat. de Baptism. [p] In Psal. lxvi
[q] De Exterminat. Schism.
[r] Lib. 3. de Bapt. c. 16.

sacrum chrismo non præbent. Quocirca qui ex hac hæresi corpori ecclesiæ conjunguntur, benedicti patres ungi jusserunt :" so Theodoret.[a] For that reason only the Novatians were to be confirmed upon their conversion, because they had it not before. I find also they did confirm the converted Arians ; but the reason is given in the first council of Arles, "quia propriâ lege utuntur," "they had a way of their own :" that is, as the gloss saith upon the canon " de Arianis Consecrat. dist. 4." " their baptism was not in the name of the holy Trinity ;" and so their baptism being null, or at least suspected, to make all as sure as they could, they confirmed them. The same also is the case of the Bonasiaci in the second council of Arles, though they were (as some of the Arians also were) baptized in the name of the most holy Trinity ; but it was a suspected matter, and therefore they confirmed them : but to such persons who had been rightly baptized and confirmed, they never did repeat it. Πνεύματος ἁγίου σφραγῖδα δώῃ ἀνεξάλειπτον, "The gift of the Spirit is an indelible seal," saith St. Cyril ;[t] —ἀνεπιχείρητον St. Basil calls it, it is "inviolable." They who did rebaptize, did also reconfirm. But as it was an error in St. Cyprian and the Africans to do the first, so was the second also, in case they had done it ; for I find no mention expressly that they did the latter but upon the forementioned accounts, and either upon supposition of the invalidity of their first pretended baptism, or their not using at all of confirmation in their heretical conventicles. But the repetition of confirmation is expressly forbidden by the council of Tarracon,[u] cap. 6. and by Pope Gregory the Second : and "sanctum chrisma collatum et altaris honor propter consecrationem (quæ per episcopos tantùm exercenda et conferenda sunt) evelli non queunt," said the fathers in a council at Toledo ;[x] "confirmation and holy orders, which are to be given by bishops alone, can never be annulled, and therefore they can never be repeated." And this relies upon those severe words of St. Paul : having spoken of "the foundation of the doctrine of baptisms and laying on of hands,"[y] he says, "if they fall away, they can never be renewed ;"[y] that is, the ministry of baptism and confirmation can never be repeated. To christians that sin after these ministrations, there is only left a νήψατε, "expergiscimini," that they "arise from slumber," and stir up the graces of the Holy Ghost. Every man ought to be careful that he "do not grieve the Holy Spirit ;" but if he does, yet let him not "quench" him, for that is a desperate case. Φύλαττε τὸν φυλακτικόν· The Holy Spirit is the great conservative of the new life ; only "keep the keeper ;" take care that the Spirit of God do not depart from you : for the great ministry of the Spirit is but once ; for as baptism is, so is confirmation.

I end this discourse with a plain exhortation out of St. Ambrose, upon those words of St. Paul, "He that confirmeth us with you in Christ, is God ;" "Repete quia accepisti signaculum spirituale, spiritum sapientiæ et intellectûs, spiritum consilii atque virtutis, spiritum cognitionis atque pietatis, spiritum sancti timoris, et serva quod accepisti. Signavit te Deus Pater, confirmavit te Christus Dominus :" "Remember that thou (who hast been confirmed) hast received the spiritual signature : the spirit of wisdom and understanding, the spirit of counsel and strength, the spirit of knowledge and godliness, the spirit of holy fear : keep what thou hast received. The Father hath sealed thee, and Christ thy Lord hath confirmed thee, by his Divine Spirit ;"—and he will never depart from thee, εἰ μὴ δι᾽ ἔργων φαυλότητα ἡμεῖς ἑαυτοὺς ταύτης ἀποξενώσωμεν, "unless by evil works we estrange him from us."[z] The same advice is given by Prudentius.

Cultor Dei, memento
Te fontis et lavacri
Rorem subiisse sanctum,
Et chrismate innotatum.[a]

Remember how great things ye have received, and what God hath done for you : ye are of his flock and his militia ; ye are now to fight his battles, and therefore to put on his armour, and to implore his auxiliaries, and to make use of his strengths, and always to be on his side against all his and all our enemies. But he that desires grace, must not despise to make use of all the instruments of grace. For though God communicates his invisible Spirit to you, yet that he is pleased to do it by visible instruments, is more than he needs, but not more than we do need. And therefore since God descends to our infirmities, let us carefully and lovingly address ourselves to his ordinances : that as we receive remission of sins by the washing of water, and the body and blood of Christ by the ministry of consecrated symbols ; so we may receive the Holy Ghost "sub ducibus christianæ militiæ," by the prayer and imposition of the bishop's hands, whom our Lord Jesus hath separated to this ministry. "For if you corroborate yourself by baptism," (they are the words of St. Gregory Nazianzen,[b]) "and then take heed for the future, by the most excellent and firmest aids consigning your mind and body with the unction from above," (viz. in the holy rite of confirmation,) "with the Holy Ghost, as the children of Israel did with the aspersion on the door-posts in the night of the death of the first-born of Egypt, what (evil) shall happen to you ?" (meaning, that no evil can invade you :) "and what aid shall you get ? If you sit down, you shall be without fear ; and if you rest, your sleep shall be sweet unto you."—But if when ye have received the Holy Spirit, you live not according to his Divine principles, you will lose him again ; that is, you will lose all the blessing, though the impression does still remain, till ye turn quite apostates : "in pessimis hominibus manebit, licèt ad judicium" (saith St. Austin[c]) ; "the Holy Ghost will remain," either as a testimony of your unthankfulness unto condemnation, or else as a seal of grace, and an earnest of your inheritance of eternal glory.

---

[a] Lib. 3. Hæret. Fabul.   [t] Cyril. Hieros. in Procatech.
[a] Apud Gratian. de Consecrat. dist. 5. cap. Dictum est, et cap. de Homine.

[x] Concil. Toletan. 8. can. 7.   [y] Heb. vi. 6.
[u] Zonar. in Can. Laodicen. 48.   [a] Innovatum.
[b] Orat. in Sanct. Lavac.   [c] Lib. 2. cont. Lit. Petil. c. 104.

A Select Bibliography

Arminian Magazine. 1778 – 1798.

A Collection of Letters, written by the late Rev. John Wesley and several Methodist Preachers in Connection with him, to the Late Mrs. Eliza Bennis, with her Answers, Chiefly Explaining and Enforcing the Doctrine of Sanctification. Philadelphia: B Graves, 1809.

Austin, *Anointing with the Spirit, The Rite of Confirmation.* New York: Pueblo Publishing Company, 1985.

Bangs, Nathan. *A History of the Methodist Episcopal Church.* 4 vols. New York: G. Lane and C. B. Tippett, 1845.

_____. *An Original Church of Christ: or, A Scriptural Vindication of the Orders and Powers of the Ministry.* New York: T. Mason and G. Lane, 1837.

Baker (Frank) collection of Wesleyana and British Methodism M. Rubenstein Rare Book & Manuscript Library, Duke University.

Baptism, Eucharist and Ministry, Faith and Order Paper no. 111. Geneva: World Council of Churches, 1982.

Barth. Karl. *Church Dogmatics.* Edited by G. W. Bromiley and T. F. Torrance. Translated G. W. Bromiley. 5 vols. Edinburgh: T. & T. Clark, 1969.

Benson, Joseph. *The Papers of Joseph Benson.* Catalogued in 1991. Published by John Rylands University Library of Manchester and Methodist Archives and Research Center.

Binney, Amos. *A Theological Compend of Christian Doctrine.* Nashville: Southern Methodist Publishing House,1840.

Bulmer, Agnes. *Memoir of Mrs. Elizabeth Mortimer* New York: Mason and Lane, 1836.

Campbell, Ted. *John Wesley and Christian Antiquity.* Nashville: Kingswood Books, 1991.

Candler, Warren A. *Life of Thomas Coke.* Nashville: Publishing House M.E., South, 1923.

Chilcote, Paul W. *She Offered Them Christ: The Legacy of Women Preachers in Early Methodism.* Nashville : Abingdon Press, 1993.

Clarke, Adam, editor. *Memoirs of the Late Eminent Mrs. Mary Cooper of London.* Halifax: Nicholson and Sons, 1814.

Clarke, Adam. *An Account of the Infancy, Religious, and Literary Life of Adam Clarke* (autobiography), edited J. B. B. Clarke. 3 vols. New York: B. Waugh and T. Mason, 1833.

Coke, Thomas. *A Commentary on the New Testament.* London: G. Whitfield, 1803.

Collins, Kenneth. *The Theology of John Wesley.* Nashville: Abingdon Press, 2007.

Coke, Thomas. *Funeral Sermon, Preached in Spitafields-Chapel, London, on Sunday, Oct. 26, 1794 on the Death of Mrs. Hester Ann Rogers* Birmingham: J. Belcher, 1975.

Crookshank, C. H. *History of Methodism in Ireland.* Belfast: R. S. Allen,Son & Allen-University House, 1885.

Cully, Kendig Brubaker, ed. *Confirmation: History, Doctrine, and Practice.* Greenwich, Conn, 1962.

Dallimore, Arnold A. *George Whitefield, The Life and Times of the Great Evangelist of the Eighteen Century Revival.* 2 vols. London: Banner of Truth, 1970.

Dayton, Donald. *The Theological Roots of Pentecostalism.* Grand Rapids: Francis Asbury Press, 1987.

Dieter, Melvin E. *The Holiness Revival of the Nineteenth Century.* Metuchen, New Jersey: The Scarecrow Press, Inc., 1980.

_____. ed. *The Nineteenth Century Holiness Movement.* Volume 4 of *Great Holiness Classics.* Kansas City, MO: Beacon Hill Press.

Dix, Gregory. *Confirmation. Or Laying on of Hands?* London: S.P.C.K., 1936.

_____. *The Theology of Confirmation in Relation to Baptism.* Westminster: Dacre Press, 1946.

Forsaith, Peter. *'Unexampled Labours,' Letters of the Revd John Fletcher to leaders in the Evangelical Revivial,* ed., with an introduction by Peter Forsaith, with additional notes by Kenneth Loyer. London: Epworth, 2008.

Fletcher, John William. "Doctrine of the New Birth, as it is stated in these sheets, is directly or indirectly maintained by the most spiritual divines, especially in their sacred poems." *The Asbury Theological Journal.* 50.1 (Spring, 1998):35-56.

_____. "Language of the Father's Dispensation," *The Asbury Theological Journal,* 53.1 (Spring, 1998): 65- 78.

Works of John Fletcher, ed. Joseph Benson. 10 Volumes. London: Richard Edwards, 1806.

Heitzenrater, Richard P. *Mirror and Memory.* Nashville: Kingswood Books, 1989.

Hurst, John Fletcher. *The History of Methodism.* 7 vols. New York: Eaton & Mains, 1902-04.

Jackson, Thomas. *The Life of Charles Wesley.* London: John Mason, 1849.

_____. *Memoirs of Charles Wesley.* London: John Mason, 1848.

Lampe, G. W. H. *The Seal of the Spirit.* Second Edition. London: SPCK, 1967.

Lenton, John. *John Wesley's Preachers* Eugene, Oregon: Wipf & Stock, 2009.

Lloyd, Gareth. *Charles Wesley and the Struggle for Methodist Identity.* Oxford: Oxford University Press, 2007.

MacDonald, James. *Memoirs of the Rev. Joseph Benson.* New York: Bangs and T. Mason, for the Methodist Episcopal Church, 1823.

Maddox, Randy L. "Respected Founder/Neglected Guide," *Methodist History* 37 (1999), 71-88.

_____. *Responsible Grace.* Nashville: Kingswood Series, 1994.

Mason, A. J. "Introduction," *Fifty Spiritual Homilies of St. Macarius the Egyptian* London: SPCK, 1921.

Methodist Magazine (American) 1818 – 1828.

Methodist Magazine (British) 1798 – 1822.

Methodist Magazine and Quarterly Review 1830 – 1840.

Methodist Quarterly Review 1841 – 1884.

Minutes of the Conference. 15 vols. Bristol, England: Wesleyan Methodist Conference, 1802-1816.

Moore, Henry. *Life of Mary Fletcher.* New York: Hunt & Eaton, 1817.

_____. *Life of the Rev. John Wesley.* London: John Kershaw, 1825.

Oden, Thomas, and Leicester R. Longden, eds. *Essays of Albert C. Outler, The Wesleyan Theological Heritage.* Grand Rapids: Zondervan Publishing House, 1991.

O'Malley, Stephen. "Pietistic Influence on John Wesley: Wesley and Gerhard Tersteegen," *The Wesleyan Theological Journal,* 31.2 (Fall, 1996): 48-70.

Porter, Harry Boone, *Jeremy Taylor, Liturgist.* London: S.P.C.K., 1979.

Potter, J. M., Elmer T. Clark, and J. S. Payton. *Journal and Letters of Francis Asbury.* 3 vols. Nashville: Abingdon Press, 1958.

Rattenbury, Ernest J.. *The Evangelical Doctrines of Charles Wesley's Hymns.* London: Epworth Press, 1941.

Ritchie (Elizabeth) Correspondence in the Frank Baker Collection in the David M. Rubenstein Rare Book & Manuscript Library, Duke University.

Rogers, Hester Ann. *Life and Correspondence of Mrs. Hester Ann Rogers.* Introduction by Thomas O.Summers. Nashville: Publishing House of the Methodist Episcopal Church, South, 1870.

Senn, Frank C. *Christian liturgy : Catholic and Evangelical.* Minneapolis, MN: Fortress Press, 1997.

Steele, Daniel. *A Defense of Christian Perfection or A Criticism of Dr. James Mudge's "Growth in Holiness Toward Perfection."* New York: Hunt and Eaton, 1896.

_____. *Half-Hours with St. Paul.* Boston: the Christian Witness Company, 1895.

Streiff, Patrick Philipp. "Jean Guillaume de la Fléchère John William Fletcher 1729-1785." Thesis, Th. D, Bern University, 1983, and subsequently published at Frankfurt am Main: Peter Lang, 1984.

_____. *Reluctant Saint? A Theological Biography of Fletcher of Madeley*. Translated by G. W. S Knowles. Peterborough: Epworth, 2001.

Thurian, Max, ed. *Churches Respond to BEM: Official Response to the "Baptism, Eucharist and Ministry" Text.* 6 vols. Geneva: W.C.C., 1986-88.

Tyerman, Luke. *The Life and Times of the Rev. John Wesley*. 3 vols. New York: Harper and Brothers, 1872.

_____. *Wesley's Designated Successor*. New York: Phillips and Hunt, 1883.

John Tyson, *Charles Wesley on Sanctification*. Grand Rapids: Zondervan, 1986.

_____. Editor. *Charles Wesley: A Reader*. Oxford University Press, 1989.

Vickers, John. *Thomas Coke, Apostle of Methodism*. Nashville: Abingdon, 1969.

Wesley, Charles. Published and manuscript copies of poetry and hymns available online at The Center for Studies in the Wesleyan Tradition, Duke Divinity School. https://divinity.duke.edu/initiatives/cswt/research-resources#citation

_____. *Manuscript Journal of the Reverend Charles Wesley, M.A*, ed. S. T. Kimbrough, Jr., and Kenneth G. C. Newport, 2 volumes. Nashville: Kingswood Books, 2008.

_____. Unpublished Letters. Transcribed by Gareth Lloyd. the Methodist Archives and Research Center (MARC), John Rylands University Library of Manchester, England,

Wesley, Charles, *The Letters of Charles Wesley, A Critical Edition, with Introduction and Notes, Volume I, 1728–1756*, ed. Kenneth G. C. Newport and Gareth Lloyd. Oxford: University Press, 2013.

_____. *The Unpublished Poetry of Charles Wesley*. Editors, S T Kimbrough Jr. & Oliver A. Beckerlegge. 3 volumes. Nashville: Kingswood Books, 1988-92).

Wesley, Charles and John. *Hymns and Sacred Poems*. Bristol: Farley, 1940, 1942.

Wesley, John. *John Wesley, A Library of Protestant Thought*. Edited by Albert Outler. New York: Oxford University Press, 1964.

_____. *John Wesley's Sunday Service in North America*. Edited with an introduction by James F. White. Nashville: The United Methodist Publishing House, 1984.

_____. *The Works of John Wesley*. Edited by Thomas Jackson. 14 vols. London: Wesleyan Conference Office, 1872; reprinted Grand Rapids: Baker Book House, 1978.

_____. *The Works of John Wesley*. Begun as "The Oxford Edition of *The Works of John Wesley*" Oxford: Clarendon Press, 1975-1983; continued as "The Bicentennial Edition of *The Works of John Wesley*." 35 volumes. Nashville: Abingdon Press, 1984–

Wood, Laurence. *The Meaning of Pentecost in Early Methodism, Rediscovering John Fletcher as John Wesley's Vindicator and Designated Successor*, 2002.

Index

A farther grace 1, 3, 5, 7, 9, 11, 13, 15, 17, 19, 21, 23, 25, 27
a true, living faith 22
abiding witness of the Spirit 2, 40, 50, 52, 97, 98, 110-112, 123, 129, 168, 176, 202, 226
Aldersgate experience 21, 25, 29, 30, 37, 39, 47, 186
almost Christian 96, 145
annual conference of John Wesley and his preachers 4, 89, 104, 174, 181, 194, 198, 202, 224, 243
Arminian Magazine 6, 16, 88, 118, 119, 130, 134, 135, 149, 153, 159, 171, 175-78, 182, 189, 190, 191, 195, 198, 199, 202, 204, 206, 210, 212, 223, 229, 235-36, 243, 255, 279
    Fletcher mentioned in almost every annual volume for one hundred years 235
Asbury Theological Seminary 118, 140, 231, 273
Asbury, Francis 6, 137, 205, 228, 233, 235-36, 242, 243-44, 255, 277
Austin, Gerard 261

Bangs, Nathan 7, 222, 238-39, 243, 257, 277
    The first serious American Methodist theologian 257
baptism with the Holy Spirit 4-5, 10, 12-13, 16, 31-32, 61, 88, 103, 105, 108-109, 115-16, 122, 143-44, 146, 148, 152, 154, 157-59, 161, 165-67, 171-72, 175-76, 181-82, 188, 194-206, 208, 210, 212, 215-16, 218, 222-24, 227, 233, 235-36, 237-38, 240-42, 245, 249-50, 252, 258-59, 262-63, 267, 269, 273, 278
    A sampling of the expression in Methodist history 233
    defined as perfect love in a letter from a Methodist preacher to John Wesley 121
    definition of the baptism with the Spirit as Christian perfection 241, 244
    John Wesley carefully nuanced 268
    John Wesley on the promise of baptism with the Spirit and circumcision of heart in baptism and the fulfillment of that promise in personal faith 267
    John Wesley's multiple sermons on "Baptized with the Holy Spirit" 193
    Pentecost moments 269
Barth, Karl 261-63, 278
    baptism with the Spirit signified the perfection of the Christian life 262
    baptism with water symbolized beginning of the Christian life in regeneration representing Easter event 74, 262
Baxter, Richard 251, 270, 276
    called for the restoration of confirmation 251
    the Holy Spirit is promised as a "fundamental right" in baptism 251
Bennis, Eliza 122, 133, 157-58, 160
    personal Pentecost of full sanctification 122
Benson, Joseph 28, 41, 87, 139, 142-46, 149-50, 152, 156, 158-59, 169, 171, 175, 187, 189, 200, 206-207, 210, 214-15, 225, 228-30, 234, 240, 256, 267, 271-72, 279
    baptism of the Holy Spirit 211

Benson never altered his idea 206
encouraged his future wife to be baptized with the Spirit 210
no disagreement among Methodists about the meaning of the baptism with the Spirit 207
worried that Fletcher exaggerated the status of those in the pre-Christian dispensation 207
worried that some might misinterpret the miraculous expectation of having a personal Pentecost 207

Binney, Amos 2
Bishop of London 94
Bishops' Pastoral Address to the General Conference of the Methodist Episcopal Church 270
Böhler, Peter 14, 24–26, 29, 35, 39, 41, 47
Book of Common Prayer 247, 250–52, 254–56, 261, 266, 276–77
Borgen, Ole 104, 120
born again 6, 21, 25, 50–51, 63, 97–98, 105, 125–26, 181, 208, 248, 270
Bosanquet, Mary 123, 146, 172, 183, 188, 207–208, 210, 215–17, 222, 228, 254, 271, 279
    Charles Wesley said a model of "pure and perfect love" 124
Bourdaloue, Louis 212, 229
Bramwell, William 222, 231
Bray, John 33, 39, 51
Bristol 3, 4, 16, 17, 26, 27, 28, 36, 59, 61, 66–67, 88, 89, 97, 115, 134–35, 150, 159, 167–69, 181, 190, 193–94, 195–96, 203, 209, 221–22, 231
Bristol Society 59
Brooks, Phillips 273
Bruner, Dale 261, 278
Bultmann, Rudolf, 68, 76, 267

Calvinism 114, 185
Cell, G. C. 142
Chapel-en-le-Frith 4
Chilcote, Paul W. 183, 191
Christian perfection 1
    "baptize me now with fire" 58
    "Come, Holy Ghost, all Quickening fire," 58
    confirmation 9
    constant fruits of faith 113
    full kingdom in the Holy Spirit 58
    full sanctification 1, 3, 12, 43, 51, 88, 97, 115–16, 122, 125, 127–28, 143, 145, 163, 176, 180, 196, 199, 206, 227, 237, 240, 242, 256–57, 268–69, 271
    never a terminal point 2
    "O that the Comforter would come" 58
    Pentecost as an infusion of pure love for God 74
    perfect love 1
    personalized interpretation of the Anglican Rite of Confirmation 10
    Plain Account of Christian Perfection 10–11, 17, 27, 82, 117, 144, 150, 176, 189, 224, 255
    Promise of the Father 5, 11, 14–15, 29, 56, 63, 73, 78, 91, 97–98, 154, 162, 166, 172, 174, 177–78, 197, 208–209, 216, 221, 227, 2346
    purity of intent 2, 10, 247
    sanctification after justification embedded deeply in their Anglican heritage 10
    "seal of my sins in Christ forgiven, earnest of love, and pledge of heaven" 57
    second blessing 9–10, 58, 66, 113–14, 240, 270
    second gift 5, 9–10, 19, 58, 63, 66, 98, 129, 270
    "the earnest of my heaven!" 105
    the farther rest 9
    the indwelling Spirit 58
circumcision of heart 21, 26–27, 78, 116, 120, 124, 130, 134–35, 253, 267
    entails witness of the Spirit 130
City Road Methodist Chapel 140, 149
Clarke 1, 6, 116, 159, 193–99, 203–204, 223, 225–27, 231–32, 254, 271, 276, 283
Clement of Alexandria 252
Coke, Thomas 31, 36, 176, 181, 188, 194–96, 199, 203, 205, 205, 216, 221–22, 225, 226, 228, 231, 233, 242, 255, 277

Fletcher's *Checks* "acknowledged and disseminated by John Wesley" and officially "recognized by the [British] Methodist Conference" 205
Collins, Kenneth J. 276n45
Comforter 11, 14–15, 30, 33, 38, 42, 52–53, 57–58, 63–66, 91, 99, 103, 105, 114, 128–33, 146–47, 158, 176, 183, 201, 226, 236, 247–48
Confirmation 245
   a proposal for today 245
   an implicit catechism 255
   Anglican ritual of confirmation 251
   baptized with water and the Spirit in John Wesley's *Sunday Service* 266
   Christian perfection as the Rite of Confirmation Felt 245
   Confirmation deleted 254
      Sunday Service 254
   confirmation service for today 272
   early twentieth-century ecumenical liturgical studies 258
   Fletcher proposed that John Wesley be allowed to confirm Methodists 245
   John Fletcher's Idea of Confirmation 246
   Puritans rejected Book of Common Prayer 251, 252, 278
   ratifying, strengthening, or sanctifying? 250
   recent ecumenical liturgical developments 260
   Roman Catholic catechism 256
   The Apostolic Tradition of St. Hippolytus of Rome 259, 260, 262, 264, 278
      revealed the practice of baptism from the time of the primitive church 260
   the two gestures of baptism in the Primitive Church 248
   United Methodist Church Book of Worship 265
   a service of baptism, confirmation, and renewal 265
   The United Methodist Hymnal 265
Cooper, Mary 225–26, 230–31
case study of the Pentecost preaching of the early Methodists 225
Cornelius 78, 99, 155
Cranmer, Thomas 250–52, 256, 261, 276
Cyprian 252

Darcy, Lady Maxwell 213
David, Christian 14, 37, 39–43, 44, 46–47, 49, 51, 92, 97, 106, 116, 162, 165, 167, 195, 245
   full assurance of faith comes through "the indwelling of the Spirit" 42
   the disciples' pre-Pentecost and Pentecost experience as a pattern 42
Dieter, Melvin E. 241–42, 244
   The Holiness Revival of the Nineteenth Century 241
dispensationalism of Fletcher as soteriological and not to be confused with the eschatological dispensationalism of the Plymouth Brethren and John Darby 242
Dix, Gregory 249, 258, 266, 269, 276, 278
   The Theology of Confirmation in Relation to Baptism 259
   traced the history of the rite of confirmation 249
Dublin 2, 87, 110, 122, 158, 181–82, 199, 223
Dunn, James D. G. 263, 278
   rejected the priority of the primitive liturgy 263
   relied on abstract biblical exegesis 263

Epworth 17, 20, 28, 36, 61, 149, 159, 169, 203, 275, 277
evolutionary biology 253

Family Hymns 133
filled with the Holy Spirit 16, 32–33, 51, 55, 58, 80, 92, 97–98, 100–104, 115–16, 137, 142, 144–46, 155, 171–77, 179–80, 182, 184, 186, 194–95, 198–99, 205–206, 210–14, 216, 218, 237, 239–40, 272–73
   Wesley "explained and applied" 218

John Wesley cited Elizabeth Ritchie as an example of being filled with the Spirit 218
John Wesley said to be perfected in love is being filled with the Holy Spirit 144
defined as Christian perfection 104
Fisk, Wilbur 235, 237, 241
Fletcher, John 4, 7, 10, 24, 28, 31, 35-36, 41, 58, 87, 89, 98, 102-103, 116, 118-119, 121-22, 133-34, 137-39, 141-42, 145, 149-52, 157-61, 163, 166, 169, 171-73, 176, 181, 183, 185, 187-206, 211, 213-216, 218-219, 223-24, 228-29, 231-32, 234-37, 240-41, 243-47, 249, 256, 265, 268-71, 276, 278, 279
baptism of the Spirit "of late years gloriously revived by Mr. Wesley" 123
Checks to Antinomianism 88, 121, 122 137, 138-40, 151, 173, 234, 255
consensus between John Wesley and John Fletcher 171
correspondence with Charles Wesley on baptism with the Spirit 161
did John Wesley really change his mind? 145
encouraged Charles Wesley to join him "after the example of the Apostles" 163
Essay on Truth 28, 88, 103, 153, 155-57, 167, 173, 186, 191, 196, 199, 204, 237, 240, 271, 275
exploratory ideas about the baptism with the Spirit to Charles Wesley 152
Fletcher resigned as president of Trevecca College 143
"Fullness" corresponded to John Wesley's idea of a higher degree as distinct from a lower degree of sanctifyng grace 145
inconsistency in John Wesley's theology 151
Ireland, James 152
John and Charles Wesley edited, corrected, and published his manuscripts 162
John Wesley said "no secrets between us" 139
John Wesley said had superior "intellectual abilities" 139
John Wesley, "I do not perceive [now with your changes] that there is any difference between us" 161
John Wesley's special abridged edition 153
memorialized as a "genius" in City Road Chapel 140
our views of Christian Perfection are a little different 161
"My friend [John Wesley] . . . chiefly rests the doctrine of Christian perfection on being baptized and filled with the Spirit" 172
Portrait of St. Paul 140
progressive order of salvation from the lowest to the highest 154
proleptic idea of the dynamic interflow of grace throughout salvation history 151
proposed to Charles Wesley "a Methodist Church" 247
proposed to John Wesley that Methodism be "a daughter church of our holy mother, the Church of England" 245
seemed to disagree with Benson and Fletcher on the baptism with the Spirit 143
soteriological doctrine of dispensations 154
theme of *Last Check* was for Christ to "baptize with the Holy Spirit" 157
to Charles Wesley: "New Baptisms are Necessary From Time to Time" 151
Vicar of Madeley 88, 123, 137, 138, 140, 185, 189
Fletcher, Mary 4, 7, 161, 168, 181-82, 185, 190-91, 203, 205, 210, 215-16, 218-19, 223, 231, 254, 276
Forsaith, Peter 117, 138, 148-49
fullness of the Spirit 2, 87, 117, 129, 142, 172, 177, 199, 208-212, 216, 235, 242, 252, 268-69

Garrettson, Freeborn 2, 7
Gibbons, Edward 20
Gilpin, Joshua 137
Gradin, Arvid 41, 49
Gray's Inn Walks 91
great salvation 1, 91, 97, 110
    full salvation 1, 2, 197, 220-21, 239
Gwynne, Sarah (Wesley) 110, 112
    Charles Wesley desired that she be baptized with the Spirit for perfect love 111

half-Christians 3
half-Methodist 1
Haslam, Peter 237
Heitzenrater, Richard 7, 17, 23, 26-27, 29, 159, 185, 191, 203
Herrnhut 22, 24, 34, 41, 41-45, 49, 91-93, 118, 122, 154, 225
    Charles Wesley's view of the "plan of salvation" changed after John's visit to Herrnhut 44
    the reason why John Wesley went for a visit 39
Heylyn, John 16, 29-31, 36, 43, 97, 102-103, 115, 133, 177, 179, 194, 195, 218, 252, 269, 273
    baptism with the Spirit 31
    John Wesley heard his Pentecost sermon on the same day as Charles Wesley's personal Pentecost 30
    Pentecost Sermon and Charles Wesley's Pentecost Conversion 29
    Theological Lectures 31, 36, 115, 276
holiness 1, 2, 3-15, 17, 19-21, 23, 25-28
    full assurance 2, 5, 11, 14, 23-26, 30, 33-34, 37, 39-41, 44-47, 49, 55, 60, 104, 106, 110, 112, 123, 125, 147, 150, 154-55, 166, 185
    holiness after forgiveness 3
    holiness after Justification 49
    perfect holiness 5, 75, 108, 146-47, 212, 216, 254
Holy Communion 3, 32, 194, 226, 256, 271
Holy Spirit as Comforter 15, 33, 42, 52
Huntingdon, Countess, Lady 4, 7, 99, 137, 142-43, 150-51, 159, 162, 168, 172, 252
Hurst, J. F. 190-91, 203, 228, 232, 243, 247, 275-76
Hymns and Sacred Poems 16-7, 26, 36, 39, 46-47, 49-50, 56, 61, 66, 84, 89, 97-98, 175-18, 120, 129-30, 135, 146, 150, 192, 275, 279

indwelling Comforter 15, 63, 65, 103, 128-29, 132, 146-47
indwelling of the Spirit 19, 40-41, 45, 66, 97-98, 108, 116, 125, 129-30, 146-48, 152, 185, 226, 259, 268
"indwelling Spirit sealed" 130
instructions on how Christian believers today can be filled with the Spirit 32

Jacob, Edmond 73
Jones, E. Stanley 273
justification by faith 3, 5-6, 21, 23, 24-25, 33, 35, 39, 42-43, 50-51, 56, 91-92, 104-105, 108, 112, 116, 123-26, 130, 132, 135, 141, 145-46, 156, 167, 172, 184-85, 223, 240, 245, 259, 267

Kinghorn, Kenneth 140
Kingswood 3, 7, 26-28, 97, 231

Lampe, G. W.H. 259
Law, William 19
    A parent of Methodism 20
    A Practical Treatise upon Christian Perfection 19
    the missing ingredient 24
Lawton, George 140, 149, 275
life-threatening storm 22
Lindström, Harald 1
Lloyd, Gareth 3, 4, 7, 28, 118, 134, 168, 199, 204
    corrected the dismissive role of Charles Wesley given by earlier Methodist writers 3
London 3-4, 6-7, 16-17, 20, 24, 26, 28, 36, 59, 61-62, 87-89, 91, 94, 110, 118-19,

121–22, 124, 135, 140, 149–50, 156, 159, 167, 169, 172, 174, 182, 189–92, 199, 203–205, 219–20, 222, 224, 227–232, 235, 243, 247, 275, 276–77, 278, 279
Luther, Martin 37, 184, 250

Macarius (pseudo-Macarius) 189, 245, 259-60, 275
  preached the baptism with the Holy Spirit 24
Maddox, Eileen F. xiii
Maddox, Randy xiii
Mason, A. J. 259
  The Relation of Confirmation to Baptism 259
Maxfield, Thomas 124
  Bell, George 124
  extreme claims about the gifts of the Spirit 124
Merritt, James 241
Methodist Episcopal Church in America 2, 228, 233, 242, 254, 277
Methodist Magazine 6, 89, 119, 139, 149, 174, 189–90, 203–204, 227, 229, 232, 234–35, 237–39, 243–44, 279
Moltmann, Jürgen 264
Moore, Henry 28, 40, 47, 92, 117, 119, 167, 169, 182, 187, 191–92, 203, 219, 223–26, 230–31, 238
Moravians 14, 22–25, 29, 30, 33, 35, 37, 39, 44, 45, 51, 92, 100, 125
  English Moravians 43, 91
  German Moravians 44, 49, 91
Moses 68–72, 74, 78, 112, 154, 178–79, 183–85
  restoration theme 72
Mudge, James 240, 244

new birth 5, 15, 22–23, 25, 35–36, 50–51, 61, 63, 108–109, 119, 124–26, 134, 169, 172, 189, 203–204, 206– 210, 228–29, 248, 256, 258, 265, 276–77
  "born again of the Spirit" as Christian perfection 25
  born of God 26, 30, 34–35, 42, 44, 50–51, 59, 61, 80, 82, 127, 207
  John Wesley later defined as the moment of justifying faith 25
  marks of the new birth 125

O'Malley, J. Steven vii, xiii
One Thing Needful 6, 21–22, 26–27, 42, 87, 97–98, 104, 106, 110–112
Outler. Albert 2, 6– 7, 17, 26–28, 36, 47, 61, 88–89, 102, 117–20, 125, 134–35, 140, 149, 185, 189–192, 203, 270, 275, 277, 279

Palmer, Phoebe 240, 244
  editor of *Guide to Holiness* 241
Pannenberg, Wolfhart 261, 264
  Pannenberg came to accept confirmation as the sealing of the Spirit, catechism, and a reaffirmation of water baptism. 264
Pawson, John 222
Pilmore, Joseph 88–89, 237, 238, 243
Prince William and Kate Middleton 109
"Principles of a Methodist" 97, 117, 134
Promised Land 43, 67–68, 70, 74–75, 77, 80–82
  a new conquest 72
  a new exodux 72, 79
  Canaan of perfct love 80, 202–203
  Let us hasten to enter that rest 81
  rest 3, 9, 11, 37, 43, 50, 57, 66–67, 76–78, 80, 83, 87–89, 101, 105–107, 110–111, 148, 173, 177, 185, 207, 210, 214, 217, 224, 239, 242, 252, 257, 275
  von Rad, Gerhad 6, 80, 88–89

Quaker 104, 106, 110, 113

Rattenbury, J. Ernest 15, 34–36, 51, 61, 99,18, 125–126, 135, 163, 169, 271
Richardson, Alan 73
Ritchie, Elizabeth 145, 156–157, 160, 189, 198, 205, 214–20, 230, 268, 271
  After reading Fletcher doctrine of dis-

pensations, she said "I am athirst for the Perfection of my dispensation" 157
close friends with John and Mary Fletcher 215
Elizabeth Ritchie said to John Wesley: "I long for the Spirit's fullest Baptism 157, 198, 205, 214-20, 230, 268, 271
John Wesley's dearest friend and band leader 156
"Mr. Fletcher has given us a wonderful view of the different dispensations" 156
Rogers, Hester Ann 203, 205, 215, 220-22, 230-31, 268, 271, 276
letter to John Wesley on Pentecostal outpouring 220
Rogers, James 220
Rutherford, Thomas 223
Christian Perfection, An Extract from John Fletcher 224

Sabin, Elijah 237
sanctification
begun 1
by the power of the Holy Spirit 2
Christian perfection 2
entire sanctification 1
fullness of sanctification 2
interchangeable with Christian perfection 2
never-ending process of further growth 2
sermons themes 3
distinction between justification and holiness 3
justifying faith and sanctifying grace. 3, 21, 44
Spirit of holiness 1, 3, 5, 7, 9, 11, 13, 15, 17, 19, 21, 23, 25, 27, 55, 79, 97, 99, 148
St. Paul's Cathedral 254
Steele, Daniel
founding president of Syracuse University 240
professor of theology of Boston University 240
wrote a critique of Mudge 240

Streiff, Patrick 149, 165, 168-169
Sudgen, E. H. 119, 145

Taylor, Jeremy 6, 9-12, 14-17, 49, 98, 104, 106, 109, 118, 126, 248, 251-52, 256-57, 266, 269, 272, 276
A Discourse of Confirmation 10, 16
a high church interpretation of Confirmation 251
baptism of the Holy Spirit 12
baptism with water distinct from baptism with the Spirit 12
confirmation and the witness of the Spirit 14
descent of the Holy Spirit 12
gift and reception of the Holy Spiri 13
John Wesley reported about him "no great genius on earth" 10
Pentecost repeatable for all subsequent generations 15
power from on high 12
receive the Holy Spirit in confirmation 14
Rule and Exercises of Holy Living 10
sanctification and confirmation 12
seal of the Spiri 12
the bestowal of the Spirit to the Samaritans 13
Tennent, Timothy C. xiii
Thompson, Sarah 210
Treffry, Richard 206, 227-28, 232
Trevecca 87, 142-44, 152, 161, 172, 175, 206-208, 213, 237
Trinity 86, 131-33, 135, 147, 150, 220, 264, 279
Tyerman, Luke 142, 149, 169, 188-89, 203, 228
Tyson, John 15, 26, 28-29, 36, 51, 56, 61-62, 125, 134
Charles Wesley's contribution to Wesleyan pneumatology 29

United Methodist General Board of Discipleship 273
Watson, Richard 140-41, 227, 232, 239

baptism of the Spirit 227
Wesley, Charles
   a penetrating lyrical commentator on Scripture. 5
   behind-the-scenes activities 4
   Charles Wesley's personal Pentecost 33
   Charles' reliance upon his brother 44
   co-founder of Methodism 3, 4
   co-ordinate authority with John 3
   confirmation 98
   daughter, Sally, 5
   Ephesians were "wholly sanctified" with receiving the Holy Spirit in Acts 19 129
   Groaning for the Spirit of Adoption 103
      baptism with Spirit means perfect love 105
   "Have ye received the Holy Spirit, since ye believed?" 99
   "He dwelleth with you, and shall be in you" (John 14:7) 130
   health issues 4
   highlighted in Charles Wesley's journal and hymns 6
   Hymns for Love 146
   identification of the Pentecost-bestowal of the Spirit with Christian perfection 66
   "Love Divine, all Loves excelling"—Prayer for Spirit of Pentecost to sanctify in perfect love 109
   loyalty to the Church of England 4
   our day of Pentecost is nigh 65
   process of sanctification 5
   Samuel Bradburn, Funeral Preacher 4
   "The pure baptismal Fire . . . perfect holiness" 108
   "Thy sanctifying Spirit pour" 67
   "To cleanse in the baptismal flood [baptism of the Spirit]," 15
Wesley, John
   a justified person has some measure of the indwelling of the Spirit 127
   "a sort of faith" equivalent to the faith of the disciples of the earthly Jesus who "had not then 'the [Pentecost] faith that overcometh the world'" 23
   "A Treatise on Baptism," 253
   approved John Fletcher's writings 123
   Baptism as "washing away the guilt of original sin" and "circumcision of heart" 253
   "Be 'baptized with the Holy Spirit and with fire' . . . till the love" 91
   changed his view about not being converted when he went to Georgia 23
   Clarke heard John Wesley preach two sermons on the baptism with the Holy Spirit within three months 194
   disciples sanctified on the day of Pentecost 91, 97
   "Farther Appeal to Men of Reason and Religion," 103, 152
      "the baptism with the Spirit" as the "inward baptism" 103
   filled with the Holy Spirit and made holy on day of Pentecost 96
   his day of Pentecost 121
   impossibility of being half a Christian 20
   inner circle 205
   letter to William Law 108
   meaning of the need to save his own soul 21
   "men attain perfect love" through being "baptized with the Spirit and fire" 103
   missionary to Georgia 21
   "'must be baptized with the Holy Spirit' implies this and no more" 91, 108, 116, 152
   "On Sin in Believers" 126
   Pentecost is a pattern for believers for all times 92
   "Salvation by Faith" 24, 25, 26, 28, 33, 118, 125, 155
   "Scriptural Christianity" 101–102, 103, 199
   sermon on "Christian perfection" 102
   the Apostles justified before the death of Christ 96

"Circumcision of Heart" and William Law 21

"The Holy Spirit was not yet given in his sanctifying graces 91

The Explanatory Notes upon the New Testament 114, 257
- disciples before Pentecost were justified and enjoyed a measure of God's love 114

the Holy Spirit is given in a lower degree to all justified believers, the full baptism with the Holy Spirit is given to believers perfected in love 182

"They were all filled with the Holy Spirit" 16

William Law, "One Thing Needful" 21

Wesley, Samuel 47
- John and Charles answered to their older brother 46

Wesley, Susanna 10, 16, 47, 60, 62

Wesleyan theology
- traditional Wesleyan theology rejected toward the end of the 19th Century 240

Wesleyan-Methodist Magazine 239

Westminster Shorter Catechism 254

Whitefield, George 20, 49, 51, 61, 113, 114, 185

Wrestling Jacob 84, 86–87, 214

Zinzendorf, 39, 91–92, 94, 13, 192
- debate with John Wesley, 92
- Charles Wesley's reaction, 94

www.ingramcontent.com/pod-product-compliance
Lightning Source LLC
Chambersburg PA
CBHW080322170426
43193CB00017B/2871